Cedat Fortuna Peritis
(Let Fortune Yield to Experience)
A History of the Field Artillery School

By

Boyd L. Dastrup

Field Artillery Branch Historian's Office

US Army Field Artillery School

Fort Sill, Oklahoma

FIELD ARTILLERY SCHOOL

Brigadier General Thomas S. Vandal — Commandant
Colonel Matt R. Merrick — Assistant Commandant
Dr. Boyd L. Dastrup — Field Artillery Branch Historian

Published by Books Express Publishing
Copyright © Books Express, 2011
ISBN 978-1-78039-566-1

Books Express publications are available from all good retail and online booksellers. For publishing proposals and direct ordering please contact us at: info@books-express.com

Foreword

From its humble beginnings as the School of Fire for Field Artillery in 1911, the Field Artillery School emerged as a worldwide leader in training and educating field artillerymen and developing fire support tactics, doctrine, organizations, and systems. Recognizing the inadequate performance of the Army's field artillery during the Spanish-American War of 1898, the emergence of modern field artillery, and indirect fire, President Theodore Roosevelt directed the War Department to send Captain Dan T. Moore of the 6th Field Artillery Regiment to Europe in 1908-1909. While there, Moore observed European field artillery training and found the German Artillery School at Juterborg with its emphasis on practical exercises, new methods of shooting, and testing new material to be particularly impressive. Based on this, Moore enthusiastically encouraged the War Department to develop a field artillery school along the lines of the German school and received the mission to establish the School of Fire for Field Artillery at Fort Sill.

Although the School of Fire experienced a few rocky years after opening in September 1911, the passage of time validated its efforts. During World War I, the school trained officers in observed and unobserved indirect fire for duty in France using classroom instruction and practical field exercises. According to the Chief of Field Artillery, Major General William J. Snow who served as commandant of the school in 1917, the school produced officers who performed with distinction in France and provided the core of the Army's field artillery training.

Following the war, the school, redesignated as the Field Artillery School in 1919, continued employing innovative training techniques in the classroom and the field in the 1920s-1930s. While the classroom instruction provided theoretical training, practical exercises honed the skills of field artillerymen in realistic field settings. Besides providing classroom gunnery training, Major Carlos Brewer and Major Orlando Ward, who were directors of the Gunnery Department early in the 1930s, pressed to make observed indirect fire more responsive by developing the fire direction center. Along with the graphic firing table introduced in 1939 and the portable radio, the fire direction center provided unprecedented, flexible massed fires during World War II.

After the war, the Field Artillery School retained its leadership in training and participated in key combat developments. While undergoing name changes in the 1940s and 1950s, the school trained officers and enlisted soldiers on emerging conventional and nuclear field artillery systems as part of The Artillery Center, which included the Antiaircraft Artillery School at Fort Bliss, Texas, renamed the Air Defense Artillery School in 1957. Such training complemented the school's involvement in the development of the Field Artillery Digital Automated Computer to make the school a leader in Army automation and the airmobile artillery concept used in the Vietnam War of the 1960s.

Although the Vietnam War caused the Field Artillery School's operational tempo to increase and to focus on fire support in counterinsurgency warfare, it returned to conventional warfare in the 1970s. Through the remaining years of the 20th century, the school introduced counterfire and the fire support team, among other doctrinal and force structure changes, and played a key role in developing the Multiple-Launch Rocket System, the Paladin M109 self-propelled howitzer, and other field artillery systems.

As it helped modernize the Field Artillery, the school updated its classrooms and instructional methodologies. It adopted advanced information technology for classroom instruction and distributed learning to deliver instruction beyond the school house, introduced small group instruction to develop adaptive leaders, and strengthened its ties with the reserve components through the Total Army School System.

As the school moved into the 21st century, Operation Enduring Freedom in Afghanistan and Operation Iraqi Freedom shaped more change. To support those operations, the school introduced practical exercises on counterinsurgency warfare, trained students in precision fires to minimize collateral damage, and trained officers and soldiers to employ non-lethal effects, such as electronic warfare and tactical information operations, to complement lethal effects.

During the Field Artillery School's centennial year of 2011, it carried on the traditions established by the School of Fire for Field Artillery many years ago. Constantly adjusting to meet the nation's defense requirements, the school trained Army and Marine field artillerymen and other nations' field artillerymen to be technically and tactically proficient and to provide lethal and non-lethal effects in support of full spectrum operations. As a key member of the progressive Fires Center of Excellence at Fort Sill, a product of the Base Realignment and Closure 2005 which collocated the Air Defense Artillery School on Fort Sill, the school became a partner in producing fires officers and soldiers for the 21st century.

Artillery Strong!

Thomas S. Vandal

Brigadier General, USA

Commandant

Preface

Over the years, the Field Artillery School transformed itself to meet the needs of the Army. During the 20 years preceding the opening of the School of Fire for Field Artillery at Fort Sill, Oklahoma, in 1911, the War Department candidly acknowledged the requirement for trained field artillerymen, but training had been sporadic and ineffective since the American Civil War because artillery schools opened and closed with regularity and furnished little training even when opened. While the Artillery School at Fort Monroe, Virginia, renamed the Coast Artillery School in 1907, focused on coast artillery training, the garrison schools concentrated on drill and ceremony and rote memorization but not firing.

The Mounted Service School at Fort Riley, Kansas, was created by the War Department in 1907 to replace the ineffective School of Practice for Cavalry and Field Artillery at Fort Riley that had opened in 1892. It operated under several names over the years with the mission of teaching equitation and field artillery tactics, but it failed to fill the void created by the Coast Artillery School's decision to furnish coast artillery instruction exclusively.

Inadequate training, modern field guns, indirect fire that was supplanting direct fire, and the Field Artillery's poor performance in the Spanish-American War of 1898 prompted the War Department to organize a school devoted to training field artillerymen. On 15 September 1911, the School of Fire for Field Artillery opened its doors.

Outside forces continued shaping the school following World War I, which caused the school to expand its operations. Facing the imperative of improving indirect fire tactics, techniques, and procedures to make fire support more responsive on a more mobile battlefield, the school developed the fire direction center to facilitate massing and shifting fires more rapidly than ever before. The school also participated in testing motor-drawn and self-propelled artillery, and played a role in the adoption of organic field artillery aerial observation.

During the four decades after World War II, pressures beyond the school reinforced the need to adapt. The shortage of field artillery and antiaircraft artillery officers and the Army's push to save money generated the need for flexibility in officer assignments. This caused the school to conduct cross training in the late 1940s to the 1960s during which field artillery and antiaircraft artillery officers were trained in both artillery branches so that they could serve in either. Meanwhile, the Army entered the atomic and nuclear age, forcing the school to develop courses and doctrine for a conventional and nuclear battlefield. Subsequently, the Vietnam War of the 1960s and 1970s prompted the school to shift its focus from conventional and tactical nuclear warfare to guerilla warfare, while the Army's return to Europe in the 1970s rekindled interest in conventional and nuclear warfare and suitable weapons and equipment.

National and international events during the last decade of the 20th century and the first decade of the 21st century once again sculpted the school. Fearful that the Army would become irrelevant in the small wars springing up around the world, General Eric K. Shinseki, Chief of Staff of the Army, tore the Army and school away from a Cold War orientation with its emphasis on heavy units and moved training to lighter and more mobile units for fighting throughout the world. The War on Terrorism following the terrorist attacks of 11 September 2001 pulled the Army and school even further from the Cold War moorings.

Although the school trained soldiers and officers to fight on the conventional battlefield, non-standard missions in Operation Iraqi Freedom and Operation Enduring Freedom in Afghanistan – patrolling, civil affairs, and psychological warfare, among others – during the early years of the 21st century eroded field artillerymen's core fire support skills. Non-standard missions also stimulated the school to emphasize resetting (retraining) the field artillery force in its core field artillery competencies and to adopt non-lethal effects – tactical information operations and electronic warfare – as core competencies.

Although outside forces drove the school's program of instruction and involvement in combat developments, individual efforts did not go unnoticed in an organization devoted to team play. Against tremendous odds, Captain Dan T. Moore opened the School of Fire for Field Artillery in 1911. Years later in the 1920s and 1930s, Major Carlos Brewer, as a director of the Gunnery Department, reformed gunnery techniques to mass fires more rapidly, while his successor, Major Orlando Ward, created the fire direction center. Lieutenant Colonel H.L.C. Jones, director of the Gunnery Department, subsequently improved upon the center and paved the way for its acceptance throughout the field artillery community. Starting out as an early advocate of cross training late in the 1940s, Major General Thomas E. de Shazo, the Commandant of the US Army Artillery and Missile School late in the 1950s, became an outspoken opponent of cross training after witnessing its deleterious impact on officers and unsuccessfully pushed to revoke it. Only the Vietnam War ended that disastrous program.

Major General David E. Ott developed the fire support team to facilitate coordinating fires from attack helicopters, tactical aircraft, mortars, naval guns, and field artillery and counterfire to engage enemy indirect fire systems in the 1970s to overcome the numerically superior ground forces of the Soviet Union and Warsaw Pact. Years later, Major General David C. Ralston initiated reset efforts to retrain field artillerymen in their core fire support skills that had deteriorated after serving in non-standard missions in Operation Iraqi Freedom and Operation Enduring Freedom (Afghanistan) during the first years of the 21st century. These individuals and others met the changing demands placed upon the school to train high quality field artillerymen and develop new field artillery systems.

This book starts with the school at the beginning of the 20th century and carries the story through the first decade of the 21st century. Although the school's early years fell short of Captain Dan T. Moore's vision of creating a field artillery school comparable to the German one at Juterborg, the ensuing ones saw the rise of a first-rate institution that fulfilled the captain's dream.

I would like to thank Mark Megehee of the Field Artillery Museum at Fort Sill, Dan Scraper who has played a key role in developing training for field artillery officers, and

David A. Christensen, the Air Defense Artillery School historian, for taking time to read the manuscript and offer suggestions for improvement. I would also like to acknowledge Dr. Donald P. Wright and Jody Becker of the Combat Studies Institute, Fort Leavenworth, Kansas, for their outstanding attention to detail and advice during the editing process. Any errors in fact are mine.

Boyd L. Dastrup, Ph.D.
US Army Field Artillery School

To my wife, Karen, for all of her support.

Contents

Foreword iii
Preface v
Contents xi
Chapter One: A New, Isolated Fort 1
Chapter Two: A New Mission 15
Chapter Three: The War to End All Wars 45
Chapter Four: Peace and Transition 69
Chapter Five: Another War: 1939-1945 103
Chapter Six: Early Cold War Years: 1945-1971 131
Chapter Seven: Back to Europe 173
Chapter Eight: Moving toward the New Century 209
Chapter Nine: The New Century 251
Conclusion 301
Glossary 303
Names of Field Artillery School 307
Field Artillery School Commandants 309
Chiefs of Field Artillery 311
Bibliography 313
Index 327

Chapter One
A New, Isolated Fort

During the 19th century, white Americans steadily expanded the boundaries of the United States of America. From the original 13 colonies along the Atlantic Ocean, they flowed westward across the American continent in search of economic opportunities and land and conquered and displaced Native Americans tribes as they moved. Upon reaching the Trans-Mississippi West by the 1820s, they encountered the Great Plains where the scarcity of water, the relentless summer heat, and the thick indigenous grasses that were difficult to plow created unfavorable conditions for traditional farming methods based upon an abundant water supply and moderate summers. Prompted by the unforgiving conditions of the Great Plains, they migrated to Texas, California, or Oregon where more hospitable climates and better opportunities existed. Although trappers, traders, and explorers saw potential in Indian Territory, present-day Oklahoma, the American preoccupation with Texas in the 1830s and 1840s, the discovery of gold in California in 1849, the aridity and scorching summers of the Great Plains, and the American Civil War of 1861-1865 discouraged serious migration onto the Great Plains.

However, immigrant overland trails to Oregon, California, and Utah, cutting through the heart of the Great Plains, alarmed Native American tribes about the white settlers' intentions and led to the Fort Laramie Treaty of 1851 between the federal government and Native Americans. The treaty promised the Northern Plains tribes annuities of food and clothing. In exchange, they would permit the immigrant wagon trains to travel safely across their territory.

Meanwhile, the allure of riches enticed other Anglos to traverse the Great Plains. To the south of Fort Laramie in present-day Wyoming, the discovery of gold in the Rocky Mountains, near present-day Denver, Colorado, in 1859 aggravated the uneasy truce between the Native Americans tribes in the area and the Anglos. Anglos rushed into the area in search of gold, causing a rapid growth of communities in Colorado to support the gold seekers and armed clashes between the tribes and whites.

Following the passage of the Homestead Act of 1862 with its provisions for purchasing land at a relatively inexpensive price and the end of the American Civil War that allowed the country to shift its attention once again to the West, the rapidly growing white population now equipped with steel plows with the ability to cut through the thick plains grasses to get to the rich soil beneath and improved windmills to pump water to the water-starved soil moved onto the Great Plains in search of arable farm land. This wave of settlers also intensified the simmering confrontation between the Native Americans and whites, produced an armed, bloody conflict, and eventually led to the establishment of Fort Sill in 1869 to maintain peace in the region.

Laying a Foundation

Although the white population avoided the Great Plains in its search for suitable farmland before the American Civil War, explorers, trappers, hunters, and traders did not. After purchasing the Louisiana Territory from France in 1803, President Thomas Jefferson commissioned several expeditions to gather as much information as possible about the newly acquired land. In 1804, President Jefferson dispatched Captain Meriwether Lewis and Lieutenant William Clark, both of the US Army, to find a route to the Pacific Ocean, to strengthen American claims to the Oregon Territory, and to gather information about the indigenous inhabitants, flora, and fauna. With the able assistance of Sacagawea, a Shoshoni who was a captive of the Dakota tribes, the Lewis and Clark expedition, composed of Army officers, enlisted personnel, and even Clark's African-American slave York, explored thousands of square miles of the country, made important scientific observations, established friendly relations with Native American tribes along the route of travel, and returned to St. Louis, Missouri, in September 1806.[1]

As Lewis and Clark trekked through the northern portion of the Louisiana country, Lieutenant Zebulon Montgomery Pike rose to prominence as an explorer. In the fall of 1805, he pushed northward from St. Louis to find the source of the Mississippi River. After reaching Leech Lake in present-day Minnesota which he determined to be the source of the Mississippi River, he started back to St. Louis, arriving there in April 1806. Pike set out again on another journey in July 1806. With a party of 20 men, he ventured westward along the Missouri and Osage Rivers and turned south to the Arkansas River and followed it into present-day Colorado. For two months he explored the Colorado country, unsuccessfully tried to climb a peak that later bore his name, and hunted vainly for the headwaters of the Red River. In the spring of 1807, Spanish soldiers captured him and his party, escorted them to Chihuahua, Mexico, for intensive questioning, and then marched them to Natchitoches, originally established by the French in 1714 as an outpost at the head of navigation on the Red River for trading with the Spanish in Mexico. Here, the Spanish deposited him on the American side of the Louisiana Territory border.[2]

Meanwhile, President Jefferson proposed sending out other expeditions to unlock additional secrets of the territory. One would explore the Platte and Kansas Rivers. A second would traverse the Des Moines River. A third would scout the Upper Mississippi and Minnesota Rivers, while a fourth party would ascend the Red River to its source and explore the headwaters of the Arkansas River. Lacking President Jefferson's zeal and practical interest in the Louisiana Territory, however, Congress granted only enough money to fund one of the expeditions. At President Jefferson's direction, William Dunbar, a noted scientist from Natchez, Mississippi, and John Hunter, a Philadelphia chemist, received the intimidating task of leading a team up the Red River to its source. The small party left Natchez in October 1804, but Spanish soldiers prevented it from traveling up the river. Undeterred by this failure, President Jefferson wrung more money from Congress and dispatched Thomas Freeman, a surveyor and astronomer, with a body of 37 people in 1806 to explore the Red River to its source. Freeman's party entered the Red River in May 1806, expecting to ascend the river in boats. Like Dunbar's ill-fated expedition, this endeavor also faltered. Spanish soldiers forced Freeman's company to turn back before it could find the source of the Red River. Thus far, official government explorers floundered in their attempts to fulfill the ambitious dream of President Jefferson of scouting and mapping the

Louisiana country in detail. The source of the Red River remained obscure, and most of present-day Oklahoma remained a mystery to the white man. Only the Native American tribes knew the region.[3]

Years passed before any serious undertakings succeeded in present-day Oklahoma. Although Lieutenant James R. Wilkinson who was the son of Major General James Wilkinson, the governor of the Louisiana Territory, traveled through the site of present-day Ponca City, Oklahoma, in 1806, although R.B. Sparks visited northern present-day Oklahoma in 1806, and although George C. Sibley attempted to find the source of the Red River in 1811, Major Stephen H. Long of the US Army left the most enduring legacy following his exploration of the West. Between 1817 and 1819, Long's expedition constructed Fort Smith on the Arkansas River in present-day Arkansas, while Colonel Henry Leavenworth's expedition built Fort Snelling at the junction of the Mississippi and Minnesota Rivers. In 1819, Long and Colonel Henry Atkinson left St. Louis for the Mandan villages on the Missouri River, but their steamboat broke down so frequently that they traveled no farther than Council Bluffs where they erected Fort Atkinson at the junction of the Missouri and Platte Rivers in present-day Nebraska. After this abortive attempt, the US Army shifted its attention south to the Red River. In June 1820, Long and his small party left Fort Atkinson to explore the sources of the Red, Platte, and Arkansas Rivers. After reaching the Rocky Mountains without locating the source of the Platte River, Long divided his command. Part descended the Arkansas River, while the other under Long searched for the Red River. Long's small band followed the Purgatory and Cimarron Rivers until they merged into a larger river that Long believed to be the Red River.

After following this river downstream, he learned to his dismay when his band reached the Arkansas River that it had been descending the Canadian River which ran through the heart of present-day Oklahoma. He continued to follow the Arkansas River until he reached Fort Smith. Although his groups took extensive notes on the flora, fauna, geology, Native American tribes, and agricultural potential, Long's most lasting contribution focused on his uncomplimentary appellation of the explored area and that beyond his travels. Believing the land to be worthless for traditional agriculture, he labeled the entire Great Plains as "The Great American Desert." His term was nothing new as far as government officials were concerned because it echoed an earlier description about the region by Pike after his expedition into the West. However, the official map of Long's journey incorporated the expression for the first time and established the psychological barrier to white settlement for years to come.[4] Although government explorers opened the Louisiana Territory by mapping and traversing it, traders created the conditions for permanent settlement. Moving to tap the vast potential of trade with Santa Fe, Mexico, and northern Mexico, which lacked manufacturing centers and begged for American goods, Jean Pierre Chouteau, a French trader, constructed a trading post on the Three Forks around 1802 where the Grand, Verdigris, and Arkansas Rivers joined in present-day eastern Oklahoma. From this post, shipments of raw materials could be floated down the Arkansas River to the Mississippi River to New Orleans or up the Mississippi River to St. Louis. Years later in 1817, Chouteau's son, Auguste Pierre Chouteau, established a trading post on the Grand River, near present-day Salina, Oklahoma. Together, the Chouteau trading posts and other trading posts furnished excellent starting points for transporting manufactured goods to Santa Fe. As might be expected, farmers and settlers soon ventured onto the land near Chouteau's trading posts and the others in the region. To protect the expanding white population from raids and reprisals from the Native Americans, the federal government built Fort Gibson in 1824 at the fork of the Verdigris, Arkansas, and Grand Rivers and erected Fort Towson in 1824, near the mouth of the Kiamichi River to the south. Together, these two forts stood as twin sentinels to replace Fort Smith as guardians of the vast untapped region.[5]

As the creation of Fort Gibson and Fort Towson suggested, explorers, traders, farmers, and settlers albeit in small numbers moved onto land occupied by Native Americans and created the conditions for conflict. Throughout the colonial period, white settlers appropriated the lands of eastern Native Americans and pushed them farther west onto lands already populated by other Native American tribes.[6] Upon acquiring the Louisiana Territory in 1803, President Jefferson envisioned the possibility of moving Native Americans there. If the Native Americans east of the Mississippi River could be voluntarily relocated west of the river onto lands undesired by the white population, the friction between the two peoples could be eliminated. Equally important, valuable lands currently occupied by Native Americans in the East could be opened up to white settlement with less opposition.

This line of thinking persisted for the next 20 years and prompted the haphazard removal of portions of Native American tribes from the East to the West. Upon being elected president in 1828, Andrew Jackson, who championed removal with unprecedented enthusiasm, found willing support for his cause in Congress. In 1830, Congress passed the Indian Removal Act. The act ended the inconsistent nature of the removals of the first three decades of the 19th century, accelerated their pace, made the forced removal of Native American tribes an official government policy, and led to the creation of a gigantic Indian Territory stretching from the Red River in the south to the Missouri River in the north and extending west from the 95th Parallel. From 1830 onward, the northern Native American tribes moved involuntarily into northern Indian Territory (present-day Nebraska and Kansas), while the Five Civilized Tribes of the southeastern United States were transferred into southern Indian Territory (present-day Oklahoma).[7]

Forcefully displacing the relatively sedentary Five Civilized Tribes who were replicating much of the Anglo's life style brought them into contact with the nomadic Southern Plains tribes (the Osages, Comanches, Kiowas, and Wichitas) to create a serious confrontation. Already feeling the pressure of the expanding white population, the Southern Plains tribes resented the intrusion of other Native American tribes onto their land, insisted that the territory granted to the Five Civilized Tribes was still their own, and launched terrifying raids against the Five Civilized Tribes. Located the farthest west in Indian Territory, the Chickasaws experienced more violent raids by the Southern Plains tribes than the other civilized tribes. To avoid conflicts with those nomadic tribes, the Five Civilized Tribes stayed east of the Arbuckle Range in central Indian Territory even though they had rights to land to the west.[8]

To protect the Five Civilized Tribes from the Southern Plains tribes, the War Department signed treaties with the indigenous tribes and established additional forts in Indian Territory.

The First Dragoon Regiment under Major General Henry Leavenworth, who had founded Fort Leavenworth in 1827 along the Missouri River, moved into southwest Indian Territory to acquire guarantees from the native tribes. He wanted them to stop harassing the newly arriving Five Civilized Tribes, traders, hunters, and trappers and to permit safe passage along the trade routes through Indian Territory to Santa Fe. The regiment marched from Fort Gibson to the vicinity of the confluence of the Washita and Red Rivers. Mortally ill, Leavenworth turned over his command to Colonel Henry Dodge to complete the mission. On 16 July 1834, Dodge conferred with a group of Comanches along Cache Creek near present-day Fort Sill and later met with the Wichitas to the west of the Wichita Mountains. As a result of the meetings, the federal government signed treaties at Fort Gibson with the Comanches in 1835 and the Wichitas in 1837 to create a temporary but uneasy peace to the territory until the mid-1860s and later built Fort Washita on the Washita River in 1842 to assist Fort Gibson and Fort Towson in protecting the Five Civilized Tribes from the Plains tribes. Captain Randolph B. Marcy, with his company of the 5th Infantry, explored present-day Oklahoma, producing outstanding maps. He founded an outpost in April 1851 that was subsequently named Fort Arbuckle in honor of General Matthew Arbuckle, a frontier Army officer who had died of cholera. The fort remained in use until 1870 when the establishment of Fort Sill rendered it unnecessary.[9]

Onto the Southern Plains

Following the American Civil War of 1861-1865, the US Army found the Southern Great Plains ablaze with violence and bloodshed between two conflicting cultures – the Native Americans fighting for self-preservation and the white settlers seeking complete domination of the region. Feeling the escalating pressure from the encroaching white population sweeping onto the Southern Plains in quest of land, adventure, and commerce, the Kiowa-Apache, Comanche, Kiowa, Cheyenne, Arapaho, and other Native American tribes aggressively fought to defend and preserve their homelands and way of life. The federal government dispatched a peace commission in October 1867 to end the fierce warfare that had been unleashed with the Sand Creek Massacre in November 1864 in southeastern Colorado near the Arkansas River where Colonel John M. Chivington's Colorado volunteers had ruthlessly butchered Black Kettle's peaceful Cheyenne village. Consisting of Major General William S. Harney, Major General Alfred H. Terry, other army officers, and civilians, the commission conferred with the hostile Southern Plains tribes at Medicine Lodge Creek in southern Kansas to formulate a lasting peace treaty.[10]

After exhaustive and heated discussions, the commission and the Native Americans finally reached an agreement and signed the Medicine Lodge Creek Peace Treaty in late October 1867. The treaty concentrated the signatory tribes on two reservations in Indian Territory that had been reduced in size to present-day Oklahoma following the passage of the Kansas-Nebraska Act of 1854. One reservation was dedicated to the Kiowas, Comanches, and Kiowa-Apaches; and the other was for the Southern Cheyennes and Arapahos.[11] The treaty permitted the Southern Cheyenne to hunt north of the Arkansas River until the buffalo had been all killed off but committed them and the other tribes to remain peaceful. The treaty also allowed white emigrant travel over the trails, permitted private companies to build railroads across the trackless plains, stipulated converting the Native Americans into farmers and Christians, and prohibited the tribes from raiding off the reservations into Texas, Kansas, and Colorado. In return, the federal government promised to protect the tribes from white hunters who were indiscriminately killing the buffalo, to provide schools, churches, farms, and agricultural implements to civilize the people, and to issue annuities of food, blankets, and clothing to offset the loss of the buffalo as the major source of food, clothing, and shelter. Basically, the treaty spelled an end to the Native Americans' way of life and meant the forced adoption of the white man's lifestyle.[12] Relocating the nomadic Southern Plains tribes onto reservations in western Indian Territory and pacifying them presented a challenge. Some bands reluctantly accepted reservation status and government rations during the scarcity of the winter months but returned to raiding in the milder months. Others, such as the Southern Cheyenne, rejected the Medicine Lodge Creek Peace Treaty out of hand. They maintained their hostility and resisted any attempts to confine them to the reservations. The poor living conditions on the reservations and the continued killing of buffalo by white hunters drew elements of the Comanches and Kiowas back to war and encouraged them to step up their raids into Kansas, Colorado, and Texas in retaliation for broken promises.[13]

Influenced by the intensity of the raids on white settlements in Kansas, Lieutenant General William T. Sherman, commander of the Division of the Missouri and noted Civil War commander, assigned Major General Philip H. Sheridan, another famous Civil War general, to end the depredations with military force as required. After peaceful means had failed, Sheridan laid the groundwork for a military campaign with Sherman's blessing. Sheridan concentrated vast stores of supplies at Fort Gibson in eastern Indian Territory and Fort Larned in Kansas for forwarding to Fort Arbuckle and Fort Cobb, both in Indian Territory. Once the preparations had been completed, Sheridan opened his punitive, three-pronged winter offensive late in 1868 to drive hostile Native Americans from their winter camps to the Native American agency at Fort Cobb where the friendly bands were assembling for rations and protection under Colonel (Brevet Major General) William B. Hazen. Hazen commanded the Southern Indian Military District that covered all of Indian Territory and supervised and controlled the issuance of goods and supplies to the tribes in western Indian Territory. One prong under Major Andrew W. Evans marched east from Fort Bascom, New Mexico, along the South Canadian River. Another under Major (Brevet Brigadier General) Eugene A. Carr moved southeast from Fort Lyon, Colorado. Together, the two columns had the mission of blocking any hostile bands that were attempting to escape from the third column that was driving south from Fort Dodge, Kansas, with the assignment of striking the killing blow if needed and punishing the Native Americans who had been raiding into Kansas.[14]

Commanded by Lieutenant Colonel Alfred M. Sully and composed of 1,700 soldiers, including infantry and cavalry, the third and largest of the columns left Fort Dodge early in November 1868 and moved slowly south into Indian Territory where it established Camp Supply near the North Canadian River as a base of operations. At Camp Supply, Sully directed Lieutenant Colonel (Brevet Major General) George A. Custer's 7th Cavalry Regiment to find and strike at the Native Americans. After marching through deep snow from Camp Supply for almost three days in search of unfriendly Native Americans, especially those who had been raiding into Kansas, Custer slowed down his advance upon reaching the Canadian River, also called the South Canadian, on 26 November 1868. There, he dispatched his second in command, Major Joel Elliott, with three troops of cavalry and a few Native American scouts to reconnoiter upstream for any signs of Native Americans while he moved downstream to find a suitable location for a camp.

Elliott soon found a recently abandoned camp and fresh pony tracks in the new fallen snow leading to the south and sent a scout to report this finding to Custer. Concluding that the tracks were made by the belligerent Native Americans returning from recent raids into Kansas, Custer rapidly transmitted orders to Elliott via a scout to follow the trail and to halt and wait at dark for the main body. Custer left his supply wagons on the Canadian River to improve his mobility and led a hasty march with his main column of cavalry, seven ammunition wagons, and one ambulance to catch up with Elliott. On the morning of 27 November 1868, Custer found Black Kettle's camp of Cheyennes on the Washita River, near present-day Cheyenne, Oklahoma, divided his command into four columns, and attacked at the break of dawn. During the course of the ensuing battle, Custer's 7th Cavalry Regiment slaughtered more than 800 ponies and mules, killed many Native Americans, including Black Kettle, took many women and children as prisoners, and burned the village to the ground before retreating toward Camp Supply.

Custer made a weak attempt to find Elliott's command in his rush to retire from the battlefield to protect his tenuous supply line from a growing number of restive warriors from neighboring Kiowa, Arapaho, and Cheyenne camps downstream who were gathering on ridges surrounding Black Kettle's destroyed village and appeared to be eager to join the fight. Custer subsequently left Elliott's command to fend for itself. At the start of the fight, Elliott had led one of the four attack columns and then subdivided it when he took 17 men to chase escaping warriors who were attempting to break through the Army's lines for help. Elliott and his small detachment quickly found themselves outnumbered and surrounded by Arapahos, gallantly defended themselves, but were eventually killed.[15] After Custer had jubilantly returned to Camp Supply to boast of his resounding victory, Sheridan continued to maintain military pressure on the hostile bands. On 7 December 1868, Sheridan led a column of cavalry south from Camp Supply toward the Wichita Mountains with the intent of rounding up various bands of hostile Kiowas and Comanches. During the remaining days of December 1868 and the first days of January 1869, the general gathered them up and forcibly herded them to Fort Cobb.[16]

Meanwhile, six cavalry troops under Evans marched out of Fort Bascom along the South Canadian River into the Texas panhandle, as seven 5th Cavalry Regiment troops commanded by Carr drove southeastward from Fort Lyon toward the headwaters of the Red River and into Indian Territory. Of the two, only Evans' command saw any significant action. At Soldier Springs on the west side of the Wichita Mountains in southwest Indian Territory, Evans' column attacked a Comanche village on Christmas Day, suffered only one casualty, seriously damaged their food and shelter, killed 22 Comanches, and compelled them to return to the reservation on Indian Territory.[17] As he was conducting his mopping up action in his winter campaign, Sheridan searched for a strategic location to establish a military post closer to the center of southwest Indian Territory to protect the exposed Texas frontier from future Native American raids. In December 1868, Sheridan selected Colonel (Brevet Major General) Benjamin H. Grierson to pick a site for the new post.[18] Grierson previously had led an expedition from Fort Gibson, Indian Territory, into the region to the south of Fort Cobb in the summer of 1868 to determine the defensive needs of the territory in light of the raids by Cheyennes and Arapahos into Kansas. For the new post, Grierson found an excellent spot near Medicine Bluff, a cliff formation not far from the base of the Wichita Mountains. On 8 January 1869, Sheridan staked out his new post on the site identified by Grierson and called it Camp Wichita. Against the wishes of the 7th Cavalry Regiment that wanted the post named Fort Elliott after Major Joel Elliott who had been killed at the Washita after he had been abandoned by Custer, Sheridan subsequently renamed the camp Fort Sill on 1 August 1869 in honor of Brigadier General Joshua W. Sill. A classmate of Sheridan's at West Point, Sill was killed during the Civil War leading a Union brigade in Sheridan's division at the Battle of Murfreesboro (Stones River), Tennessee, on 31 December 1862.[19]

The New Fort and Its Mission

Fort Sill quickly became a base for future operations against hostile Native Americans, and subsequently assumed the mission of keeping the peace in Southwest Indian Territory. In 1869, soldiers erected temporary wooden buildings using roughhewn logs cut from the heavy timber along Medicine Creek and bricks and carpentry tools transported from Fort Arbuckle about 40 miles east. Later in 1870, with picks and shovels, African-American soldiers of the 10th Cavalry Regiment commanded by Grierson hacked out blocks of stone from nearby limestone outcroppings to construct a permanent fort while other soldiers guarded against attacks from any warlike Native Americans in the area. With the consent of the Department of the Interior, Lieutenant L.H. Orleman of the 10th Cavalry Regiment formally surveyed Fort Sill in August 1871; and later on 7 October 1871, President Ulysses S. Grant officially declared Fort Sill to be an Army fort.[20]

Besides serving as a Native American agency beginning early in 1869, when Albert Gallatin Boone arrived to become the first agent, and ending in 1901, when the federal government closed the agency with the opening of the Kiowa, Comanche, and Apache reservations to white settlement, Fort Sill stood as a lonely sentinel in southwest Indian Territory. Surrounded by both friendly and hostile Native Americans, Fort Sill was more than 300 miles from the nearest railhead at Fort Harkness, Kansas. High water, bad weather, and Native American attacks often interrupted communications with Fort Harkness and other frontier army posts and left Fort Sill isolated from the outside world. The little garrison received its mail by wagon from Boggy Depot, a trading center and post office about 100 miles to the east on the Clear Boggy, a tributary of the Red River in the Indian Territory, while communications between the post and the War Department often required 10 to 14 days.[21]

During the early 1870s, the fort's garrison fluctuated in size between 300 to 800 soldiers and had the unenviable task of maintaining peace in southwest Indian Territory. With assistance from Fort Reno to the north as needed, Fort Sill's small garrison supervised 6,000 to 8,000 Native Americans and frequently encountered difficulties with the Comanches, Kiowas, and Southern Cheyennes who disliked reservation life and resisted assimilation. Many opposed the white man's religion and cattle ranching, which the federal government and assimilationists saw as a middle ground between the nomadic lifestyle of the plains tribes and the desired sedentary yeoman lifestyle of Anglo America. Cattle ranching would be a stage through which the Native Americans would pass on their way to total assimilation into the dominant or white man's culture. Restive portions of these tribes who resisted assimilation raided into Kansas and Texas at will, stole horses and mules, destroyed white settlements, and returned to their sanctuaries in Indian Territory where civil and military authorities could not touch them.[22]

To end the depredations and pacify the region permanently, the US Army launched the Red River Campaign of 1874-1875. From Fort Sill and frontier forts in Texas and New Mexico, columns of troops relentlessly pursued hostile bands of Comanches, Kiowas, and Southern Cheyennes. One column under Lieutenant Colonel John W. Davidson of the 10th Cavalry Regiment operated westward from Fort Sill. Exhausted by the chase, the hostile bands eventually surrendered piecemeal and returned to the reservations to join friendly Native Americans who had not participated in the depredations. The Red River War of 1874-1875, or Indian Territory Campaign as the War Department officially called it, completed the subjugation of the Southern Plains tribes that Sheridan had initiated in 1868-1869 with his three-pronged, winter offensive.[23]

With the conclusion of the Native American wars in Indian Territory when Quanah Parker, an influential Comanche chief and part white by virtue of his white mother, Cynthia Anne Parker, surrendered to the Army in June 1875, Fort Sill assumed the peacetime mission of policing Southwest Indian Territory for the next 26 years. Besides supervising the cattle trails, such as the Chisholm, running from Texas through Indian Territory to the railheads in western Kansas where the cattle were shipped to lucrative eastern markets, Fort Sill troops hunted bands of white outlaws, poachers, whiskey peddlers, and a few renegade Native Americans in an effort to maintain law and order in the lawless land and simultaneously attempted to prevent white settlers and cattlemen from encroaching into western Indian Territory. Perhaps, the post's most glamorous responsibility came with the arrival of Geronimo and his Chiricahua Apaches from Mount Vernon Barracks, Alabama, in October 1894 for confinement as prisoners of war and conversion to the white man's way of life. Under the guidance of Captain Hugh L. Scott, who was sympathetic to their plight and later Chief of Staff of the Army from 1914 to 1917, the Chiricahua Apaches learned to build houses, raise crops, and herd cattle. To accommodate the prisoners of war, the federal government enlarged Fort Sill from its original size of 23,000 acres to 51,400 acres in 1895 by annexing lands from the Kiowas, Comanches, and Kiowa-Apaches with their consent and even promised to make the post the permanent home for the Fort Sill Apaches as the prisoners of war were often called.[24]

As the Chiricahua Apache were slowly adjusting to their new life, national events transformed Fort Sill's mission. Succumbing to pressure to open the Comanche, Kiowa, and Apache reservations to white settlement, Congress sent a commission composed of David H. Jerome, Alfred M. Wilson, and Warren G. Sayre in 1892 to meet with members of the affected tribes to discuss selling a portion of their land to the federal government. Upon hearing the commission's proposal, most of the Native Americans opposed it. However, some, such as Quanah Parker of the Comanches, realized the inevitability of the sale. Led by Stumbling Bear, Big Tree, Poor Buffalo, and Komalty of the Kiowas, White Man and Chewathlanie of the Kiowa-Apaches, and Quanah Parker and White Wolf of the Comanches, the Native Americans entered into tense negotiations with the Jerome Commission. After three days of heated discussions at the Red Store trading complex just to the south of Fort Sill over the selling price and the amount of land to be sold, the Jerome Commission and the Native Americans finally reached an agreement on 6 October 1892 that required Congressional ratification to be effective. Under the terms of the agreement, the federal government would allot 160 acres to each tribal member and would establish a plot of 480,000 acres, called Big Pasture, between present-day Lawton, Oklahoma, and the Red River for the Native Americans to use as they pleased but would be open to leasing by Texas cattlemen. The federal government would also buy surplus reservation land from the tribes and open it to white settlement.[25]

Opposition to the agreement immediately surfaced to stall ratification. Although the adult males of the tribes signed the agreement, they claimed trickery and deceit on the part of the commission and refused to give up their land. Equally important, they insisted that the interpreter, Joshua Givens, had made false or incorrect translations of what they had said and written. Army Captain Hugh L. Scott, a long-time friend and defender of the Native Americans around Fort Sill, James Mooney of the Smithsonian Institution in Washington D.C., and others sympathetic to the Native Americans' cause concurred. Insisting that commissioners had used bribery and fraud to obtain Native American signatures on the agreement, they helped resist ratification. Scott and Mooney soon gained unlikely allies with their own agenda. Powerful ranchers living across the Red River in Texas and holding inexpensive grazing leases on Big Pasture also challenged the agreement because they feared losing their inexpensive leases. Together, the efforts of Scott and the ranchers and the fervent support of Sen. Matt Quay of Pennsylvania obstructed ratification of the agreement for eight years. After Quay died and Scott was sent to Cuba in 1900 to be a part of an occupying military force after the Spanish-American War, Congress approved the agreement in July 1900 to make it effective. As a result, the Comanches, Kiowas, and Apaches received less than a dollar an acre for their lands and rightfully felt cheated.[26]

Ratification set in motion a series of events that culminated in the founding of Lawton in 1901. In keeping with the provisions of the agreement, the federal government made the allotments of land to the Native Americans for personal use, established the Wichita Mountain Reserve of 58,000 acres to the west of Fort Sill, enlarged Fort Sill to 56,000 acres, abolished the grazing leases, and set aside Big Pasture of 480,000 acres for Native American use. Subsequently, Congress passed the Lottery Opening Act of March 1901 as a means of distributing the surplus land. Under the act's provisions, the federal government divided the land into present-day Comanche, Kiowa, and Caddo counties, surveyed the land into 160-acre plots, set aside 320 acres in each county for a county seat that would be surveyed, platted, and subdivided as a town site with lots being sold at auction to pay for courthouses, jails, roads, bridges, and government expenses. Equally important, the act opened the surplus land for white settlement upon a proclamation of the President of the United States. Rather than allowing the settlers to select their land by making a "run" as had been the practice when opening other Native American lands in present-day Oklahoma, the Lottery Opening Act prescribed a lottery to distribute the lands. This would prevent conflicting claims and contests over land as had occurred in the earlier land runs in present-day Oklahoma.[27]

Following the proclamation of 4 July 1901 by President William H. McKinley that opened the reservation to white settlement and divided it into two districts with a land office at El Reno for the northern district and one at Fort Sill for the southern district, homesteaders rushed to both sites to register for the lottery. About 29,000 homesteaders converged on Fort Sill by horse, wagon, buggy, or foot where registration for the south district was scheduled to take place. Upon arriving, they erected a tent city patrolled by Fort Sill soldiers to maintain the peace and waited for the registration and later the drawing. When the land office opened on 10 July 1901, the eager homesteaders formed a line stretching across the post and running out onto the prairie, hoping to get lucky with the land lottery. On 29 July 1901, the drama heightened with the first drawing at El Reno where the Fort Sill registration cards had been delivered. Out of the Fort Sill cylinder, James T. Wood of Weatherford, Oklahoma, was the first name drawn, and the second was Mattie Beal of Wichita, Kansas. Eight days later on 6 August 1901, government officials auctioned off lots in present-day Lawton. Within years, Lawton, named after Major General Henry W. Lawton who had been a quartermaster at Fort Sill years earlier, had earned a Medal of Honor, and had participated in the capture of Geronimo, became a community where cattlemen, traders, gamblers, soldiers, and others mingled and walked the dusty streets, while cultivated fields and fenced pastures quickly replaced open range in southwest Oklahoma. Only Fort Sill with its old stone buildings remained untouched and stood as a link to the past. The opening of Native American lands for white settlement and the subsequent founding of Lawton as the county seat of Comanche County closed an era for Fort Sill. Together, they ended the post's isolation and concluded its responsibilities for policing the frontier.[28]

After being constructed by the US Army in 1869-1870 to bring peace to southwest Indian Territory after years of unrest, Fort Sill served as a frontier post for more than 30 years. After the exhilarating military campaigns of the 1870s had driven the hostile Native Americans, especially the Comanche, Kiowa, and Southern Cheyenne, back onto the reservations in Indian Territory, Fort Sill soldiers settled into monotonous peacekeeping duties and essentially served as giant sheriff's posses chasing outlaws and others who disturbed the peace in the territory. As significant as bringing and maintaining peace to the area were, unfolding international events promised to change Fort Sill's mission.

Notes

1 Edwin C. McReynolds, *Oklahoma: A History of the Sooner State* (Norman, OK: University of Oklahoma Press, 1964), pp. 51-54; Ray M. Billington, *Westward Expansion: A History of the American Frontier* (New York: Macmillan Publishing Company, Inc., 1974), pp. 372-76; Jerome O. Steffen, "William Clark," in Paul A. Hutton, ed., *Soldiers West: Biographies from the Military Frontier* (Lincoln, NB: University of Nebraska Press, 1987), pp. 11-24; see Stephen E. Ambrose's *Undaunted Courage: Meriwether Lewis, Thomas Jefferson, and the Opening of the American West* (New York: Touchstone Books, 1996) for an excellent discussion of the Lewis and Clark expedition.

2 Billington, *Westward Expansion*, pp. 376-77.

3 Billington, *Westward Expansion*, p. 376; Morris Swett, *Fort Sill: A History*, photocopy, (Fort Sill, OK: 1921), p. 1, UF25 H673 S59, Morris Swett Technical Library (MSTL), US Army Field Artillery School; Duane Gage, "Oklahoma: A Resettlement Area for Indians," *Chronicles of Oklahoma*, Autumn 1969, p. 284.

4 Billington, *Westward Expansion*, p. 378; Swett, Fort Sill, p. 1, UF25 H673 S59, MSTL; Roger L. Nichols, "Stephen H. Long," in Paul A. Hutton, ed., *Soldiers West: Biographies from the Military Frontier* (Lincoln, NB: University of Nebraska Press, 1987), pp. 33-35; M. David Stevens, *Lawton-Fort Sill: A Pictorial History* (Norfolk, VA: The Donning Company, 1990), p. 17; Gage, "Oklahoma," p. 285; McReynolds, Oklahoma, pp. 65-68.

5 Billington, *Westward Expansion*, p. 382; McReynolds, *Oklahoma*, pp. 62-65, 72-73; H. Wayne Morgan and Anne Hodges Morgan, *Oklahoma: A Bicentennial History* (New York: W.W. Norton and Company, Inc., 1977), p. 20; Gage, "Oklahoma," p. 291.

6 Morgan and Morgan, *Oklahoma*, pp. 20-21; Billington, *Westward Expansion*, pp. 219-20, 266-67, 273-75, 396; Gage, "Oklahoma," p. 288; McReynolds, *Oklahoma*, pp. 132-33.

7 Gage, "Oklahoma," pp. 290-94; Billington, *Westward Expansion*, pp. 297-316, 396; Morgan and Morgan, *Oklahoma*, pp. 20-29.

8 Billington, *Westward Expansion*, pp. 397-99; Berlin B. Chapman, "Establishment of the Wichita Reservation," *Chronicles of Oklahoma*, Mar-Dec 1933, p. 1044; Gage, "Oklahoma," p. 294; John W. Morris and Edwin C. McReynolds, *Historical Atlas of Oklahoma* (Norman, OK: University of Oklahoma Press, 1965), p. 13; Morgan and Morgan, *Oklahoma*, p. 28; Wilbur S. Nye, *Carbine and Lance: The Story of Old Fort Sill* (Norman, OK: University of Oklahoma Press, 1974), p. 17. See Grant Foreman's *Indian Removal: The Emigration of the Five Civilized Tribes of Indians* (Norman, OK: University of Oklahoma Press, 1972) and Grant Foreman's *The Five Civilized Tribes: Cherokee, Chickasaw, Choctaw, Creek, and Seminole* (Norman, OK: University of Oklahoma Press, 1974) for extensive discussions of the removal of the Five Civilized Tribes to Oklahoma.

9 Nye, *Carbine and Lance*, pp. 7-17; Stevens, Lawton-Fort Sill, pp. 17-19; W.B. Morrison, "Fort Arbuckle," *Chronicles of Oklahoma*, Mar 1928, pp. 26-34.

10 Paul H. Hutton, *Phil Sheridan and His Army* (Lincoln, NE: University of Nebraska Press, 1985), pp. 29-30; Jerome A. Greene, *Washita: The US Army and the Southern Cheyennes, 1867-1869* (Norman, OK: University of Oklahoma Press, 2004), pp. 3-24, 34-37. For more on the Sand Creek Massacre, see Reginald S. Craig's *The Fighting Parson: The Biography of Colonel John M. Chivington* (Los Angeles: Westernlore Press, 1959). This book is a sympathetic interpretation of Chivington and his role in the Sand Creek Massacre.

11 Greene, *Washita*, p. 37. The Indian Removal Act of 1830 gave the President of the United States authority to designate specific lands as Indian Territory for the Native Americans that were being removed from their homelands in southeastern United States. Initially, Indian Territory

included present-day Oklahoma, Kansas, and Nebraska. With the creation of the territories of Kansas and Nebraska in 1854, only Oklahoma remained as Indian Territory. As white settlers moved onto the Southern Great Plains during the four decades after the Civil War, pressure mounted to open Indian Territory for white settlement. The federal government finally opened Indian Territory to white settlers through a series of land runs between 1889 and 1901 and created the state of Oklahoma in 1907. Initially, Indian Territory was the home to the Five Civilized Tribes (Cherokee, Creek, Seminole, Choctaw, and Chickasaw) from the southeastern United States. Eventually, the federal government moved other tribes from their homelands into Indian Territory to make room for the expanding white population.

12 Greene, *Washita*, pp. 37-38; Hutton, *Sheridan and His Army*, pp. 33-34; Gillette Griswold, "Fort Sill, Oklahoma: A Brief History," unpublished manuscript, pp. 2-3, in Historical Research and Document Collection (HRDC) Field Artillery Branch Historian's Office, US Army Field Artillery School; Andrew Denson, "Unite With Us to Rescue the Kiowas: The Five Civilized Tribes and Warfare on the Southern Plains," *The Chronicles of Oklahoma*, Winter 2003-04, pp. 458-79; Nye, *Carbine and Lance*, p. 45

13 Denson, "Unite with Us to Rescue the Kiowas," pp. 458-60; Greene, *Washita*, pp. 38-41.

14 Greene, *Washita*, pp. 43-76; Hutton, *Phil Sheridan and His Army*, pp. 41-53; Nye, *Carbine and Lance*, pp. 55-58; Denson, "Unite with Us to Rescue the Kiowas," p. 460; Stan Hoig, T*he Battle of the Washita: The Sheridan-Custer Indian Campaign of 1867-69* (Lincoln, NE: University of Nebraska Press, 1976), pp. 74, 75, 86, 87.

15 Greene, *Washita*, pp. 117-62; Hutton, *Phil Sheridan and His Army*, pp. 56-76, 80-90; Nye, *Carbine and Lance*, pp. 51-54, 59-78, 84-89, 100.

16 Hutton, *Phil Sheridan and His Army*, pp. 56-76, 80-90; Stevens, *Lawton-Fort Sill*, pp. 3-4; Nye, *Carbine and Lance*, pp. 51-54, 59-78, 84-89, 100.

17 Hoig, *The Battle of the Washita*, pp. 74-75, 168.

18 Hutton, *Phil Sheridan and His Army*, pp. 90-91; Greene, *Washita*, p. 54.

19 Hutton, *Phil Sheridan and His Army*, pp. 100-01; Nye, *Carbine and Lance*, p. 100.

20 "A Brief History of Fort Sill and the Field Artillery School," *Field Artillery Journal*, Nov-Dec 1933, pp. 528-29; Nye, Carbine and Lance, pp. 101, 105.

21 McReynolds, *Oklahoma*, pp. 170, 214, 256; Nye, *Carbine and Lance*, p. 55; Gillette Griswold, "Fort Sill, Oklahoma," unpublished manuscript, p. 5, HRDC; Riley Sunderland, *History of the Field Artillery School: 1911-1942* (Fort Sill, OK: Fort Sill Printing Plant, 1942), p. 31; "A Brief History of Fort Sill and the Field Artillery School," pp. 528-29.

22 "A Brief History of Fort Sill and the Field Artillery School," pp. 528-29; Todd Leahy, "Beef Instead of Bayonets: Cultural Mores and the Failure of Assimilation on the Kiowa-Comanche Reservation," *The Chronicles of Oklahoma*, Winter 2005-2006, pp. 490-99.

23 Hutton, *Phil Sheridan and His Army*, pp. 245-261; "A Brief History of Fort Sill and the Field Artillery School," p. 530; Griswold, "Fort Sill, Oklahoma," pp. 3-9, HRDC; See Nye's *Carbine and Lance* for a full discussion of early Fort Sill and William H. Leckie's *The Buffalo Soldier: A Narrative of the Negro Cavalry in the West* (1967) for a solid account of African-American soldiers at Fort Sill.

24 Nye, *Carbine and Lance*, p. 298; Griswold, "Fort Sill, Oklahoma," p. 9, HRDC; Brenda L. Haes, "Fort Sill, The Chiricahua Apaches, and the Government's Promise of Permanent Residence," *The Chronicles of Oklahoma*, Spring 2000, pp. 28-43; "A Brief History of Fort Sill and the Field Artillery School," p. 534; H. Henrietta Stockel, *Shame and Endurance: The Untold Story of the*

Chiricahua Apache Prisoners of War (Tucson, AZ: The University of Arizona Press, 2004), pp. 101-53. See John A. Turcheneske's *The Chiricahua Apache Prisoners of War: Fort Sill, 1894-1914* (1997) for a penetrating, in-depth analysis of the Apache prisoners of war.

    25 Monta Rae Collins, "The History of the City of Lawton, Oklahoma," unpublished master's thesis, University of Oklahoma, 1941, p. 8; Joe Looney and Vivian Wilson Looney, *The History of Comanche County, Oklahoma* (Lawton, OK: Southwest Genealogical Society, 1985), pp. 17-18; Arthur R. Lawrence, *Lawton: A Golden Anniversary, 1901-1951* (Lawton, OK: Arthur R. Lawrence, 1951), p. 4; Leahy, "Beef Instead of Bayonets," pp. 490-99.

    26 Collins, "History of the City of Lawton, Oklahoma," p. 8; Looney and Looney, *The History of Comanche County, Oklahoma*, p. 18; Nye, *Carbine and Lance*, pp. 303-04; Lawrence, *Lawton: A Golden Anniversary*, p. 4.

    27 Collins, "History of the City of Lawton, Oklahoma," pp. 8-12; Nye, *Carbine and Lance*, p. 304; Looney and Looney, *The History of Comanche County, Oklahoma*, p. 19.

    28 McReynolds, *Oklahoma*, pp. 304-05; Collins, "A History of Lawton, Oklahoma," pp. 12-25; Looney and Looney, *The History of Comanche County, Oklahoma*, pp. 20-21; Nye, *Carbine and Lance*, pp. 304-07; Noel Edwards, "Some Facts about Lawton, Oklahoma," ca. 1902, pp. 1-14, Lawton Public Library; MG Robert M. Danford, "Morris S. Simpson," *Field Artillery Journal*, Nov-Dec 1944, pp. 765-67.

Chapter Two
A New Mission

Following the opening of western Indian Territory to white settlement in 1901, Fort Sill converted from a cavalry post to a field artillery post during the first decade of the 20th century. Although the first field artillery unit arrived at Fort Sill in 1902 and the last cavalry unit left in 1907, the transition from one branch to another culminated when the War Department created the School of Fire for Field Artillery in 1911 to train field artillerymen in the latest techniques of their branch that were growing more sophisticated with the introduction of new weapons and indirect fire. Captain Dan T. Moore, the school's first commandant, and his successor, Lieutenant Colonel Edward L. McGlachlin, overcame insufficient funding by the War Department, instructor and staff shortages, and inadequate facilities to produce competent field artillerymen and to lay the foundation for future growth.

The School of Fire for Field Artillery

Pressured by the United States' expanding commercial interests throughout the world and its newly acquired overseas possessions following the Spanish-American War and influenced by the intensifying imperial rivalries among European countries over colonies in the first decade of the 20th century, the War Department faced the imperative of transforming its Army. It had to convert the Army from a frontier constabulary to an armed force capable of fighting on the modern battlefield. To do this, the War Department confronted the necessity of eliminating the long-standing division of command between the Commanding General and the Secretary of War that had existed through most of the 19th century and that had been so disruptive during the Spanish-American War. While the Commanding General exercised discipline and control over the troops, the Secretary of War provided administrative support and supervised fiscal matters through the military bureau chiefs. Secretary of War Elihu Root, who was appointed to this office in 1899 to institute reforms, wanted to establish a chief of staff and general staff and to reduce the independence of the War Department's bureau chiefs. At Root's recommendation, Congress overcame some die-hard opposition in 1903 when it created the Chief of Staff to replace the Commanding General and to serve as the chief army advisor to the President of the United States through the Secretary of War and organized a general staff to prepare war plans, make policy, and make the War Department more efficient and attune to the 20th century. However, Congress retained some of the bureaus, such as the Adjutant General. Although hostility to the reforms existed for several years, the newly organized general staff issued the Army's first field service regulations in 1905 to govern and organize troops in the field, drew up plans for an expeditionary force to be sent to Cuba in 1906, designed plans for three permanent divisions composed of Regular Army and National Guard regiments in 1910 that were never formed because troubles on the Mexican border led to the creation of temporary divisions in 1911, and equipped the Army with state-of-the-art weapons and equipment for combat on the modern battlefield.[1]

Equally important, the War Department introduced a comprehensive, sequential education system that ran from the garrison schools to the Army War College to raise the standards of professional training of officers. In 1901, the War Department directed that the educational system for officers would be the US Military Academy at West Point, a school at each post for elementary instruction in theory and practice, five service schools (the Artillery School, the Engineer School of Application, the School of Antisubmarine Defense, the School of Application for Cavalry and Field Artillery, and the Army Medical School), the General Staff and Service College, and the Army War College. As the requirement for specialized training grew with the introduction of new weapons and equipment, the War Department opened the Signal School in 1905, the School of Fire for Field Artillery in 1911, and the School of Musketry in 1913.[2]

Organizing the School of Fire for Field Artillery capped the changes in the Field Artillery that had been underway for several years. A Congressional act of February 1901 expanded the Infantry from 25 to 30 regiments and dissolved the Artillery's regimental organization that had been in place since the Reorganization of 1821, which mixed coast and field artillery units together in the same regiment and rotated officers between the two artilleries. The 1901 act established an Artillery Corps of Coast Artillery with 126 companies and Field Artillery with 30 batteries that included field, mountain, and horse batteries under a Chief of Artillery and to serve on the Army General Staff with Brigadier General William F. Randolph being the first chief. Yet, the act failed to divorce the Field Artillery from the Coast Artillery totally and preserved the wasteful practice of rotating officers between two artilleries that had no tactical relationship with each other. This hurt both branches by hindering the efficiency of either and produced a generic artillery officer just at the time that field artillery and coast artillery technology was growing more sophisticated and different from each other.[3]

Although the first field artillery unit, the 29th Field Artillery Battery, organized in Havana, Cuba, in 1901 with Captain Edward E. Gayle as commander in response to the Congressional act of February 1901, transferred to Fort Sill on 9 January 1902 and initiated the slow process of converting the post from a cavalry to a field artillery installation, a more significant development came several years later.[4] Impressed with Fort Sill's size and varied terrain that was suitable for field artillery training, Lieutenant General Adna R. Chaffee, the Chief of Staff of the Army, decided early in 1905 to station a provisional field artillery regiment of two battalions there. Under the command of Colonel Walter Howe, the provisional regiment would consist of the 2d, 8th, 13th, 14th, 15th, and 21st batteries of field artillery and would have the mission of training officers and enlisted personnel in the latest field artillery tactics and techniques, meaning indirect fire. The regiment's first units arrived on 29 June 1905 and established a camp where Colonel (Brevet Major General) Benjamin H. Grierson's 10th Cavalry Regiment had camped in 1868 and 1869. Economy measures unfortunately caused the War Department to disband the regiment along with its fellow provisional field artillery regiment at Fort Riley, Kansas, in November 1905.[5]

Notwithstanding this decision, the War Department's endeavor to modernize its combat forces to fight a European-style enemy carried on and eventually led to creating the Field Artillery on a permanent basis. In 1904, the Chief of Artillery, Brigadier General

Joseph P. Story, urged forming the Field Artillery into permanent battalions and regiments during peacetime. By doing this, the Field Artillery could support the Infantry and Cavalry on the mobile battlefield more effectively and could eliminate the striking organizational deficiencies highlighted during the Spanish-American War when the War Department could only muster a provisional battalion of four field batteries equipped with obsolete equipment for combat duty in Cuba.[6] In his annual report for 1904, Story emphatically noted, "Divisions, corps, and armies should have their chiefs of artillery, who should be in actual command of all of their field artillery, and they should be provided with adequate staffs. . . . Field Artillery should in time of peace be organized into tactical units" to prepare for war.[7] In an even more trenchant indictment about the inadequate state of preparedness and the need for reforming the Field Artillery, Story added, "There is no first-class power which has so systematically neglected its field artillery as the United States."[8]

Echoing these sentiments and going one step further, Story's successor, Brigadier General Arthur Murray, discussed the differing missions of the two artilleries. He explained in 1906 that the Coast Artillery existed solely for harbor defense and had no tactical relation to the "active forces of infantry, cavalry, or field artillery, the three fighting elements of a mobile army."[9] Murray advised the War Department, "It is a sound military principle that only such arms of the service as have a fighting or tactical relation with each other should be combined for organization purposes."[10] Both generals concurred that the Field Artillery and the Coast Artillery should be separated because they had entirely different tactical missions and needs.[11]

After much prodding by concerned officers in the War Department, especially Story and Murray, Congress finally acknowledged the differences between the two artilleries and took appropriate action. On 25 January 1907, a Congressional act separated the Coast Artillery and the Field Artillery into independent branches. The act permitted establishing permanent field artillery regiments and battalions; allowed the War Department to develop officers, noncommissioned officers, and enlisted personnel with field artillery expertise; and ended the damaging policy of rotating personnel between the two artilleries.[12]

Several months later, the Field Artillery became a reality. War Department General Orders No. 118 of 31 May 1907 formed the Field Artillery into six regiments (three mounted, two mountain, and one horse) of two battalions each. With the passage of the January 1907 act and the subsequent War Department General Orders of 31 May 1907, the Field Artillery achieved a new status within the War Department by becoming an official combat arms branch. Before, it had been subordinate to the Coast Artillery that had received most of the money and attention because it defended the country's vulnerable harbors against enemy naval attacks.[13]

The separation of the two artilleries directly influenced Fort Sill. In May 1907, the Chief of Staff of the Army, Major General J. Franklin Bell (1906-1910), moved the last cavalry regiment (13th Cavalry Regiment) from Fort Sill and replaced it with the 1st Field Artillery Regiment that had been created after the separation. Transferring the last cavalry unit to another post and concentrating the 1st Field Artillery Regiment at Fort Sill in June 1907 eliminated the last vestiges of the frontier army and started the process of turning the post into a home for field artillery.[14]

To accommodate the field artillery regiment and to fulfill his desire to make Fort Sill into a brigade or division post but not solely a field artillery post as part of the overall drive to modernize, Bell outlined an ambitious construction program. He contemplated spending $20 million to make Fort Sill a military show place for the country and envisioned building new facilities along the south boundary of the reservation as far west as Signal Mountain. Bell also wanted to build an electric railroad between Lawton and the post, to construct a hotel atop Signal Mountain, and to tear down the old limestone buildings erected by the 10th Cavalry Regiment in the 1870s. As might be expected, Bell met stiff resistance from romantics, including Secretary of War William H. Taft, when he suggested razing Fort Sill's historic limestone buildings. Although Taft and his fellow idealists supported modernizing and expanding Fort Sill, they wanted to maintain the limestone buildings as a memorial of the post's frontier days. Taft even visited the post and then decided to retain the limestone buildings.[15]

Influenced by Taft and preservationists and based upon a report by the Corps of Engineers that opposed expanding the post along its southern boundary where the soldiers would have easy access to whiskey peddlers and other unsavory people from the neighboring town of Lawton, Bell picked a more isolated location for his post. Erected on the 1869 site of Custer's 7th Cavalry Regiment's parade ground about one mile to the west of the original post, New Post as it was called to distinguish it from the original post, now known as Old Post where the old limestone buildings stood, consisted of brick and concrete buildings. Construction began in 1909 and was completed in 1911.[16]

As critical as the arrival of the 1st Field Artillery Regiment and the construction of New Post were, the opening of the School of Fire for Field Artillery on 15 September 1911 played an even more pivotal role of moving the post away from its cavalry roots and into the 20th century. The separation of the Coast Artillery and the Field Artillery in 1907 deprived field artillerymen of desperately needed formal training on sophisticated weapons that were being introduced and new gunnery techniques. Through 1906, field artillery and coast artillery personnel received formal training at the Artillery School, Fortress Monroe, Virginia, where they pointed their field artillery pieces out into the ocean and aimed at floating barrels employing direct fire techniques. This training, even though it was rudimentary and better than none, met the requirements for training field artillerymen to employ direct fire and to engage immobile objects. Anticipating a separation of the two artilleries in the near future and recognizing that the Field Artillery and Coast Artillery were actually two different branches with dissimilar missions, the Artillery School, renamed the Coast Artillery School in 1907 to reflect its new orientation, eliminated all field artillery training from its curriculum in 1906 and focused its attention on training coast artillerymen on the latest coast artillery tactics and techniques.[17]

This restructured curriculum at the Coast Artillery School, the creation of two independent artilleries in 1907, the adoption of sophisticated field artillery weapons, the push to introduce indirect fire that was slowly replacing direct fire, and poor gunnery scores by field artillerymen reinforced the requirement for field artillery training. Not even the Mounted Service School at Fort Riley, Kansas, created by the War Department in 1907 to replace the ineffective School of Practice for Cavalry and Field Artillery at Fort Riley that had opened in 1892 and operated under several names over the years with the mission of teaching equitation and field artillery tactics, filled the void created by the Coast Artillery School's decision to furnish coast artillery instruction exclusively. The Fort Riley schools failed to train field artillerymen because they stressed equitation at the expense of field artillery instruction. Created by the War Department in 1902 to train lieutenants and captains, to replace the ineffective post lyceums, and to serve as the foundation of a progressive education system, the garrison schools with their emphasis on rote memorization, military discipline, military administration, and theoretical instruction also fell short in developing trained field artillerymen. Basically, the War Department did not have a formal institution to pick up the slack of training field artillerymen after 1907.[18]

Congressional fiscal thriftiness also influenced the quality of field artillery training. Although the War Department was abandoning its small garrisons in the makeshift forts built during the campaigns in the Trans-Mississippi West against the Native Americans in the later decades of 19th century and concentrating its forces in large numbers, advocating professional education, modernizing its equipment, and creating a general staff, limited Congressional funding restricted the impact of the educational and training reforms and led to ammunition shortages to curtail firing practice for field artillerymen.[19]

Commenting upon this state of training for field artillerymen, an anonymous writer in the *Field Artillery Journal* lamented. He wrote in mid-1911:

> We now have schools of many kinds, but none for the field artillery. We even have a school of musketry. . . There is no school of fire. . . Such a school is needed not to teach the enlisted men how to shoot, but to teach the officers the observation and application of the fire of their batteries.[20]

Without the availability of standardized technical and tactical training at a school of fire of some kind, this writer and other concerned field artillery officers understood that their branch's future was at risk. Field artillerymen would have difficulties acquiring the requisite skills to operate the new weapons, to employ indirect fire, and to fight on the new battlefield; and the shortcomings with the Field Artillery highlighted by the Spanish-American War would persist.[21]

An editorial in the *Field Artillery Journal* of July-September 1915 also recalled the dire situation of the Field Artillery during the first decade of the 20th century. It pointed out:

> The technical training of our field artillery officers depended entirely upon chance. Some officers had no training at all. . . . Others were fortunate enough to serve under superiors who were able and willing to impart the knowledge which they themselves had acquired solely through their own efforts. But there was no system whatsoever. It was apparently a matter of indifference to the War Department whether the field artillery was able to make good use of its materiel or not.[22]

As this editorial emphatically reinforced, field artillerymen lacked suitable training to make them competent on the modern battlefield as it existed at the time and learned their trade by happenstance. Although field artillery units were consolidated into six regiments after 1907, the small branch was still scattered over 10 posts across the continental United States that were generally commanded by an infantry or cavalry officer who had little interest or knowledge in field artillery issues and centered their energies on parade ground drill and other time-consuming duties that were irrelevant to combat. Only the 6th Field Artillery Regiment at Fort Riley with all of its units stationed at one post published an annual training schedule for its two battalions. With the exception of the 6th Field Artillery Regiment, field artillerymen rarely trained in units larger than the battery and never learned the techniques of employing indirect fire. Not even the 6th Field Artillery Regiment and the leading field artillery intellectuals of the time, such as Captain William J. Snow who later became the Chief of Field Artillery (1918-1927) and Captain Fox Conner who later served as the chief of the Operations Section of the General Headquarters, American Expeditionary Force in World War I and was a brilliant student of warfare, stressed indirect fire techniques. They emphasized fighting in the open by employing direct fire even though they understood the revolutionary nature of indirect fire and the compelling need to adopt it.[23]

Major General William J. Snow
Chief of Field Artillery
1918-1927

Such circumstances led to action. In 1908, the Chief of Coast Artillery, Major General Arthur Murray, recommended creating a school of fire for field artillery. It would fill the void created by the separation of the two artilleries and teach modern field artillery fire direction techniques more thoroughly than conditions at the time allowed. About the same time, President Theodore Roosevelt and a group of progressive field artillery officers, including Major William J. Lassiter who was detailed as a field artillery officer to the Inspector General's Office, took up the banner of reform. They criticized the Field Artillery's poor performance in the Spanish-American War and backwardness compared to its counterparts in foreign armies and also understood the serious limitations of field artillery training of the time. If the War Department wanted to stay abreast of foreign armies in an age characterized by growing imperial rivalries over colonies that could easily erupt into a major war, it required trained field artillerymen to support the other combat arms on the mobile battlefield. This demanded formal training and a large military installation with sufficient space for target practice and field maneuvers.[24]

At President Roosevelt's direction, the War Department sent Captain Dan T. Moore of the 6th Field Artillery Regiment, who was educated in Switzerland and Germany and was a former aide to the President, to Europe in 1908-1909 to observe how the Europeans trained their field artillery officers and enlisted personnel. During those years, he visited field artillery schools in Austria, Hungary, Holland, England, and Italy and actually studied at the German Field Artillery School at Juterborg.[25] The German field artillery school especially impressed Moore. It taught officers how to shoot, developed and improved methods of fire, tested new material, and emphasized practical firing and tactical exercises, among other things. Moreover, the Prussians founded their school under circumstances replicating those in the American army of the early 20th century. New rifled, breech-loading field artillery appearing in the 1850s and 1860s and the poor performance of Prussian field artillery in the Austro-Prussian War of 1866 had prodded the Prussians to open the Juterborg school in 1867. Likewise, the appearance of new weapons, the existence of inadequately trained field artillerymen, the disappointing performance of field artillery units in the Spanish-American War, and the introduction of indirect fire demanded the formation of a field artillery school in the United States.[26]

Captain Dan T. Moore
Field Artillery School Commandant
19 Jul 1911-15 Sep 1914

Using the German field artillery school as a model and acting under the direction of Colonel Edwin St. Greble of the Office of the Chief of Staff in the War Department, headed by Major General Leonard Wood, Moore traveled to Fort Sill in November 1910 to begin laying the foundation for a field artillery school at the isolated Oklahoma post. Although the War Department was still considering other sites for a school, Fort Sill favorably impressed Moore as it had done Murray several years earlier in 1906. The post's wide expanse of land and varied terrain provided sufficient room for target practice and the tactical handling of field artillery. Along with the area's mild climate that would permit training all year, these factors led Moore to determine that Fort Sill would be worth its cost many times over to the government. As part of a board composed of Lieutenant Colonel D. J. Rumbaugh of the 1st Field Artillery Regiment who was replaced by Colonel Henry M. Andrews of the 1st Field Artillery Regiment in March 1911 and Captain Jesse Langdon of the 1st Field Artillery Regiment, Moore started drafting a concept plan for a field artillery school at Fort Sill in January 1911.[27]

Critical obstacles soon raised the issue about the suitability of the post. As of 1911, Chiricahua Apache prisoners of war occupied much of the post. They grazed cattle on the proposed firing ranges.[28] Apprehensive about this potentially dangerous situation and a conflict with the Chiricahua Apaches, Moore frequently wrote St. Greble, seeking consolation and guidance.[29] On 16 March 1911 Moore explained, "[Chiricahua Apache] villages are now scattered in such a way that many miles of the reservation cannot be used for target practice without shooting over or near one of them."[30] Also, the Chiricahua Apache cattle wandered freely around the post, trampled gardens and lawns, and even tipped over garbage cans.[31] Acknowledging this, the Adjutant General of the War Department, Major General Fred C. Ainsworth, refused to give permission to develop firing ranges on Fort Sill unless the "lives and property" of the Chiricahuas' were protected; and this position presented a serious barrier to surmount.[32]

Thus, in the eyes of Moore, the War Department wanted to use Fort Sill for two contradictory purposes, prompting him to propose a solution. The War Department desired to open a school of fire for field artillery there, while maintaining Chiricahua Apaches on the same land. To overcome this, Moore suggested setting aside a certain amount of land for the Native Americans for farming and grazing their cattle and dedicating the rest of the land for military purposes. As Moore conceded, this proposal would force the Native Americans to reduce the size of their cattle herd because grazing and growing hay for feed for the winter months would be seriously restricted by the reduction in the amount of available land and would mean eventual relocation. This solution basically split Fort Sill into two areas. While one would be set aside for military use, the other would be occupied and used by the Native Americans.[33]

Moore noted another serious drawback in establishing the school at Fort Sill.[34] During the dry season in the summer months, conducting target practice would be impossible without setting fire to the prairie grass that would easily burn out of control. He spelled out vividly, "These fires would cause more damage to the Indians indirectly, than any other cause, by burning up the feed of their cattle."[35] Interestingly, the Chiricahua Apaches cut and baled hay for income; and the fires caused by field artillery projectiles would potentially reduce their income. In fact, the Chiricahua Apaches cut and baled publicly-owned hay and sold it to the government. The government then issued the same hay back to the Native Americans for free to feed their stock.[36]

Notwithstanding the possibility of field artillery target practice setting fire to acres of hay, the thorny and controversial hay business, and the existence of Native Americans on the post, Moore championed establishing a field artillery school on Fort Sill because its size and varied terrain outweighed the installation's limitations. On 17 March 1911 he pleaded, "This is such a magnificent reservation for artillery work that it would be a shame to lose it — so we have to just got to get the matter fixed up in some way."[37]

In a letter dated 23 March 1911, St. Greble responded to Moore's concerns. "The War Department will probably decide what is to be done with the Apache prisoners and I think that they will probably be removed from the reservation," he advised.[38] This would eventually eliminate one worry. Trying to provide a perspective, St. Greble then added that Native Americans' property rights and lives had been protected in the past and that ways to safeguard them in the future could be found. He failed to acknowledge that field artillery firing practice had been nonexistent before the arrival of field artillery units at the beginning of the century with their requirements for ranges. Thus, protecting property and lives had been relatively easy when Fort Sill had been a cavalry post and when the need for large firing ranges was nonexistent.[39] Addressing the anxiety about fire, St. Greble added, "In firing you can easily prevent fires by cutting the grass on the zones which you will use or by back burning it."[40]

Such words undoubtedly reassured Moore about the future of the school at Fort Sill but at the same time informed him that he would have to work around the Native Americans at least temporarily until the War Department could decide what to do with them. In view of this, Moore decided to confine the firing ranges to south of Medicine Creek and west of the railroad tracks to minimize contact between the Chiricahua Apaches and the Army. This reduced the number of firing positions available to the students and had the potential of downgrading the quality of the instruction at the same time. Essentially, this decision restricted a portion of Fort Sill to military uses and further strengthened the War Department's determination to move the Chiricahua Apaches off the post.[41]

With these issues being resolved at least for the time being, Moore and the rest of the board pressed forward with developing the school. As they battled funding constraints established by the War Department in an era of limited Congressional budgets for the military, Moore and his colleagues encountered another critical problem that overshadowed the challenge presented by the Native Americans and the potential of fire and that threatened to prevent opening the school at Fort Sill.[42] The post lacked sufficient water to support the anticipated expanded operations, especially during a drought.[43] Writing St. Greble on 14 June 1911, Moore commented, "The question that is worrying me, is whether or not we are going to have enough water for the needs of the School, and whether under the present conditions it is advisable to establish it here at considerable expense to the Government with the possibility of having to abandon the whole plant on account of lack of water."[44] Moore wrote four days later, "We cannot count on getting more than 40,000 gallons a day from every available source, and I believe that this is a large estimate."[45] Reflecting upon the serious predicament, Moore even suggested curtailing the size of the garrison to support the school and dropping all plans for assembling the 5th Field Artillery Regiment at Fort Sill to support training.[46]

From Moore's perspective, the neighboring City of Lawton contributed to the water shortage. Shortly after it had been founded in 1901, the city constructed a dam on Medicine Bluff Creek for a source of water and obtained permission from the War Department to build a pipeline across Fort Sill to carry water from the artificial lake, Lake Lawtonka, created by the dam, to the city. Unfortunately, the dam greatly lowered the level of the creek. In fact, Moore wrote St. Greble on 29 June 1911, "Medicine Creek is now dry and has been for two years."[47] Moore commented that the fort's water supply would remain critical until the rain and runoff had filled the dam and caused it to overflow.[48]

To aggravate matters even more, the owners of Medicine Park to the north of Fort Sill erected two dams across the Medicine Creek for bathing and boating even though state laws prohibited private citizens from building dams on streams.[49] This further decreased the flow of the creek and prevented Fort Sill from benefiting from "all of our own water shed," according to Moore.[50] Without these dams Fort Sill would have plenty of water, and furnishing water for the additional personnel required to staff the School of Fire for Field Artillery would be easy. Fortunately, Fort Sill found a solution. It started borrowing water from Lawton's 10-inch pipeline and drawing water from old wells. Although the shortage still existed, the school could at least open with sufficient water to support operations. Later in the summer, runoff nearly filled Lake Lawtonka to improve the water situation.[51]

Against this difficult backdrop, Moore expressed his thoughts about the significance of the school. On 25 May 1911 he penned, "On the other hand all you can expect is value received for your money, and this I claim the School will give, not only to us field artillerymen but to the army at large."[52] He wrote:

> I say the army at large, because in event of war the Infantry and Cavalry will be the ones that will pay in blood for the mistakes made by our arm, through the lack of opportunity [training] given to its officers. A field artillery captain who cannot direct the fire of his battery is a useless impedimenta to any army, and the worst point is that the other fellow, generally the infantry men, pay for his mistakes.[53]

As his missive to St. Greble clearly noted, Moore understood the importance of fire support in combined arms warfare, the challenge of teaching officers and soldiers indirect fire, and the requirement for tactically and technically competent field artillerymen. Without qualified officers the Field Artillery would have difficulties supporting the Infantry and Cavalry on the modern battlefield, and countless number of lives would be needlessly lost. In view of recent European and American wars, growing international rivalries over colonies, and the emergence of the United States as a significant economic power and a challenger to European dominance throughout the world, the War Department could ill afford to cling to the old haphazard ways of training field artillerymen. It had to develop competent and efficient officers and enlisted soldiers, in this case, field artillerymen, in peacetime to keep abreast of foreign military developments. The Europeans, the Russians, and the Japanese were busily training their armies in the latest techniques, tactics, and procedures and adopting state-of-the-art lethal weapons and equipment. In view of the arms race, the United States could not fall further behind militarily. Thus, in Moore's mind, a field artillery school at Fort Sill was important and could not be dismissed as a luxury. Improvements in modernizing American field guns and howitzers with their attending limbers and caissons, which were generally as good as their European counterparts, compelled developing skilled field artillerymen.[54] Given this scenario and his understanding of American strategic interests, Moore assumed personal responsibility for the school's success.[55] On 3 June 1911 Moore wrote St. Greble, "I now feel that the School is well started and that if we do not succeed it will be our own fault."[56]

To produce officers and enlisted personnel that could furnish fire support required obtaining a capable staff and faculty for the School of Fire. On 30 March 1911, Moore composed a letter to St. Greble about the need for an African-American detachment to serve as mounted orderlies and janitors. In that same communiqué, Moore explained the necessity for a white detachment to serve as blacksmiths, mechanics, carpenters, and painters and to operate the target ranges.[57] Over the next several weeks, Moore repeatedly urged the War Department to detail the most capable officers to the school to serve as instructors and commanders of the instruction batteries.[58]

On 10 April 1911, St. Greble answered one of Moore's initial queries about personnel. "Your scheme for the personnel would be beautiful if you know of any way by which you can get them: I do not unless Congress will legislate in the matter," St. Greble impatiently retorted.[59] He then sarcastically suggested getting the President of the United States to authorize increasing the strengths of field batteries to create a surplus that could be drawn upon to fill the school's staff and faculty and observed that the War Department would probably not approve of Moore's list of desired officers anyway.[60]

Early on, obtaining qualified personnel for the school staff, faculty, and instruction batteries to support and train the students posed a vexing problem for Moore as St. Greble's comments suggested. In 1911, the Army had fewer than 300 field artillery officers; everyone had to be utilized to the best advantage. Using officers as instructors did not seem to be wise because the War Department had a shortage of officers and enlisted personnel. Sending people to staff the school, even though the War Department wanted to do so, meant stripping them from operational units and intensifying existing personnel shortages in field batteries and battalions. This certainly was not a desired end-state for the operational force and meant sacrificing it for the training institution.[61]

In spite of the Army-wide personnel shortages, Moore continually pressed the urgency of staffing the school with proficient officers and encountered stiff opposition from the War Department.[62] In correspondence with the War Department on 3 June 1911, Moore recommended specific officers for duty as a detachment commander and instructors in the school. He wanted First Lieutenant Ralph M. Pennell to command the school detachment and to direct the target department.[63] As permitted by the Army Appropriation Act of 1909 and War Department general orders, the War Department authorized forming school detachments to support training, but shortages of personnel forbade sending the desired officers.[64] The War Department approved only one of his requests when it agreed that Pennell could serve as the school's secretary and even recommended having him serve as a battery commander at the same time as an economy measure.[65]

Moore found the War Department's actions to be unacceptable and complained. In a stinging letter of criticism to St. Greble on 18 June 1911, Moore wrote, "Your letter of June 14th just received, and evidentally (sic) we have been working at cross purposes as far as the Captains of the instruction batteries are concerned."[66] Moore persisted passionately, "What I want is men placed in command of these organizations, who are efficient as they can be. You must realize that the success of this School is going to depend in great part upon the efficiency of the instruction batteries."[67] As far as Moore was concerned, the officers sent so far simply failed to meet his high standards for competency and jeopardized the school's training mission, causing him to ask the War Department for his choices once again. He desired Captain Louis T. Boiseau and Captain Fred T. Austin who later became a major general and the Chief of the Field Artillery in 1927-1930 as instructors.[68]

Failing to get these two officers, Moore again wrote St. Greble on 28 July 1911 about the low caliber of the ones detailed to the school. He complained, "One of the present captains [of the instruction batteries] who has had his battery for over four years does not know what a bracket is and has absolutly (sic) no idea as to how the fire of a battery should be conducted."[69] Acknowledging that the shortage of officers hindered getting highly qualified officers as instructors, Moore finally resigned himself to the dire situation and resolved to make unskilled officers competent.[70]

Finding quality people for the instruction batteries proved to be no less challenging. In a letter to St. Greble on 8 August 1911, Moore lamented that A and B Batteries of the 5th Field Artillery Regiment were untrained and composed of new recruits when they arrived at Fort Sill on 8 July 1911.[71] In that same communication Moore described them as being "mobs" that had to be whipped into shape by 15 September 1911 when the first class started.[72] Moore then grumbled, "The men . . . have never fired the guns before and were therefore gun shy and nervous, and the officers although they attended practice before were practically ignorant of the prescribed methods of conducting fire."[73] In view of the significance that he attached to the school and the role that it should play in modernizing the field army, especially the Field Artillery, Moore resented receiving untrained and incompetent officers and soldiers as school cadre and being forced to train them.[74]

As his correspondence to St. Greble during the months prior to September 1911 implied, Moore faced seemingly insurmountable odds. The post lacked sufficient water to support the additional personnel required to operate the school and had Chiricahua Apaches and their cattle occupying much of the post, restricting the land available for firing ranges. On top of this, the poor quality of the officers and enlisted personnel being sent to serve in the instruction batteries and the shortages of ammunition and equipment added to Moore's frustration and threatened to delay opening the school or to prevent it from opening at all. Responding to the gloomy situation, feeling the pressure to succeed, and fearing failure, he wrote St. Greble on 8 August 1911, "If it [the school] is not a success they [War Department and field artillery officers] are going to cuss me out in chorus. . . . If they [instruction batteries] are not trained and able to deliver the goods by September 15th, yours truly will get it where the chicken got the ax."[75] Moore questioned the ability of the school to thrive under such difficult circumstances and feared failure and stinging criticism from his peers and superiors. Nothing so far pointed toward success.[76]

Undoubtedly, the War Department's fiscal thriftiness during an era of limited congressional budgets for the military contributed to Moore's problems. In Moore's view, the War Department had to spend more money to obtain the proper facilities and equipment to support effective training. Also, the limited funding created a shortage of qualified officers and enlisted personnel for the school detachment and the instruction batteries. Reflecting on the personnel shortages, Moore wrote on 9 February 1912, "On September 15th the School Detachment, out of an authorized strength of 42 men, had 17 for duty and most of these men had only been with the detachment for a short period of time and were therefore not trained in the duties which they were to perform."[77] This situation fortunately changed. By the end of the first course that lasted from 15 September 1911 to 15 December 1911, the school detachment had 38 personnel.[78]

In February 1912, Moore reported about the progress of the instruction batteries. "Considering the short period of time available for the training of the two instruction batteries, they did remarkably well and although at the commencement of the course [September 1911], the work of the gun detachments was somewhat faulty, this cannot be said of the latter part of the course."[79] Improvement was shown as the gun detachments learned their duties and responsibilities. Even so, Moore believed that the personnel should have arrived trained.[80] Despite the obstacles, Moore and the other members of the board organized the School of Fire for Field Artillery over several months. At the end of August 1911, Moore had a few ill-prepared instructors, understrength and inadequately trained instruction batteries, and some equipment and ammunition to begin training in September 1911. In view of the situation, the school's future looked problematic with the desired goal of producing competent field artillerymen being difficult to attain.

Growing Pains

Undeterred, Moore opened the School of Fire for Field Artillery as directed by the War Department to satisfy the pressing need for trained field artillerymen to support the other combat arms in a world that was growing increasingly more dangerous. In General Orders No. 72 of 3 June 1911, the War Department established the School of Fire for Field Artillery, directed it to furnish practical instruction, outlined the courses of instruction; and later in General Orders No. 73 of 5 June 1911 the War Department made the school an official part of its professional educational system that included the US Military Academy, post schools for enlisted personnel, garrison schools for officers, and branch service schools for branch and technical training and that intended to raise training standards.[81] Shortly afterward, the War Department dissolved the board that had designed the school and designated Moore as commandant on 19 July 1911.[82] When the school opened its doors on 15 September 1911, its official birth ended "the day of haphazard methods and accidental efficiency" and marked the beginning of standardized instruction and training in gunnery and some instruction in tactics for field artillery officers and enlisted personnel.[83]

The School of Fire began operations with a staff and faculty consisting of Captain Dan T. Moore, First Lieutenant Ralph M. Pennell, First Lieutenant Roger S. Parrott, and First Lieutenant John C. Maul. Interestingly, only Moore had any experience as a field artillery officer. Parrott had recently transferred from the Field Artillery to the Ordnance to give him minimal field artillery expertise. While Pennell was a cavalry officer, Maul was an infantry officer who had been borrowed from the 5th Field Artillery Regiment.[84] As a team, these officers set out to "teach officers by actual practical exercise. . .the general principals in conducting fire. . . [and] the tactical employment field artillery" with a clear emphasis on gunnery.[85]

Yet, none of these officers had any real expertise in indirect fire as their backgrounds indicated to reflect the overall state of the Field Artillery in 1911. Like so many field artillery officers in various armies with the exception of the Japanese and the Russians who had demonstrated proficiency with indirect fire in the Russo-Japanese War of 1904-1905, the Americans would have to teach themselves indirect fire through trial and error without the benefit of having someone with more knowledge and experience leading the way. As such, Moore and the other officers found themselves on the cutting edge. They had the task of teaching field artillerymen observed indirect fire which was more complicated than direct fire. Employing direct fire, the gunner aimed at a clearly seen target by looking down the cannon tube as though he were aiming a rifle. With indirect fire, field artillerymen used a forward observer to locate the target, an aiming point, and a compass to hit the unseen target.[86]

As prescribed by the War Department, the school offered four courses. Captains and lieutenants took Course A. Field officers attended Course B. Noncommissioned officers registered in Course C. Militia officers enrolled in Course D. Among other student officers, Captain Henry W. Butner who served as the Commandant of the Field Artillery School in 1934-1936, Captain Augustine McIntyre who was the Commandant of the Field Artillery School in 1936-1940, and Major Ernest Hinds who became the Chief of Artillery for the American Expeditionary Force during World War I and Commandant of the Field Artillery School in 1919-1923 reported for Course A on 15 September 1911. Like the other courses, Course A consisted of gunnery, panoramic sketching to identify targets, battery drill, practical ballistics, and critiques by instructors and fellow students and minimal instruction on field artillery tactics. The short three-month length of the course simply precluded teaching more than gunnery and some rudimentary tactics even though a few officers in the War Department pressed Moore to include more tactics in the program of instruction to make the course more comprehensive and to make the School of Fire a true field artillery school and not just a gunnery school.[87]

Responding to this criticism about the school's narrow focus on gunnery, Moore explained the predicament. In a letter of 16 December 1911 to St. Greble, Moore wrote about the course material for the first class of the fall of 1911 being too advanced for the average student. The officers arrived at the school poorly prepared to learn the intricacies of indirect fire and battery operations because they still viewed gunnery from the perspective of the direct fire days.[88] Reflecting on the caliber of the students in that first class, Moore later lamented on 12 January 1912 about the Americans lagging far behind the Europeans in the quality of their field artillerymen "that it really makes one shudder."[89] He continued this theme in another letter to St. Greble on 16 January 1912:

> I have never have had such a hopeless feeling in my life as I had during the latter part of the last course [September-December 1911], when I found out that the student officers hadn't ever grasped the elements and the firing they did was rotten. In fact, they did not seem to even grasp the rudiments, it was simply pitiful.[90]

Moore found the American field artillerymen to be incompetent. They lacked a solid foundation in the basics and as a result had difficulties learning indirect fire that was more sophisticated than direct fire. In fact, student officers attending the course in the fall were deficient in the elementary knowledge of gunnery, could not locate targets, and wasted ammunition.[91]

Interestingly, Moore expected more of the students than they could give and ignored an important reality. For American field artillerymen, observed indirect fire was totally new and a critical break with direct fire that was relatively easy to learn and to apply.[92]

Only a few days into the first course that had been designed on the assumption that the students would have a working knowledge of adjusting fire and other basic aspects of indirect fire, Moore faced the undesirable task of revamping instruction. To overcome inadequately prepared students who reflected decades of neglected gunnery training, Moore eliminated all advanced subjects that had been agreed upon by the school's founders and the War Department and shifted the school's focus to the basics for the rest of the first course and for the course scheduled for the spring of 1912. He essentially had to overcome the fruits of the preceding decades when training had emphasized rote memorization, military discipline, and administration at the expense of practical exercises and when the Army had been scattered around the Trans-Mississippi West in small garrisons that also hampered effective training. Equally important, Moore had to abandon his assumption about the state of training for incoming personnel. They did not understand the rudiments of observed indirect fire as he had hoped.[93]

With the revised curriculum for the spring course of 1912 as a model, Moore and the school's staff and faculty implemented the course for September-December 1912. During the first month of the course for the fall of 1912, the students spent time with flash targets, preparing firing data, and various methods of adjusting fire on a target. After training in these fundamentals, the students then proceeded to firing field guns and learned how to bracket a target. They also learned panoramic sketching, technical and tactical battery drill, and practical ballistics and went through critiques conducted by the instructors and fellow students. Along with more competent officers who were beginning to attend the school and were better prepared, the revised course for the fall of 1912 produced better qualified graduates although they fell short of Moore's ideal of being experts in observed indirect fire techniques who could train their colleagues in the regiments. Like the previous two classes, the class of fall of 1912 was handicapped by shortages of ammunition and personnel in the instruction batteries and depended upon old guns, carriages, and other obsolete equipment.[94]

At the close of the fall class of 1912, Moore expressed his thoughts about the quality the students. On 2 December 1912 he composed, "If we teach our officers how to shoot, we will have accomplished our object and three months devoted exclusively to this subject isn't enough. Therefore let us devote all our energy and time here to teaching them how to shoot."[95]

Moore's practical experience with inadequately prepared student officers influenced his view of the school's mission and hindered turning the School of Fire into a true field artillery school along the lines of the German field artillery school in Juterborg. Yet, the school's curriculum reflected the reality of 1911-1912. The pressing need to teach basic observed indirect fire techniques to officers and noncommissioned officers with limited gunnery skills certainly overrode teaching tactics, other related field artillery subjects, and advanced subjects. The school existed to teach field artillerymen how to shoot on the open, mobile battlefield. With the aid of a forward observer who would be positioned as close as possible to the enemy to locate targets and to adjust fire, field artillery officers had to learn how to shift fires rapidly and effectively around the battlefield to engage enemy personnel and materiel targets in the open that hindered the infantry advance. The school's envisioned fluid, open battlefield not only reflected the recent American experience in Cuba and the Philippines but also underscored the rationale for Moore's insistence on computing firing data quickly and accurately and engaging a target with a minimum number of rounds. Unless field artillery officers could compute technical fire direction rapidly and accurately, they would be unable to provide effective close support on a mobile battlefield.[96]

In his report of 25 June 1912, Moore noted another disappointing characteristic of the students. "Upon the arrival at this School a great majority of the student officers seemed convinced that the amount of ammunition and time consumed in obtaining the necessary adjustments was not of importance," he wrote.[97] They failed to comprehend the need to respond rapidly and effectively to a call for fire from the forward observer to maximize surprise and success on the open battlefield and objected to the requirement to compute data quickly and correctly.[98]

Despite the handicaps, Moore wrote in his a report on 27 June 1913 how the modest increases in the ammunition allotted to the school during the past year had helped to train students to shoot better and hit targets more rapidly and accurately than their predecessors, while more and better equipment had significantly enhanced the quality of instruction. Even with minimal support from the War Department, the school was making progress. Although infantry and cavalry officers were impressed with the ability of the graduates to deliver effective observed indirect fire, Moore's attitude still reflected ambivalence about his view on the state of the school and his frustrations. Refusing to acknowledge his accomplishments and the school's steady improvement in two years, he bemoaned the need for more and better instructors and more ammunition before serious improvements in the quality of the instruction and the graduates could be made.[99]

Although St. Greble supported Moore and the school had improved its curriculum and produced better graduates in 1913 than in 1911, Moore's focus on the basics, such as gunnery, as late as 1913 fueled criticism. Desiring more instruction on tactics, Moore's opponents censured him for being absorbed on teaching the basics. Yet, those same officers conceded that the school was making progress under his tutelage because recent graduates could shoot and hit targets better than their predecessors could. Basically, they wanted more out of the school than Moore was prepared to give in view of the quality of the students, staff, and faculty.[100]

LTC Edward F. McGlachlin, Jr.
Field Artillery School Commandant
15 Sep 1914-26 Jun 1916

In the face of continuing disapproval from opponents over the school's program of instruction and mounting exhaustion caused by juggling the demands of being the school commandant, an instructor, a firing battery commander, and member of the Field Artillery Board, Moore requested to be relieved of his responsibilities. On 15 September 1914, Lieutenant Colonel Edward F. McGlachlin, who later served as the commanding general of the 1st Division in the American Expeditionary Force in France from November 1918 to August 1919, replaced Moore as commandant of the school.[101] Although he acknowledged the requirement for additional instructors and more ammunition, McGlachlin found the school to be in better shape in 1914 than it had been in 1911 and recognized that better prepared students led to better graduates. This assessment was borne out by a memorandum for the Chief of Staff of the Army, Major General Hugh L. Scott, signed by the Chief of the War College Division, Brigadier General M.M. Macomb, on 18 December 1914. The memorandum credited the improved firing efficiency of the Army's field batteries to the school.[102]

With better prepared students enrolling in the school, McGlachlin instituted critical curriculum reforms during his tenure as commandant from 1914-1916. Explaining his reforms of 1914-1915, he wrote on 1 July 1915, "More thorough instruction [this past year] has been given in the subjects of communications and practical ballistics, more attention given to tactics of fire and tactics of maneuver and . . . more emphasis . . . on reconnaissance and occupation of position."[103] The school required student officers to fire under difficult tactical and technical conditions. By taking these steps, he made the school's curriculum more comprehensive than it had been under Moore and produced a more broadly trained graduate. Even though McGlachlin expanded the program of instruction with the inclusion of additional subjects, gunnery still remained the core subject and the school's reason for being. The requirement to teach observed indirect fire gunnery techniques for combat on the open, mobile battlefield dictated that orientation of the curriculum.[104]

Against this backdrop, the School of Fire struggled to find a permanent home on Fort

Sill. In 1911, the post furnished the school with a small, wooden building on the southeast corner of Old Post (Bldg 432 in 2010) for the office of the commandant, secretary, and sergeant major. The classroom (Bldg 435 in 2010) was located in the stone barracks across the street. In the fall of 1911, Moore moved his office into the more spacious old post headquarters building (Bldg 437 in 2010) that had been vacated by the post commander upon the completion of New Post about one mile to the west of Old Post. The school soon outgrew these modest facilities on Old Post and moved into the new unoccupied barracks (Bldg 1616 in 2010) on New Post in September 1912 at the direction of the post commander, Colonel Granger Adams, formerly of the 5th Field Artillery Regiment. Nearby where Lieutenant Colonel (Brevet Major General) George A. Custer had camped with his 7th Cavalry Regiment in 1869, student officers framed and netted tents for use as quarters and erected a temporary structure for a mess hall.[105] In an article in the *Field Artillery Journal* in 1912, Captain W.H. Burt described the students' austere living accommodations. He ambiguously wrote, "The quarters available for student officers at Fort Sill are poor, but comfortable enough."[106]

Although the War Department moved the Chiricahua Apaches off Fort Sill in mid-1913 to give the school more land for firing ranges and tactical exercises and to end discussion over their safety, the debate over the quality of the school's physical facilities raged on.[107] Shortly after becoming the commandant in September 1914, McGlachlin complained that the school's facilities were entirely unsuited for comfortable and effective study during the windy and inclement weather experienced during part of the school term.[108]

As a result of this criticism, the school moved its facilities once again. In the middle of the fall class of 1914, Adams transferred the school from New Post back to Old Post in October 1914 with the arrival of a battery of the 5th Field Artillery Regiment. Adams housed the commandant's office, the secretary's office, the library, and the classrooms in stone barracks (Bldg 441 in 2010) on the southwest corner of Old Post that had formerly been inhabited by cavalry troops and by Satanta, Satank, and Big Tree when they were Army prisoners in the 1870s. In a letter to the War Department, McGlachlin pointed out the unsuitability of the new accommodations and the problems associated with moving the school around.[109]

McGlachlin later learned that the stone barracks on Old Post would not be home to the school for long. Upon assuming command of the post in February 1915, Colonel Richard M. Blatchford pressed to invigorate the moribund School of Musketry that had been relatively inactive since its arrival at Fort Sill in 1913 because troubles on the Mexican border repeatedly drew students away from the school. Based upon his seniority, Blatchford directed McGlachlin to move the School of Fire out of its stone barracks on Old Post to make room for the School of Musketry. Trying to mollify an irate McGlachlin, Blatchford told him about his plan to build temporary wooden buildings to house the school. Realizing the inadequacy of such a proposal, McGlachlin purchased the Old Trader's Store of William H. Quinette for $1,500 for use as a school house with the permission from the War Department. McGlachlin renovated it and moved the school into it in July 1915. Fortunately, school was out for the summer, and no classrooms were required for the time being. A one-story, one-room wooden building that was located to the west of Old Post and that dated to the 1870s, the Old Trader's Store was even less suitable for a school house than the stone barracks and was the last place of refuge. In the meantime, the school detachment lived in tents, ate in a tent mess hall, and suffered through unbearable heat in the summer.[110]

In his report to the War Department signed on 1 July 1915, McGlachlin officially objected to Blatchford's plan. In disapproving language he pointed out, "The situation of the school now is most unsatisfactory. . . . The school proper has no place to go, no suitable storage room for its valuable equipment, no satisfactory arrangements for carrying on its routine or for preparing to accomplish its functions during the next term [fall of 1915]."[111] The frequent moves over the past two years interrupted course work and forced the students to live in tents; and the temporary accommodations were inadequate.[112]

Several weeks after McGlachlin had moved the school, Brigadier General William A. Mann who had just replaced Blatchford as the Commandant of the School of Musketry and commander of Fort Sill actually followed through with his predecessor's plan for a new building for the school. Mann secured the funds for two long, one-story shacks just south of the Old Trader's Store and moved the school's classrooms, print shop, photo shop, and school detachment into them in September 1915. The school's library remained in the Old Trader's Store, and students occupied tents in the vicinity. In this forbidding setting, the school taught the fall class of 1915. The heat was so intense in the shanties that even the instructors worked in undershirts. Captain Fox Conner, an instructor, sought to relieve the situation by having a false roof built over the classrooms with airspace between the two roofs, trying to improve air circulation. Although the buildings were supposed to be temporary, the school utilized them for one purpose or another until 1934 when they were torn down to make room for new officers' quarters.[113]

In the April-June 1915 edition of the *Field Artillery Journal*, the editor, Captain Marlborough Churchill, complained about the school's facilities. "The School of Fire for Field Artillery is practically homeless," he commented.[114] ". . . it is evident," he added, "that it cannot continue unless it is properly organized, efficiently administered and decently housed."[115]

To provide adequate facilities for the School of Fire, McGlachlin, in the meantime, reaffirmed a solution in his report of 1 July 1915 that had been discussed earlier in the year.[116] He suggested, "Immediate steps should be taken unless, as is believed, they have already been taken, to obtain the funds and to start permanent construction at the earliest possible date of buildings especially planned . . . [for] the School and its personnel."[117] Only buildings specifically constructed and dedicated to the school would solve the problem with the facilities. Budget constraints, however, prevented erecting the desired permanent facilities that would be located on the site of the Old Trader's Store.[118]

The revolution in Mexico soon overshadowed the controversy over the school's facilities and location. In a telegram on 23 August 1915, Secretary of War Lindley M. Garrison informed McGlachlin about his intention to send all officers to the Mexican border and

The first administration building for the School of Fire for Field Artillery.

to close the school if necessary. Shortly afterward, the War Department shipped two field batteries from the school to the border. At the recommendation of the War Department, McGlachlin and Mann cancelled classes for their respective schools for the fall of 1915 so that students could return to the units but hoped to restart classes sometime in 1916.[119]

Of the two schools, only the School of Fire reopened when it started instructing 14 officers and 24 noncommissioned officers in February 1916.[120] Immediately, the simmering controversy of consolidating the School of Musketry and the School of Fire to teach combined arms warfare arose again as an attempt to reopen the former. Early in 1916, Mann started pushing the virtues of consolidation – the ability to teach combined arms warfare – as he had done in the fall of 1915.[121] Although some field artillery officers supported such action, they conceded that the merger should not come at the expense of the School of Fire for Field Artillery but failed to present a convincing argument for maintaining the independence of each school.[122]

The most vocal of the opponent of a merger proved to be McGlachlin probably because he feared that the School of Musketry would be the dominant partner in view of Mann's seniority. In June 1916 he wrote, "It is not necessary, however, it seems to me, that such instruction [combined arms training] should take place. . . . Such combined training can be given only with considerable bodies of troops and should have for its object the training of troops, rather than the instruction of students."[123] He then added, "Such training should be given, I think, at field maneuvers yearly throughout the service."[124] According to McGlachlin, merging the schools to facilitate teaching combined arms warfare would not be beneficial for either branch and would detract from gunnery training for field artillerymen.[125]

Once again the crisis on the Mexican border eclipsed any attempt to reopen the schools permanently and to join them for combined arms training. On 9 May 1916 the Fort Sill commander, Brigadier General Granger Adams, wired the Adjutant General, Major General Henry P. McCain, and urged closing the school and sending all officers to the border. Requiring more troops for the border, the War Department approved Adams' recommendation that very day. Adams closed the School of Fire on 9 May 1916. Although his intention was to furnish troops for duty on the border, Adams' action also ended the debate over combining the School of Fire and the School of Musketry into one school. The last field artillery officer left on 9 July 1916; the School of Fire did not open again until World War I.[126]

Closing the School of Fire led to a bitter recrimination. In the editorial section of the *Field Artillery Journal* of January-March of 1917, the editor wrote, "A year ago it was a school of which our service could well be proud. The technique of field artillery fire was there taught in a manner not excelled by that of any other school of its kind in the world."[127] Continuing, the editor pointed out:

> Its effects were felt throughout the Field Artillery in the improvement of firing, the material progress that officers of all grades were making in their profession, and in a marked advance in the general efficiency of the arm. . . . For the future efficiency of the Field Artillery arm it is to be hoped that the School of Fire will be reopened at once and kept in operation until all officers of the army shall have had the benefits of the instruction.[128]

Unquestionably, the school's efforts of 1911-1916 improved the efficiency of the Field Artillery as a whole as the editorial implied and provided a valuable service to the Army.[129]

By closing the school, the War Department sacrificed training for operational considerations as it had done frequently in the past to meet wartime needs with a small force. The War Department closed the Artillery School at Fortress Monroe in the 1830s to send students to fight the Seminoles in southeastern United States and suspended the school's operations during the Civil War of 1861-1865 and the Spanish-American War of 1898 to dispatch troops to the front. Personnel shortages, among other issues, generated by the Filipino Insurrection compelled the War Department to close the School of Application for Cavalry and Light Artillery at Fort Riley, Kansas, in 1899. In reality, the War Department took the only viable course of action. With war threatening, the War Department only had a small, partially trained field army for duty on the Mexican border and took steps to enlarge it.[130]

Closing the school to provide field artillerymen for duty on the Mexican border abruptly ended the school's first five years of existence. Poorly prepared students, inadequate facilities, and shortages of ammunition and equipment hampered the initial progress and forced the school to focus on the basics at the expense of teaching advanced gunnery techniques under Moore. Better prepared students who had received some training in their regiments by school graduates began attending the school in 1913-1914. Such students permitted McGlachlin to initiate reforms late in 1914 to make the school's curriculum more advanced and comprehensive than before even though adequate facilities still remained a dream and shortages of ammunition persisted to limit the frequency of live-fire exercises. Notwithstanding these limitations, the School of Fire for Field Artillery still created a small cadre of trained field artillery officers and enlisted soldiers that could train the rest of the Field Artillery as required.

Notes

1   Maurice Matloff, ed., *American Military History* (Washington, D.C.: US Army Center of Military History, 1985), pp. 349-50.

2   Matloff, *American Military History*, pp. 347-49; Edward M. Coffman, *The Regulars: The American Army, 1898-1941* (Cambridge, MA: The Belknap Press of the Harvard University Press, 2004), pp. 176-82. See Graham A. Cosmas, *An Army for Empire: The United States Army in the Spanish-American War* (Columbia, MO: University of Missouri Press, 1971) for a solid discussion of the War Department's deficiencies in mobilizing ground forces for the Spanish-American War.

3   Boyd L. Dastrup, *King of Battle: A Branch History of the US Army's Field Artillery* (Fort Monroe, VA: Office of the Command Historian, US Army Training and Doctrine Command, 1992, reprinted by the US Army Center of Military History, 1994), pp. 63-64, 156-57; War Department, General Order No. 66, 13 May 1901; War Department, General Order No. 15, 13 Feb 1901; War Department, General Order No. 9, 6 Feb 1901; Matloff, ed., *American Military History*, p. 154.

4   War Department, General Orders No. 78, 6 Jun 1901; War Department, General Orders No. 116, 3 Sep 1901.

5   War Department, General Orders No. 152, 14 Sep 1904; War Department, General Orders No. 89, 14 Jun 1905; Annual Report, War Department, 1905, 2: 260-61; Dastrup, *King of Battle*, p. 152; Wilbur S. Nye, *Carbine and Lance: The Story of Old Fort Sill* (Norman, OK: University of Oklahoma Press, 1974), p. 315.

6   Annual Report of the Chief of Artillery, 1904, p. 14; Dastrup, *King of Battle*, p. 138.

7   Annual Report of the Chief of Artillery, 1904, p. 14.

8   Annual Report of the Chief of Artillery, 1904, p. 14.

9   Annual Report of the Chief of Artillery, 1906, p. 8.

10   Annual Report of the Chief of Artillery, 1906, p. 8.

11   Annual Report of the Chief of Artillery, 1904, p. 14; Annual Report of the Chief of Artillery, 1906, p. 8.

12   War Department, General Order No. 24, 2 Feb 1907; War Department, Special Order No. 132, 6 Jun 1907; Annual Report, War Department, 1907, 2:189, 216, 217; House of Representatives, Resolution No. 17347, File No. 107347, Record Group (RG) 94, National Archives; Memo for Secretary of War, subj: Proposed Order for the Organization of the Field Artillery into Six Regiments, 16 May 1907, File No. 1242815, RG 94.

13   War Department, General Order No. 118, 31 May 1907; War Department, Special Order No. 132, 6 Jun 1907; War Department, File No. 1242815, RG 94; Annual Report, War Department, 1907, 2:189, 216, 217; Annual Report, War Department, 1908, 2:217.

14   "A Brief History of Fort Sill and the Field Artillery School," *Field Artillery Journal,* Nov-Dec 1933, pp. 528-41; Dastrup, *King of Battle*, p. 152; Gillette Griswold, "Fort Sill, Oklahoma: A Brief History," unpublished manuscript, pp. 9-10, Historical Research and Documents Collection (HRDC), Field Artillery Branch Historian's Office, US Army Field Artillery School, Fort Sill; Griswold, "Fort Sill, Oklahoma: A Chronology of Key Events," unpublished manuscript, p. 7, HRDC; Russell F. Weigley, *History of the United States Army* (Bloomington, IN: Indiana University Press, 1984), p. 596; Nye, *Carbine and Lance*, pp. 315-16.

15   *Nye, Carbine and Lance, pp. 315-16.*

16   *Nye, Carbine and Lance, p. 319;* "A Brief History of Fort Sill and the Field Artillery

School," pp. 528-41; Griswold, "Fort Sill, Oklahoma," p. 9, HRDC.

17 Dennis P. Mroczkowski, "Artillery School at Fort Monroe," in William E. Simon, ed., *Professional Military Education in the United States: A Historical Dictionary* (Westport, CT: Greenwood Press, 2000), pp. 68-71; Paul S. Morando and David J. Johnson, *Fort Monroe* (Charleston, SC: Arcadia Publishing, 2008), p. 8.

18 Mroczkowski, "Artillery School at Fort Monroe," pp. 68-71; Nye, *Carbine and Lance*, p. 320; Boyd L. Dastrup, "School of Application for Cavalry and Light Artillery," in *Professional Military Education in the United States*, pp. 284-86; Riley Sunderland, *History of the Field Artillery School, 1911-1942* (Fort Sill, OK: Field Artillery School Printing Plant, 1942), p. 28; Shelford Bidwell and Dominick Graham, *Firepower: British Army Weapons and Theories of War, 1904-1945* (London: George Allen and Unwin, 1982), pp. 12-13; Frank E. Comparato, *Age of Great Guns: Cannon Kings and Cannoneers Who Forged the Firepower of Artillery* (Harrisburg, PA: The Stackpole Company, 1965), p. 118; War Department, Document 507, Study on the Development of Large Caliber, Mobile Artillery, and Machine Guns in the Present European War, in War Department, *Statement of A Proper Military Policy for the United States* (Washington: Government Printing Office, 1916), pp. 3-4; Hew Strachan, *European Armies and the Conduct of War* (London: George Allen and Unwin, 1983), pp. 138-39; H.A. Bethel, *Modern Artillery in the Field* (London: Macmillan and Company Limited, 1911), pp. 2, 151; Dastrup, *King of Battle*, p. 153; Theodore Roosevelt, *An Autobiography* (New York: The Macmillan Company, 1919), p. 276; "Dan Tyler Moore, Captain Field Artillery," *Field Artillery Journal*, Oct 1945, p. 600; James E. Hewes, *From Root to McNamara: Army Organization and Administration, 1900-1963* (Washington, DC: Center of Military History, US Army, 1975), p. 386; Steven A. Stebbins, "Indirect Fire: The Challenge and Response in the US Army, 1907-1917," unpublished master's thesis, University of North Carolina, 1993, pp. 37-39; Edward M. Coffman, *The Regulars: The American Army, 1898-1941* (Cambridge, MA: The Belkap Press of Harvard University Press, 2004), p. 176-77; Morando and Johnson, *Fort Monroe*, p. 8.

19 Nye, *Carbine and Lance*, p. 320; Edward M. Coffman, *The Old Army: A Portrait of the American Army in Peacetime, 1784-1898* (New York: Oxford University Press, 1986), pp. 269-82; Weigley, *History of the United States Army*, pp. 325-26; War Department, General Orders No. 73, 5 Jun 1911.

20 "Firing Schools," *Field Artillery Journal*, Apr-Jun 1911, pp. 187-88.

21 Mroczkowski, "Artillery School at Fort Monroe," pp. 68-71; Nye, *Carbine and Lance*, p. 320; Dastrup, "School of Application for Cavalry and Light Artillery," pp. 284-86; Sunderland, *History of the Field Artillery School*, p. 28; Bidwell and Graham, *Firepower*, pp. 12-13; Comparato, *Age of Great Guns*, p. 118; War Department, Document 507, pp. 3-4; Strachan, *European Armies and the Conduct of War*, pp. 138-39; Bethel, *Modern Artillery in the Field*, pp. 2, 151; Dastrup, *King of Battle*, p. 153; Roosevelt, *An Autobiography*, p. 276; "Dan Tyler Moore, Captain Field Artillery," *Field Artillery Journal*, p. 600; Hewes, *From Root to McNamara*, p. 386.

22 "The Needs of the School of Fire," *Field Artillery Journal*, Jul-Sep 1915, pp. 459-60.

23 "The Needs of the School of Fire," pp. 459-60; Stebbins, "Indirect Fire," pp. 31-32, 36-40, 47-48; William J. Snow, "The Functions and Training of Field Artillery," thesis, Army War College, 1908.

24 Nye, *Carbine and Lance*, p. 320; Sunderland, *History of the Field Artillery School*, p. 28; Bidwell and Graham, *Firepower*, pp. 12-13; Comparato, *Age of Great Guns*, p. 118; War Department, Document 507, pp. 3-4; Strachan, *European Armies and the Conduct of War*, pp. 138-39; Bethel, *Modern Artillery in the Field,* pp. 2, 151; Dastrup, *King of Battle*, p. 153; Roosevelt,

An Autobiography, p. 276; "Dan Tyler Moore, Captain Field Artillery," p. 600; Hewes, *From Root to McNamara*, p. 386; Annual Report of the Chief of Artillery, 1906, pp. 27-28; CPT Steven A. Stebbins, "To Teach a Man to Shoot: Dan T. Moore and the School of Fire, 1909-1914," *Field Artillery Magazine*, Aug 1994, pp. 10-13.

25 Memorandum, subj: The School of Fire at Juterbog, Germany, 26 Jul 1909, UF73 J7M7 1909, MSTL; Report, subj: Austrian School of Field Artillery Fire, Dutch School of Field Artillery Fire, English School of Field Artillery Fire, Italian School of Field Artillery Fire, 1909, UF55 M7 1909, MSTL; Morris Swett, "The Forerunners of Sill: A History of Artillery Schools in the United States," *Field Artillery Journal,* Nov-Dec 1938, pp. 453-63; Ltr, SGT Lynn Boggs to MG Ralph M. Pennell, 24 May 1957, in Webster Allyn Capron, "Recollections of the Early Days of the School for Fire for Field Artillery," manuscript, UF25 H673 C2, MSTL; CPT David T. Zabecki, "Dan T. Moore: Founder of the Field Artillery School," *Field Artillery Journal*, Nov-Dec 1981, pp. 58-60.

26 Sunderland, *History of the Field Artillery School*, pp. 28-29; Memorandum, subj: The School of Fire at Juterbog, Germany, 26 Jul 1909, UF73 J7M7 1909, MSTL.

27 Zabecki, "Dan T. Moore," pp. 58-60; Nye, *Carbine and Lance*, p. 321; "Dan Tyler Moore, Captain FA," p. 600; Sunderland, *History of the Field Artillery School*, p. 30; Annual Report of the Chief of Artillery, 1906, pp. 27-28.

28 Morris Swett, "History of Artillery School in the United States (extract)," unpublished manuscript, 1938, p. 38, HRDC.

29 Ltr, Moore to Greble, 18 Jan 1911, in Correspondence 1911-1914, UF25 S372 C6, MSTL; Ltr, Moore to Greble, 17 Mar 1911, in Correspondence 1911-1914, UF25 S372 C6, MSTL.

30 Ltr, Moore to Greble, 16 Mar 1911, in Correspondence, 1911-1914, UF25 S372 C6, MSTL.

31 Ltr, Boggs to Pennell, 24 May 1957, in Webster Allyn Capron, "Recollections of the Early Days of the School of Fire for Field Artillery," manuscript, UF25 H673 C2, MSTL.

32 Ltr, Moore to Greble, 17 Mar 1911, in Correspondence 1911-1914, UF25 S372 C6, MSTL.

33 Ltr, Moore to Greble, 17 Mar 1911.

34 Ltr, Moore to Greble, 18 Jan 1911, in Correspondence 1911-1914, UF25 S372 C6, MSTL; Ltr, Moore to Greble, 17 Mar 1911, in Correspondence 1911-1914, UF25 S372 C6, MSTL.

35 Ltr, Moore to Greble, 17 Mar 1911.

36 Nye, *Carbine and Lance*, p. 322.

37 Ltr, Moore to Greble, 17 Mar 1911, in Correspondence 1911-1914, UF25 S372 C6, MSTL.

38 Ltr, Greble to Moore, 23 Mar 1911, in Correspondence 1911-1914, UF25 S372 C6, MSTL. As Greble predicted, the problem with the Native Americans disappeared. To make room for the School of Fire for Field Artillery, the federal government gave the Chiricahua Apaches in 1913 the choice of returning to their homeland in Arizona and New Mexico or receiving allotments of land near present-day Apache to the north of Fort Sill. Although many left for Arizona and New Mexico, some took the allotments. Regardless of the decision, the Chiricahua Apaches moved off Fort Sill, freeing land for target practice and eliminating the possibility of killing cattle and even Chiricahua Apaches with field artillery rounds. See Nye, *Carbine and Lance*, p. 302.

39 Ltr, Greble to Moore, 23 Mar 1911, in Correspondence 1911-1914, UF25 S372 C6, MSTL.

40 Ltr, Greble to Moore, 23 Mar 1911.

41 "Dan Tyler Moore, Captain FA," p. 600; Swett, "History of the Artillery Schools in the United States," pp. 38, 41, HRDC.

42   Ltr, Moore to Greble, 4 Apr 1911, in Correspondence 1911-1914, UF25 S372 C6, MSTL; Ltr, Greble to Moore, 10 Apr 1911, in Correspondence 1911-1914, UF25 S372 C6, MSTL; Ltr, Greble to Moore, 11 Apr 1911, in Correspondence 1911-1914, UF25 S372 C6, MSTL; Ltr, Greble to Moore, 25 Apr 1911, in Correspondence 1911-1914, UF25 S372 C6, MSTL.

43   Ltr, Moore to Greble, 14 Jun 1911, in Correspondence 1911-1914, UF25 S372 C6, MSTL.

44   Ltr, Moore to Greble, 14 Jun 1911.

45   Ltr, Moore to Greble, 18 Jun 1911, in Correspondence 1911-1914, UF25 S372 C6, MSTL.

46   Ltr, Moore to Greble, 29 Jun 1911, in Correspondence 1911-1914, UF25 S372 C6, MSTL.

47   Ltr, Moore to Greble, 29 Jun 1911.

48   Ltr, Moore to Greble, 29 Jun 1911; Sunderland, *History of the Field Artillery School*, p. 36.

49   Sunderland, *History of the Field Artillery School,* p. 36; Swett, "History of Artillery Schools in the United States," pp. 42-43.

50   Ltr, Moore to Greble, 29 Jun 1911, in Correspondence 1911-1914, UF25 S372 C6, MSTL.

51   Sunderland, *History of the Field Artillery School*, p. 36.

52   Ltr, Moore to Greble, 25 May 1911, in Correspondence 1911-1914, UF25 S372 C6, MSTL.

53   Ltr, Moore to Greble, 25 May 1911.

54   Paddy Griffith, *Forward into Battle: Fighting Tactics from Waterloo to Vietnam* (Sussex, UK: Antony Bird Publications, LTD, 1981), pp. 43-74; Larry H. Addington, *The Patterns of War since the Eighteenth Century* (Bloomington, IN: Indiana University Press, second edition, 1994), pp. 102-33; William H. McNeill, *The Pursuit of Power: Technology, Armed Force, and Society since A.D. 1000* (Chicago: University of Chicago Press, 1982), pp. 262-306; Paul Kennedy, *The Rise and Fall of the Great Powers: Economic Change and Military Conflict from 1500 to 2000* (New York: Random House, 1987), pp. 194-249.

55   Kennedy, *The Rise and Fall of the Great Powers,* pp. 194-249.

56   Ltr, Moore to Greble, 3 Jun 1911, in Correspondence 1911-1914, UF25 S372 C6, MSTL.

57   Ltr, Moore to Greble, 30 March 1911, in Correspondence 1911-1914, UF25 S372 C6, MSTL.

58   Numerous letters in Correspondence 1911-1914, UF25 S372 C6, MSTL.

59   Ltr, Greble to Moore, 10 Apr 1911, in Correspondence 1911-1914, UF25 S372 C6, MSTL.

60   Ltr, Greble to Moore, 10 Apr 1911.

61   Ltr, Greble to Moore, 10 Apr 1911; Ltr, Greble to Moore, 25 Apr 1911, in Correspondence 1911-1914, UF25 S372 C6, MSTL; Ltr, Moore to Greble, 20 May 1911, in Correspondence 1911-1914, UF25 S372 C6, MSTL; Ltr, Moore to Greble, 14 Jun 1911, in Correspondence 1911-1914, UF25 S372 C6, MSTL; Ltr, Moore to Greble, 18 Jun 1911, in Correspondence 1911-1914, UF25 S372 C6, MSTL; Ltr, Moore to Greble, 3 Jun 1911, in Correspondence 1911-1914, UF25 S372 C6, MSTL.

62   Ltr, Moore to Greble, 21 Apr 1911, in Correspondence 1911-1914, UF25 S372 C6, MSTL; Ltr, Greble to Moore, 25 Apr 1911, in Correspondence 1911-1914, UF25 S372 C6, MSTL; Ltr, Moore to Greble, 14 Jun 1911, in Correspondence 1911-1914, UF25 S372 C6, MSTL.

63   Ltr, Moore to Greble, 3 Jun 1911, in Correspondence 1911-1914, UF25 S372 C6, MSTL; Ltr, Greble to Moore, 25 Apr 1911, in Correspondence 1911-1914, UF25 S372 C6, MSTL; Ltr, Greble to Moore, 14 Jun 1911, in Correspondence 1911-1914, UF25 S372 C6, MSTL; Ltr, Moore to Greble, 18 Jun 1911, in Correspondence 1911-1914, UF25 S372 C6, MSTL.

64 Ltr, Moore to Greble, 14 Apr 1911, in Correspondence 1911-1914, UF25 S372 C6, MSTL; Ltr, Greble to Moore, 18 Apr 1911, in Correspondence 1911-1914, UF25 S372 C6, MSTL; Ltr, Moore to Greble, 21 Apr 1911, in Correspondence 1911-1914, UF25 S372 C6, MSTL; Ltr, Greble to Moore, 31 May 1911, in Correspondence 1911-1914, UF25 S372 C6, MSTL; Ltr, Moore to Greble, 21 May 1911, in Correspondence 1911-1914, UF25 S372 C6, MSTL; Ltr, Moore to Greble, 23 May 1911, in Correspondence 1911-1914, UF25 S372 C6, MSTL; Sunderland, *History of the Field Artillery School*, p. 35.

65 Ltr, Moore to Greble, 21 Apr 1911, in Correspondence 1911-1914, UF25 S372 C6, MSTL; Sunderland, *History of the Field Artillery School*, p. 35; Memorandum for the Adjutant General, 17 Jul 1911, in Correspondence 1911-1914, UF25 S372 C6, MSTL; Ltr, Greble to Moore, 10 Jul 1911, in Correspondence 1911-1914, UF25 S372 C6, MSTL.

66 Ltr, Moore to Greble, 18 Jun 1911, in Correspondence 1911-1914, UF25 S372 C6, MSTL.

67 Ltr, Moore to Greble, 18 Jun 1911.

68 Ltr, Moore to Greble, 3 Jun 1911, in Correspondence 1911-1914, UF25 S372 C6, MSTL; Ltr, Moore to Greble, 18 Jun 1911, in Correspondence 1911-1914, UF25 S372 C6, MSTL.

69 Ltr, Moore to Greble, 28 Jul 1911, in Correspondence 1911-1914, UF25 S372 C6, MSTL.

70 Ltr, Moore to Greble, 28 Jul 1911.

71 Ltr, Moore to Greble, 8 Aug 1911, in Correspondence 1911-1914, UF25 S372 C6, MSTL.

72 Ltr, Moore to Greble, 8 Aug 1911.

73 Ltr, Moore to Greble, 8 Aug 1911.

74 Ltr, Moore to Greble, 8 Aug 1911.

75 Ltr, Moore to Greble, 8 Aug 1911.

76 Ltr, Moore to Greble, 8 Aug 1911. A careful reading of Moore's correspondence with Greble revealed Moore's pessimistic outlook on the success of the school.

77 Report, School of Fire for Field Artillery, 9 Feb 1912, p. 1, UF23.5 E1, MSTL.

78 Report, School of Fire for Field Artillery, 9 Feb 1912, p. 1, UF23.5 E1, MSTL.

79 Report, School of Fire, 24 May 1912, in Rpt of School of Fire for Field Artillery, 1911-1912, UF23.5 E1, MSTL.

80 Report, School of Fire, 24 May 1912.

81 War Department, General Orders No. 72, 3 Jun 1911; War Department, General Orders No. 73, 5 Jun 1911; "The School of Fire for Field Artillery," *Field Artillery Journal*, Jan-Mar 1912, pp. 116-19.

82 "Dan Tyler Moore: Captain FA," p. 600; Sunderland, *History of the Field Artillery School*, p. 37; Nye, *Carbine and Lance*, p. 323; "A Brief History of Fort Sill and the Field Artillery School," p. 537; Memorandum for Adjutant General, 17 Jul 1911, in Correspondence, 1911-1914, UF25 S372 C6, MSTL.

83 Sunderland, *History of the Field Artillery School*, p. 37; Swett, "History of Artillery Schools in the United States," p. 45, HRDC; Nye, *Carbine and Lance*, p. 323; Ltr, Greble to Moore, 15 Jul 1911, Correspondence, 1911-1914, UF25 S372 C6, MSTL.

84 Sunderland, *History of the Field Artillery School*, p. 37.

85 Ltr, Moore to COL H.L. Scott, 22 Oct 1911, in Correspondence 1911-1914, UF25 S372 C6, MSTL.

86 Dastrup, *King of Battle*, p. 153; Boyd L. Dastrup, *The Field Artillery: History and Sourcebook* (Westport, CT: Greenwood Press, 1994), p. 45.

87 War Department, General Orders No. 72, 3 Jun 1911; Sunderland, *History of the Field Artillery School,* p. 37; 2001 US Army Field Artillery Center and Fort Sill (USAFACFS), Annual Command History (ACH), p. 133; Memorandum for Adjutant General, 17 Jul 1911, in Correspondence 1911-1914, UF25 S372 C6, MSTL ; "The School of Fire for Field Artillery," pp. 116-19; Ltr, Moore to Greble, 2 Dec 1912, in Correspondence 1911-1914, UF25 S372 C6, MSTL; Rpt, School of Fire Fire for Field Artillery, 25 Jun 1912, p. 1, in Reports, School of Fire for Field Artillery, 1911-1912, UF23.5 E1, MSTL, Ltr, Moore to H.L. Scott, 22 Oct 1911, Correspondence, 1911-1914, UF25 S372 C6, MSTL.

88 Ltr, Moore to Greble, 16 Dec 1911, in Correspondence 1911-1914, UF25 S372 C6, MSTL; Sunderland, *History of the Field Artillery School*, p. 38.

89 Ltr, Moore to Greble, 12 Jan 1912, in Correspondence 1911-1914, UF25 S372 C6, MSTL.

90 Ltr, Moore to Greble, 16 Jan 1912, in Correspondence 1911-1914, UF25 S372 C6, MSTL.

91 Ltr, Moore to Greble, 16 Jan 1912.

92 Ltr, Moore to Greble, 16 Jan 1912.

93 Sunderland, *History of the Field Artillery School*, pp. 38-40; Rpt, School of Fire, 27 Jun 1916, p. 2, UF25.5 E1, MSTL; MAJ Richard C. Burleson, "Some Observations Concerning the Use of Accompanying Batteries During the World War with Some Personal Experiences," *Field Artillery Journal*, Dec 1921, p. 525; Rpt, 24 May 1912, pp. 1-2, in Rpts, School of Fire for Field Artillery, 1911-1912, UF23.5 E1, MSTL; Swett, "History of Artillery Schools in the United States," p. 49, HRDC; Stevens, "Indirect Fire," p. 58; Nye, *Carbine and Lance*, p. 320; Coffman, *The Old Army*, pp. 269-82; Weigley, *History of the United States Army*, pp. 325-26; War Department, General Orders No. 73, 5 Jun 1911.

94 Sunderland, *History of the Field Artillery School*, pp. 39-40; Swett, "History of Artillery Schools in the United States (Extract)," p. 57, HRDC; "The School of Fire for Field Artillery," *Field Artillery Journal*, Jan-Mar 1912, pp. 116-17; Rpt, School of Fire for Field Artillery, 25 Jun 1912, pp. 5, 8, UF23.5E1; MSTL; Rpt, School of Fire for Field Artillery, 27 Jun 1913, p. 12, UF23.5 E1, MSTL; Rpt, School of Fire for Field Artillery, 9 Feb 1912, pp. 6, 15, UF23.5 E1, MSTL.

95 Ltr, Moore to Greble, 2 Dec 1912, in Correspondence 1911-1914, UF25 S372 C6, MSTL.

96 Ltr, Moore to Greble, 2 Dec 1912; Sunderland, *History of the Field Artillery School*, p. 37; CPT W.H. Burt, "Notes on the Course at the School of Fire," *Field Artillery Journal*, Apr-Jun 1912, pp. 235-36; "The School of Fire for Field Artillery," pp. 116-19; "The Mission of the School of Fire for Field Artillery," *Field Artillery Journal,* Oct-Dec 1917, pp. 383-90; Stebbins, "Indirect Fire," p. 61.

97 Rpt, School of Fire, 25 Jun 1912, p. 6, UF23.5 E2, MSTL.

98 Rpt, School of Fire, 25 Jun 1912, p. 6.

99 Annual Report, School of Fire for Field Artillery, 27 Jun 1913, pp. 4, 12, UF23.5 E1, MSTL; Ltr, Department Commander, HQ Eastern Department, Governors Island, New York, to MG Leonard Wood, Chief of Staff, War Department, subj: Field Artillery School of Fire, Fort Sill, OK, 5 Jun 1913, in Correspondence 1911-1914, UF25 S372 C6, in MSTL; "The Needs of the School of Fire," *Field Artillery Journal*, Apr-Jun 1915, pp. 459-61; Nye, *Carbine and Lance*, p. 325; Stebbins, "Indirect Fire," p. 59.

100 "The Needs of the School of Fire," pp. 459-61; Nye, *Carbine and Lance*, p. 325.

101 Nye, *Carbine and Lance*, p. 325; Stebbins, "Indirect Fire," p. 60.

102 Sunderland, *History of the Field Artillery School*, pp. 46-47; "The Needs of the School of Fire," pp. 459-61.

103 Rpt, School of Fire, 1 Jul 1915, p. 2, UF23.5 E1, MSTL.

104 Rpt, School of Fire, 1 Jul 1915, p. 2; Memorandum for Adjutant General of the Army, subj: School of Fire for Field Artillery and School of Musketry, 1 Sep 1915, attached to Rpt, School of Fire, 1 Jul 1915, UF23.5 E1, MSTL; Rpt, School of Fire, 27 Jun 1916, p. 2, UF23.5 E1, MSTL.

105 Nye, *Carbine and Lance*, p. 325; Rpt, School of Fire for Field Artillery, 27 Jun 1913, p. 18, UF23.5 E1, MSTL; O. Willard Holloway, *Post Commanders of Fort Sill: 1869-1940* (Fort Sill, OK: US Army Artillery and Missile Center, n.d.), p. 1; Sunderland, *History of the Field Artillery School*, p. 45.

106 Burt, "Notes on the Course at the School of Fire," p. 235.

107 Rpt, School of Fire for Field Artillery, 30 Jun 1914, p. 4, UF23.5 E1, MSTL.

108 Sunderland, *History of the Field Artillery School*, p. 49; Nye, *Carbine and Lance*, p. 325.

109 Sunderland, *History of the Field Artillery School*, p. 49; "A Brief History of the Field Artillery School," pp. 537-38; Nye, *Carbine and Lance*, p. 325.

110 War Department, General Orders No. 28, 18 May 1915; "The Needs of the School of Fire," pp. 459-61; "A Brief History of the Field Artillery School," p. 538; Sunderland, *History of the Field Artillery School*, pp. 36, 49-50; Ltr, COL Webster A. Capron to MG Ralph M. Pennell, 8 May 1957, in Webster Allyn Capron, "Recollections of the Early Days of the School for Fire for Field Artillery," unpublished manuscript, UF25 H673 C2, MSTL; Nye, *Carbine and Lance*, pp. map section, 326-27; Rpt, School of Fire, 1 Jul 1915, p. 4, UF23.5 E1, MSTL; Ltr, Cdr, Fort Sill, to Adjutant General, subj: School of Fire for Field Artillery and School of Musketry, 1 Sep 1915, UF23.5 E1, MSTL; "The School of Fire for Field Artillery and the School of Musketry," *Field Artillery Journal*, Jul-Sep 1915, p. 630.

111 Rpt, School of Fire for Field Artillery, 1 Jul 1915, p. 4, UF23.5 E1, MSTL.

112 Rpt, School of Fire for Field Artillery, 1 Jul 1915, p. 4; Sunderland, *History of the Field Artillery School*, p. 49; "A Brief History of the Field Artillery School," pp. 537-38; Nye, *Carbine and Lance*, p. 325

113 *Nye, Carbine and Lance,* pp. 326-27.

114 "The Needs of the School of Fire," p. 461.

115 "The Needs of the School of Fire," p. 461.

116 "The Needs of the School of Fire," p. 461.

117 Rpt, School of Fire for Field Artillery, 1 Jul 1915, p. 4, UF23.5 E1, MSTL.

118 Rpt, School of Fire for Field Artillery, 1 Jul 1915, p. 4; "The Needs of the School of Fire," p. 461.

119 Sunderland, *History of the Field Artillery School*, pp. 50-51; Rpt, subj: School of Fire for Field Artillery and School of Musketry, 1 Sep 1915, UF23.5 E1, MSTL; Rpt, subj: Reports of the School of Fire, 18 Feb 1928, UF23.5 E1, MSTL; Hewes, *From Root to McNamara*, p. 403.

120 Sunderland, *History of the Field Artillery School*, pp. 50-51; Rpt, subj: School of Fire for Field Artillery and School of Musketry, 1 Sep 1915, UF23.5 E1, MSTL; Rpt, subj: Reports of the School of Fire, 18 Feb 1928, UF23.5 E1, MSTL; Hewes, *From Root to McNamara,* p. 403.

121 Swett, "History of the Artillery Schools in the United States," Extract, pp. 61-63, HRDC;

Rpt, subj: School of Fire for Field Artillery and the School of Musketry, 1 Sep 1915, UF23.5 E1, MSTL; Sunderland, *History of the Field Artillery School,* pp. 50-51; Holloway, *Post Commanders of Fort Sill*, code number 49. Mann served as post commander from 16 May 1915 to 17 Nov 1915 and 1 Jan 1916 to 28 Apr 1916 and was replaced by Colonel Granger Adams on 29 Apr 1916.

122 "The School of Fire for Field Artillery and the School of Musketry," p. 630.

123 Rpt, School of Fire, 27 Jun 1916, p. 4, UF23.5 E1, MSTL.

124 Rpt, School of Fire, 27 Jun 1916, p. 4.

125 Rpt, School of Fire, 27 Jun 1916, p. 5; Swett, "History of Artillery Schools in the United States," Extract, pp. 61-62, HRDC; Sunderland, *History of the Field Artillery School*, pp. 50-51; Rpt, subj: School of Fire for Field Artillery and School of Musketry, 1 Sep 1915, UF23.5 E1, MSTL; Rpt, subj: Reports of the School of Fire, 18 Feb 1928, UF23.5 E1, MSTL; Hewes, *From Root to McNamara*, p. 403.

126 Sunderland, *History of the Field Artillery School*, pp. 50-51; Rpt, subj: School of Fire for Field Artillery and School of Musketry, 1 Sep 1915, UF23.5 E1, MSTL; Rpt, subj: Reports of the School of Fire, 18 Feb 1928, UF23.5 E1, MSTL; Hewes, *From Root to McNamara*, p. 403.

127 "The School of Fire," *Field Artillery Journal*, Jan-Mar 1917, p. 73.

128 "The School of Fire," p. 73.

129 "The School of Fire," p. 73.

130 Mroczkowski, "Artillery School at Fort Monroe," pp. 68-71; Dastrup, "School of Application for Cavalry and Light Artillery," pp. 284-86; Matloff, *American Military History*, p. 366; Weigley, *History of the United States Army*, pp. 347-48.

44

Chapter Three
The War to End All Wars

Following the United States' declaration of war on Germany and Central Powers on 6 April 1917, the School of Fire for Field Artillery rapidly adjusted to satisfy wartime field artillery training requirements. After being closed for little over a year in response to the crisis on the Mexican border, the school reopened in July 1917, developed a wartime course of instruction for officers and a course for aerial observers, and enlarged its physical facilities through new construction to accommodate the increased number of students to be trained. The school also played a vital role as a part of the War Department's comprehensive training program for field artillerymen that extended far beyond Fort Sill.

Girding for War

The political turmoil in Mexico that created instability along the US-Mexican border, the uncertain course of the war in Europe, the Allied propaganda campaign about German atrocities, the German violation of Belgium neutrality, and the growing tension with Germany over its aggressive submarine attacks upon American merchant shipping in the Atlantic Ocean prompted the Congress to shore up the country's security by passing the National Defense Act of June 1916. Among other things, the act authorized increasing the peacetime strength of the Regular Army from 108,000 to 175,000 men over a period of five years, established a wartime strength of 286,000 men for the Regular Army, and created tactical divisions and brigades with three brigades to each division and three regiments to a brigade.[1]

Retaining the tradition of the citizen soldier that dated to the militia of Colonial America, the National Defense Act concurrently provided for National Guard and Voluntary Army formations to support the Regular Army. Bolstered by federal funds, increased federal supervision, federal standards for training that dictated the number of drill periods a year and number of field training days a year, and officers and enlisted personnel who swore to obey the President and defend the Constitution of the United States, the National Guard would expand fourfold to more than 400,000. In addition, the act clearly delineated the Guard's preeminence as the country's principle trained reserve, prescribed standards for Guard officers, and allocated 12 National Guard field artillery brigades in peacetime. To ensure that additional officers and soldiers would be trained in peacetime, the act placed the Officers' Reserve Corps and the Reserve Officers' Training Corps in the nation's colleges and universities on a firmer basis and created an Enlisted Reserve Corps. Of equal importance, the act permitted the creation of the Voluntary Army in time of war.[2]

For the Field Artillery of the Regular Army, the National Defense Act granted a salutary increase from six to nine regiments during peacetime and to 21 regiments during war. As might be anticipated, the Field Artillery's peacetime expansion of 1916-1917 from six regiments to nine regiments led to understrength units.[3] For example, the Field Artillery in the Regular Army had 246 officers and 5,470 enlisted soldiers in June 1916. When the United States declared war on Germany in April 1917, it had 408 officers and 8,253 enlisted personnel filling nine regiments that were far below their authorized peacetime strength and were inadequately trained.[4] Wartime expansion to 21 regiments in 1917-1918 further eroded the training base and intensified personnel shortages in the regiments.[5]

Augmenting the Regular Army, the Field Artillery of the National Guard and the National Army, called the Volunteer Army by the National Defense Act of 1916 and composed of draftees and recruits, reflected the same state of readiness as their Regular Army cousins did in 1917. The National Guard had 541 field artillery officers and 12,275 enlisted soldiers when war was declared. At the time, the National Guard Field Artillery consisted of six regiments, 19 separate battalions, and 79 separate batteries, and was understrength and inadequately trained. Eighteen months later in November 1918 when the armistice was signed to end the war, the National Guard had 51 field artillery regiments. Meanwhile, the National Army's field artillery grew from no regiments in April 1917 to 138 regiments in November 1918. Training this field artillery force that swelled virtually overnight from 949 officers and 20,528 enlisted soldiers in April 1917 to 22,392 officers and 439,760 enlisted soldiers in November 1918 fell to Regular Army field artillery officers who possessed only a rudimentary understanding of the latest field artillery tactics and techniques. They also thought in terms of providing fire support with light field pieces on a mobile battlefield with an emphasis on flanking, enveloping, and annihilating even though combat in Europe suggested that such tactics were ill-suited for trench warfare on the Western Front. Remarkably by the time that US forces had reached the Western Front, a war of movement was beginning to reemerge, though at first in retrograde.[6]

Besides highlighting the inadequate state of training and readiness in the Field Artillery, mobilization for World War I energized the School of Fire for Field Artillery that had been closed since May 1916 to release officers and soldiers for duty on the US-Mexican border. Early in July 1917, the School of Fire for Field Artillery consisted of a caretaker detachment under the command of Colonel Robert M. Blatchford, an infantry officer and the commander of Fort Sill. On 10 July 1917, Blatchford received a brief telegram from the War Department, notifying him about its plan to reopen the School of Fire for Field Artillery to train field artillery officers to meet wartime requirements. Five days later on 15 July 1917, 21 student officers met by Sergeant Morris Swett, the school's librarian, stepped off a train from Oklahoma City, Oklahoma, for training. For school facilities, they saw nothing but the Old Trader's Store to the west of the Old Post, the two frame shanties built in 1915, and some tents. In addition, the students found no instructors, no training plans, no field artillery, and no texts when they reported for training on 16 July 1917. Under such bleak and discouraging circumstances, the senior officer organized the class to maintain military discipline. The students occupied their time studying the local terrain, basically doing nothing, until the staff and faculty arrived.[7]

Slowly, the instructors who had been handpicked by the incoming Commandant of the School of Fire for Field Artillery, Colonel William J. Snow, and school staff drifted in. On 19 July 1917, Lieutenant Colonel F.E. Hopkins arrived to serve as the first instructor. Within a few days, Lieutenant Colonel Fred T. Austin who was later the Chief of Field Artillery from 1927 to 1930, Captain Robert M. Danford who was the Chief of Field Artillery from 1938 to 1942, Captain Cliff Andrus who served as the Commandant of the Field Artillery School from 1946 to 1949, and other Regular Army field artillery officers joined Hopkins to form the core of the school's instructor staff. Subsequently on 3 August 1917, a small contingent of French field artillery officers with combat experience on the Western Front reported for duty as instructors with the objective of teaching French doctrine and tactics to the inexperienced Americans.[8]

Meanwhile, Snow reported for duty on 27 July 1917, to replace Colonel (later Brigadier General) Adrian S. Fleming who had been bombarding the War Department with letters and telegrams about the difficulties of reestablishing the School of Fire for Field Artillery, and also assumed the position of post commander. Charged with training field artillerymen for combat, Snow found Fleming struggling to organize a school with little or no resources.[9] In fact, the small cadre of instructors lectured out of the *Field Artillery Drill and Service Regulations of 1916* to a motley class of students. Enlarged in number from the initial 21 officers to 108 officers, zero class as this class was known to distinguish it from the regular wartime classes that began in October 1917 lived and attended classes in tents. Some officers were Regular Army cavalry and coast artillery officers who had been transferred to the Field Artillery to fill out shortages. Some were National Guard officers; some were former noncommissioned officers who had just been commissioned. Regardless of their rank, few knew anything about field artillery tactics, techniques, and procedures.[10]

Although the overall lack of competency of the incoming officers forced Fleming and Snow to focus on the basics and to build from the ground up, they never designed a course of instruction for zero class.[11] Improvisation ruled. In his wartime memoirs, Snow explained, "We . . . felt our way along. I held daily meetings of the instructors, and based on the reports they made each day as to how the students had or had not absorbed that day's instruction we planned the next day's work."[12] As Snow further recalled, "I do not think that we were ever able to plan, even tentatively, more than three days' work in advance until we got the class well grounded. After this was accomplished, we made remarkable progress."[13] Even with this impromptu and haphazard arrangement, the students from zero class eventually learned the basics of field artillery gunnery before leaving for combat duty in France in the fall of 1917.[14]

As Snow's experience suggested, the school had an inauspicious wartime beginning. In a few terse but eloquent sentences, Snow encapsulated the somber mood and demoralizing situation at the school in August 1917. "As I remember," he reflected years later in 1941, "there were plenty of students to be instructed but no means of imparting the instruction."[15] In a serious indictment of the War Department's lack of preparedness during peacetime and flawed mobilization, Snow added, "It seemed that the plan to start the School had been first to send the students, then the commandant, then the instructors, and equipment from time to time afterwards."[16] The War Department unwisely shipped students to the school before sending the commandant and instructors to prepare a suitable program of instruction. The curriculum should have been prepared before the first students arrived, but the urgency to get some training underway caused the War Department to transpose the process and create confusion. This action reflected the lack of a mobilization plan to furnish trained men to fill out the American Expeditionary Forces for duty in Europe.[17]

To his dismay, Snow quickly learned that the school had to compete for scarce facilities and ranges at Fort Sill with the School of Musketry that had reopened in 1917 under Colonel Charles S. Farnsworth who later became the Chief of Infantry after World War I.[18] Together, Farnsworth and Snow tried to coordinate the use of the post for both schools so that each could train their respective students. They even created a joint board of infantry and field artillery officers to help supervise where each branch would conduct training each day.[19] "Try as we would we were continually stepping on each other's toes in spite of the fact that we were good friends," Snow remembered.[20]

Subsequent developments added to Snow's and Farnsworth's frustrations. In 1917, the Air Service, then part of the Signal Corps, constructed an airdrome south of Fort Sill and called it Henry Post Army Airfield after Lieutenant Henry B. Post who had been killed in an airplane accident near San Diego, California, in 1914 in an attempt to establish an altitude record. Although army aviation first arrived at Fort Sill in 1915 when the First Aero Squadron was sent to the Oklahoma post to conduct experiments in aerial observation for field artillery, the War Department sent the 3d Aero Squadron and others in 1917. Subsequently, the War Department opened the School for Aerial Artillery Observers in the fall of 1917 and later the Air Service School in August 1918 to train field artillery aerial observers. To reduce the strain on Fort Sill's limited resources generated by these new missions and the potential for future conflict over facilities, the War Department transferred the School of Musketry to Camp Benning, Georgia, in October 1918 at the recommendation of a War Department board that had been convened to find a suitable site for infantry training.[21]

As post commander, Snow encountered other issues that complicated reestablishing the School of Fire for Field Artillery. When he arrived, the 36th Division composed of Oklahoma and Texas National Guard units and commanded by Major General Edwin John St. Greble was already training on the huge National Army cantonment, Camp Doniphan, that was under construction on Fort Sill and that had been named after Colonel Alexander W. Doniphan of Mexican War fame. The cantonment occupied the prairie west and south of New Post where Snow had hoped to establish firing ranges. This situation forced Snow to use valuable time selecting different sites for firing ranges that could have been spent in training. Although the War Department shipped the 36th Division to Camp Bowie, Texas, in August 1917 for further training before sending it to Europe, it mobilized the 35th Division comprising Kansas and Missouri National Guard units at Camp Doniphan in September 1917 which included the future President of the United States, Captain Harry S. Truman of the 129th Field Artillery Regiment, for training. The War Department also directed Snow to find a site for a hospital and a remount depot and to supervise their construction. Fortunately, the post quartermaster, Colonel George D. Guyer, relieved Snow of most of the burden by overseeing the construction.[22]

Although these construction projects and other pressing duties as post commander could have detracted Snow from his primary mission of reviving the School of Fire for Field Artillery, they did not. As he and his instructors developed the curriculum and obtained the requisite training aids and equipment, Snow explored enlarging the school's physical facilities to accommodate the projected number of officers that would be going through it to fill out the large, conscript armies being organized. Much to his delight, he learned at an instructor's meeting late in July 1917 that Danford and another instructor, Captain Francis W. Honeycutt, had been working on a plan to do that very thing. The three combined their efforts into one expansion plan. The Snow Plan, as it was called, outlined enlarging the school's physical facilities to accommodate 1,200 students at one time with 100 students entering the school each week, developing a wartime course of 12 weeks, organizing the school into six departments (Artillery Tactics, Liaison, Engineering, Practical Ballistics, Artillery Materiel, and Artillery Transportation), furnishing the necessary housing, increasing the number of the school troops to support the training, and forming a larger school detachment.[23]

On 15 August 1917, Snow left for Washington D.C. to sell the War Department on the ambitious plan.[24] To Snow's disappointment, the Chief of Staff of the Army, Major General Hugh L. Scott, who had worked with the Chiricahua Apaches at Fort Sill in the 1890s, believed that "there should be no schools during this war, and that the proper way to learn war was in fighting the enemy!"[25] Shocked by such a naive remark but undeterred by Scott's irreversible position and lack of sympathy for formal training, Snow wrote, "Imagine pitting a raw, untrained, undisciplined army against the Germans, with their most efficient army in the world."[26] Despite Scott's outrageous comment that reflected an archaic 19th century attitude held by many senior army officers about formal training, the Adjutant General, Major General Henry P. McCain, approved Snow's plan on 12 September 1917 and allotted $750,000 for construction.[27]

Shortly afterward, the War Department allocated the money and awarded contracts to the Selden-Breck Construction Company of St. Louis, Missouri. In less than 40 days during the fall of 1917, about 3,000 workers raised wooden buildings for class and lecture rooms and cantonment barracks for school troops on the plateau northwest of Old Post. The school's central facility, later named Snow Hall after Snow who became the first Chief of Field Artillery on 15 February 1918, housed the Office of the Administrator, eight large lecture rooms with the capacity of 200 people each, a room to show movie pictures, and small class rooms with a capacity of 50 people each. Specially-designed rooms were apportioned to the Photographic and Drafting Departments. Other buildings included barracks for each class complete with a lavatory, a shower facility, a dining room, and two large sleeping quarters; a large library; a mess hall and barracks for instructors; and shops for tailors and barbers. Streets were named, and buildings numbered to create a small town that was located about 300 yards northwest from the School of Musketry on Old Post.[28]

Until the school buildings could be completed late in 1917, students and instructors suffered through primitive learning conditions. To make room for the ongoing construction, the students frequently moved their tents used as shelters while instructors held classes under trees or in the shade of buildings whenever it was possible to get out of the hot

Oklahoma sun. It was customary for junior instructors to pray that the senior instructors would be ordered to other posts or France so that they might inherit the trees or shady sides of buildings for their classes.[29]

In the midst of this construction bedlam and the austere living and training conditions, the first wartime class arrived on 27 September 1917 and assembled on 1 October 1917 to begin 12 weeks of training that had been developed by a team of American and French field artillery officers. Composed of Regular Army, National Guard, and National Army officers, ranging from second lieutenant to colonel, the class received its introduction to the school in a weather-beaten structure, known as the Old Trader's Store that also served as the administration building and the school library.[30]

On the first day of class, these students and those that followed through the rest of the war attended an introductory lecture by the commandant of the school, Fleming who assumed the position on 26 September 1917 upon the departure of Snow to join the 156th Field Artillery Brigade at Camp Jackson, South Carolina, after being promoted to brigadier general.[31] In a lecture to the school's second wartime class that reported late in October 1917, Fleming provided a brief overview of the course of instruction and its objective.[32] "The need of even partially educated field artillery officers is so urgent that the School term has been reduced to a minimum. Tactics and the broad knowledge necessary for the proper emplacement and use of artillery you must learn elsewhere," he bluntly informed the students.[33] Fleming added, "Practical liaison with the other arms you must also learn subsequently, except that some opportunity will be afforded for exercises, in conjunction with the Infantry School of Arms. . . . Also you will receive considerable instruction in air liaison in cooperation with the School of Aerial Artillery Observers establishment."[34] This school conducted its first course on 18 September 1917 to train airplane and balloon observers.[35]

Although students would learn about air liaison with aerial observers who would be trained in the details of aerial observation from fixed wing aircraft and balloons, the School of Fire's main mission focused on gunnery. In the *Field Artillery Journal* of October-December 1917, Fleming wrote, "And since the ultimate reason for the existence of artillery is to shoot, our primary and final object is to teach you the techniques of shooting."[36] The pressing requirement for trained field artillery officers dictated that the school would be first and foremost a gunnery school and that tactics and liaison techniques would be learned on the job in the heat of combat in France.[37]

Fleming's article which was also an address to incoming students also outlined the school's expectations of them. He told them plainly:

> If you graduate from this School you will, upon your return to your regiments, be expected to instruct both officers and enlisted men and to prove your ability to do this. You must acquire a working knowledge of the various things which must be taught here. This includes the determination and use of firing data, observation of fire, communications, reconnaissance, field engineering, field gunnery, materiel, and transportation.[38]

While they had the ultimate purpose of learning the art of shooting as Fleming expressed, the graduates had the obligation of teaching their fellow officers upon returning to their units. As Snow explained, after joining or rejoining their regiments, Fort Sill graduates would serve as instructors, "thus spreading the gospel of open warfare . . . and leavening the mass of field artillery officers."[39] Reflecting this thinking, Snow dispatched three recent graduates to train National Guard field artillery officers in response to a brigade commander's request, thus pressing graduates with a cursory knowledge of gunnery and indirect fire into the role of trainers in an army that was rapidly expanding and preparing for combat duty.[40]

To train field artillerymen, the school instituted a strict regimen. During the first five weeks, all officers received the same instruction. The daily class schedule ran from 7:30 a.m. to 11:30 a.m. and from 1:30 p.m. to 5:30 p.m. On Saturday mornings, the school tested students on their mastery of the instruction of the past week. Those students who failed the examinations went before a board of officers to determine their future status in the school. Repeated failures in the tests meant sending the student back to his regiment without graduating. Beginning in the fifth week of the course, students going to light artillery units (horse-drawn) conducted firing practice on light artillery, generally 75-mm. and 3-inch field guns. At the same time, officers with assignments to heavy artillery units (tractor-drawn) fired 155-mm. field guns and howitzers, 4.7-inch howitzers, and 6-inch howitzers. Some officers even trained on heavy trench mortars. Generally, they fired every other day.[41]

During the last week of the course, the school held its culminating training event to give students the opportunity to conduct unobserved indirect fire using maps and observed indirect fire from trenches modeled after those in France for realism.[42] Constructed on the north side of Fort Sill, the American trench system ran south from Ketch Hill on the north to Chrystie Hill, named after Captain Phineas P. Chrystie of the 312th Field Artillery Regiment who was killed on 6 February 1918 when a 155-mm. howitzer exploded, and then to Heyl Hill on the south. This line was complete with battery positions, dugouts, front-line shelters, concrete shelters, and observation posts, among other things, and faced the enemy line to the north. Running virtually parallel to the friendly line, the enemy line included Rabbit Hill and Barbed Wire Hill complete with barbed wire entanglements that the school used to demonstrate how barbed wire could be cut by field artillery fire. Enemy lookout and listening posts, observation posts, command posts, and communication trenches gave the enemy line added realism. From observation posts on Rumbough, Heyl, and Chrystie Hills, student officers directed fire onto enemy targets, ranging from emplaced batteries to mockup tanks that were supporting an infantry advance, with help from aerial and ground observers.[43]

Unlike the American Expeditionary Force schools in France that taught trench warfare with its attending unobserved map fire techniques patterned after the French method, the School of Fire of Field Artillery stressed maneuver warfare and observed indirect fire even though many officers, including American, insisted that it was obsolete.[44] According to the American concept of open warfare taught at the school, the battle would begin with short preparatory field artillery fire barrage employing observed indirect fire to achieve mastery over enemy field artillery. Once ascendancy over enemy field artillery had been gained, the infantry would attack. At this time part of the field guns would be moved forward with the infantry advance to suppress enemy small arms fire, including machine guns, with direct fire and to engage any exposed enemy field batteries. With these field guns serving primarily as moral support, massed infantry small arms fire would drive the enemy out of its defensive positions. Once the objective had been secured, all field guns would be moved forward as fast as possible to repel any enemy counterattacks.[45]

This tactical doctrine supported by many American field artillerymen, such as Major Charles P. Summerall and Captain Oliver L. Spaulding, Jr., gave little attention to bombarding the rear area to disrupt command and control, logistics, or reserve formations even though indirect fire would permit engaging such deep targets. While American observers saw the European war as instructive and wrote about the technological advances in warfare, they clung tightly to observed indirect fire for an open battlefield or war of movement with its dependence upon infantry charges and disparaged unobserved map fire of trench warfare as practiced on the Western Front. Equipped with unreliable target acquisition and communications systems, the Americans paid little attention to delivering field artillery fires beyond the visible front-line. In the midst of a war with its emphasis on field artillery firepower, the American army and School of Fire for Field Artillery continued teaching field artillery employment as it had been taught for years and dispatched graduates to operational field artillery units where they would teach the American concept of observed indirect fire, even though pressure by the Allies to abandon open warfare for trench warfare intensified.[46] Discussing the debate over observed indirect fire versus unobserved indirect fire, Snow wrote, "In fact, this pressure was continuous during the entire war. However, I could not bring myself . . . to the conviction that our principles underlying the use of field artillery were wrong or out of date."[47]

Following the guidance of the Commanding General of the AEF, General John P. Pershing, a strong advocate of open warfare and an ardent opponent of trench warfare, the School of Fire for Field Artillery found itself wedded to teaching open warfare doctrine in 1917-1918 that relied on the rifles and bayonets of self-reliant, aggressive infantrymen and a nominal amount of field artillery fire. Basically, American field artillery would be light, would gallop into action, would set up in the open if necessary, and would fire off a rapid volley to smash any pocket of resistance. Ironically, the school trained field artillery officers for a more difficult style of fighting than unobserved indirect fire. Observed indirect fire demanded initiative, resourcefulness, and judgment – skills that were not easily or quickly taught to new officers in a short course of instruction. In contrast to trench warfare and unobserved indirect fire where skills were used repeatedly and where time was available to plan in great detail, open warfare or maneuver warfare required field artillerymen to employ myriad skills and to execute missions rapidly with a minimal amount of planning.[48]

Although the professional journals, including the *Field Artillery Journal*, and American advisors such as Summerall who were monitoring the war, discussed the importance of trench warfare, the American army endorsed employing observed indirect fire on a mobile battlefield where flanking, enveloping, and annihilating were critical. With this view of the battlefield, the Americans and School of Fire for Field Artillery envisioned field artillery in a supportive role to aggressive and self-reliant infantry charges and advocated the economic use of field artillery ammunition. According to Pershing and other senior American army officers, if used properly, open warfare tactics would permit the American army to break the enemy formations even if they were entrenched and then rout them with a determined pursuit.[49]

Brigadier General Lesley J. McNair, the senior field artillery officer on the AEF staff, reflected Pershing's thinking. In November 1918, he vehemently criticized European unobserved map firing techniques and advocated the superiority of the American doctrine of observed fire. He explained that the Europeans concentrated on unobserved indirect fire rather than focusing on observed fire and pushing field artillery forward to support the infantry advance. A strong sponsor of observed indirect fire, McNair wrote that unobserved map firing was causing too many infantry casualties because it seldom engaged obstacles to the infantry advance as observed fire could. Whereas observed indirect fire offered flexibility, unobserved fire was rigid and prohibited adjusting to meet changing tactical requirements like observed fire could, making American technique superior.[50]

The American rapid advances on the Western Front in the fall of 1918 seemed to validate the school's, McNair's, Snow's, and Pershing's advocacy of observed indirect fire and war of maneuver in the face of unsuppressed infantry and field artillery fire. Yet, they failed to recognize that field artillery firepower and observed and unobserved indirect fire permitted the war of maneuver because it paralyzed the enemy throughout its tactical depth.[51]

As anticipated, the American emphasis upon open warfare created tension between the French liaison officers detailed to the school and American instructors. One French field artillery officer with no experience with open warfare but with trench warfare experience strongly advocated reorganizing the school's curriculum to stress trench warfare techniques. Along with the other French field artillery officers, he found the school and Snow to be unreceptive and adamant about teaching open warfare techniques. In fact, Snow wrote after the war about the French attempt to subvert the school's effort to teach open warfare and the intense pressure to force the Americans to abandon open warfare for trench warfare.[52]

Although he was willing to concede about crafting adaptations to make open warfare more consistent with trench warfare, Snow did not buckle under the pressure to change field artillery tactics and doctrine. While Snow continued to emphasize open warfare at the expense of trench warfare, the School of Fire for Field Artillery wrote and printed its own texts that emphasized open warfare rather than using the countless British and French texts that were available for training.[53]

On the eve of the World War I, European armies ironically embraced observed indirect fire for a war of movement that they condemned the Americans for advocating. The Europeans taught that the battle would begin with a field artillery duel from guns in concealed positions for observed indirect fire. Once enemy field artillery had been silenced, the infantry would advance under the cover of continuous shrapnel fire from field guns that would be moved from their hidden positions for observed indirect fire into the open for direct fire engagements if necessary. The Europeans even promoted pushing the guns forward with the infantry advance and moving them within small arms range to press home the infantry attack.

As in the days of Napoleon, field artillery fire was important, but an aggressive infantry attack would still decide the battle. Although the Russo-Japanese War of 1904-1905 dispelled this and indicated that infantry attacks were suicidal in the face of devastating indirect fire from well-placed field guns and small arms fire, European armies continued making field artillery fire subordinate to infantry maneuver following the Russo-Japanese War. Field artillery batteries had to adjust their fire to the infantry advance by shifting their fire around the battlefield to meet the needs of the attacking infantry and then had to close within small arms range for direct fire to help the infantry attack succeed. The Europeans also taught the importance of counterbattery fire but found it to be impractical on a mobile battlefield against defiladed batteries. As their American cousins, European armies wanted to flank, envelop, and annihilate the opponent, a system of fighting that had existed in Europe for years.[54]

The opening battles of World War I demonstrated the futility of flanking, enveloping, and annihilating and employing aggressive infantry tactics with minimal field artillery fire for support and forced alterations. While complex technical fire direction computation methods prevented shifting observed fire around the battlefield effectively to support the infantry advance, inadequate communication systems hampered coordinating infantry and field artillery action. To minimize the need to communicate between infantry formations and field artillery batteries and to simplify computing technical fire direction, the Europeans developed unobserved map fire that was dependent upon detailed fire plans. Concealed and covered batteries fired long preliminary bombardments designed to destroy everything, furnished inflexible rolling barrages in front of the advancing infantry to keep the defenders under cover until the infantry could reach enemy lines, and furnished counterbattery fire to protect the infantry from enemy field artillery fire until the supporting infantry field guns could be moved forward. Such tactics inverted the historic relationship between infantry maneuver and field artillery fire. Rather than compelling batteries to adjust to infantry action, the infantry attack had to conform to the field artillery barrages.[55]

The European armies eventually modified this concept of fighting. By the time that the Americans entered the war in 1918, unobserved map fire depended upon aerial photographs and other target acquisition means, such as sound and flash ranging, to locate key enemy targets, including hidden batteries and command posts, and discarded massed unobserved indirect fires that were characterized by long bombardments and that had sacrificed surprise in 1914-1917. Influenced by Captain André Lafarge of the French army and Colonel Georg Bruchmüller of the German army, European armies adopted predicted fire where registration fire was not used or kept to a minimum to enhance surprise. Predicted indirect fire minimized the employment of observers to adjust fire onto a target, emphasized placing fires on a target at the right moment for improved effectiveness, and used mathematics to determine the direction and distance to the target. Basically, predicted fire included a barrage of fire that moved in front of the infantry to force the defender to go underground or undercover, the simultaneous attack with field artillery fire on strong points, communications, and reserves throughout the depth of the enemy's defenses, and counterbattery fire using gas and high-explosive steel shell. Counterbattery fire would protect the advancing infantry from hostile field artillery fire until friendly accompanying field guns could be moved forward to engage enemy field artillery. Besides stressing attacking the entire depth of the enemy's battlefield simultaneously, which the old method did not, this new style of warfare emphasized breaking through the enemy front with a minimal amount of preparatory fires and devastating the full depth of the enemy with field artillery firepower. A paralyzing breakthrough employing predicted fire, not flanking and enveloping, became the object, and indirect fire was the key. This formula almost gave Germany a victory in the spring of 1918.[56]

Meanwhile, the School of Fire for Field Artillery supplied aerial observation training because it was growing more important to see the rear areas. The school conducted a two-week course at Henry Post Field that covered field artillery organization, targets, tactics, and the principles of observation for field artillery officers. While some of the students in the two-week course were graduates of the school's wartime course, other field artillery officers attending the short course were not. Upon successful completion of this course, the graduates along with other field artillery officers attended the School of Aerial Artillery Observers at Henry Post Field. All graduates of the School of Aerial Artillery Observers were sent to the Air Service and never returned to their field artillery regiments.[57]

Snow found this practice to be unsatisfactory because officers received the necessary aerial observer training, left their field artillery regiments, and did not return to them. Basically, the Field Artillery lost some of its best trained officers to the fledgling Air Service. This procedure produced 25 new aerial observers a week but irritated regimental commanders who reluctantly sent young officers for aerial observer training that was becoming more important as the range of field artillery increased and as the need for striking behind front lines escalated. After lengthy and heated discussions between Snow and the Air Service to eliminate the problem, both finally agreed to keep the officers in the Field Artillery and to detail them to the Air Corps that controlled the Air Service. Also, Snow and the Air Service decided to develop a seven-week aerial observer course for flying cadets and field artillerymen with the first class beginning on 25 August 1918. At the time of the armistice in November 1918, the school was producing 100 field artillery aerial observers a week. The flying cadets received Air Service commissions, and field artillerymen became aerial observers and stayed in field artillery units.[58]

Between September 1917 and April 1919 when the School of Fire for Field Artillery ended its wartime course and initiated its peacetime course, the school expanded rapidly.[59] Using Snow's plan as a framework, the school built new facilities to handle an increased student load, designed a wartime course for officers that produced 3,215 graduates, emphasized observed indirect fire for a war of movement, and trained 515 officers to be aerial observers. The only courses taught at the school – the field artillery officer course and the air observer course – trained field artillerymen and observers for duty on the battlefields on the Western Front and centered their instruction on furnishing observed indirect fire for the open warfare with its stress on closing with the enemy with aggressive infantry charges.[60]

As Snow recorded in his wartime memoirs and annual report, the School of Fire for Field Artillery started from scratch in July 1917, making its wartime achievements even more impressive. When Snow and his instructors arrived, they had nothing to build upon. Stripping the school of instructors and students and closing it during the crisis on the Mexican border in 1916-1917 left only a small garrison without any field artillerymen at Fort Sill. This gave Snow, Fleming, and their instructors the opportunity to write programs of instruction without being encumbered by existing lesson plans. Basically, they could take the school in any desired direction without the imperative of revising.

Beyond the School House

Even with the rapid expansion of 1917-1918, the School of Fire for Field Artillery lacked the capacity of producing the required number of qualified field artillery officers for combat in Europe even though it was the "only bright star in the whole Field Artillery firmament." Recognizing the need for more field artillery officers than the school could turn out and also enlisted soldiers, the War Department hastily designed a makeshift training program in the summer of 1917 and eventually adopted Snow's recommendation of 1918 for a comprehensive training system to mass produce field artillerymen.[61]

Following the declaration of war in April 1917, the pressing need for officers to fill the National Guard and National Army formations being created prompted the War Department to create officer candidate camps which provided a three-month course for reservists and civilians in the summer of 1917.[62] While the first two officer training camps drew their candidates directly from civilian life, the third and fourth took their candidates from the enlisted ranks of the first draft. After cursory training, the graduates were commissioned with a rank up to major depending upon their standing in the class and then reported to their regiments or brigades to pick up field artillery training as the circumstances would permit. The regiments and brigades conducted night school, but the lack of equipment and skilled field artillery officers to serve as instructors quickly demonstrated that a reliable and trained field artillery officer corps would not be created using this system.[63] Officers who were products of these camps and schools were not qualified for a commission. But the system satisfied the immediate need of getting officers to operational units rapidly as possible.[64]

To take over the load of the officer candidate camps that were deemed a temporary expedient, the War Department directed each National Army and National Guard division to form their own schools to train officers for the combat arms. When the draftees arrived, the divisions hurriedly assigned them to a branch of the service according to their vocations, hoping for a good match. The lack of training space, an insufficient amount of proper equipment, and the cursory training prevented the division schools from graduating

School of Fire for Field Artillery in World War I

qualified field artillery officers. Incompetent instructors who were generally reservists with little training also figured prominently to the inability to create proficient graduates. The War Department could not spare Regular Army field artillery officers, who in reality did not have much more expertise than the reservists, as instructors, so untrained reservists bore the responsibility of training field artillery officers for the National Army and National Guard.[65]

Snow voiced severe criticism of the officer candidate camps and schools.[66] Early in 1918 upon becoming the Chief of Field Artillery, he commented:

> There were thus 15 or more schools – all more or less uncoordinated, all with different standards, and facilities for instruction. The only uniformity they possessed was in a wholly inadequate course of instruction, and incompetent instructors with insufficient equipment. The instructors were, in nearly all cases, reserve officers, who knew only what field artillery they had acquired in a similar previous school.[67]

Venting his frustration, Snow noted, "It was truly a case of the 'blind leading the blind' and each succeeding crop of field artillery officers was less competent than its predecessor."[68]

Meanwhile, a haphazard system arose to train enlisted Regular Army, National Guard, and National Army field artillery soldiers and units. Early in the mobilization effort, division and brigade camps provided the specialized training based upon guidance from the War Department issued in July 1917.[69] The July 1917 guidance allotted 16 weeks for rigorous training, assigned the subjects to be covered, prescribed the number of hours for each, outlined a daily training schedule, and tasked brigade and regimental commanders to implement the training. In many instances, field artillery brigade commanders were infantry officers and did not understand the needs of the Field Artillery, while the lack of standardization permitted the quality of training to vary from camp to camp. Moreover, few units had their appropriate complement of equipment, and most lacked trained instructors. This situation led to inconsistent field artillery training in the citizen formations for the rank and file. In the meantime, the widely scattered condition of Regular Army field artillery regiments prevented coordinating instruction for enlisted personnel. This format of training continued into 1918, failing to produce qualified field artillery enlisted soldiers.[70]

To be sure Snow found this system of training field artillery officers, enlisted personnel, and units to be inadequate and broken. After the war Snow wrote in his annual report for 1919, "Conditions in the Field Artillery in January, 1918, may be characterized as chaotic."[71] He explained, "Training was almost at a standstill. Equipment and material was negligible."[72] In an article in the *Field Artillery Journal* in November-December 1940, Snow reflected, "I was thoroughly disgusted with the Division Schools."[73]

Interestingly, Colonel Alfred A. Starbird of the Inspector General's Office condemned National Guard field artillery units even more strongly than Snow did. In a report of December 1917 that he compiled after visiting 15 National Guard field artillery brigades, he found their training to be deplorable. Most of the training deficiencies stemmed from insufficient personnel caused by the replacement system that was constantly transferring the most experienced personnel to operational units and by the lack of equipment.[74]

After becoming the Chief of Field Artillery when the position was created on 10 February 1918, Snow submitted a comprehensive plan to the War Department on 27 March 1918. It abolished the existing training system by centralizing all field artillery training under the newly formed Office of the Chief of Field Artillery. Confidently believing in his plan, he recommended establishing a Field Artillery Replacement Depot at Camp Jackson, South Carolina, increasing graduate production at the School of Fire for Field Artillery even more than it had been, organizing brigade firing centers, forming specialist schools in the divisions, establishing a system of training and coordination through inspector-instructors who would help and inspect the training of brigades, and opening a Field Artillery Central Officers' Training School. Such a school would ensure uniformity in training field artillery officers, establish standards for commissioning, reduce the number of instructors required, guarantee qualified instructors, and replace the division schools. For Snow, this was particularly critical because unqualified reserve officers who had practically no experience other than that gained at a preceding training camp were serving as instructors in National Guard and National Army training facilities and serving in operational units.[75]

Although the acting Director of the War Plans Division, War Department, Colonel D.W. Ketchum, and the Adjutant General, Major General Henry P. McCain, opposed centralizing field artillery training under the Chief of Field Artillery and wanted to preserve the existing chaotic system, Snow presented his plan to the Chief of Staff of the War Department,

Major General Tasker H. Bliss, on 27 March 1918. After careful consideration, Bliss finally approved a portion of Snow's plan on 14 April 1918. He supported everything but creating a Field Artillery Central Officers' School for commissioning enlisted soldiers as officers because the process would separate them from their units. For training officers, he approved continuing the division training schools.[76]

Within one month after gaining approval of his plan, Snow started implementing it. On 8 May 1918, the first field artillery replacement depot opened at Camp Jackson under Brigadier General Robert M. Danford, a former instructor in the School of Fire for Field Artillery. Prompted by the success of Camp Jackson, its own inability to provide the requisite number graduates, and the recognition of the necessity of such a camp, the War Department started a second one on 25 June 1918 at Camp Zachary Taylor, near Louisville, Kentucky, under Brigadier General Fred T. Austin, another former School of Fire for Field Artillery instructor. During the course of the war, the two replacement depots trained more than 8,000 officers and 35,000 enlisted soldiers in the essential duties of soldiers and various field artillery specialties, such as automobile mechanics, truck driving, and tractor driving, among others, to fill in as replacements. Upon completion of their training, the officers transferred to the School of Fire for Field Artillery for advanced field artillery training before moving to their units. In comparison, the enlisted soldiers who had received specialized training went directly to their first unit of assignment.[77]

To fill a noticeable training gap that stemmed from the lack of materiel and space to train and that had prevented many field artillery brigades from training as a unit before shipping to France, to train field artillery brigades still in the United States in the shortest time possible, and to reduce the amount of training required overseas, the War Department subsequently established brigade firing centers as Snow recommended under its control.[78] In the summer of 1918, the War Department opened brigade firing centers at Camp Doniphan, Fort Sill; Camp Jackson; Camp Knox, Kentucky; and Camp McClellan, Alabama; along the lines of the brigade firing centers in France with the idea that they would be "finishing schools" for unit training.[79]

Requiring even more training capacity, the War Department initiated new construction at Camp Knox and Camp Jackson to replace the temporary facilities and purchased 135,000 acres at Camp Bragg near Fayetteville, North Carolina, in 1918 to supplant the brigade firing center at Camp McClellan; but the war ended before the construction of cantonments at Camp Bragg for six field artillery brigades could be completed.[80]

Unfortunately, the brigades arrived at the brigade firing centers with insufficient training to make them finishing schools as Snow desired. For the most part, the officers had graduated from the old officer training camps of the first days of the war or division officer candidate schools and lacked adequate training in field artillery tactics and techniques. In the case of National Guard brigades, 31 percent of the officers had received a direct commission from a state governor and had no military training at all. Such a state of training forced Snow and Colonel Edmund L. Gruber who helped pioneer the brigade firing center concept to abandon their original plans. Before providing advanced training as they had initially planned, they had to furnish elementary training at the firing centers for the brigades.[81]

Basically, the brigades went through one to five weeks of elementary instruction and then intensive, advanced practical training. Altogether, training for field artillery brigades lasted three months and covered general instruction in field artillery tactics and battery, battalion, and brigade firing problems that included preparations for an attack and advance and preparations for retirement to a secondary position and relief. For the most part, combat experienced officers served as instructors and furnished intensive practical training between June 1918 when the American Expeditionary Force first saw combat and November 1918 when the armistice was signed to end the war. Altogether, six brigades went through the four field artillery brigade firing centers prior to the armistice before being shipped to France with eight brigades undergoing training when the armistice was signed in November 1918.[82]

Concurring with the War Department's Inspector observations, Snow found the training at the firing centers to be indispensable.[83] Based upon the training schedules, the employment of combat experienced instructors, and the concentration of equipment at the centers, Snow concluded, "It may be truly said that only those brigades which had passed through these firing centers were properly trained and organized upon their departure from this country for France."[84]

Gruber commented about the brigade firing center concept in October 1918 when he addressed the training program at Camp Doniphan that he had designed. Camp Doniphan's 10- to 12-week course supplied intensive, practical field artillery training for officers and enlisted personnel. Moving from the least difficult to the most difficult subjects and tasks, the course began with three to four weeks of preliminary instruction, then four weeks of battery instruction and firing practice, two weeks of battalion field exercises and firing, and two or three weeks of brigade exercises and firing in a trench system constructed east of Signal Mountain with help from the School of Fire for Field Artillery. In the brigade firing exercise, field artillerymen organized fires and liaison, did everything that they would do on the front, and learned unobserved map fire and observed fire techniques.[85]

Although Bliss approved Snow's overall plan for training field artillerymen on 14 April 1918 as mentioned, he preserved the existing decentralized training system for field artillery officers and unwisely rejected the Central Officers' Training School concept. Conditions, however, dictated changing the system because the divisions were being shipped overseas, leaving their schools stranded stateside without any command support and the ability to train and commission field artillery officers as replacements. This meant that the flow of new field artillery officers as replacements would come to a halt in the near future. Also, the surplus of 2,000 to 3,000 field artillery officers that had existed early in 1918 disappeared virtually overnight because of the overseas deployments and turned into a deficit of more than 2,000 by May 1918. Under such circumstances, General Peyton C. March, who was the acting Chief of Staff of the Army, faced the imperative of approving Snow's Field Artillery Central Officers' Training School concept to ensure the availability of competent field artillery officers.[86]

Influenced by this and the projected need for 15,000 new field artillery officers by January 1919 and continual pressure from Snow, the War Department adopted Snow's Field Artillery Central Officers' Training School on 20 May 1918 and opened it on 15 June 1918 under Lieutenant Colonel Arthur H. Carter at Camp Zachary Taylor, Kentucky. The school replaced the division officer candidate training camps, standardized training, and focused its training on only "the absolute essentials" to equip the graduate with the background to perform his duties as a commissioned officer upon graduation.[87] Organized into five main departments (Fire Discipline and Materiel, Gunnery, Mounted Instruction, Reconnaissance, and Miscellaneous Instruction), headquarters personnel, and 10 batteries of school troops, the school, with help from the Military Training Camp Association that organized committees in cities around the country to recruit men for the Field Artillery, received select enlisted soldiers and civilians each week for a course of 12 weeks of instruction on military fundamentals that all officers needed to know and the principles of field artillery. At the end of the course, the school graduated the students with the rank of sergeant or commissioned them as a second lieutenant in the Field Artillery depending upon their qualifications. Students who failed to graduate as either a sergeant or a second lieutenant were sent to a replacement depot where their skills could be used. Those graduating as a second lieutenant then attended the School of Fire for Field Artillery. Between June 1918 and November 1918 when the school ceased operations, the school produced 8,737 graduates. Of those, about 5,214 received commissions as second lieutenants in the Field Artillery of the US Army. The rest received commissions in the Field Artillery Reserve Corps in accordance with the provisions of the National Defense Act of 1916. Basically, the Field Artillery Central Officers Training School took large groups of untrained candidates in an emergency situation and turned them into officers capable of handling enlisted soldiers and sufficiently qualified in the fundamentals of field artillery to serve in a battery and become battery commanders.[88]

Snow initially wanted the Field Artillery Central Officers' Training School to be part of a progressive and sequential officer training system that ran from basic to advanced training. In his comprehensive plan of March 1918, Snow sought eight months of training for all field artillery officers. They would spend three months at the Field Artillery Central Officers' Training School, two months at a Replacement Depot to learn the actual handling, feeding, training, clothing, and caring for soldiers, and three months at the School of Fire for Field Artillery to learn advanced field artillery tactics, techniques, and procedures. Coupled with the late start of Snow's training program, the increasing demand for field artillery officers prevented the ideal from being attained. Few officers went through eight months of training. Generally, they had five to six months of training at the most. With a few exceptions they went from either the Field Artillery Central Officers' Training Center or the Replacement Training Depots to the School of Fire for Field Artillery and received little practical training in leading soldiers.[89]

Recognizing the need for technicians in field artillery units, the War Department also created schools to train them. It established schools for aerial observers; radio officers, motor and tractor specialists; telephone, liaison, and orienting officers; and even staff officers.[90]

Even though the War Department implemented Snow's ambitious plan, the expansion from nine inadequately trained Regular Army field artillery regiments in April 1917 to 21 Regular Army field artillery regiments, 138 National Guard field artillery regiments, and 51 National Army field artillery regiments in November 1918 taxed the training system. In 20 months, 21,984 officers (3,215 officers trained at the School of Fire for Field Artillery) and 431,507 enlisted soldiers went through the field artillery training system. Reflecting upon the magnitude of the training effort, Snow concluded correctly that the task of training field artillerymen in 1917-1918 was unprecedented in the history of the country with the School of Fire for Field Artillery playing a key role.[91] "Without question this school contributed more to the success of the Field Artillery operations in this war than any other Artillery activity," Snow recorded in his annual report for 1919.[92]

Yet, Snow acknowledged a striking shortcoming even with his system. He wrote in October 1919, "It is an incontrovertible fact that even with the most intensive training and the greatest of incentives, it is impossible to train properly field artillerymen in two to four months."[93] Although Snow created a comprehensive training program to mass produce qualified field artillerymen for the battlefields of France, the demands of the war prevented the objective from being achieved and forced many field artillerymen to learn their trade through on-the-job training in the trenches of France.[94]

Notwithstanding Snow's observation about the difficulty of training field artillerymen in a short period of time and their questionable competency, the School of Fire for Field Artillery certainly rose to the occasion in 1917-1918. During the war, it formed the core of an extensive field artillery training program and trained officers to assume positions of command and high responsibility in field artillery units in the American Expeditionary Force and to employ open warfare and trench warfare tactics with an emphasis upon the former although it remained primarily a gunnery school.

Endnotes

1   Annual Report of the Chief of Field Artillery, 1919, p. 7; Maurice Matloff, ed., *American Military History* (Washington, DC: Center of Military History, US Army, 1985), p. 367; Russell F. Weigley, *History of the United States Army* (Bloomington, IN: Indiana University Press, 1984), p. 348.

2   Weigley, *History of the United States Army*, pp. 348-49; Matloff, *American Military History*, p. 367; Annual Report of the Chief of Field Artillery, 1919, p. 8.

3   Riley Sunderland, *History of the Field Artillery School: 1911-1942* (Fort Sill, OK: Fort Sill Printing Plant, 1942), p. 53.

4   Annual Report of the Chief of Artillery, 1919, pp. 17-18.

5   Annual Report of the Chief of Field Artillery, 1919, p. 7; Matloff, *American Military History*, p. 367.

6   Annual Report of the Chief of Field Artillery, 1919, pp. 7-9, 16, 17, 19; Sunderland, *History of the Field Artillery School*, p. 53; *The Mil*, 1922, p. 7, UF25 C615 A7, Morris Swett Technical Library (MSTL), US Army Field Artillery School. *The Mil* was the yearbook for the battery officer class after World War I.

7   Sunderland, *History of the Field Artillery School*, p. 53; Annual Report of the Chief of Field Artillery, 1919, pp. 10, 106; MG William J. Snow, *Signposts of Experience: World War I Memoirs* (Washington DC: United States Field Artillery Association, 1941), pp. 141, 143, 144; Wilbur S. Nye, *Carbine and Lance: The Story of Old Fort Sill* (Norman, OK: University of Oklahoma Press, 1974), p. 328; CPT E. Durette, "Fort Sill in Wartime," *Field Artillery Journal*, May-Jun 1923, pp. 239-45; Morris Swett, "History of Artillery Schools in the United States," unpublished manuscript, 1938, pp. 64-87, Historical Research and Document Collection (HRDC), Field Artillery Branch Historian's Office, US Army Field Artillery School.

8   Sunderland, *History of the Field Artillery School*, p. 53; Annual Report of the Chief of Field Artillery, 1919, pp. 10, 106; Snow, *Signposts of Experience*, pp. 141, 143, 144, 164; Nye, *Carbine and Lance*, p. 328; Durette, "Fort Sill in Wartime," pp. 239-45; MG William J. Snow, History of Office, Chief of Field Artillery, draft manuscript, 1933, UF23 A1S5

9   Sunderland, *History of the Field Artillery School*, p. 53; Snow, History of Office Chief of Field Artillery, pp. 90-94, UF23 A1S5, MSTL; Snow, *Signposts of Experience*, p. 143.

10   Snow, *Signposts of Experience*, pp. 143-44.

11   Snow, *Signposts of Experience*, pp. 144, 328; Sunderland, *History of the Field Artillery School*, p. 54; Annual Report of the Chief of Field Artillery, 1919, p. 110; "A Brief History of Fort Sill and the Field Artillery School," *Field Artillery Journal*, Nov-Dec 1933, pp. 528-41.

12   Snow, *Signposts of Experience*, p. 143.

13   Snow, *Signposts of Experience*, p. 143.

14   Snow, *Signposts of Experience*, p. 143.

15   Snow, *Signposts of Experience*, p. 143.

16   Snow, *Signposts of Experience*, p. 143.

17   Snow, *Signposts of Experience*, p. 143..

18   Snow, *Signposts of Experience*, p. 145; MG William J. Snow, "Field Artillery Firing Centers," *Field Artillery Journal*, Nov-Dec 1940, p. 450; MG William J. Snow, "Origin of the

Field Artillery School," *Field Artillery Journal*, Feb 1941, p. 102.

19 Snow, "Origin of the Field Artillery School," p. 102.

20 Snow, *Signposts of Experience*, p. 145.

21 Gillette Griswold, "Fort Sill, Oklahoma: A Brief History," unpublished manuscript, pp. 11-12, HRDC; Nye, *Carbine and Lance*, pp. 326, 330-31; MG William J. Snow, History of Office, Chief of Field Artillery, pp. 93-95, UF23 A1S5, MSTL; Snow, *Signposts of Experience*, pp. 145-46; Griswold, "Fort Sill, Oklahoma: A Chronology of Events," unpaginated chronology, HRDC; Snow, "Origin of the Field Artillery School," p. 102.

22 Snow, History of Office, Chief of Field Artillery, pp. 93-95, UF23 A1S5, MSTL; Snow, *Signposts of Experience*, pp. 145-46; Nye, *Carbine and Lance*, pp. 330-31; Griswold, "Fort Sill, Oklahoma: A Chronology of Events," unpaginated chronology, HRDC; Griswold, "Fort Sill, Oklahoma: A Brief History," draft history, pp. 10-11, HRDC; Snow, "Origin of the Field Artillery School," p. 102.

23 Sunderland, *History of the Field Artillery School*, pp. 54-55; Snow, *Signposts of Experience*, pp. 152-53.

24 Durette, "Fort Sill in Wartime," pp. 239-45; Snow, *Signposts of Experience*, p. 147.

25 Snow, *Signposts of Experience*, p. 147.

26 Snow, *Signposts of Experience*, p. 147.

27 Annual Report of the Chief of Field Artillery, 1919, p. 106; Snow, *Signposts of Experience*, p. 153; James E. Hewes, Jr., *From Root to McNamara: Army Organization and Administration, 1900-1963* (Washington DC: US Army Center of Military History, 1975), p. 403; Sunderland, *History of the Field Artillery School*, pp. 54-58.

28 Sunderland, *History of the Field Artillery School*, p. 55; Nye, *Carbine and Lance*, p. 329; Annual Report of the Chief of Field Artillery, 1919, p. 106; Durette, "Fort Sill in Wartime," pp. 240-41.

29 Nye, *Carbine and Lance*, p. 329; Annual Report of the Chief of Field Artillery, 1919, p. 106.

30 *On-the-Way: First Class, School of Fire for Field Artillery, Fort Sill, Oklahoma* (Salt Lake City, UT: The Deseret News Publishing Company, n.d.), p. 16; Durette, "Fort Sill in Wartime," pp. 239-45. CPT Durette was the senior French officer at the School of Fire during the war courses.

31 Durette, "Fort Sill in Wartime," pp. 239-45.

32 Snow, *Signposts of Experience*, pp. 14, 154; Snow, "Origin of the Field Artillery School," p. 103.

33 "The Mission of the School of Fire for Field Artillery," *Field Artillery Journal*, Oct-Dec 1917, p. 384.

34 "The Mission of the School of Fire for Field Artillery," p. 384.

35 Durette, "Fort Sill in Wartime," p. 241; Griswold, "Fort Sill, Oklahoma: A Chronology of Key Events," HRDC; Jean Schucker, "Henry Post Army Airfield: First Home of Army Aviation," *US Army Aviation Digest*, May-Jun 1992, pp. 18-21.

36 "The Mission of the School of Fire for Field Artillery," p. 385.

37 "The Mission of the School of Fire for Field Artillery," p. 385.; Sunderland, *History of the Field Artillery School*, p. 68; Schucker, "Henry Post Army Airfield," pp. 18-21.

38 "The Mission of the School of Fire for Field Artillery," p. 388.

39 Snow, *Signposts of Experience*, p. 157.

40 "The Mission of the School of Fire for Field Artillery," p. 388; Snow, History of Office, Chief of Field Artillery, p. 105, UF23 A1S5, MSTL.

41 "The Mission of the School of Fire for Field Artillery," pp. 389-90; Durette, "Fort Sill in Wartime," pp. 239-45; Sunderland, *History of the Field Artillery School*, pp. 58, 63, 68; MAJ Harrison Fuller, "The Apache Gate Sector," *Field Artillery Journal*, Jan-Mar 1919, pp. 7-16; Griswold, "Fort Sill, Oklahoma: A Brief History," p. 12, HRDC. See Peter B. Kyne, "The Artillery Mill at Old Fort Sill," *The Saturday Evening Post*, 9 Nov 1918, pp. 15, 49, 50, 52, for an interesting look into training at the School of Fire and Fort Sill during World War I.

42 Snow, *Signposts of Experience*, p. 45; Sunderland, *History of the Field Artillery School*, pp. 63-64; Fuller, "The Apache Gate Sector," pp. 7-16.

43 Fuller, "The Apache Gate Sector," pp. 7-16.

44 Snow, History of Office, Chief of Field Artillery, p. 100, UF23 A1S5, MSTL; Mark E. Grotelueschen, *Doctrine under Trial: American Artillery Employment in World War One* (Westport, CT: Greenwood Press, 2001), p. 11; LTC John B. Anderson, "Are We Justified Discarding 'Pre-War' Methods of Training," *Field Artillery Journal*, Apr-Jun 1919, pp. 222-30; Department of Gunnery, School of Fire, "American Drill Regulations and Artillery Firing," *Field Artillery Journal*, Jul-Sep 1918, pp. 363-69; Field Artillery Brigade Firing Center, Fort Sill, Instruction Pamphlet No. 22, Field Artillery Fire in the Present War, 1918, in Instruction Pamphlets, Field Artillery Brigade Firing Center, UF23.5 S6U51, MSTL; Snow, "Origins of the Field Artillery School," p. 104.

45 Steven A. Stebbins, "Indirect Fire: The Challenge and Response in the US Army, 1907-1917," unpublished master's thesis, University of North Carolina, 1993, pp. 18-23, 40, 68-71, 78-80, 84; Richard L. Pierce, "A Maximum of Support: The Development of US Army Field Artillery Doctrine in World War One," unpublished master's thesis, Ohio State University, 1983, p. 18.

46 Stebbins, "Indirect Fire," pp. 18-23, 40, 68-71, 78-80, 84; Pierce, "A Maximum of Support," p. 18.

47 Snow, History of Office, Chief of Field Artillery, p. 100, UF23 A1S5, MSTL.

48 J.B.A. Bailey, *Field Artillery and Firepower* (Annapolis, MD: Naval Institute Press, 2004), pp. 214-66; J.B.A. Bailey, "The First World War and the Birth of Modern Warfare," in Macgregor Knox and Williamson Murray, eds. *The Dynamics of Military Revolution, 1300-2050* (New York: Cambridge University Press, 2004), pp. 132-53; Grotelueschen, *Doctrine under Trial*, pp. 18-19; Department of Gunnery, School of Fire, "American Drill Regulations and Artillery Firing," p. 363.

49 Grotelueschen, *Doctrine under Trial*, p. 5.

50 Sunderland, *History of the Field Artillery School*, p. 64.

51 Bailey, *Field Artillery and Firepower*, p. 269; Grotelueschen, *Doctrine under Trial*, pp. 144-52.

52 Snow, *Signposts of Experience*, p. 45; Sunderland, *History of the Field Artillery School*, pp. 63-64; Fuller, "The Apache Gate Sector," pp. 7-16; Bailey, *Field Artillery and Firepower*, p. 266; Snow, History of Office, Chief of Field Artillery, p. 100, UF23 A1S5, MSTL.

53 Snow, "Origin of the Field Artillery School," pp. 104-05.

54 Bailey, *Field Artillery and Firepower*, pp. 218-19, 228, 231, 238; Bailey, "The First World War and the Birth of Modern Warfare," p. 151.

55 Bailey, *Field Artillery and Firepower*, pp. 240-54; Bailey, "The First World War and the Birth of Modern Warfare," pp. 133-40; Grotelueschen, *Doctrine under Trial*, p. 20; Stebbins,

"Indirect Fire," p. 87; Pierce, "A Maximum of Support," p. 65.

56   Bailey, "The First World War and the Birth of Modern Warfare," pp. 140-51; Grotelueschen, *Doctrine under Trial*, p. 5; Bailey, *Field Artillery and Firepower*, pp. 258-70.

57   Sunderland, *History of the Field Artillery School, 1911-1942*, p. 68; Schucker, "Henry Post Army Airfield," pp. 18-21; Annual Report of the Chief of Field Artillery, 1919, p. 77.

58   Sunderland, *History of the Field Artillery School,* pp. 56, 68; Annual Report of the Chief of Field Artillery, 1919, p. 77; Snow, *Signpost of Experience*, p. 167.

59   Sunderland, *History of the Field Artillery School*, p. 73; Annual Report of the Field Artillery School, 13 Aug 1920, p. 1.

60   Sunderland, *History of the Field Artillery School*, p. 72.

61   Snow, *Signposts of Experience*, p. 49; Snow, History of Office, Chief of Field Artillery, p. 40, UF23 A1S5, MSTL.

62   Annual Report of the Chief of Field Artillery, 1919, pp. 69-71, 75-76; Sunderland, *History of the Field Artillery School, 1911-1942*, pp. 68-69.

63   Annual Report of the Chief of Field Artillery, 1919, pp. 69-70; Sunderland, *History of the Field Artillery School, 1911-1942,* pp. 68-70.

64   Annual Report of the Chief of Field Artillery, 1919, pp. 8, 75-77; Snow, History of Office, Chief of Field Artillery, p. 111, UF23 A1S5, MSTL; Sunderland, *History of the Field Artillery School*, p. 69.

65   Annual Report of the Chief of Field Artillery, 1919, pp. 69-70, 75-77; Snow, History of Office, Chief of Field Artillery, p. 111, UF23 A1S5, MSTL; Sunderland, *History of the Field Artillery School*, p. 69.

66   Report of the Chief of Field Artillery, 1919, pp. 69-76.

67   Snow, History of Office, Chief of Field Artillery, p. 110, UF23 A1S5, MSTL.

68   Snow, History of Office, Chief of Field Artillery, p. 110.

69   Annual Report of the Chief of Field Artillery, 1919, pp. 70-71.

70   Annual Report of the Chief of Field Artillery, 1919, pp. 71-72, 76-77; Snow, History of Office, Chief of Field Artillery, p. 45, UF23 A1S5, MSTL.

71   Annual Report of the Chief of Field Artillery, 1919, p. 9.

72   Annual Report of the Chief of Field Artillery, 1919, p. 13.

73   Snow, "Field Artillery Firing Centers," p. 452.

74   Annual Report of the Chief of Field Artillery, 1919, pp. 55, 73, 74; Snow, *Signposts of Experience*, p. 23.

75   Annual Report of the Chief of Field Artillery, 1919, pp. 9, 13, 74; Sunderland, *History of the Field Artillery School*, pp. 68-71; Hewes, *From Root to McNamara*, p. 403; Snow, History of Office, Chief of Field Artillery, pp. 40-45, UF23 A1S5, MSTL; Raymond Walters, *et al, The Story of the Field Artillery Central Officers Training School, Camp Zachary Taylor, Kentucky* (New York: The Knickerbocker Press, 1919), pp. 9-10.

76   Snow, History of Office, Chief of Field Artillery, pp. 43-44, UF23 A1S5, MSTL; Annual Report of the Chief of Field Artillery, 1919, p. 79.

77   Annual Report of the Chief of Field Artillery, 1919, pp. 9-14, 77-147; Snow, *Signposts of Experience*, pp. 70-165; Walters, *et al, The Story of the Field Artillery Central Officers' Training*

School, pp. 484-503; "The Field Artillery Central Officers' Training School," *Field Artillery Journal*, Jul-Sep 1918, pp. 370-80; "Field Artillery Training in the United States," *Field Artillery Journal*, Jul-Sep 1918, pp. 427-29; Report, subj: Field Artillery Replacement Depot, Camp Zachary Taylor, Kentucky, undated, UF23.66 E11, MSTL; Sunderland, *History of the Field Artillery School: 1911-1942*, p. 70; "Current Notes," *Field Artillery Journal*, Jul-Sep 1918, p. 427; Hewes, *From Root to McNamara*, p. 403; Snow, "Field Artillery Firing Centers," p. 452; Snow, History of Office, Chief of Field Artillery, pp. 59-67, UF23 A1S5, MSTL.

78 Snow, History of Office, Chief of Field Artillery, p. 125, UF23 A1S5, MSTL.

79 Snow, History of the Office, Chief of Field Artillery, p. 126.

80 Annual Report of the Chief of Field Artillery, 1919, pp. 9-14, 115-47; Snow, *Signposts of Experience*, pp. 70-165; Walters, *et al, The Story of the Field Artillery Central Officers' Training School*, pp. 484-503; "The Field Artillery Central Officers' Training School," pp. 370-80; "Field Artillery Training in the United States," *Field Artillery Journal*, Jul-Sep 1918, pp. 427-29; Report, subj: Field Artillery Cantonment Camp Bragg, Fayetteville, North Carolina, Jul 1919, p. 1, F262 B8U5, MSTL; Report, subj: Field Artillery Replacement Depot, Camp Zachary Taylor, Kentucky, undated, UF23.66 E11, MSTL. Construction on the brigade firing centers at Fort Bragg was completed in February 1919 with the idea that they could be utilized during peacetime to prepare for wartime.

81 Snow, *Signpost of Experience*, pp. 84-89; Annual Report of the Chief of Field Artillery, 1919, p. 115.

82 Annual Report of the Chief of Field Artillery, 1919, pp. 9-14, 115-47; Snow, *Signposts of Experience*, pp. 70-165; Walters, *et al, The Story of the Field Artillery Central Officers' Training School,* pp. 484-503; "The Field Artillery Central Officers' Training School," pp. 370-80; "Field Artillery Training in the United States," *Field Artillery Journal*, Jul-Sep 1918, pp. 427-29; Report, subj: Field Artillery Cantonment Camp Bragg, Fayetteville, North Carolina, Jul 1919, p. 1, F262 B8U5, MSTL; Report, subj: Field Artillery Replacement Depot, Camp Zachary Taylor, Kentucky, undated, UF23.66 E11, MSTL.

83 Annual Report of the Chief of Field Artillery, 1919, p. 116.

84 Annual Report of the Chief of Field Artillery, 1919, p. 10.

85 Sunderland, *History of the Field Artillery School*, p. 71; Annual Report of the Chief of Field Artillery, 1919, pp. 117-26.

86 Snow, History of Office, Chief of Field Artillery, pp. 111-14, UF23 A1S5, MSTL.

87 Snow, History of Office, Chief of Field Artillery, p. 114; Walters, *et al, The Story of the Field Artillery Central Officers Training School,* p. 11.

88 "Field Artillery Center Officer's Training School," pp. 370-74; Walters, *et al, The Story of the Field Artillery Central Officers' Training School,*" pp. 484-503; John Kirby, "Colonel Carter Explains Aims of Artillery School," *Field Artillery Journal*, Jul-Sep 1918, pp. 374-79; Annual Report of the Chief of Field Artillery, 1919, pp. 78-106; Snow, History of Office, Chief of Field Artillery, pp. 115-20, UF23 A1S5, MSTL; Snow, "Field Artillery Firing Centers," pp. 447-55; Walters, *The Story of the Field Artillery Central Officers Training School,* pp. 14, 30-36, 39, 54.

89 Snow, "Field Artillery Firing Centers," pp. 452, 455; Annual Report of the Chief of Field Artillery, 1919, pp. 9-14, 77-147; Snow, *Signposts of Experience*, pp. 70-165; Walters, "The Field Artillery Central Officers' Training School," pp. 484-503; "The Field Artillery Central Officers' Training School," pp. 370-80; "Field Artillery Training in the United States," pp. 427-29; Report, subj: Field Artillery Replacement Depot, Camp Zachary Taylor, Kentucky, undated, UF23.66 E11,

MSTL; Sunderland, *History of the Field Artillery School*, p. 70; "Current Notes," *Field Artillery Journal*, Jul-Sep 1918, p. 427; Hewes, *From Root to McNamara*, p. 403; Snow, History of Office, Chief of Field Artillery, pp. 120-22, UF23 A1S5, MSTL.

90 Annual Report of the Chief of Field Artillery, 1919, pp. 9-14, 77-147; Snow, *Signposts of Experience*, pp. 70-165; Walters, *et al, The Story of the Field Artillery Central Officers' Training School*, pp. 484-503; "The Field Artillery Central Officers' Training School," pp. 370-80; "Field Artillery Training in the United States," pp. 427-29; Report, subj: Field Artillery Replacement Depot, Camp Zachary Taylor, Kentucky, undated; Snow, History of Office, Chief of Field Artillery, p. 134, UF23 A1S5, MSTL.

91 Annual Report of the Chief of Field Artillery, 1919, p. 188.

92 Annual Report of the Chief of Field Artillery, 1919, p. 10.

93 Annual Report of the Chief of Field Artillery, 1919, p. 188.

94 Annual Report of the Chief of Field Artillery, 1919, p. 188.

Chapter Four
Peace and Transition

Although World War I validated the School of Fire for Field Artillery's reason for being, peacetime brought uncertainty and change. Following the war, the United States rapidly demobilized and returned to its historical reliance upon a small military force in peacetime. For the school, this meant reduced funding, smaller classes, and possible transfer of the school to a more suitable location. Notwithstanding this, the school had to prepare for the next war by incorporating the lessons from recent combat action into tactics, doctrine, and training even though pacifism and isolationism promised to keep America out of another war.

Adjusting to Peace

Over a period of several months, the School of Fire for Field Artillery transitioned from wartime to peacetime operations for the first time in its short history. It abandoned its wartime course for officers, developed peacetime courses for officers and enlisted soldiers, underwent a name change, became part of a progressive educational system and participated in the debate over the appropriate fire support doctrine to be taught and employed by the Field Artillery.

Within months after the armistice of November 1918 had been signed, the wartime Army disintegrated. In the first month of demobilization, the Army released nearly 650,000 soldiers and within nine months nearly 3,250,000. By January 1920 only 130,000, mainly Regular Army soldiers, remained to maintain a token military occupation of Coblenz, Germany, and to carry on normal peacetime duties.[1]

In the midst of this rapid demobilization, the Chief of Field Artillery, Major General William J. Snow (1919-1927), started preparing the Field Artillery for a future war. Acknowledging the requirement to maintain a skilled body of officers and soldiers in peacetime who would form the nucleus for wartime expansion and help modernize the Field Artillery, Snow designed a comprehensive educational system. With support from the War Department, Snow organized Reserve Officers' Training Corps field artillery units at 22 colleges and universities throughout the United States to develop a pool of qualified reserve field artillery officers; divided them into batteries, battalions, and regiments; and planned to conduct annual Reserve Officer Training Corps summer camps of 12 weeks broken into two six-week sessions where the students would participate in field exercises during the summer after their freshman and junior years. Upon graduation from college and successful completion of Field Artillery Reserve Officer Training Corps training, the individual would be commissioned a second lieutenant in the Field Artillery Reserve Corps and be ready for mobilization as required.[2]

Concurrently, Snow designed a field artillery school system in 1919 that ran from basic to advanced courses for Regular Army and National Guard officers and soldiers. Less experienced Regular Army and National Guard field artillery officers would attend the Field Artillery Basic School at Camp Zachary Taylor, Kentucky (formerly the Field Artillery Central Officers' Training School during the war and renamed the Field Artillery School, Camp Zachary Taylor, Kentucky, Basic Course, on 22 November 1919), where they would receive instruction in basic military skills and field artillery subjects that all field artillery first and second lieutenants should know and that had taken pre-war officers from five to seven years to master serving in a battery and attending a garrison school. In the summer of 1920, the War Department transferred the school to Camp Knox, Kentucky.[3] Captains and field grade officers would attend the Battery Officers' Course at the School of Fire for Field Artillery at Fort Sill, Oklahoma. Renamed the Field Artillery School on 21 April 1919 and tasked to train Regular Army and National Guard officers and soldiers, the school would focus its instruction on general technical training, furnish some instruction in the handling of a battery to prepare officers for battery command, and conduct enlisted specialist courses in mechanics, horseshoeing, saddlery, carpentry, and other subjects. To augment basic and battery-level training, Snow planned to open a field artillery tactical school for advanced field artillery subjects at Camp Bragg, North Carolina, during the last half of 1920 for senior field artillery officers.[4]

As Snow pushed his education and training program to avoid the wartime training debacle of 1917-1918, the War Department acted. Notwithstanding the rapid demobilization and the revival of the country's historical reliance upon a small army in peacetime, the War Department could not discount the possibility of a future war along the lines of the one just fought and took measures to be better prepared than it had been in 1917. This apprehension prodded the War Department to propose a permanent Regular Army of 500,000 that would be organized as an expansible force and be filled out by draftees in time of war. Uneasy about a large standing army, Congress balked at such a proposal because it ran counter to the American tradition of a small army in peacetime and resembled German militarism that the country had just defeated.[5]

After months of debate over the nature of the military force and the War Department's proposal, Congress passed the National Defense Act of June 1920 to replace the National Defense Act of 1916. In this 1920 act that governed the country's military establishment through 1950, Congress rejected the War Department's expansible Regular Army that Regular Army officers had advocated since the days of the Secretary of War John C. Calhoun in the 1820s. Congress established the Army of the United States with three components: the Regular Army, the civilian National Guard, and the civilian Organized Reserves (Officers' and Enlisted Reserve Corps). Each component would be regulated in peacetime so that it could contribute its appropriate share in a war emergency. The Regular Army with an authorized strength of 17,000 officers and 280,000 soldiers would be a combat-ready, balanced, standing force rather than the skeletonized structure under the expansible army concept. It had the mission of training the citizen components, serving as a model for the citizen formations, and furnishing garrisons for coastal fortifications and overseas possessions. The 435,000-person National Guard would form the second line of defense. Although the Guard would remain under state control, it would receive its training from the Regular Army. Upon mobilization, the National Guard would fall under federal control, while the Organized Reserves, the counterpart of the National Army of 1917-1918, would provide the third line of defense and be trained by the Regular Army.[6]

As a part of the National Defense Act of 1920, Congress revamped the War Department's education system to ensure preparedness in peacetime, recognizing the complexities of modern war, even though it refused to create a large, peacetime Regular Army.[7] Specifically, the act outlined an extensive system of training and education for the regular and reserve forces. The United States Military Academy and Reserve Officer Training Corps would furnish most of the basic military education and training for new officers, while the branch schools, such as the Field Artillery School, would supply branch technical training for Regular Army, National Guard, and Organized Reserve officers and soldiers. Field artillery officers would attend the Basic Course at Camp Knox early in their careers, then the Battery Officers' Course at the Field Artillery School, and finally the Advanced Course at Camp Bragg, while National Guard and Organize Reserve field artillery officers would enroll in extension courses and take abbreviated on-site versions of the Regular Army's Basic Course, Battery Officers' Course, and Advanced Course. Upon completing these branch schools, select Regular Army officers from the Field Artillery and other branches of the Army would attend the Command and General Staff College at Fort Leavenworth, Kansas, to prepare them for divisional command and staff positions. Senior officers with demonstrated abilities for higher command and staff responsibilities would attend the Army War College in Washington, D.C.[8]

Against this backdrop of reform that delineated a progressive and sequential education system to ensure the availability of competent Army officers and soldiers upon mobilization, the Field Artillery School composed of the Department of Gunnery, the Department of Tactics, the Department of Materiel, the Department of Research that conducted research projects and experiments for the Chief of Field Artillery and Field Artillery Board at Camp Bragg, and the Department of Equitation completed its last wartime course on 4 April 1919. Following guidance from Colonel Robert M. Danford (later Chief of Field Artillery, 1938-1942) of the Office of the Chief of Field Artillery in the War Department, the school implemented a peacetime Battery Officers' Course of 45 weeks that ran from January through December and covered the technical and tactical aspects of field artillery and that reflected Snow's wartime dictum that training a field artilleryman in two to four months was impossible and unwise.[9]

On 21 April 1919, the course, composed of 40 officers ranging from second lieutenants to colonels, began training. So that the course would end in December as scheduled, the school squeezed 45 weeks of instruction into 35 weeks. During that shortened time, the students attended classes from 0800-1130 and 1330-1600 daily, studied in the evening, and underwent 1,800 hours of intensive instruction. Of those hours, the students received 400 hours in gunnery where they learned to compute technical firing data, studied ballistics and other technical subjects and had 590 hours of tactics, 570 hours on materiel, and 240 hours of equitation (horse riding). As the breakdown of the course's program of instruction revealed, the Field Artillery School assumed the trappings of a true field artillery school by devoting more than 75 percent of its program of instruction to tactics and other field artillery subjects. This curriculum contrasted significantly with previous ones. Prior to and during the war, the students received only a few hours of tactics and spent the bulk of their time on gunnery.[10]

Gunnery, however, proved to be the most difficult subject. Acknowledging this, the Director of the Gunnery Department, Colonel Cortlandt Parker, on 5 November 1919 requested the Commandant of the School, Brigadier General Ernest Hinds (1919-1923), to allot more hours to gunnery instruction than in the current class. To teach field artillery officers how to work with infantry officers and to reaffirm the necessity of team work between the Field Artillery and the Infantry, Parker also recommended creating a Department of Liaison to enhance combined arms warfare by improving the ability of the Infantry and Field Artillery to work together and adding three hours of instruction on sound and flash ranging to engage hidden batteries for counterbattery work to permit infantry soldiers to advance without being impeded by enemy indirect fire.[11]

Although curtailed funding prevented allocating additional hours for gunnery instruction and creating a Department of Liaison, the school made other critical changes over the next several months. The school formed the Enlisted Division, later called the Enlisted Specialists' School, in December 1919. By 1921, eight enlisted courses of varying lengths for master sergeants, battery clerks, battery mechanics, motor mechanics, horseshoers, saddlers, stable sergeants, and communications specialists were operating at full capacity. The master sergeants course, for example, covered everything that officers learned in the Basic Officers' Course at Camp Knox with the exception of ballistics and theoretical gunnery and qualified master sergeants to be officers during time of war to signal the requirement and desire to create a pool of trained personnel in peacetime to support rapid mobilization of the officer corps during war.[12]

Because the enlisted courses took soldiers away from their units and because many officers and soldiers failed to recognize the need for standardized technical training during peacetime for the enlisted ranks, many soldiers refused to attend the school's enlisted courses. They wanted to return to the old ways where noncommissioned officers learned their trade on the job and failed to see any reason to change this method of training. To counter this spurious thinking, Hinds and school instructors waged an aggressive campaign to convince commanders and soldiers of the utility of formal technical training in a school and the necessity of attending enlisted courses because the increased complexity of combat as the recent war indicated required being prepared in peacetime through effective training. As attested by increased attendance in the enlisted courses during the following years that jumped from no enlisted soldiers enrolled in them in 1919 to 191 in 1920 and 146 in 1921, they succeeded. Over a period of 20 years from 1919 to 1939, an average of 117 enlisted soldiers graduated from the school annually.[13]

The school restructured its academic year after creating the Enlisted Division, integrating classroom instruction on sound and flash ranging that had been developed during the war to detect concealed batteries for counterbattery work into the Battery Officers' Class in January 1920, initiating a National Guard Officers' Course of three months in September

1920 that emphasized the fundamentals of field artillery tactics, techniques, and procedures and gunnery, and creating a 13-week aerial observer course in January 1920 for select graduates of the Battery Officers' Course.[14] To match the calendars of other Army schools and to avoid the searing Oklahoma summer in the days before air conditioning, the school changed its academic year in 1921. Rather than running classes from January through December, it launched a school year that ran from September through June. Although this schedule overlapped two calendar years, the change permitted teaching theoretical work indoors during the fall and winter and conducting practical exercises outdoors in the spring. To implement this modification, the school reduced the Battery Officers' Course for the Regular Army that had begun in January 1921 from nine months to six months, closed it on 2 July 1921 without eliminating any subjects, and decreased the length of its enlisted courses which had theoretical and practical training so that new ones could start in September 1921.[15]

In the midst of these curriculum and organizational reforms, a controversy over the focus of gunnery and tactics instruction erupted in the school and the Field Artillery. Proponents of trench warfare and unobserved indirect fire and the advocates of open warfare and observed indirect fire disputed the direction that the school should take in the postwar years and the appropriate training. As the War Department and the Field Artillery School pressed forward searching for the relevant lessons from the recent war for incorporation into tactics and doctrine and instruction, the sponsors of trench warfare envisioned themselves as modernists and purveyors of future warfare and championed unobserved map firing and predicted fire as it had been conducted during the recent war. They proclaimed open warfare where infantrymen relied upon their rifles and bayonets and where forward observers were attached to the infantry and conducted observed indirect fire by designating the target on a map by using prominent terrain features or grid coordinates when maps were available and adjusting fire onto the target to be obsolete.[16]

Open warfare supporters quickly countered this argument. They insisted that the infantryman with his rifle was still the most important element on the battlefield and that field artillery units should shift observed fire around a mobile battlefield to engage any obstacles that obstructed the infantry advance. Observed fire advocates also found observed fire to be more accurate and effective in support of advancing infantry than methodical, inflexible unobserved indirect map firing with its emphasis upon detailed fire plans and highly choreographed schedules as practiced during the war. As a result, observed fire should be the primary method of engaging targets.[17]

Addressing this escalating debate over the future of field artillery tactics and doctrine and also over training, Brigadier General Dwight E. Aultman, a veteran field artillery officer, pointed out the strengths of the two. Unobserved map fire permitted massing fire, engaging concealed targets beyond the front line of troops, and attacking targets throughout the depth of the battlefield as combat during the last year of the war had demonstrated. However, unobserved map fire relied upon mathematical and mechanical accuracy, hindered flexibility, and neglected observed fire. In comparison, observed fire hampered massing fires, prevented hitting concealed targets beyond the front line of troops, such as enemy batteries, focused on attacking the visible enemy front line, but promoted flexibility by permitting the battery commander to shift fire to satisfy changing conditions on the battlefield.[18] Based upon this reasoning, Aultman found middle ground. He insisted, "Both methods should be taught, observation of fire should be stressed, and all artillery officers should be so trained that, when the emergency is upon them, they may be prepared to meet it in the most effective manner."[19] Field artillery officers had to be flexible and have the ability to employ both methods of fire direction because each had strengths and weaknesses.[20]

A combat veteran of World War I, Lieutenant Colonel John B. Anderson joined the debate with his article in the *Field Artillery Journal* in 1919. After discussing the soundness of observed fire for open warfare, he cautioned, "Trench warfare methods are auxiliary and improved methods to be used when a battery is in position for long periods, and the battery commander has the time to make careful corrections and computations."[21] He then noted, "But in the open the battery commander must return to rapid calculation of data, observed fire, and rapid and numerous changes of position."[22] The Field Artillery and Field Artillery School had to teach observed fire for a war of movement "to deliver telling blows to the enemy forces" in the open.[23]

Caught up in this debate, Hinds, who had also served as Chief of Artillery for the American Expeditionary Force in 1917-1918, expressed his ideas on the matter. In an article in the *Field Artillery Journal* late in 1919, he wrote:

> Map firing is frequently of great value, but it should not replace observed fire where the latter is practicable. The barrage is a necessity where the resistances are practically continuous, everywhere powerful, and clearly known to the attacker. When the resistance becomes irregular the barrage should no longer be employed. Artillery support must take the form of fire applied promptly and exactly where needed.[24]

For Hinds, both types of fire had their place. Field artillerymen had to exploit the strengths of each.[25]

Upon becoming commandant of the Field Artillery School in October 1919, Hinds continued this line of thought. In a letter to Snow on 22 November 1919, he acknowledged the school's efforts to teach both types of warfare to student officers to prepare them for their assignments upon graduation from the school.[26] In a subsequent letter to Snow on 17 December 1919 and in his speech to the first postwar class that graduated on 19 December 1919, Hinds advocated the primacy of open warfare over trench warfare. To determine if the school's instruction reflected this orientation, Hinds ordered the Assistant Commandant of the School, Major Augustine McIntyre, in December 1919 to survey the school's courses to determine the weight being attached to each form of warfare. Much to the general's shock, McIntyre concluded after his investigation that the right doctrine, meaning open warfare, was being taught but that it needed to be hammered home to the students even more. Twenty-seven percent of the time spent on gunnery firing problems was devoted to observed fire and open warfare with the rest of the time being spent on trench warfare techniques and unobserved map firing, while 50 percent of the tactical problems focused on trench warfare. While this orientation was undoubtedly a lingering impact of the war and reflected the ambivalence about the nature of the future battlefield and the absence of clear guidance from the commandant of the school, instructors found teaching gunnery for trench warfare to be easier than teaching gunnery for mobile warfare and chose the easier path. Solving gunnery problems for trench warfare did not require calculating data rapidly for an ever-changing battlefield. As Hinds learned, gunnery instruction in the school failed to reflect the thinking of Snow and March on open warfare and observed fire to the exclusion of trench warfare and unobserved fire and tried to accommodate both trench warfare and mobile warfare techniques with the former clearly having precedence.[27]

Pressed by Snow who along with other high-ranking officers in the War Department believed that open warfare methods had won the war and that the Americans had employed the right doctrine and were determined to ensure stressing it, Hinds changed the school's focus beginning with the Battery Officers' Course that started in January 1920. In a training circular distributed to all students, he dispelled any lingering confusion and debate about the proper doctrine.[28]

Upon greeting the students on 10 January 1920, he informed them about the school's position on open warfare and its intention to devote more instructional hours to it.[29] "The foundation of all Field Artillery training then lies in open warfare. Trench warfare is merely an application of the principles of open warfare to a peculiar case," Hinds emphasized.[30] He continued that open warfare was the preferred form of fighting.[31] Reinforcing this point, he noted:

> The foundation of all Field Artillery training then lies in open warfare...All instruction will be primarily in open warfare tactics: the refinements of trench warfare will not be taught until the principles of open warfare have been thoroughly mastered.[32]

In this terse statement, Hinds unmistakably settled the school's orientation on fire direction and gunnery. Without any question, the school would focus its instruction on observed fire using ground and aerial observers for open warfare and would relegate unobserved indirect fire to a distance second in priority.[33] In fact, the restructured course focused 75 percent of its classroom instruction and practical exercises on open warfare and observed fire during the remaining time of Hinds' tenure as commandant and used the aerial observer course that started in January 1920 to teach officers how to locate targets from the air and to adjust fire onto them.[34]

In a letter to Snow on 15 January 1920, Hinds, however, exposed his ambivalence about the proper warfare doctrine. Trench warfare methods of unobserved fire to mass fire and to hit concealed targets remained pertinent, he wrote, because trench warfare could not be ruled out in the future and because field batteries had to have the ability to engage targets beyond the terrestrial observer's eyesight. Although the school should not lose sight of the recent combat lessons where observed indirect fire techniques often precluded massing fires and unobserved indirect fire proved to be the only reliable way of massing fires, an article of faith for field artillerymen, Hinds continued, open warfare on a mobile battlefield and observed fire represented the future of warfare and should be accentuated. After reemphasizing the strengths of observed indirect fire, Hinds then explained, "Besides the teaching of the refinement necessary where unobserved fire must be employed, it is intended also to inculcate at the same time a very valuable lesson as to its inefficiency as compared with observed and well adjusted fire."[35] In the future, forward observers, called liaison officers, would identify enemy targets and shift fires around the battlefield to support the other combat arms as they advanced.[36]

As the debate over open warfare and trench warfare indicated, the Field Artillery School found itself caught up in the contest over the vision of the future battlefield. By teaching the preeminence of open warfare with its attending observed indirect fire over trench warfare with its unobserved indirect fire, the school clung tightly to pre-war doctrine as its foundation of training, simultaneously shaped the orientation of future field artillery leaders, and reinforced its drive to move beyond being only a gunnery school as it had been throughout most of its short history. Gunnery still remained a critical aspect of instruction, but teaching tactics and other field artillery subjects to support open warfare and participating in the development of doctrine had assumed a more important role than previously.

Consolidation and a New Lease on Life

As the Field Artillery School was settling into its peacetime routine and organizing its programs of instruction based upon open warfare and lessons learned from the war, its future at Fort Sill quickly became questionable. In a letter on 31 March 1921, Hinds made a passing reference to the possibility of closing the Field Artillery School at Fort Sill founded upon rumors that he had heard floating around the War Department about the need to restructure officer education in the face of declining budgets. With little information to go on, Hinds pressed ahead with ambitious plans for the school. He projected that the Basic Course at Camp Knox would be transferred to Fort Sill and that the Field Artillery School would remain open. To handle the increased student load produced by the expansion, he solicited help from Snow on 19 July 1921 to enlarge the size of the school detachment that supported training, to remodel school barracks, and to obtain additional funding.[37] In the face of uncertainty and with little information to go on, Hinds demonstrated confidence about the Field Artillery School's future at Fort Sill, even foresaw additional courses coming to the school, and urged Snow to keep him informed about the "probabilities" of the Camp Knox course moving to Fort Sill.[38]

Months later, the rumors about revamping the War Department's officer education system and the future of the Field Artillery School turned to fact. Early in 1922, War Department reached the conclusion that its existing officer education system composed of its branch schools, the Command and General Staff College, and the Army War College was cumbersome, produced overlapping courses, did not satisfy postwar conditions, was too expensive in an era of declining military budgets, and took officers away from the troops too frequently and too long. Based upon this and his own conclusions about the inadequacies of the existing school system, the Chief of Staff of the Army, General of the Armies John J. Pershing, formed a board of senior officers to examine it and make proposals for changes. Above all, Pershing wanted the board to simplify the education system by consolidating branch courses at one location wherever possible to save money as postwar budget cuts began to erode the War Department's funding.[39]

Headed by Brigadier General Edward F. McGlachlin, the former commandant of the School of Fire for Field Artillery from 1914 to 1916, the board scrutinized the existing school system, the possibility of consolidating or coordinating field artillery courses, the proper doctrine to teach, the appropriate amount of formal training in the school house, the need to curtail expenses, the integration of lessons learned from the war into the programs of instruction, and the requirement for correspondence courses for the Organized Reserves and National Guard as delineated by the National Defense Act of 1920.[40]

At the time the War Department had a decentralized field artillery training system. It conducted field artillery training in the Basic Course at Camp Knox, the Battery Officers' Course at Fort Sill, and the Field Officers' Course at Camp Bragg and tried to coordinate their programs of instruction with the General Service School's curriculum at Fort Leavenworth, Kansas. This effort proved to be difficult, cumbersome, and inefficient and prompted the War Department to consider consolidating the three field artillery schools at one location with Camp Bragg and Fort Sill being the leading contenders for the new Field Artillery School. Advocates for Camp Bragg, such as Brigadier General Albert J. Bowley who commanded the 2d Brigade in the American Expeditionary Forces during the latter months of the war and became the Chief of Artillery for the 6th Corps in 1919 identified Camp Bragg's eastern location, its proximity to civilian and military educational centers, its large military population, and its moderate climate as key reasons for moving all field artillery training to the North Carolina installation.[41]

Fort Sill also had its supporters. They pointed to the post's superior terrain, the Field Artillery School's existing facilities, and a permanent water and sewage plant, among other critical facilities, as reasons for consolidating all field artillery training at the Oklahoma post. Above all, the proponents of Fort Sill, especially Hinds who also advocated consolidation, noted the high costs of constructing permanent facilities at Camp Bragg.[42] In a lengthy letter on 5 May 1922 to Snow, Hinds wrote, "It will take you years of time and millions of money to duplicate it [the Field Artillery School's facilities] at Bragg."[43]

Yet, Hinds conceded Camp Bragg's superiority to Fort Sill. He stated, "If we had to build from the bottom up[,] I should certainly not select Sill."[44] Although he failed to provide a solid endorsement for Fort Sill and to elucidate upon his reasoning, he hinted at the post's isolated location as a reason but believed economic issues to be more important than terrain and location. Constructing the appropriate facilities to support field artillery training at Camp Bragg would be time consuming and expensive. To Hinds, Fort Sill was not the ideal location for field artillery training, but economic considerations dictated consolidating training there, especially as military spending began shrinking seriously as a result of Congressional action.[45]

After visiting Camp Knox, Camp Bragg, and Fort Sill and hearing the various arguments from Hinds, the War Department, and others, the McGlachlin board reached its own conclusions. While Fort Sill's facilities were the best, the post's central location in the United States seemed to be its most attractive feature because it would cut travel time and costs for students. In view of this, the McGlachlin board voted to consolidate the three field artillery courses under the Field Artillery School but recommended moving the school to Camp Benning, Georgia, as soon as funds could be obtained to erect a permanent field artillery post there. Like Hinds, the board did not see Fort Sill as the ideal location. It was a temporary solution until money was available to move the school to a better location.[46]

Backed by this recommendation, the War Department subsequently selected Fort Sill as a short-term expedient until a better site, such as Camp Benning, could be found and directed consolidating the field artillery courses there immediately. Only economic considerations kept the Field Artillery School at Fort Sill because Camp Bragg offered more and better terrain for training field artillerymen and a more hospitable climate.[47]

In mid-1922, the War Department took action with its field artillery courses to reduce expenses during an era of austere budgets and to simplify training. At the direction of the War Department, the Field Artillery School merged the Basic Course from Camp Knox with its Battery Officers' Course to form the Battery Officers' Course for second lieutenants and first lieutenants and redesignated the Field Officers' Course that had moved from Camp Bragg as the Advanced Course for senior captains and field grade officers, typically majors. Starting in the fall of 1922, Fort Sill's Field Artillery School began teaching a nine-month Battery Officers' Course for Regular Army field artillery officers, a nine-month Advanced Course for Regular Army field artillery officers, and a two-month Refresher Course for high-ranking Regular Army field artillery officers. The school also instituted a five-month course for Infantry and Cavalry field officers who were detailed to the Field Artillery for at least four years, a three-month National Guard Officer Course, a three-month Organized Reserve Officers' Course, and Regular Army, National Guard, and Organized Reserve enlisted courses of varying lengths. The school also furnished correspondence courses that paralleled the old Basic Course, the Battery Officers' Course, and the Advanced Course for Organized Reserve and National Guard officers who were unable to attend the resident courses. By 1925, 599 National Guard officers, 2,024 Organized Reserve officers, and 98 other individuals were taking the correspondence courses. All courses, with the exception of the extension courses for the reserve components which only taught theory, furnished theoretical and practical instruction. For example, the new Battery Officers' Course included 1,372 hours of instruction with 475 hours in gunnery, 427 hours on tactics, 216 hours on equipment, and 254 hours on animal transport. Meanwhile, the Advanced Course furnished 1,311 hours with 98 hours on gunnery, 1,069 hours on tactics, 88 hours on equipment, and 56 hours on animal transport.[48]

The Assistant Commandant of the School, Colonel Henry W. Butner, commented in *The Shrapnel* – the school's yearbook – in 1923 about the school's crucial role in professional education and the importance of the organizational reforms of 1922. According to Butner, graduation from the Field Artillery School marked just the beginning of a career. He counseled:

> The subject of Field Artillery is a life study and the school hopes to lay the foundation on sound principles for such study. The Artillery officer must continue the study of his profession, or he will fail when the time comes to practice it. And failure in war, means failure in life, for the soldier.[49]

Butner called upon the graduates to be professionals and to continue studying their profession seriously after leaving the school so that they would be successful in war when it came.[50]

Snow likewise recognized the school's significant contribution to the branch. Writing in his annual report for 1923-1924 about the impact of the restructured school, Snow commented, "Training at the Field Artillery School is considered of incalculable importance, not only in developing the individual students in the technique of artillery, but in the standardization of field artillery training as well."[51] Based upon his pre-war experience with the lack of training for the Field Artillery as a whole, he found training during peace for war to be critical. To Snow's way of thinking, the Field Artillery School's significance should be clearly understood because it provided standardized training to Regular Army, National Guard, and Organized Reserve field artillery officers and soldiers to prepare them for war during peacetime.[52]

About the same time, Hinds echoed similar thinking. Speaking at the graduation of the Battery Officers' Course of 1923-1924, he noted on 14 June 1924:

> Due to the training of the field artillery officers here, the training of officers of other arms at their special service schools, and training of all arms at Fort Leavenworth, a very marked improvement is evident in the technical and tactical handling of organizations in our manoeuvers (sic)."[53]

For Hinds as well as for other prominent officers in the War Department, the Field Artillery School produced competent graduates and formed part of an invaluable peacetime training experience so that the Army, in this particular case, the Field Artillery, would be prepared for war and would not have to scramble like it had done in 1917-1918.[54]

Butner's, Snow's, and Hinds' comments reflected the progress that the school had made since the war. As the senior instructor in the Department of Tactics, Lieutenant Colonel Daniel F. Craig wrote in his report to the Commandant of the Field Artillery School, Major General George LeR. Irwin (1923-1928), on 15 June 1924, "The experience gained in the last few years is resulting in well balanced and coordinated courses for all the classes which receive instruction under this Department."[55]

During the academic year of 1923-1924, the school increased the number of field exercises over past years. Such training gave Regular Army officers and National Guard and Organized Reserve officers who attended the school full-time the opportunity to apply the theoretical knowledge learned in the classroom to field conditions, to work on low-level combined arms warfare with the infantry battalion assigned to Fort Sill, to adjust observed indirect fire using ground and aerial observers, and to serve in command and staff positions. During practical exercises, officers in the Advanced Course played the role of battalion commanders, while officers in the Battery Officers' Course led batteries.[56]

Over the next several years, the school continued stressing practical exercises in the field with troops. In 1925-1926, the school increased the time spent in field exercises where student officers shifted fires around the battlefield using ground and aerial observers to spot targets and adjusted fire in keeping with the drive to teach open warfare. Reflecting the emphasis upon open warfare during the academic year of 1925-1926, the Department of Tactics pointed out, "Fires must be delivered when and where asked for; and that delays in opening fire are unpardonable."[57] Four years later, the Commandant of the Field Artillery School, Brigadier General William M. Cruikshank (1930-1934), reported:

> The courses are being developed constantly as a result of experience, improved methods of instruction, changes in organization, regulations and governing doctrines, and inventions and other developments in the military art. There has been and will be a continuing effort to shape the courses so that the instruction in the methods peculiar to the World War will not be unduly emphasized at the expense of the methods which would be more appropriate for war under other conditions.[58]

In view of a battlefield that was growing more mobile with the advent of the motor vehicle and the conclusion about the trenches of the Great War being an aberration, Cruikshank emphasized the imperative of shifting observed fires responsively around the battlefield to provide fire support when and where the maneuver arms needed it and accentuated the necessity of abandoning any thoughts about employing unobserved fire in the future. To this end the school improved gunnery methods and conducted practical exercises so that field artillery officers could engage mobile targets, including tanks, more effectively.[59]

While practical exercises remained a critical aspect of all officer and enlisted courses into the 1930s, the school adapted them to meet the changing needs of the Field Artillery. Beginning in 1936, the school's practical exercises involved the employment of field artillery with mechanized forces and taught student officers how to conduct envelopments and how to defend against envelopments. During the school year of 1936-1937, the school converted 27 tactical problems and practical exercises based upon the old square-division of World War I to the experimental triangular division under development. In 1939, the school introduced practical exercises for sound and flash ranging for Regular Army and National Guard courses for the first time to complement classroom instruction using the 1st Observation Battalion that had transferred on a temporary basis from Fort Bragg to Fort Sill.[60]

Over a period of 20 years beginning in 1919 and ending in 1938, more than 6,000 reserve and active component officers and soldiers graduated from the Field Artillery School where they underwent theoretical training and practical exercises. While 2,084 Regular Army field artillery officers graduated from the Basic Officers' Course and the Advanced Course which were consolidated to form the Regular Course in 1934 in response to budget reductions, 1,342 National Guard and Organized Reserve field artillery officers completed the resident courses with an untold number finishing the correspondence courses. In the meantime, 2,739 soldiers learned skills in shorthand, motor mechanics, horse shoeing, saddlery, communications, or cooking in resident courses.[61]

During the 1920s and 1930s, the Field Artillery School unswervingly fulfilled its assigned mission of training field artillerymen. It added more instruction on tactics without detracting from teaching gunnery, emphasized fighting a war of movement and observed indirect fire, developed resident instruction around classroom activities and practical exercises, and designed and distributed correspondence courses for National Guard and Organized Reserve officers and soldiers.

The Infrastructure

Upon arriving at Fort Sill to attend the Field Artillery School in the 1920s and 1930s, students encountered an interesting blend of old and new buildings and simultaneously came face to face with the stark reality of the War Department's neglect of the school's facilities caused by limited funding and indecisiveness of a permanent location for the school. As a memorandum for the Chief of Field Artillery explained, construction over the years had divided Fort Sill into the Old Post, the New Post, the Henry Post Field, and the Field Artillery School that was composed of wood buildings erected during the war.[62]

In response to the inadequacies of the World War I wood buildings and after the decision had been made to consolidate all field artillery training at Fort Sill, Hinds pressed for new construction for the school. He wrote in his report of 16 June 1923, "It is earnestly recommended that the permanent building program be started. Several of the school's buildings are in such poor condition due to the temporary nature of their construction that they can no longer be properly or economically maintained. They are rapidly becoming unfit for occupancy."[63] Hinds empathetically added, "The extreme fire hazard has been reported several times and remedial action has been requested. The school administration building caught fire three times during the past winter [1922-1923]."[64]

One year later, Hinds's successor, Major General George LeR. Irwin (1923-1928), repeated the warning about the quality of the temporary buildings. He reported, "During each cold snap, the plumbing throughout the area freezes, resulting in much damage to government and personal property."[65] Hinds and Irwin painted a bleak picture of the school's buildings and envisioned only one solution – new construction.[66]

After conducting an inspection of the Field Artillery School and Fort Sill, the Inspector General of the War Department, Major General Eli A. Helmick, meanwhile added his own plea for permanent construction to replace the unsatisfactory temporary buildings. In a four-page letter to Snow on 10 May 1923, Helmick wrote about the small, poorly designed temporary quarters for the families of student officers. The buildings were not fit for the hot climate during the summer months. Helmick also noted:

> The most pressing need of this school, as you undoubtedly know, is the
> necessity for continuing the proposed building project. The entire school

area, as at present, is either temporary buildings, which are a constant fire hazard, or old buildings unfitted [sic] for the present purposes. Families are living in buildings that constantly endanger their lives should a fire break out.[67]

Continuing his biting critique about the dire condition of the school's physical facilities, Helmick composed, "Considering the above, in connection with the fact that everything connected with the School should be a model to the student officers, the necessity for the constant pressure for improvements on the War Department and Congress is apparent."[68] Although Snow concurred with these sentiments and pressed for action, the War Department's failure to designate Fort Sill as the permanent home of the Field Artillery School caused Congress to decline to appropriate funds for permanent construction during the early 1920s and for maintenance on the old buildings.[69]

Although Congressional appropriations would probably be doubtful, Irwin nevertheless designed a comprehensive housing plan in 1924 with backing from Helmick and Snow. Irwin reported on 30 June 1925 to the Chief of Field Artillery, "The housing situation for Officers is still far from satisfactory. Most of the Student Officers are forced to live in temporary buildings where living conditions are not conducive to contentment nor to the possibility of study."[70] Irwin further noted:

> It is well realized that under present policies [budget cuts] little can be done to better this situation, but it is hoped the needs of the School will be borne in mind when the construction schemes made possible by the money obtained from the sale of Obsolete Military Lands are being worked out.[71]

Although he acknowledged a lack of funding, Irwin moved forward and encouraged Snow to approve his plan for permanent construction.[72]

Pushing to make at least some minor improvements, Irwin partially implemented his plan. Over a period of several years, Fort Sill under Irwin's direction built a new riding hall with soldier labor in 1925, erected some fireproof buildings in 1925, installed steam heat in many buildings that same year to reduce the hazard of fire, built a fireproof annex to the school library in 1926, and completed construction of a few bungalows for battery officers and a post hospital in 1928 with small appropriations from Congress.[73]

As Irwin clearly noted, the lack of funding from Congress prohibited the proper maintenance of the existing facilities or the implementation of a desperately needed extensive construction program. Notwithstanding Irwin's efforts, inadequate funding caused the school's facilities to continue deteriorating during the rest of the 1920s and prevented the total realization of Irwin's permanent building plan.[74]

The situation with the school's facilities became so bleak that Cruikshank responded. On 8 July 1930 he observed:

> The old war time cantonment buildings on this post used for quarters and storage have more than outlived their economic usefulness. Each year it costs more to keep these buildings in even a fair state of repair than it did the year

Snow Hall fire of 1929

        before. . . . Buildings are being used for quarters and storage which are neither suitable nor safe.⁷⁵

Despite Cruikshank's passionate plea for permanent buildings to reduce maintenance costs and to house the school and students properly, the War Department reduced funding for maintenance and construction more as budgets became tighter as Congress continued to decrease military spending early in the 1930s.⁷⁶

    A series of fires further aggravated the situation with the school's obsolete facilities. Between 1921 and 1926 19 fires burned down many of the temporary wood frame buildings constructed during the war. The fires razed the school library, ordnance shops, motor shops, and other buildings. In his annual report for 1924-1925, Snow described the Field Artillery School's facilities as a fire risk "such as no city in the United States would tolerate within its limits."⁷⁷ In reports to the Chief of Field Artillery on 11 June 1926 and 3 July 1926, Irwin buttressed Snow's observation by writing that a major fire on 17 June 1925 burned down 106 officer quarters and forced many married students and their families to live in Lawton to south of the post at great inconvenience. Living in Lawton proved to be costly to the soldiers whose rent and pay allowances often did not cover the added expenses. Some even had to live in unsatisfactory rental apartments. Fortunately, there was no loss of life in the 17 June 1925 fire because the students had graduated five days earlier and were gone, leaving the quarters empty. Later in 1926, another fire destroyed $1 million worth of ordnance maintained in a storehouse. Although faulty coal-burning stoves played a prominent role in the fires, arsonists set some of them. On 11 October 1926, 13 enlisted soldiers were found guilty of arson and received prison sentences ranging from two years to 32 years.[78]

The greatest loss psychologically came when Snow Hall that was named after Major General William J. Snow and that was the main academic building burned down on 8 August 1929. Snow Hall housed the Field Artillery School headquarters and a majority of the classrooms. This left the school with only two frame buildings of wartime construction, a row of shacks that had been built for the School of Fire for Field Artillery in 1915 and the Old Trader's Store and compelled the school and Fort Sill to rely even more heavily upon temporary facilities to start classes in September 1929.[79]

Reflecting upon the 1929 fire, Cruikshank warned the War Department in his annual report in July 1930. He pled, "It is to be emphasized in connection with the instructional plant, that in case of another serious fire, it would be impossible to rehabilitate the plant as was done in this case for want of existing buildings, in other words, the last reserve of buildings had been utilized," and another fire would force the school to close down until new buildings could be erected to replace those burned down.[80]

Along with the lack of maintenance being performed on the buildings which caused rapid deterioration and certainly detracted from creature comfort, the fires created cramped classrooms and hazardous living conditions, demanded an extensive rebuilding program, and even persuaded the War Department to investigate the possibility of transferring the school to another military post.[81] To find a suitable permanent home for the Field Artillery School, the War Department convened a board under Brigadier General William M. Cruikshank in January 1930 just before he became the Commandant of the Field Artillery School in February 1930. After examining the possibilities of Jordan Narrows, Utah; Brady, Texas; and Camp Knox, Kentucky; and other locations and experiencing intensive lobbying by various interest groups pushing a particular site, the Cruikshank board narrowed its options to Fort Sill and Fort Bragg. Fort Bragg had more rain and more snow, was a larger reservation (120,454 acres), and was an extremely attractive place for firing long-range field guns scheduled to be introduced in the next few years. In contrast, Fort Sill had more housing facilities, more varied terrain than Fort Bragg, and an elaborate firing range, but the installation was small (51,292 acres) with a warmer, drier, windier, and sunnier climate than Fort Bragg's. Although Fort Sill's climate was not the most comfortable, it permitted outdoor instruction almost every day. However, Fort Sill lacked a good water supply, and this certainly deterred making the post a permanent location for the school.[82]

Upon hearing that the lack of a good water supply and the size of the post stood in the way of locating the school permanently at Fort Sill, Lawtonians came to the rescue. In May 1930, they passed a bond of $600,000 to improve the quality of the water supply by making enhancements to the dam that formed Lake Lawtonka, the major source of water for Fort Sill and Lawton. Based upon this and the Cruikshank board's position of the fall of 1930 that Fort Sill's overall advantages outweighed Fort Bragg's, Secretary of War Patrick J. Hurley, who was born in Indian Territory and had sympathetic feelings for Fort Sill, ended years of indecision about the Field Artillery School's permanent location. On 10 December 1930 he designated Fort Sill as the permanent home for the school.[83]

Anticipating that Fort Sill would become the permanent site of the Field Artillery School even before Hurley's announcement based upon the Cruikshank board's favorable recommendation, the post formed a board composed of Colonel Charles M. Bundel, Lieutenant Colonel Lesley J. McNair, Major George M. Peck, and Major John M. Mellon to draw up a building program for the school. After considerable work the board completed its proposed $11 million construction program in November 1930 and submitted it to the Chief of Field Artillery, Major General Harry G. Bishop (1930-1934), who endorsed it in December 1930. Bishop then forwarded the program to the Adjutant General, Major General Charles H. Bridges, on 22 December 1930 for approval. Because of Bridges' endorsement that came on 10 February 1931, the support from the local Lawton community, and Hurley's decision to locate the school permanently at Fort Sill, Congress subsequently appropriated funding in 1932 for the construction of permanent buildings on the Oklahoma post for the first time since 1910-1911 when New Post had been erected. In 1932-1933, Fort Sill employed this windfall to build quarters for Air Corps personnel at Henry Post Field, officer quarters, noncommissioned officer quarters, and two large barracks on the west end of the parade ground of New Post.[84]

Meanwhile, the Field Artillery School submitted estimates to the War Department for additional building projects. Using these estimates, the War Department requested money from the Public Works Administration, a New Deal agency created by the National Industrial Recovery Act of 1933. On 21 September 1933, the War Department announced that the Public Works Administration had allocated $4,392,000 for more permanent construction on Fort Sill. Using these funds, Fort Sill built barracks, noncommissioned officer quarters, officer quarters, and other much needed facilities in 1933-1935, including a school administration building, eventually named after Lieutenant General Lesley J. McNair who was killed in the European Theater of Operations in 1944. Still requiring more facilities, especially housing, the Commandant of the Field Artillery School, Brigadier General Augustine McIntyre (1936-1940), sent a new five-year, $6 million housing plan to the Chief of Field Artillery, Major Robert M. Danford (1938-1942), in November 1936 for approval. But it was never adopted. Almost two years passed before Fort Sill received more money for the school. In June 1938, the Bureau of the Budget approved $1.29 million to construct additional barracks, noncommissioned officer quarters, and other buildings to combat the recession of 1937-1938. Besides building more barracks and noncommissioned officer quarters, the post constructed an addition to the school's administration building, bachelor officer quarters, a movie theater, a hospital, and other facilities of modified Spanish architecture using Works Progress Administration (another New Deal agency created in 1935 and later renamed Works Projects Administration in 1938) labor to complement the earlier construction projects.[85]

The extensive construction programs of the 1930s gave the school its first dedicated permanent buildings in its short history. Since Captain Dan T. Moore opened the school in 1911, the school had moved from facility to facility like an itinerant or depended upon temporary wooden structures for classroom and administrative space even though it was the War Department's sole source for field artillery instruction after 1922. Along with the recognition that the temporary wooden buildings were a fire hazard and the decision to locate the school at Fort Sill permanently in 1930, New Deal construction in the 1930s transformed the school by permitting it to move into state-of-the-art facilities and end its vagabond lifestyle.

More Than Training and Facilities

Although the school dissolved the Department of Research in September 1922, the Field Artillery School's role in combat developments complemented its training mission.[86] In cooperation with the Field Artillery Board that moved from Fort Bragg to Fort Sill in 1922, the school helped evaluate developmental towed howitzers and guns, self-propelled howitzers and guns, signal equipment, sights, and other field artillery equipment over the next several years. In 1928-1929, the school, for example, tested portee field artillery where light field pieces were loaded onto the beds of trucks or trailers for rapid transportation over paved or unpaved roads and cross country, but the school failed to reach any firm conclusions about its suitability and never made any recommendations about adopting it. Later in 1933-1934, the school tested an experimental battalion of truck-drawn field artillery at the direction of Bishop. Completed in 1935, the school's study demonstrated the maneuverability of motor-drawn (towed) field artillery, found it to be less vulnerable and less subject to fatigue than horse-drawn units, and urged continued motorization especially as engineering and technical deficiencies with motor vehicles were eliminated.[87]

Notwithstanding its hesitancy to adopt motor vehicles as prime movers without any qualifications, the school's involvement with motor vehicles continued. Three years after completing the study on motorization, the Field Artillery School participated in selecting the proper field artillery systems for the division. Prompted by the growing controversy in the War Department over the division's proposed field artillery armament of 75-mm. field guns and 105-mm. howitzers to replace the 75-mm. field gun and 155-mm. howitzer mix of World War One, Danford directed the school in June 1938 to conduct a study to determine the best combination of weapons. Specifically, he wanted to know if the 105-mm. howitzer and the 75-mm. gun combination which furnished mobility at the expense of firepower should still be companion pieces in the division as recommended by the Westerfelt Board headed by Brigadier General William I. Westerfelt and often called the Caliber Board that the War Department had convened in 1919 to determine the preferred guns and howitzers for each echelon of command.[88]

In a lengthy report in September 1938 that concluded two months of testing various gun and howitzer combinations, the school responded. It categorically rejected replacing the 155-mm. howitzer with the 105-mm. howitzer as a companion piece for the 75-mm. gun in the division because the 105-mm. howitzer and 75-mm. gun combination only offered mobility and lacked sufficient firepower for the modern battlefield. As the school explained, recent experience with the 155-mm. howitzer demonstrated the weapon's mobility when towed by a truck or tractor and suitability for employment as a general support weapon in the division. Continuing, the school noted, "To replace it [the 155-mm. howitzer] piece for piece by the 105-mm. howitzer would be at the sacrifice of much artillery fire-power, which we can ill afford to lose, and at a gain which is, in the main illusory."[89]

Understanding that World War I and the Spanish Civil War of the late 1930s reaffirmed the importance of firepower, the Field Artillery School strongly advocated a 155-mm. howitzer and 105-mm. howitzer mix in the division. With the advent of tractors and trucks as prime movers to pull 155-mm. howitzers, such a howitzer combination offered mobility and firepower. Yet, the surplus of 75-mm. guns and ammunition from the war stood in the way of scrapping the gun in the division. Even though the school and many field artillery officers pressed for 155-mm. and 105-mm. howitzers for the division and even though tests of the triangular division in 1938-1939 with the 2d Division demonstrated the lack of firepower offered by 105-mm. howitzers and 75-mm. guns, the War Department stubbornly retained that combination. Besides believing that the 75-mm. gun was an all-purpose weapon, the War Department noted the surplus 75-mm. ammunition from the war and the expense associated with replacing the 75-mm. gun with the 105-mm. howitzer, causing it to refuse adopting a 155-mm. towed howitzer and 105-mm. towed howitzer combination for the division. Even Chief of Staff of the Army, General George C. Marshall (1939-1945), was reluctant to spend money on new weapons in a time of peace when a war surplus existed. By demonstrating the mobility of tractor- and truck-drawn 155-mm. howitzers and 105-mm. howitzers, the war in Europe in 1939-1940 finally prompted the War Department and Marshall to abandon 75-mm. guns and 105-mm. howitzers for 105-mm. howitzers and 155-mm. howitzers respectively in the division in 1940. However, the 155-mm. howitzer and 105-mm. mix did not replace the 105-mm. howitzer and 75-mm. gun combination until 1943 when sufficient numbers of the 105-mm. howitzer had been produced.[90]

The Field Artillery School study of September 1938 on the preferred combination of weapons for division artillery also addressed the desired characteristics for a 105-mm. howitzer. In that report, the school urged designing a 105-mm. howitzer with an elevation of 45 degrees, a variable length recoil system to eliminate digging a recoil pit for high-angle fire missions, and a traverse of 45 degrees. The school wanted 45 degree elevation to hit the reverse side of a slope and 45 degree traverse to cover broader fronts and to minimize shifting trails and relaying the weapon as often to hit mobile targets. These characteristics would make the howitzer more responsive than its predecessors. When it was introduced in 1943, the M2 105-mm. towed howitzer had an elevation of 64 degrees to exceed the school's recommendation and a traverse of 45 degrees.[91]

Meanwhile, the school examined the possibility of restructuring field artillery organization to increase firepower. During 1939, it conducted an extensive test of a six-gun battery and a four-battery battalion. In a report of 2 August 1939, the school concluded that the six-gun battery furnished more firepower than a four-gun battery and better fire support to the infantry during displacement because more field pieces were available for close support than with the current four-gun battery. However, the school found the larger battery to be more cumbersome and difficult to manage and conceal than the smaller battery and preferred expanding the battalion to four firing batteries even though this option was more resource intensive than the three firing batteries in the existing battalion. In view of this and command and control problems with the six-gun battery, the War Department retained the four-gun battery for the infantry division through World War II.[92]

In the meantime, the Field Artillery School explored new fire direction doctrine to make the Field Artillery relevant to the new age and to exploit the increased mobility and firepower of field artillery weapons being introduced.[93] Although the school taught trench warfare doctrine and unobserved indirect fire during the 1920s, open warfare doctrine and observed indirect fire from the battery which was the primary conductor of fire and the battalion which had responsibility for both observed and unobserved fire dominated instruction. In its officer courses, the school advocated attaching a forward observer, called a liaison officer, to infantry units and using him to adjust observed fire onto enemy targets by a descriptive reference to a prominent terrain feature on a map or by giving the target's coordinates to the batteries for them to plot. This practice permitted the forward observer to shift fires from a battalion around the battlefield in support of the infantry advance. As long as maps were available, the battalion could do this relatively effectively. Without maps, the battalion's three firing batteries had to adjust observed fire individually onto the target; this was time consuming and ineffective and violated the principle of massing fire.[94]

In his report to the acting Commandant of the School in June 1929, the Assistant Commandant of the School, Lieutenant Colonel William P. Ennis, questioned these methods of locating targets. "Unless there is some prominent object recorded on the map which is close to the enemy target, the chance of any liaison officer [during the heat of battle] being able to give the coordinates with accuracy . . . is very doubtful," he asserted.[95] To locate a target accurately required employing the grid coordinate and the prominent terrain feature together; World War I and Ennis's experience with practical exercises in the school during the 1920s showed employing the two together to be extremely difficult. Yet, other than insisting that the observer had to stay as close as possible to the infantry, he failed to offer a solution to replace the current method of adjusting observed fire.[96]

As might be expected, Ennis's strongest criticism about observed fire focused on the inability of observers to communicate effectively with the batteries and battalion. Even if the target could be accurately designated by the liaison officer using grid coordinates or a prominent terrain feature, the chances of the observer maintaining effective communication in battle with the batteries or battalion remained slight in view of existing communications systems – the field telephone – especially in a war of movement. He lamented, "I believe our most difficult problem in the field artillery today is communication. Little progress has been made . . . since the war. We do not carry nearly enough wire . . . and our radio equipment is far behind that now used in commercial pursuits."[97] The state of communications technology in 1929 therefore presented the greatest obstacle to responsive observed indirect fire.[98]

As Ennis and other field artillery officers indicated, the methods of massing fire in 1929 had not changed from what they had been in 1918. If all battery forward observers could identify the target by descriptive reference or locate it on a map, the problem of massing fire was relatively easy. If the target was obscure, the non-firing batteries would watch for the bursts of the adjusting battery to try to spot the target. If the target could be located on a map, coordinates could be passed to the batteries for them to plot and compute data. However, if there was no map or if only one observer could see the target, then massing fire from a battalion was problematic.[99]

Besides concurring with Ennis's trenchant analysis about the deficiencies of observed fire from a battalion, the Director of the Gunnery Department, Major Carlos Brewer, recognized the general dissatisfaction within the Army at the Field Artillery's ineffective close support to the Infantry during the war and the inadequate postwar attempts to improve close support and took upon himself to eliminate that notable shortcoming. Inspired by Lieutenant Colonel Neil Fraser-Tytler's *Field Guns in France* (1929) where he described his ability to shift fire around the battlefields of World War I and supported by his instructors and staff, Brewer pushed to make field artillery fire more responsive than it had been in the war. Early in 1931, Brewer and his instructors concluded that the problem of unresponsive close support in 1917-1918 stemmed from the practice of massing the fire of a battalion by descriptive reference to terrain features or by the grid coordinate when maps were available. To eliminate this weakness, Brewer introduced a firing chart on which a base point had been plotted with accuracy and adopted the practice of locating battery positions by survey and designating targets with reference to the base point. In the spring of 1931, the Gunnery Department successfully demonstrated massing battalion fire on a target by using this method after registering one battery on the target without all of the forward observers being able to see the target and without maps. Yet, Brewer did not centralize computing firing data at the battalion even though some field artillery officers advocated this. He kept this function in the battery because he could not find a rapid method of centralizing computing firing data at the battalion to make it a firing unit.[100]

Continuing the work, Brewer's successor, Major Orlando Ward, eventually solved the problem of massing fire rapidly and accurately. In 1932-1934, Ward and his instructors developed the fire direction center to centralize computing firing data in the battalion. They advocated using the battalion commander as the director of fire whenever fire control could be centralized because he identified the targets to be engaged and employing the battery commander as the conductor of fire. The battalion commander would dispatch forward observers from the batteries and the battalion who would report their observations back to the fire direction center using radios rather than telephones. The fire direction center would then compute the technical firing data rather than the forward observer who had done this in the American army since the inception of observed indirect fire, apply the necessary corrections, conduct the adjustments, and synchronize fire on the most dangerous target even if only one observer could see the target. With accurate maps the battalion fire direction center could mass fire within 10 minutes after receiving a call for fire, while a battery could provide fire within five minutes. Without maps, the fire direction center generally took longer to mass fires. Even though fire direction center only could handle observed indirect fire, it surpassed anything in Europe.[101]

However, the school ran into stiff opposition selling the fire direction center to the War Department and the Field Artillery community. The Chief of Field Artillery, Major General Upton Birnie, Jr. (1934-1938), proved to be the biggest obstacle. Along with other senior field artillery officers, he opposed taking any prerogatives away from the battery commander who had been the director of fire during the war and giving them to the battalion commander who had become the director of fire with the development of the fire direction center. Other field artillery officers voiced different objections. While some wanted the forward observer to talk directly to the battery doing the firing as the practice had been, many insisted that massing a battalion fire on a single target by adjusting a single battery was impossible. Such fiery resistance and conservatism caused the War Department to reject the fire direction center.[102]

With help from his staff and instructors, Lieutenant Colonel H.L.C. Jones, who became director of the Gunnery Department in 1939, refined the fire direction center and paved the way for its acceptance. Based upon his experience as a battalion commander of the 2d Battalion, 77th Field Artillery Regiment, Jones centralized all fire direction computation for observed and unobserved fire in the battalion, increased the number of people in the fire direction center to handle the additional task, but also left observed fire to the battery commander. In fast-moving situations, Jones required the battery to handle observed fire. As soon as the situation stabilized, the battalion assumed responsibility for observed and unobserved fires. Subsequently, Jones initiated computing observed and unobserved fires from the same fire direction chart. After demonstrating his refinements early in 1941 to the Commandant of the Field Artillery School, Brigadier General George R. Allin (1941-1942), Jones finally convinced him to accept the fire direction center and the battalion as the firing unit.

The War Department subsequently adopted the fire direction center after the Chief of Staff of the Army, General George C. Marshall, had witnessed a four-battalion shoot on 10 April 1941. On that day the 18th Field Artillery, acting as division artillery, massed fires upon a particular target at Fort Sill and then shifted fires to other targets selected by Marshall. Subsequently in a demonstration for Danford in October 1941, Jones employed the fire direction center to mass fires without the benefit of a map and with only one observer seeing the target and converted him to employing the fire direction center.[103]

Coupled with the graphic firing table, a special slide rule introduced in 1940 especially for computing technical fire direction, and the portable radio, the fire direction center revolutionized fire support. It gave field artillery units the ability to shift massed fires rapidly and effectively around the battlefield and to disperse their weapons to protect them from counterbattery fire and represented a significant breakthrough with observed fire which had been difficult to provide during the recent war and had been the subject of much criticism.[104]

Published between 1935 and 1938 by the school at the direction of the Chief of Field Artillery, distributed free to all Regular Army officers, and sent to National Guard and Organized Reserve officers at a nominal fee, *The Digest of Field Artillery Developments* also reflected the school's growing participation in the development and dissemination of doctrine. *The Digest of Field Artillery Developments* examined new tactics, techniques, and procedures that were not covered by official publications to permit field artillerymen to keep abreast of the latest developments and thinking.[105] Writing in the first edition, Birnie noted:

> It will treat . . . subjects, which because of incomplete treatment in the Field Artillery Field Manual and Training Regulations, require expansion and . . . methods, which, by reason of recent changes in materiel and equipment . . . have been . . . developed by the Field Artillery School or the Field Artillery Board, or developed elsewhere. . . .[106]

Although the development of tactics, techniques, and procedures and doctrine was a group effort by many War Department agencies, Birnie openly acknowledged the Field Artillery School's leading role and sanctioned the principles and techniques published in *The Digest of Field Artillery Developments*.[107]

As much as publishing *The Digest of Field Artillery Developments*, developing the fire direction center and graphic firing table, advocating new tactics, techniques, procedures, and doctrine, conducting courses on motor maintenance, and studying the appropriate howitzer combination for the division reflected the school's efforts to embrace modernization, the school's ties with the horse remained strong. Horse shows, polo matches, and fox hunts continued to be a staple for officers and exposed a school imbued with the upper-class traditions of the gentleman soldier. In fact, the school believed the horse shows and polo matches to be legitimate training activities and even formed polo teams that participated in national and international polo competitions during the 1920s and 1930s, making those decades the heyday of polo at Fort Sill, while the school's annual report devoted more space to horse shows and the Field Artillery polo team after 1937 than before when it became evident that the motor vehicle would eventually replace the horse. This illustrated the school's efforts to stay connected to its heritage and maintain interest in equestrian activities. Basically, the school cautiously abandoned the tried and proven horse as a prime mover for the motor vehicle to demonstrate its unswerving loyalty to the horse, the cultural traditions that surrounded the animal, and the intellectual and emotional difficulty of adopting motor vehicles as prime movers.[108]

Formal courses in advanced horsemanship for officers and saddlers and horseshoer courses for enlisted personnel also reflected the reluctance to abandon the horse totally for unreliable motor vehicles and presented an interesting picture of a branch, a school, and an officer corps that were trying to move into the modern era of motor vehicles while dutifully clinging to the past. Like many Army officers of the time, field artillery officers found themselves uneasily straddling two eras. One was the horse-drawn, and the other was the motor vehicle.[109]

Outside of the development of the fire direction center, the school's efforts at modernizing the Field Artillery ironically bore little fruit to advance it beyond 1918. As Europe was marching off to war in 1939, a few farsighted field artillery officers had tried to move the school and the branch forward by advocating the adoption of motorized (towed) field artillery, but limited funds and conservatism restricted serious progress, leaving the school's intellectual orientation more closely attune to 1918 than 1939. Although the Field Artillery School had become a true field artillery school fulfilling Captain Dan T. Moore's dream of 1911 of creating a field artillery school along the lines of the German field artillery school at Juterborg, assumed a critical role in combat developments, and became permanently located at Fort Sill, the school found its lingering ties to the horse-drawn army too emotionally difficult to sever.

Notes

1 Russell F. Weigley, *History of the United States Army* (Bloomington, IN: Indiana University Press, 1984), pp. 395-96; Maurice Matloff, ed., *American Military History* (Washington, D.C.: Center of Military History, United States Army, 1985), pp. 405-06.

2 Annual Report of the Chief of Field Artillery, 1920, pp. 7, 20-22, UF23 A2, Morris Swett Technical Library (MSTL), US Army Field Artillery School; Raymond Walters, "Field Artillery in American Colleges," *Field Artillery Journal*, Nov-Dec 1919, pp. 543-55.

3 Annual Report of the Chief of Field Artillery, 1920, pp. 16-17, 20, UF23 A2, MSTL; "A Proposed Scheme of Officers' Schools for Field Artillery," *Field Artillery Journal*, Apr-Jun 1919, pp. 207, 209; Raymond Walters, *et al, The Story of the Field Artillery Central Officers Training School, Camp Zachary Taylor, Kentucky* (New York: The Knickerbocker Press, 1919), p. 94.

4 Annual Report of the Chief of Field Artillery, 1920, pp. 1, 5, 6, 14, 15, 16, 31, UF23 A2, MSTL; Report, subj: Report of the Commandant, Field Artillery School, 13 Aug 1920, p. 1, UF23.5 E1, MSTL; Riley Sunderland, *History of the Field Artillery School:1911-1942* (Fort Sill, OK: Field Artillery School Printing Plant, 1942), p. 94; Walters, *et al, The Story of the Field Artillery Central Officers' Training School*, p. 94.

5 Weigley, *History of the United States Army*, pp. 396-97; Matloff, *American Military History*, pp. 407-08.

6 Gillette Griswold, "Fort Sill, Oklahoma: A Brief History," unpublished manuscript, p. 9, Historical Research and Document Collection (HRDC), Field Artillery Branch Historian's Office, US Army Field Artillery School; Matloff, *American Military History* , p. 409; Weigley, *History of the United States Army*, p. 399; William O. Odom, *After the Trenches: The Transformation of US Army Doctrine, 1918-1939* (College Station, TX: Texas A&M University Press, 1999), pp. 16-17; Annual Report of the Field Artillery School, 13 Aug 1920, p. 1, UF23.5 E1, MSTL; Annual Report of the Chief of Field Artillery, 1920, pp. 30-32, UF23 A2, MSTL; Sunderland, *History of the Field Artillery School*, pp. 85-87; *The Mil*, 1922, UF25 C616A7, 1922, p. 38, MSTL. *The Mil* was the class yearbook for the battery officer course at the Field Artillery School

7 Annual Report of the Chief of Field Artillery, 1920, pp. 30-31, UF23 A2, MSTL; Sunderland, *History of the Field Artillery School*, p. 85; Annual Report of the Chief of Field Artillery, FY 1922, in *Field Artillery Journal*, Nov-Dec 1922, pp, 462-63.

8 Griswold, "Fort Sill, Oklahoma: A Brief History," HRDC; Matloff, *American Military History*, p. 409; Odom, *After the Trenches*, pp. 16-17; Annual Report of the Field Artillery School, 13 Aug 1920, p. 1, UF23.5 E1, MSTL; Annual Report of the Chief of Field Artillery, 1920, pp. 30-32, UF23 A2, MSTL; Sunderland, *History of the Field Artillery School*, pp. 85-87; *The Mil*, 1922, UF25 C616A7, 1922, p. 38, MSTL.

9 Lecture, MG Ernest Hinds, Commandant, Field Artillery School, 10 Jan 1920, in Miscellaneous Correspondence pertaining to Fort Sill, 1911-1924, UF25 H673 M4, MSTL; Annual Report of the Field Artillery School, 13 Aug 1920, p. 1, UF23.5 E1, MSTL; Annual Report of the Field Artillery School, 4 Jan 1921, p. 2, UF23.5 E1, MSTL; Sunderland, *History of the Field Artillery School*, pp. 74-75; *The Mil*, 1922, pp. 27-31, 80, UF25 C615A7, MSTL.

10 See note 9.

11 Annual Report of the Field Artillery School, 13 Aug 1920, Appendix F, UF23.5 E1, MSTL.

12 *The Mil*, 1922, pp. 80-81, UF25 C615A7, MSTL; Sunderland, *History of the Field Artillery School*, pp. 82, 84, 94, 118, 147, 190; Annual Report of the Field Artillery School, 11 Jul 1921, pp. 3-7, UF23.5 E1, MSTL; Robert S. Rush, "The Evolution of NCOs in Training Soldiers," unpublished

paper, p. 8, HRDC; The Field Artillery School, School Catalogue, 1920, unpaginated, UF23.5 Q7, MSTL.

13 *The Mil*, 1922, pp. 80-81, UF25 C615A7, MSTL; Sunderland, *History of the Field Artillery School*, pp. 82, 84, 94, 118, 147, 190; Annual Report of the Field Artillery School, 11 Jul 1921, pp. 3-7, UF23.5 E1, MSTL; Rush, "The Evolution of NCOs in Training Soldiers," p. 8, HRDC; The Field Artillery School, School Catalogue, 1920, unpaginated, UF23.5 Q7, MSTL.

14 Annual Report of the Field Artillery School, 4 Jan 1921, pp. 1, 2, 6, Appendix D, UF23.5 E1, MSTL; Annual Report of the Field Artillery School, 11 Jul 1921, pp. 1, 2, UF23.5 E1, MSTL; Sunderland, *History of the Field Artillery School*, pp. 80-81; The Field Artillery School, School Catalogue, 1920, UF23.5 Q7, MSTL.

15 Annual Report of the Field Artillery School, 13 Aug 1920, p. 2, UF23.5 E1, MSTL; Annual Report of the Field Artillery School, 4 Jan 1921, pp. 1, 2, UF23.5 E1, MSTL; Annual Report of the Field Artillery School, 11 Jul 1921, pp. 1, 2, UF23.5 E1, MSTL; Sunderland, *History of the Field Artillery School*, pp. 80-81.

16 "Discussions," *Field Artillery Journal*, Apr-Jun 1919, pp. 218-30; LTC John B. Anderson, "Are We Justified in Discarding 'Pre-War' Methods of Training?" *Field Artillery Journal*, Apr-Jun 1919, p. 222; Annual Report of the Commandant, The Field Artillery School, 28 Jun 1929, p. 8, UF23.5 E1, MSTL; Richard L. Pierce, "A Maximum of Support: The Development of US Army Field Artillery Doctrine in World War One," unpublished master's thesis, 1983, Ohio State University, pp. 126, 130; Steven A. Stebbins, "Indirect Fire: The Challenge and Response in the US Army, 1907-1917," unpublished master's thesis, University of North Carolina, 1993, p. 87; Odom, *After the Trenches*, pp. 44-45.

17 "Discussions," *Field Artillery Journal*, Apr-Jun 1919, pp. 218-30; Anderson, "Are We Justified in Discarding 'Pre-War' Methods of Training?" p. 222; Annual Report of the Commandant, The Field Artillery School, 28 Jun 1929, p. 8, UF23.5 E1, MSTL; Pierce, "A Maximum of Support," pp. 126, 130; Stebbins, "Indirect Fire," p. 87; Odom, *After the Trenches*, pp. 44-45.

18 BG Dwight E. Aultman, "Maps and Map Firing," *Field Artillery Journal*, Jul-Aug 1920, pp. 380-81; "Discussions," *Field Artillery Journal*, Apr-Jun 1919, pp. 218-30; Annual Report of the Commandant, The Field Artillery School, 28 Jun 1929, p. 8, UF23.5 E1, MSTL; Pierce, "A Maximum of Support," pp. 126, 130; Stebbins, "Indirect Fire," p. 87.

19 Aultman, "Maps and Map Firing," p. 381.

20 Aultman, "Maps and Map Firing," p. 381.

21 Anderson, "Are We Justified in Discarding 'Pre-War' Methods of Training?" p. 224.

22 Anderson, "Are We Justified in Discarding 'Pre-War' Methods of Training?" p. 224.

23 Anderson, "Are We Justified in Discarding 'Pre-War' Methods of Training?" p. 230.

24 MG Ernest Hinds, "The Training of Artillery in France," *Field Artillery Journal*, Sep-Oct 1919, p. 381.

25 Hinds, "The Training of Artillery in France," p. 381.

26 Ltr, Hinds to MG William J. Snow, 22 Nov 1919, in Miscellaneous Correspondence pertaining to Fort Sill, 1911-1924, UF25 H673 M4, MSTL; Remarks to Graduating Class, School of Fire, 19 Dec 1919, in Miscellaneous Correspondence pertaining to Fort Sill, 1911-1924, UF25 H673 M4, MSTL.

27 Ltr, Hinds to Snow, 22 Nov 1919, in Miscellaneous Correspondence pertaining to Fort Sill, 1911-1924, UF25 H673 M4, MSTL; Remarks to Graduating Class at the School of Fire, Fort

Sill, Oklahoma, 17 Dec 1919, by MG Ernest Hinds, in Miscellaneous Correspondence pertaining to Fort Sill, 1911-1924, UF25 H673 M4, MSTL; Ltr, Hinds to Snow, 15 Jan 1920, in Miscellaneous Correspondence pertaining to Fort Sill, 1911-1924, UF25 H673 M4, MSTL; Sunderland, *History of the Field Artillery School,* p. 80; David E. Johnson, "From Frontier Constabulary to Modern Army: The US Army Between the Wars," in Harold R. Winton and David R. Mets, eds., *The Challenge of Change: Military Institutions and New Realities, 1918-1941* (Lincoln, NE: University of Nebraska Press, 2000), pp. 166-68.

28   Lecture by MG Ernest Hinds, 10 Jan 1920, in Miscellaneous Correspondence pertaining to Fort Sill, 1911-1924, UF25 H673 M4, MSTL; Odom, *After the Trenches*, pp. 75-76.

29   Lecture, Hinds, 10 Jan 1920, in Miscellaneous Correspondence pertaining to Fort Sill, 1911-1924, UF25 H673 M4, MSTL; Sunderland, *History of the Field Artillery School*, pp. 78-79.

30   Lecture, Hinds, 10 Jan 1920, in Miscellaneous Correspondence pertaining to Fort Sill, 1911-1924, UF25 H673 M4, MSTL.

31   Annual Report of the Field Artillery School, 13 Aug 1920, Appendix A, UF23.5 E1, MSTL.

32   Lecture, Hinds, 10 Jan 1920, p. 3, in Miscellaneous Correspondence pertaining to Fort Sill, 1911-1924, UF25 H673 M4, MSTL.

33   Lecture, Hinds, 10 Jan 1920, p. 3; Report of Commandant, Field Artillery School, 13 Aug 1920, Appendix A, UF23.5 E1, MSTL; Annual Report, 11 Jul 1921, Appendix D, UF23.5 E1, MSTL; Annual Report, 4 Jan 1921, p. 2, UF23.5 E1, MSTL.

34   Sunderland, *History of the Field Artillery School*, p. 78; Annual Report, 4 Jan 1921, p. 6, UF23.5 E1, MSTL.

35   Annual Report, 4 Jan 1921, p. 6.

36   Annual Report, 4 Jan 1921, p. 6.

37   Ltr, Hinds to Snow, 31 Mar 1921, in Miscellaneous Correspondence pertaining to Fort Sill, 1911-1924, UF25 H673 M4, MSTL; Annual Report of the Field Artillery School, 16 Jun 1923, p. 1, UF23.5 E1, MSTL; Ltr, Hinds to Snow, 19 Jul 1921, in Miscellaneous Correspondence pertaining to Fort Sill, 1911-1924, UF25 H673 M4, MSTL; Ltr, Hinds to Snow, 16 Jan 1922, in Miscellaneous Correspondence pertaining to Fort Sill, 1911-1924, UF25 H673 M4, MSTL.

38   Ltr, Hinds to Snow, 19 Jul 1921, in Miscellaneous Correspondence pertaining to Fort Sill, 1911-1924, UF25 H673 M4, MSTL.

39   Ltr, Hinds to Snow, 16 Feb 1922, in Miscellaneous Correspondence pertaining to Fort Sill, 1911-1924, UF25 H673 M4, MSTL; Griswold, "Fort Sill, Oklahoma: A Brief History," p. 13, HRDC; "A Brief History of Fort Sill and the Field Artillery School," *Field Artillery Journal*, Nov-Dec 1933, pp. 528-41; Sunderland, *History of the Field Artillery School*, pp. 84-91; Robert R. Palmer, Bell I. Wiley, and William R. Keast, *The Procurement and Training of Ground Combat Troops* (Washington, D.C.: Office of the Chief of Military History, Department of the Army, 1948), p. 259.

40   Ltr, Hinds to Snow, 16 Feb 1922, in Miscellaneous Correspondence pertaining to Fort Sill, 1911-1924, UF25 H673 M4, MSTL; Griswold, "Fort Sill, Oklahoma: A Brief History," p. 13, HRDC; "A Brief History of Fort Sill and the Field Artillery School," pp. 528-41; Sunderland, *History of the Field Artillery School*, pp. 84-91; Palmer, Wiley, and Keast, *The Procurement and Training of Ground Combat Troops*, p. 259.

41   Annual Report of the Chief of Field Artillery, 1923, in *Field Artillery Journal*, Jan-Feb 1923, 31-32, 50-51; Ltr, Hinds to Snow, 22 Feb 1922, in Miscellaneous Correspondence pertaining

to Fort Sill, 1911-1924, UF25 H673 M4, MSTL; Portrait of BG Albert J. Bowley, *Field Artillery Journal*, Sep-Oct 1921, p. 426.

42 Annual Report of the Chief of Field Artillery, 1923, in *Field Artillery Journal*, Jan-Feb 1923, 31-32, 50-51; Ltr, Hinds to Snow, 22 Feb 1922, in Miscellaneous Correspondence pertaining to Fort Sill, 1911-1924, UF25 H673 M4, MSTL; Portrait of BG Albert J. Bowley, p. 426; Sunderland, *History of the Field Artillery School*, p. 86; Memorandum for Hinds, subj: Field Artillery Schools and Their Location, 17 Feb 1922, in File of Correspondence for 1936, UF25 S372 FA, MSTL.

43 Ltr, Hinds to Snow, 5 May 1922, in Miscellaneous Correspondence pertaining to Fort Sill, 1911-1924, UF25 H673 M4, MSTL.

44 Ltr, Hinds to Snow, 5 May 1922.

45 Ltr, Hinds to Snow, 5 May 1922.

46 Sunderland, *History of the Field Artillery School*, p. 86; Memorandum for Hinds, subj: Field Artillery Schools and Their Location, 17 Feb 1922, in File of Correspondence for 1936, UF25 S372 FA, MSTL.

47 Wilbur S. Nye, *Carbine and Lance: The Story of Old Fort Sill* (Norman, OK: University of Oklahoma Press, 1974), p. 332; Griswold, "Fort Sill, Oklahoma: A Brief History," p. 13, HRDC; "A Brief History of Fort Sill and the Field Artillery School," pp. 528-41; Sunderland, *History of the Field Artillery School*, pp. 84-91, 95-97; Annual Report of the Chief of Field Artillery, 1923, in *Field Artillery Journal*, Jan-Feb 1924, pp. 50-51; Report of the Field Artillery School, 16 Jun 1923, pp. 1-4, UF23.5 E1, MSTL; Ltr, Post Cdr to Adj Gen, subj: Funds for Completion of Building One-Seventeen, 30 Jun 1922, in Miscellaneous Correspondence pertaining to Fort Sill, 1911-1924, UF25 H673 M4, MSTL; *The Shrapnel for 1925*, p. 147, UF25 C615 A7, MSTL; *The Shrapnel for 1923*, p. 14, UF25 C615 A7, MSTL; Palmer, Wiley, and Keast, *The Procurement and Training of Ground Combat Troops*, p. 259.

48 Nye, *Carbine and Lance*, p. 332; Griswold, "Fort Sill, Oklahoma: A Brief History," p. 13, HRDC; "A Brief History of Fort Sill and the Field Artillery School," pp. 528-41; Sunderland, *History of the Field Artillery School*, pp. 84-91, 95-97; Annual Report of the Chief of Field Artillery, 1923, in *Field Artillery Journal*, Jan-Feb 1924, pp. 50-51; Report of the Field Artillery School, 16 Jun 1923, pp. 1-4, UF23.5 E1, MSTL; Ltr, Post Cdr to Adj Gen, subj: Funds for Completion of Building One-Seventeen, 30 Jun 1922, in Miscellaneous Correspondence pertaining to Fort Sill, 1911-1924, UF25 H673 M4, MSTL; *The Shrapnel for 1925*, p. 147, UF25 C615 A7, MSTL; *The Shrapnel for 1923*, p. 14, UF25 C615 A7, MSTL; Palmer, Wiley, and Keast, *The Procurement and Training of Ground Combat Troops*, p. 259.

49 *The Shrapnel for 1923*, p. 10, UF25 C615 A7, MSTL.

50 *The Shrapnel for 1923*, p. 10.

51 Annual Report of the Chief of Artillery for 1923-1924, in *Field Artillery Journal*, Jan-Feb 1925, p. 24.

52 *Annual Report of the Chief of Field Artillery for 1923-1924*, p. 24.

53 Hinds, "Graduation Address to the Classes at the Field Artillery School, June 14, 1924," *Field Artillery Journal*, Sep-Oct 1924, p. 469; Annual Report of the Chief of Field Artillery for 1923-1924, in *Field Artillery Journal*, Jan-Feb 1925, p. 24.

54 Hinds, "Graduation Address to the Classes at the Field Artillery School, June 14, 1924," p. 469.

55 Memorandum for Cmdt, subj: Annual Report, 15 Jun 1924, in Annual Report for School

Year 1923-1924, UF23.5 E1, MSTL.

56 Memorandum for Cmdt, subj: Annual Report, 15 Jun 1924.

57 Annual Report for School Year 1925-1926, pp. 21, 24, UF23.5 E1, MSTL.

58 Annual Report of the Field Artillery School, 8 Jul 1930, p. 2, UF23.5 E1, MSTL.

59 Annual Report of the Field Artillery School, 8 Jul 1930, pp. 2-3; Sunderland, *History of the Field Artillery School,* p. 103; Edwin P. Parker, "The Regular Course, The Field Artillery School," *Field Artillery Journal*, May-Jun 1934, pp. 202-06; The Field Artillery School, Description of Courses, 1930-1931, pp. 6, 7, 9, 10, UF23.5 Q7, MSTL; The Field Artillery School, Description of Courses, pp. 6, 7, 9, UF23.5 Q7, MSTL.

60 Parker, "The Regular Course, The Field Artillery School," pp. 202-06; The Field Artillery School, Description of Courses, 1930-1931, pp. 6, 7, 9, 10, UF23.5 Q7, MSTL; The Field Artillery School, Description of Courses, pp. 6, 7, 9, UF23.5 Q7, MSTL; Annual Report of the Chief of Field Artillery for 1925-1926, in *Field Artillery Journal*, Nov-Dec 1926, p. 584; Annual Report of the Chief of Field Artillery for 1926-1927, in *Field Artillery Journal* Nov-Dec 1927, p. 560; Annual Report of the Chief of Field Artillery for 1928, in *Field Artillery Journal,* Nov-Dec 1928, p. 579; "The Regular Course, The Field Artillery School," *Field Artillery Journal*, May-Jun 1934, pp. 202-06; Annual Report of the Commandant, The Field Artillery School, 29 Jun 1934, p. 1, UF23.5 E1, MSTL; Annual Report of the Commandant, The Field Artillery School, 10 Jul 1935, p. 1, UF23.5 E1, MSTL; Annual Report of the Academic Division, The Field Artillery School, 4 Jun 1929, pp. 1-2, in Annual Report of the Commandant, The Field Artillery School, 28 Jun 1929, UF23.5 E1, MSTL; Annual Report of the Commandant, The Field Artillery School, 25 Jun 1935, p. 13, UF23.5 E1, MSTL; Annual Report of the Field Artillery School, 24 Jul 1937, p. 25, UF23.5 E1, MSTL; Annual Report of the Field Artillery School, 20 Jul 1939, p. 2, UF23.5 E1, MSTL; Sunderland, *History of the Field Artillery School*, pp. 140-41; Report of Operations of Field Artillery School, 24 Jul 1937, pp. 23-24, UF23.5 E1, MSTL.

61 Report of Operations of the Field Artillery School, 24 July 1937, pp. 2-3; Report of Operations of the Field Artillery School, 20 Jul 1939, p. 3, UF23.5 E1, MSTL; Sunderland, *History of the Field Artillery School*, pp. 84, 94, 118, 147, 190.

62 Sunderland, *History of the Field Artillery School*, pp. 75-76.

63 Report of the Field Artillery School, 16 Jun 1923, p. 7, UF23.5 E1, MSTL.

64 Report of the Field Artillery School, 16 Jun 1923, p. 7.

65 Report of the Field Artillery School, 19 Jun 1924, p. 6, UF23.5 E1, MSTL.

66 Report of the Field Artillery School, 19 Jun 1924, p. 6.

67 Ltr, Helmick to Snow, 10 May 1923, in Miscellaneous Correspondence pertaining to Fort Sill, 1911-1924, UF25 H673 M4, MSTL.

68 Ltr, Helmick to Snow, 10 May 1923

69 Nye, *Carbine and Lance*, p. 332; Parker, "New Construction at Fort Sill," Jan-Feb 1934, pp. 5-14.

70 Annual Report of the Field Artillery School, 30 Jun 1925, p. 6, UF23.5 E1, MSTL.

71 Annual Report for the School Year 1924-1925, pp. 6-7, UF23.5 E1, MSTL.

72 Annual Report for the School Year 1924-1925, pp. 2-3.

73 Sunderland, *History of the Field Artillery School*, p. 114; Annual Report of the Field Artillery School, 30 Jun 1925, pp. 1-7, UF23.5 E1, MSTL; Annual Report of the Field Artillery

School, 3 Jul 1926, p. 2, UF23.5 E1, MSTL; Ltr, BG Dwight E. Aultman, FAS Cmdt, to MG Fred T. Austin, Chief of Field Artillery, 13 Nov 1928, in Miscellaneous Correspondence pertaining to Fort Sill, 1925-1930, UF25 H673 M4, MSTL; Reports of Commandant, 21 Jun 1929, p. 5, UF23.5 E1, MSTL.

74   Edwin P. Parker, Jr., "New Construction at Fort Sill," *Field Artillery Journal*, Jan-Feb 1934, p. 5; Annual Report of the Commandant, 8 Jul 1930, pp. 1-2, UF23.5 E1, MSTL.

75   Annual Report of the Commandant, 8 Jul 1930, p. 8.

76   Annual Report of the Commandant, 8 Jul 1930, p. 8.

77   Annual Report of the Chief of Field Artillery for 1924-1925, in *Field Artillery Journal*, Mar-Apr 1926, p. 196.

78   "Snow Hall Burns Down," *Field Artillery Journal*, Sep 1929, p. 584; Sunderland, *History of the Field Artillery School*, pp. 114-17; Griswold, "Fort Sill, Oklahoma: A Brief History," pp. 13-14, HRDC; Nye, *Carbine and Lance*, pp. 332-33; Paul McClung, "Lawton, Fort Sill Forge Early Successful Combination," Lawton *Constitution*, 5 Aug 1976, p. 9G; "A Brief History of Fort Sill and the Field Artillery School," pp. 528-41; Report of the Field Artillery School, 3 Jul 1926, p. 2, UF23.5 E1, MSTL; Report of the Field Artillery School, 11 Jun 1926, p. 42, UF23.5 E1, MSTL; Annual Report of the Commandant of the Field Artillery School, 8 Jul 1930, p. 1, UF23.5 E1, MSTL.

79   "Snow Hall Burns Down," p. 584; Sunderland, *History of the Field Artillery School*, pp. 114-17; Griswold, "Fort Sill, Oklahoma: A Brief History," pp. 13-14, HRDC; Nye, *Carbine and Lance*, pp. 332-33; Parker, "New Construction at Fort Sill," pp. 5-14; McClung, "Lawton, Fort Sill Forge Early Successful Combination," p. 9G; "A Brief History of Fort Sill and the Field Artillery School," pp. 528-41; Report of the Field Artillery School, 3 Jul 1926, p. 2, UF23.5 E1, MSTL; Report of the Field Artillery School, 11 Jun 1926, p. 42, UF23.5 E1, MSTL; Annual Report of the Commandant of the Field Artillery School, 8 Jul 1930, p. 1, UF23.5 E1, MSTL; Annual Report of the Chief of Field Artillery for 1924-1925, in *Field Artillery Journal*, Mar-Apr 1926, p. 196.

80   Annual Report of the Field Artillery School, 8 Jul 1930, p. 2, UF23.5 E1, MSTL.

81   "Snow Hall Burns Down," p. 584; Sunderland, *History of the Field Artillery School*, pp. 114-17; Griswold, "Fort Sill, Oklahoma: A Brief History," pp. 13-14, HRDC; Nye, *Carbine and Lance*, pp. 332-33; McClung, "Lawton, Fort Sill Forge Early Successful Combination," p. 9G; "A Brief History of Fort Sill and the Field Artillery School," pp. 528-41; Report of the Field Artillery School, 3 Jul 1926, p. 2, UF23.5 E1, MSTL; Report of the Field Artillery School, 11 Jun 1926, p. 42, UF23.5 E1, MSTL; Annual Report of the Commandant of the Field Artillery School, 8 Jul 1930, p. 1, UF23.5 E1, MSTL; Annual Report of the Chief of Field Artillery for 1924-1925, in *Field Artillery Journal*, Mar-Apr 1926, p. 196.

82   War Department, Special Orders No. 4, 8 Jan 1930, in Miscellaneous Correspondence pertaining to Fort Sill 1925-1930, UF25 H673 M4, MSTL; Sunderland, *History of the Field Artillery School*, pp. 116-17; Report, subj: Summary of the Water Situation, Fort Sill, Oklahoma, undated, Miscellaneous Papers on the Location of Field Artillery School, 1930, UF25 S372 M4, MSTL; Ltr, COL George P. Tyner, Acting Cmdt, to GEN Cruikshank, 30 Jan 1930, in Miscellaneous Papers on the Location of the Field Artillery School, 1930, UF25 S372 M4, MSTL. This file contains interesting correspondence supporting Fort Sill as the permanent location of the Field Artillery School. Also see letters in Correspondence Pertaining to Fort Sill 1925-1930, UF25 H673 M4, MSTL, written by several interest groups to have the school located at their chosen site.

83   Sunderland, *History of the Field Artillery School*, p. 117; "Fort Sill to be Permanent Home

of the Field Artillery School," *Field Artillery Journal*, Jan-Feb 1931, pp. 96-97.

84   Parker, "New Construction at Fort Sill," pp. 5-11; Sunderland, *History of the Field Artillery School*, pp. 121, 176-79; Annual Report of the Chief of Field Artillery, in *Field Artillery Journal*, Nov-Dec 1931, pp. 583-84.

85   Nye, *Carbine and Lance*, pp. 332-34; Parker, "New Construction at Fort Sill," pp. 5-13; Sunderland, *History of the Field Artillery School*, pp. 121, 176-79; Annual Report of Operations, the Field Artillery School, 10 Jun 1935, p. 14, UF23.5 E1, MSTL; Annual Report of Commandant, The Field Artillery School, 29 Jun 1934, pp. 1, 8, 9, UF23.5 E1, MSTL; Ltr, Commandant, Field Artillery School, to Chief of Field Artillery, 4 May 1937, in Miscellaneous Files on Fort Sill, 1937-1938, UF25 S372 M4, MSTL; Ltr, Commandant, Field Artillery School to Chief of Field Artillery, 24 Jan 1938, in Miscellaneous Files on Fort Sill, 1937-1938, UF25 S372 M4, MSTL; Ltr, Office of the Quartermaster to Commandant, Field Artillery School, 31 Dec 1937, in Miscellaneous Files on Fort Sill, 1937-1938, UF25 S372 M4, MSTL; Ltr, Commandant, Field Artillery School, to Commanding General, Eighth Corps Area, Fort Sam Houston, TX, 14 Oct 1937, in Miscellaneous Files on Fort Sill, 1937-1938, UF25 S372 M4, MSTL; Ltr, Chief of Field Artillery to Commandant, Field Artillery School, 3 Feb 1938, in Miscellaneous Files on Fort Sill, 1931-1938, UF25 S372 M4, MSTL; Ltr, Chief of Field Artillery to Representative Johnson, House of Representatives, 12 Jan 1937, in Miscellaneous Files, 1931-1938, UF25 H673 M4, MSTL; Ltr with atch, Chief of Field Artillery to Commandant, Field Artillery School, 30 Apr 1938, in Miscellaneous Files, 1931-1938, UF25 H673 M4, MSTL; Ltr, Office of the Chief of Staff, War Department, to Commandant, Field Artillery School, 10 Jun 38, in Miscellaneous Files, 1931-1938, UF25 H673 M4, MSTL; Ltr, Commandant, Field Artillery School, to Chief of Field Artillery, 18 Nov 1938, in Miscellaneous Files 1931-1938, UF25 H673 M4, MSTL; Ltr, Chief of Field Artillery to Commandant, Field Artillery School, 29 Nov 1938, in Miscellaneous Files 1931-1938, UF25 H673 M4, MSTL; Ltr, Commandant, Field Artillery School, to Chief of Field Artillery, 6 Dec 1938, in Miscellaneous Files 1931-1938, UF25 H673 M4, MSTL; Ltr with atch, Chief of Field Artillery to Commandant, Field Artillery School, 23 Dec 1938, in Miscellaneous Files 1931-1938, UF25 H673 M4, MSTL; Ltr, Commandant, Field Artillery School, to Chief of Field Artillery, 24 Feb 1936, in Miscellaneous Files 1931-1938, UF25 H673 M4, MSTL.

86   Sunderland, *History of the Field Artillery School*, pp. 91-92.

87   Sunderland, *History of the Field Artillery School, pp. 125-26, 173-76*; Annual Report of the Commandant, The Field Artillery School, 28 Jun 1929, pp. 8, 14, UF23.5 E1, MSTL; Annual Report of the Commandant, The Field Artillery School, 1 Jul 1932, p. 3, UF23.5 E1, MSTL; Annual Report of the Academic Division, 16 Jun 1935-30 Jun 1936, p. 14, in Report of Operations of the Field Artillery School for the School Year, 1935-1936, 23 Jul 1936, UF23.5 E1, MSTL; Annual Report of the Field Artillery School, 19 Jun 1933, Enclosure 1, UF23.5 E1, MSTL; Annual Report of the School Troops Division, Field Artillery School, 15 Jun 1934, in Annual Report of Commandant, The Field Artillery School, 29 Jun 1934, UF23.5 E1, MSTL; Annual Report of Operations, The Field Artillery School for the School Year 1934-1935, 10 Jul 1935, p. 6, UF23.5 E1, MSTL; Report of Operations of the Field Artillery School for the School Year 1936-1937, 24 Jul 1937, p. 2, UF23.5 E1, MSTL; Report of Operations of the Field Artillery School for the School Year 1937-1938, 15 Jul 1938, pp. 6-7, UF23.5 E1, MSTL; Report of Operations of the Field Artillery School for the School Year 1938-1939, 20 Jul 1939, pp. 3-4, UF23.5 E1, MSTL.

88   Annual Report of the Chief of Field Artillery, 1920, p. 6; War Department, Report of the Board of Officers Convened Pursuant to the Following Order (Westervelt Board): SO No. 289, 11 Dec 1918, pp. 4, 24-29; Constance M. Green, Harry C. Thomson, and Peter C. Roots, *The Ordnance Department: Planning Munitions for War* (Washington: Office of the Chief of Military History,

1955), p. 171; The Field Artillery School, *Field Artillery Materiel* (Fort Sill, OK: The Field Artillery School, 1934), pp. 16-22. Note: The Westervelt Board recommended a 75-mm. to 3-inch gun and a 105-mm. howitzer mix for the division because this would support fighting on a mobile battlefield. The War Department opted for the 75-mm. gun in 1920 rather than the 3-inch gun in the drive to build its field artillery system around the metric system for standardization purposes and planned to substitute the existing 155-mm. howitzer and 75-mm. gun combination for a 105-mm. howitzer and 75-mm. gun mix as soon as a suitable 105-mm. howitzer could be fielded.

89 The Field Artillery School, A Study of the 105-mm. howitzer with particular regard to the practical aspects of certain features of design, Sep 1938, pp. 1-2, UL303 A4 1938, MSTL, hereafter called Study of the 105-mm. howitzer.

90 Study of the 105-mm. howitzer, pp. 2, 19, 42, UL303 A4 1938, MSTL; Chief of Field Artillery, MG Upton Birnie, Lecture, US Army Command and General Staff College, 13 May 1937, UF23 B6 1937, MSTL; Janice McKenney, "More Bang for the Buck in the Interwar Army: The 105-mm. Howitzer," *Military Affairs*, Apr 1978, pp. 82-85; Jonathan M. House, "Designing the Light Division," *Military Review*, May 1984, pp. 41-47; Maj Jay M. MacKelvie, Quartermaster School, 12 Jan 1941, UF23 M3 Rare, MSTL.

91 Study of the 105-mm. howitzer, UL303 A4 1938, MSTL; Sunderland, *History of the Field Artillery School*, pp. 154-55; Field Artillery School, Characteristics of Major Field Artillery Weapons, Jan 1943, UL303 U5, MSTL; G.M. Barnes, *Weapons of World War II* (New York: D.Van Nostrand Company, Inc., 1947), pp. 118-19.

92 Sunderland, *History of the Field Artillery School*, p. 159; Report, Seventh Army, subj: Seventh Army Artillery Officer's Conference, 9-10 Jun 1945, UF7.5 A5 1945, MSTL; Boyd L. Dastrup, *King of Battle: A Branch History of the US Army's Field Artillery* (Fort Monroe, VA: Office of the Command Historian, US Army Training and Doctrine Command, 1992, reprinted by US Army Center of Military History in 1993), p. 195, 213, 241.

93 Sunderland, *History of the Field Artillery School*, p. 106; Annual Report of the Commandant of the Field Artillery School, 8 Jul 1930, p. 2, UF23.5 E1, MSTL; Memorandum from School Troops Division to Commandant of the Field Artillery School, subj: Annual Report, 10 Jun 30, UF23.5 E1, MSTL; Ltr, BG Dwight E. Aultman to MG Fred T. Austin, 13 Nov 1928, in correspondence pertaining to Fort Sill 1925-1930, UF25 H673 M4, MSTL.

94 Reports of the Commandant, Field Artillery School, 21 Jun 1929, Appendix D, p. 8, UF23.5 E1, MSTL; LTC Frank G. Ratliff, "The Field Artillery Battalion Fire-Direction Center – Its Past, Present, and Future," *Field Artillery Journal*, May-Jun 1950, p. 117.

95 Reports of the Commandant, Field Artillery School, 21 Jun 1929, p. 9, UF23.5 E1, MSTL.

96 Reports of the Commandant, Field Artillery School, 21 Jun 1929, p. 9.

97 Reports of the Commandant, Field Artillery School, 21 Jun 1929, p. 9.

98 Reports of the Commandant, Field Artillery School, 21 Jun 1929, Appendix D, p.8; Sunderland, *History of the Field Artillery School*, p. 129.

99 Riley Sunderland, "Massed Fire and the FDC," *Army*, May 1958, pp. 56-59.

100 Sunderland, "Massed Fires and the FDC," pp. 56-59; Sunderland, *History of the Field Artillery School*, pp. 129-30; Dastrup, *King of Battle*, p. 197. See the footnotes 73-75 on pages 196-97 for a complete list of the relevant primary sources.

101 Dastrup, *King of Battle*, pp. 197-98. See the footnotes on those pages for the primary sources used; "Fire Direction in the Battalion," *The Digest of Field Artillery Developments*, 1935, pp. 1-17; Russell A. Gugeler, *Major General Orlando Ward: Life of A Leader* (Oakland, OR: Red

Anvil Press, 2009), pp. 94-114.

102 Dastrup, *King of Battle,* pp. 196-98; Ratliff, "The Field Artillery Battalion Fire-Direction Center," p. 118.

103 Dastrup, *King of Battle*, Footnote 81, pp. 197-99, see footnotes on these pages for primary sources used; Ltr, BG Allin to MG Danford, 10 Apr 1941, Miscellaneous Correspondence File, 1941, UF25 S372 M4, 1941, MSTL; Sunderland, *History of the Field Artillery School*, pp. 210-11; Ratliff, "The Field Artillery Battalion Fire-Direction Center," p. 118; Sunderland, "Massed Fire and the FDC," pp. 56-59; "Fire Direction in the Battalion," pp. 1-17.

104 Dastrup, *King of Battle*, Footnote 81, p. 199; Ltr, Allin to Danford, 10 Apr 1941, Miscellaneous Correspondence File, 1941, UF25 S372 M4, 1941, MSTL; Sunderland, *History of the Field Artillery School*, pp. 210-11; Ratliff, "The Field Artillery Battalion Fire-Direction Center," p. 118; Sunderland, "Massed Fire and the FDC," pp. 56-59; "Fire Direction in the Battalion," pp. 1-17; Dastrup, *King of Battle*, pp. 197-98, see the footnotes on those pages for the primary sources used.

105 Sunderland, *History of the Field Artillery School*, pp. 136-37, 169; Forward, *The Digest of Field Artillery Developments*, Sep 1937. The Field Artillery School ceased publishing the *Digest* in 1938 because the Chief of Field Artillery, MG Robert M. Danford, decided to use the *Field Artillery Journal* to disseminate new information that was not yet in field artillery training manuals.

106 Forward, *The Digest of Field Artillery Developments*, Sep 1935; Forward, *The Digest of Field Artillery Developments*, Sep 1936.

107 Forward, *The Digest of Field Artillery Developments*, Sep 1935.

108 Sunderland, *History of the Field Artillery School*, pp. 125-26, 173-76; Annual Report of the Commandant, The Field Artillery School, 28 Jun 1929, pp. 8, 14, UF23.5 E1, MSTL; Annual Report of the Commandant, The Field Artillery School, 1 Jul 1932, p. 3, UF23.5 E1, MSTL; Annual Report of the Academic Division, 16 Jun 1935-30 Jun 1936, p. 14, in Report of Operations of the Field Artillery School for the School Year, 1935-1936, 23 Jul 1936, UF23.5 E1, MSTL; Annual Report of the Field Artillery School, 19 Jun 1933, Enclosure 1, UF23.5 E1, MSTL; Annual Report of the School Troops Division, Field Artillery School, 15 Jun 1934, in Annual Report of Commandant, The Field Artillery School, 29 Jun 1934, UF23.5 E1, MSTL; Annual Report of Operations, The Field Artillery School for the School Year 1934-1935, 10 Jul 1935, p. 6, UF23.5 E1, MSTL; Report of Operations of the Field Artillery School for the School Year 1936-1937, 24 Jul 1937, p. 2, UF23.5 E1, MSTL; Report of Operations of the Field Artillery School for the School Year 1937-1938, 15 Jul 1938, pp. 6-7, UF23.5 E1, MSTL; Report of Operations of the Field Artillery School for the School Year 1938-1939, 20 Jul 1939, pp. 3-4, UF23.5 E1, MSTL; Annual Report for 1937-1938, 15 Jul 1938, pp. 5-7, Appendix A, UF23.5 E1, MSTL; Annual Report for 1938-1939, 20 Jul 1939, pp. 3-4, Appendix A, UF23.5 E1, MSTL; Annual Report for 1939-1940, 11 Jul 1940, pp. 1-4, UF23.5 E1, MSTL.

109 Annual Report for 1937-1938, 15 Jul 1938, pp. 5-7, Appendix A, UF23.5 E1, MSTL; Annual Report for 1938-1939, 20 Jul 1939, pp. 3-4, Appendix A, UF23.5 E1, MSTL; Annual Report for 1939-1940, 11 Jul 1940, pp. 1-4, UF23.5 E1, MSTL.

Chapter Five
Another War: 1939-1945

Although the training reforms and increased involvement in equipment and force structure design and doctrine development during the 1920s and 1930s gave the Field Artillery School a comprehensive mission unlike its almost exclusive focus on gunnery prior to World War I, World War II spawned far-reaching changes in the school that altered it forever and dragged it away from its slow-pace, nine-month school year. To satisfy wartime graduate requirements, the school revamped its school year, increased the number and kinds of courses, took on the mission of supervising the Field Artillery Officer Candidate School, and expanded its physical facilities. More importantly, the war forced the school to sever its ties with horse-drawn artillery for motor-drawn and self-propelled artillery.

A Fitful Transition

The European diplomatic crisis of the late 1930s with the specter of war looming on the horizon prodded the War Department to improve its readiness to avoid being caught unprepared for war as it had been in 1917. Chief of Staff of the War Department General Malin Craig immediately directed a study of mobilization plans in October 1935 after succeeding General Douglas A. MacArthur, who had taken steps to improve readiness by focusing on equipping and training combat units for mobile warfare. Craig wanted to determine whether the forces that they contemplated could be mustered in the time proposed. As he anticipated, the study concluded that they could not. This prompted Craig to direct the revision of existing mobilization plans to establish attainable goals, to make the most of limited military resources, and to secure the strongest possible force at the outset of war. In doing so, he returned to the basic premise of the National Defense Act of 1920 that the Army should train recruits and simultaneously be ready to fight. In view of this, the Protective Mobilization Plan of 1937 outlined the process of expanding and equipping the Army and providing training centers, unit and individual training programs, and training manuals. Equally as important, the plan called for inducting the National Guard onto active duty to furnish the Regular Army with an initial force of about 400,000. Along with the Navy, this force would protect the country while the Army expanded in an orderly fashion. The Protective Mobilization Plan of 1939, the successor to the 1937 version, called for a two-phase expansion. The first phase prescribed a small emergency force, called the Initial Protective Force of 400,000 Regular Army and National Guard troops, to be available within 30 days after mobilization and to supply security during general mobilization. The second phase or general mobilization involved expanding to 1,150,000 in the active force within 240 days after mobilization had been declared.[1]

With the Protective Mobilization Plan of 1937 and especially its 1939 revision and the Chief of Field Artillery's Protective Mobilization Plan of 1939 as guides, the Field Artillery School became involved in the mobilization planning. To satisfy field artillery mobilization requirements the Chief of Field Artillery, Major General Robert M. Danford

(1938-1942), directed the Field Artillery School to develop a refresher course for officers and an officer candidate course for enlisted personnel who desired to be officers so that the officer ranks could expand orderly and rapidly. These two courses would begin 15 days after mobilization began and would reach a peak load of 4,000 students within 110 days after mobilization had started. On 24 March 1939, Danford subsequently expanded the school's mobilization mission when he tasked the Commandant of the School, Brigadier General Augustine McIntyre (1936-1940), to submit plans for enlisted specialist courses of 75 days, an officer refresher course of one month, and an officer candidate course of 12 weeks. Much to McIntyre's and the Field Artillery School's distress, Danford's guidance of March 1939 failed to address the potential number of students that would be attending the school and the fate of the school's peacetime courses, such as the Regular Course that had been the heart and soul of the school for several years. Even though the numbers were still unknown, Danford's assignment at least implied developing mobilization courses and retaining the peacetime courses.[2]

In view of Danford's general direction that permitted the school to design courses with a minimal amount of supervision, the school's concern over the number of students to be taught, the frequency of the courses, and the future of the Regular Course and other peacetime officer and enlisted courses persisted over the next several months as the War Department struggled to define the Army's role in any potential war or conflict. With one eye to reelection in 1940 and another one on the country's isolationistic mood, President Franklin D. Roosevelt heightened the sense of urgency to mobilization planning and furnished some focus. On 8 September 1939 just days after Germany had invaded Poland, the President proclaimed a limited national emergency. This allowed expanding the Regular Army from an authorized strength of 210,000 to 227,000 and the National Guard from 200,000 to 235,000 and directed the military to step up the pace of training. The proclamation also sanctioned activating reserve officers to augment Regular Army officers and implied that mobilization would be more than just a drill or exercise.[3]

Roosevelt's limited national emergency naturally influenced Danford's personnel projections. On 7 September 1939, the General informed the Field Artillery School that the Army would expand to 280,000 men, that the Field Artillery would increase in size second only to the Air Corps, and that Fort Sill would double in troop strength based upon the provisions of the National Defense Act of 1920 that governed mobilization. Because Roosevelt's declaration of 8 September 1939 would only enlarge the Army by 17,000 men, Danford reduced his projected size of the field artillery force on 9 September 1939. With rumors circulating in the War Department about the Army's eventual expansion to 280,000 in keeping with the National Defense Act of 1920, he subsequently amended his figures upward later in September 1939 to be consistent with the 280,000 figure. The limited national emergency failed to end the confusion over mobilization and the debate over the size of the force. As a result, the Field Artillery School found itself in a perplexing circumstance through the early fall of 1939. It did not know the size of the field artillery force to be trained and therefore did not know how much it would have to expand. Notwithstanding this confusion and receiving little oversight, the school started writing mobilization courses to complement its peacetime courses.[4]

On 6 October 1939, additional guidance came, but it was not what was desired nor expected. That day the War Department told the school to terminate its Regular Course for officers and its advanced courses in Horsemanship and Motors for officers on 1 February 1940 rather than in June 1940 which had been the traditional end of the school year. This would permit some instructors and students to participate in the first genuine corps and army maneuvers in American military history that were scheduled for the spring of 1940 as part of the Protective Mobilization Plan of 1939 to prepare the Army for combat action and to test new force structure, doctrine, and tactics against early reports on German combat methods. Yet, the War Department failed to address the status of the school's mobilization courses that were being developed and the future of its peacetime courses. As a result, the ambiguity about the Field Artillery School's training mission continued.[5]

For the school's Regular Course, reducing its length to support the corps and army maneuvers had far-reaching implications. When the official word finally came from the War Department on 21 October 1939 to end the course by 1 February 1940, thereby cutting its length, students had already attended six weeks of the 35-week course. To meet the deadline, the school condensed almost seven months of the remaining training schedule into three months by teaching classes eight hours a day, holding classes during the Christmas break of December 1939, and eliminating less critical subjects. With these adaptations the revised course covered only about 52 percent of the normal peacetime course, addressed the "bare essentials" that a battery commander should know, and produced a less qualified graduate than the peacetime Regular Course of 35 weeks had done.[6]

The spring maneuvers influenced the school in other ways. With the exception of the 18th Field Artillery Regiment, all of the school troops – the 1st Field Artillery Regiment and 77th Field Artillery Regiment – participated in the maneuvers at the direction of the War Department. This left the school with the 18th Field Artillery Regiment (horse-drawn) and an insufficient number of school troops to support training and made teaching the enlisted courses and the National Guard and Organized Reserve Officers' Course in the spring of 1940 difficult. In fact, dispatching school troops to the maneuvers came just at the time when the number of students in the enlisted courses had expanded from 152 in the spring of 1939 to 182 in the spring of 1940 for a modest increase and when the National Guard and Organized Reserve Officers' Course had grown from 45 students in the spring of 1939 to 131 students in the spring of 1940 as the school began to feel the impact of the limited national emergency declared by Roosevelt in September 1939. To accomplish its training mission, the school improvised a truck-drawn battalion from one of the horse-drawn battalions of the 18th Field Artillery Regiment. Ultimately, supporting the maneuvers caused the school to sacrifice quality in its officer and enlisted courses by stripping it of skilled instructors.[7]

Additionally, the maneuvers forced the school to revise its Protective Mobilization Plan of 1939 that outlined its priorities and activities to convert from a peacetime to a wartime institution and the units that would depart from Fort Sill to the theater of operations and those that would remain as school troops.[8] Ironically, the school's Protective Mobilization Plan of 1939 failed to provide for any school troops – a glaring omission – to support training during mobilization. This explained why the school lost so many troops to the maneuvers and struggled to furnish training in the spring of 1940. To eliminate this deficiency the school revamped its Protective Mobilization Plan of 1939 in the spring of 1940 and submitted it to the War Department for approval. For school troops the revised plan called for making the 18th Field Artillery Regiment a three-battalion organization – one battalion of truck-drawn 75-mm. guns less ammunition trains, one battalion of truck-drawn 155-mm. howitzers less ammunition trains, and one battalion of horse-drawn 75-mm. guns. On 18 April 1940, the War Department endorsed the plan and designated the 18th Field Artillery Regiment as school troops that could not be taken from the school to satisfy an emergency or another unit's training needs.[9]

As it staffed its protective mobilization plan for approval and wrote mobilization courses, the school began working on peacetime courses for the academic year of 1940-1941. Under the direction of McIntyre, the Assistant Commandant of School, Brigadier General Leroy P. Collins (1938-1941), submitted a detailed proposal in December 1939 to the Office of the Chief of Field Artillery for a four-month advanced course for "higher field artillery commanders and staff officers."[10] The proposed advanced course had a one-month phase to refresh students on the basics and a three-month phase on higher field artillery studies. As the Field Artillery School, McIntyre and Collins pointed out, the course would train field artillery officers being sent to the divisions being activated on the proper employment of field artillery in the new triangular division and to the corps that would be activated.[11]

Preparation for the academic year continued into January 1940. Without any specific guidance from the War Department about the length of the peacetime academic year, Collins recommended teaching a full-length Regular Course of 35 weeks and even proposed ending it in March 1941, thinking that the War Department would prefer a shorter year to accommodate the possibility of spring maneuvers. Eventually on 8 February 1940, the school officially planned offering a full-length Regular Course of 35 weeks that would run from September 1940 to June 1941 if maneuvers did not interfere. To accommodate maneuvers if they were held, the course would run from August 1940 to April 1941. If the Regular Course's length was cut, the school planned to offer an Advanced Gunnery Course. For 1940-1941 Collins also suggested a National Guard and Reserve Officers' Course for the fall and spring, a 39-week Advanced Horsemanship Course for officers, a 19-week Advanced Motors Course in the fall and spring for officers, and an Advanced Communications Course in the fall and spring for officers. To ensure that qualified field artillery soldiers were available, Collins projected a full series of enlisted courses for sergeant instructors in the fall, motor mechanics in the fall and spring, horseshoers in the fall and spring, saddlers in the fall and spring, communications specialists in the fall and spring, and battery mechanics in the spring and even included a enlisted horsemanship course. All enlisted courses would be the usual 19 weeks in length except for the sergeant instructor course which would be its usual 13 weeks.[12]

At his own discretion, Collins preserved the *status quo* since the school had taught his recommended courses for years and failed to take into consideration mobilization requirements beyond the proposed advanced course for "higher field artillery commanders and staff officers" which could be used as a mobilization course if necessary. In defense of Collins, the United States was still technically at peace early in 1940 and was trying to preserve its neutrality in the European war. Moreover, only a few reserve officers were scheduled to report to the Field Artillery School for training in 1940-1941. The need to change the school's curriculum was not clearly envisioned by anyone.[13]

Shortly afterward, Danford responded to the school's projected plan for the academic year of 1940-1941. On 15 February 1940, he established the closing date of June 1941 for the Regular Course. He also disapproved the Advanced Communication Course for officers because an officer shortage prevented taking them away from their units, limited the enlisted horsemanship course to Fort Sill personnel because the War Department lacked the funds to bring them in from other posts, and delayed making a decision on the advanced course for the fall of 1940.[14]

After the German invasion of the Low Countries and France in May 1940 that stepped up the War Department's pace of mobilization and heightened the sense of urgency, McIntyre revised the school's program of instruction for 1940-1941 by devising a comprehensive mobilization plan to support a war effort to end all speculation about the school's mobilization efforts. McIntyre created short mobilization courses for officers and enlisted soldiers and special courses for field grade officers that could be implemented quickly upon mobilization, outlined operating the entire year if required by abandoning the existing nine-month school year, and concurrently prepared to teach the normal peacetime courses for the coming academic year of 1940-1941. By taking these measures, McIntyre gave the school the flexibility to teach either mobilization or peacetime courses or to teach both simultaneously and provided the ability to adjust rapidly to a fluid situation.[15]

As the War Department embarked upon a large expansion program in the summer of 1940, instructions from Danford clarified the school's path for the coming months and reaffirmed the wisdom of McIntyre's actions, removing some of the uncertainty about the future. In a letter of 12 June 1940, Danford told McIntyre to start teaching mobilization courses for Organized Reserve officers and Regular Army enlisted specialists on 1 July 1940 and to initiate a three-month basic course on field artillery fundamentals for newly commissioned regular officers from the US Military Academy and Reserve Officer Training Corps. Danford also wanted the one-month refresher course for Organized Reserve officers to accommodate as many as 150 students at a time and outlined teaching the course six times during the remaining months of 1940. For enlisted soldiers, Danford desired a communications course, a battery mechanics course, a motor mechanics course, a saddlers course, and a horseshoers course and established a three-month (12 weeks) limit on the length of the courses. Through these officer and enlisted courses that would generate more graduates than the peacetime courses would furnish, Danford pressed to meet the anticipated growing requirement for more field artillery officers and soldiers to fill out Regular Army units that were expanding to meet their wartime strengths in 1940 or that were being created. At the time the Regular Army had 14,000 officers, required more officers for planning, training, administration, and potential combat, and had to tap the

National Guard and Organized Reserve for officers to fill out its rapidly growing force.[16]

Based upon rumors that were floating around the War Department, Danford concurrently advised McIntyre that the Field Artillery School's Regular Course which had been a staple for officers since 1934 and its advanced courses (Communications and Motors) for officers would last no longer than three months if they were even authorized. For the Regular Course, this meant cutting it from nine to three months, while the Communications and Motors Courses would be reduced from five to three months. As the guidance indicated, Danford proposed serious modifications to the school's curriculum by reducing the length of the Regular Course and advanced courses to ensure that the school would meet the needs of a rapidly expanding army and suggested the possibility of teaching mobilization and peacetime courses of reduced lengths concurrently. However, Danford directed the school in mid-1940 to focus its attention on mobilization courses with the implication that peacetime operations would be eliminated soon.[17]

Shortly after the school initiated its Refresher Course for the Organized Reserve officers on 10 July 1940, a War Department directive resolved the vagueness about the academic year of 1940-1941. With serious mobilization getting underway to defend the continental United States and the rest of the Western Hemisphere from any hostile armed forces, the War Department outlined its training plans on 27 July 1940. It authorized four types of training courses to be taught in its service schools. It sanctioned refresher courses for select officers of all Army components, a special basic course for newly commissioned officers coming from the US Military Academy or Reserve Officer Training Corps, specialist courses for select officers, and specialist courses for key enlisted personnel. Concurrently, the War Department discontinued all nine-month peacetime courses, shutting down the Field Artillery School's Regular Course, and limited all course lengths to no more than 12 weeks to get trained officers and soldiers to the field rapidly and in large numbers. For the Field Artillery School, this tasking of 27 July 1940 provided the first serious guidance from the War Department and signaled that mobilization was underway even though the United States was still officially at peace and that the leisure pace of peacetime training was ending.[18]

Following this guidance, the Field Artillery School cancelled all plans for teaching its Regular Course and other traditional peacetime courses for the academic year of 1940-1941 and launched its recently designed 12-week mobilization courses in August 1940. On the first of the month, the school initiated officer specialist courses in communications, motors, and horsemanship of 12 weeks each. Eight days later on 9 August 1940, the Basic Course for US Military Academy and Reserve Officer Training Corps honor graduates who were commissioned in the Field Artillery began. On 15 August 1940, the school launched its Battery Officers Course (Special) to train National Guard and Army Reserve battery grade officers in the duties of field artillery batteries and battalion staffs. This course replaced the one-month Refresher Course for reserve officers that had been implemented on 10 July 1940 in accordance with the Chief of Field Artillery's Protective Mobilization Plan of 1939 because the Refresher Course was too short and failed to cover the needs of the reserve officers being activated. Three months later on 14 November 1940, the Advanced

Course began training field artillery officers for battalion and higher echelons of command, but it was discontinued in February 1942 because too many of the officers attending the course lacked the appropriate field artillery background and because 60 percent of the students were National Guard officers who were being shipped back to their units where their training would not be used. On 10 July 1941, the school instituted an 8-week Field Officers Course for select battalion and regimental commanders and senior staff officers to teach them the tactics and techniques of the field artillery battalion that neither the Battery Officers Course nor the Advanced Course addressed. These officer courses complemented six 12-week enlisted courses – communications, motor mechanic, battery mechanic, horseshoer, saddler, and horsemanship – each that got underway in August 1940.[19]

Reflecting upon this rapid transition from peacetime to mobilization operations that lacked any precedence as a model, Colonel W.C. Potter, the executive officer for the Office of the Chief of Field Artillery, wrote the Bureau of Public Relations in the War Department on 7 July 1941 about the Field Artillery School's efforts to satisfy mobilization requirements. Over a period of about one year, the school completely reorganized all of its instruction into short, intensive courses for all grades, specialties, and skills that would be required for the officer's and the enlisted soldier's next assignment and that would accommodate a growing student population.[20]

The school's rapid expansion of 1940-1941 that included opening the Field Artillery Officer Candidate School in July 1941 and the mobilization of the 45th Infantry Division of the Oklahoma National Guard under Major General William S. Key in September 1940 at Fort Sill created two interesting problems. They forced the installation to address its inadequate water supply once again and simultaneously taxed the existing physical facilities.[21]

Although Fort Sill and Lawton had increased the quantity of water between 1930 and 1935, the post and city continued campaigning to raise the height of the dam that formed Lake Lawtonka to furnish more water and sought financial assistance from the federal government to do so. The federal government approved the city's and Fort Sill's proposal but failed to provide any funding. In August 1936, McIntyre reacted by writing the Chief of Field Artillery about the urgent need to increase the post's water supply because he anticipated an imminent growth in the military population at the school in response to the political unrest in Europe and Japan. Again, the federal government refused to help. With rumors circulating about troop increases in 1937, Fort Sill and Lawton considered enlarging the water filter plant at Lake Lawtonka that was running at full capacity and noted the requirement for increased water storage capacity at the lake. In 1938, the city and fort examined the possibility of raising the height of the dam again and pressured the federal government for financial assistance. Although the federal government promised funding through the Works Projects Administration, a New Deal organization that had been created in 1935 to provide meaningful jobs in the public sector for the unemployed during the Great Depression, Lawton still had to raise $90,000 to pay its share of the expansion costs. When construction finally began in 1939, engineers had to lower the level of the water in the reservoir. Along with a drought in the summer of 1939, lowering the reservoir's level compounded the existing water crisis that led to emergency measures. Lawton laid a pipeline from Lake Rush to Lake Jed Johnson to Lake Thomas and dug more wells, while Fort Sill placed a new pump at Ambrosia Springs into operation to furnish 200,000 gallons of water a day. Yet, the emergency measures failed to solve the water shortage caused by construction.[22]

Writing Danford on 22 August 1940 just after becoming commandant of the Field Artillery School, Brigadier General Donald C. Cubbison (August 1940-December 1940) reinforced the urgency of solving the perennial water shortage by enlarging the dam. Bluntly, he wrote Danford that mobilizing the 45th Infantry Division would stress the post's water supply system.[23]

An encouraging report of 23 August 1940 by the Lawton City engineer, Wayne Hendricks, subsequently suggested that the water supply would be improved by raising the height of the dam. Hendricks reported that 936 million gallons of water had accumulated in Lake Lawtonka since April 1940 for the exclusive use of Fort Sill, that this was being augmented by 500,000 gallons of water a day from Medicine Bluffs Creek, and that Lawton was drilling additional wells.[24]

One week later on 30 August 1940 after reading the report, Cubbison optimistically wrote Danford about the improving water situation:

> The first of the new water wells in Lawton appears today to be a very fine well. . . . If it approves to be as favorable as is now indicated and the second drilling does equally well, then it would appear that we shall have sufficient water, provided always that the water table stands up to its present height.[25]

Although he believed that the measures being taken would solve the water shortage, Cubbison cautiously but optimistically viewed the water situation.[26]

Time bore out even Cubbison's guarded confidence. The combined effort started in 1939 by Fort Sill and Lawton and completed late in 1940 finally raised the Lake Lawtonka dam another 10 feet to provide both an ample supply of water. While the federal government spent $323,000 on the expansion project through the Works Projects Administration, Lawton provided $90,000.[27] With the help of a wetter than normal fall and the additional wells, raising the height of the dam ended the water shortage and eliminated the fear about insufficient water to support mobilizing and training the 45th Infantry Division at Fort Sill between September 1940 and February 1941 when it departed for additional training at Camp Berkeley, Texas, in preparation for participation in the Louisiana Maneuvers later in 1941.[28]

Accommodating the school and the 45th Infantry Division also compelled the federal government to rebuild the Concurrent Camp Area (Camp Doniphan) that had been erected on Fort Sill during the World War I to house and train the 35th and 36th Divisions, that was about two miles southwest of Old Post and had been allowed to deteriorate over the years, and to consider purchasing additional land. As early as December 1938, the War

Department and Fort Sill projected the need to refurbish Camp Doniphan as a potential mobilization site, but the lack of money and any sense of urgency at the time prevented them from taking any concrete action. This situation eventually changed. On 28 June 1939, Danford wrote McIntyre about the War Department intention of allotting $400,000 to rehabilitate Camp Doniphan. One year later in July 1940, Works Projects Administration laborers completed erecting warehouses, repair shops, and other needed facilities; the camp which could accommodate about 5,500 soldiers was ready for use just as Fort Sill's training load began rapidly expanding.[29]

Unfortunately, the new construction failed to meet the needs of the 45th Infantry Division. During its time at Fort Sill, the division occupied a part of Camp Doniphan. Despite new construction, the post lacked enough permanent buildings to handle the division and the Field Artillery School's growing training load. This circumstance forced the division to erect hundreds of tents to house its soldiers. Some tents were staked on bare ground, while others were staked on concrete floors. Row after row of stakes marked imaginary streets with a kitchen at one end and a latrine at the other.[30]

Concurrent with this expansion, the school noted the need for new construction to accommodate the Field Artillery Officer Candidate School that was scheduled to open on 1 July 1941. Beginning in the fall of 1940, Fort Sill let contracts for new temporary barracks and completed most of them by mid-1941. The Field Artillery School, however, recognized the need for additional facilities to handle the projected expansion of Field Artillery Officer Candidate School in 1942 to meet the growing demands for officers. Specifically in October 1941, the Field Artillery School anticipated the requirement for 10 63-person barracks, two recreational buildings, six administration buildings, a 1,000-person mess hall, and 12 motor repair shops, among other facilities, to house the increased number of Officer Candidate School candidates.[31] A couple of months later in December 1941, Allin noted Fort Sill's inability to accommodate the current student population adequately. At the time, incoming Officer Candidate School students were being placed in tents. In view of these unfavorable circumstances, Allin reinforced Fort Sill's requirement for adequate mess halls, housing better than tents, more instructors, better training aids, and sufficient school troops to maintain high standards of instruction for Field Artillery School and Officer Candidate School students. Fortunately, tarpaper and frame barracks replaced the tents in 1942.[32]

Meanwhile, Fort Sill faced the necessity of acquiring additional land to support mobilization. During the first half of 1940, Frank L. Ketch, the owner of the Ketch Ranch, his associates, other local ranchers, and the War Department tensely negotiated to purchase the land.[33] To speed up the discussions that had stalled, representatives of the Quartermaster General visited Fort Sill in August 1940 to inspect the land and threatened to condemn it so that the War Department could purchase it quickly with little opposition if talks failed.[34]

Subsequent to the visit on 3 September 1940, Cubbison reinforced the imperative of buying the Ketch Ranch and the lands to south of post to expand the firing ranges. "If we secure the new land we have in mind, this ought to give them [45th Infantry Division] plenty of terrain for training and would [prevent interference] with the school program," he commented in a letter to Danford on 3 September 1940.[35] As Cubbison clearly understood,

Fort Sill required more land for training so that the activities of the 45th Infantry Division and the school would not interfere with each other and degrade training. Based upon this strong recommendation and the pressing requirement to expand the post's training facilities, the War Department finally purchased the Ketch Ranch and other land in 1941 to make Fort Sill contiguous to the Wichita Mountains National Wildlife Refuge on the west. Buying the Ketch Ranch that the installation had wanted for more than 10 years and the additional property enlarged Fort Sill from 51,242 acres to 74,600 acres.[36]

Over a period of 15 months beginning in August 1940 and continuing to the eve of the Japanese attack on Pearl Harbor on 7 December 1941, the Field Artillery School and Fort Sill experienced unprecedented growth as the War Department mobilized in response to a series of international crises. Between 1919 and 1939, for example, the Field Artillery School trained 5,789 students from the Regular Army, National Guard, and Organized Reserve during an academic year of nine months and had the capacity of training a peak load of 575 field artillerymen during a year if required. In comparison, the school trained 7,354 officers and enlisted personnel between August 1940 when mobilization began and December 1941 to reflect the tremendous expansion as the school geared for possible war while Field Artillery Officer Candidate School commissioned 462 second lieutenants between July 1941 and January 1942.[37]

Virtually overnight, mobilization transformed the Field Artillery School. By abandoning lengthy peacetime courses, replacing them with shorter mobilization courses, teaching them frequently, assuming responsibility for the Field Artillery Officer Candidate School, and adopting year-around operations, the school shifted from its leisure peacetime training pace of the 1920s and 1930s to a high-tempo schedule that produced more but less qualified graduates while Fort Sill purchased more land and built new facilities to support that growth.

Accelerated Growth and More Missions

As mobilization intensified, the Army modified its training system. Through early 1941 the Army relied upon its field units to furnish basic military training and its service schools, such as the Field Artillery School, for advanced and specialized training for individuals, both enlisted and officer. In view of the anticipated immense influx of trainees generated by the Selective Service Act of 1940, mass production assumed an unprecedented importance. This requirement led to the establishment of replacement training centers in March 1941 for basic military training, relieving the Army's field units of that burdensome task, and assigned them to the Chiefs of Ground Combat Arms (Infantry, Cavalry, Field Artillery, and Coast Artillery) to give the chiefs responsibility for training individuals in the replacement training centers and the service schools. In the meantime, General Headquarters, War Department that had been created with the War Department reorganization of 1921 to serve as a command post for the field forces and that had been activated on 26 July 1940 supervised training tactical units. This organization separated training individuals from training tactical units. After July 1941, the General Headquarters and the Army Air Forces, which was created on 20 July 1941 and supervised by the General Staff, shared responsibility for training tactical units.[38]

Within months of the Japanese attack on Pearl Harbor on 7 December 1941, the Chief of Staff of the Army, General George C. Marshall, pushed through a sweeping reorganization of the War Department on 9 March 1942 to facilitate staff coordination and enhance mobilization that ultimately influenced training. Among other actions, Marshall's reforms created the Army Ground Forces and the Services of Supply, later renamed the Army Services Forces, which became the Army's central agency for supply under Lieutenant General Brehon B. Somervill and made the Army Air Forces an independent command with its own chief and staff. The Army Ground Forces commanded by Lieutenant General Lesley J. McNair, a noted field artillery officer and former assistant commandant of the Field Artillery School (1929-1930), assumed the training mission for individuals and units, absorbed the ground combat arms, took over the responsibilities of the Chiefs of Infantry, Field Artillery, Cavalry, and Coast Artillery, inactivated their offices, and delegated training to the Replacement and School Command, a subordinate command under Major General Courtney H. Hodges, former Chief of Infantry, at Birmingham, Alabama. The command controlled the training replacement centers and the service schools, thus centralizing all training under one organization.[39]

In the midst of this reorganization that restructured training to meet the needs of a country at war, the Field Artillery School's training tempo grew more hectic to prepare officers and soldiers for combat. The Field Artillery School's student load jumped from 1,935 in December 1941 to 7,750 in December 1942.[40] During the course of the war, a basic course (officer basic course or officer candidate school) and an advanced course comprised the core of officer training in the Army and the Field Artillery School although it taught other officer courses as needed. Initially, the War Department required every officer to have at least six months of training with four to six months between the basic course and the advanced course. Through July 1943, field artillery senior first lieutenants and captains received 12 weeks of training in the Officers Basic Course, formerly called the Battery Officers Course until December 1942, for duty in field artillery batteries and assignments on battalion staffs. Pressed to improve the quality of battery grade officers, the War Department lengthened the Officers Basic Course in July 1943 from 12 weeks to 17 weeks to permit more extensive training. Meanwhile, senior captains and above attended 12 weeks of advanced training in the Field Grade Officers Course (advanced course) to prepare them for service as battalion commanders and staff officers in the field artillery battalion, division artillery, and corps artillery.[41]

The opening of officer candidate schools in July 1941 throughout the Army significantly influenced the basic courses in the various branch service schools.[42] Initially, the Field Artillery School intended its Officers Basic Course to be the core of its officer training because all officers would be required to attend it. After the Army opened the Field Artillery Officer Candidate School under the Field Artillery School on 8 July 1941 for enlisted soldiers and warrant officers who wanted to be officers to fill the growing need for officers, the number of graduates of the Officers Basic Course declined precipitously from a high of 216 with Class Eight (6 March 1941-28 May 1941) to 53 in Class 12 (26 June 1941-15 September 1941). From Class 12 through Class 124 which graduated on 27 May 1944, the Officers Basic Course averaged 61 graduates per class.[43]

For the most part, the 12-week and the 17-week Officers Basic Course and the 12-week Field Artillery Officer Candidate School course provided the same instruction with the latter furnishing more leadership training because the students in the Officers Basic Course usually had some military experience as officers, while Officer Candidate School students usually had less because they only had to have six months in the Army before they could apply to the school. As directed by the War Department, only senior first lieutenants and captains who had not graduated from Field Artillery Officer Candidate School attended the Officers Basic Course after the attack on Pearl Harbor. As time went by, more and more officers graduated from Field Artillery Officer Candidate School to lessen the need for the Officers Basic Course. In fact, the student load of Field Artillery Officer Candidate School almost doubled early in 1942 with classes starting each week. Before July 1942, the school had an average of 102 graduates per class. Afterward, it climbed to an average of 191 graduates per class with a high of 456 graduates in Class 59 (14 January 1943-8 April 1943).[44]

Because of these circumstances and the declining requirement for officer basic courses by early 1944, the Army discontinued them in September 1944. Upon completing its last Officers Basic Course in May 1944, the Field Artillery School inaugurated an Officers Special Basic Course of 10 weeks for officers transferring from other branches to the Field Artillery. The principal source of students for the Officers Special Basic Course came from the Antiaircraft Artillery because Allied domination of the air by late 1943 had reduced the requirement for antiaircraft artillery.[45]

Meanwhile, the demographics of the Field Grade Officers Course shifted.[46] As the need for field artillery officers to fill high command positions grew during the course of the war, the importance of advanced training increased. The number of graduates from the Field Artillery School's Field Grade Officers Course swelled from 455 in 1942 to 1,068 in 1943 to 1,678 in 1944.[47] To meet the mounting need for more officers, the War Department altered the Field Grade Officers Course prerequisites. After April 1943, any field artillery officer from a first lieutenant up with the requirement for training for an upcoming assignment could attend the course. The War Department also abandoned the prerequisite of graduation from the basic course for admission to the Field Grade Officers Course and started allowing officers with considerable troop time who had not graduated from a basic course to attend. With these changes, rank and previous training no longer played a role in attendance because the Field Grade Officers Course was opened to any officer above first lieutenant with proper qualifications. In practice, however, only a small percentage of first lieutenants attended the Field Grade Officers Course.[48]

In keeping with the transformation in student demographics, the Field Artillery School changed the course's name to the Officer Advanced Course (12 weeks) in April 1943 and shifted its focus from training officers to become battalion commanders and staff officers at the battalion and higher to become battery commanders and commanders and staff officers of field artillery battalions, groups, and brigades, and division artillery. Thus, the Officer Advanced Course assumed a broader mission than its predecessor, the Field Grade Officer Course.[49]

McNair Hall housed the school from the late 1930s to 1954.

Officers attending the basic and advanced courses fit into a larger body of students. Although the expansion during 1940 and 1941 dramatically increased the Field Artillery School's training load and the number of graduates, the war generated even greater growth. Authorized by the War Department, the school added officer and enlisted courses as needed to augment the officer basic and advanced courses to meet the Army's requirements. With the exception of Field Artillery Officer Candidate School that was initially overseen by the Chief of Field Artillery through March 1942 when the position was dissolved and its responsibilities for training were absorbed by the Army Ground Forces, the school commandant had the authority to cancel any class with sufficient reason or to establish courses to train personnel under his control. On several occasions, the commandant cancelled a class especially during the waning months of the war because insufficient numbers of students reported for training to justify offering the course.[50]

During the war, the school graduated 108,999 students, conducted 72 officer and enlisted courses at Camp Doniphan that was approximately two miles southwest of Old Post, the cantonment area immediately south of Old Post, McNair Hall (the school house), or Henry Post Airfield that was about two miles south of Old Post, and taught as many as 35 courses concurrently. Of the 108,999 graduates, 35,031 were officers; the rest were enlisted personnel. The student population grew rapidly from 1,935 in December 1941 to a peak of 8,902 in February 1943 to dwarf the enrollment of 409 in July 1940 just before serious mobilization got underway. Meanwhile, the staff and faculty increased from 1,441 in December 1941 to a peak of 3,473 in September 1944.[51]

115

As it started producing more graduates, the Field Artillery School received the Field Artillery Officer Candidate School mission. Pre-war planning for officer candidate schools originated in 1934. A War Department letter of 3 May 1934 addressed the requirement for opening officer candidate schools upon mobilization and conducting other training activities under the nine geographical corps that administered and commanded the field forces in the United States. The following year, the War Department designed a three-month officer candidate course for mobilization purposes and placed it under the geographical corps commanders. Placing officer candidate schools under a corps went unchallenged until 1937. That year, the War Department started questioning the wisdom of maintaining nine schools and sought to consolidate and standardize officer candidate training. Out of this thinking came the decision to place the Chiefs of the Combat Arms in charge of officer candidate training as the Chief of Field Artillery, Major General Upton Birnie (1934-1938), explained to McIntyre in 1937. Fierce resistance from corps commanders who feared losing a mission caused the issue to stall; two years passed before the War Department aligned the schools under the combat arms branch chiefs.[52] This new arrangement meant that school graduates would be trained to fill officer positions in a particular combat arm and would not receive all-purpose training that would have been provided by the geographical corps commander and applicable to any branch.[53]

In the fall of 1940, the War Department started opening officer candidate schools as a part of mobilization to convert enlisted soldiers and warrant officers to commissioned officers in a short period of time. Ironically, the Chiefs of Infantry, Cavalry, Field Artillery, and Coast Artillery, the only branches concerned in the early planning, unanimously opposed the schools because a shortage of officers did not exist at the time. They failed to see the schools' necessity and opposed expanding the Officers' Reserve Corps unless the need became urgent. Unlike the branch chiefs, Marshall supported the officer candidate school concept because officers would be needed in 1941 when most of the 50,000 reserve officers who had been called to extended active duty of one year in 1940 would start returning to civilian life. Marshall overrode stiff opposition from his staff and the combat arms branch chiefs. On 15 January 1941, the Adjutant General directed establishing five officer candidate schools (Infantry, Field Artillery, Coast Artillery, Cavalry, and Armor) with the first class reporting to each school on 1 July 1941.[54]

Subsequent to this tasking on 24 January 1941, the War Department requested the Field Artillery School to design a field artillery officer candidate school course that was similar to the one provided in the War Department's 1939 Protective Mobilization Plan and to forward it for approval. Rather than following guidance, the Field Artillery School developed a two-phase officer candidate school course that took advantage of the existing mobilization Battery Officers Course and involved less planning to create. The school recommended a four-week basic course to weed out the unsatisfactory students. Those that passed this course would attend the mobilization Battery Officers Course of 12 weeks that had been taught since August 1940. Because this two-phase format of 16 weeks would exceed the 12-week maximum length of an officer candidate school course, the War Department rejected it early in 1941 and directed the creation of a one-phase, 12-week officer candidate school.[55]

As tasked by the War Department, 125-man classes entered officer candidate schools at six-week intervals with classes overlapping so that 250 candidates would be in school at any given time. Each combat arm trained warrant officers and enlisted soldiers from their respective branches who had at least six months of army service before applying, who were United States citizens between the ages of 21 and 36, had earned a score of 110 on the Army General Classification Test and received a score of 115 on either of two officer candidate tests. Basically, the school converted warrant officers and enlisted soldiers into officers to meet mobilization requirements for commissioned officers in the company grades that could not be filled with Regular, Reserve, and National Guard officers and excluded civilians. Pressed by the requirement for more officers, the War Department subsequently modified the age guidelines in January 1942 when it established age limits from 18 to 46 to make them conform to Selective Service age limits for enlistment but retained qualification boards to select candidates to ensure that only the most competent people attended an officer candidate school.[56]

For added flexibility, the War Department issued Circular 48 on 19 February 1942 that abolished the short-lived practice of restricting a branch from enrolling only enlisted soldiers and warrant officers from its own ranks branch to fill its quotas. Students could now be taken from other branches. Because the rapid activations outran supply and left units with serious shortages of enlisted personnel available early in 1942 for an officer candidate school, the War Department approved recruiting civilians beginning in the summer of 1942 and therefore abandoned its policy of securing new officers exclusively from the enlisted or warrant officer ranks.[57]

Meanwhile, established in the Field Artillery School as directed by the War Department, the Field Artillery Officer Candidate School had a commandant of candidates, an executive officer, an adjutant, and supply officer on its staff and received its first class of 126 students on 8 July 1941. Besides working in mess halls and functioning as charge of quarters in the class mailroom and battalion headquarters and being observed dutifully by the tactical officer, the students from this class and successive classes underwent formal instruction in military courtesy, close order drill and ceremonies, close combat, customs of the service, discipline, and education and served as company commanders, company executive officers, platoon leaders, and other leaders. Rotating through these positions on a weekly or semi-weekly basis, the students had to make decisions, give commands, maintain discipline, make corrections, anticipate problems, and cope with emergencies. Such training permitted the school's staff to judge candidates on their leadership skills and other qualities that were not directly related to academic performance and to eliminate those who lacked the capacity for leadership.[58] The school utilized faculty boards to recycle candidates or to weed out those with academic failures and leadership deficiencies.[59]

In addition, the Field Artillery Officer Candidate School prepared officers to serve as field artillerymen. Specifically, it trained them to fill assignments as a platoon leader in a firing battery, a field artillery staff officer, or a tactical officer at the Field Artillery School based upon the Army doctrine that every officer should be qualified to fill any position in a particular branch commensurate with the rank. Besides receiving training on each field artillery weapon, the field artillery officer candidate conducted firing problems and participated in tactical exercises with the 105-mm. howitzer which was the basic piece by 1940 and was the one that the graduate would most generally use.[60]

Analyzing the initial Field Artillery Officer Candidate School class, Danford observed in the fall of 1941 that it was similar to the Battery Officers Course that had started in August 1940 as a part of the school's mobilization program even though officer candidate school candidates were held to more rigid academic standards than commissioned officers in the Battery Officers Course. In fact, the gunnery instruction portion of the Field Artillery Officer Candidate School program of instruction was substantially the same as the gunnery instruction in the Battery Officers Course. With this in mind, Danford wanted the Officer Candidate School to focus more on field artillery basics with some work in mathematics, mess management, and the duties of an executive officer and to reduce the time spent on gunnery because he expected graduates to return to Fort Sill for the Battery Officers Course where they would learn gunnery. Because of this, he pressed the Commandant of the Field Artillery School, Brigadier General George R. Allin (1941-1942), to restructure the officer candidate course to fit his desired model.[61]

Allin quickly demurred. In a letter to Danford, Allin explained that the gunnery portion of the Officer Candidate School was identical to the Battery Officers Course for a critical reason. Along with his staff, Allin did not expect school graduates to attend the Battery Officers Course because operational requirements would prevent this. Students therefore had to have gunnery instruction, or they would be unable to function as field artillery officers.[62]

As time revealed, Allin correctly assessed the situation. Wartime pressures prohibited very few if any graduates of the Field Artillery Officer Candidate School to take the Battery Officers Course or its successor, Officer Basic Course. After July 1941 when the first Officer Candidate School course began, the number of graduates from the Battery Officers Course dropped precipitously from a high of 204 in August 1941 to 55 in September 1941, while graduates from the Officer Candidate School climbed from 79 in October 1941 to a high of 481 in October 1942. When the Field Artillery Officer Candidate School ceased operations on 12 December 1946 with the graduation of Class 179, over 26,000 men had received commissions as field artillery second lieutenants.[63]

Although the rapid expansion of officer candidate schools in 1942 failed to eliminate the shortage of officers, it did generate a sharp decline in the quality of candidates, forcing the War Department to find a suitable way of weeding out the undesirable and unfit but satisfying the growing need for officers at the same time. Out of this conundrum emerged the preparatory school and recycling policy. In mid-1942, the War Department organized a preparatory school course of one month in the Field Artillery Replacement Center on Fort Sill that had opened on 28 November 1942 as a tent city just to west of Henry Post Field with the exception of recreation buildings, post exchanges, mess halls, bath houses, and a headquarters building which were constructed of wood. The center furnished field artillery basic training for selective service inductees and shipped them to tactical units that were well advanced in their training for the development of teams from the company level to the division level. The preparatory school also provided basic field artillery training for individuals who had been accepted to the Field Artillery Officer Candidate School but lacked basic military training. During the course, instructors taught the applicants weapons handling, small-unit tactics, map reading, drill, and other subjects and conducted daily inspections of quarters, daily inspections in ranks, and weekly uniform inspections. If the officer candidate successfully completed the preparatory school, the individual then attended the Field Artillery Officer Candidate School.[64]

At the direction of Danford who opposed dismissing any candidate with a reasonable prospect of becoming an officer and urged recycling students with academic and leadership deficiencies to later classes, the Field Artillery School also organized a salvage school course in September 1942 for candidates reporting to the Officer Candidate School without attending the preparatory school and for students who struggled to keep up their classmates in the Officer Candidate School.[65] Begun by the Commandant of Troops of the Field Artillery Officer Candidate School, Lieutenant Colonel Craig Krayenbuhl, the salvage school course lasted four weeks. It provided basic instruction in gunnery, gun drill, tactics, and mathematics. Those students who used the salvage school course to overcome difficulties encountered in the Officer Candidate School enrolled in a new Officer Candidate School class that was doing the work that they were doing at the time of transferring to the salvage school course.[66]

Although the preparatory school and the salvage school courses reduced the number of dismissals from the Field Artillery Officer Candidate School and removed students who would have slowed down the pace of their classmates, they enabled the school to absorb several hundred students during the critical period of 1942-1943 when so many men were being sent to Fort Sill without benefit of an adequate background. Equally as important, the two courses prolonged candidate training by one to four months, absorbed facilities that could have been devoted to training first-rate candidates, and did not ensure the graduation of recycles. Only the sheer necessity of producing officers justified the preparatory school and salvage school.[67]

Even so, these corrective measures failed to produce the necessary number of qualified field artillery officers and prompted the War Department to explore other alternatives. In April 1943 the War Department examined a proposal by the Army Service Forces to make the officer candidate school a four-month course (seventeen weeks). Although the Army Ground Forces opposed extending the school from three to four months and wanted the additional training to be completed in the officer's first unit as had been the tradition, the War Department decided on 18 May 1943 to lengthen training in the school from three months to four months beginning on 1 July 1943 to improve the quality of the graduates.[68]

On 2 July 1943 the Field Artillery School expanded its Field Artillery Officer Candidate School training to seventeen weeks and continued the block system of instruction that had begun with the initial class of July 1941. Tactical officers and select officers from the Department of Tactics utilized the first two weeks to provide instruction on army administration, military law, mess management, and other general military subjects. During the next two weeks, the Department of Motors conducted instruction on motors.

After that the Department of Material taught one week of field artillery equipment and weapon systems. Next, the students went through six weeks of gunnery instruction by the Department of Gunnery and then two weeks of instruction by the Department of Communications. For the last four weeks, the Department of Tactics taught tactics. Beginning with Class 125, the school started integrating gunnery instruction with tactics instruction during the last four weeks of training.[69]

From July 1941 when it began operations through 12 December 1946 when the Army closed its doors, the Field Artillery Officer Candidate School provided rigorous training regardless of the length of its course. The school turned enlisted personnel, warrant officers, and civilians into field artillery officers who were well grounded in the tactics, techniques, and procedures of the Field Artillery and were prepared serve in operational units.

Organic Aerial Observation and Horses

Although expanding course offerings, including the Field Artillery Officer Candidate School, to meet the requirements of the growing student population occupied much of its attention during the war, the Field Artillery School also played a major role in the development of organic field artillery aerial observation which had a lasting impact beyond the war years and ended its close association with horse-drawn field artillery. Despite focusing primarily on the need for new field artillery weapons, the Hero Board of 1918-1919 established by Major General Ernest Hines, the Chief of Artillery for the American Expeditionary Forces during World War One, and chaired by Brigadier General Andrew Hero, Jr., examined field artillery performance during World War One. The board concluded that aerial observation failed to meet the needs of field artillery units. Poor liaison between field artillery units and the Aviation Section of the Signal Corps, lack of field artillery training for observers, ground commanders' habit of making aerial reconnaissance missions secondary to combat missions, airfields that were too far from the front lines to permit field artillery officers and aviators to get to know each other and to gain the others' confidence, and the Signal Corps' control of observation assets prevented field artillery commanders from getting aerial observation when and where they needed and wanted it.[70]

Although these problems hampered effective aerial observation, field artillery officers still found it to be critical for conducting indirect fire and attacking deeply defiladed targets and batteries. Brigadier General Albert J. Bowley of the 6th Corps Artillery for example wrote in 1918, "Aerial observation in my experience has been conspicuous by its absence. . . . Aerial observation is very essential and should be developed."[71] Likewise, Brigadier General Adrian S. Fleming of the 158th Field Artillery Brigade noted, "The only solution I see is to assign certain aeroplanes and balloons to the artillery for the purpose of observing and permit them to do no other work."[72] With these perspectives and others in mind, the Hero Board published its thoughts. It urged placing aerial observation under the charge of field artillery units and employing field artillery officers as observers to ensure effective control by field artillery commanders. In other words, organic field artillery aerial observation was the key.[73]

Field Artillery School ca. 1940

Although the concept of organic field artillery air observation received little attention during the 1920s with the rise of strategic airpower as conceived by airpower enthusiasts, such as Brigadier General Billy Mitchell, to avoid the stalemate and mass slaughter that had characterized close combat in World War One, Chiefs of Field Artillery revived interest in it in the 1930s.[74] In light of aerial observation practices in World War One and the imperative of destroying or neutralizing deeply defiladed, camouflaged batteries and other enemy targets that could only be found with aerial observation, the former Chief of Field Artillery, Major General Harry G. Bishop (1930-1934), expressed his opinion in 1935-1936. He openly criticized using Air Corps personnel as aerial observers because they did not know the needs of field artillery units. As many other field artillery officers of the time advocated, Bishop wanted the observers to be field artillerymen because they understood the requirements of their branch. However, he did not explicitly advocate organic field artillery aerial observation even though he strongly implied its relevance. Basically, Bishop was searching for a way to make aerial observation more effective and responsive to the needs of the Field Artillery.[75]

Upon becoming Chief of Field Artillery in 1938, Danford unequivocally pushed organic field artillery aerial observation unlike Bishop. The following year, Danford laid out the Field Artillery's position to the Chief of the Air Corps, Major General Henry

H. Arnold who was a close confidant of Brigadier General Billy Mitchell in the 1920s. Danford wanted the Air Corps to supply the Field Artillery with light aircraft, pilots, and ground crews and advocated assigning aircraft directly to field artillery units rather than to corps headquarters as outlined by Army doctrine. Organic field artillery aerial observation would resolve the problem of unresponsive aerial observation by placing it under field artillery commanders rather than other commanders, including ground force commanders who would pursue their own interests at the expense of field artillery units. As might be expected, Arnold vigorously opposed organic field artillery aerial observation. He favored centralized control of all aviation assets under an air force commander to ensure focusing airpower on strategic bombing and disagreed with placing it under a ground commander who would fail to appreciate airpower's unique capabilities of attacking deep, strategic targets.[76]

Undeterred by Arnold's vocal, stubborn opposition and vision of airpower, Danford continued pushing organic field artillery aerial observation. On 26 September 1939 he directed McIntyre to convene a committee, eventually called the Air-Ground Procedures Board, to test existing aerial observation procedures and to provide alternatives. During the school year of 1939-1940, the board developed gunnery and communications procedures that would permit one airplane to direct the fire of more than one battalion of field artillery. Although its final report was completed in May 1940 but was not published until August 1941, the board advocated organic aerial field artillery observation as the only solution to the arm's requirement for over-the-horizon organic observation.[77]

Another study also conducted by the Field Artillery School reinforced this conclusion. Completed in May 1941 under the direction of Colonel P.N. Hanson, the study reaffirmed organic field artillery aerial observation as the only viable answer for meeting the arm's aerial observation needs. The increased mobility of the ground forces since 1919 compounded the difficulties of ground observation's ability of maintaining sight of mobile ground combat forces and threatened the Field Artillery's capacity to provide responsive close support and to engage targets beyond the sight of ground observers. Organic field artillery air observation would also permit locating more targets than ground observation could. Equally important, it would facilitate exploiting the newly created fire direction center's ability to shift and mass fires.[78]

Shortly after the Hanson report of May 1941 and Major William W. Ford's article entitled "Wings of St. Barbara," in the *Field Artillery Journal* of April 1941 that strongly advocated organic aerial observation, Danford initiated a chain of events on 8 October 1941 that led to the creation of organic field artillery aerial observation. On that day he petitioned the War Department for organic field artillery aerial observation by arguing that the time was right to provide it. Although he initially encountered stiff resistance from Arnold, the airpower enthusiast eventually relented and started supporting using light aircraft for organic field artillery aerial observation. With the last major obstacle removed when Arnold finally acknowledged the usefulness of the concept, Danford obtained approval from the War Department on 10 December 1941 to test organic field artillery aerial observation in February and March 1942. Using various models of light aircraft, the experiments at Camp

Blanding, Florida, and Fort Sam Houston, Texas, demonstrated the timeliness and reliability of organic field artillery air observation and subsequently prompted the War Department to issue a directive on 6 June 1942 that established organic field artillery aerial observation. Directed by the War Department, the Field Artillery School created the Department of Air Training under Lieutenant Colonel William W. Ford on 6 June 1942 to guarantee a force of adequately trained pilots-observers and mechanics, to train students how to land small aircraft on roads, short, improvised landing strips, and open fields, and to observe fire from the air, among other critical skills. Beginning in August 1942 and ending early in 1946, the department trained 2,939 students in its Field Artillery Pilot-Observer Course and 2,359 students in its Field Artillery Air Mechanic Course. Along with the Danford and overseas field artillery battalions with organic aerial observation, the Department of Air Training in the Field Artillery School played a vital role in shaping organic field artillery aerial observation doctrine after 1942.[79]

Just as momentous as the organization of the Department of Air Training was, the school ended its long-standing relationship with horses during World War Two. During the latter years of the 1930s, the Department of Animal Transport expanded its activities beyond formal instruction in equitation and polo matches to organizing horse shows. Fort Sill rebuilt its equestrian stadium and named it after Lieutenant Colonel William H. Rucker. Here, the school and Fort Sill held informal horse shows and other equestrian activities and even formed a horse show team. Composed of members of the Department of Animal Transport, the horse show team competed in horse shows throughout the United States, Europe, and Mexico, won acclaim and distinction, and even prepared to take part in the 1940 Summer Olympics at Helsinki, Finland. The outbreak of World War Two in 1939 caused the International Olympic Committee to cancel the 1940 Summer Olympics and prompted the school to dissolve its horse show team in 1940.[80]

Even so, the school did not abandon the horse quite yet. In the summer of 1942, the school quit teaching its Officer Specialist Course (Horsemanship) and Enlisted Specialist Course (Horsemanship), as the Army started phasing out horse-drawn artillery in favor of motor-drawn (towed) artillery and self-propelled artillery and started increasing the number courses on motor engines and motor vehicle maintenance. The school, however, retained its Officers' Pack Artillery Course, Enlisted Packmaster Course, Enlisted Saddler Course, and Enlisted Horseshoer Course because pack artillery was still required in some areas of the world. This combination of launching the Department of Air Training in 1942, ending courses on horsemanship and related courses, even though some courses, such as those that supported pack artillery remained through 1944 when the last pack artillery courses were taught, and inactivating the Department of Animal Transport in 1944 signaled the closing of an era. The school as well as the Army gradually ended its dependence upon horses and mules for motor vehicles.[81]

Although the Field Artillery School added new missions by supervising the Field Artillery Officer Candidate School and organizing the Department of Air Training to teach aerial observation during World War II and abandoned the horse over several years, its wartime mission remained consistent with the pre-war years. It still trained officers and enlisted personnel in the latest field artillery tactics, techniques, and procedures and played a key role in the development field artillery tactics and doctrine. This latter function assumed a broader dimension with the creation of the Department of Air Training to train organic field artillery aerial observers and aircraft mechanics. As with the development of the fire direction center in the 1930s, establishing the Department of Air Training reflected the school's drive to make the Field Artillery more responsive to the needs of the other combat arms, while closing the Department of Animal Transport in 1944 ended ties with the horse.

Notes

1   Frank N. Schubert, "Mobilization," US Army Center of Military History Commemorative World War Two Pamphlet, undated, No. 72-32, pp. 5, 7-10; Russell F. Weigley, *History of the United States Army* (Bloomington, IN: Indiana University Press, 1984), pp. 415-19; Riley Sunderland, *History of the Field Artillery School: 1911-1942* (Fort Sill, OK: Field Artillery School Printing Plant, 1942) pp. 186-87; Annual Report of Field Artillery School for 1939-1940, 11 Jul 1940, pp. 1, Appendix A, UF23.5 E1, Morris Swett Technical Library (MSTL), US Army Field Artillery School, Fort Sill; *History of the Field Artillery School: World War II* (Fort Sill, OK: Field Artillery School Printing Plant, 1946), pp. 8-9; Mark Skinner Watson, *Chief of Staff: Prewar Plans and Preparations* (Washington, D.C.: Historical Division, US Army, 1950), pp. 30, 78, 153, 154; Stetson Conn, "Highlights of Mobilization, World War II, 1938-1942," draft manuscript, US Army Center of Military History, p. 2; Maurice Matloff, ed., *American Military History* (Washington, D.C.: Center of Military History, US Army, 1985), pp. 416-17.

2   Sunderland, *History of the Field Artillery School*, pp. 186-87; Annual Report of Field Artillery School for 1939-1940, 11 Jul 1940, pp. 1, Appendix A, UF 23.5 E1, MSTL; *History of the Field Artillery School: World War II*, pp. 8-10; Watson, *Chief of Staff*, pp. 30, 78, 153, 154; Conn, "Highlights of Mobilization, World War II, 1938-1942," p. 2.

3   Weigley, *History of the United States* Army, p. 424; Conn, *Highlights of Mobilization, World War II*, Introduction; Schubert, "Mobilization," pp. 9-10.

4   Sunderland, *History of the Field Artillery School*, pp. 186-87; Annual Report of Field Artillery School for 1939-1940, 11 Jul 1940, pp. 1, Appendix A, UF 23.5 E1, MSTL; *History of the Field Artillery School: World War II*, pp. 8-9; Weigley, *History of the United States Army*, pp. 423-24; Matloff, ed., *American Military History*, p. 418; Schubert, "Mobilization," pp. 9-10.

5   Sunderland, *History of the Field Artillery School*, pp. 186-87; Annual Report of Field Artillery School for 1939-1940, 11 Jul 1940, pp. 1, Appendix A, UF 23.5 E1, MSTL; *History of the Field Artillery School: World War II*, pp. 8-9; Conn, "Highlights of Mobilization," p. 4.

6   Annual Report of the Field Artillery School for 1939-1940, 11 Jul 1940, p. 2, UF 23.5 E1, MSTL; Sunderland, *History of the Field Artillery School*, p. 190.

7   Annual Report of the Field Artillery School for 1939-1940, 11 Jul 1940, p. 2, Sections XVI, XVII, and XVIII, UF 23.5 E1, MSTL.

8   Ltr, Danford to Cubbison, 24 Aug 1940, Miscellaneous Correspondence, 1939-1945, UF25 H673 M4, MSTL.

9   Ltr, Field Artillery School to Adjutant General, subj: Approval of Table of Organization for Field Artillery School Troops, P.M.P, 26 Mar 1940, Miscellaneous Correspondence, 1939-1945, UF25 H673 M4, MSTL; Sunderland, *History of the Field Artillery School*, pp. 193-95; Mobilization Plan of Mobilization Center, Fort Sill Area, Oklahoma, 5 Mar 1937, UF25 S372 M6U6, MSTL.

10   Sunderland, *History of the Field Artillery School,* p. 188.

11   Sunderland, *History of the Field Artillery School*, p. 188.

12   Sunderland, *History of the Field Artillery School*, p. 189; Field Artillery School, Description of Courses, 1939-1940, p. 3, UF23.5 Q7, MSTL.

13   Sunderland, *History of the Field Artillery School*, p. 189; Field Artillery School, Description of Courses, 1939-1940, p. 3, UF23.5 Q7, MSTL.

14   Sunderland, *History of the Field Artillery School*, pp. 188-89.

15   Sunderland, *History of the Field Artillery School*, p. 196; *History of the Field Artillery School: World War II*, p. 9; Report of Operations of the Field Artillery School for School Year 1939-1940, 11 Jul 1940, p. 9, UF23.5 E1, MSTL.

16   Robert R. Palmer, Bell I. Wiley, and William R. Keast, *The Procurement and Training of*

Ground Combat Troops (Washington, D.C.: Office of the Chief of Military History, Department of the Army, 1948), p. 91; Ltr with atch, Danford to McIntyre, 12 Jun 1940, Miscellaneous Correspondence, 1939-1945, UF25 H673 M4, MSTL; Sunderland, *History of the Field Artillery School*, p. 197; Annual Report of the Field Artillery School for 1939-1940, 11 Jul 1940, Appendix, UF23.5 E1, MSTL.

17   Ltr with atch, Danford to McIntyre, 12 Jun 1940, Miscellaneous Correspondence, 1939-1945, UF25 H673 M4, MSTL; Sunderland, *History of the Field Artillery School*, pp. 9, 10, 37, 38; Annual Report of the Field Artillery School for 1939-1940, 11 Jul 1940, Appendix, UF23.5 E1, MSTL.

18   Palmer, Wiley, and Keast, *The Procurement and Training of Ground Combat Troops*, pp. 260-61, 266; Sunderland, *History of the Field Artillery School*, p. 196.

19   *History of the Field Artillery School: World War II*, pp. 9-10, 29-33, 37-38, 42-43, 64-68, 102-04, 127; Ltr with atch, Chief of Field Artillery to Director, Bureau of Public Relations, War Department, subj: Summary of Accomplishments During the Past Year, 7 Jul 1941, Miscellaneous Correspondence, 1939-1945, UF25 H673 M4, MSTL; Sunderland, *History of the Field Artillery School*, p. 213; LTC Ross B. Warren, "Advanced Course (Special) Number Two," *Field Artillery Journal,* Aug 1941, p. 554; Report, subj: Visit of News Correspondents, 18-19 Nov 1940, UF25 H673 N2 1940, MSTL.

20   Ltr with atch, Chief of Field Artillery to Director of Bureau of Public Relations, War Department, subj: Summary of Accomplishments during the Past Year, 7 Jul 1941, Miscellaneous Correspondence, 1939-1945, UF25 H673 M4, MSTL; Sunderland, *History of the Field Artillery School*, pp. 84, 118, 147, 190.

21   Ltr, McIntyre to Danford, 2 Apr 1940, Miscellaneous Correspondence, 1939-1945, UF25 H673 M4, MSTL.

22   Wilbur S. Nye, *Carbine and Lance: The Story of Old Fort Sill* (Norman, OK: University of Oklahoma Press, 1974) p. 336; Arthur R. Lawrence, *Lawton Golden Anniversary: 1901-1951* (Lawton, OK: Arthur R. Lawrence, 1951), p. 16; Sunderland, *History of the Field Artillery School*, pp. 179, 180, 191, 192; Ltr, McIntyre to Danford, 2 Apr 1940, Miscellaneous Correspondence, 1939-1945, UF25 H673 M4, MSTL.

23   Ltr, Cubbison to Danford, 22 Aug 1940, Miscellaneous Correspondence, 1939-1945, UF25 H673 M4, MSTL. Nye, *Carbine and Lance*, p. 336; Lawrence, *Lawton Golden Anniversary*, p. 16; Sunderland, *History of the Field Artillery School*, pp. 179, 180, 191, 192.

24   Sunderland, *History of the Field Artillery School*, pp. 192-93.

25   Ltr, Cubbison to Danford, 30 Aug 1940, Miscellaneous Correspondence, 1939-1945, UF25 H673 M4, MSTL.

26   Ltr, Cubbison to Danford, 30 Aug 1940.

27   Ltr, Cubbison to Danford, 22 Aug 1940, Miscellaneous Correspondence, 1939-1945, UF25 H673 M4, MSTL. Nye, *Carbine and Lance*, p. 336; Lawrence, *Lawton Golden Anniversary*, p. 16; Sunderland, *History of the Field Artillery School*, pp. 179, 180, 191, 192.

28   Ltr, Cubbison to Danford, 22 Aug 1940, Miscellaneous Correspondence, 1939-1945, UF25 H673 M4, MSTL; Ltr, BG G.R. Allin to Danford, 7 Feb 1941, Miscellaneous Correspondence, 1941, UF25 S372 M4, MSTL; Nye, *Carbine and Lance*, p. 336; Lawrence, *Lawton Golden Anniversary*, p. 16; Sunderland, *History of the Field Artillery School,* pp. 179, 180, 191, 192, 193, 220, 221; Kenny A. Franks, *Citizen Soldiers: Oklahoma's National Guard* (Norman, OK: University of Oklahoma Press, 1984), pp. 40, 53-56, 140.

29   Ltr, Danford to McIntyre, 28 Jun 1939, Miscellaneous Correspondence, 1939-1945, UF25 H673 M4, MSTL; Ltr, Danford to McIntyre, 2 Aug 1939, Miscellaneous Correspondence, 1939-1945, UF25 H673 M4, MSTL; Sunderland, *History of the Field Artillery School*, pp. 178-79;

Report, subj: Visit of News Correspondents, 18-19 Nov 1940, UF25 H673 N2 1940, MSTL.

30 Franks, *Citizen Soldiers*, pp. 40, 53-56, 140; *History of the Field Artillery School: World War II)*, p. 1.

31 Sunderland, *History of the Field Artillery School*, pp. 221, 234-35; Ltr, Allin to Danford, 6 Nov 1941, Miscellaneous Correspondence, 1939-1945, UF25 H673 M4, MSTL.

32 Sunderland, *History of the Field Artillery School*, pp. 200-02, 214, 221, 234, 235, 239, 240; *History of the Field Artillery School: World War II*, 29-42, 70, 109, 121, 131, 134, 136; Ltr, Allin to Danford, 6 Nov 1941, Miscellaneous Correspondence, 1939-1945, UF25 H673 M4, MSTL.

33 Ltr, Elmer Thomas to Frank L. Ketch, 20 Apr 1940, Miscellaneous Correspondence, 1939-1945, UF25 H673 M4, MSTL; Ltr, Cubbison to Danford, 15 Aug 1940, Miscellaneous Correspondence, 1940, UF25 S372 M4, MSTL; Ltr, Cubbison to Danford, 30 Aug 1940, Miscellaneous Correspondence, 1939-1945, UF25 H673 M4, MSTL.

34 Ltr, Cubbison to Danford, 11 Jan 1940, Miscellaneous Correspondence, 1941, UF25 S372 M4, MSTL; Ltr, Cubbison to Danford, 22 Aug 1940, Miscellaneous Correspondence, 1939-1945, UF25 H673 M4, MSTL.

35 Ltr, Cubbison to Danford, 3 Sep 1940, Miscellaneous Correspondence, 1939-1945, UF25 H673 M4, MSTL.

36 Ltr, Cubbison to Danford, 3 Sep 1940; Ltr, Allin to Danford, 4 Apr 1941, Miscellaneous Correspondence, 1941, UF25 S372 M4, MSTL; Ltr, Allin to Chief, Construction Branch, War Department General Staff, 7 May 1941, Miscellaneous Correspondence, 1939-1945, UF25 H673 M4, MSTL; Ltr, COL S.J. Chamberlain, Chief, Construction Branch, War Department General Staff, to Allin, 14 Jun 1941, Miscellaneous Correspondence, 1939-1945, UF25 H673 M4, MSTL; Ltr, Allin to Danford, 4 Apr 1941, Miscellaneous Correspondence, 1941, UF25 S372 M4, MSTL; Ltr, Allin to Honorable Jed Johnson, House of Representatives, 4 Apr 1941, Miscellaneous Correspondence, 1941, UF25 S372 M4, MSTL; Nye, *Carbine and Lance*, p. 336; Gillette Griswold, "Fort Sill, Oklahoma: A Brief History," unpublished manuscript, p. 15, Historical Records and Document Collection (HRDC), Field Artillery Branch Historian's Office, US Army Field Artillery School, Fort Sill; Ltr, Allin to Danford, 7 May 1941, Miscellaneous Correspondence, 1941, UF25 S372 M4, MSTL.

37 Sunderland, *History of the Field Artillery School*, pp. 200-02, 214, 221, 234, 235, 239, 240; *History of the Field Artillery School: World War II*, 29-42, 70, 109, 121, 131, 134, 136, 214; Ltr, Allin to Danford, 6 Nov 1941, Miscellaneous Correspondence, 1939-1945, UF25 H673 M4, MSTL; School Graduation Statistics, HRDC.

38 William R. Keast, Provision of Enlisted Replacements, Army Ground Forces Study Number 7, 1946, p. 2; William R. Keast, The Procurement and Branch Distribution of Officers, Army Ground Forces Study Number 6, 1946, p. 7; William H. Willis, The Replacement and School Command, Army Ground Forces Study Number 33, 1946, p. 1; Kent R. Greenfield and Robert R. Palmer, Origins of the Army Ground Forces General Headquarters, United States Army, 1940-1942, Army Ground Forces Study Number 1, 1946, pp. 1-7; Matloff, *American Military History*, pp. 429-30.

39 Keast, Provision of Enlisted Replacements, p. 2; Keast, The Procurement and Branch Distribution of Officers, p. 7; Willis, The Replacement and School Command, 1946, p. 1; Greenfield and Palmer, Origins of the Army Ground Forces General Headquarters, United States Army, 1940-1942, pp. 1-7; Matloff, *American Military History*, pp. 429-30.

40 *History of the Field Artillery School: World War II*, p. 266.

41 Palmer, Wiley, and Keast, *The Procurement and Training of Ground Combat Troops*, pp. 270-71, 358; *History of the Field Artillery School: World War II*, pp. 29, 30, 34, 37, 214.

42 Palmer, Wiley, and Keast, *The Procurement and Training of Ground Combat Troops*, pp. 270-71, 358; *History of the Field Artillery School: World War II*, pp. 29, 30, 34, 214.

43 *History of the Field Artillery School: World War II*, pp. 30, 31, 214, 215-18; Palmer, Wiley, and Keast, *The Procurement and Training of Ground Combat Troops*, p. 263; Sunderland, *History of the Field Artillery School*, p. 234; Keast, The Procurement and Branch Distribution of Officers, p. 7.

44 See endnote 43.

45 Palmer, Wiley, and Keast, *The Procurement and Training of Ground Combat Troops*, pp. 270-71, 358; *History of the Field Artillery School: World War II*, pp. 29, 30, 34, 214.

46 Palmer, Wiley, and Keast, *The Procurement and Training of Ground Force Troops*, p. 267; *History of the Field Artillery School: World War II*, pp. 39-41.

47 Palmer, Wiley, and Keast, *The Procurement and Training of Ground Combat Troops*, pp. 266-71; *History of the Field Artillery School: World War II*, pp. 39-41.

48 See endnote 47.

49 See endnote 47.

50 *History of the US Army Artillery and Missile School, 1945-1957* (Fort Sill, OK: Fort Sill Printing Plant, 1957), pp. 6, 8; *History of the Field Artillery School: World War II*, pp. 266-67; Palmer, Wiley, and Keast, *The Procurement and Training of Ground Troops*, p. 430; Report of the Department of the Army Board to Review Army Officer Schools, Feb 1966, Vol 2, p. 131, U408 H2U4, MSTL.

51 *History of the US Army Artillery and Missile School, 1945-1957*, pp. 6, 8; *History of the Field Artillery School: World War II*, pp. 266-67; Palmer, Wiley, and Keast, *The Procurement and Training of Ground Troops*, p. 430; Report of the Department of the Army Board to Review Army Officer Schools, Feb 1966, Vol II, p. 131, U408 H2U4, MSTL.

52 Sunderland, *History of the Field Artillery School*, p. 221.

53 Sunderland, *History of the Field Artillery School*, pp. 221, 234; Palmer, Wiley, and Keast, *The Procurement and Training of Ground Troops*, pp. 330-31.

54 Sunderland, *History of the Field Artillery School*, p. 222.

55 Sunderland, *History of the Field Artillery School*, pp. 223, 234; Palmer, Wiley, and Keast, *The Procurement and Training of Ground Combat Troops*, pp. 325-28; *History of the Field Artillery School: World War II*, pp. 197-98.

56 *History of the Field Artillery School: World War II, ., p. 198.*

57 Palmer, Wiley, and Keast, *The Procurement and Training of Ground Combat Troops*, pp. 104, 107, 108, 325-28; Sunderland, *History of the Field Artillery School*, pp. 222, 234; *History of the Field Artillery School: World War II*, pp. 197-98.

58 Palmer, Wiley, and Keast, *The Procurement and Training of Ground Troops*, pp. 334, 338; Sunderland, *History of the Field Artillery School*, p. 224.

59 Field Artillery School, Description of Courses, Jul 1941, p. 33, UF23.5 Q7, MSTL.

60 Sunderland, History of the Field Artillery School, pp. 221, 234; Palmer, Wiley, and Keast, *The Procurement and Training of Ground Troops*, pp. 330-31.

61 Sunderland, *History of the Field Artillery School*, p. 229.

62 Sunderland, *History of the Field Artillery School*, p. 229.

63 *History of the Field Artillery School: World War II*, pp. 30, 214-18.

64 Palmer, Wiley, and Keast, *The Procurement and Training of Ground Combat Troops*, p. 351; Keast, Provision of Enlisted Replacements, p. 2; Keast, The Procurement and Branch Distribution of Officers, pp. 18-19; LTC Edwin P. Parker, Jr., "Field Artillery Replacement Centers," *Field Artillery Journal*, Feb 1941, pp. 83-86; LTC Edwin P. Parker, Jr. "They Start to Roll," *Field Artillery Journal*, May 1941, pp. 273-76; LTC O.F. Marston, "The Camp Roberts Replacement

Center," *Field Artillery Journal*, Mar 1941, pp. 178-79; Report, subj: National Defense Installations Tour, 21-22 Mar 1941, UF25 H673 N2 1941, MSTL.

65 Palmer, Wiley, and Keast, *The Procurement and Training of Ground Combat Troops*, p. 351; Parker, "Field Artillery Replacement Centers," pp. 83-86; Parker, "They Start to Roll," pp. 273-76; Marston, "The Camp Roberts Replacement Center," pp. 178-79.

66 Sunderland, *History of the Field Artillery School*, p. 243; Palmer, Wiley, and Keast, *The Procurement and Training of Ground Combat Troops*, pp. 353-56.

67 Sunderland, *History of the Field Artillery School*, pp. 243-44.

68 Palmer, Wiley, and Keast, *The Procurement and Training of Ground Combat Troops,* pp. 358-59.

69 *History of the Field Artillery School: World War II*, pp. 206, 244-58.

70 US Army AEF, Report of the Board to Study the Experience Gained by the Artillery of the AEF, 1918, pp. 1, 3, 10, 25, hereafter cited as Hero Board Report, Defense Technical Information Center (DTIC) ADA 161150; Edgar F. Raines, Jr., *Eyes of Artillery: The Origins of Modern US Army Aviation in World War II* (Washington, D.C.: Center of Military History, US Army, 2000), pp. 15-16, 33; Dastrup, *King of Battle*, pp. 179-80.

71 Hero Board Report, DTIC ADA 161150, p. 663.

72 Hero Board Report,, p. 664.

73 Hero Board Report, pp. 25-26, 665-71, 823-40; Dastrup, *King of Battle*, p. 181.

74 Raines, *Eyes of Artillery*, pp. 14-29.

75 Harry G. Bishop, *Field Artillery: King of Battle* (Boston: Houghton Mifflin Company, 1936), pp. 130-35; Raines, *Eyes of Artillery*, p. 16; Dastrup, *King of Battle*, p. 206.

76 Raines, *Eyes of Artillery*, pp. 31-32.

77 Raines, *Eyes of Artillery*, pp. 36-37, 106-08; Report of Operations of the Field Artillery School for the School Year 1939-1940, 11 Jul 1940, p. 10, UF 23.5 E7, MSTL; Memorandum, subj: Final Report of the Air-Ground-Procedure Board, 19 Aug 1941, in Office of the Chief of Field Artillery, Air Observation for Field Artillery, Tab F, UL502.9 A3U5 1941a, MSTL.

78 Field Artillery School, Committee Study, subj: The Observation Aviation Required for Artillery Missions, 14 May 1941, U421 Q71A311, MSTL.

79 LTC William W. Ford, "Wings for St. Barbara," *Field Artillery Journal,* Apr 1941, pp. 232-34; *History of the Field Artillery School: World War II*, pp. 3, 5, 169-70; Raines, *Eyes of Artillery*, pp. 66-78, 106-08; Boyd L. Dastrup, *King of Battle: A Branch History of the US Army's Field Artillery* (Fort Monroe, VA: Office of the Command Historian, US Army Training and Doctrine Command, 1992, reprinted by US Army Center of Military History, 1993), pp. 207-08. See footnotes on those pages for the primary sources.

80 Sunderland, *History of the Field Artillery School,* pp. 173-76.

81 *History of the Field Artillery School: World War II*, pp. 3, 64-69, 125-34 .

Chapter Six

Early Cold War Years: 1945-1971

Although the Field Artillery School anticipated returning to the slow-paced operations characteristic of the 1920s and 1930s following World War II, circumstances beyond its control prevented the fruition of that wistful dream. The organization of The Artillery School in 1946, the introduction of cross training and cross assignments to save money and promote flexibility in assigning officers, the inactivation of the Coast Artillery in 1950, the consolidation of the Field Artillery and the Antiaircraft Artillery, a former branch of the Coast Artillery, in 1950, the internal reorganizations in the school, and, of course, the Cold War forever altered the school.

Shifting Gears

In the fall of 1945, President Harry S. Truman issued a directive to Secretary of War Robert T. Patterson authorizing him to reorganize the War Department and the Army to simplify command and staff operations, to establish clear cut command channels, and to economize in the face of demobilization and budget cuts. Tasked by Patterson and General Thomas T. Handy, the Deputy Chief of Staff for the Army, on 30 August 1945 to scrutinize overall Army organization and operations, the Board of Officers on the Reorganization of the War Department chaired by Lieutenant General Alexander M. Patch launched its inquiry. On 18 October 1945, the Patch Board submitted its lengthy report. To achieve economies, it recommended Congressional legislation to abolish the Chiefs of Infantry, Cavalry, Field Artillery, and Coast Artillery that had been vacant since 9 March 1942 when their powers had been transferred to the Chief of Army Ground Forces as a part of a broad reorganization of the War Department. Among other proposals, the Patch Board also urged combining the Cavalry and Armor forces to create the Armor Branch and merging the Coast Artillery with its antiaircraft artillery mission and the Field Artillery into one artillery branch as a cost-saving measure and as a means of gaining flexibility in officer assignments by permitting them to serve in any one of the three artilleries.[1]

When Patch unexpectedly died in December 1945, the Army reconvened the board under Lieutenant General William H. Simpson. Given the same mandate of saving money and simplifying organization, the Simpson Board – as it was now called – reaffirmed the conclusions of the Patch Board about necessity of consolidating the Field Artillery and the Coast Artillery into a single artillery. The board based its rationale upon the World War II experience where all three (the Coast Artillery, Antiaircraft Artillery, and Field Artillery) artilleries had employed cannons, had accompanied the infantry, and had supplemented or performed each others' missions. Based upon this, members of the Patch and Simpson Boards saw a blurred distinction among the three artilleries and found consolidation to be a logical step. It would save money, promote flexibility within the artillery officer corps by permitting them to serve in all three artilleries, provide positions for coast artillery officers who were potentially out of a job with the rumored demise of the Coast Artillery, and support a small peacetime military establishment that would surely be created in keeping with the country's military tradition.[2]

As the Patch Board before it, the Simpson Board also addressed transferring antiaircraft artillery to the Army Air Force which was seeking complete independence from the Army and its own air defenses. Early in 1945, the Army Air Force proposed creating a large antiaircraft artillery establishment under its supervision and control to ensure antiaircraft artillery support to the air forces. Although the Patch Board strenuously objected to this recommendation, fearing the loss of antiaircraft artillery support for the ground forces, the Simpson Board reflected this apprehension even more. It vehemently opposed transferring antiaircraft artillery to the Army Air Force because the ground forces would lose control over it and tendered consolidating the Coast Artillery and the Field Artillery into one branch as a means of staving off this possible transfer.[3]

Influenced by the Patch Board, the Simpson Board, and the Artillery Conference of March 1946 at Fort Sill that also urged merging the artilleries into one as a cost-saving measure, the Army submitted its recommendation to Congress in mid-1946 to combine the Coast Artillery and the Field Artillery into one artillery branch. Flexible artillery officer assignments that would broaden the officer's military knowledge, would permit moving officers among the three artilleries, and would improve the promotion potential for coast artillery and antiaircraft artillery officers to general officer certainly influenced the push to combine the artilleries. However, the budget reductions caused by the huge drawdown after the war more than anything prompted the consolidation proposal.[4] As the Chief of Staff of the Army, General Dwight D. Eisenhower, clearly directed on 22 August 1945, the Army had to find ways to reduce overhead and save money; consolidation fit neatly with his guidance.[5]

Before Congress could act on the recommendations, the Army combined what it legally could in its drive to reduce overhead.[6] In a letter of 17 September 1946, Headquarters Army Ground Forces, commanded by Lieutenant General Jacob L. Devers, directed the Replacement and School Command at Birmingham, Alabama, to form a board of officers to draft a detailed plan to consolidate the Field Artillery School, the Antiaircraft Artillery School, and the Coast Artillery School into one school to "effect economies of funds and personnel."[7] As a part of this plan, the board had to determine the physical costs of the required moves, the costs of constructing new facilities, and the savings generated by a consolidation.[8]

Thirteen days later on 30 September 1946, the board started its work. Over a period of about one month, it visited the three schools, examined their programs of instruction, and obtained data on the size of each installation and the costs associated with moving each school and new construction. Based upon its extensive examination, the board found merging the three artillery schools to be feasible and desirable. While the Coast Artillery School would be renamed the Seacoast Artillery Branch of The Artillery School, would move from Fort Monroe, Virginia, to Fort Winfield Scott, California, and would conduct instruction on submarine mines and seacoast artillery radar, the Antiaircraft Artillery School at Fort Bliss, Texas, would be designated as the Antiaircraft and Guided Missile Branch of The Artillery School and provide all antiaircraft artillery training. The Field Artillery School would become The Artillery School and have the responsibility for teaching all common artillery subjects and theoretical instruction on guns of all calibers and the firing of field pieces. With this reorganization The Artillery Center at Fort Sill would assume control of the three artillery schools even though they would remain at their present locations and would become the hub of artillery training.[9]

Accordingly, the merger offered promise and opportunities. It would reduce overhead and personnel requirements for staff and faculty, would streamline operations, and would improve promotion opportunities for officers in the Coast Artillery, including Antiaircraft Artillery, by giving them more command opportunities than they had had during the war, meaning that they could command field artillery batteries and battalions if required. Equally as important, the merger would fend off losing antiaircraft artillery to the Army Air Force which would be disastrous in the eyes of ground force officers and would create a common ground for mutual understanding and language among the artilleries.[10]

Before the board could submit its far-reaching proposals to Headquarters Army Ground Forces for consideration, Brigadier General Bruce C. Clarke, the operations officer (G-3) for the Army Ground Forces, presented his plan. Deferring to Clarke, Headquarters Army Ground Forces dissolved the board and implemented the general's recommendations for overhauling Army Ground Force schools.[11] Effective 1 November 1946, the command established The Armored Center at Fort Knox, Kentucky, for all armored instruction, The Artillery Center at Fort Sill for all fire support training, The Infantry Center at Fort Benning, Georgia, for infantry and airborne training, placed these three centers and service schools under Headquarters Army Ground Forces, and discontinued the Replacement and School Command.[12]

As Colonel Thomas E. de Shazo of The Artillery School explained early in 1947, The Artillery Center oversaw The Artillery School which was the consolidation of the Field Artillery School, the Seacoast Artillery School, and the Antiaircraft Artillery School, all Army Ground Force troops stationed at Fort Sill, and post activities. The Artillery School would teach all subjects common to the three artilleries and field artillery subjects, while the Seacoast Artillery School and the Antiaircraft Artillery School would teach subjects specific to their branches.[13]

Subsequent to the creation of The Artillery Center, the Commanding General, Major General Clift Andrus, and The Artillery School presented their belated views on the new organization. Finding the merger of the three artillery schools to be unsatisfactory by failing to relocate them to one site, Andrus urged taking the restructuring even further. In a letter to Devers on 20 November 1946, he suggested totally eliminating the Coast Artillery School and Antiaircraft Artillery School and replacing them with a Department of Harbor Defense and a Department of Antiaircraft Firing in The Artillery School to achieve even more economies and actual physical consolidation. Equally important, Andrus urged purchasing or leasing land near Childress, Texas, about 180 miles west of Fort Sill for antiaircraft artillery firing ranges. After considering these controversial proposals, Devers responded in a terse letter to Andrus on 23 December 1946 where he explained his reasons for rejecting the plan. Devers found Andrus's concept to be too disruptive, expensive, and radical. He also noted that Fort Sill lacked sufficient land to conduct all of the projected artillery training. As a result, neither the Coast Artillery School nor the Antiaircraft Artillery School was abolished as Andrus urged for the reasons outlined by Devers. War Department General Order Number 11, dated 22 January 1947, officially redesignated the Coast Artillery School as the Seacoast Artillery School as a branch of The Artillery School, the Antiaircraft Artillery School as a branch of The Artillery School, and Field Artillery School as The Artillery School.[14]

Together, these three schools formed a crucial part of an extensive Army school system for officers. Newly commissioned officers would first attend the Ground General School at Fort Riley, Kansas, for 17 weeks of basic branch-immaterial training. They would subsequently attend their branch's basic course and their branch's advance course later in their careers. After completing the advance course, select officers would attend the Command and General Staff College at Fort Leavenworth, Kansas.[15]

As the Field Artillery School went through this major reorganization, it shifted from wartime to peacetime operations. Between September 1945 and December 1945, the number of students dropped from 2,321 to 1,014. Concurrently, the school lost experienced instructors to overseas assignments or separation from the Army, and grew more dependent upon inexperienced instructors in the classroom. Meanwhile, the US Army Ground Forces Replacement and School Command which had supervised the Army's combat arms schools since 9 March 1942 furnished its first peacetime training guidance.[16] In a conference for school commandants, assistant commandants, and other key leaders on 6-7 November 1945, the Replacement and School Command directed starting interim peacetime courses for officers and enlisted soldiers by January 1946. The schools would teach these courses until September 1946 when they would initiate their regular peacetime courses, implying that the pre-war academic year of September-May would be revived and that year-around operations would cease.[17]

At the same time, the Replacement and School Command tasked its service schools to offer two unique courses – a Professor of Military Science and Tactics Orientation Course and an Ex-Prisoner of War Orientation Course. While the former would train select officers for duty as professors of military science and tactics in Reserve Officer Training Corps programs at American universities to create a pool of trained reserve officers for mobilization and deployment if necessary, the latter would start in June 1946 and be required for all company grade officers who had been captured by enemy forces prior to 1 December 1944. Former prisoner-of-war officers who were captains and below would attend the service school of their arm or branch to be brought up to date on the weapons, vehicles, equipment, and doctrine of their respective arm. In December 1945, Devers modified this guidance. Regardless of rank, all former prisoner-of-war officers would spend two weeks each at the Infantry School, Armor School, Cavalry School, Field Artillery School, and Antiaircraft Artillery School for instruction on the latest tactics, techniques, and procedures of each combat arm.[18]

OCS: The Makers of Officers.

At the beginning of 1946, the Field Artillery School, therefore, encountered a daunting challenge as it started shifting from wartime to peacetime operations. Designing and teaching interim courses and concurrently developing peacetime extension and regular courses for officers and soldiers with the goal of starting them by September 1946 completely overshadowed the Ex-Prisoner of War Orientation Course and the Professor of Military Science and Tactics Orientation Course. In fact, the school taught the Ex-Prisoner of War Orientation Course through September 1946 when it was discontinued and only taught a couple of iterations of the Professor of Military Science and Tactics Orientation Course before terminating it late in 1946. From September 1946 onward, the school focused its attention on its peacetime courses. That month it returned to the September-May academic year reminiscent of the pre-war years when it initiated eight officer courses and 10 enlisted courses and geared itself for a small student load as a result of demobilization. For example, the basic officer course of 26 weeks for newly commissioned Regular Army field artillery second lieutenants would be taught once a year and produce 109 graduates annually, while the Regular Army advanced officer course of 41 weeks for field artillery captains would be taught once a year and generate 60 graduates. Meanwhile, the Associate Basic Course for National Guard and Organized Reserve field artillery second lieutenants would produce about 800 officers annually with five classes being taught between September and May, while the Associate Advanced Artillery Course for National Guard and Organized Reserve field artillery captains would turn out 400 graduates annually with four classes being taught between September and May. With the exception of the air mechanic course for soldiers which would be divided into seven classes and taught between September and May, all enlisted courses would be offered once a year. Over the next four years, these courses formed the heart and soul of the school's curriculum with other courses being taught as needed. As de Shazo, the assistant commandant of The Artillery School, implied in the *Field Artillery Journal* in the March-April 1947 edition, the school clearly expected to return to the slow pace of the 1920s and 1930s by limiting instruction to nine months out of the year even though the anticipated annual graduate production figures would exceed those of the 1920s and 1930s.[19]

The emerging Cold War soon dictated that the United States had to expand its armed forces, compelling the school to adopt year-around operations to satisfy the requirement for more graduates. Signed by President Harry S. Truman on 24 June 1948, the Selective Service Act committed the country to enlarging its military forces in peacetime through a draft with the goal of increasing the Army from about 600,000 to 900,000 soldiers by 1 July 1949. In response, The Artillery School immediately launched preparations to receive an influx of students, expecting the average monthly student load in all classes to climb from 440 in 1947 to 890 by October 1948 and even higher to 1,450 by March 1949.[20]

Such a projected rapid escalation in students prompted the school to outline options to handle the load. It could create new courses or modify the existing courses to manage more students. Regardless of the option selected, more instructors would be needed. To accommodate the growth, the school developed its "Plan for Expansion of The Artillery School" where it outlined raising the capacity of each course. On 1 October 1948, the school delivered its plan to the Chief of Staff of the Fourth Army and the Office of the Chief of Army Field Forces at Fort Monroe, Virginia, for approval. Specifically, the plan included 10 officer and 11 enlisted courses and an instructor staff of 963 which represented a dramatic augmentation of instructors from 404 in the summer of 1948.[21]

By the end of November 1948, the desired number of instructors had not arrived. Reflecting the stress associated with the much expected expansion and the shortage of instructors, Andrus wrote urgent letters in November 1948 to the Office of the Chief of Army Field Forces that supervised and directed training but lacked command authority and Headquarters Fourth Army which exercised command authority informing them about the school's dire need for more instructors. Although the Fourth Army increased the number of instructor requirements, Army-wide personnel shortages prevented filling them. Thus, the shortages persisted, but fortunately circumstances changed.[22]

Shortly after the school had petitioned for more instructors, the newly created Department of Defense completed reevaluating the number of trained soldiers required in light of the national economy in December 1948 and reduced the planned expansion of the Army downward. It now estimated the need for 677,000 soldiers rather than the previous forecast of 900,000. This decrease nullified any serious growth in the student load because the Army already had around 600,000 soldiers in uniform and concurrently prompted the school to withdraw its request for additional instructors. Other than normal fluctuations caused by personnel rotations, the school's number of staff and faculty remained fairly constant from early 1949 to June 1950, ranging between 626 in 1947 and 722 in 1950 when the Korean War broke out, while its student load per month grew from 430 in 1947 to 1,196 in 1950. This gradual expansion came from the addition of specialist courses to train antiaircraft artillery enlisted soldiers that was part of the consolidation of the artillery schools in 1946.[23]

Meanwhile, the Army established organic aviation for the Infantry, Armor, Cavalry, Tank Destroyer, and Engineer branches to expand the concept beyond the Field Artillery that had pioneered organic aviation prior to the war. To train the necessary number of liaison aircraft pilots and mechanics, the Army Ground Forces redesignated the Field Artillery School's Department of Air Training as the Army Ground Forces Air Training School on 7 December 1945 and placed the school under the Commandant of Field Artillery School with an assistant commandant directly in charge. The Army Ground Forces then made Brigadier General William W. Ford, a flying enthusiast, a key participant in the development of organic field artillery aerial observation in the 1930s and 1940s, and the first director of the Department of Air Training from 1942 to 1943, the assistant commandant. This action caused the Field Artillery School to discontinue its Field Artillery Pilot Course and Field Artillery Air Mechanic Course early in 1946 and to initiate the Army Ground Forces Air Mechanic Course in January 1946 and the Army Ground Forces Airplane Pilot Course in March 1946.[24]

Although the reorganization expanded pilot and mechanics training beyond field artillerymen, both courses provided the same training that the school's wartime pilot and mechanics courses had furnished with one major exception: the courses tailored training for each branch. During the last weeks of instruction, for example, engineers received additional training in aerial photography. When the Air Training School was discontinued in November 1946 as part of the major Army service school reorganization that led to the creation of The Artillery School, The Artillery School reestablished the Department of Air Training that same month and taught mechanic and pilot courses through 1 July 1953 for all the branches of the Army that had organic aviation. On that date the school discontinued the Department of Air Training and transferred its records and files to the Army Aviation School established by the Department of the Army on 16 January 1953 at Fort Sill to supply all of the Army's aviation training. Because the school's rapid growth strained Fort Sill's resources, created crowded living and training conditions, and forced the use of substandard facilities for aviation training, the Army transferred it to Fort Rucker, Alabama, in August 1954.[25]

Directed by Headquarters, Army Ground Forces on 28 August 1946, the Field Artillery School, the Coast Artillery School, and the Antiaircraft Artillery School, meanwhile, developed cross training or training officers in all three artilleries to facilitate a true merger of the artilleries. They designed an integrated basic course for all newly commissioned second lieutenants to teach them fundamentals of field artillery, coast artillery, and antiaircraft artillery and created an integrated advance course for officers with three to 10 years of experience where they would undergo additional training in the three artilleries. As seen by the War Department, these integrated courses would be a critical step toward the consolidation of the three branches by creating a body of officers who could serve in all three artilleries and would promote flexibility in assigning officers. Equally important, cross training would save money, another crucial objective.[26]

The emergence of cross training stemmed from the Army's World War II experience. After the Allies had gained air supremacy, antiaircraft artillery officers were frequently transferred to field artillery units, and heavy coast artillery guns served by coast artillerymen often functioned as field artillery especially against heavily fortified enemy defenses. Officers, however, lacked the requisite training to function effectively outside of their branches and often went through on-the-job training if transferred to another branch. The need for a well-balanced artillery force with officers who could perform field artillery, antiaircraft artillery, and coast artillery duties and the requirement to conserve money and manpower resources in the face of personnel shortages dictated cross training and cross assignment or moving officers among the three branches. With the recent past as prologue, the present and future would require artillery officers with qualifications in the employment of the three artilleries. This would minimize the impact of officer shortages and promote flexibility by permitting the Army to assign artillery officers where they were needed the most.[27]

Soon, the fruits of the cross training effort appeared. On 17 January 1947, the Officer's Advance Course, Class Number One, completed field artillery training at Fort Sill, transferred to Fort Bliss for antiaircraft training, and then to Fort Winfield Scott for coast artillery training on submarine mines and seacoast artillery radar. Three weeks later on 6 February 1947, the Officer's Basic Course, Class Number One, finished instruction at The Artillery School and moved to the Antiaircraft Artillery School and then to the Seacoast Artillery School before graduating on 18 April 1947.[28] Such training held out much promise and seemed to be the wave of the future for training artillery officers.[29]

In an open letter in the September-October 1947 edition of the *Field Artillery Journal* subsequent to the graduation of classes from the first integrated courses, Devers explained his rationale and advocacy of cross training and cross assignment. He considered all antiaircraft, field artillery, and coast artillery officers to be ground force officers first and artillery officers second. Integrated training would give them a well-rounded knowledge of field, coast, and antiaircraft artillery employment, permit them to serve in all artillery units, and provide them with a valuable foundation for command and staff positions. Besides providing future artillery officers with a general knowledge of all artillery weapons and a specialized knowledge of some, cross training would create a closely knit artillery component of the Army Ground Forces and give every artillery officer a better opportunity for advancement, echoing one of the Army's reasons for integrating the artilleries.[30]

Reality quickly clashed with the dreams of Devers, the Assistant Commandant of The Artillery School, de Shazo, and other Army officers who endorsed cross training. Addressing the separate school locations, The Artillery School found the movement of students from one school to the other to be financially costly and disruptive during the academic year of 1947-

1948. To end this unproductive practice, it urged physically consolidating the Antiaircraft Artillery School and The Artillery School at Fort Sill, but ignored the Seacoast Artillery School's future because modern naval guns and aircraft had made coastal artillery obsolete and because it faced closure. To accommodate physical consolidation, The Artillery School advised building additional quarters to house the student officers, constructing more office space on Fort Sill, acquiring more land for ranges because of the longer ranges of the new weapons, and introducing air conditioning in classrooms to make training bearable in the summer because the traditional academic year would have to be jettisoned to accommodate the increased number of students.[31]

In its annual report for the academic year of 1948-1949, The Artillery School reiterated its complaint about transferring students from one school to another one as being counterproductive and a waste of time and money. Rather than furnishing artillery training at separate locations, The Artillery School recommended once again combining field artillery and antiaircraft artillery training at one location and discounted the existence of the Seacoast Artillery School again because its future was questionable.[32] Consolidating the Field Artillery School and Antiaircraft Artillery School at one location – Fort Sill – would save travel expenses for students and instructors by ending the practice of moving them from school to school, improve instruction, eliminate lost training time, facilitate cross training, and further promote the complete unification of the Field Artillery and Antiaircraft Artillery as one artillery branch.[33] Yet, the school cautioned, "If The Artillery School is to remain at Fort Sill, additional land should be acquired to add to the existing range and maneuver areas. This increase in size of the reservation is justified in the increase of ranges of new weapons."[34]

Subsequently, a board of officers appointed by the Department of the Army to examine any physical consolidation concurred with The Artillery School's position in a report on 1 November 1949 but disagreed with the location. The board insisted that the separate school houses would continue to foster a divided artillery, interests, and allegiances and would support undesirable specialization within the arm. Because "the interchangeability of personnel is mandatory" in view of the World War II experience and existing funding levels, collocation was desirable.[35] The board found Fort Bliss to be the practicable, economical, and logical site. The Texas installation had sufficient land for ranges and maneuver sites whereas Fort Sill did not. Moreover, physical consolidation would contribute to the complete merger of the two artilleries.[36] However, the cost of co-locating the two schools as the military's annual budget declined prohibited physical consolidation.[37]

As The Artillery School, the US Army Field Forces, formerly called the Army Ground Forces until 1948, and the Army explored the possibility of physically merging the two schools to improve training and streamline overhead and command structure costs and integrating the artilleries, The Artillery School began challenging the competency of the graduates of the basic and advance officer courses. In its annual report for 1949-1950, the school complained about the incompetent graduates from the integrated officer courses and clamored for devoting more training time to branch peculiar material. The limited length of the advance course of 41 weeks and the basic course of 26 weeks prevented devoting sufficient time to field artillery or antiaircraft artillery training. Limited training in their specialty produced officers who were considered to be either field artillery or antiaircraft artillery officers to be ill-prepared for combat and command in either branch. They knew a little about both branches and more importantly lacked sufficient training to be competent in their own branch.[38]

Upon becoming the Commandant of The Artillery School in 1950, Major General Arthur M. Harper (1950-1953) entered the debate. Also arguing that cross training produced an inadequately prepared officer, Harper pressed to end it especially during war in favor of short, specialized courses to qualify the maximum number of officers for their combat mission. In a memorandum to the Chief of Army Field Forces on 22 June 1950 on the eve of the Korean War, Harper wrote, "The resultant product [of cross training] is an officer who, in the event of mobilization in the next few years, is not technically qualified to the degree necessary to enable him to train efficiently a unit of his specific arm."[39] Continuing, he pointed out:

> Antiaircraft artillery and field artillery officers have received almost identical courses of instruction. As a result, the branch material subject matter for each arm is not covered thoroughly.... It is, however, regrettably apparent that neither the antiaircraft artillery nor the field artillery officer receives sufficient basic branch material knowledge to produce an officer well grounded in his specific arm.[40]

With this in mind, Harper urged separate training for the two branches during peacetime because their missions, techniques, equipment, tactics, and organizations were distinctly different and because heavy antiaircraft artillery guns would never be employed in the surface role. He also believed that field artillery officers required more time than allotted to gain a detailed knowledge of the functioning of the tank, infantry, and field artillery team, that the antiaircraft artillery officer needed meticulous training on attacking air targets, and that the time available prevented providing sufficient training in each artillery branch. Basically, Harper considered cross training to be a folly and unsatisfactory and became one its major detractors.[41]

Notwithstanding Harper's and other artillery officers' genuine concerns, Congress passed the Army Reorganization Act of July 1950. The act confirmed the powers of the Secretary of the Army to administer departmental affairs. Under the secretary, the Army Chief of Staff was responsible for the Army's readiness and operational plans. The chief was also responsible for carrying out the approved plans and policies of the department. Below the Chief of Staff was the Chief of Army Field Forces who had the responsibility for developing tactical doctrine, controlling the Army's school system, and training field units. Equally important, the act gave the Infantry, Artillery, and Armor statutory recognition, inactivated the Coast Artillery, and allowed the Army to merge the Antiaircraft Artillery, formerly a part of the Coast Artillery, and the Field Artillery legally to form one artillery branch. Basically, the act legitimized the Army's artillery organization that had existed since the fall of 1946 and indicated that cross training and assignment would continue.[42]

Snow Hall classroom in the 1950s

Although the Congress and Army merged the two artillery branches, Harper's recommendation of June 1950 to end cross training, the general belief throughout the Army, especially the artillery community, about cross training's failure to turn out technically competent officers, and the Korean War that reinforced the need for specialized training caused the US Army Field Forces to reevaluate artillery training. In a message of 14 August 1950, US Army Field Forces approved separate training for each artillery branch beginning with the school year of 1951-1952. Specifically, it authorized a separate battery officer's course for new field artillery and antiaircraft artillery second lieutenants to provide them with the basics of their respective branches. In addition, the command sanctioned a separate advance course for career field artillery and antiaircraft artillery officers with five to 12 years of experience. The advance course would no longer teach remedial subjects as part of its core curriculum and would focus its attention on subjects required for captains.[43]

Despite this measure, Harper continued his assault on cross training and cross assignment, fearing their return. In a terse sentence in the school's annual report of November 1950, Harper commented, "The present separation of the courses [during the war] should be continued indefinitely."[44] Given the Army's devotion to cross training during peacetime and the desire for flexible officer assignments in recent years, he rightfully worried about their revival after the war to stay within declining postwar budgets and personnel strengths to retain flexibility in assigning artillery officers.[45]

Besides causing the demise of cross training and assignment, the Korean War simultaneously generated a dramatic increase in student load and graduate production. On 1 July 1950 when American armed forces entered the hostilities on the Korean peninsula, the Army's strength stood at 593,000. One year later it had 1,531,000 in uniform. As might be expected, Fort Sill and The Artillery School acutely felt the rapid mobilization. On 31 July 1950 just a few days after the North Korean invasion of South Korea, the Chief of Army Field Forces, General Mark W. Clark, directed the school to intensify and accelerate training by making sweeping revisions in its programs of instruction, lesson plans, and general operations to graduate more students. To accomplish this, the school extended its training week from 40 hours to 44 hours with authorization to place certain specialist courses on a 48 hour week, decreased the number of holidays from seven to four, abandoned the two-week Christmas break, reduced the length of its courses by eliminating nonessential subjects to permit teaching classes more frequently, increased the number of students in each class, made training more realistic by integrating lessons learned, and taught classes the year around. The school also increased the number of students in its Associate Reserve Officer Advance Course from 65 to 120 per class and Associate Reserve Battery Officer Course from 101 to 400 per class, added courses for Army Reserve and National Guard personnel and non-Army personnel being called to active duty, and assumed the responsibility for training Army Reserve and Army National Guard field artillery units that were being mobilized at Fort Sill.[46]

Student production figures reflected these actions. The school produced 1,895 graduates in 1949, 3,247 graduates in 1950, and 13,061 graduates in 1951 with the monthly student load climbing from 1,185 in June 1950 to a high of 4,100 in January 1952. All of the expansion in student load, however, was accomplished in the face of a serious shortage of qualified instructors because they were being reassigned to deploying units. As of 1 December 1950, the school had 100 fewer instructors than it had on 1 April 1950 to teach a student load that had more than doubled. The shortage caused Harper to authorize withdrawing student officers from the Officer Advance Course for duty as instructors and to inform the US Army Field Forces about the school's growing difficulties of meeting the required graduate numbers. To reduce the shortages which had become acute by the end of 1950, the Army authorized additional instructor and staff positions on 1 February 1951 and started filling them in the spring of 1951 with reservists, Marines, and civilians. This action raised the school's staff and faculty from 1,289 in June 1950 to 3,097 in June 1951. Unfortunately, the school often received unqualified, low-ranking, non-school graduates as potential instructors and had to take time to train them to prevent instruction standards from dropping even further. Fortunately, the student load dropped to 11,952 in 1952 and the rapid expansion of the mission ceased as the situation in Korea stabilized and reduced some of the personnel turbulence and instructor shortages. Yet, instructor shortages persisted throughout the rest of the war, forcing the school to continue employing inexperienced and unqualified officers which degraded the quality of training.[47]

In the middle of the severe staff and faculty shortages and turnover of instructors that had hindered training since 1945 and that were intensified by the Korean War, Clark directed The Artillery School to submit a plan to reopen the Field Artillery Officer Candidate School that had closed in December 1946. The school tendered its plan on 14 December 1950 that called for a class of 115 students to enter every four weeks, among other things. Upon the approval of Clark with minor changes, The Artillery School activated the Field Artillery Officer Candidate School on 21 February 1951 with 53 officer candidates attending the first course. More than 3,500 second lieutenants graduated from the school during the Korean War.[48]

To be sure, the rapid expansion of The Artillery School, the reestablishment of the Field Artillery Officer Candidate School, and the creation of the Field Artillery Replacement Training Center in 1950 for basic combat training overloaded training facilities to meet mobilization requirements and stepped up the drive to expand and improve the school's physical plant. Fort Sill refurbished buildings on the westernmost part of the post that had been used by the school during World War II, rented classrooms in downtown Lawton, and even examined the possibility of new construction. This latter consideration led to the selection of an officer to coordinate an extensive building program. When it became apparent that a single individual could not manage such a vast effort, the Assistant Commandant of The Artillery School, Brigadier General William H. Colbern (1950-1952), appointed a board of officers to study the school's classroom and housing requirements and make recommendations. The board found Fort Sill to have sufficient facilities to handle the required training load except for the Field Artillery Officer Candidate School. In view of this, Fort Sill transformed mess halls, post exchanges, and recreation halls left over from World War II into classrooms, barracks, and administrative space for the school.[49]

In the midst of this construction, Fort Sill rejuvenated its interest in a new school house to replace McNair Hall as the main academic and administration facility for The Artillery School. As early as 1948, the decentralized nature of the classrooms in the cantonment area south of Old Post and the concurrent camp area (Camp Doniphan) about one mile southwest of Old Post created transportation and scheduling problems and prodded Fort Sill to urge the Army to build a modern school house with state-of-the-art acoustics, classrooms, broadcasting systems, and air conditioning to accommodate year-around training that was already underway. A new facility would permit centralizing training and replacing McNair Hall as the main school house facility. Postwar economy measures even in the face of the heightening Cold War, however, prevented the construction of a new facility.[50]

Started in December 1952 when funding became available, completed in 1954, and named after Major General William J. Snow, the first Chief of Field Artillery (1918-1927) and former commandant of the School of Fire for Field Artillery (1917), Snow Hall was the new school house. It contained administrative offices and classrooms, held almost 2,000 students at one time, housed all officer courses, was air conditioned which was a major innovation at the time to make possible year-around instruction, and completed a dream of a new school house.[51]

Notwithstanding this construction program to meet the needs of The Artillery School during the Korean War and the completion of Snow Hall in 1954, turbulence characterized the school's operations between 1945 and 1953. The rapid demobilization of 1945-1946 caused the loss of staff and faculty, forced the school to write and teach temporary courses as it was developing peacetime programs of instruction, and encouraged economy measures that led to consolidating the three artillery schools and designing cross training and cross assignment to create flexibility in assigning officers and to save money. Just as these initiatives were getting underway, the Korean War compelled The Artillery School to expand its operations virtually overnight to meet the Army's need for trained field artillerymen, straining staff, faculty, and physical facilities alike.

Sustained Military Readiness

Although the end of the Korean War brought about by the July 1953 armistice promised cuts in the military's budget and training requirements, the Cold War with its attending arms race promoted military readiness over the next two decades. For The Artillery School, the Cold War of the 1950s and 1960s led to the introduction of courses to support atomic and nuclear artillery systems, a growing number of graduates after a decline of five years during the modest demobilization after the Korean War, and the acquisition of additional land to accommodate rocket and missile training.

During the 1950s, The Artillery School (1946-1955) which was redesignated as the Artillery and Guided Missile School (1955-1957), the US Army Artillery and Guided Missile School (1957), and the US Army Artillery and Missile School (1957-1969) played a key role in the introduction of cannons, rockets, and guided missiles with the abilities of carrying a conventional, atomic, or nuclear warhead. In May 1955, the US Army Continental Army Command, formerly the US Army Field Forces, charged the Artillery and Guided Missile School with developing doctrine and training for all surface-to-surface artillery weapons, including cannon artillery, rockets, and missiles, and the Antiaircraft Artillery and Guided Missile School with the responsibility of designing doctrine and training for surface-to-air artillery weapons. In support of this reorganization, the Army transferred all surface-to-surface missile courses from Fort Bliss to Fort Sill in 1956 and 1957 to join the Honest John courses already being conducted at the Oklahoma installation and moved two Corporal battalions from Fort Bliss to Fort Sill in 1955-1956 to support the training. Basically, these actions recognized the critical divergence of the two artilleries' weapon systems, made the school with the primary tactical interest in a weapon responsible for training and doctrine, and reaffirmed the existence of two *de facto* artilleries – something that cross training and cross assignment and the Army conveniently ignored in the quest for flexibility and monetary savings.[52]

Introducing atomic and nuclear artillery courses had a two-fold impact on the Fort Sill school and a significant effect on Fort Sill. First, it arrested the decline in the school's student production after the mid-1950s. Student production dropped from 13,061 in 1951 at the height of the Korean War to 6,602 in 1958 and started climbing the following year to reach 8,221 in 1962 as the courses started coming on board.[53] Second, the courses ushered the school into the atomic and nuclear age and diversified its training mission beyond conventional field artillery. To meet the needs of the new weapons, the school integrated instruction on nuclear cannons, rockets, and guided missiles into the Artillery Officer

Advance Course for regular army artillery officers in 1955-1956, added comparable training to the Associate Field Artillery Officer Advance Course for reserve officers in 1956-1957, adopted specialty courses on nuclear warheads for officers and soldiers, introduced courses on the characteristics of atomic and nuclear weapons, and instituted a nuclear weapons employment course for officers in 1961.[54]

Besides teaching students about the blast and thermal and radiation effects of atomic and nuclear weapons, special weapons as they were called, on the battlefield, the nuclear weapons employment course taught their tactical employment. School instructors emphasized that the ideal atomic or nuclear target was of such size, density, composition, or tactical importance that the use of atomic or nuclear weapons was necessary to achieve the desired results and that the tactical advantage gained by its destruction would ensure or materially assist in the accomplishment of the commander's mission.[55]

The addition of 280-mm cannon course and rocket and missile courses also forced Fort Sill to adjust. For example, the Honest John free flight rocket, the 280-mm. cannon, and the guided missiles had ranges that measured in miles rather than yards that had been means of determining range for years. To carry out its training and combat development missions in the nuclear era, Fort Sill required more land than its current 74,000 acres. In 1955, the post initiated action to acquire 31,020 acres – 10,700 acres from the Wichita Mountains Wildlife Refuge that was managed by the Department of the Interior and abutted the northern edge of the installation and 20,320 acres in Comanche County west of Fort Sill that was owned by private individuals. Such a land acquisition would assure adequate space for cannon, rocket, and missile training not only in the present but also in the foreseeable future. Despite support from Oklahoma senators, Robert S. Kerr and Mike Monroney, and Representative Victor Wickersham of the Sixth Congressional District in Oklahoma where Fort Sill was located, private citizens with backing from the Wichita Landowners Association, the Oklahoma Farm Bureau, and the Oklahoma Cattleman's Association fought back. They deluged Congress with letters and petitions to prevent transferring land from the refuge to Fort Sill. Opposed to despoiling the refuge, many people urged the Army to fire their rockets and missiles elsewhere. Despite this vocal resistance, Congress passed legislation on 2 August 1955 to permit transferring the 10,700 acres from the refuge and allocated funding for purchasing the 20,320 acres of privately-owned land.[56]

Several years passed before Congress finally reached a compromise agreement for the refuge land on 6 September 1957. It authorized military maneuvers and training activities under restrictions and stipulations that preserved the recreational and wildlife value of the refuge. Essentially, the agreement set aside 3,600 out of the 10,700 acres of the refuge as a buffer zone with firing only along the outer perimeter of these acres, preserved the integrity of the refuge, and assured no further expansion of Fort Sill onto the refuge.[57]

Although Congress approved purchasing 20,320 acres of privately-own land and appropriated funding and although Cold War imperatives encouraged enlarging the Oklahoma installation even more, Fort Sill meanwhile ran into resolute opposition from local landowners in its quest for the land. Many people in the small communities surrounding Fort Sill opposed selling their land to the Army, disliked the possibility of missiles and rockets straying off course and landing on their property, preferred continuing the practice of sending Fort Sill soldiers and students to the White Sands Missile Range, New Mexico, where there was plenty of land to fire live rockets and missiles, but they lost the fight. On 1 January 1957, the US Army District Engineer Office at Tulsa, Oklahoma, officially transferred 20,320 acres of privately-owned land to Fort Sill to give the post 94,000 acres (its size in 2010).[58]

As the Commanding General of Fort Sill, Major General Thomas E. de Shazo candidly acknowledged in 1957 that the post saw purchasing the 20,320 acres as a step in the right direction and ultimately wanted to purchase an additional 273,000 acres in Kiowa and Caddo Counties to support rocket and missile live-fire training. Championed by retired Major General James C. Styron, commander the 45th Infantry Division of the Oklahoma Army National Guard in the Korean War, a cotton buyer, and a resident of Hobart to the northwest of Fort Sill, the landowners resisted. They formed the Southwest Oklahoma Survival Association to present a unified front to prevent the government from taking their land and in doing so gained support from an entirely unexpected ally.[59]

Although acquiring the 273,000 acres for training soldiers on cannon, rockets, and guided missiles certainly fit into the Army's priorities, the Eisenhower administration and Congress focused their attention and funding on massive retaliation that revolved around strategic bombing by the Air Force, especially after the Soviets launched *Sputnik* in October 1957, and allotted the Army a minor role in national defense. Based upon this priority, Fort Sill's proposal for the additional land beyond the 20,320 acres never received any serious consideration by the Eisenhower administration, the Pentagon, and Congress in 1957-1959 even though de Shazo outlined a cogent rationale for expansion. As a result, the Army and Fort Sill eventually yielded to the obvious. In 1959, Fort Sill abandoned any plans to acquire more acres and announced that the firing portion of rocket and missile training for officers and enlisted personnel would remain at White Sands Missile Range near Fort Bliss because it had plenty of land.[60]

If anything, the battle for more land to accommodate training on long-range atomic and later nuclear field artillery weapons reflected a critical dilemma for the school as it moved into the atomic and nuclear age. At the beginning of the 1950s, Fort Sill lacked the requisite land for live-fire training on such weapons with their ranges measured in miles and not yards and aggressively fought for it. Seeking to play a greater role in national defense that nuclear-capable cannons, rockets, and missiles would bring, the installation acquired land from the Wichita Wildlife Refuge and some private-owned land but never got the additional 273,000 acres desired. This restricted the US Army and Missile School's ability to provide training on nuclear weapons and made it dependent upon the White Sands Missile Range, something that de Shazo and his successors did not want.

The Folly of Integrated Training

Meanwhile, at the direction of the Army Field Forces, The Artillery School reinstituted cross training to reduce costs and promote flexible officer assignments in the face of acute career artillery officer shortages.[61] In May 1951, a board of officers from Fort Sill and Fort Bliss developed an integrated Artillery Officer Advance Course of about 11 months for Fiscal Year 1952 which began in July 1951 to train 200 regular army field artillery officers with at least five years of experience, 100 regular army antiaircraft artillery officers, 50 Marine officers, and 50 allied students on field artillery and antiaircraft artillery tactics, techniques, and procedures and weapons. Out of the 11-month course, nine months of training would be at Fort Sill with the rest at Fort Bliss.[62]

Almost nine months later on 22 March 1952, Clark expanded the integrated training initiative beyond the advance course. He directed The Artillery School and Antiaircraft Artillery School to develop an integrated Associate Battery Officer Course for newly commissioned regular army or reserve component second lieutenants, an integrated Associate Officer Advance Course for reserve component officers or regular army officers who required refresher training, and an integrated Battery Officer Course for regular army officers with at least two years of experience to complement the integrated Artillery Advance Officer Course for regular army officers beginning with the academic year of 1952-1953. Subsequently, a board of officers assembled in the summer of 1952 to determine the proper long-range program of education for artillery officers and endorsed Clark's guidance on cross (integrated) training to promote flexible assignments and to furnish a broad training experience for artillery officers in accordance with the one-branch concept advocated by the Army's Career Management Division. Thus, integration was institutionalized once again even though it produced unqualified officers prior to the Korean War and even though the war was still being fought which placed a premium on qualified and competent officers who possessed subject matter expertise in field artillery or antiaircraft artillery.[63]

As directed by Clark, the school started teaching the integrated Associated Battery Officer Course, the integrated Associated Officer Advance Course, the integrated Officer Advance Course of 36 weeks, and the integrated Battery Officer Course of 25 weeks for the academic year of 1952-1953 to give officers a broad background in artillery tactics and employment. In 1954, the Army added a non-integrated basic course of 17 weeks for all newly commissioned artillery officers. Depending upon their first unit assignment, officers attended the basic course at either Fort Sill for field artillery training or Fort Bliss for antiaircraft artillery training. The continuing shortage of officers later led to integrating the basic course in 1956. The creation of the basic course whether it was integrated or not gave the Artillery and Guided Missile School a three-tier officer education system. In 1955-1956, the school conducted an integrated 17-week Officer Basic Course, an integrated 28-week Battery Officer Career Course, and an integrated 39- week Officer Advance Course with 10 weeks of transition training for antiaircraft artillery officers in field artillery and similar training for field artillery officers in antiaircraft artillery.[64]

Although integration seemed to meet the needs for broadly trained artillery officers who could serve in either antiaircraft artillery or field artillery units, to save money and to mitigate officer shortages, serious objections to cross training reemerged. On 9 February 1955, the Commanding General of the US Continental Army Command (formerly US Army Field Forces through February 1955), General John S. Dahlquist, questioned the wisdom of cross training in light of the complexity of field artillery and antiaircraft artillery equipment and weapons and the differing specialized techniques for the two artilleries. Basically, he recognized the existence of two *de facto* artillery branches with their separate weapon systems, tactics, organizations, and missions. Because some officers left the service after completing their initial obligation and only required training in one of the branches, he also wanted to abandon integrated training in the basic and battery courses but to retain it in the advance course for career officers. Later in March 1955, the Deputy Chief of Staff for Logistics, Lieutenant General W.B. Palmer, also criticized cross training. He wrote that the techniques practiced by both artilleries were becoming so diversified that it was impossible for any officer to be skilled in one let alone two artilleries. In view of Dahlquest's, Palmer's, Fort Sill's, and Fort Bliss's opposition to cross training, Major General Paul D. Adams, Acting Assistant Chief of Staff for Operations for the Army, announced the Army's decision on 11 June 1955 to establish separate Field Artillery and Antiaircraft Artillery Battery Officer Courses in Fiscal Year 1956 (July 1955-June 1956) and separate field artillery and antiaircraft artillery officer basic courses in Fiscal Year 1956.[65]

Although personnel shortages prevented initiating these actions in Fiscal Year 1956 as intended, the Chief of Staff of the Army, General Maxwell D. Taylor, reinforced the Army's commitment to separate basic and battery courses and simultaneously elucidated his conditional opposition to cross training on 29 March 1956. While the Artillery and Guided Missile School at Fort Sill would focus on developing tactical and training doctrine for surface-to-surface artillery, the Antiaircraft Artillery and Guided Missile School would center its attention on developing tactical and training doctrine for surface-to-air artillery. Cross training second and first lieutenants would be abolished by 1957. However, it would remain for captains in the advance course.[66]

With the issue of integration still lingering and controversial, the US Continental Army Command rejoined the debate. In June 1957, it announced its disagreement with cross training because the two artilleries had fundamentally different doctrine, tactics, and techniques for employment and had different responsibilities on the battlefield. Equally important, cross training produced a "group of jack-of-all trades and masters-of-none." As a result, the command only endorsed cross training for captains in the advance course for the same reasons that Dahlquist had enumerated two years earlier.[67]

The Artillery and Guided Missile School also voiced its opposition to cross training. It found cross training to be wasteful of travel funds, instructors, school facilities, talent, and time. The monetary cost alone for student travel and temporary duty for the advance course was almost $90,000 a year. Moreover, as the two artilleries were becoming more technical, cross training became less effective and produced less qualified officers. In fact, tests conducted by the Artillery and Guided Missile School in 1956 reaffirmed this. Officers lacked the basic knowledge required by antiaircraft artillery officers and field artillery officers in their respective branches, while moving officers between the two artilleries further complicated gaining any professional expertise in either branch and produced a generalist just when specialists were required.[68]

Snow Hall, pictured from 1957, has been the school house since 1954

As the Fort Sill school noted, the Korean War also reinforced the futility of cross training. During the war, officers usually did not move between antiaircraft artillery and field artillery assignments. If an antiaircraft artillery officer was assigned to a field artillery unit, the individual generally served in the S-1 (operations), S-4 (supply), the headquarters and headquarters battery, or service battery. An antiaircraft artillery officer very seldom served in a firing battery where the knowledge of field artillery gunnery was an imperative. As a result, any training in field artillery for antiaircraft artillery officers was not fully utilized and was wasteful. Also, as surface-to-air missiles and surface-to-surface missiles were becoming operational in the mid-1950s, the need for greater specialization grew. The complexity of the new weapons, the differing techniques required, and the economic limitations placed upon the length of time in training dictated a new training strategy. For these reasons along with the inclusion of redundant refresher instruction in the Officer Advance Course, the Artillery and Guided Missile School recommended on 8 May 1956 to create separate basic, battery, and advance courses and even proposed forming separate artilleries.[69]

In a letter to the Commanding General of the Antiaircraft Artillery and Guided Missile School in October 1956, Major General Robert J. Wood, and the Commandant of the Artillery and Missile School, Major General Thomas E. de Shazo (1956-1959), explained additional reasons for abandoning cross training. Although he endorsed cross training when he was the assistant commandant of The Artillery School late in the 1940s, he now opposed it. He wrote, "So far integration (cross training) has not been successful in accomplishing the objectives assigned it."[70] De Shazo added, "Comments from Artillery Commanders who have had the responsibility of supporting infantry and armor in ground combat have, over the last few years, indicated a rather shocking lack of technical knowledge by junior field artillery officers."[71] In unambiguous language he then noted,

> "No longer can we expect the officer to be technically qualified in cannon type AAA [antiaircraft artillery] and FA [field artillery] as well as in SAM [surface-to-air missiles] and SSM [surface-to-surface missiles]. As a matter of fact it is my understanding that it has proven virtually impossible to cross-train effectively the majority of antiaircraft artillery officers in the weapon systems of their own arm alone"[72]

The general also pointed out, "As the artilleries have become more technical cross-training has become more difficult until today the effective cross-training of artillery officers has become virtually impossible."[73]

De Shazo raised other arguments against cross training. In a letter to Wood on 16 May 1956, he explained that it was wasteful of travel funds, talent, and time, destroyed *esprit de corps* among field artillery officers and antiaircraft artillery officers, hampered unit readiness, and produced unqualified field artillery officers.[74] Cross training also decreased professional qualifications. For these reasons, he urged separating the artilleries and abolishing cross training and cross assignments.[75]

Despite de Shazo's cogent argument and the Army's decision of 1955 to end integrated training in Fiscal Year 1957, personnel shortages deterred separation and caused integration to remain a vital part of instruction. The Army and Guided Missile School retained responsibility for all surface-to-surface artillery training which included guided missiles, such as the Corporal missile, and free-flight rockets, such as the Honest John, below the advance course level; the Fort Bliss school kept responsibility for all surface-to-air artillery training below the advance course level. Newly commissioned officers graduating from the US Military Academy and Distinguished Military Graduates from the Reserved Officer Training Corps attended a non-integrated basic course of 22 weeks beginning in 1958. A non-integrated battery officer course for artillery officers with two to five years of experience followed the basic course. An integrated advance course came afterward for artillery officers with five to 12 years of experience.[76]

However, this training system for junior officers soon changed. The Career Management Division of the Department of the Army recommended abandoning the three-tier education system for junior officers for a two-tier system consisting of a basic course and an advance course to save money and reduce the time spent in training. At the time a regular army artillery officer went through 85 to 92 weeks of training in comparison to a regular army infantry officer who had 48 weeks of training and a regular army armor officer who had 52 weeks of training. Upon implementing the Career Management Division's recommendations in 1959, the US Continental Army Command abandoned the battery course, adopted a non-integrated basic artillery course for newly commissioned officers, and retained the integrated advance course for career artillery officers with three to eight years of experience to promote flexible assignments to overcome the acute shortage of career artillery officers and to permit cross assignment. Although the experts wanted to abandon integrated training totally and favored specialized branch training, personnel officers who supported flexible assignment capabilities and career officer shortages convinced the Army to retain integrated training and cross assignments for captains and above. Thus, the needs of the personnel system with its emphasis upon flexible assignment procedures and economy measures won even though the officer education system was producing artillery officers of doubtful qualifications.[77]

As projected by the Army Artillery and Missile School, integrated training in the Officer Advance Course failed to produce competent career field artillery or antiaircraft artillery officers. In a letter in July 1962, just three years after the reforms of 1959 had eliminated cross training from all artillery officer education except for the Officer Advance Course, the Assistant Commandant of the US Army Artillery and Missile School, Brigadier General Edwin S. Hartshorn (1959-1962), complained to the Commandant, Major General Lewis S. Griffing (1961-1964), about the poor quality of the graduates of the school's integrated Officer Advance Course. The course duplicated instruction from the non-integrated Officer Basic Courses to give antiaircraft artillery-oriented captains some background in field artillery and field artillery-oriented captains some training in antiaircraft artillery. Repeating instruction from the basic courses prevented allotting sufficient to time for detailed instruction on field artillery and antiaircraft artillery weapons and created incompetent captains.[78]

Hartshorn's concerns and similar ones by the US Army Antiaircraft Artillery and Guided Missile School led to an extensive study in 1963 under the direction of the Commanding General of the US Continental Army Command, General John K. Waters, to examine separating the two artilleries and creating a US Continental Army Command position on the issue. The study group found that integration failed to produce any significant economies and did not create a viable base of trained and competent officers in adequate numbers to work in both the Field Artillery and the Antiaircraft Artillery, renamed the Air Defense Artillery in 1957 to reflect its dual mission of antiaircraft and antimissile defense. In view of these conclusions, the study group urged separating the two artilleries. The acting Commanding General of the US Continental Army Command, Lieutenant General E.J. Messinger, concurred and proposed discontinuing cross training and cross assignment below the grade of lieutenant colonel. Although most of the Army's staff agreed with Messinger, the Office of Personnel Operations vigorously contested the study's conclusions because it advocated assignment flexibility in all grades to meet mobilization requirements along the lines of World War II; the move for separation stalled. Basically, the influence of World War II where the Coast Artillery, Antiaircraft Artillery, and Field Artillery often performed each others' missions and where antiaircraft artillery officers had often transferred from antiaircraft artillery units to field artillery units once the air war had been won still dominated the thinking of the Office of Personnel Operations and many senior officers outside of the Artillery. Flexibility was more important than competency.

Cross training and assignment for artillery officers with five to 12 years of experience continued even though the experts in the Artillery advised to abolish the practices.[79]

Appointed by Department of the Army orders of 23 June 1965, the Board to Review Army Officer Schools under Lieutenant General Ralph E. Haines, Jr., commonly called the Haines Board, reexamined cross training and reached the same conclusions that Hartshorn had arrived at a few years earlier and that had generated the US Continental Army Command study of 1963. Over a period of seven months beginning in July 1965, the board assiduously assembled information and conducted interviews with key Army officials closely involved in officer education. The board also analyzed the results of the board headed by Lieutenant General Leonard T. Gerow in 1945 that had established the post-World War II education system for officers, the board chaired by Lieutenant General Manton S. Eddy in 1948 that had reviewed the Gerow board recommendations, and the board led by Lieutenant General Edward T. Williams in 1958 that had evaluated officer education to determine its strengths and weaknesses. In its report of February 1966, the Haines Board questioned the validity of cross training career artillery officers. In the Officer Advance Course artillery officers received 24 weeks of instruction at the US Army Artillery and Missile School where they went through common artillery instruction and field artillery instruction and underwent eight weeks of air defense artillery instruction at the US Army Air Defense Artillery School. As the Haines Board observed, 76 hours of instruction in the Officer Advance Course at Fort Sill overlapped the gunnery, survey, and artillery transport instruction taught in the Field Artillery Officer Basic Course. This training proved to be redundant for field artillery officers because they had received it in the basic course but it was also required for air defense artillery captains. At the Air Defense School, the Haines Board found 83 hours of instruction in the advance course to be unwarranted for air defense artillery officers who had graduated from the Air Defense Artillery Officer Basic Course but necessary for field artillery captains. More seriously, those students who had been cross-trained had 10 weeks of unneeded instruction.[80]

Based upon these findings, the Board advised eliminating this refresher training and offering remedial training only to those officers who required it. All incoming student officers would take a test to determine their competency in field artillery or air defense artillery depending upon their branch assignment. Only those who failed the test would receive remedial training in the appropriate subject area. As a result, qualified officers would spend more time on advanced work and would not be slowed down by refresher training. Basically, the Officer Advance Course with its extensive amount of refresher training in both artilleries failed to produce competent captains to serve as battery commanders because it spent too much time on basic instruction, taught basic field artillery and air defense artillery skills, and did not devote sufficient training on advanced subjects in either artillery.[81]

Although the Haines Board recommendations failed to prod the Army to abandon cross training, the continued outcries over redundant training and the fallacies of cross training and cross assignment sharpened during the Vietnam War where they were tested under combat conditions for the second time, found to be wanting, leading to serious reform.

Indications of the shortcomings of integration emerged in 1965-1966 and caused cross assignments to be severely restricted which was reminiscent of the pattern established in the Korean War when integration basically did not exist. The challenging field artillery gunnery problems encountered, the short tours that emphasized the need for officers to arrive in Vietnam fully competent as field artillery officers, and the personnel policies that stressed cross training and cross assignment and concurrently decreased the combat efficiency of field artillery units prompted the Army to form a study group in 1966.[82]

Under Colonel A.D. Pickard, Chief of the Artillery Branch, Officer Personnel Directorate, Office of Personnel Operations, the study group investigated the impact of current officer personnel policies upon the combat efficiency of units and upon the proficiency of the individual artillery officer. Echoing the Haines Board report, Pickard's study, known as The Artillery Branch Study of 1966-1967, concluded, "Integration of artillery training has spawned mediocrity. The Advanced Course has been necessarily oriented to officers who cannot assimilate the desired level of instruction without first being provided the basics. The cross training for at least 70 percent of the class represents time, money and effort which will never be recovered."[83] The study continued:

> The officer facing cross assignment after graduation, will still require additional training to qualify for the new assignment. . . . The field artillery commanders in Vietnam have identified three areas needing improvement within the officer corps of the branch. Artillery officers: must be better ground in gunnery, must be proficient and able to operate upon arrival in Vietnam and should not be Air Defense officers.[84]

As the study pointed out, the one-year tour of duty in Vietnam left little time for on-the-job training in the basic techniques of field artillery and required captains to arrive fully trained and competent to command in decentralized field artillery operations. Cross training and cross assignment simply degraded the quality of the career field artillery officers arriving for duty in Vietnam.[85]

As the Artillery Branch Study concluded, cross training and cross assignments never lived up to the dreams of their originators. Although the designers of the 1940s and 1950s were combat-experienced officers, they proposed a system based upon conditions during and immediately after World War II and the perception that once the air war had been won there would not be any need for antiaircraft artillery and that this situation would permit transferring antiaircraft artillery officers to field artillery units. The designers also failed to foresee the accelerated development of technology that divided the two artilleries into totally separate branches or the Korean War where the cross assignment of officers was minimal. While cross training attempted to train officers with five to eight years of experience in all artillery subjects to permit flexible assignments, cross assignment placed them in positions for which they lacked the qualifications and concurrently degraded unit readiness.[86]

Based upon the recommendations of The Artillery Branch Study of 1966-1967 to abolish cross training and cross assignment, the pressure to send competent field artillery captains to Vietnam for battery command, and the recognition that the doctrines, missions, equipment, and techniques of air defense artillery and field artillery widely diverged and required different skills, the Army restructured the two artilleries in 1968. Acknowledging the futility of training officers in the employment of both, the Army divided the Artillery into the Air Defense Artillery and the Field Artillery on 28 May 1968. Later, Department of the Army orders of 20 January 1969 officially redesignated the US Army Artillery and Missile School as the US Army Field Artillery School and the US Army Antiaircraft Artillery and Guided Missile School as the US Army Air Defense Artillery School to reflect the total separation of the two.[87]

This action ended cross training and cross assignments, both of which were dismal failures. While the former produced career officers without any solid credentials in their specialty as field artillery or antiaircraft artillery officers, the latter certainly did not promote expertise either by rotating officers between the two artilleries and creating generalists notwithstanding the specialty courses and hurt unit readiness. Fortunately, the separation advanced specialization in an era of growing technological sophistication to end the attempt to produce a generic artillery officer who could serve in either branch but not well.

Building the Future Force

As it struggled to reform officer education to match the reality of the new technology, The Artillery School (1946-1955) and its successors meanwhile actively participated in the Army's modernization effort. Although it abolished the Department of Research and Analysis on 31 October 1949 which had a combat developments mission, the school assumed the lead for the Army in the 1950s and 1960s in writing field artillery doctrine, developing tactics, designing field artillery force structure, formulating materiel requirements, and forecasting future needs.[88] Doctrinally, the US Army Artillery and Missile School (1957-1969) revised the Field Artillery's cornerstone doctrinal manual, *Field Manual 6-20, Artillery Tactics and Techniques*, in 1958 to ensure responsive fire support on the emerging nuclear battlefield.[89]

To implement doctrine, the school understood the imperative of introducing improved target acquisition systems, weapon systems, command and control systems, and support systems. Acknowledging that forward observation was limited to daylight hours with good visibility and that existing sound ranging and flash ranging systems were unsuitable for mobile warfare, the school saw the need for better target acquisition systems. Specifically, it wanted systems with the ability to detect hostile batteries beyond 20,000 yards in all weather and on all terrain, hoped to develop a target acquisition system with the capability of locating enemy indirect fire systems, especially nuclear artillery, before they could fire, and even investigated employing radar and drone aircraft to complement ground and aerial observers. Although the Army employed the SCR 784 radar effectively during World War II to find enemy indirect fire systems, primarily mortars, the pressure for more accurate target location information and faster response times for a battlefield that was growing more mobile led to the development of the AN/TPQ-10 Countermortar Radar in 1952 and the AN/TPQ-4 Countermortar Radar in 1958 to supplant the SCR 784. While the Q-4 replaced the AN/TPQ-10 Countermortar Radar in the countermortar role, the Q-10 retained its counterartillery mission. The Q-4 and Q-10 radars were more mobile, could locate enemy indirect fire systems much faster and more accurately, and could scan a larger search sector than the SCR 784 and World War II vintage sound ranging and flash ranging technology could do.[90]

Once targets had been located, towed and self-propelled artillery had to respond rapidly. Observing the requirement for greater dispersion and mobility to improve survivability on the tactical nuclear battlefield, the school's Department of Gunnery under Colonel W.E. Showalter pointed out in 1957 the imperative of attacking targets in any direction with speed and effectiveness. This meant developing a firing chart that permitted shooting in a complete circle (6400 mils/360 degrees) to support the Pentomic infantry, armor, and airborne divisions under development because existing ones provided only 3200-mil capabilities and were designed for a linear battlefield.[91] Without an urgent need, the Gunnery Department, however, failed to make any serious progress designing a 6400-mil chart during the remaining years of the 1950s. The Vietnam War of the 1960s with its dispersed battery operations furnished the pressing requirement for providing fires in a complete circle at fire support bases and finally caused the Gunnery Department to create a firing chart in 1966 with 6400-mil coverage.[92]

Fighting on the future battlefield with 6400-mil capabilities involved more than developing new firing charts and gunnery methods. Initially, field artillerymen improvised by adapting existing technology to fire in a complete circle. Building upon the initial efforts of First Lieutenant Nathaniel Foster of the 8th Battalion, 6th Field Artillery in Vietnam, the Gunnery Department developed a speed shift pedestal for the towed M114 155-mm. howitzer in 1964-1965 to permit rapid traverse through 6400 mils with a field artillery piece designed for only 872 mils. Field artillerymen would have to improvise because existing field artillery lacked 6400-mil traverse capabilities.[93]

Fortunately at the same time that Showalter saw the need for a chart with 6400-mil capabilities, the Army, with the US Army Artillery and Missile School (1957-1969) playing a key role, established the requirements and characteristics for a new family of field artillery weapons that were fielded early in the 1960s (the towed M102 105-mm. howitzer, the self-propelled M107 175-mm. gun, the self-propelled M108 105-mm. howitzer, the self-propelled M109 155-mm. howitzer, and the self-propelled M110 8-inch howitzer). These weapon systems had increased traverse, more mobility and firepower, and better survivability and lethality than their predecessors and promised to furnish effective fire support on the tactical nuclear battlefield. While the M107 and M110 lacked 6400-mil capabilities, the M102 with a pedestal firing platform under its carriage and a roller tire attached to the trail assembly and the M108 and M109 with their turrets had the ability to traverse through 6400 mils, making them ideal for the future battlefield, and allowed fire direction centers to exploit the new 6400-mil firing chart.[94]

The search for more responsive firepower, meanwhile, sparked interest in aerial rocket artillery (helicopters armed with rockets and machine guns) and air assault artillery (towed artillery airlifted by helicopters). In view of the tests of the 11th Air Assault Division being conducted at Fort Benning, Georgia, to determine the feasibility of the air mobility concept where men and equipment would be transported by air, including field artillery, the Commandant of the US Army Artillery and Missile School, Major General Lewis S. Griffing (1961-1964), obtained CH-34 (Choctaw) helicopters in January 1963 and equipped them with 4.5-inch rockets and machine guns to determine the viability of transporting field artillery weapons by air and firing them from aerial platforms if necessary. Under the direction of the Committee for Aerial Artillery Test and Evaluation composed of representatives from each of the school's departments, the US Army Artillery Board, and the US Army Combat Developments Command Artillery Agency, the 1st Aerial Artillery Battery, a provisional unit organized in April 1963, evaluated the aerial rocket artillery concept. During 1963-1964, the battery fired more than 13,000 rounds of ammunition, flew more than 1,200 hours, and demonstrated the practicality of mounting rockets and machine guns on an aerial platform for use in air-to-ground and even ground-to-ground fire.[95]

While these tests persuaded the school of the ability of aerial rocket artillery to furnish fire support on the future battlefield, the 11th Air Assault Division tests that included airlifting towed 105-mm. howitzers by helicopter, a concept that had been tested at Fort Sill late in the 1950s, led the school to see the utility of air assault artillery.[96] In fact, Colonel Samuel Ross, director of the Gunnery Department, pointed out in 1964, "The School is convinced that aerial artillery [aerial rocket artillery and air assault artillery] will fill a vital role in future skirmishes. Its value will undoubtedly be noted in mountain, jungle, and delta operations where, as in all warfare, we [field artillerymen] must maintain a balance between firepower and mobility."[97]

The success of these tests with aerial rocket artillery and air assault artillery along with the other tests with the 11th Air Assault Division led to redesignating it as the 1st Cavalry Division in 1964. Division artillery was initially composed of towed 105-mm. howitzers that would be airlifted from position to position by helicopter (CH-47 Chinook and UH-1 Iroquois), aerial rocket artillery, and the Little John rocket system that could carry a conventional or nuclear warhead. When the Little John was dropped as general support artillery in 1965 to make the division even more mobile, the 1st Cavalry Division's field artillery thereafter consisted of towed howitzers for direct support and aerial rocket artillery for general support. Such air-transportable capabilities freed field artillery units from the tyranny of the terrain and permitted moving them rapidly around the battlefield.[98]

The drive for more responsive field artillery also prompted the development of automated technical fire direction. As early as 1950, The Artillery School had reached the conclusion about the necessity of automating technical fire direction to achieve rapid, first-round accuracy without registration, to take advantage of long-range field artillery systems, especially rockets and guided missiles, scheduled for fielding during the next decade, and to eliminate human error. This led to the M15 analog computer of the mid-1950s.[99]

Dissatisfied with the M15's inability to compute firing data for field artillery weapons with ranges beyond 15,000 yards and more than one weapon system, the US Continental Army Command joined the search for a suitable computer. In a letter to the Deputy

Chief of Staff for Military Operations in July 1956, the US Continental Army Command outlined its interest in employing automatic data processing systems in field operations and subsequently directed its subordinate commands to provide recommendations where they might be effectively employed. In a reply to this tasking, the Artillery and Guided Missile School proposed automating technical fire direction, target analysis, the volume and quantity of fire to place on a target, post-strike analysis, fire planning, survey data processing, target acquisition, and ammunition status. After considering this input, the command told the school to perform a system analysis study for the field artillery functions of fire control, survey, and ammunition status to determine how automation would improve fire support in these areas.[100]

The school's subsequent study and other comparable Army studies led to the development of the M18 Field Artillery Digital Automated Computer with advocates boasting at the beginning of the 1960s that it would give them first round hits and provide the requisite surprise on the tactical nuclear battlefield. Although the Field Artillery Digital Automated Computer never supplied first-round hit capability and failed to eliminate the manual computation of fire direction data as desired, it supplanted the M15 analog computer and reduced fatigue and errors by fire direction center personnel in Vietnam. The shortage of spare parts, however, caused the computer to be inoperable much of the time and prompted field artillerymen of all ranks to question its utility.[101]

As its involvement with the development of the Field Artillery Digital Automated Computer and other field artillery systems indicated, The Artillery School and its successors played an invaluable role in combat developments to complement its training mission. Moving into the mid-1960s, the school began to realize the fruits of its labors with the fielding of new radar target acquisition systems, the M102, M107, M108, M109, and M110 howitzers, and the Field Artillery Digital Automated Computer. Ironically, cross training and assignment limited the impact of the advancements in doctrine, weapons, and equipment because they failed to produce competent field artillery officers, especially captains, with the abilities to exploit the new technology.

Rice Paddies and Jungles

As the US Army Artillery and Missile School worked to introduce new weapons and field artillery systems to support a tactical nuclear battlefield, the United States advisory effort in Vietnam began in September 1950 when United States Military Assistance Advisory Group opened its headquarters in Saigon to buttress up a failing French military endeavor. During the 1950s and early 1960s, the American advisory endeavor evolved from a modest effort to a more involved one. For example, at first most field artillery advisors were at the highest levels of the Military Advisory Assistance Group. After the French left in 1954, Military Assistance Advisory Group advisors helped reorganize and train the Army of the Republic of Vietnam but rarely had any contact with individual field artillery units. Following President John F. Kennedy's decision of late 1961 to send more advisors, thereby increasing the American commitment to the Republic of South

Vietnam, field artillery advisors began working directly with field artillery battalions and division and corps artilleries as a part of the Military Assistance Command, Vietnam which replaced the Military Advisory Assistance Group in 1962, but they focused their efforts at the battalion. A three-man team composed of a captain, first lieutenant, and staff sergeant assisted the Vietnamese unit commander and his staff with administrative procedures, personnel management, logistics, communications, and operations with the emphasis on the tactical employment of field artillery and maintenance, among other responsibilities. Specifically, the officers furnished advice on all matters concerning unit effectiveness, while the noncommissioned officer concentrated on planning, organizing, and supervising training of the firing battery and individual gun sections.[102]

The Army only picked the best to serve on advisory teams. Both officers and noncommissioned officers were professional, knowledgeable, and aggressive. However, they learned quickly that they could only advise and not lead which often meant that their advice was rejected by the Vietnamese commander who had often received field artillery training at Fort Sill. In fact, 663 Vietnamese officers went through field artillery training between 1953 and 1973 with the peak attendance coming in 1960-1964 when yearly attendance exceeded 60 per year.[103]

Before assuming their duties, all advisors attended the Military Assistance Training Agency course at Fort Bragg, North Carolina. Here, they became acquainted with Vietnam and its people, government, and history and received basic language training to prepare them for their duties. In the Fort Bragg course, field artillery advisors also underwent training in Vietnamese methods of employing field artillery and after 1962 attended resident courses at Fort Sill.[104]

To prepare field artillerymen for duty as advisors and the unique combat circumstances in South Vietnam that differed significantly from Europe where the Army's focus had been since 1953 following the Korean War, the US Army Artillery and Missile School integrated instruction on guerrilla and jungle warfare into its programs of instruction beginning in August 1961. By 1962, all officer and enlisted courses contained basic theoretical instruction on guerrilla warfare that covered the doctrinal foundations of communist guerrilla warfare, the characteristics of communist guerrilla operations, and defense against guerrilla warfare. Jungle warfare classes dealt with the general considerations of jungle operations, jungle weather, terrain, and vegetation, the effects of a jungle environment on operations, including field artillery, and the tactical modifications required to fight in a jungle. Unlike its other officer and enlisted courses with their focus on theory, the school's Officer Advance Course provided a practical exercise in infantry brigade operations and field artillery support in special warfare and jungle operations. Even with these additions to the program of instruction, the school's main focus still centered on fighting in Europe against the armored and mechanized forces of the Soviet Union and Warsaw Pact. Jungle warfare was on the periphery of instruction.[105]

In August 1961 in an article in *Artillery Trends*, Captain C.R. Leach of the Tactics/Combined Arms Department provided the school's rationale for the instruction in guerrilla warfare. He explained, "Artillerymen must be prepared to render effective fire support whenever and wherever needed."[106] This involved adjusting traditional methods and recognizing the impact of guerrilla tactics upon the effectiveness of field artillery fire support. For the most part, fire support, even though it would inflict little material damage, would be critical because it would demoralize the guerrilla forces. Fighting guerrilla forces meant taking the "initiative . . . in situations which called for immediate action."[107] Officers had to be aggressive. Leach added, "Of course, the destruction of the guerrilla forces must of necessity be carried on by the infantry and cavalry reconnaissance units. The mission of the artillery will be to provide fire support to these forces. Frequently, there will be nothing to shoot at."[108]

Forecasting future combat action for American field artillery in Vietnam, Leach pointed out in 1961 potential operational scenarios. The battery might be broken down into platoons or even a single howitzer section, while helicopters might provide the required mobility.[109] He concluded:

> The traditional role of the US artillery will remain that of providing effective fire support for the forces engaged in counterguerrilla operations. Equipment can be tailored and men can be trained to do the job, but the effectiveness of the support which the artillery will be called upon to provide will be directly proportional to the leadership and flexible thinking of the artillery commanders at all levels.[110]

As Leach strongly suggested with support from the school's leadership, field artillery leaders, both officer and noncommissioned officers, had to be adaptive and adjust to tactical circumstances that differed from tactics, techniques, and procedures for fighting in Europe that still predominated instruction and practical exercises in the school. Officers had to look beyond the current field manuals for guidance and had to be innovative.[111]

In an article in *Artillery Trends* in August 1961, Major Richard M. Jennings of the Tactics/Combined Arms Department reiterated Leach's message and expressed his own thoughts. Tactical employment centered upon decentralized field artillery units and called for a quick reaction to engage fleeting targets with fires.[112] Jennings then warned, "The Artillery must be prepared to participate in jungle warfare. . . . If artillery units are properly trained in jungle fighting, artillery fire support will be fast and accurate and will contribute decisively to the success of the battle."[113]

Over the next several years, special warfare and jungle warfare gradually assumed greater interest in the school and pushed conventional warfare or high intensity warfare into the background. "Of special concern to the United States has been a small country considered to be one of the last road-blocks halting Communism in Asia – South Vietnam," the school recorded in 1964.[114] In view of this, the school expanded the number of classes in 1964 on "jungle-type" warfare being fought in Vietnam in its programs of instruction to prepare field artillerymen to serve as military advisors there with the Tactics/Combined Arms Department furnishing the majority of the instruction on counterinsurgency operations, unconventional warfare, and psychological warfare.[115]

From 1965, the "Vietnam Crisis" absorbed most of the school's attention and time.[116]

As to be expected, this transition caused the school to revamp its programs of instruction to reflect the combat situation in Southeast Asia. In its Officer Advance Course it added instruction on internal defense and initiated night illumination shoots in 1965. One year later, the school adopted practical exercises on airmobile operations, designed and built a Vietnamese village on Fort Sill's East Range, called Tran Hoa, for training exercises. One section of the village was "friendly," while the other was a Viet Cong or guerrilla village complete with booby traps, tunnels, and huts with secretive escape doors. That same year, the school commenced instruction on battery defense, developed a new firing chart to simplify 6400-mil coverage to facilitate fire support from fire bases, used practical exercises to train officers and enlisted soldiers how to fire in a complete circle, trained students on the preparation of a landing zone with field artillery fires, taught soldiers how to adjust fire by sound, and tripled the size of its Field Artillery Radar Operator's Course to meet the need for more radar technicians in Vietnam. The school also constructed two fire support bases for practical exercises to provide students with a realistic full-scale preview of combat action in Vietnam, taught riverine operations (the use of landing craft of varying sizes to transport combat forces, including field artillery, along rivers), furnished counterinsurgency packets for Army-wide distribution, and expanded its Noncommissioned Officer Candidate School in 1968 to produce more graduates to meet the growing demand for more noncommissioned officers in Vietnam. In March 1968, the Office of the Director of Instruction added a five-week Field Artillery Officer Vietnam Orientation Course for all field artillery officers before they went to Vietnam to review field artillery subjects and teach special procedures, such as zone-to-zone transfer, 6400-mil firing chart, and other tactics, techniques, and procedures that were unique to combat in Vietnam.[117]

To keep these classes, commanders, and units current on the latest developments and tactics, techniques, and procedures, the school took aggressive measures. First, it corresponded with field artillery commanders in South Vietnam and integrated the information gained into its curriculum. By 1968, information gleaned from letters, official reports, after-action reports, and even 35-mm. color slides formed the basis of lessons learned for the program of instruction. Second, the school dispatched liaison teams to South Vietnam to solicit lessons learned for dissemination. In September 1967, the Commandant of the US Army Artillery and Missile School, Major General Charles P. Brown (1967-1970), led one such team. The team conducted extensive interviews at all levels of command and returned with critical information. Although his team learned that overall field artillery employment was excellent, Brown found the need for more Vietnamese-specific training and requirement for the increased emphasis on 6400-mil fire direction procedures. Third, the school sent training teams to stateside units to keep them abreast of the latest doctrine, trends, developments, and equipment in the field artillery.[118]

For the school, the liaison teams, training teams, and correspondence with commanders in Vietnam revealed a critical shift in emphasis. From 1965 through 1971 when American involvement in the Vietnam War began winding down, all of the school's teaching departments stressed counterinsurgency and jungle warfare in their programs of instruction. This contrasted remarkably with the pre-Vietnam war years. Since the mid-1950s, the school had emphasized fighting on a tactical nuclear battlefield in Europe against a heavily mechanized and armored force. Although it increased instruction and training on guerrilla warfare and jungle warfare, the school never totally abandoned training field artillerymen for the tactical nuclear battlefield by furnishing some instruction specially designed for Europe.[119]

Concurrently, the commitment in Vietnam forced the US Army Artillery and Missile School to step up the pace of its operations to meet the requirement for trained field artillerymen in the midst of a shrinking staff and faculty. In 1965, experienced field artillery captains were being pulled from instructor positions and being sent to Vietnam. Along with other school personnel being shipped to Vietnam, this triggered staff and faculty turbulence. More importantly, the loss of experienced captains as instructors compelled the school to turn to inexperienced first lieutenants and later civilians. In response to the loss of instructors, the school wrote, "Vietnam is affecting everyone. As the world watches the growing crisis in Southeast Asia, the impact of Vietnam is felt hardest among military agencies, and the United States Army and Missile School is no exception" as its staff and faculty declined in numbers. Interestingly, the school had a difficult time retaining gunnery instructors because operational units in Vietnam required their skills.[120]

Although the instructor drain continued into 1966-1967 with more and more officers and enlisted personnel deploying to Vietnam, returning Vietnam veterans offered singular opportunities to offset the losses. To take advantage of their experience, the school made them instructors and augmented them with select graduates of officer courses who had demonstrated exceptional proficiency in gunnery. After 1967, as the instructor pool continued to shrink, the school even used enlisted soldiers who displayed mathematical skills and a proficiency in fire direction as gunnery instructors. The main source of gunnery instructors, however, remained graduates of the Field Artillery Officer Candidate School. Of the 257 gunnery instructors in 1967, 118 were second lieutenants right out of the school.[121]

Against this backdrop of personnel instability caused by the rapid turnover in staff and faculty, the school experienced a significant increase in student population that taxed its shrinking faculty base. The number of graduates grew from 12,550 in 1965, to 19,000 in 1966, to 22,600 in 1967, to more than 23,000 in 1968, representing the peak number of students during the Vietnam War. The Field Artillery Officer Candidate School, which was a part of the school, also felt the strain. In 1967, it commissioned 6,287 second lieutenants to eclipse the previous high of 1,932 established in 1952 during the Korean War. To accommodate this overnight growth, the US Army Artillery and Missile School enlarged the Field Artillery Officer Candidate School from two to six battalions, constructed an additional 13 barracks and five buildings to house battalion headquarters and supply facilities, and renovated about 80 barracks and classrooms in 1966. This focus on combat in Vietnam started declining in 1970 as the United States increased its emphasis on Vietnamization, where the South Vietnamese took more responsibility for their own defense, and came to a final end in 1975 when the last of the combat units left, permitting the school to shift its attention back to Europe.[122]

During the 28 years following World War II, the Cold War compelled The Artillery

School and its successors to maintain a hectic pace that was more frantic at times than other times as the Vietnam War years attested. The student load and number of graduates rose and fell depending upon the temperature of the Cold War, creating a roller coaster effect. Despite this, the school remained focused on training officers and soldiers for the tactical nuclear battlefield and after the early 1960s for Vietnam, introduced new tactics and doctrine, and participated in developing new equipment, and weapons.

Notes

1   Artillery Branch Study of 1966-1967, pp. 30-31, UF23.5 L12A41, Morris Swett Technical Library (MSTL), US Army Field Artillery School, Fort Sill; "Reorganization of the War Department and the Army," *Field Artillery Journal*, Jun 1946, pp. 339-43.

2   Artillery Branch Study of 1966-1967, pp. 30-31, UF23.5 L12A41, MSTL; Russell M. Weigley, *History of the United States Army* (Bloomington, IN: Indiana University Press, 1984), pp. 487-88; William F. Brand, Jr., "A Re-examination of the Integration of the Artilleries," unpublished thesis, US Army War College, 1963, p. 2; James E. Hewes, Jr., *From Root to McNamara: Army Organization and Administration, 1900-1963* (Washington, D.C.: Center of Military History, US Army, 1975), pp. 146-53; "Reorganization of the War Department and the Army," pp. 339-43; Report, subj: Integration of the Artillery, 8 May 1956, in Consolidation of the Artillery Schools, UF23.5 L12U6, MSTL; Ltr for CG, Continental Army Command, subj: Integration of the Artillery, 16 May 1956, in Consolidation of the Artillery, UF23.5 L12U6, MSTL; BG Charles E. Hart, "Integration of the Artilleries," *Military Review*, Nov 1949, pp. 17-22; John Hamilton, "Common Ground: The Antiaircraft and Field Artillery Merger of 1950," *Air Defense Artillery Magazine*, Apr-Jun 2006, pp. 23-28.

3   Brand, "A Re-examination of the Integration of the Artilleries," pp. 7-8.

4   Memorandum with atch, subj: Report on Study of Artillery Branch Separation, undated, UF320.3 U6, MSTL; Ltr with atch, CG, Fort Sill, to CG, Fort Bliss, undated, in Correspondence between MG T.E. de Shazo, Ft. Sill, and MG Robert J. Wood, Ft. Bliss, UF23.5 L12C6, MSTL.

5   Artillery Branch Study, 1967, pp. 31-32 UF23.5 L12A41, MSTL; Memorandum (Extract), subj: Enforcement of Economics, 22 Aug 1946, in Consolidation of the Artillery Schools, 1956, UF 23.5 L12U6, MSTL; Brand, "A Re-examination of the Integration of the Artilleries," p. 9.

6   Memorandum for Commanding General, Replacement and School Command, subj: Consolidation of Artillery School, 17 Sep 1946, in Consolidation of Artillery Schools, 1956, UF23.5 L12U6, MSTL; Memorandum, subj: Integration of the Artillery, 8 May 1956, in Consolidation of the Artillery, 1956, UF23.5 L12U6, MSTL; Ltr, War Department to CG, Army Air Forces and Army Ground Forces, subj: Enforcement of Economies, 22 Aug 1946, in Consolidation of the Artillery Schools, 1956, UF23.5 L12U6, MSTL; Brand, "A Re-examination of the Integration of the Artilleries," pp. 2-9; Artillery Branch Study of 1966-1967, pp. 30-31, UF23.5 L12A41, MSTL; *History of the US Army Artillery and Missile School, 1945-1957* (Fort Sill, OK: Fort Sill Printing Plant, 1957), p. 17; Memorandum, subj: Integration of the Artillery, 8 May 1956, in Consolidation of the Artillery Schools, 1956, UF23.5 L12U6, MSTL; Report, subj: Study of Artillery Integration, 1963, p. 1, UF320.3 U6, MSTL.

7   Memorandum, subj: Integration of the Artillery, 8 May 1956, in Consolidation of the Artillery Schools, 1956, UF23.5 L12U6, MSTL; Ltr, HQ Army Ground Forces to CG Replacement and School Command, subj: Consolidation of Artillery Schools, 17 Sep 1946, in Correspondence between de Shazo and Wood, UF23.5 L12C6, MSTL; William R. Keast, Army Ground Forces Study Number Seven, Provision of Enlisted Replacements, 1946, p. 2.

8   Memorandum for Commanding General, Replacement and School Command, subj: Consolidation of Artillery Schools, 17 Sep 1946, in Consolidation of Artillery Schools, 1956, UF23.5 L12U6, MSTL; Ltr, HQ Army Ground Forces to CG Replacement and School Command, subj: Consolidation of Artillery Schools, 17 Sep 1946, in Correspondence between de Shazo and Wood, UF23.5 L12C6, MSTL.

9   Memorandum, subj: Historical Information, 9 Dec 1946, in Memorandum, subj: Historical Information, 18 Jul 1946, UF23.5 E1, MSTL; Memorandum, subj: History of the Artillery School, 30 Nov 1946, in Memorandum, subj: Historical Information, 18 Jul 1946, UF23.5 E1, MSTL; *History of the US Army Artillery and Missile School, 1945-1957*, p. 18; Report of Activities of The

Artillery School and Center from 1 Sep 1945-1 Apr 1949, p. 3, UF23.5 E11U4, MSTL; Hamilton, "Common Ground," pp. 23-28.

10 See endnote 9.

11 *History of the US Army Artillery and Missile School, 1945-1957*, p. 18; Report of Activities of The Artillery School and Center from 1 Sep 1945-1 Apr 1949, p. 3, UF23.5 E11U4, MSTL.

12 Memorandum for Commanding General, Replacement and School Command, subj: Consolidation of Artillery School, 17 Sep 1946, in Consolidation of Artillery Schools, 1956, UF23.5 L12U6, MSTL; Memorandum, subj: Integration of the Artillery, 8 May 1956, in Consolidation of the Artillery, 1956, UF23.5 L12U6, MSTL; Ltr, War Department to CG, Army Air Forces and Army Ground Forces, subj: Enforcement of Economies, 22 Aug 1946, in Consolidation of the Artillery School, 1956, UF23.5 L12U6, MSTL; Brand, "A Re-examination of the Integration of the Artilleries," pp. 2-9; Artillery Branch Study of 1966-1967, pp. 30-31, UF23.5 L12A41, MSTL; Telephone Call Transcript, 7 Oct 1946, in Correspondence between de Shazo and Wood, UF23.5 L12C6, MSTL.

13 COL Thomas E. de Shazo, "The Artillery School," *Field Artillery Journal*, Mar-Apr 1947, pp. 95-98; Oral History Interview with Bruce C. Clarke by Jerry N. Hess, 14 Jan 1970, Truman Library; *History of the US Army Artillery and Missile School: 1945-1957,* p. 18.

14 War Department General Order No. 11, 22 Jan 1947; Memorandum, subj: Organization of The Armored, The Artillery, The Infantry, The Ground General School, and The Antiaircraft and Guided Missile Centers, 16 Jan 1948, in Integration of the Artillery Schools, UF23.5 L12U6, MSTL; *History of the US Army Artillery and Guided Missile School, 1945-1957*, pp. 19, 86; Study of the History of The Artillery School, 1 Nov 1946-31 Dec 1946, 16 Jan 1947, in Memorandum, subj: Historical Information, 18 Jul 1946, UF23.5 E1, MSTL; Report, subj: Consolidated Board Report, 1 Nov 1949, US23.5 L12U6, MSTL; de Shazo, "The Artillery School," pp. 95-98; "Going to School," *Field Artillery Journal*, Mar-Apr 1947, p. 92.

15 War Department General Order No. 11, 22 Jan 1947; Memorandum, subj: Organization of The Armored, The Artillery, The Infantry, The Ground General School, and The Antiaircraft and Guided Missile Centers, 16 Jan 1948, in Integration of the Artillery Schools, UF23.5 L12U6, MSTL; *History of the US Army Artillery and Guided Missile School, 1945-1957*, pp. 19, 86; Study of the History of The Artillery School, 1 Nov 1946-31 Dec 1946, 16 Jan 1947, in Memorandum, subj: Historical Information, 18 Jul 1946, UF23.5 E1, MSTL; Report, subj: Consolidated Board Report, 1 Nov 1949, UF23.5 L12U6, MSTL; de Shazo, "The Artillery School," pp. 95-98; "Going to School," p. 92; *History of the Field Artillery School: World War II* (Fort Sill, OK: Fort Sill Printing Plant, 1945), p. 267; *History of the US Army Artillery and Missile School: 1945-1957*, pp. 10, 12, 17-21, 174; Riley Sunderland, *History of the Field Artillery School: 1911-1942* (Fort Sill, OK: Fort Sill Printing Plant, 1942), p. 190; War Department General Order No. 11, 22 Jan 1947; Gillette Griswold, "Fort Sill, Oklahoma: A Brief History," p. 16, unpublished manuscript, Historical Research and Document Collection (HRDC), Field Artillery Branch Historian's Office, US Army Field Artillery School; Melvin L. Whiteley, "History of the Field Artillery School," unpaginated, unpublished manuscript, MSTL; "Reorganized AGF School System," *Field Artillery Journal*, Nov-Dec 1946, pp. 644-45; Memorandum, subj: Historical Information, 18 Jul 1946, UF23.5 E1, MSTL. In the spring of 1947, the Army established the Ground General School to conduct the Officer Candidate School, among other responsibilities, LTC Wheeler G. Merriam, "The Ground General School," *Field Artillery Journal*, Mar-Apr 1947, pp. 93-94.

16 *History of the US Army Artillery and Missile School, 1945-1957*, pp. 8-9; Memorandum, subj; Historical Information, 18 Jul 1946, UF23.5 E1, MSTL; *History of the Field Artillery School: World War II*, pp. 266-67.

17 *History of the US Army Artillery and Missile School, 1945-1957*, pp. 6, 9-10; Memorandum,

subj: Historical Information, 18 Jul 1946, UF23.5 E1, MSTL; Report of the Department of the Army Board to Review Army Officer Schools, Feb 1966, Vol II, p. 131, U408 H204, MSTL; Maurice Matloff, ed., *American Military History* (Washington, D.C.: Center of Military History, United States Army, 1985), p. 430; Robert R. Palmer, Bell I. Wiley, and William R. Keast, *The Procurement and Training of Ground Combat Troops* (Washington, D.C.: Office of the Chief of Military History, Department of the Army, 1948), p. 173.

18 *History of the US Army Artillery and Missile School, 1945-1957*, pp. 6, 9-10; Memorandum, subj: Historical Information, 18 Jul 1946, UF23.5 E1, MSTL; Report of the Department of the Army Board to Review Army Officer Schools, Feb 1966, Vol 2, p. 131, U408 H204, MSTL; Matloff, ed., *American Military History*, p. 430; Palmer, Wiley, and Keast, *The Procurement and Training of Ground Combat Troops*, p. 173.

19 Memorandum, subj: Historical Information, 18 Jul 1946, UF23.5 E1, MSTL; Memorandum, subj: Historical Information, 7 Aug 1946, in Memorandum, subj: Historical Information, 18 Jul 1946, UF23.5 E1, MSTL; *History of the US Army Artillery and Missile School: 1945-1957*, pp. 15-16, 23, 174-77, 203-22; COL Thomas E. de Shazo, "The Artillery School," *Field Artillery Journal*, Mar-Apr 1947, pp. 95-98.

20 *History of the US Army Artillery and Missile School: 1945-1957*, pp. 28-31; John L. Romjue, Susan Canedy, and Anne W. Chapman, *Prepare the Army for War: A Historical Overview of the Army Training and Doctrine Command, 1973-1993* (Fort Monroe, VA: Office of the Command Historian, United States Army Training and Doctrine Command, 1993), pp. 5-6.

21 *History of the US Army Artillery and Missile School: 1945-1957*, pp. 28-31; Romjue, Canedy, and Chapman, *Prepare the Army for War*, pp. 5-6.

22 *History of the US Army Artillery and Missile School: 1945-1957*, pp. 28-31; Romjue, Canedy, and Chapman, *Prepare the Army for War:* pp. 5-6.

23 *History of the US Army Artillery and Missile School, 1945-1957*, pp. 27-32, 171, 173; Weigley, *History of the United States Army*, p. 600.

24 Memorandum, subj: Historical Information, 18 Jul 1946, UF23.5 E1, MSTL; Memorandum, subj: Historical Information, 7 Aug 1946, in Memorandum, subj: Historical Information, 18 Jul 1946, UF23.5 E1, MSTL; Memorandum for Commanding General Replacement and School Command, subj: Historical Information, 18 Jul 1946, UF23.5 E1, MSTL; Richard P. Weinert, Jr., *A History of Army Aviation: 1950-1962* (Fort Monroe, VA: Office of the Command Historian, US Army Training and Doctrine Command, 1991), pp. 95-99; Wilbur S. Nye, *Carbine and Lance: The Story of Old Fort Sill* (Norman, OK: University of Oklahoma Press, 1974), p. 340; *History of the US Army Artillery and Missile School: 1945-1957*, pp. 61, 84, 86, 87, 96; Report of Activities of The Artillery School and Center, 1 Sep 1945-1 Apr 1949, p. 2, UF23.5 E11U4, MSTL.

25 Memorandum, subj: Historical Information, 18 Jul 1946, UF23.5 E1, MSTL; Memorandum, subj: Historical Information, 7 Aug 1946, in Memorandum, subj: Historical Information, 18 Jul 1946, UF23.5 E1, MSTL; Memorandum for Commanding General Replacement and School Command, subj: Historical Information, 18 Jul 1946, UF23.5 E1, MSTL; Weinert, *A History of Army Aviation*, pp. 95-99; Nye, *Carbine and Lance*, p. 340; *History of the US Army Artillery and Missile School: 1945-1957*, pp. 61, 84, 86, 87, 96; Report of Activities of The Artillery School and Center, 1 Sep 1945-1 Apr 1949, p. 2, UF23.5 E11U4, MSTL.

26 Memorandum, subj: Information on the Artillery, 8 May 1956, in Consolidation of the Artillery Schools, UF23.5 L12U6, MSTL; de Shazo, "The Artillery School," pp. 95-98.

27 Memorandum, subj: Information on the Artillery, 8 May 1956, in Consolidation of the Artillery, 1956, UF23.5 L12U6, MSTL; Memorandum, subj: Annual Report for School Year 1947-1948, undated, UF23.5 E1, MSTL; Memorandum, subj: Integration of the Artillery, 1956, in Integration of the Artillery School, 1956, UF23.5 L12U6, MSTL; *History of the US Army Artillery*

and Missile School, 1945-1957, pp. 39-40, 202; Brand, "A Re-examination of Integration of the Artilleries," pp. 10-11; "Courses of Instruction at the F.A. School," *Field Artillery Journal*, Jun 1946, pp. 348-50; de Shazo, "The Artillery School," pp. 95-98; Memorandum for The Adjutant General, subj: Annual Report for School Year 1947-1948, undated, UF23.5 E1, MSTL.

28 Memorandum, subj: Information on the Artillery, 8 May 1956, in Consolidation of the Artillery, 1956, UF23.5 L12U6, MSTL; Memorandum, subj: Annual Report for School Year 1947-1948, UF23.5 E1, MSTL; Memorandum, subj: Integration of the Artillery, 1956, in Integration of the Artillery School, 1956, UF23.5 L12U6, MSTL; *History of the US Army Artillery and Missile School, 1945-1957*, pp. 39-40, 202; Brand, "A Re-examination of Integration of the Artilleries," pp. 10-11; "Courses of Instruction at the F.A. School," pp. 348-50, UF23 Q7, MSTL.

29 de Shazo, "The Artillery School," pp. 95-98; Memorandum for The Adjutant General, subj: Annual Report for School Year 1947-1948, undated, UF23.5 E1, MSTL.

30 GEN Jacob L. Devers, Statement on Artillery Integration, undated, in Consolidation of the Artillery Schools, 1956, UF23.5 L12U6, MSTL; GEN Jacob L. Devers, "Artillery Integration," *Field Artillery Journal*, Sep-Oct 1947, p. 303.

31 *History of the US Army Artillery and Missile School, 1945-1957*, p. 25; Memorandum with atch, subj: Consolidation Board Report, 1 Nov 1949, in Consolidation of the Artillery Schools, UF23.5 L12U6, MSTL; Memorandum for the Adjutant General, subj: Annual Report for School Year 1947-1948, undated, UF23.5 E1, MSTL; Organization and Mission of The Artillery School, 1 Aug 1951, p. 9, UF25 S372 U6 1951, MSTL.

32 Department of the Army, General Order Number 24, 27 July 1950, deactivated the Seacoast Artillery Branch of The Artillery School.

33 Memorandum, subj: Annual Report for School Year 1948-1949, 23 Sep 1949, UF23.5 E1, MSTL; *History of the US Army Artillery and Missile School, 1945-1957*, p. 25; Memorandum for the Adjutant General, subj: Annual Report for School Year 1947-1948, undated, UF23.5 E1, MSTL; MG Charles E. Hart, "Integration of the Artilleries," *Military Review*, Nov. 1949, pp. 17-22.

34 Memorandum, subj: Annual Report for School Year 1948-1949, 23 Sep 1949, UF23.5 E1, MSTL.

35 Memorandum for LTG Manton S. Eddy, Cmdt, Command and General Staff College, subj: Consolidated Board Report, 1 Nov 1949, in Consolidation of the Artillery Schools, UF23.5 L12U6, MSTL.

36 Memorandum for Eddy, subj: Consolidated Board Report, 1 Nov 1949, in Consolidation of the Artillery Schools, UF23.5 L12U6, MSTL; Memorandum for CG, The Artillery Center, subj: Report of the Board of Officers, 15 Oct 1949, in Consolidation of the Artillery Schools, UF23.5 U12U6, MSTL.

37 Memorandum for Eddy, subj: Consolidated Board Report, 1 Nov 1949, in Consolidation of the Artillery Schools, UF23.5 L12U6, MSTL.

38 Memorandum for Adjutant General, subj: Annual Report for School Year 1949-1950, 17 Nov 1950, UF23.5 E1, MSTL; *History of the US Army Artillery and Missile School, 1945-1957*, pp. 202, 221.

39 Memorandum for Chief, Army Field Forces, subj: Integration of the Artilleries, 22 Jun 1950, in Integration of the Artilleries, UF 23.5 L12U61, MSTL.

40 Memorandum for Chief, Army Field Forces, subj: Integration of the Artilleries, 22 Jun 1950, in Integration of the Artilleries, UF 23.5 L12U61, MSTL.

41 Memorandum for Chief, Army Field Forces, subj: Integration of the Artilleries, 22 Jun 1950, in Integration of the Artilleries, UF 23.5 L12U61, MSTL.

42 Matloff, *American Military History*, p. 541; US Army Field Artillery School (USAFAS), An Institutional Self-Study for Initial Accreditation, Dec 1979, p. 1-4, UF23.5 A2U511, MSTL;

Weigley, *History of the United States Army*, p. 495; Hamilton, "Common Ground," pp. 23-28.

43 Memorandum, subj: Annual Report for School Year 1949-1950, 17 Nov 1950, pp. 2-3, UF23.5 E1, MSTL; *History of the US Army Artillery and Missile School: 1945-1957*, pp. 39, 204, 205, 221, 222.

44 Memorandum for the Adjutant General, subj: Annual Report for School Year 1949-1950, 17 Nov 1950, UF23.5 E1, MSTL.

45 Memorandum for the Adjutant General, subj: Annual Report for School Year 1949-1950, 17 Nov 1950, UF23.5 E1, MSTL.

46 *History of the US Army Artillery and Missile School: 1945-1957*, pp. 36-51, 164-65, 177-79; Memorandum for Chief, Army Field Forces, subj: Annual Report for School Year 1950-1951, 14 Jan 1952, UF23.5 E1, MSTL; Organization and Mission of The Artillery School, 1 Aug 1951, p. 9, UF25 S372 U6 1951, MSTL; Units Mobilized at Fort Sill File, HRDC; USAFAS Accreditation Self-Study Report, May 1976, p. 1a, UF23.5 A2U5, MSTL; James E. Hewes, Jr., *From Root to McNamara: Army Organization and Administration, 1900-1963* (Washington, D.C.: Center of Military History, United States Army, 1975), p. 408; The Artillery Center, Record of Events, 1 Jun 1950-31 Oct 1950, Section 2, UF25 H673 U6 R, MSTL.

47 *History of the US Army Artillery and Missile School: 1945-1957*, pp. 36-51, 164-65, 177-79; Memorandum for Chief, Army Field Forces, subj: Annual Report for School Year 1950-1951, 14 Jan 1952, UF23.5 E1, MSTL; Organization and Mission of The Artillery School, 1 Aug 1951, p. 9, UF25 S372 U6 1951, MSTL; Units Mobilized at Fort Sill File, HRDC; USAFAS Accreditation Self-Study Report, May 1976, p. 1a, UF23.5 A2U5, MSTL; The Artillery School, Record of Events, 1-30 Nov 1950, Section I, UF25 H673 U6 R, MSTL; The Artillery School, Record of Events, 1-28 Feb 1951, Section 2, UF25, H673 U6 R, MSTL; The Artillery School, Record of Events, 1-30 Sep 1951, Section I, UF25 H673 U6 R, MSTL; The Artillery School, Record of Events, 1 Jun 1950-31 Oct 1950, Section 2, UF25 H673 U6 R, MSTL; The Artillery School, Record of Events, 1-31 Dec 1950, Section II, UF25 H673 U6 R, MSTL; The Artillery School, Record of Events, 1-31 Mar 1951, Sections II and X, UF25 H673 U6 R, MTSL.

48 LTC William B. Lee, "US Army Training Center, Field Artillery," *Artillery Trends*, Feb 1960, pp. 28-35; LT James J. Dorsey, "This Patch Needs A Sleeve," *Artillery Trends*, Dec 1963, pp. 34-39; "USAAMS Extension Courses Provide Many Benefits," *Artillery Trends*, Apr 1965, p. 2; *History of the US Army Artillery and Missile School: 1945-1957*, pp. 47, 59, 69, 70, 71, 94, 95, 106; *History of the US Army Artillery and Missile School: 1958-1967* (Fort Sill, OK: Fort Sill Printing Plant, 1967), p. 93; 1973 USAFAS Annual Historical Supplement, unpaginated; *History of the US Army Artillery and Missile School: 1945-1957*, pp. 11, 13, 14, 24, 44-49, 52, 94, 171, 327; The Artillery School, Record of Events, 1 Jun 1950-31 Oct 1950, Section II, UF25 H673 U6 R, MSTL; The Artillery School, Record of Events, 1-31 Dec 1950, Section II, UF25 H673 U6 R, MSTL; The Artillery School, Record of Events, 1-31 Mar 1951, Sections II and X, UF25 H673 U6 R, MTSL.

49 *History of the US Army Artillery and Missile School: 1945-1957*, pp. 48, 51, 52, 54, 66; The Artillery Center, Record of Events, 1-30 Nov 1950, Section IX, UF25 H673 U6 R, MSTL.

50 *History of the US Army Artillery and Missile School: 1945-1957*, pp. 25, 31.

51 *History of the US Army Artillery and Missile School: 1945-1957,* pp. 60, 66.

52 *History of the US Army Artillery and Missile School: 1945-1957*, pp. 24, 25, 48, 52, 63, 64, 67-71, 161; Nye, *Carbine and Lance*, p. 339; Hamilton, "Common Ground," pp. 23-28; USAFAS, An Institutional Self-Study for Initial Accreditation, Dec 1979, pp. 1-4 - 1-5, UF23.5 A2U511, MSTL; Melvin L. Whiteley, "History of the Field Artillery School," unpublished manuscript, unpaginated, UF25 S372 W5, MSTL; *History of the US Army Artillery and Missile School: 1945-1957*, pp. 24, 25, 48, 52, 63, 64, 67-71, 161.

53 Nye, *Carbine and Lance*, p. 339; *History of the US Army Artillery and Missile School:*

1945-1957, pp. 24, 25, 48, 52, 54, 63, 64, 67-71, 161; "1951-1961," Lawton *Constitution*, 5 Aug 1976, p. 2h; *History of the US Army Artillery and Missile School: 1958-1967*, pp. v-vi. When The Artillery School started teaching rocket and missile courses, the Army changed its name to the Artillery and Guided Missile School in 1955 to reflect the change in mission and later in January 1957 changed the school's name to the US Army Artillery and Guided Missile School. In July 1957 the Army dropped guided from the school's name. Over a period of 10 years, the school introduced the 280-mm. atomic warhead course in 1952, Honest John rocket courses in 1954, the 8-inch howitzer atomic projectile assembly course in 1956, Corporal missile courses in 1957, Redstone missile courses in 1957, Lacrosse missile courses in 1959, Little John missile courses in 1961, Sergeant missile courses in 1962, and Pershing missile courses in 1962.

54 Memorandum, subj: Annual Report for School Year 1950-1951, 12 Feb 1952, in Annual Report for 1950-1951, UF23.5 E1, MSTL; COL F.T. Unger, "Special Weapons Instruction," *Trends in Artillery for Instruction*, Apr 1957, pp. 22-23; MAJ Burris C. Dale, "Atomic Targets of Opportunity – Definition and Brief Discussion," *Trends in Artillery for Instruction*, Oct 1957, pp. 100-03; "Nuclear Weapons Department," *Artillery Trends*, Jul 1960, pp. 3-8; *History of the US Army Artillery and Missile School: 1958-1967*, pp. 107, 113-51; *History of the US Army Artillery and Missile School: 1945-1957*, p. 71; Lee, "US Army Training Center, Field Artillery," pp. 28-35; Dorsey, "This Patch Needs A Sleeve," pp. 34-39; "USAAMS Extension Courses Provide Many Benefits," *Artillery Trends*, Apr 1965, p. 2; *History of the US Army Artillery and Missile School: 1945-1957*, pp. 47, 59, 69, 70, 71, 94, 95, 106; *History of the US Army Artillery and Missile School: 1958-1967*, p. 93; 1973 USAFAS Annual Historical Supplement, unpaginated.

55 Memorandum, subj: Annual Report for School Year 1950-1951, 12 Feb 1952, in Annual Report for 1950-1951, UF23.5 E1, MSTL; Unger, "Special Weapons Instruction," pp. 22-23; Dale, "Atomic Targets of Opportunity," pp. 100-03; "Nuclear Weapons Department," pp. 3-8; *History of the US Army Artillery and Missile School: 1958-1967*, pp. 107, 113-51; *History of the US Army Artillery and Missile School: 1945-1957*, p. 71.

56 Richard Lowitt, "Fort Sill Enters the Missile Age," *Chronicles of Oklahoma*, Winter 2005-2006, pp. 389-402.

57 Lowitt, "Fort Sill Enters the Missile Age," pp. 402-03.

58 Lowitt, "Fort Sill Enters the Missile Age," pp. 389-402; *History of the US Army Artillery and Missile School, 1945-1957*, p. 70.

59 Lowitt, "Fort Sill Enters the Missile Age," p. 404.

60 Griswold, "Fort Sill, Oklahoma: A Brief History," p. 17, unpublished manuscript, HRDC; "1951-1961: The Korean Threat," Lawton *Constitution*, 5 Aug 1976, p. 2h; McClung, "Lawton, Fort Sill Forge Early Successful Combination," Lawton *Constitution*, 5 Aug 1976, p. 9g; Jim Downing, "Ft. Sill's Future is Keyed to Expansion," Tulsa *Tribune*, 8 Aug 1959, HRDC; *History of the US Army Artillery and Missile School: 1945-1957*, pp. 62-73, 161; Fort Sill Economic Impact for Fiscal Year 1994, p. 16, HRDC; Edward R. Ritenbaugh and Glenn O. Brown, "Fort Sill: World's Crossroad," p. 5, unpublished manuscript, MSTL; Lowitt, "Fort Sill Enters the Missile Age," pp. 402-30.

61 Ltr, Inspector of Artillery to MG Arthur M. Harper, 18 Apr 1952, in Plans for the Integration of Field Artillery and Antiaircraft Officer Training, undated, UF23.5 L12U5, MSTL.

62 Ltr, Chief of Army Field Forces to Assistant Chief of Staff, G3, subj: Integrated Education of Artillery Officers, 22 Mar 1952, in Plans for the Integration of Field Artillery and Antiaircraft Officer Schooling, undated, UF23.5 L12U5, MSTL; *History of the US Army Artillery and Missile School: 1945-1957* pp. 202-22; Report, Board of Officers, subj: Long-Range Program of Education of Artillery Officers, 16 Aug 1952, pp. 6-8, in Report of Proceedings by Board of Officers, UF23.4 C2R3, MSTL; Hamilton, "Common Ground," pp. 23-28; The Artillery School, Record of Events,

1-30 May 1951, Section I, UF25 H673 U6 R, MSTL.

63 Ltr, Chief of Army Field Forces to Assistant Chief of Staff, G3, subj: Integrated Education of Artillery Officers, 22 Mar 1952, in Plans for the Integration of Field Artillery and Antiaircraft Officer Schooling, undated, UF23.5 L12U5, MSTL; *History of the US Army Artillery and Missile School: 1945-1957* pp. 202-22; Report, Board of Officers, subj: Long-Range Program of Education of Artillery Officers, 16 Aug 1952, pp. 6-8, in Report of Proceedings by Board of Officers, UF23.4 C2R3, MSTL; Hamilton, "Common Ground," pp. 23-28; The Artillery School, Record of Events, 1-30 May 1951, Section I, UF25 H673 U6 R, MSTL.

64 Report, subj: Study of Artillery Branch Separation, 1963, p. A-3, UF320.3 U6, MSTL; Report, subj: Integration of the Artillery, 8 May 1956, p. 8, in Correspondence between de Shazo and Wood, UF23.5 L12C6, MSTL; Brand, "A Re-examination of the Integration of the Artilleries, 1963," p. 11; *History of the US Army Artillery and Missile School: 1945-1957*, pp. 202-22; Memorandum for CG Continental Army Command, subj: The Artillery and Guided Missile School, 30 Apr 1956, in Consolidation of the Artillery Schools, UF23.5 L12U6, MSTL.

65 Ltr, CG, CONARC to Assistant Chief of Staff, G3, subj: Training and Assignment of Artillery Officers, 9 Feb 1955, in Consolidation of the Artillery School, UF23.5 L12U6, MSTL; Memorandum for CG, Continental Army Command, subj: The Artillery and Guided Missile School, 30 Apr 1956, in Consolidation of the Artillery Schools, UF23.5 L12U6, MSTL; The Artillery Branch Study, 1967, p. 41, UF23.5 L12A41, MSTL; Memorandum to CG, Continental Army Command, subj: Training and Assignment of Artillery Officers, 11 Jan 1955, in Consolidation of the Artilleries, UF23.5 L12U6, MSTL; *History of the US Army Artillery and Missile School: 1945-1957*, pp. 24, 25, 48, 52, 63, 64, 67-71, 161; Nye, *Carbine and Lance*, p. 339; Hamilton, "Common Ground," pp. 23-28.

66 Memorandum for CG, Continental Army Command, subj: The Artillery and Guided Missile School, 30 Apr 1956, in Consolidation of the Artillery Schools, UF23.5 L12U6, MSTL.

67 The Artillery Branch Study, 1967, pp. 42-43, UF23.5 L12A41, MSTL; Memorandum for CG, Continental Army Command, subj: The Artillery and Guided Missile School, 30 Apr 1956, in Consolidation of the Artillery Schools, UF23.5 L12U6, MSTL.

68 Memorandum, subj: Integration of the Artillery, 8 May 1956, in Consolidation of the Artillery Schools, UF23.5 L1U26, MSTL; Report, subj: Integration of the Artillery, 8 May 1956, in Correspondence between de Shazo and Wood, UF23.5 L12C6, MSTL.

69 Report, subj: Integration of the Artillery, 8 May 1956, in Correspondence between de Shazo and Wood, UF23.5 L12C6, MSTL; Ltr with atch, de Shazo to Wood, Oct 1956, in Correspondence between de Shazo and Wood, UF23.5 L12C6, MSTL; Report, subj: Integration of the Artillery, 8 May 1956, pp. 8-10, in Correspondence between de Shazo and Wood, UF23.5 L12C6, MSTL; The Artillery Branch Study, 1967, p. 39, UF23.5 L12A41, MSTL; *History of the US Army Artillery and Missile School, 1945-1957*, pp. 67-68.

70 Ltr, de Shazo to Wood, ca October 1956, in Correspondence between MG T.E. de Shazo and MG Robert J. Wood, UF23.5 L12C6, MSTL.

71 Ltr, de Shazo to Wood, ca. October 1956, in Correspondence between MG T.E. de Shazo and MG Robert J. Wood.

72 Ltr, de Shazo to Wood, ca. October 1956.

73 Ltr with atch, de Shazo to Wood, undated, in Correspondence between de Shazo and Wood, UF23.5 L12C6, MSTL.

74 Ltr with atch, de Shazo to Wood, undated.

75 Memorandum for CG Continental Army Command, 16 May 1956, in Consolidation of the Artillery Schools, UF23.5 L12U6, MSTL.

76 *History of the US Army Artillery and Missile School, 1945-1957*, pp. 203-222; Brand, "A

Re-examination of Integration of the Artilleries," pp. 11-12, 31-33; The Artillery Branch Study, 1967, pp. 41-44, UF23.5 l12A41, MSTL.

77 *History of the US Army Artillery and Missile School, 1945-1957,* pp. 203-222; Brand, "A Re-examination of Integration of the Artilleries," pp. 11-12, 31-33; The Artillery Branch Study, 1967, pp. 41-44, UF23.5 l12A41, MSTL; Report of the Department of the Army Board to Review Army Officer Schools, Feb 1966, Vol II, p. 308, U408 H2U4, MSTL. LTG Ralph E. Haines, Jr., chaired the board.

78 The Artillery Branch Study, 1967, pp. 45-46, UF23.5 L12A41, MSTL; Ltr, Waters to MG Lewis S. Griffing, Cmdt, US Army Artillery and Missile School, 17 Jun 1963, in Report on Study of Artillery Branch Separation, UF320.3 U6, MSTL; Report on Study of Artillery Branch Separation, pp. 1-12, UF320.3 U6, MSTL; *History of the US Army Artillery and Missile School: 1945-1957,* p. 68: "AAA Now Air Defense Artillery," *Artillery Trends,* Jun 1958, p. 59.

79 See endnote 78.

80 Report of the Department of the Army Board to Review Army Officer Schools, Feb 1966, Vol I, pp. 4, 5, 9, 34, 177, Vol III, pp. 448-49, 528, U408 H2U4, MSTL; Report of the Department of the Army Board on Educational System for Officers (Manton S. Eddy Board), 26 Oct 1949, U408 J68 1949, MSTL; Report of the Department of the Army Officer Education and Training Review Board (Edward T. Williams Board), 1958, U408.3 U547 1958, MSTL.

81 Report of the Department of the Army Board to Review Army Officer Schools, Feb 1966, Vol I, pp. 4, 5, 9, 34, 177, Vol III, pp. 448-49, 528, U408 H2U4, MSTL;

82 The Artillery Branch Study, 1967, pp. 1-4, UF23.5 L12A41, MSTL.

83 The Artillery Branch Study, 1967, p. 93.

84 The Artillery Branch Study, 1967, pp. 93-94.

85 The Artillery Branch Study, 1967, pp. 95, 107.

86 The Artillery Branch Study, 1967, pp. 115-20.

87 Nye, *Carbine and Lance,* pp. 341-42; 1969 USAFAS Annual Historical Supplement, p. 1; USAFAS Accreditation Self-Study Report, May 1976, p. 1a, UF23.5 A2U5, MSTL.

88 *History of the US Army Artillery and Missile School: 1946-1957,* pp. 64, 90-100; *History of the US Army Artillery and Missile School: 1958-1967,* p. 25. Department of Research and Analysis (1947-1949), The Artillery Board (1951-1952), Department of Combat Development (1952-1960), Office of Combat Development and Doctrine (1960-1962), and US Army Artillery Combat Development Agency (1962-1969).

89 LTC Kenneth B. Stark, "Revision of Field Manual, 6-20, Artillery Tactics and Technique," *Trends in Artillery for Instruction*, Feb 1958, pp. 19-20; CPT William A. Naugher, "ROCID Artillery FDC," *Trends in Artillery for Instruction*, Feb 1958, pp. 36-39; LTC Kenneth B. Stark, "Methods of Deploying Cannon and Missile Field Artillery," *Artillery Trends*, Jun 1958, pp. 5-8; MAJ William W. Madison, "The First Round," *Artillery Trends*, Oct 1958, pp. 30-32; MAJ John P. O' Connell, "Organization and Tactics for Field Artillery Missile Units," *Artillery Trends*, Feb 1959, pp. 11-14; LTC William J. Wood, "Tactical Employment of the New Division Artillery," *Artillery Trends*, Mar 1959, pp. 23-36; 1LT Thoren J. Schroeck, "Developing Future Artillery," *Artillery Trends*, Dec 1959, pp. 3-6.

90 "Department of Combat Developments," *The Artillery Quarterly*, Jan 1957, p. 2; "Drones in the Future," *Artillery Trends*, Mar 1959, pp. 61-62; MAJ John C. Marschhausen, "New Eyes for the Countermortar Teams," *Artillery Trends*, Jun 1958, pp. 3-5; CPT W. Thomas Reeder, "Exercise Your Radar," *Artillery Trends*, Jun 1959, pp. 38-39;. Schroeck, "Developing Future Artillery," pp. 3-6; *History of the US Army Artillery and Missile School: 1946-1957*, p. 64.

91 COL W.E. Showalter, "An All Around Problem," *Trends in Artillery for Instruction*, Jun 1957, pp. 16-18.

92 Showalter, "An All Around Problem," pp. 16-18; MG David E. Ott, *Field Artillery: 1954-1973* (Washington, D.C.: Department of the Army, 1975), pp. 32, 70-72; *History of the US Army Artillery and Missile School: 1945-1957*, p. 186; 1966 USAAMS Annual Historical Supplement, p. 7.

93 Showalter, "An All Around Problem," pp. 16-18; Ott, *Field Artillery*, pp. 32, 70-72; *History of the US Army Artillery and Missile School: 1945-1957*, p. 186; 1966 US Army Artillery and Missile School (USAAMS) Annual Historical Supplement, p. 7; "New Family of Weapons," *Trends in Artillery for Instruction*, Apr 1957, pp. 17-18; "Weapon System: 1970," *Artillery Trends*, Feb 1962, pp. 4-37; Dastrup, *King of Battle*, p. 277.

94 "New Family of Weapons," *Trends in Artillery for Instruction*, Apr 1957, pp. 17-18; "Weapon System: 1970," *Artillery Trends*, Feb 1962, pp. 4-37; Dastrup, *King of Battle*, p. 277.

95 1964 USAAMS Annual Historical Supplement, pp. 1-2; 1965 USAAMS Annual Historical Supplement, pp. 1-2; *History of the US Army Artillery and Missile School: 1958-1967*, pp. 172-73; COL William A. Becker, "A Bold New Look," *Artillery Trends*, Apr 1965, pp. 6-8; CPT Robert W. Arnold, CPT Ira E. Greeley, and CPT Lawrence O. Zittrain, "Aerial Rocket Artillery," *Artillery Trends*, Apr 1965, pp. 20-25.

96 "The Flying Artillery," *Artillery Trends*, May 1960, pp. 12-28; LT R.N. Tredway, "The H-2C in Artillery Employment," *Artillery Trends*, Jul 1962, pp. 42-48.

97 1964 USAAMS Annual Historical Supplement, p. 2.

98 Becker, "A Bold New Look," pp. 6-8; Arnold, Greeley, and Zittrain, "Aerial Rocket Artillery," pp. 20-25; MAJ Robert G. Custer, "Air Assault Artillery Finale," *Artillery Trends*, Nov 1965, pp. 12-16; "Air Assault to Airmobile," *Artillery Trends*, Nov 1965, pp. 27-30; CPT Morris J. Keller, "Little John: The Mighty Mite," *Artillery Trends*, Jul 1960, pp. 20-25; "Air Assault," *Artillery Trends*, Apr 1963, pp. 49-54; MAJ Steven M. Leonard, "One Man's Vision: The Evolution of Airmobile Artillery," *Field Artillery Journal*, Jul-Aug 1999, pp. 24-28.

99 CPT Donald C. Fox, "Automatic Data Processing Systems," *Trends in Artillery for Instruction*, Feb 1958, pp. 14-16; Showalter, "An All Around Problem," pp. 16-18; "Need for Electronic Computers," *Trends in Field Artillery for Instruction*, Jun 1957, pp. 19-21; "Automatic Data Processing Systems," *Trends in Field Artillery for Instruction*, Feb 1958, pp. 33-35; "New Eyes for Countermortar Teams," *Trends in Artillery*, Jun 1958, pp. 3-5.

100 See endnote 99.

101 LT Robert C. Cahalane, "Field Artillery Gun Data Computers," *Trends in Artillery for Instruction*, Feb 1958, pp. 32-34; "First Round Hits with FADAC," *Artillery Trends*, Sep 1960, pp. 8-15; "The Computer Story: Speed and Accuracy," *Artillery Trends*, Sep 1960, pp. 30-38; Dastrup, *King of Battle*, p. 287.

102 CPT Leslie A. Belknap, "The Unsung Heroes: Redleg Advisory Efforts in Vietnam, 1965-1969," *Field Artillery Journal*, April 1991, pp. 14-17; Ott, *Field Artillery*, pp. 22-37, 239.

103 Ott, *Field Artillery*, pp. 25-26.

104 [104]Ott, *Field Artillery*, pp. 22-37, 239.

105 "Guerrilla, Jungle Instruction Increased," *Artillery Trends*, Aug 1961, p. 30; *History of the US Army Artillery and Missile School: 1958-1967*, p. 175.

106 CPT C.R. Leach, "Special Warfare," *Artillery Trends*, Aug 1961, p. 16.

107 Leach, "Special Warfare," p. 16.

108 Leach, "Special Warfare," p. 17.

109 Leach, "Special Warfare," p. 20.

110 Leach, "Special Warfare," p. 21.

111 Leach, "Special Warfare," p. 21.

112 MAJ Richard M. Jennings, "Special Warfare," *Artillery Trends*, Aug 1961, pp. 22-30.

113 Jennings, "Special Warfare," p. 30.

114 1963-1964 USAAMS Annual Historical Supplement, p. 4.

115 1963-1964 USAAMS Annual Historical Supplement, pp. 4-5; 1965 USAAM Annual Historical Supplement, p. 1.

116 1963-1964 USAAMS Annual Historical Supplement, p. 4; 1966 USAAMS Annual Historical Supplement, p. 2.

117 1963-1964 USAAMS Annual Historical Supplement, p. 5; 1965 USAAMS Annual Historical Supplement, pp. 1-6; 1966 USAAMS Annual Historical Supplement, pp. 1-7, 11, 12; 1967 USAAMS Annual Historical Supplement, pp. 1-11; 1968 USAAMS Annual Historical Supplement, pp. 1-6; COL Richard A. Crecelius and MAJ Henry A. Pedicone, "Nuclear Firepower," *Artillery Trends*, Jul 1965, pp. 30-45; "Counterinsurgency Operation Classes," *Artillery Trends*, Jul 1965, p. 27; CPT Charles W. Jackson, Jr., "Adjust by Sound," *Artillery Trends*, Jan 1968, pp. 28-34; Ott, *Field Artillery*, pp. 84, 134-36; Virgil Gaither, "Sill's Vietnam Village Shows What It's Like," Lawton *Constitution-Morning Press*, 5 Nov 1967, p. 10b; US Continental Army Command, Training Hints, 31 Jan 1967, pp. 8-16, UF133 U4, MSTL.

118 1963-1964 USAAMS Annual Historical Supplement, p. 5; 1965 Annual USAAMS Annual Historical Supplement, pp. 1-6; 1966 USAAMS Annual Historical Supplement, pp. 1-7, 11, 12; 1967 USAAMS Annual Historical Supplement, pp. 1-11; 1968 USAAMS Annual Historical Supplement, pp. 1-6; Crecelius and Pedicone, "Nuclear Firepower," pp. 30-45; "Counterinsurgency Operation Classes," *Artillery Trends*, Jul 1965, p. 27; Jackson, "Adjust by Sound," pp. 28-34; Ott, *Field Artillery*, pp. 84, 134-36.

119 1963-1964 USAAMS Annual Historical Supplement, p. 5; 1965 USAAMS Annual Historical Supplement, pp. 1-6; 1966 USAAMS Annual Historical Supplement, pp. 1-7, 11, 12; 1967 USAAMS Annual Historical Supplement, pp. 1-11; 1968 USAAMS Annual Historical Supplement, pp. 1-6; Crecelius and Pedicone, "Nuclear Firepower," pp. 30-45; "Counterinsurgency Operation Classes," p. 27; Jackson, "Adjust by Sound," pp. 28-34; Ott, *Field Artillery*, pp. 84, 134-36.

120 1965 USAAMS Annual Historical Supplement, p. 1.

121 1965 USAAMS Annual Historical Supplement, pp. 5-6; 1966 USAAMS Annual Historical Supplement, pp. 1-3; *History of the US Army Artillery and Missile School: 1958-1967*, pp. 174-90; Installation Population Figures, HRDC; 1973 USAFAS Annual Historical Summary, unpaginated.

122 1965 USAAMS Annual Historical Supplement, pp. 5-6; 1966 USAAMS Annual Historical Supplement, pp. 1-3; *History of the US Army Artillery and Missile School: 1958-1967*, pp. 174-90; Installation Population Figures, HRDC; 1973 USAFAS Annual Historical Summary, unpaginated.

Chapter Seven
Back to Europe

As the Vietnam War receded into the background in the 1970s, the Army turned its attention back to Europe where it encountered the Soviet Union's and Warsaw Pact's imposing, modernized ground forces. Based upon this impressive threat, the US Army Field Artillery School (1969-present) shifted its program of instruction from concentrating on fire support in guerrilla and jungle warfare to armored and mechanized warfare supported by self-propelled howitzers to prepare officers and soldiers to fight Soviet and Warsaw Pact ground forces. Simultaneously, it embarked upon an intensive effort to modernize tactics, doctrine, organization, and equipment to prepare officers and soldiers for combat in Europe.

Retooling the Classroom and Training

In 1971-1973, United States' Vietnamization program not only diminished the country's military role in Vietnam significantly but also altered the US Army Field Artillery School's operational tempo and focus. As the Army of Republic of South Vietnam's role in fighting the People's Army of Vietnam and the People's Liberation Front (Viet Cong) increased, the Army's combat effort declined, reducing the requirement for trained officers and soldiers. This prompted the school to cut the number of classes for each officer and enlisted course being taught and to shift from a six-day training week to a five-day training week.[1]

The decreasing requirement for officers also caused closing the Field Artillery Officer Candidate School that had been a vital element of the Field Artillery School over the years in producing officers. The first Field Artillery Officer Candidate School class graduated on 2 October 1941. When it became apparent that the need for field artillery officers was less critical following World War II, the Army Ground Forces shut down the school on 12 December 1946 with the graduation of Class 179. After the Korean War broke out, the Army reopened the Field Artillery Officer Candidate School on 21 February 1951 as a part of The Artillery School (1946-1955). Even with the armistice of 1953 that ended the Korean War and lessened the demand for field artillery officers, the Army kept the school open for the next 20 years to satisfy Cold War needs for field artillery officers. Following the graduation of Field Artillery Officer Candidate School class 4-73 on 7 July 1973, the Army closed the school after 22 years of continuous operations because it needed fewer field artillery officers, it no longer saw the requirement for branch-specific officer candidate schools, and it activated the branch immaterial Officer Candidate School at Fort Benning, Georgia, on 6 July 1973.[2]

Concurrently, the Field Artillery School abandoned its focus on fire support in counterinsurgency, guerilla, and jungle warfare for fire support in conventional warfare, often called mid- to high-intensity warfare, in Europe. After January 1971, all courses started emphasizing the use of the mechanized infantry-armor-field artillery team operating in the Federal Republic of Germany and guarding the Fulda Gap against a heavily mechanized, armored threat. Influenced by the destructiveness of the Arab-Israeli War of October 1973, the school envisioned the imperative of being prepared to fight and win the first battle of the next war. In view of this, the school concentrated its efforts in 1974-1975 on preparing active and reserve component officers and soldiers to be ready for combat without additional training. Even with this reorientation, the Field Artillery Officer Basic Course and Field Artillery Officer Advance Course still provided some instruction in low-intensity warfare outside of Europe.[3]

Although this shift in focus was critical in the effort to prepare the Army for armed conflict in Europe, the Army, the Field Artillery School, and the newly organized US Army Training and Doctrine Command (TRADOC) that replaced the Continental Army Command in 1973 recognized the necessity of additional reforms. For example, they acknowledged the negative impact of the Vietnam War upon training. During the war, quantity victimized quality as the Field Artillery School, its predecessors, and the Continental Army Command increased the number of graduates and rushed them to Vietnam by decreasing the course lengths which in turn prevented officers from mastering essential skills. With the end of the ground commitment in 1973, the Army required fewer troops, opening the opportunity to improve the quality of training, simultaneously advocated a "back to basics" approach in training, and launched an exhaustive effort to improve officer, warrant officer, and noncommissioned officer training and education to meet the demands of the modern, lethal battlefield as illustrated by the Arab-Israeli War of October 1973.[4]

For the Field Artillery School, training officers, warrant officers, and enlisted soldiers underwent a significant transformation as the Army pushed to make training relevant for the modern battlefield by adding more hands-on, equipment-oriented realistic training. In January 1973, the school introduced student highlights of training in its Field Artillery Officer Basic Course for second lieutenants. It was a one-day, live-fire field training exercise presented during the first week of the course. By limiting formal lecture instruction to two to three minutes, the training exercise provided students with a fast-moving, dynamic field exercise and gave them hands-on training early in their training. Although the school phased it out over the next several years, the short-lived practical exercise signaled the direction that the school was heading. From the school's perspective, practical exercises held the key for enhancing the quality of training especially for second lieutenants. For example, the Field Artillery Officer Basic Course stressed student performance in the field and conducted several graded field exercises. As of 1976, the school provided 10 observed fire shoots for each officer basic course class, planned to add more practical exercises in the coming year, and trained its second lieutenants to be a forward observer, a battery fire direction officer, and a firing battery executive officer using practical exercises as well as classroom instruction.[5]

In the midst this curriculum reform for second lieutenants with its emphasis on fighting in Europe against a well-equipped armored ground force, the Army implemented the Officer Personnel Management System in 1974, forcing the school to adjust its officer programs of instruction to satisfy new personnel and training requirements. The Officer Personnel Management System centralized command selection, designated command tours, and created primary and secondary specialties for officers, among other things. To align its basic course with the objectives of the Officer Personnel Management System, the school had to train newly commissioned second lieutenants in the basics of field artillery and qualify them in a specialty in Career Management Field 13 (Field Artillery). After two years of serious work, the school replaced its officer basic course of 13 weeks for a two-phase course in 1976. Phase one (10 weeks) taught second lieutenants the basics of field artillery tactics, techniques, and procedures, manual and automated gunnery, and firing battery operations to make them a proficient forward observer, battery fire direction officer, and battery executive officer.[6]

Following graduation from the first phase which qualified them as field artillery officers, the second lieutenants attended a specialty course (phase two) of varying lengths (four to six weeks). They attended the Field Artillery Cannon Battery Officer Course, Lance Missile Officer Course, Pershing Officer Course, or Field Artillery Target Acquisition/Survey Course. Here, they received their branch specialty training. Together, both phases prepared the new second lieutenants for their first duty assignment but did not cause them to spend an excessive length of time in training. This permitted the Army to get trained second lieutenants to their first duty assignments as soon as practical which was crucial because of a shortage of junior officers.[7]

As the school began implementing its restructured Field Artillery Officer Basic Course, the Army announced its plans to revamp its officer basic courses even more. In August 1977, the Chief of Staff of the Army, General Bernard Rogers, directed that a Review of Education and Training of Officers be conducted to find better ways to train officers. Published in June 1978 under the direction of Major General Benjamin L. Harrison, the study recommended, among other things, the requirement to expand the length of the Army's officer basic courses to ensure giving young second lieutenants the requisite skills and training to perform competently in their first duty assignment. They had to have the ability to think critically and had to perform specific duty positions. In other words, the Army's officer basic courses had to be more functional than they had been in the past and had to develop critical thinking skills in the young officers. For the Field Artillery School, the functional orientation reinforced the direction that it had taken in 1976 when it started training second lieutenants to be a battery executive officer, forward observer, and fire direction officer and did not portend a serious restructuring of its instructional philosophy or program of instruction.[8]

However, the school faced adjusting the number of weeks for the course. After examining the Review of Education and Training of Officers study, the Army decided in 1980 to increase the length of its officer basic courses by 1984. The expanded officer basic courses would add instruction in command skills and provide additional time for crucial socialization of second lieutenants by giving them more time to get to know their fellow officers. In keeping with this guidance, the Field Artillery School structured its Field Artillery Officer Basic Course program of instruction in 1980 to furnish 19 weeks and four days of training. The school combined its Field Artillery Officer Basic Course that had been initiated in 1976 and its Field Artillery Cannon Battery Officer Course that had been started that same year.⁹

Approved in 1981 by TRADOC and implemented in 1983 when the necessary resources finally became available, this new format trained second lieutenants in the basics of field artillery and gave them a general knowledge of a cannon weapon system. Specifically, the course focused on the skills and knowledge of observed fire, fire direction, and management of individual training to prepare second lieutenants to be a fire support team chief who led a team of forward observers, a cannon battery fire direction officer, and a battery executive officer, making it a functional course. After the Field Artillery Officer Basic Course all second lieutenants who did not go to a cannon unit received specialty training of varying lengths in the Field Artillery Target Acquisition Course, the Survey Officer Course, the Pershing Officer Course, or the Lance Officer Course. While the Field Artillery Officer Basic Course focused on functional training, the follow-on courses furnished specialty training of varying lengths on a particular weapon system other than a cannon to qualify them for their first duty assignment. In reality, the school preserved the two-phase approach for training second lieutenants and merely increased the length of training to satisfy TRADOC guidance.¹⁰

Pushing to expand the number of subjects taught in its officer basic course and to accommodate the 52 hours of common core instruction in leadership, ethics, military justice, military history, and other subjects mandated by TRADOC in 1984 for all second lieutenants, the school planned to increase the number of weeks from 19 to 21 in 1986 even before the current course had been tried and proven. Before plans could be laid for such a revision, the Chief of Staff of the Army, General John A. Wickham, intervened.¹¹

Anticipating a declining budget in the near future, Wickham sent TRADOC a message in July 1985 that directed reducing all officer basic training to 15 weeks and two days to cut costs and get second lieutenants to operational units faster. For the Field Artillery School, Wickham's instruction meant reversing the trend of the past several years of expanding officer basic training to include more subjects and would force the elimination of less critical training to stay within the prescribed length. As the school looked for ways to reduce the length of its basic course, TRADOC came to the rescue by devising a basic course of 19 weeks and four days that included a common core of subjects that all second lieutenants should know and sent it to the Army for approval early in 1986. Upon authorization from the Army, TRADOC started implementing its officer basic course model over the next several years. While part of the 19-week, four-day course would be devoted to common core topics, another part would be branch-specific training.¹²

Based on this guidance, the Field Artillery School created a two-phase Field Artillery Officer Basic Course for 1986. Phase one lasted 12 weeks and two days, covered the common core subjects, and focused on war fighting skills, observed fire, manual gunnery, field artillery fundamentals, and principles of fire support. During the second phase of seven weeks and two days, student officers received cannon, Lance missile, or Multiple-Launch Rocket System training depending upon their initial duty assignment. When this format failed to prepare second lieutenants for a cannon assignment following a tour of duty with a Lance missile or Multiple-Launch Rocket System unit, the school revamped its 19-week and four-day course in 1991 to focus on the fundamentals of cannon artillery as well as TRADOC common core subjects. This format ensured a well-rounded officer, prepared second lieutenants to be a fire direction officer, a fire support team chief, and a battery executive officer and afforded greater flexibility in assignments. Students with assignments to either a Lance or a Multiple-Launch Rocket System unit received training on those weapon systems after graduation from the basic course.[13]

Meanwhile, rising training costs and a shortage of captains prodded the Army to decrease the length of time that an officer would be away from the troops. Directed by the Army's Officer Personnel Management System, TRADOC cut the length of its officer advance courses from 36 weeks to 26 weeks in 1976. This caused the Field Artillery School to eliminate less critical training, such as writing and some field training exercises, from its Field Artillery Officer Advance Course and to focus the course on preparing captains to serve as a battery commander, battalion fire direction officer, and maneuver battalion/brigade fire support officer on the mid-intensity battlefield. Concurrently, the school increased the number of instructional hours on observed fire and registration. Gunnery instruction accounted for 33 percent of the course with more emphasis than before placed upon automated gunnery to teach student officers how to use the Field Artillery Digital Automated Computer, forcing the reduction in the time devoted to manual gunnery. As in the Field Artillery Officer Basic Course, advance course students underwent instruction on Soviet doctrine and organization of ground forces; the capabilities, limitations, and vulnerabilities of Soviet equipment and weapons; and the offensive and defensive tactics employed by Soviet ground forces from company to regimental levels to prepare them for possible combat in Europe. The school also divided the course into two phases – a technical proficiency phase of 22 weeks and an application phase of four weeks composed of practical exercises, seminars, and other activities where the student officer applied the acquired knowledge.[14]

Late in 1976, the Commandant and Assistant Commandant of the School reflected upon the changes to the advance course. In a draft letter for incoming students in 1976, the Commandant of the Field Artillery School, Major General David E. Ott (1973-1976), described the Field Artillery Officer Advance Course as a compact, fast-pace course that required students to begin with a higher level of knowledge of field artillery than ever before because the basics that had been learned in the Field Artillery Officer Basic Course would not be reviewed. The shortened length of the course simply precluded refresher instruction in the basics.[15] Along the same lines of thinking, the Assistant Commandant, Brigadier General Albert B. Akers (1975-1978), wrote in November 1975, "The 26-week advanced course must be limited to hardcore training. It is directed towards providing you [the student] with a master's degree in the techniques of battery command, fire support planning and coordination, and gunnery procedures."[16]

This 26-week format filled with practical exercises remained constant until January 1984. To meet the needs of the operational commands and to cut training costs with the emphasis on the latter, the Army told TRADOC to reduce its officer advance courses for all branches to 20 weeks, to make them functional courses, and to feature a core curriculum of common tasks that every captain should know to perform effectively at the company level. For officers requiring more specialized training, they would attend a follow-on course of not more than six weeks after completing the advance course.[17]

TRADOC followed up with additional guidance. Discussing the orientation of the revamped officer advance course, the Commanding General of TRADOC, General William R. Richardson, said in February 1984 that it would be a hands-on, performance-oriented course and focus on technical and tactical proficiency to prepare captains to lead, train, fight, and maintain units because the existing branch officer advance courses were too lectured oriented. Subsequently in March 1984, TRADOC announced dividing its officer advance courses into common core on combined arms subjects and other training mandated (leadership, writing, ethics, and military history, among other subjects) by the Army and TRADOC and branch-specific training. Common core instruction would last six weeks and be followed by 14 weeks of branch-specific training. As an alternative to providing the instruction in common core and branch-specific phases, TRADOC permitted integrating common core and branch subjects to eliminate two distinct phases.[18]

For the Field Artillery School, TRADOC's guidance meant cutting six weeks of instruction from its Field Artillery Officer Advance Course to get down to the 19-week and four-day format and developing follow-on courses. To reduce the length, the school eliminated less critical instruction and trimmed branch-specific training. At the same time it designed follow-on courses – Fire Direction Officer Course, Pershing Officer Course, Lance Officer Course, Tactical Fire Direction System Officer Course, Nuclear Warhead Detachment Course, Cannon Systems Qualification Course, Nuclear/Chemical Target Analysis Course, and Multiple-Launch Rocket System Course. By the time that the revisions had been implemented in 1985, the school's Field Artillery Officer Advance Course trained captains to be a fire support officer, staff officer, and battery commander who were technically and tactically competent to fight on the European battlefield.[19]

Meanwhile, the school revamped its warrant officer education program. Prior to 1968, warrant officers had no formal progressive military education system. Over the next four years, the Army gradually implemented basic or entry level training, intermediate or mid-career training, and advanced training. In 1973 the Army redesignated the levels of training as entry, advanced, and senior. Even with this formal education program in place, the Army still appointed noncommissioned officers as warrant officers based upon their training and experience. Understanding that this method had little quality control, the Army revamped it. Effective on 1 October 1984, all potential warrant officers had to go through a "Triple Check" system. Check one involved the administrative application process, verification of qualifications, and board selection to attend the Warrant Officer Entry Course. Check two included attending the entry course which was a mandatory high-stress leadership and ethics course designed to enhance and develop officer qualities in the warrant officer candidates. Check three consisted of military occupational specialty training (Warrant Officer Basic Course) for branch certification. This system ended the practice of direct appointments and provided better guidelines for selecting warrant officer candidates.[20]

On 3 August 1983, TRADOC meanwhile approved the Field Artillery School's pilot

Warrant Officer Entry Course and established a starting date of 5 January 1984 for the course. Between August 1983 and January 1984, the school created a branch-immaterial, six-week course, refined it, and then implemented it as a standard training program in February 1986 at TRADOC's direction rather than as an experimental one as initially planned. Subsequently in March 1986, TRADOC directed its other service schools to pattern their entry courses after Fort Sill's.[21]

As the school was implementing its course, TRADOC made a significant announcement about warrant officer training. Seeking to save money in the face of declining budgets and to standardize warrant officer entry courses, Richardson directed Fort Rucker, Alabama; Aberdeen Proving Ground, Maryland; and Fort Sill in May 1985 to study combining all courses at Fort Rucker. After several months of study, options emerged in the fall of 1985. TRADOC could consolidate all entry courses at Fort Rucker, Fort Sill, or Aberdeen Proving Ground; could combine all non-aviation entry courses at Aberdeen Proving Ground; or could continue studying the preferred method of implementing warrant officer training. Based upon the study, TRADOC announced its intention in January 1986 to consolidate all warrant officer – Warrant Officer Entry Course, Warrant Officer Basic Course for military occupational specialty certification, and Warrant Officer Advance Course – training at one location to save money. Later in March 1986, pressured by a declining budget and the requirement to ensure competent warrant officers, TRADOC reversed this position and decided to consolidate only the generic entry courses at one location after concluding that the branch service schools should handle branch qualification and advance training.[22]

After lengthy studies in 1986 and 1987, TRADOC subsequently announced its site for its entry course. Initially, it selected Fort Jackson, South Carolina, because it could provide the least expensive entry course. When Fort Rucker revised its costs downward for its entry course, TRADOC subsequently picked it and started the course in 1988. This decision left the Field Artillery School with a basic and advance course for field artillery warrant officers.[23]

Concurrently, the Army developed a three-tier Noncommissioned Officer Education System in 1971 to formalize and upgrade noncommissioned officer training and education. In 1948, the Army formulated a career development program for enlisted soldiers to take them from a basic recruit through retirement because World War II had highlighted the need for competent noncommissioned officers. This program based recommendation for promotion to the next higher grade on a system of competitive examinations, evaluation reports, and promotion boards without regard to unit vacancies. Just as this program was being implemented, the Korean War cut it short. Although Army organizations, meanwhile, created noncommissioned officer academies with the first being organized in Germany in 1947 to train noncommissioned officers for constabulary duty, most went out of existence by the end of the 1950s because attendance was not mandatory and because many noncommissioned officers failed to see the need to attend. With the failure to revive a career development program for enlisted soldiers after the Korean War and the collapse of noncommissioned officer academies in the 1950s, training for the noncommissioned officer corps languished.[24]

The Vietnam War forced the Army to reassess the need for a career development program for noncommissioned officers and noncommissioned officer academies. Noncommissioned officers with long years of service left the Army because of the repeated tours of duty in Vietnam, prompting the Army to create a stop-gap measure with the organization of noncommissioned officer candidate courses at Fort Sill, Fort Knox, Kentucky; and Fort Benning, Georgia; where soldiers graduated as a sergeant team leader or staff sergeant squad leader. Notwithstanding this effort that produced noncommissioned officers, the noncommissioned officer corps was still in a shambles at the end of the war.[25]

As the Army started the transition from a draftee force to a voluntary force, it recognized the requirement to improve training for enlisted soldiers and noncommissioned officers and to create a career development program. Through the 1960s, enlisted soldier training focused on a "hands-on" experience and learning through osmosis. An old soldier using the manual could show the young soldier how to put on a uniform, to clean weapons and equipment, and to pack but not much else. Based upon this and the need for a professional noncommissioned officer corps, the Army adopted the Enlisted Personnel Management System in February 1972 to foster professionalism, to provide a career development program, to furnish the Army with trained noncommissioned officers, and to enhance career attractiveness to keep soldiers in the Army. The system grouped enlisted military occupational specialties called career management fields together that were related and were manageable from a personnel and manpower standpoint. The system also outlined five skill levels for each military occupational specialty that were tied to rank to provide logical progression from private (E1) to sergeant major (E9) in one field. However, only skill levels two through five were part of the Noncommissioned Officer Education System. One of these career management fields was 13 (Field Artillery) which was a consolidation of the old Field Artillery career management fields of 13 and 15.[26]

To support the Enlisted Personnel Management System and its skill levels, TRADOC established a sequential and progressive education program for noncommissioned officers that was patterned after the officer education system. The Army initiated a basic course in 1972, an advanced course in 1972, and a senior course in 1973 to produce noncommissioned officers who could train, lead, and direct the men under their command. However, graduation from them was not mandatory for promotion.[27]

Recognizing the requirement for professional development as outlined by various studies on the noncommissioned officer with the most recent one completed in December 1985, the Army made graduation mandatory for promotion. On 1 October 1989, completion of the Primary Leadership Development Course became compulsory for promotion to sergeant (skill level two). It taught young soldiers the basic tenets of leadership. One year later on 1 October 1990, graduation from the Basic Noncommissioned Officer Course which trained sergeants as a squad, crew, or section leader became a requirement for promotion to staff sergeant (skill level three), while on 1 October 1993, completion of the Advanced Noncommissioned Officer Course became obligatory for promotion to sergeant first class (skill level four). This course emphasized technical and advanced leadership skills required to train soldiers at the platoon level. On that same day, graduation from the

Sergeants Major Academy became a requirement for promotion to sergeant major (skill level five).[28]

Fulfilling the vision of 1948, the Enlisted Personnel Management System gave noncommissioned officers and enlisted soldiers their first real standardized career progression program with required training for promotion and encouraged professional development. In 1993, the noncommissioned officer education system therefore featured four integrated levels of training – primary, basic, advanced, and senior. Unlike the courses for officers and specialized courses designed to meet the officer's next unit of assignment, enlisted soldiers attended the Primary Leadership Development Course, Basic Noncommissioned Officer Course, and Advanced Noncommissioned Officer Course for their particular military occupational specialty, such as cannon crew member, to prepare them to perform duties required for assignments of progressively greater responsibility in that specialty.[29]

As with the officer courses, the main objective of the noncommissioned officer education system in the Field Artillery School focused on helping the student master the skills and knowledge necessary for the real world performance of the jobs or tasks to an acceptable standard. A vital part of this was the skill qualification test that replaced the military occupational specialty test in 1977. A formally administered test with written and hands-on sections, the skill qualification test measured a soldier's proficiency in a military occupational specialty. To be awarded the next skill level and to be eligible for promotion, soldiers (privates through corporals) had to achieve a score of 80 percent on the skill qualification test while a score of 60 to 79 percent verified the soldier's ability to perform in the military occupational specialty. However, a score of 80 percent or better did not guarantee a promotion because the soldier still had to receive high performance evaluations on enlisted evaluation reports, meet time-in-service and time-in-grade requirements, and be recommended by the individual's commander.[30]

For the Field Artillery School, a sequential and progressive noncommissioned officer education system represented a major breakthrough. For years, the school had taught everything that an enlisted soldier needed for an entire career in one course. As a result, many enlisted soldiers never received additional formal training upon graduation from advance individual training while some attended a school to learn the job that they were performing. With the new education system the school taught the appropriate skills for each level of responsibility, such as staff sergeant on a cannon crew. This basically meant that a new soldier learned the skills required for the first job and returned to school to learn skills required to function in a higher rank.[31]

As it revamped individual training in the school house, the Field Artillery School developed the Army Training and Evaluation Program for collective training for operational units. Initiated by TRADOC, the Army Training and Evaluation Program was a new performance-oriented program that required elements from platoon through battalion, their soldiers, and officers to perform tasks to a standard and not just put in training hours and replaced the time-oriented Army Training Program in use since World War II. The Army Training and Evaluation Program defined specified missions, tasks, conditions, and the standards to be met. At the same time, it placed responsibility for executing the training program directly on the unit and was structured to allow units to train as they would fight, to evaluate the results of their training, and to use the lessons learned to improve training.[32]

The program reflected a significant training development. Achieving the standard became even more important than before. All soldiers and units would be tested to demonstrate their skills and have to meet an established standard, while the tests would be as realistic as possible to determine the soldiers' and units' ability to perform their required tasks in a combat environment. Like the rest of the training revolution of the 1970s, the Army Training and Evaluation Program manifested the "train as we will fight" concept. Training had to be more realistic and replicate how the Army would fight on a tactical nuclear battlefield or a conventional battlefield.[33]

As critical as the individual and collective training reforms were, the introduction of small group instruction and mentoring truly transformed training in the Field Artillery School. In March 1985, Lieutenant General Charles W. Bagnal, director of the Professional Development of Officers Study Group, Department of the Army, explained the rationale for small group instruction and mentoring. Mentoring was a style of leadership that closely resembled coaching. Open communication, role modeling, and effective use of counseling and sharing of the leaders' frame of reference with their junior officers characterized this form of instruction. To implement mentoring in the Army school system, TRADOC had to abandon the traditional large group instruction format that had existed for years. Bagnal suggested reducing the faculty-student ratio at the branch service schools, providing faculty members who were the next higher grade to the students (meaning captains taught first lieutenants), supplying education and training to teach faculty members how to mentor, and guaranteeing that faculty members were quality officers, among other things.[34]

As Bagnal explained further, recent studies justified such a dramatic overhaul of officer training, especially for captains. In view of the growing sophistication of the battlefield, the Army's education and training system had to do a better job than it had done in the past by developing officers who had critical-thinking skills. Officers had to have the ability to conceptualize, innovate, synthesize disparate information, adapt to the unexpected, and be able to temper doctrine with the willingness to take a measured risk when necessary to arrest victory from almost certain defeat. Knowing what to think was insufficient. Officers had to know how to think. This involved ending the practice of "spoon-feeding" officers with facts in the classroom, requiring them to memorize the information, and then having them repeat the data back on examinations to see if they knew the information.[35]

Basically, TRADOC service schools, including the Field Artillery School, had to discard the large classroom layout of 60 or more students per instructor with its lecture format for small group instruction of about 15 students per instructor where students could be mentored and taught how to think. With this objective in mind, TRADOC directed the Combined Arms Center at Fort Leavenworth, Kansas, in July 1985 to develop a small group instruction model and conduct pilot programs at the Infantry School, Fort Benning, Georgia; the Engineer School, Fort Leonard Wood, Missouri; and the Medical Service School, Fort Sam Houston, Texas; late in 1986. Adding to this basic guidance, the

Commanding General of Combined Arms Center, Lieutenant General Robert W. Riscassi, outlined the guiding principles of small group instruction and mentoring. According to the general, the small group pilot program would set the ideal student-faculty ratio to 15 to one and would designate faculty members who were the next higher grade to the students as mentors, among other things.[36]

Envisioning a drastic change in training, the Combined Arms Center tasked TRADOC service schools to identify the full impact of small group instruction and mentoring. On 30 July 1985, the Field Artillery School responded. Mentoring had to be applied wholeheartedly since halfway measures would "simply result in grist for the mills of any detractors" who opposed abandoning tried and proven instructional methods.[37] More importantly, small group instruction would be resource intensive. In view of this, the school wrote the Combined Arms Center on 3 September 1985 about creating a high-level working committee to prioritize conflicting resource demands, to develop instructor training, to acquire additional resources to run the program, and to conduct a pilot program.[38]

Although the Field Artillery School endorsed small group instruction and mentoring in principle and although the pilot tests of small group instruction appeared to be successful, the school still stalled implementation. Lieutenant Colonel Samuel Floca's task force formed by the Commandant of the Field Artillery School, Major General Eugene Korpal (1985-1987), to examine the feasibility of the concept provided the school's real opposition. In December 1986, Floca's task force found limited resources – an insufficient number of classrooms and instructors – as valid reasons to resist initiating small group instruction and mentoring. Before the school could institute them, TRADOC had to provide the necessary resources. Basically, the school wanted more money and instructors before it would seriously consider abandoning large-group instruction.[39] In a letter to the Combined Arms Center, Korpal clarified, "The cost in manpower and facility resources . . . appears to be a major stumbling block. . . . By capitalizing on existing programs. . . [,] we can introduce 'mentoring' on a limited basis. . . ."[40] Using limited resources as an excuse, the Field Artillery School dragged its feet and resisted implementation until TRADOC provided them; but TRADOC never planned to give the school additional resources for small group instruction. The school would have to find them.[41]

At the conclusion of their pilot programs, commentary from the Infantry School, the Engineer School, and the Medical Services School reinforced the Field Artillery School's initial observations about the requisite resources. At a TRADOC conference in December 1986, the three schools stressed the resource intensive nature of small group instruction. The concept required more instructors and classrooms than large group instruction. However, they still supported small group instruction because it offered the only way of implementing mentoring and teaching critical thinking skills to officers. Retaining large group instruction of 60 or more students in a class would inhibit the development of critical thinking skills and continue the practice of rote memorization as the primary means of learning. This mixed endorsement was more than enough for TRADOC to push forward. On 10 March 1987, it directed instituting small group instruction in all officer advance courses.[42]

Although it continued to express concern about the lack of resources, the school had no other choice now but to move forward with small group instruction. In view of this situation, the Field Artillery School searched for viable options to make small group instruction work within available resources. Desiring to avoid overlapping small group instruction among the Field Artillery Officer Advance Course's seven annual classes that would make it even more resource intensive, understanding that the school's physical facilities were limited, and noting that technical subjects were unsuitable for small group instruction, the school developed a two-phase Field Artillery Officer Advance Course and started it in February 1989. Out of the 19-week and four-day Field Artillery Officer Advance Course, large group instruction where the entire class (approximately 60 students) met as a whole lasted the first eight weeks. During this phase, the school taught manual and automated gunnery and other technical skills. This was followed by small group instruction (12-15 students) phase of 12 weeks led by a field artillery major or captain who was promotable to major from the Army, Marine Corps, or an allied country. The small group phase promoted mentoring and covered leadership, maneuver tactics, synchronization of fire support, and other tactical skills to develop officers to be battery commanders, battalion or brigade fire support officers, and battalion, brigade, and division artillery staff officers.[43]

Two officers who played a key role in designing the revised course pointed out other benefits besides mentoring. As Colonel Felix Peterson, Jr., and Lieutenant Colonel Charles A. Morris wrote in the *Field Artillery Magazine* in April 1989 just after the school started small group instruction in its officer advance course, "the responsibility for learning still rests with the individual student but maximum learning occurs when a group has a common goal for learning. . ."[44] Small group instruction and mentoring placed the onus for learning on the student because the instructors had become facilitators and were no longer just purveyors of information.[45]

Although the school instituted small group instruction in its Field Artillery Officer Advance Course, it deferred implementing it in its Field Artillery Officer Basic Course and noncommissioned officer courses in 1989 because they were in the middle of major structural reforms. The noncommissioned officer courses were being moved from the school and consolidated at the Noncommissioned Officer Academy that was being formed, while the Field Artillery Officer Basic Course was being redesigned into a generic core program of 19 weeks and four days with follow-on courses of varying lengths based upon the first unit of assignment. Although the school launched small group instruction in the Basic Noncommissioned Officer Course and Advanced Noncommissioned Officer Course in 1991, it never integrated the concept into its officer basic course and warrant officer courses. Both remained in the large-group format. However, the small numbers attending the warrant officer courses made them *de facto* small group instruction oriented.[46]

Of all of the officer education system reforms since 1973, adopting small group instruction and mentoring made the most significant break with existing practices that had centered around rote memorization and large group instruction with classes of 60 or more per instructor. During the small group portion of Field Artillery Officer Advance Course, Basic Noncommissioned Officer Course, and Advanced Noncommissioned Officer Course, students actively discussed doctrine, tactics, techniques, and procedures and were forced to develop critical thinking skills by challenging their classmates' and instructor's thinking and conclusions. Introducing small group instruction and mentoring in the 1980s and 1990s certainly ranked as a more important development than the adoption of functional training (training for a specific task or job) in the Field Artillery Officer Basic Course and Field Artillery Officer Advance Course in the 1970s and 1980s which was also a major break with previous practices with their focus on generic training for field artillery officers.

As such, reforms of the 1970s and 1980s altered training and instruction in the school. Basic and advance officer training emphasized acquiring competency in a specific function, such as forward observer or battalion staff officer, and on a particular weapon system as opposed to the generic training that had dominated the school's program of instruction since 1911. More importantly, the advance course focused on developing critical thinking skills in captains through small group instruction so that they could adapt to changing battlefield conditions. Meanwhile, the reforms dramatically restructured warrant officer and noncommissioned officer training and education. For the first time, warrant officers and noncommissioned officers had a career progression path and a training program that began with the basics and ended with advanced instruction and training – something that the officers had had for years. Although the desire to improve training to enhance the competence of its graduates had been a constant drive in the school, the presence of the numerically superior and well-equipped Soviet-Warsaw Pact threat in Europe certainly furnished the impetus and sense of urgency for such sweeping training and instructional reforms of the 1970s and 1980s.

New Doctrine, Weapons, and Equipment

Meanwhile, the intensity of the Arab-Israeli War of October 1973 that was fought with American and Soviet weapons and equipment shocked the US Army, TRADOC, and the Field Artillery School by demonstrating the destructiveness of conventional weapons, especially precision munitions being introduced. Facing this harsh reality, TRADOC's three combat arms schools (Infantry, Armor, and Field Artillery) joined forces and reemphasized combined arms warfare as the best means of defeating the imposing Soviet-Warsaw Pact threat. To accomplish this, each school and combat arm made a special effort to learn the roles, missions, and capabilities of the others for better cooperation in combat. The Field Artillery School, in particular, acknowledged the need to enhance the Field Artillery's ability to furnish continuous and timely close support to the maneuver arms and to provide effective counterbattery fires to neutralize or destroy enemy indirect fire systems. As the school candidly recognized, improving fire support depended upon developing new doctrine, force structure, tactics, techniques, and procedures, new equipment, and new weapon systems.[47]

Interestingly, the formation of TRADOC in 1973 permitted the Field Artillery School to reinvigorate its role in combat developments – the systematic development of new and improved organization, equipment, weapons, and doctrine. Combat developments originated with the perception that the advent of nuclear weapons and the emergence of delivery capabilities, such as intercontinental ballistic missiles and bombers, demanded a comprehensive and systematic peacetime development of Army weapons and equipment, warfighting doctrine, and tactical organization. Beginning in 1952 and continuing over the next three years, the Office of the Chief of Army Field Forces which had the mission of combat developments created a network of offices and agencies to carry out this new function. When it replaced the Office of the Chief of Army Field Forces in 1955, the US Continental Army Command took over combat developments to complement its existing training mission. The subsequent activation of the US Army Combat Developments Experimentation Center at Fort Ord, California, in 1956 added to the proliferation of combat developments agencies that fell outside of the US Continental Army Command.

To bring the disparate agencies that worked together tenuously under one command for better supervision and coordination, the Army formed the US Army Combat Developments Command in 1962 to develop user requirements and to coordinate testing and evaluation, relieving the US Continental Army Command of its combat developments mission. This action created separate training and combat development commands that interacted with each other very little over the next several years. For the US Army Artillery and Missile School (1957-1969), the organization of the US Army Combat Developments Command ended its close involvement with combat developments because it had developed user requirements and participated in tests and evaluation since 1952. From 1962 onward, the school focused mainly on training and had only a minor involvement with combat developments.[48]

Upon its creation in 1973, TRADOC took over the combat developments mission to accompany its training mission. The alignment of combat developments and training under one command returned combat developments to the branch schools to draw upon their expertise and to coordinate combat developments and training. Once again, combat developments became an integral aspect of the Field Artillery School's (1969-present) daily operations because it furnished user requirements, monitored progress, and became actively involved in the testing and evaluation process.[49]

Although the school recognized that the next war could be an insurgency, a limited war, a full-scale nuclear war, or any other potential threat, the Soviet-Warsaw Pact threat that had assertively modernized its ground and air forces during the 1960s and early 1970s, the destructiveness of the Arab-Israeli War, and the driving imperative to modernize and rehabilitate the Army after its Vietnam war experience to fight on a mechanized and armored battlefield of the future drove combat development activities. In fact, they prompted the TRADOC commander, General William E. Depuy, to direct the writing of new doctrine. As part of the TRADOC effort, the Field Artillery School centered its attention on preparing fire support doctrine for a violent conflict of mid-intensity and short duration based upon the Arab-Israeli War precedent. To preview the changes in fire support doctrine, the school hosted a worldwide commanders' conference for senior field artillery leaders on 4-5 December 1974. The first such gathering held since the March 1946 conference that outlined the post-World War II reforms, the December 1974 conference assembled 49 division artillery, corps artillery, and group artillery commanders to exchange information, ideas, and candid reactions relating to the changes needed in field artillery doctrine, tactics, techniques, and procedures.[50]

At this conference the Commandant of the Field Artillery School, Major General David E. Ott (1973-1976), unveiled the school's new field artillery counterbattery doctrine and organization. Through 1974 the corps artillery commander had the counterbattery mission because he had the assets, primarily longer range field artillery than the division had and target acquisition systems. As Ott explained, the Field Artillery School moved counterbattery from the corps to the division and renamed it counterfire to keep it current with battlefield changes over the years. Specifically, the corps front was about 25 to 40 kilometers during World War II. Because the front was relatively small, corps artillery weapons could cover it with little difficulty. However, the corps front of the 1970s in Europe was 80 to 100 kilometers. This large front created an unmanageable number of targets, overextended communications, and made furnishing fire support difficult for corps artillery. Coupled with the extended front, field artillery in the division of the 1970s had a much longer reach and packed a heavier punch than its predecessors of World War II. With the exception of the M107 towed 175-mm. gun which was a corps asset and was being phased out and the Lance missile that was just being introduced, corps and division artillery weapons were basically the same in the 1970s.[51]

As persuasive as these reasons were for moving counterbattery from the corps to the division, "the real selling point" for developing counterfire doctrine revolved around fighting outnumbered. Under such circumstances, the division commander had to have the ability to shift back and forth between close support and counterbattery work as required. Because he would also be closer to the battle than the corps commander, he would also have a better grasp of the situation and have to determine priorities. In other words, the division commander should decide whether close support or counterbattery was the priority because he was in a better position than the corps commander to see the ebb and flow of the battle.[52]

For these reasons, the school decided to center all fire support in the division. To accomplish this, the school gave the division commander control of all field artillery in his sector, increased the size of the division artillery staff, and allotted the division artillery commander the requisite target acquisition assets to engage enemy indirect fire systems. Ultimately, giving the division commander control of all field artillery meant placing corps artillery in either a reinforcing role to a division or attaching it to a division, although the corps artillery commander would still allocate field artillery battalions. Once the battalions had been earmarked for a division, they would fall under its control. Finalized in 1975 and approved by the Army on 30 April 1976, counterfire as the school called it recognized that field artillery weapons would attack all indirect fire systems whereas counterbattery implied only engaging enemy field artillery and that command and control of fire support would be centralized in the division. Moreover, counterfire permitted the division artillery commander to manage his resources more effectively and allowed him to shift between counterfire and close support rapidly to overcome the numerical superiority of the threat.[53]

Meanwhile, Ott understood the urgency of furnishing responsive close support to the maneuver arms. The key to this focused on combining the various indirect fire systems into an effective team. To this end, Ott wrote Depuy in July 1975 about the necessity of restructuring forward observation. The growth in the size of the battlefield prevented forward observer teams from furnishing effective observed fires throughout the supported unit's sector. Also, the Army required a better method of shifting and massing fires from mortars, field artillery, attack helicopters, and tactical aircraft.[54]

Depuy shared Ott's concerns and directed the Close Support Study Group, which was formed on 29 July 1975 by Ott to examine ways of improving forward observation. In November 1975, the group issued its final report, which proposed shifting the responsibility for fire support from the maneuver company commander to the chief of the fire support team that would furnish observation for mortars, naval gunfire, close air support, naval gunfire, and field artillery. The fire support team chief would handle all fire support tasks for the company and would command, train, and supervise all observers on the fire support team, including 81-mm. and 4.2-inch mortar observers. The group also suggested making the chief as well as battalion and brigade fire support sections organic to the maneuver arms. By being organic to maneuver units, fire support experts would train with them, provide experienced fire support personnel at all times, enhance the flexibility of the field artillery battalion, and coordinate close air support, naval gunfire, field artillery, and mortars.[55]

The fire support team, which was approved in 1976, and counterfire transformed the fire support. While the fire support team tied close support to the maneuver arms more directly than before, counterfire gave the division's field artillery commander the ability to shift rapidly and effectively between close support and counterfire by placing all fire support under the division artillery commander.

Developing counterfire and the fire support team fit within a broader TRADOC effort to rewrite doctrine in general to stay abreast of changes with the battlefield. If the Arab-Israeli War of October 1973 was any indication of the future, the Army had to survive the destructiveness of the first battle of the next war against a numerically superior and well-equipped foe. Published by TRADOC in 1976, *Field Manual 100-5, Operations* served as a capstone for an entire family of doctrinal manuals. It outlined the active defense doctrine that focused on winning the first battle through violent defensive action and huge quantities of firepower and fighting outnumbered and winning.[56]

Under the umbrella of *Field Manual 100-5*, the Field Artillery School took a new approach to the school's doctrinal and training literature. It reduced the number of manuals from 50 to 30 by consolidating them, replaced all equipment-related field manuals with "user" technical manuals, and wrote one how-to-fight manual – *Field Manual 6-20, Fire Support for Combat Operations* – with three layers of manuals below it on how-to-fight. One layer centered on officers and senior noncommissioned officers. One focused on teaching enlisted soldiers how to perform their military occupational specialty. The third layer consisted of technical manuals on operating and maintaining equipment for enlisted personnel.[57]

The Field Artillery School completed *Field Manual 6-20* as the Field Artillery's capstone manual in 1978. Written for maneuver commanders, their staffs, and fire support coordinators, the manual served as the basic reference source for fire support planning and coordination.[58] In contrast to previous editions of *Field Manual 6-20*, this one was not a tactics manual. The manual provided "the first comprehensive treatment of the maneuver commander-fire support coordinator relationship and [explained] how to integrate all fire support into combined arms operations," as the Commandant of the Field Artillery School, Major General Donald R. Keith (1976-1977), related in a letter in May 1977 to the Commandant of the US Army Intelligence School and Center.[59]

Notwithstanding *Field Manual 100-5*'s significance, meanwhile, that forced *Field Manual 6-20* to be rewritten, many officers found active defense doctrine to be too conservative by stressing the defense, among other shortcomings. In 1976-1977, the Commander of V Corps in the Federal Republic of Germany, Lieutenant General Donn A. Starry, noted a critical weakness with the active defense. Because it was designed to stop a breakthrough attack, the active defense organized battalions, brigades, and even divisions to win the initial battle. However, it did not deal with the Soviet's and Warsaw Pact's second and third echelons that were an essential part of the threat's offensive doctrine and a major concern for the corps. As Starry explained, the first echelon would hit and be followed by the second and third echelons respectively. Along with the Defense Science Board, which was the senior advisory board of prominent scientists, engineers, and managers in the Department of Defense, Starry advised developing the capability of engaging the second and third echelons while fighting the first echelon.[60]

Upon becoming the Commanding General of TRADOC in 1977, Starry initiated a complete rewrite of *Field Manual 100-5*. Out of this effort emerged the 1981 edition of *Field Manual 100-5* which outlined AirLand Battle doctrine where the Army and Air Force would fight all three echelons simultaneously. As the Army was fighting the first echelon, air and ground forces, including field artillery, would engage the second and third echelons to slow them down and reduce their numbers. By doing this, the ground forces could recover from fighting the first echelon before encountering the depleted second and the third echelons.[61]

Countering the enemy's echeloned formations successfully underscored the imperative of Army-wide force structure modernization. Cognizant of the need to abandon the Reorganization Objective Army Division of the 1960s, Starry initiated the Division 86 Study in 1978 to follow up where the Division Restructuring Study of 1977-1978 had left off. To defeat the Soviet and Warsaw Pact ground forces, the Division 86 Study emphasized creating a heavy division with the ability of fighting the close and deep battles.[62]

After digesting the recommendations of the Division Restructuring Study and the Division 86 Study, TRADOC developed a heavy division design with input from the Field Artillery School and other service schools. Approved by the Chief of Staff of the Army, General Edward C. Meyer, in August 1980, the new heavy division had 20,000 officers and soldiers and six tank battalions and four mechanized battalions in its armored version or five tank battalions and five mechanized battalions in its mechanized infantry version. The heavy division's field artillery consisted of three direct support battalions of M109 155-mm. self-propelled howitzers (seventy-two) and one general support battalion of M110 8-inch self-propelled howitzers (sixteen) and a battery of Multiple-Launch Rocket System M270 launchers (nine). Because the personnel resources would not be available for the Division 86 heavy division, its successor, the Army of Excellence effort of the mid-1980s, subsequently reduced personnel requirements but still retained 10 maneuver battalions, three direct support field artillery battalions (72 M109 howitzers), and one general support battery of M270 launchers (nine). As with the Division Restructuring Study and Division 86 Study, the Army of Excellence built the division around a weapon system rather than integrating a new weapon system into existing organization as had been the practice for years.[63]

Although the potential of fighting a low- to mid-intensity conflict had existed, the Iranian Islamic fundamentalist revolution of 1979 and the Soviet invasion of Afghanistan that same year prompted the United States to broaden its strategic interests beyond Europe. Based upon this, the Army directed TRADOC to draw up plans for a light division to meet its future strategic requirements. To satisfy this, TRADOC devised three light divisions – airborne, air assault, and infantry – in 1979-1980. TRADOC's first effort with Infantry Division 86 produced a light division of 14,000 officers and soldiers and a division artillery of three battalions of M198 towed 155-mm. howitzers (72) for direct support and a battalion of M198 howitzers, M110 eight-inch howitzers, and Multiple-Launch Rocket System M270 launchers for general support. Because this division with its North Atlantic Treaty Organization reinforcement mission was too heavy, TRADOC redesigned the light division still as a part of its Infantry Division 86 effort. Division 86 had three direct support battalions of M198 howitzers (72) and a general support battery of nine M270 launchers. Conceptually, this light division would arrive early and buy time for the heavier forces to follow and would reinforce heavy divisions in scenarios and terrain – cities, forests, and mountains – where it could be more effective than the heavy division. Eventually, the Army of Excellence infantry division replaced Infantry Division 86. The Army of Excellence light division's primary mission focused on supporting worldwide contingency operations with a collateral mission of reinforcement of heavy divisions in Europe but only if terrain and circumstances called for it.[64]

As it restructured its force and doctrine, the Army launched the most massive equipment and weapon modernization program in its history to offset the Soviet-Warsaw Pact's modernized ground forces. Although these equipment and weapon systems had their beginnings in the Vietnam drawdown of the late 1960s and early 1970s, they were eventually fielded early in the 1980s. At the top of the list, the Army placed a new attack helicopter, followed by a new utility helicopter, a new tank, a new surface-to-air missile, a new heavy infantry antitank weapon, a service-wide digital tactical communications system, improved conventional munitions, and an integrated command and control system. By 1974, decreasing budgets reduced the list to a new tank (Abrams), a new infantry fighting vehicle (Bradley), a new surface-to-air missile (Patriot), a new attack helicopter (Apache), and a new utility helicopter (Black Hawk), commonly called the "Big Five."[65]

Although the Field Artillery's requirements did not make the top five, the Army modernized the branch with the Field Artillery School leading the way by developing the requirements. To make the fire support team function effectively in the heavy division called for a track vehicle with the necessary communications and laser designation capabilities. As Keith noted in 1976, the Field Artillery needed a Bradley Infantry Fighting Vehicle based system to permit the fire support team to stay abreast of the maneuver arms' tanks and infantry fighting vehicles. Obtaining a Bradley-based fire support team vehicle, however, was out of the question until the Infantry's and Cavalry's needs had been met. For the Field Artillery, this meant waiting at least 10 years or more, using the modified M113 armored personnel carrier, and lacking the capability to keep up with faster moving armored vehicles.[66]

Obtaining a new fire support team vehicle only partially met forward observation requirements for close support on the new battlefield. To counter the Warsaw Pact's massive field artillery barrages, the Field Artillery School had to improve locating enemy indirect fire systems. This led to the acquisition of the AN/TPQ-36 countermortar radar and AN/TPQ-37 counterbattery radar in the 1970s to replace the AN/TPS-4A radar and caused the Field Artillery to abandon sound and flash ranging in the 1980s. Called Firefinder radars, the Q-36 and Q-37 located enemy indirect fire systems by tracking a projectile's trajectory with a radar beam and automatically furnishing the location to the Tactical Fire Direction System that was developed to compute technical and tactical fire direction and replaced the Field Artillery Digital Automated Computer in the 1980s. Both systems were descendents of the Electrical Numerical Integrator Calculator, an electrical digital computer, of the 1940s that had been designed to compute ballistic firing tables. Working in concert, the Q-36 and the Tactical Fire Direction System were so effective that gun crews could shell an enemy mortar battery before its rounds landed on friendly positions.[67]

Because these radars did not provide over-the-horizon observation capabilities and could only detect active enemy indirect fire systems, because the Arab-Israeli War reinforced the difficulty of flying manned aircraft into enemy airspace defended by sophisticated air defenses, and because manned aircraft were becoming more expensive, the Field Artillery School and the Army lacked the luxury of depending upon manned aircraft, loitering near or over enemy territory for reconnaissance and target acquisition as they had done since World War II. This noted deficiency prompted the school and the Army to initiate work in 1974 on a remotely piloted vehicle called the Aquila. Upon fielding, the Aquila would provide real-time target acquisition information and lase targets for the Cannon-Launched Guided Projectile, commonly called Copperhead, a precision 15-mm. munition under development. Although the initial tests revealed the Aquila's ability to provide reconnaissance and to acquire and designate targets for Copperhead, escalating costs and technical problems eventually forced the Army to abandon the Aquila in 1987 for less expensive but more reliable unmanned aerial vehicles.[68]

Meanwhile, the Army and the school examined the need for a new scout helicopter for field artillery and other missions. In October 1979, the Advanced Scout Helicopter Special Study Group outlined the requirement for a real-time information, reconnaissance, security, aerial observation, and target acquisition/designation system with the ability to operate 24 hours a day in all kinds of weather. The Army System Review Council of November 1979 subsequently reaffirmed the group's findings. However, fielding a new helicopter would be too expensive, prompting the council to recommend upgrading an existing helicopter as a less expensive alternative.[69]

Although some Army aviators strongly advocated obtaining a new helicopter, the Army heeded the council's advice by formulating the Army Helicopter Improvement Program. When a series of competitive fly offs between Bell Helicopter's OH-58D and Hughes's OH-6 demonstrated the former's superiority, the Army chose the OH-58D as its Advanced Helicopter Improvement Program helicopter to carry a laser rangefinder for designating targets for Hellfire (attack helicopter missiles), Copperhead, and other precision-guided munitions. Of the 578 OH-58D helicopters to be purchased, the Army conceded that attack and air cavalry units had the higher priority and would receive 545 helicopters, leaving the Field Artillery only 33.[70]

Further testing of the OH-58D in 1984-1985 prompted the Defense System Acquisition Council to reverse fielding priorities late in 1985. Although the tests failed to support employing the helicopter to lase targets for attack helicopter antitank missiles and to scout the battlefield for air cavalry units, the tests validated the helicopter's ability to perform field artillery missions.[71]

However, additional testing, budget cuts that reduced the number of OH-58Ds to be purchased, Operation Prime Chance in the Persian Gulf in 1987-1988 where the OH-58D provided aerial cover for merchant convoys, and the decision to arm the helicopter undermined employing it in a field artillery role. This caused the Army to drop the field artillery mission as its top priority for the helicopter even though the Commandant of the Field Artillery School, Major Raphael J. Hallada (1987-1991), strenuously objected. In October 1989, the Army decided to employ armed OH-58D helicopters in armed reconnaissance roles in air cavalry units and unarmed OH-58Ds in multi-purpose light helicopter roles in the XVIII Airborne Corps and the 82d Airborne Division. Any remaining OH-58Ds would be divided between corps target acquisition reconnaissance companies and training commands. More importantly, OH-58A/C model aircraft would eventually supplant all field artillery OH-58Ds. These series of decisions cost field artillery units the ability to lase over-the-hill targets with organic assets. Coupled with the termination of the Aquila program, the loss of the OH-58D brought the school's efforts to introduce state-of-the-art aerial target acquisition systems to a halt. Ultimately, field artillery units would have to depend upon another branch for aerial observation for the foreseeable future.[72]

To complement new target acquisition systems and doctrine, the Field Artillery still required modern munitions and weapons to stop a massed Soviet and Warsaw Pact attack. From the Field Artillery School's perspective, the Army could increase the number of indirect fire weapons or develop more deadly munitions. Although the Army had improved its conventional field artillery munitions during the 1950s and 1960s, it introduced the Dual Purpose Improved Conventional Munition that consisted of a carrier projectile that ejected explosive anti-personnel and anti-armor submunitions upon detonation. As promising as the munition appeared to be upon fielding in the 1980s, the Field Artillery School found it to be wanting. The munition did not resolve the inherent inaccuracy of field artillery weapons, forcing the branch to expend huge amounts of ordnance to destroy an armored target and to increase the number of field artillery weapons on the battlefield.[73]

The school's Fire Support Mission Area Analysis of 1974 outlined the imperative of acquiring precision munitions to reduce the amount of ordnance required to destroy a target, especially moving armored targets, and the size of the attending logistical tail. Addressing the deficiencies of existing munitions, including the Dual Purpose Improved Conventional Munition, the study pointed out that about 50 conventional high-explosive 155-mm. rounds were required to hit a stalled tank and that even a greater number were needed to hit a moving tank in World War II. Because Warsaw Pact and Soviet massed armored formations presented a grave threat, qualitative improvements in munition accuracy would be required. Such thinking and the recent success of precision munitions in the Vietnam War and Arab-Israeli War reinforced the school's and the Army's vision of precision munitions as the wave of the future.[74]

Within a few years, the drive for precision munitions produced fruit. Initially conceived in 1970, Copperhead took on added significance. A fin-stabilized projectile fired from a 155-mm. howitzer and guided to the target by a laser designator from either an aerial or ground observer, the munition was fielded in the 1980s. Meanwhile, early in the 1980s, the school became involved in the development of the Search-and-Destroy Artillery Munition, later renamed the Sense-and-Destroy Armor Munition. In contrast to the Copperhead, the Sense-and-Destroy Armor Munition would not depend upon a laser designator to hit a target and would be a fire-and-forget munition. It would consist of three to four submunitions in a carrier projectile that would be dispensed above armored formations. A specially designed parachute would open to stabilize each submunition, control the descent rate, and cause it to rotate. Each submunition would carry a millimeter wave sensor and a slug of metal. Upon detecting a target, the sensor would detonate the charge to send the slug hurling toward the target. Although technological problems slowed down the munition's development with fielding coming in the 21st century, the Search-and-Destroy Armor Munition and Copperhead offered the potential of engaging one target with one munition and reducing excessive ammunition expenditures to destroy an armored target.[75]

Modernizing weapons complemented precision munitions. Concerned with Soviet and Warsaw Pact field artillery with greater ranges than American field artillery, the Field Artillery School replaced the M114 towed 155-mm. howitzer of World War II origins with the M198 towed 155-mm. howitzer beginning in 1979. The M198 had a range of 30 kilometers with rocket-assisted projectiles twice the range of the M114 and could be airlifted by a helicopter or carried by an Air Force C-130 aircraft. Meanwhile, the Army increased the range of the M109 self-propelled 155-mm. howitzer from 18.5 to 23.7 kilometers in 1979, redesignated it as the M109A2/A3, and boosted the range of the M110 self-propelled 8-inch howitzer from 20 to 23 kilometers.[76]

Although the M109A2/A3 would have better range and increased ammunition carrying capabilities than earlier M109s, the Enhanced Self-Propelled Weapon System Study of

1979 still identified critical limitations. The study determined the requirement for tube artillery to be capable of continuous operations and to possess high rates of fire to support emerging AirLand Battle doctrine. Tube artillery also had to generate greater firepower at reduced personnel costs and to have greater speed to keep up with the new armored vehicles (Abrams tank and Bradley infantry fighting vehicle) scheduled for fielding in the 1980s. The M109A2/A3 simply failed to meet future needs, especially in mobility and survivability. When it became evident that costs would prohibit developing a new self-propelled 155-mm. howitzer to replace the M109A2/A3, TRADOC and the US Army Materiel Command initiated the Howitzer Extended Life Program in 1980.[77]

Meanwhile, the Army chartered the Division Support Weapon System Special Study Group in 1980 to pick up where the Enhanced Self-propelled Artillery Weapon System Study left off. Published in July 1981, the study challenged the Howitzer Extended Life Program howitzer's maintainability and air transportability, among other issues. More importantly, it found the howitzer to be too slow to stay abreast of the Abrams tank and Bradley infantry fighting vehicle. Based upon these deficiencies and others and the Army Vice Chief of Staff's tasking to develop an enhanced howitzer, TRADOC initiated the Howitzer Improvement Program as a follow-on to the Howitzer Extended Life Program howitzer. Integrating the latest technology, the Howitzer Improvement Program howitzer would upgrade the M109A2/A3 by including Howitzer Extended Life Program improvements, would reduce the crew size, and would have the ability to stay abreast of the maneuver arms, among other key enhancements. Aware that the two programs were concurrent and ongoing, the Army Vice Chief of Staff, General Maxwell R. Thurman who had served at the Field Artillery School earlier in his career, combined the two into a single program in 1985 so that only one howitzer, the Howitzer Improvement Program howitzer which became the M109A6 Paladin in the 1990s would be produced.[78]

While work on the howitzer was underway, the Army, TRADOC, and the Field Artillery School pursued developing a totally new 155-mm. self-propelled howitzer. In 1984, the school announced the Army's intention of replacing the Paladin with the self-propelled 155-mm. Advanced Field Artillery System, designated the Crusader in 1994, sometime in the 1990s to satisfy Thurman's guidance of 1984 and the Division Support Weapon System Study's recommendation for a next-generation self-propelled howitzer.[79]

Soon, the Army merged the Advanced Field Artillery System into the Armored Family of Vehicles development program. In 1984, TRADOC Special Study Group Armor arrived at the conclusion that a family of armored vehicles based upon commonality of chassis was feasible and desirable to reduce costs in the face of a shrinking military budget. The following year, the Armored Combat Vehicle Science and Technology Working Group at the Army level validated the conclusions of the TRADOC study. The Defense Science Board 1985 Armor/Anti-Armor Summer Study Report subsequently endorsed a new family of armored vehicles for the turn-of-the-century battlefield, leading to the formation of the Armored Family of Vehicles Task Force in 1986 under Major General Robert J. Sunell.[80]

Renamed the Heavy Force Family of Vehicles in 1989 as part of a major program restructuring to reduce rising costs, the effort identified six systems for development.

Although the field artillery system with its resupply vehicle was the lowest priority of the six systems, field artillery combat developers in 1988-1989 fought to move up in importance. They argued that the system would incorporate leap-ahead technology to give it the capability of defeating moving and stationary enemy field artillery and armor. They lost the battle, and serious development of the system, named the Crusader in 1994, did not begin until 1992.[81]

Perhaps, the most revolutionary aspect of modernizing field artillery systems involved developing a new multiple rocket launcher. Although Army employed multiple rocket launchers in World War II, they had ranges of about 5,000 yards and were inaccurate. During the years following the war, the Army's and Field Artillery's focus on tactical nuclear weapons left the branch equipped with obsolete World War II multiple rocket launchers.[82]

Such circumstances prompted the Field Artillery School and the Army to search for a new multiple rocket launcher. Conducted in the 1960s and early 1970s, studies raised the necessity of a multiple rocket launcher to offset the enemy's superior firepower and outlined the requirement for an all-weather, conventional area fire support weapon system. Also, the Arab-Israeli War of October 1973 reinforced the need to suppress sophisticated enemy air defenses to permit manned and unmanned aircraft to cross into enemy territory to acquire targets and perform other valuable missions. Just as important, the Soviet Union and Warsaw Pact were introducing modern multiple rocket launchers early in the 1970s.[83]

Prodded by these reasons, the Field Artillery School initiated a requirement in March 1974 for a new multiple rocket launcher, called the General Support Rocket System. The rocket system would neutralize and suppress the enemy's indirect fire support and air defense systems by delivering a tremendous volume of firepower at long ranges and help offset the numerical superiority of Soviet and Warsaw Pact indirect fire systems. This would free direct and general support cannon artillery to furnish close support. Renamed the Multiple-Launch Rocket System when the program became a cooperative effort by the United States, the Federal Republic of Germany, the United Kingdom, and France in 1976, the rocket system which was fielded late in the 1970s and early 1980s furnished breakthrough fire support by supplying incredible amounts of firepower.[84]

Simultaneously, the Field Artillery School participated in the Pershing guided missile program that had its origins in the 1950s. In the middle of the decade, the Army was equipping its forces with nuclear missiles to offset Soviet manpower superiority. The missiles employed liquid fuel and were large and cumbersome. Because of this and the emergence of new technology, the Army started work on a solid-fuel ballistic missile – the Pershing I missile – with the help of private enterprise.[85]

After years of development, the Army fielded the Pershing I missile. It activated its first operational Pershing battalion at Fort Sill in 1962 and concurrently initiated resident training in the US Army Artillery and Missile School. The Pershing I missile could be moved overland or transported by helicopter or cargo plane, replaced the Redstone missile, and complemented the shorter range Honest John rocket and Sergeant missile.

Within months of the initial deployment of Pershing I to Europe in 1964, Secretary of Defense Robert S. McNamara directed the Army to enhance the missile to furnish short-notice, nuclear fire support on high-priority targets as designated by the Supreme Allied Commander in Europe. This led to the Pershing IA which had improved maintainability, mobility, and reaction time.[86]

As the Pershing IA was being fielded late in the 1960s, Soviet and American activities in Europe dramatically altered the balance of power on the continent, leading to initiatives to limit intermediate-range nuclear forces. Early in the 1970s, American strategic guarantees and North Atlantic Treaty Organization medium-range bombers, submarine-launched ballistic missiles, and tactical nuclear weapons had sufficient power to prevent Soviet aggression. With the deployment of its SS-20 missile with a longer range, greater mobility, and superior accuracy than its predecessors, SS-4 and SS-5 missiles, had, the Soviet Union overcame the North Atlantic Treaty Organization's nuclear superiority in the middle of the decade. To counter this shocking development, the United States signed the Dual-Pact Agreement with the North Atlantic Treaty Organization in October 1979 to replace the Pershing IA missile with the more sophisticated Pershing II missile and to field the US Air Force's ground-launched cruise missile.[87]

Prodded by the deployment of Pershing II in 1983, which heightened the threat of nuclear war with its pinpoint accuracy, ability to destroy hardened targets surgically, and range of 1,800 kilometers, the Soviet Union and the United States entered into negotiations to reduce their intermediate-range nuclear forces in Europe. After lengthy and heated discussions, they completed the Intermediate-Range Nuclear Forces Treaty in December 1987. In the treaty, the two superpowers agreed to eliminate their intermediate-range (1,000-1,500 miles) and shorter-range (500-1,000 miles) missiles to lessen the risk of nuclear war and strengthen international peace, security, and strategic stability.[88]

For the Field Artillery and the Field Artillery School, the treaty had critical implications. The Army had to eliminate its Pershing II, Pershing IA, and Pershing IB missiles and its Ground-Launched Cruise Missile, while the Soviet Union had to eliminate its SS-4, SS-5, SS-20, SS-CX4, SS-12, and SS-23 missiles. To ensure compliance the treaty provided for onsite inspections to verify destruction of the missile systems, their associated equipment, and training facilities. Over a period of four years beginning in 1987, the Field Artillery converted the 3d Battalion, 9th Field Artillery at Fort Sill from a Pershing to a M270 launcher unit, while the school shipped all of its Pershing II training equipment to the Pueblo Army Depot, Colorado, for storage and destruction and sent its Pershing II warhead trainers to the Sierra Army Depot in Northern California for disposal. By 1991, the school no longer had any Pershing systems or training facilities.[89]

To tie the new weapons into a system of systems, the Field Artillery School, meanwhile, participated in the development of a new command and control system to replace the Tactical Fire Direction System that was heavy and based on 1950s and 1960s technology. In response to a memorandum of 13 November 1978 from the Office of the Undersecretary of Defense for Research and Engineering which authorized a new computer for fire support command, control, and communications, the Army launched work on a successor to the system. After three years of work, the Army and the Department of Defense approved developing the Advanced Field Artillery Tactical Data System in 1981 to replace the Tactical Fire Direction System and to be a part of the Army Tactical Command and Control System which would be a family of computers, peripherals, operating systems, utilities, and software and support each individual battlefield operating system.[90] After a decade of work on the hardware and the software that was fraught with many developmental delays, the Army started fielding the Advanced Field Artillery Tactical Data System software incrementally in versions with each building on the previous to get the software to the field sooner.[91]

The school's participation in the force structure design and the introduction of new technology reflected the overall contribution that the school made to the Army in the 1970s and 1980s. During those years, it completely revamped officer, warrant officer, and noncommissioned officer training, introduced the Army Training and Evaluation Program for training field artillery units realistically, and became closely involved with combat developments once again. While the training reforms improved the quality of the school's graduates by focusing on developing critical thinking skills to improve their ability to adapt to a constantly changing battlefield, combat developments introduced new and more capable weapons and equipment and doctrine to counter the imposing Soviet and Warsaw Pact ground force. All of this bolstered the confidence of field artillerymen to fight and win on the modern battlefield.

The School and Operations Desert Shield and Storm

In the midst of this rebuilding effort, Iraq under Saddam Hussein invaded Kuwait on 2 August 1990 and provided the school with the opportunity to validate its training and combat development effort of the past two decades. In response to the attack, the United States and the United Nations launched Operation Desert Shield, a massive military buildup in the fall of 1990, to defend Saudi Arabia from Iraqi aggression and to compel Iraq to withdraw from Kuwait.[92] When Saddam Hussein failed to withdraw his military forces by the 15 January 1991 deadline established by President George H. Bush and supported by Congress and the United Nations, coalition military forces launched Operation Desert Storm on 17 January 1991 that drove Iraq out of Kuwait.[93]

Operation Desert Shield forced the Field Artillery School to step up its pace of operations. Virtually overnight, the training load expanded dramatically. To meet this, the school increased the number of classes, taught them above the maximum capacity to handle the load, initiated a six-day work week in December 1990 to speed up the training cycle, and canceled the annual two-week Christmas break to ensure the availability of trained personnel for the operational forces.[94]

Recognizing the requirement to train deploying active and reserve component (Army National Guard and Army Reserve) units, the school concurrently dispatched mobile training teams.[95] In the fall of 1990, the Target Acquisition Department under Colonel Stanley E. Griffith shipped a mobile training team of three people to Dhahran, Saudi Arabia, to train elements of the XVIII Airborne Corps on the meteorological data system being fielded and afterward sent that same team to Fort Campbell, Kentucky, to train the 196th Field Artillery Brigade of the Tennessee Army National Guard on the same equipment. In December 1990, the Director of the Gunnery Department, Colonel Thomas R. Hogan, personally led a team of 27 soldiers to train the direct support field artillery battalion of the 48th Mechanized Infantry Brigade of the Georgia Army National Guard on the latest gunnery tactics, techniques, and procedures. Altogether, seven mobile training teams from the school trained 314 personnel at other posts and 1,011 soldiers at Fort Sill.[96] As a memorandum after Operation Desert Shield and Operation Desert Storm was over noted, the Field Artillery School did not turn down "a single request for training assistance" from field artillery units. However, this came at a cost because the school stripped instructors from the classroom to fill out mobile training teams, creating an instructor shortage in the school house.[97]

Meanwhile, the Chief of Staff of the Army, General Carl Vuono, directed fully staffing all deploying units, putting additional pressure on the school's instructor base. To ensure that Fort Sill's deploying III Corps Artillery units left at full strength, Fort Sill's Adjutant General's Office post transferred soldiers from the Field Artillery School, the US Army Field Artillery Training Center that conducted basic combat training and advanced individual training, and base operations to III Corps Artillery units.[98]

To prevent losing too many training center drill instructors and support personnel, the Commander of US Army Field Artillery Training Center, Colonel Joseph P. Monko, and Hallada allowed only soldiers with certain military occupational specialties to go. This left the Field Artillery School and base operations as the major sources of filler personnel. As a result, the burden of filling vacancies fell upon them, especially the school, intensifying the existing shortages. The remaining instructors and staff had "to go that extra mile to meet all missions" by substituting for those who had left and working excessive overtime.[99] The growing shortage also forced the school to hire unqualified "contract hires."[100]

TRADOC's personnel policies further complicated the school's training mission and exacerbated the shortages.[101] On 23 August 1990, the Commanding General of TRADOC, General John W. Foss, informed the Army that he would not rely on Army National Guard or Army Reserve soldiers for relief.[102] All TRADOC training and base operation missions would be done within existing personnel resources to preserve the presidential call-up of 200,000 reserve personnel for the operational forces. Foss's policies simultaneously barred tapping the individual mobilization augmentee pool that was a part of the 200,000 call-up for instructors and was a critical aspect of Fort Sill's mobilization plans. Basically, Foss prohibited using the very resources designated by Army policy to fill instructor and staff vacancies in the school being created by the departing soldiers and civilians who were being called to active duty by their reserve or guard units.[103]

Besides this, the school lost crucial support from III Corps Artillery which had assisted the school for years, forcing critical adjustments to be made. When III Corps Artillery took its 155-mm. self-propelled howitzers to Southwest Asia, the school had to replace the corps' 155-mm. self-propelled howitzers with 105-mm. towed howitzers from its 2d Battalion, 2d

Field Artillery Regiment in field exercises that required 155-mm. self-propelled howitzers. Commenting upon this and school operations in general, Hallada explained, "We had to shift resources and continually adjust support for the school on various shoots and battery operations and exercises when . . . corps artillery units, which normally provided that support, were not there."[104]

Also, the school gave III Corps Artillery its 155-mm. self-propelled howitzers to ensure that it had its full complement upon deploying. To make up for this critical loss, the school obtained 12 surplus 155-mm. self-propelled howitzers from the US Marine Corps in the fall of 1990 after lengthy negotiations to prevent further degradation of training.[105]

Despite the repeated adjustments and equipment and instructor shortages, the Field Artillery School accomplished its training mission in support of Operations Desert Shield and Desert Storm. Shortly after the war, the Field Artillery School issued "emerging observations" in July 1991 on field artillery doctrine, organization, training, leadership, and materiel in a report to the Director of the Center for Army Lessons Learned at Fort Leavenworth, Kansas.[106]

As might be expected, the report positively addressed the Field Artillery's contributions to the resounding victory. Iraq might have had a significant edge in the number of field artillery pieces with many having superior ranges to American field artillery, but the Army's field artillery system of systems (target acquisition; command, control, communications, and computers; support and sustainment; and weapons and munitions) operated by highly trained officers and soldiers provided overwhelming fire superiority. Massed fires from the Field Artillery's system of systems silenced all of the enemy's field artillery and other indirect fire systems with responsive counterfire and knocked out its target acquisition assets to blind it and prevent it from locating targets beyond the forward line of troops. American field artillery simultaneously furnished timely close support to maneuver commanders. This permitted them to maneuver with a minimum of disruption from enemy fires.[107]

In his state of the branch address in the December 1991 edition of the *Field Artillery Magazine*, the Commandant of the Field Artillery School, Major General Fred F. Marty (1991-1993), also summed up the Field Artillery's role to the fight during Operation Desert Storm. "Our maneuver forces received lethal, timely and accurate fires in Southwest Asia. Not since World War II has fire support earned such credibility among leaders at all echelons," he wrote.[108]

As much as Marty's article and the school's report to the Center for Army Lessons Learned addressed the Field Artillery's performance during Operation Desert Storm, they also reflected the Field Artillery School's modernization and training efforts over two decades. While realistic training produced competent officers, warrant officers, noncommissioned officers, and soldiers, combat developments furnished the equipment, weapons, doctrine, tactics, techniques, and procedures to destroy the Iraqi ground forces with a minimal number of friendly casualties. Working in tandem, the Field Artillery School's training and combat development missions produced a highly effective Field Artillery that overwhelmed the Iraqi ground forces with effective, responsive fires.

Notes

1 1971 US Army Field Artillery School (USAFAS) Annual Historical Supplement, pp. 6, 23; 1972 USAFAS Annual Historical Supplemental, pp. 13, 18, 19, 20; 1973 USAFAS Annual Historical Supplement, unpaginated.

2 1973 USAFAS Annual Historical Supplement, unpaginated; 1975 USAFAS Annual Historical Supplement, p. 6.

3 1971 USAFAS Annual Historical Supplement, unpaginated; 1972 USAFAS Annual Historical Supplement, p. 11; 1975 Annual Historical Supplement, p. 1; Department of the Army (DA), *Historical Summary for Fiscal Year (FY) 1978*, p. 29.

4 John L. Romjue, Susan Canedy, and Anne Chapman, *Prepare the Army for War: A Historical Overview of the Army Training and Doctrine Command* (Fort Monroe, VA: Office of the Command Historian, US Army Training and Doctrine Command, 1993), p. 10

5 1997 US Army Field Artillery Center and Fort Sill (USAFACFS) Annual Command History (ACH), pp. 50-54; LTC Rhett A. Hernandez and MAJ Terry M. Lee, "OPMS XXI: What Does It Mean for Your Future," *Field Artillery Magazine*, Sep-Oct 1997, pp. 16-18; LTC Donna L. Coffman, "OPMS to OPMS XXI: Then, Now, and the Future - What Does It Mean to the Quartermaster Officer?" *Quartermaster Professional Bulletin,* online edition, Aug 1997; 1973 USAFAS Annual Historical Supplement, unpaginated; 1974 USAFAS Annual Historical Supplement, pp. 10, 11; 1975 USAFAS Annual Historical Supplement, pp. 6, 7, 10; 1976 USAFAS Historical Supplement, pp. 6-7; "Let's Shoot, Lieutenant," *Field Artillery Journal*, Nov-Dec 1975, pp. 24-25.

6 1997 USAFACFS ACH, pp. 50-54; Hernandez and Lee, "OPMS XXI," pp. 16-18; Coffman, "OPMS to OPMS XXI;" 1974 USAFAS Annual Historical Supplement, pp. 10, 11; 1975 USAFAS Annual Historical Supplement, pp. 6, 7, 10; 1976 USAFAS Historical Supplement, pp. 6-7; "Let's Shoot, Lieutenant," pp. 24-25; DA, *Historical Summary for FY 1974*, p. 30-31; Draft ltr, COL Robert H. Forman, Dir of Instruction, USAFAS, undated, Feb 75-Sep 1975, UF25 A31U5, Morris Swett Technical Library (MSTL) Archives, USAFAS; USAFAS Accreditation Self Study Report, May 1976, pp. 3-4, UF23.5 A2U5, MSTL.

7 1997 USAFACFS ACH, pp. 50-54; Hernandez and Lee, "OPMS XXI," pp. 16-18; Coffman, "OPMS to OPMS XXI;" 1974 USAFAS Annual Historical Supplement, pp. 10, 11; 1975 USAFAS Annual Historical Supplement, pp. 6, 7, 10; 1976 USAFAS Historical Supplement, pp. 6-7; "Let's Shoot, Lieutenant," pp. 24-25; Draft ltr, Forman, undated, Feb 1975-Sep 1975, UF25 A31U5, MSTL Archives; USAFAS Accreditation Self Study Report, May 1976, pp. 3-4, UF23.5 A2U5, MSTL.

8 Review of Education and Training of Officers (RETO), 30 Jun 1978, Vol I, pp. 1, I-3, III-3, U408 S7, MSTL; MG Edward A. Dinges, "On the Move," *Field Artillery Journal*, Jan-Feb 1981, p. 1-2.

9 RETO, 30 Jun 1978, Vol I, pp. 1, I-3, III-3, V-9, V-10; DA, *Historical Summary for FY 1984*, p. 44; Romjue, *et al, Prepare the Army for War*, p. 84; 1978 USAFAS Annual Historical Supplement, p. 3-2; 1982 USAFAS Annual Historical Summary, p. 3-1; 1983 USAFAS Annual Historical Summary, p. 3-1; Dinges, "On the Move," pp. 1-2.

10 RETO, 30 Jun 1978, Vol I, pp. 1, I-3, III-3, V-9, V-10; DA, *Historical Summary for FY 1983*, pp. 48-49; DA, *Historical Summary for FY 1984*, p. 44; Romjue, *et al, Prepare the Army for War*, p. 84; 1974 USAFAS Annual Historical Supplement, p. 11; 1982 USAFAS Annual Historical Summary, p. 3-1; 1983 USAFAS Annual Historical Summary, p. 3-1; Field Artillery Officer Basic Course (FAOBC) Program of Instruction (POI), Dec 82, UF23.5 Q71B15, MSTL.

11 DA, *Historical Summary for FY 1980*, pp. 44-45; DA, *Historical Summary for FY 1984*, p. 44; FAOBC POI, Feb 1974, UF23.5 Q71B15, MSTL; FAOBC POI, Jun 1983, UF23.5 Q71B15, MSTL; USAFAS, FY 1976 Data Sheet, Jun 1975, p. 1, in USAFAS Status Study, Sep 1975, UF23.5

C31S, MSTL; 1985 USAFACFS Annual Historical Review (AHR), pp. 37-39; MG John S. Crosby, "On the Move," *Field Artillery Journal*, Mar-Apr 1984, p. 1. Note: TRADOC initiated its common core of subjects in 1984-1985 to ensure that all second lieutenants received training in leadership, ethics, military justice, and other non-branch specific topics to make them well-rounded.

    12   DA, *Historical Summary for FY 1980*, pp. 44-45; DA, *Historical Summary for FY 1984*, p. 44; FAOBC POI, Feb 1974, UF23.5 Q71B15, MSTL; FAOBC POI, Jun 1983, UF23.5 Q71B15, MSTL; USAFAS, FY 1976 Data Sheet, Jun 1975, p. 1, in USAFAS Status Study, Sep 1975, UF23.5 C31S, MSTL; 1985 USAFAS AHR, pp. 37-39; Fact Sheet, subj: POI Scrubs, 5 Jun 1985, Historical Research and Document Collection (HRDC), Field Artillery Branch Historian's Office, USAFAS; Ltr, Cdr, USAFAS, to Cdr, US Army Combined Arms Center, Fort Leavenworth, subj: Officer Basic Course Common Core, 15 May 1985, HRDC.

    13   1978 USAFAS Annual Historical Supplement, p. 3-2; 1980 USAFAS Annual Historical Supplement, p. 3-1; 1981 USAFAS Annual Historical Supplement, p. 3-2; Briefing, subj: Restructuring of the OBC and the OAC, undated, HRDC; Interview with MAJ David Plaza, Chief, Program Management Division, Directorate of Training and Doctrine (DOTD), subj: USAFAS Course Restructure 1990, 1 Apr 1991, HRDC; FAOBC POI, 28 Feb 1991, UF23.5 Q71B15, MSTL.

    14   DA, *Historical Summary for FY 1974*, p. 31; DA, *Historical Summary for FY 1975*, p. 42; 1997 USAFAS Annual Command History (ACH), pp. 50-54; Hernandez and Lee, "OPMS XXI," pp. 16-18; Coffman, "OPMS to OPMS XXI;" 1973 USAFAS Annual Historical Supplement, unpaginated; 1974 USAFAS Annual Historical Supplement, pp. 10, 11; 1975 USAFAS Annual Historical Supplement, pp. 6, 7, 10; 1976 USAFAS Historical Supplement, pp. 6-7; "Let's Shoot, Lieutenant," pp. 24-25; Memorandum for Assistant Commandant, subj: What We Don't Teach, 20 Jul 1977, UF25 A66A3 #57B, MSTL Archives.

    15   Draft ltr to Incoming Students, MG Ott, ca Nov 1976, UF25 A66A3 #78, MSTL Archives.

    16   Memorandum, subj: Contemporary Reading Program for FAOAC 1-76, 28 Nov 1975, UF25 A566A3 #78, MSTL Archives.

    17   DA, *Historical Summary for FY* 1984, p. 44; DA, *Historical Summary for FY 1985*, p. 26; Msg, DA to AIG 7447, subj: A News Brief, 231300Z Jan 1984, HRDC; Ltr, HQ TRADOC to See Distribution, subj: Implementation of Revised Officer Advanced Course, 15 Feb 1984, HRDC.

    18   Ltr, HQ TRADOC to See Distribution, subj: Implementation of Revised Officer Advanced Course, 15 Feb 1984.

    19   Fact Sheet, subj: To Describe the Current Status of OAC Modularization, 17 Mar 1984, HRDC; Fact Sheet, subj: Revised Officer Advanced Course, 30 Mar 1984, HRDC; Memorandum for Record, subj: Revised OAC Mod, 30 Apr 1984, HRDC; Ltr, CAC to Distribution, subj: Implementation of Revised OAC, 27 Mar 1984, HRDC; Ltr, HQ TRADOC to See Distribution, subj: Implementation of Revised OAC, 15 Feb 1984, HRDC; Ltr, HQ TRADOC to See Distribution, subj: OAC Common Core, 8 May 1984, HRDC; Fact Sheet, subj: Revised OAC, 27 Aug 1984, HRDC; 1985 USAFACFS AHR, pp. 30-37; 1989 USAFACFS AHR, p. 69.

    20   DA, Total Warrant Officer Study Group, Final Report, Total Warrant Officer System, Jun 1986, pp. 76-78, HRDC; 1986 USAFAS AHR, p. 45.

    21   Disposition Form (DF), subj: WOEC, 14 Oct 1983, HRDC; DF, subj: WOEC Training Strategy, 3 Nov 1983, HRDC; Msg, Cdr, TRADOC, to Cdr, CAC, subj: Warrant Officer Candidate Training Capability, 311500Z Oct 1983, HRDC; Msg, Cdr, TRADOC, to Cmdt, USAFAS, subj: WOEC Pilot School Program of Instruction, Course Validation and Associated Milestones, 202030Z Apr 1984, HRDC; Msg, CAC to Cdr, Ft. USAVNC, subj: Warrant Officer Candidate Guide, 181420Z Mar 1986, HRDC.

    22   Msg, Cdr, TRADOC, to Cmdt, USAFAS, *et al*, subj: WOEC, 151415Z May 1985, HRDC; Msg, Cmdt, USAFAS to Cdr, USAAVNC and Cdr, USAOAC&S, subj: WOEC Consolidation

Concept Study, 081345Z Oct 1985, HRDC; DF, subj: WOEC Consolidation Concept Study, 31 Oct 1985, HRDC; DF, subj: WOEC Consolidation Study, 9 Oct 1985, HRDC; Msg, HQ TRADOC, to Cdr, USACAC, *et al,* subj: Warrant Officer Training Site Consolidation, 131326Z Mar 1986, HRDC; 1987 USAFAS Annual Historical Review, p. 50.

23 1987 USAFACFS AHR, pp. 50-51.

24 Robert S. Rush, "The Evolution of NCOs in Training Soldiers," draft manuscript, p. 10, HRDC; DA, *Historical Summary for FY 1971*, p. 35.

25 DA, *Historical Summary for FY 1971*, pp. 11-12; Larry R. Arms, edited by Patricia Rhodes, *A Short History of the NCO* (Fort Bliss, TX: US Army Sergeant Major Academy, 1991), pp. 47-48.

26 Arms, *A Short History of the NCO*, pp. 50-51; Rush, "The Evolution of NCOs in Training Soldiers," pp. 13-14; "EPMS," *Field Artillery Journal*, Nov-Dec 1977, pp. 39-43; DA, *Historical Summary for FY 1972*, p. 60.

27 Arms, *A Short History of the NCO*, pp. 50-51; Rush, "The Evolution of NCOs in Training Soldiers," pp. 13-14; Romjue, *et al, Prepare the Army for War,* pp. 36-37; COL Sam A. Brown, "EPMS and the Field Artillery," *Field Artillery Journal*, May-Jun 1977, pp. 29-33; DA, *Historical Summary for FY* 1974, p. 30; DA, *Historical Summary for FY* 1975, p. 23; DA, *Historical Summary for FY* 1977, p. 44; DA, *Historical Summary for FY 1986*, pp. 30-31; DA, *Historical Summary for FY 1987*, pp. 18-19; DA, *Historical Summary for FYs 1990 and 1991*, pp. 63-64.

28 Arms, *A Short History of the NCO*, pp. 50-51; Rush, "The Evolution of NCOs in Training Soldiers," pp. 13-14; Romjue, *et al, Prepare the Army for War,* pp. 36-37; Brown, "EPMS and the Field Artillery," pp. 29-33; DA, *Historical Summary for FY* 1974, p. 30; DA, *Historical Summary for FY* 1975, p. 23; DA, *Historical Summary for FY* 1977, p. 44; DA, *Historical Summary for FY 1986*, pp. 30-31; DA, *Historical Summary for FY 1987*, pp. 18-19; DA, *Historical Summary for FYs 1990 and 1991*, pp. 63-64.

29 Arms, *A Short History of the NCO*, pp. 50-51; Rush, "The Evolution of NCOs in Training Soldiers," pp. 13-14; Romjue, *et al, Prepare the Army for War,* pp. 36-37; Brown, "EPMS and the Field Artillery," pp. 29-33; DA, *Historical Summary for FY* 1971, p. 35; DA, *Historical Summary for FY* 1977, p. 44; DA, *Historical Summary for FY 1986*, pp. 30-31; DA, *Historical Summary for FY 1987*, pp. 18-19; DA, *Historical Summary for FYs 1990 and 1991*, pp. 63-64.

30 Arms, *A Short History of the NCO*, pp. 50-51; Rush, "The Evolution of NCOs in Training Soldiers," pp. 13-14; Romjue, *et al, Prepare the Army for War,* pp. 36-37; Brown, "EPMS and the Field Artillery," pp. 29-33; DA, *Historical Summary for FY 1977*, p. 44; DA, *Historical Summary for FY 1986*, pp. 30-31; DA, *Historical Summary for FY 1987*, pp. 18-19; DA, *Historical Summary for FYs 1990 and 1991*, pp. 63-64.

31 Romjue, *et al, Prepare the Army for War*, pp. 36-37; 1983 USAFAS Annual Historical Supplement, p. 3-2; USAFAS, Accreditation Self-Study Report, May 1976, p. 3-1, UF23.5 A2U5, MSTL; 1979 USAFAS Annual Historical Supplement, p. 3-2 - 3-3; 1980 USAFAS Annual Historical Supplement, p. 3-1; USAFAS, Accreditation Self-Study Report, Jul 1987, p. 10-3, UF23.5 A2U51, MSTL; "EPMS," pp. 39-43; LTC Daniel L. Breitenbach, "The Commander and NCO Professional Development," *Field Artillery Magazine*, Aug 1989, pp. 7-11.

32 Romjue, *et al, Prepare the Army for War*, pp. 23-24; 1974 USAFAS Annual Historical Supplement, p. 23; 1975 USAFAS Annual Historical Supplement, p. 18; 1976 USAFAS Annual Historical Supplement, p. 10; 1977 USAFAS Annual Historical Supplement, pp. 20, 36; 1981 USAFAS Annual Command History, p. 7-4; 1982 USAFAS Annual Historical Supplement, p. 7-5 - 7-7; "ARTEP," *Field Artillery Journal*, Jan-Feb 1975, pp. 52-53.

33 Romjue, *et al, Prepare the Army for War*, pp. 23-24; 1974 USAFAS Annual Historical Supplement, p. 23; 1975 USAFAS Annual Historical Supplement, p. 18; 1976 USAFAS Annual

Historical Supplement, p. 10; 1977 USAFAS Annual Historical Supplement, pp. 1, 2, 20, 36; 1981 USAFAS Annual Command History, p. 7-4; 1982 USAFAS Annual Historical Supplement, pp. 7-5 - 7-7; "ARTEP," pp. 52-53.

34 Memorandum, subj: Implementing the PDOS (Professional Development of Officers Study) recommended Pilot Mentoring Program, 22 Mar 1985, HRDC.

35 Memorandum, subj: Implementing the PDOS (Professional Development of Officers Study) recommended Pilot Mentoring Program, 22 Mar 1985.

36 Ltr, CAC to Distribution, subj: Implementation of Mentoring Strategy in TRADOC Service Schools, 14 Jul 1985, HRDC.

37 DF, subj: School Model 95, 30 Jul 1985, HRDC.

38 Ltr, USAFAS to CAC, subj: Implementation of Mentoring Strategy in TRADOC Service Schools, 3 Sep 1985, HRDC.

39 Ltr, Floca to Cdr, TRADOC, subj: SGI Model, 12 Dec 1986, HRDC; Fact Sheet, subj: SGI at Other Service Schools, 2 Mar 1988, HRDC; Briefing, subj: SGI, 28 Jan 1988, HRDC; Reorganization Study, Fort Sill 2000, Apr 1987, pp. IIIC1-IIIC8, HRDC.

40 Ltr, Korpal to Cdr, CAC, subj: Implementation of Mentoring Strategy in TRADOC Service Schools, undated, HRDC.

41 Ltr, Korpal to Cdr, CAC, subj: Implementation of Mentoring Strategy in TRADOC Service Schools, undated.

42 Trip Report, MAJ Dwight Gray, Task Force Action Officer, 23 December 1986, HRDC; Msg, Cdr, TRADOC, to AIG 891, subj: SGI, 011330Z May 1987, HRDC.

43 USAFAS 2000, Phase II, Executive Summary (Draft), undated, HRDC; Briefing, subj: School Reorganization and SGI, 30 Apr 1988, HRDC; Briefing, subj: School Reorganization and SGI, 9 May 1988, HRDC; COL Felix Peterson, Jr., and LTC Charles Morris, "Small Group Instruction in the Field Artillery School," *Field Artillery Magazine*, Apr 1989, pp. 45-47; Fact Sheet, subj: FAOAC SGI Program, 17 Mar 1989, HRDC.

44 Peterson and Morris, "Small Group Instruction at the Field Artillery School," p. 45.

45 Peterson and Morris, "Small Group Instruction at the Field Artillery School," p. 45.

46 Briefing, subj: SGI, 28 Jan 1988, HRDC; Reorganization Study, Fort Sill 2000, Apr 1987, pp. IIIC1-IIIC8, HRDC; "US Army Field Artillery School," *Field Artillery Magazine*, Dec 1991, p. 13.

47 1973 USAFAS Annual Historical Supplement, unpaginated; 1974 USAFAS Annual Historical Supplement, p. 1.

48 CPT Donald R. Klinger, "The Field Artillery Board," *Field Artillery Journal*, Sep-Oct 1982, pp. 13-18; Romjue, *et al*, *Prepare the Army for War*, pp. 6-7.

49 Klinger, "The Field Artillery Board," pp. 13-18; Romjue, *et al*, *Prepare the Army for War*, pp. 6-7.

50 Saul Bronfeld, "Fighting Outnumbered: The Impact of the Yom Kippur War on the US Army," *The Journal of Military History,* Apr 2007, pp. 465-98; An Institutional Self-Study for Initial Accreditation, USAFAS, Dec 1979, p. 1-1, UF23.5 A2 U511 R, MSTL; 1974 USAFAS Annual Historical Supplement, pp. 7-8.

51 1974 USAFAS Annual Historical Supplement, pp. 7-8; 1975 USAFAS Annual Historical Supplement, p. 15; MG David E. Ott, "Forward Observations," *Field Artillery Journal*, Nov-Dec 1975, pp. 6, 13; "Counterfire," *Field Artillery Journal*, Nov-Dec 1975, pp. 14-21; MG David E. Ott, "Forward Observations," *Field Artillery Journal*, Jul-Aug 1976, p. 3; Boyd L. Dastrup, *Modernizing the King of Battle: 1973-1991* (Fort Sill, OK: Office of the Command Historian, US Army Field Artillery Center and School, 1994, reprinted by the US Army Center of Military History, 2003), pp.

4-6.

52 1974 USAFAS Annual Historical Supplement, pp. 7-8; 1975 USAFAS Annual Historical Supplement, p. 15; Ott, "Forward Observations," pp. 6, 13; "Counterfire," pp. 14-21; Ott, "Forward Observations," p. 3; Dastrup, *Modernizing the King of Battle*, pp. 4-6.

53 1974 USAFAS Annual Historical Supplement, pp. 7-8; 1975 USAFAS Annual Historical Supplement, p. 15; Ott, "Forward Observations," pp. 6, 13; "Counterfire," pp. 14-21; Ott, "Forward Observations," p. 3; Dastrup, *Modernizing the King of Battle*, pp. 4-6.

54 Dastrup, *Modernizing the King of Battle,* pp. 5-6.

55 Dastrup, *Modernizing the King of Battle,* pp. 6-7; Ott, "Forward Observations," p. 6; BG Paul Pearson, "FIST," *Field Artillery Journal*, May-Jun 1976, pp. 7-12; 1976 USAFAS Annual Historical Supplement, p. 2.

56 Dastrup, *Modernizing the King of Battle*, pp. 2-3.

57 1975 USAFAS Annual Historical Supplement, p. 17.

58 1977 USAFAS Annual Historical Supplement, p. 1; FM 6-20, Fire Support in Combined Arms Operations, May 1977, preface; Memorandum, 1 Dec 1975, FM 6-20 File, MSTL Archives; Ltr, MG Donald R. Keith to MG John R. Thurman III, Cdr, US Army Combined Arms Center, Ft. Leavenworth, KS, 27 May 1977, Field Manual File, USAFAS, Office of the AC, MSTL Archives; Dastrup, *Modernizing the King of Battle*, p. 3.

59 Ltr with encl, Keith to BG Eugene Kelly, Jr., Cmdt, US Army Intelligence School, Ft. Huachuca, AZ, May 1977, Field Manual File, MSTL Archives.

60 Dastrup, *Modernizing the King of Battle*, pp. 13-14.

61 Dastrup, *Modernizing the King of Battle*, pp. 13-14.

62 John L. Romjue, *History of Army 86: Division 86, The Development of the Heavy Division* (Fort Monroe, VA: TRADOC Historical Office, 1982), pp. 11-41; Division 86 Final Report, Executive Summary, Oct 1981, pp. 1-13, HRDC; TRADOC Division Restructuring Study, Executive Summary, 1 Mar 1977, pp. 6, 11-14, A6-A11, MSTL; TRADOC Division Restructuring Study, The Heavy Division, 1 Mar 1977, pp. 15-18, 81-87, MSTL.

63 DA, *Historical Summary, Fiscal Year (FY) 1982,* p. 25; DA, *Historical Summary, FY 1986,* pp. 65-67; COL Robert S. Riley, "AOE: What is It?" *Field Artillery Journal,* Sep-Oct 1985, pp. 22-24; Legal Mix VI, Main Report (Extract), Jan 1985, pp. 13-14, HRDC; 1987 USAFACFS AHR, p. 86; Fact Sheet, subj: Echelon Above Corps Transition Plan, 8-inch Tradeoff for MLRS, 4 Jan 1988, HRDC; Interview, Dastrup with MAJ Ron Janowski, Force Structure Officer, DCD, 8 Mar 1988, HRDC.

64 CPT Suzann W. Voigt, "Much Ado About Something," *Field Artillery Journal,* Jul-Aug 1986, p. 29; Romjue, *A History of Army 86*, pp. 25-33, 34-57; LTC Heinz A. Shiemann, "Fire Support for the Light Division," *Field Artillery Magazine,* Oct 1987, p. 19; John L. Romjue, *The Army of Excellence: The Development of the 1980s Army* (Fort Monroe, VA: Office of the Command Historian, TRADOC, 1993), pp. 16-17; Romjue, *et al, Prepare the Army for War*, pp. 23-29.

65   Romjue, *et al, Prepare the Army for War,*, pp. 40-41.

66 Ltr, LTG (Ret) Donald R. Keith to Dastrup, 19 Jul 1993, HRDC.

67 Briefing, subj: Field Artillery Update, 18 Apr 1979, HRDC; Patrick F. Rogers, "The New Artillery," *Army*, Jul 1980, p. 31; COL William J. Harrison, "Malor," *Field Artillery Journal*, Mar-Apr 1975, pp. 30-32; Memorandum for Record, subj: The Mortar Locating Radar Development History and Status, ca 1973, HRDC; Oral History Interview, Cass with Ott, Dec 1979, pp. 29, 30, 66, 79, HRDC.

68 1985 USAFACFS AHR, pp. 69-71; 1989 USAFACFS ACH, pp. 161-64; Dastrup, *Modernizing the King of Battle*, pp. 8-9; Ltr with Encl, USAFAS to Cdr, CAC, subj: RPV Operational and Organizational Study, 8 Apr 1977, RPV Operational and Organizational Study

File, MSTL Archives; Msg, Cdr, Army Material Command, to Cdr, Army Missile Command, subj: Mini-RPVs, 111954Z Jan 1974, USAFAS, DCD File, MSTL Archives; Msg, Cdr, US Army Field Artillery Center (USAFAC), to Cdr, CAC, subj: Mini-RPV, Jul 1977, Donald R. Keith Book, Material Developments File, MSTL Archives.

69 LTC R.A. Neuwien, "How You Got It and What You Got," *US Army Aviation Digest,* Mar 1982, pp. 6-10; "OH-58D," *Army,* Aug 1990, pp. 54-56.

70 Ltr with encls, Cdr, CAC, to Cdr, USAFAS, and Cdr, USAAC, subj: OH-58D in Field Artillery Role, 18 May 1987, Annex A-1, HRDC; MG Ellis Parker, "This Vision of LHX," *US Army Aviation Digest,* Dec 1986, p. 5; Briefing, subj: To Provide Information on the AHIP as It Pertains to Field Artillery, 1987, HRDC.

71 Fact Sheet, subj: History of the Aerial Fire Support Division, 18 Feb 1988, HRDC; Fact Sheet, subj: OH-58D/AFSO Field Status, 19 Dec 1988, HRDC; Fact Sheet, subj: History of AFSC/ Proponency for Aerial Fire Support Coordinator Training, 23 Dec 1986, HRDC.

72 Msg, Cmdt, USAFAS, to Cdr, TRADOC, *et al,* subj: OH58D Retrofit and Redistribution, 031150Z Oct 1989, HRDC; Msg, Cdr, TRADOC, to Cmdt, FASCH, *et al,* subj: Revised OH58D Fielding and Employment Plan, 041558Z Oct 1989, HRDC; Fact Sheet, subj: OH-58D Distribution, 16 Apr 1990, HRDC; Fact Sheet, subj: OH-58D Fielding Status, 16 Apr 1990, HRDC; Interview, L. Martin Kaplan with MAJ George W. Chappell, Chief, Aerial Fire Support Division, Fire Support and Combined Arms Department, USAFAS, 5 Feb 1990, HRDC; Msg, Cdr, TRADOC, to Cdr, XVIII Airborne Corps, *et al,* subj: MPLH for 1st Squadron, 17th Cavalry Requirements, 041410Z Oct 1989, HRDC; Briefing, subj: AHIP, 9 Nov 1989, HRDC; Msg, Cdr, TRADOC, to Cdr, USAAVNC, *et al,* subj: OH-58D Deployment, 061742Z Oct 1989, HRDC; Briefing, subj: Armed OH-58D, 29 Dec 1989, HRDC; Interview, Dastrup with Jerry Shelley, Chief, New Systems Division, TAD, 4 Jan 1990, HRDC; Ltr with Encls, Cdr, CAC, to Cdr, USAFAS, and Cdr, USAAC, subj: OH-58D in the Field Artillery Role, 18 May 1987, HRDC.

73 J.B.A. Bailey, *Field Artillery and Firepower* (Oxford: The Military Press, 1989), p. 306; Fire Support Mission Area Analysis (C), material used is unclassified, HRDC.

74 Dastrup, *Modernizing the King of Battle*, pp. 9-10; Bailey, *Field Artillery and Firepower*, p. 307; Legal Mix V, Final Report, 17 Feb 1977, p. 1-1, HRDC; USAFAS, Operational and Organizational Concept for Copperhead, 1981-1986, p. F8; HRDC; MAJ Michael W. Hustead, "Fire Support Mission Area: Impact of Precision Guided Munitions," *Field Artillery Journal*, May-Jun 1981, pp. 19-20; Final Report, Fire Support Team Force Development Experimentation, Executive Summary, Apr-May 1984, pp. 1-8, HRDC.

75 Dastrup, *Modernizing the King of Battle*, p. 10.

76 Briefing, subj: Field Artillery Update, undated, HRDC; Truman R. Strobridge and Bernard C. Nalty, "The Roar of the 8-Incher," *Field Artillery Journal*, Mar-Apr 1980, p. 36; 1988 USAFACFS AHR, p. 129; "M198 Production Rolling," *Field Artillery Journal*, Sep-Oct 1978, p. 15; MAJ William Whelihan, "We've Got 30!" *Field Artillery Journal*, May-Jun 1979, pp. 9-12; MAJ William Whelihan, "M198," *Field Artillery Journal*, Jan-Feb 1978, p. 9.

77 MAJ Roger A. Rains, "Readiness: The Field Artillery Takes Aim," *Army*, Mar 1985, p. 41; LTC Browder A. Willis, "HELP for the M109 Self-Propelled Howitzer," *Field Artillery Journal*. May-Jun 1982, pp. 35-37; Decision Coordinating Paper, subj: 155-mm, SP Howitzer (HIP), Nov 1989, pp. 2-3, HRDC; Anthony Pokorny, "Take the Tech," *Field Artillery Journal*, Sep-Oct 1984, p. 21; Briefing, subj: Fire Support, Jan 1988, HRDC; "HELP Program Continues," *Field Artillery Journal*, Jan-Feb 1983, p. 47.

78 DSWS Main Report (S/NOFORN/WNINTEL), Extract, Jul 1983, pp. 4-2, 4-16, 4-17, 4-1 – 5-18, 10-1, material used in unclassified, HRDC; Rains, "Readiness: The Field Artillery Takes Aim," p. 41; Ltr of Agreement for the 155-mm. Self-Propelled Howitzer Improvement Program, 6

Feb 1984, HRDC; Memorandum for Record, subj: Requirements Review Committee Mtg, 31 Jan 1984, HRDC; Briefing, subj: 155-mm. Self-Propelled HIP, undated, HRDC; Memo, subj: HIP, 1 Nov 1984, HRDC; CPT James F. Janda, "Getting HELP and HIP," *Field Artillery Journal*, Sep-Oct 1985, p. 20; Fact Sheet, subj: HIP, 10 May 1988, HRDC; Briefing, subj: HIP, 2 Feb 1989, HRDC; HIP Survivability Analysis (S), Executive Summary, 2 Jun 1989, information used is unclassified, HRDC; 1989 USAFAS AHR, pp. 148-49.

79 Fact Sheet, subj: AFAS-C, 12 Sep 1988, HRDC; Fact Sheet, subj: AFAS, 15 Jul 1988, HRDC.

80 1987 USAFACFS AHR, pp. 66-67; Memorandum for See Distribution, subj: Armored Family of Vehicles Task Force Phase I Study Report, 20 Nov 1987, in AFV Task Force Phase I Report, Vol I (S), 31 Aug 1987, information used in unclassified, HRDC.

81 1987 USAFACFS AHR, p. 67; Interview, Dastrup with Paul Gross, Dep Dir, TRADOC System Manager (TSM) Cannon, Directorate of Combat Developments (DCD), 16 Feb 1990, HRDC; USAFAS Program and Project Summary Sheets, 20 Jan 1990, pp. 5-6, HRDC; The United States Army Posture Statement FY 90/91, p. 77, HRDC; DF with encls, subj: Draft AFAS-C Annex to AFV Required Operational Capabilities, 24 Mar 1988, HRDC; Briefing, subj: FA Test Bed Program, undated, HRDC; Fact Sheet, subj: AFAS, 15 Jul 1988, HRDC; COL (P) Richard W. Wharton, "The Cannon Still the King on Battlefield," *Army*, Jul 1989, p. 55; Appendix 12 AFAS-C to Annex D of the Operational and Organizational Plan for AFV, 18 Aug 1988, pp. D-12-1 – D-12-3, HRDC; Fact Sheet, subj: AFAS, 15 Jul 1988, HRDC.

82 Dastrup, *Modernizing the King of Battle*, p. 11.

83 Dastrup, *Modernizing the King of Battle*, p. 11.

84 Dastrup, *Modernizing the King of Battle*, pp. 11-12.

85 COL Myron F. Curtis, COL Thomas B. Brown, and Dr. John C. Hogan, "Pershing: It Gave Peace a Chance," *Field Artillery Magazine,* Feb 1991, p. 29.

86 Curtis, Brown, and Hogan, "Pershing," pp. 29-30; MAJ Robert L. Shearer, "Development of Pershing II," *Field Artillery Journal,* May-Jun 1980, p. 31.

87 Curtis, Brown, and Hogan, "Pershing," p. 30; Luanne Aline Turtentine, "Intermediate-Range Nuclear Force Modernization and Soviet-West German Relations," unpublished master's thesis, Naval Postgraduate School, 1984, pp. 8-12, MSTL.

88 Treaty Between the United States of America and the Union of Soviet Socialists Republics on the Elimination of their Intermediate-Range and Shorter-Range Missiles, 1987, pp. 1-4, HRDC; Msg, HQ DA to CINCUSAREUR, *et al,* subj: INF Treaty Implementation Plan Update 88-1, 122000Z Jan 1988, HRDC.

89 Annotated On-site Inspection Readiness Plan Outline, Sandia National Laboratories, 4 Jan 1988, pp. 1-2, HRDC; Briefing, subj: 1987 INF Treaty and Its Impact on Fort Sill and 3-9 FA, undated, HRDC; Memorandum for Chief of Staff with Enclosure, subj: Annual Historical Review, 1 Feb 1991, p. 7, HRDC; Staff Input, subj: Annual Historical Review for the INF Treaty Compliance Office, undated, HRDC; Interview, Dastrup with CW2 Lawrence Tompkins, INF Treaty Office, Directorate of Plans, Training, and Mobilization (DPTM), 30 Jan 1991, HRDC.

90 2000 USAFACFS ACH, pp. 148-49.

91 2000 USAFACFS ACH, pp. 149-50.

92 For extensive discussion on the modernization of the 1970s and 1980s, see Paul H. Herbert, *Deciding What Has to be Done: General William E. Depuy and the 1976 Edition of FM 100-5, Operations* (Fort Leavenworth, KS: Combat Studies Institute, US Army Command and General Staff College, 1988), John L. Romjue, *From Active Defense to AirLand Battle: The Development of Army Doctrine, 1973-1982* (Fort Monroe, VA: US Army Training and Doctrine Command Historical Office, 1984); Frank N. Schubert and Theresa L. Kraus, eds. *The Whirlwind War: The United States*

Army in Operations Desert Shield and Desert Storm (Washington, DC: Center of Military History, United States Army, 1995), and Robert H. Scales, Jr., ed., *Certain Victory: United States Army in the Gulf War* (Washington, DC: Office of the Chief of Staff, US Army, 1993). Thirty-six nations participated in the coalition by committing ground, air, or naval forces. Of the 36 nations, the Arab allies (Saudi Arabia, Egypt, and United Arab Emirates), the United Kingdom, France, and the United States contributed the most military forces. Turkey moved about 125,000 forces along its borders to deter a possible Iraqi attack. See Henry O. Malone, ed., *TRADOC Support to Operations Desert Shield and Desert Storm* (Fort Monroe, VA: Office of the Command Historian, 1992), p. 5, and "Forces Committed," *Military Review*, Sep 91, pp. 80-81, for details on the composition of the coalition forces.

93 Norman Friedman, *Desert Victory: The War for Kuwait* (Annapolis, MD: Naval Institute Press, 1991), pp. 36-40, 108, 169-96, 214-36; Malone, ed., *TRADOC Support to Operations Desert Shield and Desert Storm*, pp. 7-8; Scales, ed., *Certain Victory*, pp. 391-93; DA, *Historical Summary for Fiscal Years 1990 and 1991*, p. 24; Schubert and Kraus, eds., *The Whirlwind War*, p. 268.

94 Memorandum for Dir, DOTD, subj: Operation Desert Shield/Storm, 7 Mar 1991, HRDC; Memorandum for DPTM, subj: DOTD Significant Activities in Support of Desert Shield/Storm, 7 Mar 1991, HRDC; Report, subj: Augmenting the Training Base: The Army Reserve in Support of TRADOC, 1 Apr 1994, HRDC.

95 Memorandum for DPTM, subj: DOTD Significant Activities in Support of Desert Shield/Storm, 7 Mar 1991, in Memorandum for DPTM, subj: Field Artillery School Support of Desert Shield/Storm, undated, HRDC; Memorandum for DPTM, subj: Field Artillery School (FAS) Support of Desert Shield/Storm, undated, HRDC; Oral History Interview, Dastrup with former AC, USAFAS, COL Marshall McRee, 22 Jul 1992, p. 1, HRDC.

96 Memorandum for DPTM, subj: DOTD Significant Activities in Support of Desert Shield/Storm, 7 Mar 1991, in Memorandum for DPTM, subj: Field Artillery School Support of Desert Shield/Storm, undated, HRDC; Memorandum for DPTM, subj: Field Artillery School (FAS) Support of Desert Shield/Storm, undated, HRDC; Oral History Interview, Dastrup with McRee, 22 Jul 1992, p. 1, HRDC; Memorandum for Dir, DOTD, subj: Operation Desert Shield/Storm, 7 Mar 1991, in Memorandum for DPTM, subj: Field Artillery School Support of Desert Shield/Storm, undated, HRDC; Memorandum for See Distribution, subj: MDS Mobile Training Team to SW Asia, 17 Dec 1990, in Memorandum for DPTM, subj: Field Artillery School Support of Desert Shield/Storm, undated, HRDC.

97 Memorandum for Record, subj: USAFAS and Desert Storm, undated, HRDC.

98 Oral History Interview, Dastrup with McRee, 22 Jul 1992, pp. 4-6, HRDC; Memorandum for DPTM, subj: DOTD Significant Activities in Support of Desert Shield/Storm, undated, HRDC; Interview, Dastrup with Director, Gunnery Department, COL Thomas R. Hogan, 4 Jan 1991, HRDC; 1990 USAFACFS AHR, pp. 31-32; Report, Department of the Army, Office of the Chief, Army Reserve, subj: Augmenting the Training Base: The Army Reserve in Support of TRADOC, 1 Apr 1994, p. 13, HRDC.

99 JULLS Long Report, 27 Jul 1991, p. 24, HRDC; Memorandum for Cdr, USACATA, subj: AAR Desert Shield/Storm Phase I (Deployment/Mobilization), 10 Jul 1991, p. 5, HRDC. Most of the hiring occurred at Forts Benning, Knox, Sill, Jackson, and Dix, which were major centers for reserve component unit mobilization and individual ready reserve training. See Report, subj: Augmenting the Training Base: The Army Reserves in Support of TRADOC, 1 Apr 1994, p. 2, HRDC.

100 Report, subj: Augmenting the Training Base: The Army Reserves in Support of TRADOC, 1 Apr 1994, p. 2.

101 Oral History Interview, Dastrup with Hallada, 13 Mar 1991, p. 4, HRDC; Oral History

Interview, Dastrup and Kaplan with Cdr, 212th Field Artillery Brigade, III Corps Artillery, COL Floyd T. Banks, 19 Jun 1991, p. 5, HRDC.

102 Report, subj: Augmenting the Training Base: The Army Reserve in Support of TRADOC, 1 Apr 1994, p. 11, HRDC.

103 JULLS Long Report, 27 Jun 1991, HRDC; 1990 USAFACFS AHR, pp. 31-32; Report, Department of the Army, Office of the Chief, Army Reserve, subj: Augmenting the Training Base: The Army Reserve in Support of TRADOC, 1 Apr 1994, p. 13, HRDC.

104 Oral History Interview, Dastrup with Hallada, 13 Mar 1991, p. 10, HRDC.

105 Malone, ed., *TRADOC Support to Operations Desert Shield and Desert Storm*, p. 50; Memorandum for Record, subj: USAFAS and Desert Storm, undated, HRDC; Oral History Interview, Dastrup with Cdr, US Marine Corps Detachment, COL Kent O. Steen, 28 Aug 1992, pp. 5-6, HRDC; Oral History Interview, Dastrup with McRee, 22 Jul 1992, p. 3, HRDC; Memorandum for Chief of Staff, subj: AHR, 1 Feb 1991, HRDC

106 Memorandum for Director of Center for Army Lessons Learned (CALL), Fort Leavenworth, KS, subj: Operation Desert Storm Emerging Observations, 10 Jul 1991; Briefing, subj: Desert Storm Emerging Results, undated, HRDC.

107 E-mail with atch, subj: Manuscript Review, 8 Dec 2003, p. 9, HRDC; Memorandum for Director, CALL, subj: Operation Desert Storm Emerging Observations, 10 Jul 1991, pp. 1-2, HRDC. See Creighton W. Abrams, "The Gulf War and European Artillery," *Journal of the Royal Artillery*, Autumn 2001, pp. 41-44, for the insights from a former field artillery commander in Operation Desert Storm about combat operations.

108 MG Fred F. Marty, "State-of-the-Branch Address," *Field Artillery Magazine*, Dec 1991, p. 3.

Chapter Eight
Moving Toward New Century

Without a viable and specific threat to national security with the end of the Cold War, Congress dramatically slashed the military's budget and shifted the savings accrued to domestic social programs during the 1990s. This action, often called the peace dividend, forced the Army to decrease the number of its civilian employees and military personnel, to inactivate units, to revamp its force structure, to become more dependent upon its reserve components, to find innovative ways to maintain readiness, and to ensure the efficient use of the money appropriated by Congress. The Field Artillery School likewise had to adjust to the realities of peace and a declining budget by revising its officer, warrant officer, and enlisted courses and turning to automation as a means to enhance individual and unit training and to provide responsive and lethal field artillery on the battlefield.

Constant Change

Although Operation Desert Storm confirmed the quality of the Field Artillery School's training in recent years, keeping programs of instruction abreast of technological changes, lessons learned, and the needs of the active component and the reserve components (US Army National Guard and US Army Reserve) meant continuing modifications in the midst of declining budgets. Early in September 1991, the Assistant Commandant of the Field Artillery School, Brigadier General Tommy Franks (1991-1992), who had been the assistant division commander for maneuver in the 1st Cavalry Division during the Gulf War of 1991, organized a task force of senior officers. He directed the task force to identify the optimal Officer Advance Course without regard to resource constraints and to determine the optimal Officer Advance Course that could be reasonably implemented with existing resources. Regardless of the course of action, he desired small group leaders to have more contact with their students, more field training, and more Multiple-Launch Rocket System training, among other concerns, and the incorporation of the lessons from Operation Desert Storm into the programs of instruction. Ultimately, Franks wanted doctrine with an emphasis on the high-intensity fight to be taught first with battalion operations afterwards.[1]

As the task force examined developing an optimized Officer Advance Course without regard to resource constraints in October and November 1991, it identified key obstacles that stood in the way. The optimal course length would be 23 weeks, but the US Army Training and Doctrine Command's (TRADOC) maximum course length of 20 weeks would prevent this. Also, the school did not have enough classrooms or equipment to increase the length of small group instruction which would be a way to get small group leaders more involved with their students as mentors. As such, executing the desired optimal Field Artillery Officer Advance Course was well beyond the school's resources.[2]

With this realization, the task force designed proposals that could be realistically implemented within existing and projected resources and that presented the fewest concessions while still meeting the constraints of course length and the availability of classrooms and equipment. To do this, the task force expanded the small group instructor's time with the students beyond the small group phase by involving the instructor in every aspect of training, including large group instruction. When the students broke into small groups for practical exercises during large group instruction, the small group instructor would be involved as a mentor while the technical instructor would rotate from group to group to provide assistance as needed. This would get the small group instructor more engaged with the students without expanding the time allotted to small group instruction and committing additional resources that the school did not have. The task force also tripled the number of field exercises from five to 15 and organized instruction so that doctrine would be taught first and be the basis for instruction in tactics, techniques, and procedures rather than the reverse which had been the practice for years.[3]

The task force restructured other aspects of the advance course. It increased Multiple-Launch Rocket System operational training and provided for diagnostic testing to allow students to be placed in the appropriate skill level in computer literacy and communication skills classes. Because the task force's proposals optimized the course within existing resources and time constraints, Franks approved them in December 1991 and forwarded them to the Commandant of the Field Artillery School, Major General Fred F. Marty (1991-1993), for his approval. On 7 January 1992, Marty endorsed the recommendations for implementation as quickly as resources and circumstances would permit.[4]

No sooner had the school put into operation this optimized, two-phase officer advance course composed of small group and large group instruction in 1992 than it set out to revise the course once again in 1993 without any firm indication if the restructuring was producing competent captains. Under the optimized format that had just been initiated, phase one or total group instruction lasted seven weeks and two days, while small group instruction took 12 weeks and two days. Although the total length of 20 weeks remained constant as directed by TRADOC, the school adjusted the length of the phases to accommodate more training on automated gunnery. It increased the length of total group instruction to 10 weeks to furnish 90 hours of instruction on the Initial Fire Support Automated System and dropped training on the Tactical Fire Direction System which was scheduled for elimination from the Army's inventory during the 1990s. This forced the school to decrease small group instruction from 12 to 10 weeks. These revisions which went into effect in October 1993 with the Field Artillery Officer Advance Course Class 1-94 reinforced the need to make certain that the students were adequately trained on the latest automated systems without undermining the school's commitment of graduating officers who were qualified as battery commanders, task force and brigade fire support officers, and battalion, brigade, and division artillery staff officers.[5]

Influenced by the growing requirement for more automation instruction on the Initial Fire Support Automated System, the need for the right mix of manual gunnery and automated gunnery, the increasing demand from commanders in the field for better prepared captains, and the growing pressure to conserve declining resources, the Field Artillery School restructured its advance course again. Early in 1994, the Assistant Commandant of the

School, Brigadier General Leo J. Baxter (1994-1995), tasked school's directors to be more innovative and focus on the mission of producing captains with the abilities of performing as battalion and brigade staff officers, battery commanders, fire support officers, and fire direction officers for the high-intensity fight. The directors also had to keep the essential gunnery skills required for fire direction officers and battery commanders in the program of instruction and had to eliminate teaching skills that were already being taught in the Field Artillery Officer Basic Course.[6]

After careful consideration over a period of months, the school's department directors returned to Baxter with their suggestions. They proposed dividing the course into large group instruction of 10 weeks and small group instruction of 10 weeks. More importantly, they recommended focusing total group instruction on technical skills, such as gunnery, and centering small group instruction on the skills, knowledge, and behaviors required by battery commanders, battalion and brigade staff officers, and fire support officers. The directors also urged shifting the current focus on manual gunnery and communications from technical and operator skills and knowledge to supervisory skills and knowledge. This would eliminate redundancy because the Officer Basic Course already taught technical and operator skills and knowledge in gunnery and communications. Late in February 1995, Baxter endorsed the changes. Basically, they focused the course on new technology – the Initial Fire Support Automated System, the M109A6 (Paladin) self-propelled 155-mm. howitzer, and the Multiple-Launch Rocket System – and increased the number of practical exercises in the small groups. Subsequently in March 1995, the Commandant of the Field Artillery School, Major General John A. Dubia (1993-1995), directed putting the changes into operation in the fall of 1995.[7]

So far, the school's revisions of the Officer Advance Course represented minor changes. Nothing substantial came out of the revisions that altered the school's program of instruction or methods of instruction. While the course's basic format of small and large group instruction that dated to the late 1980s remained intact, its content and focus on the high-intensity battlefield also remained constant from revision to revision. Only the number of hours on a particular subject fluctuated. For example, when the Army started fielding the Initial Fire Support Automated System, the school increased the time devoted to training on the system and decreased time on the Tactical Fire Direction System that was being eliminated from the Army's inventory. With the pressure of declining budgets mounting, the school faced the imperative of making major changes on its own or having them imposed by higher headquarters.

Pushing to improve officer professional military education to develop innovative leaders with critical thinking skills for the future battlefield and to stay within the shrinking budgets, TRADOC, meanwhile, conducted studies with the goal of finding better ways to train and educate officers. In October 1994, the Commanding General of TRADOC, General William W. Hartzog, directed the Deputy Commandant of the Command and General Staff College, Fort Leavenworth, Kansas, to review ways to gain efficiencies in professional military education for captains. Based upon a Command and General Staff College study of 1990-1991 and the TRADOC Reengineering Study of 1993-1994,

Brigadier General R.W. House, who was the Deputy Commandant of the Command and General Staff College, developed a radical concept. He urged merging TRADOC's 20-week Officer Advance Course and its nine-week Combined Arms Services Staff School Course at Fort Leavenworth into a 20-week course which would mean seriously reducing the lengths of both courses and revamping instruction.[8]

House's study then formed the basis of the TRADOC Deputy Chief of Staff for Training Captain Professional Military Education Study of 1995-1996 that was conducted with input from the branch service schools. Among other things, the TRADOC study recommended abandoning the two-course Captain Professional Military Education system that was composed of the Officer Advance Course at the branch and service schools and Combined Arms Service Staff School Course that had begun in 1981. In its place the study proposed developing a single captain's career course to be taught at one location to reduce expenses in an era of declining budgets without sacrificing quality.[9]

Understanding the imperative of revamping professional military education for captains, Hartzog endorsed the Captain Professional Military Education Study's recommendation. Upon gaining approval from the Chief of Staff of the Army on 27 July 1996 to implement the study's proposal, Hartzog accepted an incremental approach of four phases that would provide a "glide path" and leverage technology. While phase one would preserve the two courses taught at different locations, such as at Fort Sill and Fort Leavenworth, phase two outlined the retention of the 20-week Officer Advance Course, the development of a six-week Combined Arms Services Staff School Course, and the synchronization of Officer Advance Course end dates with Combined Arms Services Staff School Course start dates to permit officers to move directly from the advance course to the staff course with minimal delay. During phase three, the Captain's Career Course would be introduced. It would employ distributive learning for common core subjects that all captains should know regardless of their branch and other appropriate subjects. The captain's career course would also synchronize the common core subjects required by TRADOC, the Officer Advance Course's program of instruction for branch training, and the Combined Arms Services Staff School Course's program of instruction for staff training to minimize redundancy. While tactical and technical training would be taught at the service schools, staff training would be conducted in the Combined Arms Services Staff School Course. Phase four would employ distance learning for common core and other appropriate subjects, would furnish tactical and technical training at the branch service schools, would use distance learning to provide staff training at the branch and service schools, and would no longer require captains to go to Fort Leavenworth for staff training. Upon complete implementation, the Captain's Career Course would reduce expenses. Specifically, field artillery captains would complete their branch training and staff training at Fort Sill with the latter being taught via distance learning from Fort Leavenworth.[10]

Only phase two directly influenced the Field Artillery School in 1996. To meet the established implementation date for phase two, the school adjusted its advance course schedule. Because Fort Leavenworth planned to have seven Combined Arms Service Staff School Course classes in Fiscal Year 1997 and because Hartzog wanted students to move directly from the advance course to the staff course without a break to minimize disruption and reduce costs, the school increased the number of advance course classes from four to seven in Fiscal Year 1997 and aligned them to match up with the Fort Leavenworth classes.[11]

By the end of 1996, the school had implemented phases one and two and started detailed planning for phases three and four. Besides synchronizing the common core subjects and forming the Officer Advance Course and the Combined Arms Service Staff School Course into an integrated course, phase three broke instruction into two weeks of common core, 16 weeks of the Officer Advance Course for branch training, and six weeks of Combined Arms Service Staff School instruction for a total of 24 weeks of training. As outlined by phase three, the Field Artillery School planned to reduce its Officer Advance Course from 20 to 18 weeks by cutting hours of instruction on manual gunnery and the number of practical exercises, among other things. Under the 18-week format, the students would go through large group instruction during the first eight weeks of the course and small group instruction during the last 10 weeks with the focus on the high-intensity fight before attending the Combined Arms Service Staff School Course.[12]

Before phase three training support packages for common core could be distributed for implementation, the Chief of Staff of the Army, General Dennis Reimer, who was the Deputy Assistant Commandant at the Field Artillery School in the 1980s, made a critical change to Captain Professional Military Education. Following a briefing at the Command and General Staff College on 31 July 1998 that outlined the transition from the two-course format to the one-course at one location format, he approved moving into phase three but not phase four. He did not want staff training to be done via distance learning because he did not want to forfeit the "immense benefit of staff group mentoring and interaction between branches that we now have in CAS3 [Combined Arms Services Staff School]."[13]

To produce the savings that phase four promised, Reimer urged TRADOC to examine the possibility of reducing the length of the Officer Advance Course if necessary. In response, TRADOC abandoned the fourth phase and created its Captain's Career Course out of Hartzog's first three phases. As of 1999, field artillery officers went through an 18-week Field Artillery Captain's Career Course that was conducted seven times a year to coincide with the Combined Arms Services Staff School Course. They attended the Field Artillery School, moved to Fort Leavenworth in a temporary duty status to complete the six-week Combined Arms Services Staff School Course, and returned to Fort Sill for graduation.[14]

Over a period of a few years, TRADOC's Captain Military Education effort driven by the need to reduce training costs fundamentally reshaped the Field Artillery School's advance course and redesignated it as the Field Artillery Captain's Career Course. For the first time in its history, the school's advance course was intimately tied to another course. The Captain's Career Course's end-dates were meshed with the Combined Arms Service Staff School Course's start dates to ensure a smooth transition from the branch course to the staff officer course while programs of instruction for both courses were coordinated to minimize redundancy. In short, the new Field Artillery Captain's Career Course was not a stand-alone course as its predecessor, the Field Artillery Officer Advance Course, had been for years because it fed directly into the Combined Arms Services Staff School Course.[15]

Meanwhile, TRADOC's Reserve Component Captain Professional Military Education effort compelled the Field Artillery School to revise its Field Artillery Officer Advance Course-Reserve Component. As of 1998, most reserve component officers completed the Field Artillery Officer Advance Course-Reserve Component through the Field Artillery Correspondence Course Program, a division of the Army Correspondence Course Program that was initiated after World War I for National Guard and Organized Reserves officers to provide professional training and that included one two-week active duty training period (summer camp). Upon completion of this training, they took the Combined Arms Staff Service School Course through correspondence, eight inactive duty training periods (weekend drills), and one two-week active duty training period (summer camp).[16]

The format of reserve component course, therefore, had serious limitations. It consisted of 17 Army Correspondence Course Program courses and active duty training. Officers worked through the correspondence courses on their own and then reported to the Field Artillery School for two weeks of active duty training. However, the correspondence program was obsolete and provided limited training because students arrived at the school unprepared, requiring a significant amount of refresher training. Essentially, this turned the two-week active duty training period into a two-week "fire hose" course to disseminate information.[17]

To avoid these striking deficiencies reserve component captains could take the resident course. Unfortunately, many could not attend the resident Field Artillery Captain's Career Course or its predecessor, Field Artillery Officer Advance Course, because they could not be released from their civilian jobs for 18 weeks.[18]

Given these limitations and the drive to standardize reserve and active component training for the Total Army, the Field Artillery School redesigned the course to eliminate the deficiencies and to support TRADOC's Reserve Component Captains Professional Military Education three-phase program. After months of work, the school introduced a strategy on 6 March 1998 for the Field Artillery Captain's Career Course-Distance Learning that would take the student two years to complete and that received endorsement from TRADOC and the National Guard Bureau.[19]

The school divided the course into three phases of asynchronous (students working alone with instructor involvement as needed), synchronous (the simultaneous participation of students and instructors via teleconferencing and the Internet), and resident training. In the first part of phase one (Phase IA), asynchronous instruction employed communications technologies, such as e-mail, multimedia data bases, and virtual libraries, consisted of common core and branch specific subjects, was performed at the officer's own pace and home station, and was completed during the first Total Army Training System year. The second part of phase one (Phase IB) included both asynchronous and synchronous instruction and relied upon communication technologies, such as desktop video teleconferencing, to enable live, real-time interaction between instructors and students, and was completed in the first six months of the second Total Army Training System year. Phase two was done during the second six months of the second Total Army Training System year with multiple active duty training periods (weekend drills) being conducted. While this phase culminated with a two-week active duty training period at Fort Sill, phase three was staff process training of eight inactive duty training periods and a two-week active duty training period.[20]

Following a pilot of the new course in 2001, the school implemented the Field Artillery Captain's Career Course-Distance Learning in 2002 to replace the existing Field Artillery Officer Advance Course-Reserve Component. This course promised to improve training for reserve component officers because it would be more intensive and challenging and produce a more tactically and technically competent reserve component captain.[21]

Meanwhile, the school's Field Artillery Officer Basic Course which focused on training second lieutenants for their first assignment encountered similar challenges as the advance course did by going through repeated revisions in the 1990s in the school's search for the optimum way to produce competent second lieutenants in the face of declining resources. Lessons from Operation Desert Storm and feedback from the combat training centers prompted the Assistant Commandant of the Field Artillery School, Brigadier General David L. Benton III (1992-1994), in the summer of 1992 to direct a comprehensive review of the Officer Basic Course to make it more relevant. Based upon input from the Fire Support and Combined Arms Department and the Gunnery Department, the school increased Multiple-Launch Rocket System and automated gunnery training and provided three full days of training on the fire support team vehicle, which was significantly more than the previous four hours of training. They also replaced the traditional orientation course where students learned to read a map and use a compass with mounted land navigation and dismounted training as a part of the observed fire block of instruction and added more hours for laser training to fill the gaps in existing training.[22]

Although the basic course had just been revamped and promised to produce a better prepared second lieutenant, deficiencies still existed, leading to more revisions. Unlike the 1992-1993 revisions with their focus on structural changes, the reforms of late 1993 and early 1994 centered on implementing training innovations to make the course more cost effective during a time of budget cuts.[23]

Under the direction of Benton, the school divided the course into three phases that were designed to reinforce the three parts of the gunnery team (forward observation, fire direction, and delivery unit operations). The phased approach logically sequenced instruction and permitted greater flexibility for remediation which was a growing challenge because failing grades were forcing more and more students to be recycled or dropped from the course; and this taxed constrained resources. While phase one (Foundation) taught the fundamentals of manual gunnery, communications, observed fire, land navigation, and leadership and culminated with a one-day, live-fire exercise that incorporated all aspects of instruction taught during the phase, phase two (Pillars) introduced automated gunnery, equipment and maintenance, basic fire planning, and combined arms operations and provided a one-day, live-fire exercise. Phase three (Capstone) furnished more combined arms training, introduced students to joint service capabilities, taught platoon leader skills and automated gunnery, furnished a battle simulation exercise where the students planned and conducted a battle, and provided a week-long field exercise. This phased approach and better synchronization of the different subjects within and between the phases made the program of instruction flow better, gave the students a better opportunity to learn the material than under the previous format, and saved money without sacrificing quality.[24]

Although the revised Field Artillery Officer Basic Course had existed for less than one year, budget reductions for Fiscal Year 1995 caused more restructuring. One significant revision replaced self-propelled howitzers with towed howitzers during field exercises to cut costs.[25] Reflecting upon this change, Brigadier General Leo Baxter, the Assistant Commandant of the School, concluded in January 1995 (1994-1995), "This reduction in the use of SP [self-propelled] systems in field training exercises allows USAFAS [US Army Field Artillery School] to train students at a significantly reduced cost, while still maintaining high standards in basic and advanced artillery skills."[26]

Even though the school retained the three phases from 1994, it decreased the number of field training exercises. It substituted the five-day war at the end of the course and eight separate one-day exercises for three, three-day training exercises and placed each three-day exercise at the end of a phase of training. This measure reduced the cost of operations while increasing field training time because the students remained in the field overnight rather than going in at the end of the day.[27]

Influenced by the introduction of new equipment, the need to improve training and conserve resources in light of continuing budget reductions, and the drive to make the basic course more attractive to newly commissioned second lieutenants, Baxter subsequently directed another major revision with the objective of implementing it in October 1995. Because manual gunnery was highly technical and taught in the first phase, some students had difficulties passing the gunnery tests, were often recycled, encountered a rough introduction to the Field Artillery, and cost the school money to recycle them. The school moved manual gunnery from the first phase to the second phase, centered the first phase on platoon leader skills, such as battery defense, communications, and observed fire, and adjusted the placement of the field training exercises in phase one. The first field training exercise occurred on the eighth day of the course where the students participated in crew drill and observed fire. The second field training exercise took place in the seventh week, covering survey/reconnaissance, selection, and occupation of position, battery defense, and observed fire. In phase three, the school taught more gunnery and fire support and concluded it with a four-day field training exercise.[28]

In 1996, the declining budget and high attrition rate caused the school to revise Officer Basic Course for the fourth time in four years. The Assistant Commandant of the School, Brigadier General William J. Lennox, Jr., (1995-1997), wanted the course to focus on fire support officer skills, fire direction officer skills, and platoon leader skills. He also desired to upgrade the level of training without increasing the length of the course and to prepare second lieutenants for duty with a light artillery unit, heavy artillery unit, or Multiple-Launch Rocket System unit without attending the mandatory follow-on course.[29]

Over a period of several months during the last of 1996, the school modularized the course and tied it to a mentoring program where experienced leaders would help new second lieutenants make the transition to Army life. Although the school retained the three phases of Foundation, Pillars, and Capstone, it divided the Officer Basic Course into four modules (fire direction officer, fire support officer, platoon leader, and common core), subdivided them into smaller modules, reduced the number of field training exercises from four to two, and abolished the follow-on courses for the Multiple-Launch Rocket System or Paladin. During the last week of the course, students attended the Multiple-Launch Rocket System, Paladin, or light artillery track, depending upon their first assignment. Besides integrating the Multiple-Launch Rocket System and Paladin training into the program of instruction, these measures, which were implemented in February 1997, saved money, produced a significantly restructured course, and invigorated the mentoring program to help second lieutenants make the transition to army life and to reduce the high recycling rate of students and high rate of terminating commissions.[30]

As the school was revamping its Officer Basic Course in 1996-1997, a video teleconference in November 1996 that included the Field Artillery School, combat training center personnel, and field commanders revealed critical deficiencies in light force training for second lieutenants because of the course's heavy force orientation. As the conference participants noted, second lieutenants had difficulties conducting land navigation, determining target location, and using indirect fires in restrictive terrain. In response, the Basic Fire Support Branch and the Combined Arms Branch in the Fire Support and Combined Arms Department introduced the Lightfighter Fire Coordination Exercise that was designed in conjunction with the Joint Readiness Training Center, Fort Polk, Louisiana, and the XVIII Airborne Corps Artillery, Fort Bragg, North Carolina. Later renamed the Dismounted Fire Support Officer Fire Coordination Exercise in June 1997, the exercise exposed second lieutenants to the intricacies of fire support in the light forces by conducting a deliberate attack, calling for fire, and adjusting fire, among other skills.[31]

With the addition of this exercise, the last of the significant revisions of the 1990s took place. At the end of the decade, the basic course consisted of three phases (Foundation, Pillars, and Capstone) with a platoon leader module, a fire direction module, a fire support module complete with the light fire support exercise, and common core instruction, such as sexual harassment, Army values, military history, and military justice, among other subjects, to prepare new second lieutenants for their first duty assignment.[32]

Just as officer training evolved during the 1990s, warrant officer training in the Field Artillery School underwent changes generated by the Army and the drive to make warrant officers tactically and technically competent and not just technically competent. Over a period of decades, technology repeatedly transformed field artillery warrant officer career fields. The Field Artillery received its first warrant officers in 1948 to serve as tactics and gunnery instructors and maintenance officers. A few years later, the branch added fire control assistants and weather warrant officers. With the introduction of rockets and missiles in the 1950s, the Field Artillery appointed warrant officers to support those new weapons systems. During the 1960s, 1970s, and 1980s, the elimination of obsolete field artillery systems, especially rockets and missiles, and the concurrent introduction of new weapon systems caused warrant officers to shuffle between opening and closing occupational specialty fields with regularity. Given this scenario, the number of warrant officers with field artillery military occupational specialties fluctuated from year to year with some lasting only a year. Of the five active field artillery military occupational specialties in the mid-1980s, only 131A, Target Acquisition Radar Technician, survived into the 1990s because the Army eliminated the others as changes in technology and weapon systems occurred.[33]

Meanwhile, other changes also profoundly affected field artillery warrant officers. Approved by the Chief of Staff of the Army in 1985, the Total Warrant Officer Study revised warrant officer career management, created the rank of Chief Warrant Officer Five, classified warrant officer requirements by rank, and redefined warrant officer responsibilities. Beginning in 1985, warrant officers had to be technically as well as tactically proficient whereas in the past they had focused their attention on technical competence. The transition from being primarily concerned with technical expertise to technical and tactical proficiency, however, moved slowly.[34]

Approved by TRADOC in February 1992, the Warrant Officer Leader Development Action Plan completely revised warrant officer training to keep it abreast with the goal of making warrant officers technically and tactically proficient. The Warrant Officer Education System replaced the Warrant Officer Training System, established quality control for the accession of warrant officers, and provided education and training at the appropriate time. To accomplish this, the plan created the Warrant Officer Candidate School to supplant the Warrant Officer Entry Course, the Warrant Officer Basic Course for Warrant Officers One and Two, the Warrant Officer Advance Course for Chief Warrant Officers Three, and the Warrant Officer Senior Staff Course for Chief Warrant Officers Four and Five. By targeting three different groups, the courses provided a logical career progression training program that emphasized leadership and technical and tactical training to move beyond the traditional emphasis upon technical proficiency.[35]

For the Field Artillery School, the plan generated major adjustments in its warrant officer military occupational specialty structure and training. On 25 November 1991 the Commandant of the Field Artillery School, Major General Fred F. Marty (1991-1993), approved restructuring the 131A Target Acquisition Radar Technician into the 131A Target Acquisition Technician over a period of four to six years and forwarded it to the Army for approval. Less than two years later on 25 May 1993, the Army endorsed the plan. As a targeting officer, the Target Acquisition Technician would be a part of targeting process in support of the combined arms commander and replace most captains and lieutenants in counterfire officer positions and field artillery intelligence officers and targeting officers from the target acquisition battery through corps artillery.[36]

To satisfy the training needs of the restructure, the school had to revamp its 131A warrant officer courses. It changed the name of its Warrant Officer Technical/Tactical Certification Course to the Warrant Officer Basic Course for Warrant Officer One. In the six-month basic course, new warrant officers received six weeks of radar tactics, three weeks of radar operations, and four months of radar maintenance training. The training also ranged from the tactical decision-making process and the intelligence preparation of the battlefield to radar tactical and technical considerations, radar theory, and basic electronics.[37]

Meanwhile, the school converted its Senior Warrant Officer Training Course to the seven-week Warrant Officer Advance Course for Chief Warrant Officers Two and Three. This course taught senior warrant officers about division fire support automated systems and the fire support and targeting process to help them develop the skills required to make targeting decisions and apply the tactical decision-making process. By 1999, both courses were in place and moving field artillery warrant officers from being technically proficient to tactically and technically proficient.[38]

Noncommissioned officer training in the Noncommissioned Officer Academy that fell under the Field Artillery School also underwent critical changes. In 1991, the Noncommissioned Officer Academy converted all Basic Noncommissioned Officer Courses and Advanced Noncommissioned Officer Courses to small group instruction in all technical tracks to comply with TRADOC guidance and focused field training exercises on leadership skills and common leader combat tasks. Five years later in October 1996, Fort Sill incorporated the Noncommissioned Officer Academy into Training Command with the Field Artillery School and the Field Artillery Training Center. Through the Primary Leadership Development Course, the Basic Noncommissioned Officer Course, and the Advanced Noncommissioned Officer Course, the academy trained field artillery soldiers throughout their careers in all Career Management Field 13 (Field Artillery) military occupational specialties, furnished progressive and sequential education and training that was directly tied to promotion, and employed the Camp Eagle Training Center on the West Range of Fort Sill for practical training exercises for the Primary Leadership Development Course. While the Primary Leadership Development Course was required for promotion to sergeant, the Basic Noncommissioned Officer Course was a prerequisite for promotion to staff sergeant; and the Advanced Noncommissioned Officer Course was mandatory for promotion to sergeant first class.[39]

More importantly, the focus of the three courses shifted after 1996 from concentrating on military occupational specialty refresher training to training on future responsibilities. Basically, the Noncommissioned Officer Academy started developing future leaders for the noncommissioned officers corps and even supplied distance learning via the First Sergeant and Battle Staff Noncommissioned Officer Courses by 1999.[40]

Of the revisions to officer, warrant officer, and noncommissioned officer training, the development of the Captain's Career Course and the new warrant officer courses represented the most significant changes. Each underwent a fundamental reorientation. While the Captain's Career Course reforms tied it to the Combined Arms Services Staff School Course to minimize redundancies for captain's training, ended the captain course's stand-alone feature that dated to the 1950s, and reflected the need to reduce costs, the warrant officer courses focused on creating technically and tactically proficient warrant officers whereas technical proficiency had been the previous standard. In the meantime, the Basic Noncommissioned Officer Course and the Advanced Noncommissioned Officer Course dropped their emphasis on military occupational specialty training for leadership training while the Officer Basic Course went through a series of changes in the 1990s as school leaders struggled to find the optimum way of training second lieutenants to prepare them for their first assignments.

Leveraging Advanced Technology

Faced with the need for standardized training throughout the Field Artillery as the Total Army grew in importance and the imperative of making training more efficient in the face of budget cuts, the Field Artillery School turned to advanced information technology. It became the lynch pin to assure the availability of quality, standardized training for active and reserve components units and soldiers and permitted augmenting the traditional ways of providing instruction and training.

During the 1990s, the Army faced a growing dependency upon its reserve components (US Army National Guard and US Army Reserve) as the active component shrank in size. In fact, the Field Artillery School projected in 1992 that two out of every three Field Artillery soldiers would be in the reserve components by 1995 when most of the drawdown would be completed. Given this scenario, the talk of "one Army – one standard" was no longer a vision to be accomplished sometime in the future. For the Total Army to accomplish its mission of fighting the nation's wars, the active and reserve components required standardized, high-quality training; this demanded a comprehensive training strategy.[41]

To address the growing concern about the critical differences between active and reserve component training that had surfaced during Operation Desert Shield and Operation Desert Storm, TRADOC outlined a strategy in 1993 of four interrelated and synergistic components: occupational training strategy, training developments, training technologies, and Future Army Schools Twenty-One. The occupational training strategy mapped individual training requirements in each military occupational specialty to furnish a training path throughout a soldier's career from initial entry into the Army to departure from the service. While training developments centered on creating a standardized program of instruction for each military occupational specialty for active and reserve components using advance information technology, training technologies leveraged state-of-the-art information technology to enhance training effectiveness and efficiency. Future Army Schools Twenty-One meanwhile aimed to create one school system for the active and reserve components. Basically, TRADOC planned to take advantage of advanced information technology to revolutionize training and education and to standardize training for the Total Army.[42]

As a key player in the implementation of the new training strategy, the Field Artillery School's training model literally started tearing down school house walls. By using advanced information technology the school set out to correct the training disparities between the active and reserve components in Career Management Field 13 (Field Artillery) so that all field artillery soldiers would follow the same career path and receive the same training.[43]

In 1993, the school introduced its occupational training strategy to produce a single program of instruction for each field artillery military occupational specialty. The school planned developing modular courses to accommodate the reserves' inactive duty training time (weekend drills) as well as active duty training time (summer camp).[44] With little guidance from TRADOC at this point, the Field Artillery School proposed employing correspondence courses, training support packages, and other exportable materials composed of various multimedia technologies, such as print, videotape, and some computer-based instruction, to train reserve components. On the whole, the school proposed to continue its reliance upon traditional methods of delivering training and instruction beyond the school house.[45]

Even before it started developing courses, advanced information technology emerged as a viable way of reaching all soldiers and units. Early in the 1990s, the Army introduced the Teletraining Network. Using a satellite, the Teletraining Network had the ability of sending and receiving training courses via the air waves. If they had access to a Teletraining Network facility, soldiers could train at their home stations to reduce expenditures and keep them in line with the declining budgets. By 1994, the school had 22 Teletraining Network sites across a seven-state area, including two at Fort Sill, and had established Fort Sill as the regional video-teletraining hub for the delivery and distribution of field artillery and other military training.[46]

The Teletraining Network extended classroom operations to 24 hours a day and seven days a week. It furnished full broadcasting quality and permitted two-way audiovisual communications with 16 sites simultaneously and any number of sites one way. It could transmit viewgraphs, videotapes, graphics, digital data, and simulations. The Teletraining Network even had a mobile camera to transmit training demonstrations from a bay area or the field.[47]

Early on, the school found the network to be particularly useful for pre-mobilization training for the reserve components. As Fort Sill moved to implement its power projection mission of mobilizing and deploying soldiers and units, it no longer had six months to deploy 69 battery-sized units as it had done during Operation Desert Shield of 1990. Rather, the installation would have only nine weeks to deploy 89 battery-size units. Faced with this imperative, Fort Sill and the Field Artillery School identified aspects of pre-mobilization training, such as reserve component instructor training and unit training on active component automated systems, loadout procedures, supply, and maintenance, to be accomplished over the Teletraining Network. Using the network, reserve component soldiers completed some training at their home stations before arriving at Fort Sill for mobilization and deployment, saving time and money in the process.[48]

Based upon guidance from Baxter and Major General John A. Dubia, the Commandant of the Field Artillery School (1993-1995), the Directorate of Training and Evaluation in the school, meanwhile, designed an extensive multimedia distance learning strategy in 1994 that went beyond employing the Teletraining Network and traditional means to distributing training via paper products to the reserve components without compromising quality and saving money at the same time. The strategy produced a single program of instruction for each military occupational specialty in Career Management Field 13 in keeping with

TRADOC's occupational training strategy. Approved by TRADOC and completed in 1995, the school's strategy relied upon computer-based instruction, video teletraining, compact disc-read only memory (CD-ROM), and the Teletraining Network.[49]

Although training for Military Occupational Specialty 13F (Fire Support Specialist) and others could be transmitted over the Teletraining Network, 13F represented the Field Artillery School's first multimedia effort using the occupational training strategy. Initiated in 1994 and completed in 1995, the 13F multimedia undertaking produced a standardized program of instruction for active and reserve component soldiers on CD-ROM. The training provided everything that an active and reserve component 13F soldier needed to know from initial entry into the military occupational specialty through retirement.[50]

In 1996, the effort to standardize training for the entire force using advanced technology grew even more expansive as by moving beyond the occupational training strategy. Approved in April 1996 by the Army Chief of Staff, the Army Distance Learning Plan tied together various ongoing training initiatives. The plan envisioned shifting from a predominantly resident training environment to a mix of distance learning, self-development, and resident training by delivering standardized individual training and portions of collective training at the right place and right time via advanced information technology to active and reserve component soldiers and units.[51]

In a brief memorandum on 29 July 1996, the Commanding General of TRADOC, General William W. Hartzog, told school commandants to redesign their courses to be consistent with the Total Army Training System format that standardized training for the active and reserve components, to establish distance learning classrooms to beam training beyond the school house, and to connect to the Internet without sacrificing quality.[52] Commandants had to incorporate video teletraining, computer-based instruction, CD-ROM, the Internet, and other advanced information technologies into training to save money and standardize active and reserve component training. Ultimately, this meant abandoning training methods that dated to World War II, that focused on resident training, that supplied nonstandard training to the active and reserve components, and that compartmentalized training into institutional, unit, and self-development training programs for career progression.[53]

As directed by TRADOC, the school published its distance learning plan in October 1996. Besides detailing the process for the development, execution, and management of distance learning programs and the consolidation of existing plans, it outlined modernizing classrooms, providing a communications infrastructure, converting all training to the Total Army Training Strategy format, creating multimedia training materials, and developing, distributing, and maintaining collective training support packages for unit training for high quality training at home stations. Also, the school would develop multimedia training modules for new equipment training for use in distance learning facilities.[54]

Over the next couple of years, the school carried out its distance learning plan. During 1997, it produced digitized lessons, interactive computer-based modules, and online training. Lessons for each military occupational specialty contained video clips of instructors teaching, demonstrations on equipment, and simulated exercises, while each module had a series of teaching objectives, practical exercises, and examinations and permitted student interaction at any point during the learning process. For example, the lessons for 13F were developed in 48 modules on 18 CD-ROMs for formal and refresher training.[55]

As it moved forward with its distance learning plan, the school eventually phased out the Teletraining Network in favor of Internet capabilities and converted enlisted and officer courses to the Total Army Training System format. By 1999, the school had transformed its 27 enlisted field artillery courses and Field Artillery Officer Advance Course to Total Army Training System courseware, digitized them, put them on the Internet, and started converting all Total Army Training System courseware to distance learning multimedia products for distribution beyond the school house so that the reserve components would receive the same training as the active component.[56]

For the reserve component, the Total Army Training System represented a significant break with the past. Through 1995, the school configured active component courses used by the reserve component to fit time, equipment, and facility constraints. Only those tasks deemed important by the proponent to prepare reservists for mobilization were included in the reserve component courses. In other words, the reserve component's training deviated significantly from the active component's training. In comparison, the Total Army Training System courseware furnished the same training to the reserve components as the active component received.[57]

The Total Army School System represented another avenue to standardize training. Established at Fort Monroe, Virginia, by the Commanding General of TRADOC, General Frederick M. Franks, Jr., in 1992, the Future Army Schools Twenty-One Task Force had the mission of establishing an effective and efficient Total Army School System of fully accredited and integrated active component and reserve component schools to furnish standardized individual training and education to the Total Army. From the outset, the task force focused on organizing active and reserve component schools into a single school system to ensure standardization while maintaining excellence.[58]

The proposed Total Army School System, renamed The Army School System in 1999, represented a major break with the past. Over the years, the active component, the Army National Guard, and the Army Reserve had developed independent school systems with separate standards. Downsizing the Army and reducing the budget in the 1990s made the three separate school systems uneconomical and unfeasible. By creating a single school system and standard, the task force hoped to abolish the old system, promote standardization, and reduce training costs.[59]

With this objective in mind, the Future Army Schools Twenty-One Task Force decided in 1992 to organize the Total Army School System around the regional schools concept. The task force divided the continental United States into seven geographical regions. Each region had six colleges (brigades/regiments) to oversee instruction in leadership, officer education, health services, combat arms, combat support, and combat service support. Below the college level, the task force placed departments (battalions) and aligned them with the proponent of a specific career management field, such as Fort Benning and the Infantry and Fort Sill and the Field Artillery.[60]

Beginning in January 1993 and continuing into 1995, the task force organized a prototype school system in Region C to test the Total Army School System model. Composed of North Carolina, South Carolina, Georgia, Florida, the Commonwealth of Puerto Rico, and the US Virgin Islands, the region had a coordinating element in Leesburg, South Carolina, that was responsible to the Army's major commands for feedback about the quality of training and established brigades/regiments and proponent-aligned battalions, using existing resources within the region.[61] Reflecting the Field Artillery School's commitment, Dubia wrote on 26 January 1995, "We fully support the Total Army School System. In anticipation of TASS [Total Army School System] implementation, we are in various stages of planning and development to ensure successful execution."[62] As an integral part of the Total Army School System, the Field Artillery School assumed the responsibility for certifying the battalions that taught field artillery subjects. Accreditation, which was required every three years, permitted field artillery school battalions and training sites to teach Field Artillery School courses and use Field Artillery School-approved courseware that was built upon the Total Army Training System and included a mixture of CD-ROM courses, correspondence courses, video monitoring, and classroom instruction.[63]

To be sure, the Total Army School System transformed training. It furnished training through a network of schools in the continental United States, simultaneously abolished the three parallel school systems of the Army Reserve, Army National Guard, and active Army that had characterized training for decades and propagated separate training standards. The Total Army School System also reduced the number of reserve component schools from 209 in 1992 to 133 schools in 1997, saved money, and exploited distance learning that was based upon advanced communication technology to disseminate individual and unit training when and where required to active and reserve component soldiers and units.[64]

One decade later, the Total Army School System had an extensive field artillery training system dedicated to training reserve component soldiers to the same standard as the active component. Accredited by the Quality Assurance Office on Fort Sill, Army National Guard field artillery subject matter experts in regional training institutes of the Total Army School System provided standardized field artillery training to reserve component soldiers and even active component soldiers as needed using Total Army Training System software.[65]

As it exploited the Internet, CD-ROM courses, and other advanced information technology to distribute training and formed The Total Army School System, TRADOC launched its classroom modernization initiative that generally fell under the rubric of Classroom XXI to take advantage of technology for training in the school house and the field. Upon receiving funding from TRADOC for classroom modernization in 1995, Training Command which was composed of the Field Artillery School, the Noncommissioned Officer Academy, and the Field Artillery Training Center outlined an ambitious plan to develop a campus area network to create one communications network to connect its subordinate organizations and a local area network that referred to the technology inside the buildings. Together, the campus area network and local area network would form the backbone of classroom modernization.[66]

In 1996, Training Command initiated work on the infrastructure. Using a fiber optics campus area network, it tied Knox Hall, I-See-O-Hall, Snow Hall, Searby Hall, Summerall Hall, and Burleson Hall – which were part of the Field Artillery School's campus – into one communications network, completed local area networks in each respective building, and implemented the Internet link.[67]

Meanwhile, modernizing the school's classrooms moved forward. In 1996, Training Command constructed 11 multimedia classrooms with multimedia overheads, access to the local area network and campus area network, video recorders, large-screen televisions, and instructor computer workstations and one student-center classroom with computer-based instruction capabilities that employed CD-ROM courseware. Training Command also completed two simulation classrooms with the Janus battle simulation system that allowed officers to plan, wargame, and fight the battles of the future without leaving the classroom and to connect with other Janus users throughout TRADOC. This initial classroom modernization effort permitted employing simulations, interactive software, and other automated capabilities as a vital portion of the learning experience, enhanced training by presenting material in an efficient multimedia format, helped students acquire an appreciation of simulation-enhanced training, reinforced classroom instruction, and provided variety.[68]

Classroom modernization of 1996-1998 reflected the school's commitment to use state-of-the-art technology to train resident students. With these new facilities in place, the school abandoned its historical dependency upon overhead viewgraphs, chalkboards, dry-erase boards, and occasional videotapes to train students in the school house.[69]

Whereas the computer-enhanced classroom improved school house training, distance learning classrooms funded by the Army delivered training to active and reserve component soldiers and civilians beyond the Field Artillery School's classrooms.[70] Once they became available early in 1999, the school put them to use. During the year, the school taught 17 distance learning classes to more than 100 students and conducted about 55 briefings, workshops, in-process reviews, video teleconferences, audio teleconferences, and Multiple Launch Rocket System 3x6 conversion training to the 5th Battalion, 113th Field Artillery Regiment of the North Carolina Army National Guard and the 2nd Battalion, 147th Field Artillery Regiment of the South Dakota Army National Guard.[71]

In the fall of 1999, Captain Robert F. Markovetz, Jr., of the 2d Battalion, 147th Field Artillery Regiment explained that distance learning was a major breakthrough, although growing pains existed. Because the South Dakota Army National Guard did not have adequate facilities, it used computer laboratories and video teleconference rooms at Northern State University, Aberdeen, South Dakota, for Multiple-Launch Rocket System crew member training and computer laboratories and video teleconference rooms at the Lake Area Technical Institute, Watertown, South Dakota, for Multiple-Launch Rocket System specialist training. Over a course of about three months, South Dakota Army National Guard soldiers completed CD-ROM-based instruction and video teleconference training. Ultimately, distance learning saved time and money, worked well, and was the wave of the future, according to Markovetz. However, the potential of distance learning in 1999 remained untapped because of the limited number of courses designed for distance learning. This changed when the Field Artillery School began producing more courses in 2000.[72]

As much as the school sincerely wanted to modernize its classrooms, the declining budgets and the Total Army concept certainly provided a sense of urgency. The school faced the imperative of standardizing training for the active and reserve components so that the Total Army worked; and advanced information technology provided the means, permitted abandoning traditional methods of training, and saved money.

Prodded by the need to facilitate effective individual and collective training, to reduce training costs, and to address the increasing public environmental concerns about noise abatement, the Field Artillery School concurrently placed a greater reliance upon simulators and simulations for training than it had in the past and participated in introducing new training aids, devices, simulators, and simulations for institutional and unit use. For years, the Army had recognized the need to integrate training the field artillery gunnery team (forward observer, fire direction specialist, and howitzer crew) by means other than expensive live-fire exercises and acknowledged this in an approved training device need statement in 1980. Seeking an alternative to live fire, the Army and the Field Artillery School turned to integrating training of the separate elements of the field artillery gunnery team with a "closed loop" training device system that would train them as a team.[73]

In the 1980s, the Field Artillery School as a result explored several different systems. The Field Artillery Tactical Engagement System and the Artillery Gunnery Team Training System were initial attempts to provide collective training to the gunnery team but did not work out. Several training aids, devices, simulators, and simulations were also developed to furnish training to selective elements of the gunnery team. However, none of these systems fully met the Field Artillery School's requirement for a closed loop system to train the gunnery team as a whole. The M31 Field Artillery Trainer, for example, required a firing range, ammunition, safety, and support provisions. Even then, the effects of changing environmental conditions on the projectile made it difficult to provide accurate predicted fire. The Training Set Forward Observation and the Guard Unit Armory Device-Full-Crew Interactive Simulation Trainer supplied effective unit and institutional training for the forward observer, but the Training Set Forward Observation which was a computer-synchronized array of slide projectors that gave forward observers a two-dimensional view of the terrain was antiquated and difficult to support, while neither the Training Set Forward Observation nor Guard Unit Armory Device-Full-Crew Interactive Simulation Trainer furnished feedback to evaluate the proficiency of the other nodes of the gunnery team. Finally, the most recent training aids, devices, simulators, simulations, and the M109A6 Paladin training package, had embedded training in the automatic fire control system, but it did not replicate the recoil function of an actual howitzer nor train crewmen in the pre-fire tasks involved in the preparation of projectiles, fuses, and charges.[74]

As a cornerstone of the Fire Support Training Strategy, which was part of the Army's

Combined Arms Training Strategy, the Closed Loop Artillery Simulation System, however, promised to capitalize on advanced technology to train the entire gunnery team while reducing training costs. From the Field Artillery School's perspective, the system represented a major turning point. It would take training field artillery soldiers and units into the 21st century by integrating target acquisition, fire direction, and weapons delivery elements together to train the gunnery team as a unit or as individual components without going to the field for live fire.[75]

The Closed Loop Artillery Simulation System soon became part of the Army's Combined Arms Tactical Trainers system. As the commandant of the school, Marty supported the idea of having initial Closed Loop Artillery Simulation System production models capable of interfacing with the Army's Combined Arms Tactical Trainer as long as developing such capabilities would not set back acquiring the Closed Loop Artillery Simulation System. Later, he directed renaming the system as the Fire Support Combined Arms Tactical Trainer and making it compatible with the Army's family of Combined Arms Tactical Trainers and forwarded his recommendation to TRADOC. On 15 March 1993, TRADOC approved redesignating the system as the Fire Support Combined Arms Tactical Trainer for the M109A5 and M109A6 155-mm. self-propelled howitzers, and developmental work began.[76]

Fielded between 1998 and 2000 to National Guard units, active component units, and the Field Artillery School to facilitate home-station training without going to the field, the Fire Support Combined Artillery Tactical Trainer consisted of the Howitzer Crew Trainer, the Collective Training Control Subsystem, and the Guard Unit Armory Device-Full-Crew Interactive Simulation Trainer. As advertised, the trainer supplied stand-alone, interactive, and closed-loop training. In the stand-alone mode, each trainer could be employed independently to train individual tasks and functions. The interactive mode permitted combined howitzer and fire direction center training. In the close-loop mode the observer's call for fire would be transmitted from the Guard Unit Armory Device-Full-Crew Interactive Simulation Trainer to the battery fire direction center with fire commands being sent to the howitzers (Howitzer Crew Trainer).[77]

The school also took part in designing the Fire Support Combined Arms Tactical Trainer-Towed for the M198 towed 155-mm. howitzer and the futuristic XM777 towed 155-mm. howitzer. Like the Fire Support Combined Arms Tactical Trainer for the self-propelled 155-mm. howitzers, the towed version fielded during the first years of the 21st century did not replace field training but augmented and enhanced it by maximizing individual, crew, and unit proficiency and could be used for institutional or unit training.[78]

To be sure, advanced information technology served as the backbone for the educational and training reforms of the 1990s. Without it the Field Artillery School could not have standardized training for the active and reserve components; the traditional methods of distributing training products which were generally paper-based would have persisted, precluding effective standardization.

Fielding a New Force

The collapse of the Soviet Union and Warsaw Pact and the growing pressures to respond to worldwide regional crises that could threaten American interests prompted American military leadership to alter its strategy. Rejecting the Cold War focus on the forward deployment of large combat forces in Europe, the New Military Strategy of January 1992, written by American military leaders, concentrated on projecting land combat power (often called power projection) from the continental United States to regional hot spots, accented strategic mobility, among other things, and required the Army to adapt with new doctrine, equipment, and weapons.

As the Army relocated much of its forces from overseas assignments, especially in Europe, to the continental United States as part of the New Military Strategy but still maintained some forward-deployed forces in certain parts of the world, Congress reduced the military's budget and personnel strength as a part of the mounting cry for a peace dividend after the Cold War.[79] Even though the Army's budget and personnel strength had been declining steadily since the mid-1980s with a temporary interruption during Operations Desert Shield and Desert Storm of 1990-1991, the shrinking budgets and personnel reductions accelerated following the collapse of the Soviet Union and the Warsaw Pact in 1989-1991. The decline in personnel strength forced the Army to drop from five corps, 18 active divisions, and 10 reserve component (Army National Guard and Army Reserve) divisions to four corps, 10 active divisions, and eight Army National Guard divisions. By the end of the decade, the Army and its reserve components were the smallest that they had been in more than 40 years.[80]

As it shrank in size, the Army faced the imperative of reallocating its combat, combat support, and combat service support units between the active component and reserve components to ensure balance. At the beginning of the 1990s, the Army National Guard had 44 percent of the combat forces, 31 percent of the combat support, and 25 percent of the combat service support. The Army Reserve had 53 percent of the combat support and combat service support and a small portion of combat forces.[81] At the conclusion of the restructuring in 1997, the Army National Guard had 55 percent of the combat units, 46 percent of the combat support, and 25 percent of the combat service support while the Army Reserve had 20 percent of the combat support, 47 percent of the combat service support, and one percent of the combat units and became primarily a support force. The active component had the remaining combat, combat support, and combat service support. This restructuring forced the active Army to grow more dependent upon its reserve components for support and gave the latter a more prominent role in national defense than previously.[82]

To be sure, the Field Artillery felt the far-reaching effects of the restructuring and declining budgets. Understanding that the constrained budgets would leave the active Army with insufficient field artillery, the Army Science Board of 1995 examined the Army National Guard's general support and direct support field artillery missions to determine the possibility of making adjustments. During Operation Desert Storm, Guard field artillery units furnished responsive and effective general support fires after a short training period before deploying to the Gulf and had the ability of maintaining proficiency with this mission in their 39 days of annual training. In comparison, maintaining competence with the more complicated direct support mission required more training time which the Guard would not have nor get. This convinced the Army Science Board to recommend abolishing the Guard's direct support field artillery mission but retaining its general support field artillery mission.[83]

Based upon this convincing logic, the Army revamped its field artillery missions. In 1990, the Army National Guard and the Army Reserve had 52 percent of the Army's direct support and general support field artillery. When the restructuring was completed at the end of the decade, the Army National Guard had 63 percent of the Army's general support field artillery and completely lost its direct support mission, while the Army Reserve lost its field artillery altogether. As a result of this realignment, one of every two field artillery brigades furnishing general support to a heavy division was in the Guard in 2000. This reallocation left the active component with the direct support and general support missions. The Army's light divisions did not fare so well. Three cannon battalions and one Multiple-Launch Rocket System battalion of the XVIII Airborne Corps provided the only active component general support for the 10th Mountain Division, the 25th Infantry Division, the 82d Airborne Division, the 101st Airborne Division, two light separate brigades, and the 3d Armored Cavalry Regiment.[84]

The Guard's expanded general support mission prompted modernization. Even before restructuring field artillery missions had started, the Army decided in 1992 to convert Army National Guard M110 eight-inch self-propelled howitzer units to Multiple-Launch Rocket System units through Congressionally-mandated procurement and the extra launchers created by the drawdown of the active force to give Guard field artillery units more mobility and lethality.[85] Upon the completion of the conversions during the first decade of the 21st century, the aging M110 was totally removed from the active and reserve components, forcing the school to train Guard and active component soldiers on the Multiple-Launch Rocket System M270 launcher using mobile training teams from the Gunnery Department.[86]

To complement this conversion, the Army decreased the number of M109A6 (Paladin) 155-mm. self-propelled howitzers in the active heavy division from 72 to 54 during the 1990s. This permitted transferring extra Paladin howitzers to the Guard to replace its obsolete M109A2/A3 self-propelled 155-mm. howitzers and some M109A5 self-propelled 155-mm. howitzers to give it a fleet of more modern M109A6 and M109A5 self-propelled 155-mm. howitzers to help it stay abreast of the active force that was being equipped with the Paladin.[87] As the Field Artillery School candidly acknowledged, the reduction of the number of Paladins in the heavy division would be risky until the introduction of the futuristic Crusader self-propelled 155-mm. howitzer, the precision Search-and-Destroy Armor Munition, the Multiple-Launch Rocket System M270A1 launcher, and the Multiple-Launch Rocket System Smart Tactical Rocket in the near future. Basically, key new systems and munition would offset the diminished number of self-propelled howitzers and enhance lethality.[88]

To compensate for the decreased number of 155-mm. self-propelled howitzers in active and reserve component heavy divisions, the Field Artillery School meanwhile submitted a detailed plan to the Chief of Staff of the Army, General Gordon R. Sullivan, in the summer of 1992 to double the number of M270 launchers from nine to 18. The school proposed organizing a Multiple-Launch Rocket System battalion of two batteries of nine M270 launchers each (2x9 force structure). Sullivan approved the concept, but funding and manpower constraints stalled implementation.[89]

Influenced by the Legal Mix VI Study of 1993 and the Army Science Board study of 1995, the Army pushed Multiple-Launch Rocket System restructuring when funding became available by announcing its intention in June 1996 to add a second battery to the heavy division beginning in 2000.[90] Subsequently, the Army divided the 18 M270 launchers into three batteries of six launchers each (3x6 force structure) to make the batteries leaner and reduce the size of the battery's battlefield footprint and logistical requirements.[91]

Similarly, the Army revamped its M198 towed 155-mm. howitzer units in the active component and the reserve component. It reduced the number of M198s in the battalion from 24 to 18 howitzers (six-howitzer batteries), freed up some M198s to replace the worst guns, and sent the worst to the depots.[92]

Designed by the Field Artillery School and approved by the Army, the restructuring of the 1990s significantly reshaped the Field Artillery. The reforms reduced the number of field artillery weapons in the division and made the Field Artillery more mobile by replacing the slow, aging M109A2/A3 and M110 howitzers for the more mobile and agile Paladin and M270 launchers.[93]

Meanwhile, the changing political realities in the world prompted the Army and the Field Artillery School to reexamine doctrine. In response to the Mutual and Balanced Force Reduction talks that ended after 16 years of debate on 2 February 1989 and reflected the growing fragmentation of Eastern Europe, TRADOC and the Field Artillery School conducted AirLand Battle-Future studies during the last three years of the 1980s to develop an umbrella concept for fighting any place in the world and one for fighting in Europe.[94]

The Conventional Forces Reduction Treaty of November 1990 ended the AirLand Battle-Future studies effort by advocating parity of military capabilities rather than a mere reduction in the number of tanks, field artillery, and infantry fighting vehicles as sponsored by the Mutual and Balanced Force Reduction talks. Because of the treaty, small military forces would defend the same amount of territory in Central Europe in the near future as the large armies had done in the past to create gaps in coverage.[95]

The Chief of Staff of the Army, General Carl E. Vuono, and the Commanding General of TRADOC, General John W. Foss, confronted this new reality by urging the Army to abandon AirLand Battle doctrine designed for fighting an echeloned Soviet-Warsaw Pact threat on a linear front for a new warfighting doctrine. While Vuono stressed destroying enemy forces as opposed to holding land as the Army had emphasized since World War II on a non-linear front, Foss advocated employing long-range intelligence systems to detect enemy forces at great distances for destruction by long-range precision fire support systems that would also cover the gaps created by the smaller forces on the emerging non-linear battlefield.[96] After the long-range precision fires had overwhelmed the enemy, the maneuver arms would attack the enemy's flanks and rear with support from organic indirect and direct fires to avoid devastating frontal assaults.[97]

Vuono's and Foss's concepts, extensive, heated discussions throughout the Army, and Operation Desert Storm lessons learned eventually led to the revision of *Field Manual 100-5, AirLand Operations*, the Army's chief warfighting manual.[98] Published in June 1993, *AirLand Operations* stressed depth and simultaneous attack throughout the depth of the battle space, non-linear maneuver warfare, and decisive army operations as part of a joint, combined, or interagency team, among other things.[99] After long-range operational fires from the different branches of the country's military services had destroyed the enemy, tactical fires from air-, land-, or sea-based delivery systems would support the maneuver forces' attack on the enemy's flanks and rear to avoid grinding frontal assaults.[100]

The Field Artillery School immediately recognized the implications of *AirLand Operations* on corps artillery. Using AirLand Battle doctrine, the corps commander fought the deep battle, mainly allocated fire support assets, and employed his field artillery brigades to reinforce division artillery as required.[101] As part of a joint forces command under AirLand Operations, the corps commander would retain control of his Multiple-Launch Rocket System and Army Tactical Missile System units and employ them to attack targets with overwhelming, long-range, operational precision fires. Fires from these systems and indirect fire systems under development would disrupt, delay, degrade, or divert enemy capabilities, would establish the conditions for future battles, and would be the major killers on the battlefield. After the operational precision fires had sufficiently destroyed the enemy, the maneuver divisions supported by their organic field artillery battalions and corps artillery as required would attack the enemy's flanks and rear. By retaining his field artillery, the corps artillery commander would fight the deep battle, simultaneously play a key role in the close battle, and no longer be an allocator of field artillery assets.[102]

As might be expected, the Field Artillery School added a significant twist to *AirLand Operations* fire support doctrine to make it significantly different from AirLand Battle's fire support doctrine. While AirLand Battle fire support doctrine was platform centric, *AirLand Operations* was effects centric. Essentially, the school envisioned abandoning fire support operations and organizations that had their roots in the first part of the 20th century for a new paradigm of effects-based fires and not source-based fires. In other words, the effect of the fires would be more important than the source, such as the M109A6 or the M270 launcher.[103]

As fire support doctrine took shape around effects-based fires with the fires effects coordination cell emerging to coordinate lethal and non-lethal fires, the Army outlined its Force XXI vision in 1993-1994. Force XXI would methodically move the Army from an industrial-age force to an information-age force to implement the *AirLand Operations* doctrine and to serve as a force projection army.[104] To reach the objective force, the Army devised three Force XXI axes. One would transform the institutional Army or the TRADOC service schools (discussed previously in this chapter). The second, commonly called Joint Venture, would turn the operational Army into a force projection force, while the third would incorporate information-age technologies, such as computers, into the institutional and operational forces to revolutionize the Army. Information-age technology would provide real-time information capabilities to improve situational awareness so that commanders and soldiers would know the location of all friendly and enemy forces on the battlefield and to minimize friendly casualties.[105]

To sustain the capabilities of the current force, minimize the cost of operating aging equipment in an era of constrained budgets, and develop a force projection Army, Force XXI's Joint Venture took advantage of the digitization experiments of TRADOC's battle laboratories, such as the Field Artillery School's Depth and Simultaneous Attack Battle Laboratory, created in 1992. Using computer simulations, a series of advanced warfighting experiments, ranging from small-scale efforts in a particular functional area to large-scale efforts, Joint Venture would develop new warfighting concepts and capabilities, determine the next step in modernization, and leverage information technology to develop a modern Army.[106]

The small-scale advanced warfighting experiments, including fire support experiments headed by the Field Artillery School, during the last years of the 1990s culminated with the Division XXI advanced warfighting experiment.[107] Conducted at Fort Hood, Texas, in November 1997 using the 4th Infantry Division (Mechanized), the Division XXI Advanced Warfighting Experiment evaluated a conceptual digitized mechanized division. Every divisional platform was equipped with a computer that was linked to the tactical Internet which was a system of computers, satellite links, radios, and other equipment. As the experiment demonstrated, digitization enhanced situational awareness, permitted the division to cover the battle space of a current corps, and enabled reducing the number of tanks, infantry fighting vehicles, and personnel in a division without sacrificing lethality and survivability.[108] Acknowledging the success of Division XXI Advanced Warfighting Experiment, General Reimer mandated fielding and testing the first operational Division XXI digitized division (4th Infantry Division) by 2001 and converting other mechanized divisions to the Division XXI design during the first decade of the 21st century.[109]

Concurrently, the Army pushed to modernize its light forces for contingency operations and force projection. The Army formed the Rapid Force Projection Initiative Advanced Concept Technology Demonstrations to move promising technologies from concept into the operational force as rapidly as possible. The success of the demonstrations led to the 10th Mountain Division's (Light Infantry) participation in the Joint Contingency Force Advanced Warfighting Experiment in September 2000 conducted by the Joint Forces Command to improve contingency force capabilities and to verify real changes to doctrine, training, and combat developments.[110]

Although the digitization of the light forces was less mature than the heavy force effort, tentative conclusions in 2000 revealed digitization's ability to improve the light forces' situational awareness and enhance their lethality and versatility by permitting them to acquire, exchange, and employ battlefield information more effectively.[111] Exploiting information supremacy through the digitization of command, control, and communication systems formed the core of the Force XXI Joint Venture initiative to ensure dominance on future battlefields.[112]

Digitization and power projection meant equipping the force with appropriate field artillery weapons and equipment.[113] Acknowledging this, the Army and the Field Artillery School observed in January 1993:

> While today's fire support systems are impressive, the requirement to keep pace in a changing world requires that we modernize continually. It is a given that the future field artillery force will be smaller. For it to remain effective, it must be more lethal with better systems and munitions, more survivable, and more deployable [than Cold War era systems].[114]

Simply put, the Field Artillery School understood the imperative of modernizing field artillery systems. However, constrained budgets appeared to be a constant factor for the near future, while an uncertain threat to national security prevented developing new weapons for a particular threat as the practice had been since the 1940s and had the potential of derailing modernization. This combination prodded the Field Artillery School to devise a fire support modernization program. It had to improve existing serviceable platforms and systems by applying information-age technologies to them, develop totally new systems only where existing systems could not be sufficiently upgraded to meet future needs, and take an active interest in acquiring light, strategically mobile field artillery systems.[115]

From the school's vantage point, *AirLand Operations* with its non-linear front placed a conspicuous burden on target acquisition systems to locate targets with better accuracy at greater ranges than ever before.[116] As the emphasis on strategic deployability grew more important with the emergence of power projection, the Field Artillery required mobile target acquisition systems and set out to enhance the AN/TPQ-36 radar. In the 1980s the school proposed placing the Q-36 on a five-ton truck for the heavy forces and downsizing the radar sufficiently for towing on a trailer behind a High Mobility Multi-purpose Wheeled Vehicle. Power projection demands of mobility and transportability forced abandoning the five-ton version in favor of the more mobile High Mobility Multi-purpose Wheeled Vehicle version. In 1994, the Army first fielded the Q-36 High Mobility Multi-purpose Wheeled Vehicle version as the Q-36 Version Seven. The second upgrade of electronic improvements produced the Q-36 Version Eight to make it suitable for the digitized battlefield of the 21st century.[117]

Meanwhile, the Army as well as the school recognized the need in 1990 to replace the 1970s vintage AN/TPQ-37. Although upgrading the Q-37 to locate rockets and field artillery at longer ranges than previous was a cost-saving measure, the Army opted to replace the Q-37 with the AN/TPQ-47 for the digitized battlefield. Upon being fielded during the first decade of the 21st century, the Q-47 would provide better tactical and strategic mobility, furnish improved accuracy, double the detection range to 60 kilometers with cannon artillery, and give targeting capabilities of 100 kilometers for rocket artillery and 300 kilometers for missile artillery.[118]

Target acquisition deficiencies for close support simultaneously attracted the Army's and the Field Artillery School's attention. The M981 Fire Support Team Vehicle employed by the fire support team lacked the mobility and speed to keep up with the maneuver arms during Operation Desert Storm that were equipped with the Abrams tank and the Bradley fighting to prod modernization. Once funding had become available and the Cavalry and Infantry had received their Bradley fighting vehicles, the Field Artillery started getting the Bradley A2 Operation Desert Storm vehicle, an improved version of the Bradley A2 employed in Operation Desert Storm, to replace the M981. The Field Artillery added a fire support team mission package to it and started fielding it to the heavy forces in 2000 as the M7 Bradley Fire Support Team Vehicle.[119]

The push to digitize the forces stimulated the Army to modernize the Bradley Fire Support Team vehicle even more. In 1995, the Army announced a plan to upgrade it to furnish information superiority. Initially designated as the Bradley Fire Support Team M7A1 but later renamed the Bradley Fire Support Team A3 (A3 Bradley Fire Support Team) in 1999, the modernization effort would add a fire support mission package to the Bradley A2A3 chassis that was a major component of the Army's digitization initiative.[120]

Through the late 1990s, the combat observation lasing team also used the M981 Fire Support Team Vehicle. Designed for the heavy and mechanized forces, the vehicle presented a unique signature in the light forces that employed High Mobility Multi-purpose Wheeled Vehicles as scout vehicles. In response to this, TRADOC approved the Field Artillery School's plan to develop a vehicle with Bradley Fire Support Team capabilities for the light forces by integrating a fire support team mission package onto a High Mobility Multi-purpose Wheeled Vehicle to provide the combat observation lasing team with unprecedented mobility, flexibility, and stealth. Scheduled for fielding early in the 21st century, the upgraded vehicle would present a common signature with other light force vehicles, save Bradley assets for fire support teams, and reduce operating costs for the combat observation lasing team.[121]

Modernization extended beyond target acquisition systems to weapon systems with the M109A6 155-mm. self-propelled howitzer replacing the M109A2/A3. Fielded early in the 1990s, the Paladin could receive a fire mission, compute firing data, select and take up its firing position, automatically unlock and point its cannon, and fire and move out without any external technical assistance. Such characteristics permitted firing the first round from the move in less than one minute to give the system a "shoot-and-scoot" capability to provide better responsiveness than the M109A2/A3 that took up to 11 minutes to respond to call to fire while on the move. The Paladin also had the ability to keep up with the Abrams tank and Bradley fighting vehicle and had secure digital and voice communications, among other enhancements, to make it more suitable for the 21st century battlefield than the M109A2/A3.[122]

Concurrently, the Army and the Field Artillery School played a key role in modernizing the rest of the Field Artillery's cannon, missile, and rocket artillery. During the 1990s, it participated in developing Advanced Field Artillery System self-propelled 155-mm. howitzer, designated the Crusader in December 1994, to replace the Paladin in the near future, improved the M992 Field Artillery Ammunition Supply Vehicle that accompanied the Paladin, upgraded the M119 towed 105-mm. howitzer, and worked to field the lightweight towed 155-mm. howitzer with digitized command and control capabilities to take the place of the aging M198 towed 155-mm. howitzer. The towed artillery digitization package would give the lightweight 155-mm. howitzer onboard digital capabilities like those in self-propelled howitzers, such as the Paladin and the futuristic Crusader, to make it fit with the emerging digital battlefield. Along with the High Mobility Artillery Rocket System M142 that would fire the Multiple-Launch Rocket System family of munitions and that was a wheeled multiple rocket launcher, the Multiple-Launch Rocket System M270A1 launcher, a longer range and more accurate Army Tactical Missile System, precision munitions, such as Search-and-Destroy-Armor Munition, and better fuses to reduce the dud rate of Operation Desert Storm, the Crusader with its own ammunition vehicle, and the lightweight 155-mm. howitzer would take the branch onto the digitized battlefield of the 21st century.[123]

To tie the field artillery's system of systems together and to improve command, control, and communications, the Army meanwhile replaced the Tactical Fire Direction System, which was introduced in the 1970s and 1980s and was obsolete, with the Advanced Field Artillery Tactical Data System (computer and software). As one of five battlefield automation systems of the Army Tactical Command and Control System, the Advanced Field Artillery Tactical Data System would facilitate coordinating field artillery fire with mortars, close air support, naval gunfire, and attack helicopters. After a decade of work that was laden with many developmental delays, the Army finally started fielding the Advanced Field Artillery Tactical Data System in 1996. To get the software to the field as soon as possible rather than waiting for the objective software to be completed, the Army introduced it in increments with the first being the least capable and with each increment having more capabilities than its predecessor.[124]

As a critical component of upgrading command and control, the Army introduced the Initial Fire Support Automation System until the Advanced Field Artillery Tactical Data System could be fielded. The Army fielded the Initial Fire Support Automation System to the active component and the Army National Guard in the 1990s. For the Guard, the system automated its fire support for the first time.[125]

As work with the Initial Fire Support Automation System, the Advanced Field Artillery Tactical Data System, and other field artillery systems suggested, the Field Artillery School played a key role in reshaping the Field Artillery. Designed by the school, new fire support doctrine and streamlined organizations which were equipped with information-age systems for improved situational awareness prepared active and reserve component field artillery units for fighting on a digital battlefield, while institutional reforms improved the quality of training and employed advanced information technology to facilitate standardized training in support of the Total Army. The school did all of this while encountering annual budget cuts and reductions in personnel strength.

Notes

1   Interview, L. Martin Kaplan with CPT David Bricker, OAC Program Manager, Directorate of Training and Doctrine (DOTD), 4 Feb 1992, Historical Research and Documents Collection (HRDC), Command Historian's Office, US Army Field Artillery School; Briefing, subj: OAC Revisions, undated, HRDC.

2   Interview, Kaplan with Bricker, 4 Feb 1992, HRDC; Briefing, subj: OAC Revisions, undated, HRDC.

3   Interview, Kaplan with Bricker, 4 Feb 1992, HRDC; Briefing, subj: OAC Revisions, undated, HRDC; Briefing, subj: Field Artillery Officer Advance Course (FAOAC), undated, HRDC; "US Army Field Artillery School," *Field Artillery Magazine*, Dec 1992, p. 14; "Training Command: FA School, FATC, and NCOA," *Field Artillery Magazine*, Dec 1993, p. 30.

4   Interview, Kaplan with Bricker, 4 Feb 1992, HRDC; Briefing, subj: OAC Revisions, undated, HRDC; Briefing, subj: Field Artillery Officer Advance Course (FAOAC), undated, HRDC; "US Army Field Artillery School," *Field Artillery Magazine*, Dec 1992, p. 14; "Training Command: FA School, FATC, and NCOA," p. 30.

5   "Azimuth Check: FAOAC Update," *Field Artillery Magazine*, Feb 1994, pp. 42-43; Briefing, subj: IFSAS Integration, 1993, HRDC; Briefing, subj: FAOAC, 1992, HRDC; Memorandum for Reorganization Task Force, subj: Comments to Statement on Noncurrence, 10 Jan 1992, HRDC.

6   Briefing, subj: FAOAC Revision Decision Brief, 22 Feb 1995, HRDC; Fact Sheet, subj: FAOAC Restructure, May 1994, HRDC; Briefing, subj: FAOAC, Jan 1996, HRDC.

7   Briefing, subj: FAOAC Revision Decision Brief, 22 Feb 1995, HRDC; Fact Sheet, subj: Proposed FAOAC New Classes and Hour Changes, 13 Feb 1995, HRDC; Briefing, subj: FAOAC Revision Decision Brief, 22 Feb 1995, HRDC; Fact Sheet with encls, subj: Battery Command Block Subjects and Sequencing, 13 Feb 1995, HRDC; Fact Sheet, subj: AR 351-1/FAOAC Position Areas of Concentration, 13 Feb 1995, HRDC; Fact Sheet, subj: FAOAC Manual and Automated Gunnery and Communications Hour Cuts, 13 Feb 1995, HRDC; Briefing, subj: FOAC Revision Decision Brief, 22 Feb 1995, HRDC; Memorandum for Record, subj: Staff Input, 12 Apr 1995, HRDC; "USAFAS Curriculum Revisions," *Field Artillery Magazine*, Sep-Oct 1995, p. 45; "Field Artillery Training Command," p. 32.

8   Memorandum for See Distribution with Encl, subj: CPT PME Action Plan, 7 Aug 1997, HRDC; LTC Joe Snow, "CAS3 [Combined Arms Staff and Service School] Anyone?" *Field Artillery Journal*, Jul-Aug 1985, pp. 34-35; Department of the Army (DA), *Historical Summary for Fiscal Year (FY) 1979*, p. 31.

9   Memorandum for See Distribution with Encl, subj: CPT PME Action Plan, 7 Aug 1997, HRDC; LTC Joe Snow, "CAS3 [Combined Arms Staff and Service School] Anyone?" pp. 34-35; Department of the Army (DA), *Historical Summary for Fiscal Year (FY) 1979*, p. 31.

10   Information Paper, subj: Review of Captains' Professional Military Education (PME), 17 Jan 1996, HRDC; Msg, TRADOC to Service School Cmdts, subj: CG Taskers-Cpt PME Brief, 21 Dec 1995, HRDC; Memorandum for TRADOC Schools, subj: CPT-PME, 29 Jan 1996, HRDC; 1996 USAFACFS ACH, pp. 56-57; Memorandum for See Distribution with Encl, subj: CPT PME Action Plan, 7 Aug 1997, HRDC; Memorandum for Cmdt, subj: Trip Report, CPT PME, Council of Colonels, Fort Leavenworth, 24 Jan 1997, HRDC. Note that the fiscal year for the federal government began on 1 October and ended in 30 September.

11   Memorandum, Dir, Warfighting Integration and Development Directorate (WIDD), subj: Synchronization of OAC End Dates with CAS3 Start Dates, 5 Feb 1996, HRDC; Memorandum for WIDD, subj: Synchronization of OAC End Dates with CAS3 Start Dates, 7 Feb 1996, HRDC;

Msg, Cdr, TRADOC to Service School Cmdts, 010800Z Aug 1996, HRDC; Memorandum for Cdr, TRADOC, subj: Synchronization of FAOAC End Dates with CAS3 Start Dates, 8 Feb 1996, HRDC.

12 Memorandum for Cmdt, subj: Trip Report, CPT PME Council of Colonels, Fort Leavenworth, 24 Jan 1997, HRDC; Briefing, subj: CPT PME FA Captains Career Course, Dec 1998, HRDC; Briefing, subj: FA Officer Training and Education, Jan 1999, HRDC; Briefing, subj: CPT PME General Officer Steering Committee, 30 Jan 1998, HRDC; Briefing, subj: FA Officer Training and Education (CG TRADOC Briefing), Jan 1999, HRDC; Memorandum for See Distribution with Encl, subj: CPT PME Action Plan, 7 Aug 1997, HRDC; Memorandum for Mel Hunt, WIDD, US Army Field Artillery School (USAFAS), subj: SME Review of Captain Professional Military Education Portion of 1998 Annual Command History, 17 Feb 1999, HRDC; "Field Artillery Training Command," *Field Artillery Magazine*, Nov-Dec 1999, p. 32.

13 Memorandum for CG, TRADOC, and DCG, TRADOC, subj: CSA Visit to CAC, 21 Sep 1998, HRDC.

14 MAJ David W. Cavitt and Melvin R. Hunt, "Captains Professional Military Education: New Technology for the New Millennium," *Field Artillery Magazine*, Nov-Dec 1999, pp. 11-13; Briefing, subj: CCC, 26 Jan 2000, HRDC; Briefing, subj: CCC, 12 Nov 1999, HRDC; Interview, Dastrup with Melvin Hunt, WIDD, 26 Jan 2000, HRDC; Fact Sheet, subj: FACCC, Apr 1999, HRDC; "Silhouettes of Steel," *Field Artillery Magazine*, Nov-Dec 1999, p. 32; USAFAS Schedule of Classes for FY99 (Extract), 25 Sep 1998, HRDC; E-mail with atch, subj: Funding for CAS3 and another ARNG Things, 3 Dec 1999, HRDC.

15 Cavitt and Hunt, "Captains Professional Military Education, pp. 11-13; Briefing, subj: CCC, 26 Jan 2000, HRDC; Briefing, subj: CCC, 12 Nov 1999, HRDC; Interview, Dastrup with Melvin Hunt, WIDD, 26 Jan 2000, HRDC; Fact Sheet, subj: FACCC, Apr 1999, HRDC; "Silhouettes of Steel," *Field Artillery Magazine*, Nov-Dec 1999, p. 32; USAFAS Schedule of Classes for FY99 (Extract), 25 Sep 1998, HRDC; E-mail with atch, subj: Funding for CAS3 and another ARNG Things, 3 Dec 1999, HRDC.

16 Cavitt and Hunt, "Captains Professional Military Education," pp. 11-13; E-mail with atch, subj: FACCC, 9 Feb 2000, HRDC; USAFAS, Accreditation Self Study Report, May 1976, p. 6-2, UF23.5 A2U5, MSTL.

17 Cavitt and Hunt, "Captains Professional Military Education," pp. 11-13; E-mail with atch, subj: FACCC, 9 Feb 2000, HRDC; USAFAS, Accreditation Self Study Report, May 1976, p. 6-2, UF23.5 A2U5, MSTL.

18 Cavitt and Hunt, "Captains Professional Military Education," pp. 11-13; E-mail with atch, subj: FACCC, 9 Feb 2000, HRDC.

19 Cavitt and Hunt, "Captains Professional Military Education," pp. 11-13.

20 Cavitt and Hunt, "Captains Professional Military Education," pp. 11-13; Draft FACCC-DL Plan, 26 Jan 2000, HRDC; E-mail, subj: Funding CAS3 and another ARNG Things, 3 Dec 1999, HRDC; Interview, Dastrup with Hunt, 26 Jan 2000, HRDC; E-mail with atch, subj: FACCC, 9 Feb 2000, HRDC; Memorandum for Dir, WIDD, subj: Coordination of 1999 USAFACFS ACH, 22 Mar 2000, HRDC.

21 See Note 20.

22 Memorandum through AC, USAFAS, for CG, USAFAS, subj: Response to Inquiry Concerning Enhanced Field Artillery Officer Basic Course (FAOBC), 28 Dec 1992, HRDC; Interview, L. Martin Kaplan with MAJ Robert Leach, Chief, Basic Fire Support Branch, Fire Support and Combined Arms Department (FSCAOD), 28 Dec 1992, HRDC; Briefing, subj: FAOBC Program Review, 14 Sep 1992, HRDC; Briefing, subj: FAOBC Program Review, 24 Sep 1992, HRDC; Ltr, BG Benton to MG William Carter III, CG, National Training Center, 28 Oct 1992, HRDC; Memorandum thru AC, USAFAS, for CG, USAFAS, subj: Response to Inquiry Concerning

Enhanced FAOBC, 28 Dec 1992, HRDC; Ltr, COL R. Gaddis to COL Sterling Richardson, 10 Nov 1992, HRDC; Ltr, BG George Fisher to Benton, undated; HRDC; Ltr, COL F.L. Turner to COL Richardson, 12 Nov 1992, HRDC; Ltr, COL Geoffrey Miller to Richardson, 12 Nov 1992, HRDC; Ltr, COL Ronald Townsend to Richardson, 13 Nov 1992, HRDC; Memorandum for Dir, FSCAOD, subj: Improvements to the Field Artillery Officer Basic Course, 13 Nov 1992, HRDC; Interview, Kaplan with Leach, 25 Oct 1992, HRDC; Fact Sheet, subj: FAOBC Program Review, 25 Oct 1992, HRDC; Briefing, subj: Fire Support Enhancements, 17 Dec 1992, HRDC.

23 "FAOBC Enhancements," *Field Artillery Magazine*, Feb 1994, p. 44; Interview, Dastrup with MAJ Daniel J. Conn, Chief, Officer Instruction Branch, Gunnery Department, 16 Feb 1994, HRDC.

24 See Note 23.

25 Interview, Dastrup with Conn, 27 Jan 1995, HRDC; Briefing (Extract), subj: FAOBC Attrition, 1994, HRDC: Memorandum for AC, subj: FAOBC Innovations, 7 Nov 1994, HRDC; Memorandum for AC, subj: Reduction in Self-Propelled Howitzer Training, 29 Dec 1994, HRDC; Memorandum for See Distribution, subj: Reduction in Self-Propelled Howitzer Training, 5 Jan 1995, HRDC.

26 Memorandum for AC, subj: Reduction in Self-Propelled Howitzer Training, 5 Jan 1995, HRDC.

27 Memorandum for AC, subj: FAOBC Innovations, 7 Nov 1994, HRDC; Briefing (Extract), subj: FAOBC Attrition, 1994, HRDC.

28 Briefing, subj: The King of Battle, 1995, HRDC.

29 Briefing, subj: FAOBC Planning Brief, Spring 1996, HRDC; Interview, Dastrup with MAJ D.A. Vindich, Officer Instruction Branch, Gunnery Department, 11 Feb 1997, HRDC.

30 Interview, Dastrup with Michael Hubbard, Dep Dir, Gunnery Department (GD), and Fred Rowzee, Dir Ops, GD, 10 Dec 1998, HRDC; Briefing, subj: Field Artillery Officer Training and Education, Jan 1999, HRDC; Msg, subj: FAOBC Input for Annual History-Reply, 19 Jan 1999, HRDC; Briefing, subj: 97 OBC Program of Instruction (POI) Progress Review Brief, 13 Nov 1996, HRDC; Briefing, subj: FAOBC Planning Brief, Spring 1996, HRDC; Briefing, subj: Gunnery Department: Standards Start Here, 1996, HRDC; Interview, Dastrup with Vindich, 11 Feb 1997, HRDC.

31 "Field Artillery Training Command," *Field Artillery Magazine*, Nov-Dec 1997, p. 32; 1997 USAFACFS ACH, pp. 28-29; Fact Sheet, subj: Fire Support Officer Lane, 27 Jan 1999, HRDC; Fact Sheet, subj: Dismounted Fire Support Officer Fire Control Exercise, Feb 1998, HRDC; "OBC: Training the New Lieutenant," *Field Artillery Magazine*, Mar-Apr 1999, p. 35; Briefing, subj: Field Artillery Officer Basic Course, 1999, HRDC; "Silhouettes of Steel," p. 32; Fact Sheet, subj: OBC Fire Support Training: A Synopsis, Apr 1999, HRDC; Memorandum for Record, subj: FAOBC, 17 Mar 2000, HRDC; Bray and Raymond, "Redleg Mentor Program," pp. 10-11; MG Randall L. Rigby, "Mapping the Future: FA State of the Branch 1996," *Field Artillery Magazine*, Nov-Dec 1996, pp. 1-6; Interview, Dastrup with MAJ John J. Sweeney, Chief, Instruction Branch, GD, 13 Jan 1999, HRDC; Interview, with Hubbard, and Rowzee, 10 Dec 1998, HRDC; Memorandum for Record, subj: Fire Support Officer, 13 Jan 1999, HRDC; Briefing, subj: FAOBC Common Core, Jan 1999, HRDC.

32 "Field Artillery Training Command," *Field Artillery Magazine*, Nov-Dec 1997, p. 32; 1997 USAFACFS ACH, pp. 28-29; Fact Sheet, subj: Fire Support Officer Lane, 27 Jan 1999, HRDC; Fact Sheet, subj: Dismounted Fire Support Officer Fire Control Exercise, Feb 1998, HRDC; "OBC," p. 35; Briefing, subj: Field Artillery Officer Basic Course, 1999, HRDC; "Silhouettes of Steel," p. 32; Fact Sheet, subj: OBC Fire Support Training: A Synopsis, Apr 1999, HRDC; Memorandum for Record, subj: FAOBC, 17 Mar 2000, HRDC; Bray and Raymond, "Redleg Mentor Program,

pp. 10-11; Rigby, "Mapping the Future: FA State of the Branch 1996," pp. 1-6; Interview, Dastrup with Sweeney, 13 Jan 1999, HRDC; Interview, with Hubbard and Rowzee, 10 Dec 1998, HRDC; Memorandum for Record, subj: Fire Support Officer, 13 Jan 1999, HRDC; Briefing, subj: FAOBC Common Core, Jan 1999, HRDC.

33 "Redlegs' Career Update: Officers, Warrant Officers, and Noncommissioned Officers," *Field Artillery Magazine*, Dec 1987, pp. 48-54; Briefing, subj: Target Acquisition in Transition, ca 1991-1992, HRDC; Briefing, subj: Fire Support, ca 1992, HRDC; Briefing, subj: Fire Support, ca 1993, HRDC; The active warrant officer MOSs were 130A, Pershing; 130B, Lance; 131A, Target Acquisition; 131B, Remotely Piloted Vehicle; and 132A, Meteorology.

34 "Redlegs' Career Update: Officers, Warrant Officers, and Noncommissioned Officers," pp. 48-54; CW3 James A. Markestad, "Warrant Officers: The New WOs for the Total Force," *Field Artillery Magazine*, Dec 1990, pp. 39-42; Memorandum for MAJ William C. Burrell, FSCAOD, USAFAS, subj: SME Field Artillery Warrant Officer Courses for the 1998 Annual Command History, 5 Mar 1999, HRDC.

35 Memorandum with Encls for CW5 Joseph Stephens, subj: Training Documents for 131A Warrant Officer Courses, 8 Dec 1992, HRDC; Memorandum with Encls for Dir, DOTD, subj: Course Administrative Data for 131A Courses, 16 Dec 1992, HRDC; DA, *Historical Summary for FY 1989*, pp. 128-29.

36 "TA Warrant Officer Restructured Approved," *Field Artillery Magazine*, Aug 1993, p. 37; Memorandum for Dir, DOTD, subj: Course Administrative Data for 131A courses, 16 Dec 1992, HRDC; Memorandum for CW5 Joseph Stephens, subj: Training Documents for 131A Warrant Officer Courses, 8 Dec 1992, HRDC; "The Radar Technician and His Role," *Field Artillery Magazine*, Jul-Aug 1996, p. 2; Msg, subj: WO Transition Course, 26 Feb 1999, HRDC.

37 "Training the Targeting Technician," *Field Artillery Magazine*, Jan-Feb 1997, p. 26; Memorandum for CW5 Joseph Stephens, subj: Training Documents for 131A Warrant Officer Courses, 8 Dec 1992, HRDC; Memorandum with Encls for Dir, DOTD, subj: Course Administrative Data for 131A Courses, 16 Dec 1992, HRDC; MG Fred F. Marty, "Developing Soldiers and Leaders for the Future," *Field Artillery Magazine*, Aug 1992, pp. 1-3.

38 See Note 37.

39 "Silhouettes of Steel," *Field Artillery Magazine*, Nov-Dec 1999, p. 32; CSM James C. McKinney, "Advice to NCOs Today: Be Patient and Professional," *Field Artillery Magazine*, Oct 1993, pp. 6-8; "Field Artillery School," *Field Artillery Magazine*, Dec 1991, p. 13; MG Fred F. Marty, "State-of-the-Branch 1991," *Field Artillery Magazine*, Dec 1991, pp. 2-3; Rigby, "Mapping the Future: State-of-the-Branch, 1996," pp. 1-6; "Field Artillery Training Command Telephone Directory," *Field Artillery Magazine*, Nov-Dec 1995, pp. 10-11; "Training Command Telephone Directory," *Field Artillery Magazine*, Nov-Dec 1999, pp. 8-10.

40 See Note 39.

41 "Multimedia Technologies to Train the Total FA," *Field Artillery Magazine*, Oct 1993, pp. 44-45; Memorandum for Record, subj: Distributed Training, Summer 1993, HRDC; TRADOC, "DTP: The Soldier's Edge," pp. 1-2, Jul 1993, HRDC.

42 TRADOC, "DTP: The Soldier's Edge," pp. 1-2, Jul 1993, HRDC.

43 Memorandum for Cdr, TRADOC, subj: USAFAS Distributed Training Program, 19 Apr 1993, HRDC; Memorandum for Record, subj: Distributed Training, 1993, HRDC; "Multimedia Technologies to Train the Total FA," pp. 44-45; Fact Sheet, subj: USAFAS Distributed Training Program, 13 Sep 1993, HRDC; Memorandum for Cmdt, USAFAS, subj: State of the Branch Report 1993, 24 Nov 1993, HRDC.

44 Fact Sheet, subj: USAFAS Distance Education Program, 28 Apr 1994, HRDC; Memorandum for Record, subj: Distributed Training, 1993, HRDC; "Multimedia Technologies

to Train the Total FA," pp. 44-45; Fact Sheet, subj: USAFAS Distance Learning Program, 2 Jan 1995, HRDC; Briefing, subj: Classroom XXI: Total Army Training, 1995, HRDC; Fact Sheet, subj: USAFAS DEP, 28 Apr 1994, HRDC; Fact Sheet, subj: TNET Satellite, 1 Sep 1994, HRDC; "Field Artillery School Builds 'Classrooms without Walls,'" Fort Sill *Cannoneer*, 2 Feb 1995, p. 6a, HRDC; Memorandum for Record, subj: Distributed Training, Summary 1993; HRDC; Fact Sheet, subj: USAFAS DEP, 28 Apr 1994, HRDC; Fact Sheet with atchs, subj: TNET, 4 May 1994, HRDC.

45 "Field Artillery Training Command," *Field Artillery Magazine*, Dec 1994, p. 30; 1994 USAFACFS ACH, p. 60; Fact Sheet, subj: The Army's TNET, 13 Sep 1993, HRDC; Fact Sheet, subj: USAFAS Distance Education Program, 28 Apr 1994, HRDC; Briefing, subj: Classroom XXI, Jan 1995, HRDC.

46 "Field Artillery Training Command," p. 30; 1994 USAFACFS ACH, p. 60; Fact Sheet, subj: The Army's TNET, 13 Sep 1993, HRDC; Fact Sheet, subj: USAFAS Distance Education Program, 28 Apr 1994, HRDC; Briefing, subj: Classroom XXI, Jan 1995, HRDC.

47 Fact Sheet, subj: USAFAS Distance Learning Program, 2 Jan 1995, HRDC; Fact Sheet, subj: TNET Satellite, 1 Sep 1994, HRDC; Interview, Dastrup with Brown, 25 Jan 1995, HRDC; "Field Artillery School Builds 'Classroom without Walls,'" p. 6a; Fact Sheet with atchs, subj: TNET, 4 May 1994, HRDC; Memorandum for Record, subj: Distributed Training, Summer 1993, HRDC; Fact Sheet, subj: USAFAS DEP, 28 Apr 1994, HRDC; Fact Sheet, subj: DTE Overview, 4 May 1994, HRDC; Fact Sheet, subj: USAFAS Distance Learning Program, 2 Dec 1995, HRDC; Briefing, subj: Training Development: Multimedia Course Redesign, Dec 1996, HRDC; "Multimedia Technologies to Train the FA," pp. 44-45; Memorandum for Record, subj: FA School Plans Training for RC Using Multimedia Technologies, 1993, HRDC; Fact Sheet, subj: The Army's TNET Satellite, 13 Sep 1993, HRDC.

48 Memorandum for Record, subj: Distributed Training, Summer 1993, HRDC.

49 1993 USAFACFS ACH, p. 64; 1994 USAFACFS ACH, p. 59; Fact Sheet, subj: DTE Overview, 3 May 1994, HRDC; Interview, Dastrup with Donald Black, WIDD, 28 Feb 1996, HRDC; Fact Sheet, subj: USAFAS Distance Learning Program, 2 Jan 1995, HRDC; Briefing, subj: Training Development: Multimedia Course Redesign, Dec 1996, HRDC; Fact Sheet, subj: The Army's TNET, 13 Sep 1993, HRDC; Fact Sheet, subj: USAFAS Distance Education Program, 28 Apr 1994, HRDC; Fact Sheet, subj: USAFAS Distance Learning Program, 2 Jan 1995, HRDC; Briefing, subj: Classroom XXI, Jan 1995, HRDC; 1995 USAFACFS ACH, Fn 20, p. 52.

50 See Note 49.

51 BG Randall L. Rigby, "Fires for Division XXI: State of the Branch 1995," *Field Artillery Magazine*, Nov-Dec 1995, pp. 1-5; Memorandum with Encl for See Distribution, subj: ADLP Implementation, 29 Jul 1996, HRDC; US Army Distance Learning Plan, Executive Summary (Extract), pp. 1-3, 19 Jan 1996, HRDC;

52 Memorandum with Encl for See Distribution, subj: ADLP Implementation, 29 Jun 1996, HRDC.

53 Army Distance Learning Training Plan, Vol 1, 3 Apr 1996, pp. 2-3, 2-11, HRDC.

54 Memorandum with Encl for AC, USAFAS, subj: Distance Learning/Classroom XXI OPLAN, 28 Oct 1996, HRDC; USAFAS Distance Learning/Classroom XXI OPLAN, Oct 1996, HRDC; MG Leo J. Baxter, "Honing the Edge: State of the Branch 1997," *Field Artillery Magazine*, Nov-Dec 1997, pp. 1-5.

55 "Field Artillery Training Command," *Field Artillery Magazine*, Nov-Dec 1997, p. 32; "Technological Advances in Training," *Field Artillery Magazine*, Mar-Apr 1997, p. 27; Memorandum for Command Historian, subj: Training Development Products for WIDD, 7 Apr 1998, HRDC; Interview, Dastrup with Sharon Dorrell, WIDD, 15 Jan 1998, HRDC; Memorandum with Encls for Cdr, TRADOC, subj: Distance Learning/Classroom XXI OPLAN, 6 Nov 1996, p. ES1.2.2., HRDC;

Memorandum for Sharon Dorrell, WIDD, subj: 1997 USAFACFS ACH, 12 Feb 1998, HRDC; Briefing, subj: Total Army Training System (TATS) Courseware Implementation Schematic Profile Update, 1998, HRDC; USAFAS Total Army Training System (Extract), 8 Feb 2000, HRDC; E-mail, subj: Distance Learning, 10 Feb 2000, HRDC; Memorandum for See Distribution with atch, subj: Coordinating Draft of the Army Distance Learning Operations Directive, 23 May 1996, HRDC.

56 "Field Artillery Training Command," *Field Artillery Magazine*, Nov-Dec 1997, p. 32; "Technological Advances in Training," *Field Artillery Magazine*, Mar-Apr 1997, p. 27; Memorandum for Command Historian, subj: Training Development Products for WIDD, 7 Apr 1998, HRDC; Interview, Dastrup with Sharon Dorrell, 15 Jan 1998, HRDC; Memorandum with Encls for Cdr, TRADOC, subj: Distance Learning/ Classroom XXI OPLAN, 6 Nov 1996, p. ES1.2.2., HRDC; Memorandum for Sharon Dorrell, WIDD, subj: 1997 USAFACFS Annual Command History, 12 Feb 1998, HRDC; Briefing, subj: TATS Courseware Implementation Schematic Profile Update, 1998, HRDC; USAFAS Total Army Training System (Extract), 8 Feb 2000, HRDC; E-mail, subj: Distance Learning, 10 Feb 2000, HRDC; Memorandum for See Distribution with atch, subj: Coordinating Draft of the Army Distance Learning Operations Directive, 23 May 1996, HRDC; Memorandum with Encl for AC, USAFAS, subj: Distance Learning/Classroom XXI OPLAN, 28 Oct 1996, HRDC; USAFAS Distance Learning/Classroom XXI OPLAN, Oct 1996, HRDC; Briefing, subj: TATS Courseware Implementation Schematic Profile Update, 1998, HRDC; Interview, Dastrup with Sharon Dorrell, WIDD, 8 Feb 2000, HRDC; USAFAS Total Army Training System, 8 Feb 2000, HRDC; Memorandum for See Distribution, subj: FY99 TASS Information Memorandum #2, 26 May 1999, HRDC.

57 Briefing, subj: TATS Courseware Implementation Schematic Profile Update, 1998, HRDC; Interview, Dastrup with Dorrell, 8 Feb 2000, HRDC; USAFAS Total Army Training System, 8 Feb 2000, HRDC; Memorandum for See Distribution, subj: FY99 TASS Information Memorandum #2, 26 May 1999, HRDC; E-mail, subj: Total Army School System, 9 Feb 2000, HRDC; Briefing, subj: TATS Courseware Implementation Schematic Profile Update, 1998, HRDC; Interview, Dastrup with Dorrell, 15 Jan 1998, HRDC; Memorandum for Sharon Dorrell, WIDD, subj: 1997 USAFACFS ACH, 12 Feb 1998, HRDC.

58 Briefing, subj: Classroom XXI: Total Army Training, Jan 1995, HRDC; TRADOC, "DTP: The Soldier's Edge," Jul 1993, p. 2, HRDC; Interview, Dastrup with Johnsie Brown, Chief, Distributed Training Division, DOTD, 26 Jan 1995, HRDC; Fact Sheet, subj: Total Army School System (TASS), 28 Apr 1994, HRDC; COL Charles E. Heller, "Educating the Army for the 21st Century," *Military Review*, Jul-Aug 1996, p. 86; Briefing, subj: Classroom XXI: Total Army Training, Jan 1995, HRDC; Fact Sheet, subj: TASS, 28 Apr 1994, HRDC; TRADOC TASS OPLAN-2 (Extract), 1 Jan 1995, pp. iv, ix-x, HRDC; Fact Sheet, subj: TASS, 28 Apr 1994, HRDC.

59 TRADOC TASS OPLAN-2 (Extract), 1 Jan 1995, p. iv, HRDC; Information Paper, subj: FAST Update, 1 Apr 1994, HRDC; Heller, "Educating the Army for the 21st Century," p. 86; 2000 USAFACFS ACH, p. 29.

60 Information Paper, subj: FAST Update, 1 Apr 1994, HRDC; TRADOC TASS OPLAN-2 (Extract), p. v, HRDC; Heller, "Educating the Army for the 21st Century," p. 86; Memorandum for Record, subj: TASS, 15 Jan 1997, HRDC; John L. Romjue, Susan Canedy, and Anne Chapman, *Prepare the Army for War: A Historical Overview of the Army Training and Doctrine Command, 1973-1993* (Fort Monroe, VA: Office of the Command Historian, US Army Training and Doctrine Command, 1993), p. 40.

61 Information Paper, subj: FAST Update, 1 Apr 1994, HRDC; TRADOC TASS OPLAN-2 (Extract), 1 Jan 1995, pp. vi, B-1, HRDC; Fact Sheet, subj: TASS, 9 Feb 1996, HRDC; Fact Sheet, subj: TASS, 28 Apr 1994, HRDC. The Field Artillery School Battalion was aligned in Region F.

62 Msg, subj: TASS, 26 Jan 1995, HRDC.

63 Memorandum for Record, subj: Staff Input for 1996 ACH, 26 Feb 1997, HRDC; Memorandum for Record, subj: TASS, 15 Jan 1997, HRDC; Interview, Dastrup with Sharon Dorrell, WIDD, 15 Jan 1998, HRDC; Interview, Dastrup with Sharon Dorrell, WIDD, 19 Jan 1999, HRDC; TRADOC Regulation 351-18 (Extract), Appendix C, HRDC; Interview, Dastrup with Sharon Dorrell, WIDD, 8 Feb 2000, HRDC; Memorandum for See Distribution, subj: FY99 TASS Information Memorandum #2, 26 May 1999, HRDC; Memorandum for Record, subj: TRADOC Integration Elements, 8 Feb 2000, HRDC; E-mail, subj: Total Army School System, 9 Feb 2000, HRDC; 2000 US Army Field Artillery Center and Fort Sill (USAFACFS) Annual Command History (ACH), p. 29. See Memorandum for Record, subj: TRADOC Integration Elements, 8 Feb 2000, for a map of the regions and their states, HRDC.

64 Fact Sheet, subj: TASS Update, 9 Feb 1996, HRDC; Memorandum for See Distribution, subj: Accreditation of TASS School Battalions in Region C, 9 Nov 1994, HRDC; Fact Sheet, subj: TASS, 7 Nov 1997, TASS File, HRDC; 1998 USAFACFS ACH, pp. 28-30; US Army Posture Statement for Fiscal Year 2000, p. 50, Posture Statement File, HRDC; Fact Sheet, subj: TASS, 6 Nov 1997, TASS File, HRDC; 1998 USAFACFS ACH, pp. 28-30; 1994 TRADOC ACH, pp. 46-48; 1995 USAFACFS ACH, pp. 41-55; 1996 USAFACFS ACH, pp. 31-53; 1997 USAFACFS ACH, pp. 17-19; 2001 USAFACFS ACH, pp. 24-25; Mark Hanna, "Task Force XXI: The Army's Digital Experiment," *Strategic Forum*, Jul 97, Force XXI File, HRDC; 2000 USAFACFS ACH, p. 29; DA, *Historical Summary for Fiscal Year 1996*, pp. 5, 67-68; 1994 TRADOC ACH, pp. 46-48; US Army Posture Statement for Fiscal Year 2000, pp. 50-51, Posture Statement File, HRDC.

65 COL Robert W. Roshell and LTC Lawrence M. Terranova, "Education for ARNG FA Officers and NCOs," *Fires Bulletin*, Jan-Feb 2009, pp. 30-34.

66 Briefing, subj: Classroom XXI, 1995, HRDC; Interview, Dastrup with LTC B.T. Palmatier, Dep Cdr, 1-30 FA, Training Command, 12 Feb 1996, HRDC; Briefing, subj: Classroom XXI, 1995, HRDC..

67 Interview, Dastrup with Bill Lodes, Training Management Division, WIDD, 22 Jan 1997, HRDC; Briefing, subj: Distance Learning Plan, 1996, HRDC.

68 "Field Artillery Training Command," *Field Artillery Magazine*, Nov-Dec 1998, p. 32; "Field Artillery Training Command," *Field Artillery Magazine*, Nov-Dec 1997, p. 32; COL David White, Cdr, 30th FA, "Cutting Edge Training Prepares Soldiers for Changing Future," Fort Sill *Cannoneer*, 27 Nov 1996, p. 6a, HRDC; Interview, Dastrup with Lodes, 22 Jan 1997, HRDC; Briefing, subj: Classroom XXI – FY96, 15 May 1996, HRDC; MG Randall L. Rigby, "CG Reflects, Reviews 1996 Goals at Fort Sill," Fort Sill *Cannoneer*, 4 Dec 1996, p. 6a, HRDC; Msg, subj: Concept Brief, 27 Aug 1996, HRDC; Briefing (Extract), subj: Classroom XXI, 1995, HRDC; USAFAS, Classroom XXI Spend Plan – FY96 (Extract), HRDC; Msg, subj: Classroom XXI Information, 21 Aug 1996, HRDC; Msg, subj: FSCAOD Input for Historical Record, 30 Jan 1997, HRDC; Memorandum for Record, subj: Classroom XXI Events for FY96, 5 Feb 1997, HRDC; Briefing, subj: Classroom XXI, Sep-Oct 1996, HRDC; Dr. Linda G. Pierce and Walter W. Millspaugh, "Simulations to Train and Develop the 21st Century FA," *Field Artillery Magazine*, Jul-Aug 1997, pp. 39-42.

69 1996 USAFACFS ACH, pp. 51-52; "Technological Advances in Training," *Field Artillery Magazine*, Mar-Apr 1997, p. 27; Msg, subj: Input for Classroom XXI History, 13 Feb 1998, HRDC; Memorandum (Extract) for Dir, WIDD, subj: Memorandum of Agreement for Classroom XXI and Distance Learning, 15 Oct 1997, HRDC; Briefing, subj: TATS Courseware Implementation Schematic Profile Update, 1998, HRDC; Memorandum for Dir, WIDD (Extract), subj: Memorandum of Agreement for Classroom XXI and Distance Learning, 15 Oct 1997, HRDC; Interview, Dastrup with Bill Lodes, WIDD, 4 Feb 1999, HRDC; Briefing, subj: Classroom XXI, Feb 1999, HRDC; Memorandum for Dir, WIDD, subj: Coordination of 1998 USAFACFS Annual Command History, 15 Mar 1999, HRDC; Interview, Dastrup with Bill Lodes, WIDD, 26 Jan

2000, HRDC; Memorandum for Record, subj: USAFAS Distance Learning Classrooms, 26 Jan 2000, HRDC; E-mail with atch, subj: Classroom XXI, 8 Feb 2000, HRDC; E-mail with atch, subj: Classroom XXI, 18 Feb 2000, HRDC; E-mail with atch, subj: Classroom XXI, 17 Feb 2000, HRDC; E-mail with atch, subj: Classroom XXI, 18 Feb 2000, HRDC.

70 Memorandum for Dir, WIDD, subj: Memorandum of Agreement for Classroom XXI and Distance Learning, 15 Oct 1997, HRDC; Interview, Dastrup with Lodes, 4 Feb 1999, HRDC; Briefing (Extract), subj: TATS Courseware Implementation Schematic Profile, 1998, HRDC; Briefing (Extract), subj: Training the Field Artillery, 28 Feb 1998, HRDC; Memorandum for Dir, WIDD, subj: Coordination of 1998 USAFACF Annual Command History, 15 Mar 1999, HRDC.

71 Interview, Dastrup with Lodes, 26 Jan 2000, HRDC; Memorandum for Record, subj: USAFAS Distance Learning Classrooms, 26 Jan 2000, HRDC; Briefing, subj: Gunnery Department, 20 Jul 1999, HRDC; Memorandum for AC, USAFAS, subj: SIGACTS, 9 Jul 1999, HRDC; Memorandum for AC, USAFAS, subj: SIGACTS, 26 Mar 1999, HRDC.

72 CPT Robert F. Markovetz, Jr., "Distance Learning: MLRS 3x6 Conversion for the Army National Guard," *Field Artillery Magazine*, Sep-Oct 1999, pp. 42-43; Memorandum for Record, subj: USAFAS Distance Learning Classrooms, 26 Jan 2000, HRDC; Interview, Dastrup with Bill Lodes, 26 Jan 2000, HRDC; Memorandum for AC, USAFAS, subj: SIGACTS, 26 Mar 1999, HRDC; Interview with atch, Dastrup with Bill Lodes, WIDD, 15 Feb 2001, HRDC; Interview, Dastrup with CPT Charles H. Akins, MLRS NET, Gunnery Dept, 12 Feb 2001, HRDC; Distance Learning Homepage, Distance Learning, 6 Feb 2001, HRDC; Training Management Division, WIDD, Homepage, 15 Feb 2001, HRDC; Msg, subj: Implementation of the Army Distance Learning Program, Feb 2001, HRDC.

73 Concept Paper, DOTD, subj: Closed Loop Training, undated, HRDC; MG Fred F. Marty, "State-of-the-Branch Address 1991," *Field Artillery Magazine*, Dec 1991, pp. 1-3; MG John A. Dubia, "Force XXI and the Field Artillery: State of the Branch 1994," *Field Artillery Magazine*, Dec 1994, pp. 1-5.

74 "US Army Field Artillery School," *Field Artillery Magazine*, Dec 1990, p. 13; Integrated Logistics Support Plan for the CLASS, undated, HRDC; 1991 USAFACFS ACH, pp. 82-83; 1993 USAFACFS ACH, p. 65; 1995 USAFACFS ACH, p. 78; 1996 USAFACFS ACH, pp. 71-80; CPT Joseph P. Nizolak, Jr., CPT William T. Drummond, Jr., and Dr. Michael J. Zyda, "FOST: Innovative Training for Tomorrow's Battlefield," *Field Artillery Magazine*, Feb 1990, pp. 46-51.

75 "US Army Field Artillery School," p. 13; Integrated Logistics Support Plan for the CLASS, undated, HRDC; 1991 USAFACFS ACH, pp. 82-83; 1993 USAFACFS ACH, p. 65; 1995 USAFACFS ACH, p. 78; 1996 USAFACFS ACH, pp. 71-80; Nizolak, Drummond, and Zyda, "FOST," pp. 46-51.

76 "MG Fred F. Marty, "Train to Win – Make the Most of Fires and Maneuver," *Field Artillery Magazine*, Oct 1992, pp. 1-3; 1993 USAFACFS ACH, pp. 76-84; Telcon, LTC Martin to COL Mengle, subj: CLASS P3I Interface with CCTT, 18 Jun 1992, HRDC; Fact Sheet, subj: Fire Support Combined Arms Tactical Trainer (FSCATT), 26 Apr 1993, HRDC; Memorandum for HQDA, subj: CLASS, 22 Mar 1993, HRDC; Memorandum for Distribution, subj: Minutes for FSCATT Phase I Test Integration Working Group, 8 Apr 1993, HRDC; Draft Msg, subj: Cdr, TRADOC to HQDA, subj: CLASS, 1993, HRDC; Memorandum for CG, subj: DCD One Liners, 30 Mar 1993, HRDC; Fact Sheet, subj: FSCATT, 25 Apr 1993, HRDC; Memorandum for See Distribution, subj: Operational Requirements Document (ORD) for FSCATT, 25 Mar 1993, HRDC.

77 Pierce and Millspaugh, "Simulations to Train and Develop the 21st Century FA," pp. 39-42; 2002 USAFACFS ACH, pp. 93, 94, 99, 100; Briefing, subj: Training Aids, Devices, Simulators, and Simulations (TADSS) Status Review, 16 Sep 2003, HRDC; Briefing, subj: 1st Annual USAFAS TADSS Conference, 16 Sep 2003, HRDC; E-mail msg with atch, subj: TADSS Input to 2003

Annual Command History, 27 Jan 2004, HRDC; E-mail msg, subj: TADSS Input to 2003 Annual Command History, 9 Feb 2004, HRDC; Msg, subj: FSCATT Fielding Plan, 1 Feb 1999, HRDC; Fact Sheet, subj: FSCATT, 10 Dec 1998, HRDC; Interview, Dastrup with Don Kraft, WIDD, 2 Feb 1999, HRDC; Fact Sheet, subj: FSCATT, Feb 1998, HRDC; Fact Sheet, subj: FSCATT, Dec 1998, HRDC; Memorandum for Record, subj: Annual Command History Inut, 25 Feb 1999, HRDC.

78 CPT Guy E. Willebrand, "FA Training Devices for the 1990s and Beyond," *Field Artillery Magazine*, Mar-Apr 1995, pp. 11-13; 2002 USAFACFS ACH, pp. 93, 94, 99, 100; Briefing, subj: TADSS Status Review, 16 Sep 2003, HRDC; Briefing, subj: 1st Annual USAFAS TADSS Conference, 16 Sep 2003, HRDC; E-mail msg with atch, subj: TADSS Input to 2003 Annual Command History, 27 Jan 2004, HRDC; E-mail msg, subj: TADSS Input to 2003 Annual Command History, 9 Feb 2004, HRDC; MG Michael D. Maples, "Ready and Relevant: The FA Now and in the Future," *Field Artillery*, Nov-Dec 2003, pp. 1-5.

79 GEN Carl E. Vuono, "Change, Continuity, and the Future of the Field Artillery," *Field Artillery Magazine*, Jun 1991, pp. 6-10; GEN John W. Foss, "AirLand Battle-Future," *Army*, Feb 1991, p. 20; Briefing, subj: Challenges for the Field Artillery, 26 Apr 1990, HRDC; Draft Trends and Implications for the US Army's Future AirLand Battle, 30 Jan 1991, pp. 1-3, HRDC; Briefing, subj: Fire Support and AirLand Battle Future, 12 Feb 1991, HRDC; US Army Modernization Plan, Vol 2, Annex G, Jan 93, pp., 2-3, G-7, HRDC; 1991 TRADOC Annual Command History (ACH), p. 6; 1992 TRADOC ACH, p. 3; US Army Posture Statement for Fiscal Year 1995, pp. 8, 18, HRDC; Department of the Army (DA), *Historical Summary for Fiscal Year 1992*, p. 14; DA, *Historical Summary for Fiscal Year 1993*, p. 42; US Army Posture Statement for Fiscal Year 1999, pp. 2, 4, Posture Statement File, HRDC; Statement on the Posture of the US Army for Fiscal Year 1997 (Extract), pp. 12-13, HRDC; "Field Artillery Units Worldwide," *Field Artillery Magazine*, Dec 1989, pullout; "Active Army and Marine Units in OCONUS," *Field Artillery Magazine*, Nov-Dec 1999, p. 21. Pages 23-54 from *Operation Desert Storm and Beyond: Modernizing the Field Artillery in the 1990s* form the foundation for pages 233-63.

80 US Army Posture Statement for Fiscal Year 2000, pp. 19-21, Posture Statement File, HRDC; US Army Posture Statement for Fiscal Year 1999, pp. x, 4-5, 42, Posture Statement File, HRDC; US Army Posture Statement for Fiscal Year 2001, p. 2, Posture Statement File, HRDC; Statement on the Posture of the US Army for Fiscal Year 1998 (Extract), pp. 4-6, Posture Statement File, HRDC; DA, *Historical Summary for Fiscal Years 1990 and 1991*, pp. 31-37, 80; DA, *Historical Summary for Fiscal Year 1987*, p. 11; DA, *Historical Summary for Fiscal Year 1996*, p. 47; DA, *Historical Summary for Fiscal Year 1992*, pp. 116-35; DA, *Historical Summary for Fiscal Year 1993*, pp. 42-43.

81 MG William F. Ward, "Performance in Panama Underscores Readiness," *Army*, Oct 1990, pp. 104-13; MG Donald Burdick, "An Essential Element of National Strategy," *Army*, Oct 1990, pp. 116-21.

82 US Army Posture Statement for Fiscal Year 1997 (Extract), pp. 7-8, Posture Statement File, HRDC; US Army Posture Statement for Fiscal Year 2000, p. 18, Posture Statement File, HRDC; DA, *Historical Summary for Fiscal Year 1996*, p. 83; DA, *Historical Summary for Fiscal Year 1994*, pp. 71-72.

83 John J. Todd and LTC James M. Holt, "Army Science Board Study: How Much Field Artillery is Enough?" *Field Artillery Magazine*, Jun 1995, pp. 20-25; MG Randall L. Rigby, "Fires for Division XXI: State of the Branch 1995," *Field Artillery Magazine*, Nov-Dec 1995, p. 3

84 E-mail with atch, subj: Manuscript Review, 8 Dec 2003, p. 50, HRDC; MG Randall L. Rigby, "3x6-2x9 MLRS Transition," *Field Artillery Magazine*, Sep-Oct 1996, pp. 18-21; Rigby, "Fires for Division XXI," p. 3; Todd and Holt, "Army Science Board Study," pp. 20-25; US Army Posture Statement for Fiscal Year 2000, p. 18, Posture Statement File, HRDC; US Army Posture

Statement for Fiscal Year 1997 (Extract), Posture Statement File, HRDC; Burdick, "An Essential Element of National Strategy," p. 118; Briefing, subj: Senior Field Artillery Advisors Council, 1995, HRDC; 1999 US Army Field Artillery Center and Fort Sill (USAFACFS) ACH, pp. 51-57; 2000 USAFACFS ACH, pp. 50-56; CPT Lawrence T. Hall and CPT Michael A. Sharp, "MLRS NET for the ARNG," *Field Artillery Magazine*, Mar-Apr 96, pp. 44-45; 2001 USAFACFS ACH, pp. 39-40.

85 MG Fred F. Marty, "State-of-the-Branch 1992," *Field Artillery Magazine*, Nov-Dec 1992, p. 1; BG William C. Bilo, "A Decisive Victory for Strategic Victory," *Field Artillery Magazine*, Mar-Apr 1995, p. 22; 1995 USAFACFS ACH, p. 69.

86 Hall and Sharp, "MLRS NET for the ARNG," pp. 44-45; 2001 USAFACFS ACH, pp. 39-40; E-mail with atch, subj: Manuscript Review, 8 Dec 03, p. 113, HRDC; Memorandum for AC, USAFAS, subj: MLRS New Equipment Training Overview, Summer 98, 21 Sep 1998, HRDC; Briefing, subj: MLRS 3x6 New Equipment Training Concept, Nov 1998, HRDC; "Ft. Sill Soldiers Train Guard," *MLRS Dispatch*, 3rd quarter, 1998, p. 3, HRDC; Memorandum for Record, subj: SME Comments on MLRS NET, 24 Feb 1999, HRDC.

87 Rigby, "3x6-2x9 MLRS Transition," pp. 18-21; Briefing, subj: AC/RC Rebalancing and TAA-11 Field Artillery Allocation Rules, 26 Aug 2003, HRDC; MG Randall L. Rigby, "1996 Senior Fire Support Conference: Focusing Fires for Force XXI," *Field Artillery Magazine*, May-Jun 1996, p. 18.

88 See Note 87.

89 Rigby, "3x6 Cannon-2x9 MLRS Transition," p. 18.

90 MG Randall L. Rigby, "Mapping the Future: State of the Branch, 1996," *Field Artillery Magazine*, Nov-Dec 1996, p. 4.

91 Information Paper, subj: MLRS, undated, in MLRS File, HRDC; FM 6-60, MLRS Operations, 23 Apr 1996, MLRS File, HRDC; Table of Organization and Equipment, 23 Apr 1999; MG Leo J. Baxter, "Meeting the Future: State of the Field Artillery 1998," *Field Artillery Magazine*, Nov-Dec 98, pp. 1-6. "Transition," *Field Artillery Magazine*, Sep-Oct 1996, pp. 18-21; Rigby, "Mapping the Future," p. 4; 1999 USAFACFS ACH, pp. 57-61; LTC Richard R. McPhee, "The Divisional MLRS Battalion in the DAWE," *Field Artillery Magazine*, May-Jun 1998, pp. 38-40; Fact Sheet, subj: M270 MLRS Self-Propelled Loader/Launchers, undated, Force XXI File, HRDC; Fact Sheet, subj: M270 MLRS Self-Propelled Loader/Launchers, undated, Force XXI File, HRDC; Fact Sheet, subj: M270 MLRS Self-Propelled Loader/Launchers, undated, Force XXI File, HRDC; Information Paper, subj: MLRS, undated, in MLRS File, HRDC; FM 6-60, MLRS Operations, 23 Apr 1996, MLRS File, HRDC; Table of Organization and Equipment, 23 Apr 1999; Briefing, subj: AC/RC Rebalancing and TAA-11 Field Artillery Allocation Rules, 26 Aug 2003, HRDC.

92 E-mail with atch, subj: Manuscript Review, 8 Dec 2003, p. 54, HRDC.

93 Interview, Dastrup with Chris Klein, Directorate of Combat Developments (DCD), 29 Jan 1997, HRDC; Msg, Chris Klein to Dastrup, subj: 3x6/2x9 Transition, 28 Feb 1997, HRDC; Msg, DA to Cdr, FORSCOM, *et al*, subj: Modernization of Field Artillery Force Structure, 241705Z Jun 1996, HRDC; Briefing, subj: 3x6 Cannon and 2x9 MLRS Transition, Jan 1997, HRDC.

94 US Arms Control and Disarmament Agency, CFE Negotiation on Conventional Arm Forces in Europe, 1989, pp. 1-2, HRDC; US Army, A Strategic Force for the 1990s and Beyond, Jan 1990, HRDC; Interview, Dastrup with Bill Rittenhouse, Concepts and Studies Division, DCD, 23 Feb 1990, HRDC; USAFAS, Conventional Forces-Europe Reductions, Initial Overview and the Field Artillery Perspective, 18 Sep 1989, pp. 5-10, HRDC; USAFAS, Fighting at Parity in Post-CFE Europe, undated, HRDC; 1999 TRADOC ACH, pp. 32-34; 1990 USAFACFS ACH, pp. 176-78; DA, *Historical Summary for FY 1989*, p. 15; John L. Romjue, *American Army Doctrine for the Post-Cold War* (Fort Monroe, VA: Military History Office, US Army Training and Doctrine Command, 1996), pp. 21-27. Romjue's book discusses in detail the transition from AirLand Battle to AirLand

Operations between 1991 and 1993. Note: Twenty-two members of NATO and the former Warsaw Pact signed the Conventional Forces Europe Treaty in November 1990 after the dissolution of the Warsaw Pact and the dismemberment of the Soviet Union.

95 US Arms Control and Disarmament Agency, CFE Negotiation on Conventional Arm Forces in Europe, 1989, pp. 1-2, HRDC; US Army, A Strategic Force for the 1990s and Beyond, Jan 1990, HRDC; Interview, Dastrup with Rittenhouse, 23 Feb 1990, HRDC; USAFAS, Conventional Forces-Europe Reductions, Initial Overview and the Field Artillery Perspective, 18 Sep 1989, pp. 5-10, HRDC; USAFAS, Fighting at Parity in Post-CFE Europe, undated, HRDC; 1999 TRADOC ACH, pp. 32-34; 1990 USAFACFS ACH, pp. 176-78; DA, *Historical Summary for FY 1989,* pp. 15, 49; Romjue, *American Army Doctrine for the Post-Cold War*, pp. 21-27.

96 Fact Sheet, subj: AirLand Battle Future, 16 Apr 1990, HRDC; Foss, "AirLand Battle-Future," pp. 20-21; C. William Rittenhouse, "Fire Support on the Non-Linear Battlefield: The Shape of Things to Come," *Field Artillery Magazine*, Oct 1990, p. 36; USAFAS, Conventional Forces-Europe Force Reductions, 18 Sep 1989, pp. 10-12, HRDC; TRADOC Pamphlet 525-5, Airland Operations: A Concept for the Evolution of AirLand Battle for the Strategic Army of the 1990s and Beyond, 1 Aug 1991, p. 1, HRDC; 1990 USAFACFS AHR, p. 178; Romjue, *American Army Doctrine for the Post-Cold War*, pp. 21-27.

97 Fact Sheet, subj: AirLand Battle Future, 16 Apr 1990, HRDC; Fact Sheet, subj: Conventional Forces in Europe Treaty, 15 Apr 1990, HRDC; Rittenhouse, "Fire Support on the Non-Linear Battlefield," Oct 1990, pp. 36-37; Foss, "AirLand Battle-Future," pp. 20-21; Briefing, subj: Challenges for the Field Artillery, 26 Apr 1990, HRDC; Briefing, subj: Fire Support and AirLand Battle-Future, 12 Feb 1991, HRDC; Interview, Dastrup with Rittenhouse, Concepts and Studies Division, DCD, 11 Feb 1991, HRDC; TRADOC Pamphlet 525-5, AirLand Operations: A Concept for the Evolution of Airland Battle for the Strategic Army of the 1990s and Beyond, 1 Aug 1991, p. 1, HRDC; 1990 USAFACFS Annual Historical Review (AHR), pp. 178-79; Memorandum for See Distribution, subj: Draft AirLand Operations Concept Paper, undated, HRDC; 1991 TRADOC ACH, pp. 57-58; Romjue, *American Army Doctrine for the Post-Cold War*, pp. 61-70.

98 See Note 97.

99 COL John W. Reitz, "A Fire Supporter's Guide to FM 100-5," *Field Artillery Magazine*, Dec 1993, pp. 10-15; Romjue, *American Army Doctrine for the Post-Cold War*, pp. 35, 37, 96-112; FM 100-5, Operations, Jun 1993.

100 Fact Sheet, subj: AirLand Battle Future, 16 Apr 1990, HRDC; Foss, "AirLand Battle-Future," p. 24; Briefing, subj: Challenges for the Field Artillery, 26 Apr 1990, HRDC; TRADOC Pamphlet 525-5, AirLand Operations: A Concept for the Evolution of AirLand Battle for the Strategic Army of the 1990s and Beyond, 1 Aug 91, pp. 16-25, HRDC; Reitz, "A Fire Supporter's Guide to FM 100-5," pp. 10-15; FM 100-5, Operations, Jun 1993, pp. 6-1 - 7-14.

101 Ltr with atch, Dastrup to MG Fred Marty, 10 Sep 2003, p. 59, HRDC; Briefing, subj: Fire Support and AirLand Battle-Future, 12 Feb 1991, HRDC; Rittenhouse, "The Shape of Things to Come," p. 38; C. William Rittenhouse, "Operation FireStrike," *Field Artillery Magazine*, Feb 1991, pp. 33-37; Interview, Dastrup with Rittenhouse, 11 Feb 1991, HRDC.

102 Ltr with atch, Dastrup to Marty, 10 Sep 2003, HRDC; Rittenhouse, "Fire Support on a Non-Linear Battlefield," pp. 37-38; Rittenhouse, "Operation Firestrike," pp. 33-37; Leighton L. Duitsman, "Army TACMS," *Field Artillery Magazine*, Jan-Feb 1991, pp. 38-41; Interview, Dastrup with Rittenhouse, 11 Feb 1991, HRDC; Briefing, subj: Fire Support and AirLand Battle-Future, 12 Feb 1991, HRDC; MG Fred F. Marty, "Deep Operations," *Field Artillery Magazine,* Apr 1993, pp. 1-2; Reitz, "A Fire Supporter's Guide to FM 100-5," pp. 10-15.

103 BG Toney Stricklin, "Fires: The Cutting Edge for the 21st Century," *Field Artillery Magazine*, May-Jun 1998, pp. 22-23; Interview, Dastrup with MAJ Gregory A. Palka, Task Force

2000, USAFAS, 30 Mar 1999, HRDC; Briefing, subj: The Effects Coordination Cell, 24 Mar 1999, HRDC; Fact Sheet, subj: Futures Fires Command and Control Concept Experimentation Program, 24 Mar 1999, HRDC.

104 DA, *Historical Summary for Fiscal Year 1996*, p. 63; Interview, Dastrup with LTC Peter R. Baker, Task Force 2000, USAFAS, 23 Mar 2000, HRDC; "Medium-weight Units to Take Advantage of Effects-based Operations," *Inside the Army*, 10 Apr 2000, pp. 6-8, HRDC.

105 1994 TRADOC ACH, pp. 17-18; "Force XXI: A Revolution and Evolution in Military Affairs," Army Link News, 17 Jul 1996, Force XXI File, HRDC; LTG Gen Paul E. Menoher, Jr., "Force XXI: Redesigning the Army through Warfighting Experiments," *Military Intelligence*, 1996, Force XXI File, HRDC; LTC Clyde Ellis, "Army Training XXI," draft article, pp. 1-2, HRDC; TRADOC Warrior XXI Campaign Plan (Extract), Nov 1995, pp. 1-2, HRDC; TRADOC, Warnet XXI Action Plan (Extract), Jan 1996, p. 2, HRDC; TRADOC, Warfighter XXI Campaign Plan (Extract), 1995, p. 2, HRDC; COL David C. White and LTC Clyde W. Ellis, "Army Training XXI," *Field Artillery Magazine*, Mar-Apr 1996, pp. 8-10.

106 US Army Posture Statement for Fiscal Year 2001, pp. 24-25, Posture Statement File, HRDC; 1992 TRADOC ACH, pp. 79-82; 1993 TRADOC ACH, pp. 92-94; 1992 USAFACFS ACH, pp. 102-06; Ltr with atch, Dastrup to Marty, 10 Sep 2003, HRDC.

107 1995 USAFACFS ACH, pp. 97-100; 1996 USAFACFS ACH, pp. 94-95; 1997 USAFACFS ACH, p. 56; Msg, subj: TF2000 Command History, 7 Feb 1997, HRDC; MAJ Vince C. Weaver, "Fires in AWE Focused Dispatch: A Step Toward Task Force XXI," *Field Artillery Magazine*, Mar-Apr 1996, pp. 38-40; Briefing, subj: Force XXI, undated, HRDC; LTC Theodore S. Russell, Jr., and MAJ Harold H. Worrell, Jr., "Focus on Light Force XXI: AWE Warrior Focus," *Field Artillery Magazine*, May-Jun 1996, pp. 36-39; Task Force XXI Final Report, Executive Summary, Oct 1997, pp. 2-3, HRDC; COL Thomas R. Goedkoop and CPT Barry E. Venable, "Task Force XXI: An Overview," *Military Review*, Mar-Apr 1997, p. 71; "TRADOC Commander Reveals Some Results of Recent Force XXI AWE," Army Link News, 8 Oct 1997, Force XXI File, HRDC; Hanna, "Task Force XXI;" US Army Posture Statement for Fiscal Year 2001, pp. 24-25, Posture Statement File, HRDC; DA, *Historical Summary for Fiscal Year 1996*, p. 4.

108 2000 USAFACFS ACH, pp. 89-91; US Army Posture Statement for Fiscal Year 2001, pp. 24-25, Posture Statement File, HRDC; Memorandum for See Distribution, subj: Division XXI AWE and First Digital Division Fielding Taskers, 22 Apr 1997, HRDC; Briefing, subj: Improving the Interim Division Design: Adjusting for Task Force XXI, undated, HRDC; Briefing, subj: Fires: The Cutting Edge, undated, HRDC; Briefing, subj: Task Force 2000 in Support of AWE, Feb 1998, HRDC; Interview, Dastrup with MAJ Henry J. Hester, Jr., and MAJ Dean Mengel, Task Force 2000, 30 Jan 1998, HRDC; Memorandum for MAJ Dean Mengel, subj: 1997 USAFACFS ACH, 12 Feb 1998, HRDC; Fact Sheet, subj: Division XXI AWE Insights, undated, in Senior Fire Support Conference Packet, 9-13 Feb 1998, HRDC; "Division AWE Will Be Basis for 21st Century Fighting Force," Army Link News, 28 Oct 1997, Force XXI File, HRDC; Director, Operational Test and Evaluation, Fiscal Year 1997 Annual Report (Extract), Battlefield Digitization: Force XXI Battle Command, Brigade and Below, and the Tactical Internet, Force XXI File, HRDC.

109 2001 USAFACFS ACH, pp. 73-74; US Army Posture Statement for Fiscal Year 2001, pp. 24-25, Posture Statement File, HRDC.

110 DA, *Historical Summary for FY 1996*, p. 65; E-mail with atch, subj: Manuscript Review, 8 Dec 2003, p. 73, HRDC; 2000 USAFACFS ACH, pp. 82-83; US Army Posture Statement for Fiscal year 2001, p. 25, Posture Statement File, HRDC. See FN 40 in the 2000 USAFACFS ACH for a complete listing of documents.

111 TRADOC System Manager (TSM) All Source Analysis System, News Letter, Oct 2000, HRDC; TSM All Source Analysis System, News Letter, Jan 2001, HRDC; US Army Posture

Statement for Fiscal Year 2001, p. 25, Posture Statement File, HRDC; MG Randall L. Rigby, "AFATDS: Learning to Interoperate--Not Just Interface," *Field Artillery Magazine*, Sep-Oct 1996, p. 1.

112 1994 TRADOC ACH, p. 132; Rigby, "AFATDS," p. 1; COL Raymond T. Odierno and MAJ Thomas L. Swingle, "AFATDS: Digitizing Fighting with Fires," *Field Artillery Magazine*, Sep-Oct 1996, pp. 12-14.

113 MG Fred F. Marty, "State-of-the-Branch 1992," *Field Artillery Magazine*, Dec 1992, pp. 1-3.

114 US Army Modernization Plan, Vol II, Annex G, Jan 1993, G27, Modernization Plan File, HRDC.

115 E-mail msg with atch, subj: Manuscript Review, 8 Dec 2003, p. 75, HRDC; U.S Army Posture Statement for FY95, p. 84, Posture Statement File, HRDC; 1991 USAFACFS ACH, p. 184; US Army Modernization Plan, Vol II, Annex G, Jan 1993, pp. G2-G6, Modernization Plan File, HRDC; 1994 TRADOC ACH, pp. 136-38.

116 Fact Sheet, subj: AN/TPQ-37 Firefinder Weapon Locating System, undated, Firefinder File, HRDC; 1986 USAFACFS Annual Historical Review (AHR), pp. 88-91; US Army Modernization Plan, Jan 1993, Vol II, G16, Modernization Plan File, HRDC.

117 LTC Robert M. Hill, "Future Watch: Target Acquisition and Precision Attack Systems," *Field Artillery Magazine*, Jan-Feb 1996, pp.18-21; "Field Artillery Equipment and Munitions Update," *Field Artillery Magazine*, Dec 1990, p. 53; Input to the Commanding General's Monthly Update to TRADOC, 15 Feb 1991, HRDC; Interview, Dastrup with Ron Anderson, TRADOC System Manager (TSM) Target Acquisition, 7 Mar 1991, HRDC; Fact Sheet, subj: Firefinder Radar Product Improvement Programs, 23 Jun 1995, HRDC; Interview, Dastrup with Ron Anderson, TSM Target Acquisition, 11 Mar 1996, HRDC; Fact Sheet, subj: Firefinder Radars, AN/TPQ-36 and 37, 21 Feb 1995, HRDC; Memorandum for BG Dean R. Ertwine, subj: Suspension of Q36(V)8 Fielding, 7 Jan 1999, HRDC; Interview, Dastrup with Ron Anderson, Firefinder Program Manager, TSM Target Acquisition, 17 Feb 1999, HRDC; Interview, Dastrup with Gordon Wehri, Chief, Target Acquisition Branch, Materiel, Requirements, and Integration Division, DCD, 6 Mar 2000, HRDC; Fact Sheet, subj: Firefinder, 21 Jan 1999, Firefinder File, HRDC.

118 Hill, "Future Watch," pp. 18-21; Baxter, "Meeting the Future," pp. 1-6; Fact Sheet, subj: ATACS/COBRA Program, 3 Sep 1991, HRDC; Fact Sheet, subj: ATACS, 14 Jan 1992, HRDC; Fact Sheet, subj: ATACS, 3 Sep 1991, HRDC; Interview, Dastrup with Anderson, 17 Feb 1999, HRDC; 1996 USAFACFS ACH, pp. 146-47; 1997 USAFACFS ACH, p. 96; Interview, Dastrup with Wehri, 6 Mar 2000, HRDC; Operational Requirements Document for the AN/TPQ-47 Firefinder Radar, Nov 1999, HRDC; Fact Sheet, subj: Firefinder AN/TPQ-47 (formerly AN/TPQ-37 P3I Block II), undated, Firefinder File, HRDC; Fact Sheet, subj: AN/TPQ-37 Firefinder Artillery Locating Radar, undated, Firefinder File, HRDC. The replacement system for the Q-37 went through several different names: the Advanced Target Acquisition Counterfire System in 1990-1991, the Advanced Firefinder System in 1992, the Firefinder AN/TPQ-37 Block II Pre-planned Product Improvement Program in 1993, the AN/TPQ-37 Block II in 1996, and the AN/TPQ -47 in 1998.

119 Fact Sheet, subj: Bradley Fighting Vehicle System, 9 Aug 2002, Bradley Fire Support Team (BFIST) File, HRDC; Fact Sheet, subj: M2/M3 Series Bradley Fighting Vehicle, 9 Aug 2002, BFIST File, HRDC; Fact Sheet, subj: Bradley Fighting Vehicle Upgrade, 26 Mar 2002, BFIST File, HRDC; Scott Gourley, "M7 Bradley Fire Support Team Vehicle," *Army*, Jul 2002, pp. 51-52.

120 Fact Sheet, subj: Bradley Fighting Vehicle (M2A3), 26 Nov 2001, BFIST File, HRDC; Fact Sheet, subj: BFIST Upgrade, 26 Mar 2002, BFIST File, HRDC; Gourley, "M7 Bradley Fire Support Team Vehicle," pp. 51-52; Fact Sheet, subj: MA2A3 and M3A3 Bradley Fighting Vehicle Systems, 9 Aug 2002, BFIST File, HRDC; Fact Sheet, subj: The A3 Bradley Fighting Vehicle,

undated, BFIST File, HRDC; E-mail, subj: BFIST/Striker, 27 Feb 2002, HRDC; Interview, Dastrup with CPT Robert S. Hribar, Material and Training Integration Division, FDIC, 19 Feb 2002, HRDC; Fact Sheet, subj: Bradley Program Overview, 5-7 Jun 2001, HRDC; Fact Sheet, subj: BFIST, 2002, HRDC; Memo, subj: None, undated, HRDC; 2000 USAFACFS ACH, pp. 141-43.

121 2000 USAFACFS ACH, pp. 144-45; 2001 USAFACFS ACH, p. 108; 2003 USAFACFS ACH, p. 108; DA, Procurement Programs (Extract), FY 2003 Budget Estimate, Feb 2002, p. 396; MG Michael D. Maples, "2002 State of the Field Artillery," *Field Artillery Magazine*, Nov-Dec 2002, p. 4; Interview, Dastrup with MAJ Neil J. Hamill, Material Requirements and Integration Division, DCD, 17 Feb 1998, HRDC; "BFIST is on the Way," *Field Artillery Magazine*, May-Jun 1997, p. 45; Msg, subj: Answers to Questions, 18 Feb 1998, HRDC; "Striker/Reconnaissance Team," *Field Artillery Magazine*, Jan-Feb 1996, p. 38.

122 Fact Sheet, subj: M109A6 Paladin Self-propelled Howitzer, undated, HRDC; Fact Sheet, subj: Paladin Self-propelled Howitzer, M109A6, undated, HRDC; Fact Sheet, subj: Paladin, undated, HRDC; Fact Sheet, subj: Paladin 155-mm. Self-propelled Howitzer, undated, HRDC; Fact Sheet, subj: M109A6 Paladin Self-propelled Howitzer, undated, HRDC; 1992 USAFACFS ACH, pp. 131-41; 1993 USAFACFS ACH, pp. 125-36; 2003 USAFACFS ACH, p. 8; LTC Kerry J. Loudenslager and CPT Ryan J. LaPorte, "Paladin Platoon Operations versus Battery Operations," *Field Artillery Magazine*, Jan-Feb 2001, pp. 16-19.

123 E-mail atch, subj: LW155, 1 Mar 2001, HRDC; Andrew Koch, "General Dynamics to Develop TAD System," *Jane's Defense Weekly*, 27 Sep 2000, p. 8, HRDC; E-mail, subj: LW 155 Info, 16 Feb 2001, HRDC; Fact Sheet, subj: Towed Artillery Digitization (TAD), undated, HRDC; "The XM777 Lightweight 155-mm. Howitzer," *Army*, Oct 2000, pp. 303-04, HRDC; Interview, Dastrup with John Yager, TSM Cannon, 16 Feb 2001, HRDC; E-mail with atch, subj: LW155, 7 Mar 2002, HRDC; Interview, Dastrup with Yager, 1 Feb 2002, HRDC; Briefing, subj: LW 155 Howitzer and TAD, 1 Oct 2001, HRDC; Interview, Dastrup with Doug Brown, Dep Dir, TSM Cannon, 4 Feb 2002, HRDC; E-mail with atch, subj: LW 155, 6 Feb 2002, HRDC; E-mail, subj: Program Manager, 6 Feb 2002, HRDC; "Name-that-Howitzer: Crusader, a Knight for the 21st Century," *Field Artillery Magazine,* Dec 94, p. 3. To minimize confusion, the new 155-mm. self-propelled howitzer will be called the Crusader.

124 2000 USAFACFS ACH, pp. 149-50; DA, *Historical Summary for FY 1989*, pp. 228-29.

125 1994 USAFACFS ACH, pp. 200-15.

Chapter Nine
The New Century

The first decade of the 21st century brought an abrupt change to the Field Artillery School. On 11 September 2001, Al Qaeda terrorists flew passenger aircraft into the Twin Towers in New York City and the Pentagon in Washington D.C., killing more than 3,000 civilian and military personnel. In response, the George W. Bush administration launched Operation Enduring Freedom (OEF) in the fall of 2001 to destroy Al Qaeda terrorist training camps in Afghanistan and the Taliban infrastructure that supported Al Qaeda, and later initiated Operation Iraqi Freedom (OIF) in 2003 to eliminate Saddam Hussein as a threat to world peace. For the Field Artillery School, OEF, OIF, the studies on officer and noncommissioned officer education conducted by the Army Training and Leader Development Panel, the overarching need to keep training and education abreast of the times, the Transformation of the Army, and the Base Realignment and Closure (BRAC) process that moved the Air Defense Artillery School from Fort Bliss, Texas, to Fort Sill caused it to restructure training and education and to participate in developing faster methods of fielding new equipment and weapons.

Training the Force

At the beginning of the new century, the US Army Field Artillery School picked up where it had left off at the end of the previous century with its two-phase Field Artillery Captain's Career Course.[1] Specifically, field artillery captains and senior first lieutenants went through a demanding 18-week course. They received the equivalent of two-weeks of common core instruction that all officers received regardless of their branch and 16 weeks of branch tactical, technical, and warfighting instruction. After seven weeks of large-group instruction with a focus on the technical aspects of fire support, such as gunnery, at the beginning of the course, the students moved into small group instruction for the last 11 weeks for tactical instruction led by a small group leader from the Army, the Marine Corps, or an allied officer from Great Britain, Australia, or Canada. The career course prepared officers to serve as a battalion and brigade fire support officer, a battalion, brigade, and division staff officer, and a battery commander. After completing 18 weeks at Fort Sill, the officers then attended the Combined Arms Service Staff Officer Course at Fort Leavenworth, Kansas, for staff officer training and returned to Fort Sill for graduation.[2]

In the meantime, the high attrition rate of captains that forced first lieutenants to become staff officers earlier than ever before and that left fewer branch-qualified captains in units, the introduction of sophisticated command and control systems, the requirement for shared training among captains of all branches, and the necessity for more hands-on training, among other things, encouraged the US Army Training and Doctrine Command (TRADOC) to reexamine its Captain's Career Course. The command had to ensure that the course met the needs of the current and future operational environment.[3]

On 1 November 2000 at a Senior Leader Institutional Transformation Conference, the Commanding General of TRADOC, General John N. Abrams, addressed these critical issues, emphasizing the need to transform the Army's officer education system. Training had to be restructured to stay abreast of the Transformation of the Army that was underway, had to be integrated across battlefield functionality, and had to be organized around the four major components of command (maneuver, maneuver support, maneuver sustainment, and battle command).[4] Although some TRADOC service school commandants were reluctant to relinquish any of their current branch responsibilities to one of the four proposed centers (maneuver, maneuver support, maneuver sustainment, and battle command) where select functions would be consolidated, the TRADOC Chief of Staff, Major General John B. Sylvester, warned, "If these functions do not migrate to Centers, the branches will not transform to a future construct that better underpins The Army Transformation."[5]

Although the details about assimilating training under the four centers remained unclear in 2000, Abrams pushed to reform the officer education system. He wanted to integrate staff instruction into the Captain's Career Course via distance learning without lengthening the course beyond 20 weeks and planned to beam it from Fort Leavenworth to all branch schools by 2004. Given TRADOC's course-length constraints, the Field Artillery School faced the imperative of reducing its Field Artillery Captain's Career Course by four weeks to fit in staff instruction. This would force the elimination of some practical exercises introduced by the Commandant of the Field Artillery School, Major General Toney Stricklin (1999-2001), to make training more rigorous, would tax existing school distance learning classrooms, and would complicate scheduling them, among other things. Equally as important, scheduling distance learning for the staff course would have to accommodate all of TRADOC's branch schools and would have to be based upon when the course could be delivered via distance learning. From the Field Artillery School's vantage point, implementing Abram's proposal seemed daunting and questionable even if it had the potential of improving the career course.[6]

Events soon overcame the Abram's proposed reforms. In May 2001, the Army Training and Leader Development Panel Study of 2000-2001 recommended developing and implementing a new Captain's Career Course. Officer education should furnish combined arms training for all captains and focus on establishing a common Army standard for fighting, leading, and training combined arms units. The career course also should teach common company command skills, should teach battalion- and brigade-level combined arms captain skills, should furnish hands-on, performance-oriented field and simulation training, and should provide captains with opportunities to train with lieutenants and noncommissioned officers. Basically, the study urged making sweeping reforms to the career course to prepare officers better for combat in the 21st century.[7]

After reviewing the study's recommendations, TRADOC outlined a two-phase Captain Officer Education System in October 2001 that made a major departure from the existing Captain's Career Course with its 18 weeks of branch-specific training and six weeks of staff training at Fort Leavenworth. Under the proposed format, all captains would attend a two-phase Combined Arms Battle Command Course. Distance learning would cover common core subjects, while resident training would teach branch-related subjects and prepare them for command. Immediately following this course, captains would attend the Combined Arms Leader Course (renamed Combined Arms Staff Course late in 2002) at Fort Leavenworth for staff and combined arms training with instruction being divided between distance learning and resident training.[8]

A couple of months later in January 2002, TRADOC restructured the sequence of the courses. To provide the right training at the right time and to focus it for the next assignment, the command reversed the order of the courses. Rather than attending Combined Arms Battle Command Course first, all captains would attend the Combined Arms Staff Course first.[9] Prior to taking command, they would attend the Combined Arms Battle Command Course for preparation as commanders. Placing the Combined Arms Staff Course first acknowledged that officers moved from staff officer positions to command and trained them accordingly whereas the previous format failed to take career progression into consideration by moving them from the Combined Arms Battle Command Course to the Combined Arms Staff Course as did the existing Captain's Career Course.[10]

At the end of 2002, TRADOC added another course of action to its Captain Officer Education System. Rather than moving from the Combined Arms Staff Course to the Combined Arms Battle Command Course which would be two separate courses, the command proposed creating one course called the Combined Arms Battle Command Course of 14 weeks. While part of the course would be conducted through distance learning, such as common core (three weeks) and branch tactical and technical training (three weeks), six weeks of combined arms operations would be held at a branch school. Subsequently, the captains would undergo training for two weeks a Combat Training Center as a temporary duty assignment and then move to the unit of assignment.[11]

Each course of action had strong points. Both synchronized a captain's training with duty position, made training available upon demand through distance learning, involved the commander more in leader development and career management than before, increased competence in staff and command positions, and reduced personnel and family turbulence. In view of this, TRADOC proposed to run pilot courses of both options with a full implementation scheduled in 2006.[12]

With support from the Chief of Staff of the Army, the new Commanding General of TRADOC, General Kevin P. Brynes, stopped work on the courses in the summer of 2003. After talking with his senior leaders who believed that the proposed education system for captains would degrade training and feeling the reduction of funding when the government started shifting resources to OIF and OEF, Byrnes directed his commandants to design a viable alternative by the middle of 2004, to continue running the existing Captain's Career Course and the staff course, and to modify and update their programs of instruction by incorporating lessons learned from OIF and OEF.[13]

Although the viable alternative was never designed, the Field Artillery Captain's Career Course underwent a significant change in May 2004. Through that month field artillery captains moved from Fort Sill to Fort Leavenworth for the Combined Arms

Services Staff School Course for generalized staff training of six weeks after completing branch training. To eliminate repetitive instruction, reduce costs, and minimize time away from operational assignments and families that this format created, Secretary of the Army Les Brownlee (2003-2004) approved merging the staff course and the career course. As a result, TRADOC discontinued the staff course after the last class graduated in May 2004 and directed its service schools to expand their career courses. Based upon this tasking, the Field Artillery School increased its career course from 18 weeks (711 hours of instruction) to 20 weeks (781 hours of instruction) by assimilating tasks from the staff course. This action ended the two-phase course and cut the Field Artillery Captain's Career Course's direct ties to Fort Leavenworth.[14]

Though the course's format remained the same over the next several years, training reflected the operational environment of OIF and OEF. After large-group instruction at the beginning of the course on gunnery, advanced fire direction officer responsibilities, the Advanced Field Artillery Tactical Data System, and the Multiple-Launch Rocket System, the students moved into the small group instruction for 13 weeks for tactical and staff instruction. In three blocks of instruction (battery, gunnery, and combined arms warfare), the career course furnished practical exercises on counterinsurgency tasks and field artillery core competencies to develop agile and adaptive leaders who were also technically proficient to serve as a battery commander, a battalion and brigade fire support officer, a field artillery battalion fire direction officer, and a battalion, brigade, division, and brigade staff officer and were capable of providing leadership in full-spectrum operations. Equally as important, the course prepared officers to integrate lethal and non-lethal effects, such as psychological operations and tactical information operations, to support the maneuver commander.[15]

Meanwhile, influenced by the requirement for more hands-on training, better digital training with the fielding of sophisticated command and control systems, and shared training opportunities by officers, the Army acknowledged the imperative of restructuring training for newly commissioned second lieutenants to keep it relevant. With this in mind, the Chief of Staff of the Army, General Eric K. Shinseki, tasked Abrams, in June 2000 to convene an Army Training and Leader Development Panel to review, assess, and provide recommendations for developing training for the 21st century. Among other recommendations, the study, released on 25 May 2001 after about 13,000 officers, soldiers, and family members had been surveyed and after extensive interviews had been conducted, urged reforming the officer education system. The Army had to facilitate career-long, progressive, and sequential leader development and prepare leaders to operate in a new strategic environment characterized by regional threats, full-spectrum operations, and information-age technology. Just as important, the quality and relevance of the Army's Officer Education System failed to meet the expectations of many officers and did not satisfactorily train them in combined arms skills or support the bonding, cohesion, and rapid team building required in full-spectrum operations. The Army missed shared training opportunities in its officer education system because training company grade officers was too branch-oriented.[16]

McNair Hall (post HQ) in 2003

To eliminate this deficiency the study urged developing and implementing a two-phase officer basic course to replace the existing officer basic course for second lieutenants. Phase one should provide basic small unit combat training and common core training to all second lieutenants at a central location and focus on warfighting and the warrior ethos. Phase two should furnish platoon-level, branch-specific training in tactical and technical skills. Ultimately, this training would create tactically and technically proficient second lieutenants (small unit leaders) with common bonds, a shared training experience, and a warrior ethos.[17]

Based upon the recommendations of an internal TRADOC study of early 2001 and the Army Training and Leader Development Panel study of May 2001, the basic course underwent critical changes in 2001. In mid-year, TRADOC announced implementing a two-phase Basic Officer Leader Course in 2003. Basic Officer Leader Course Phase One would immediately follow commissioning. Newly commissioned second lieutenants would attend it. Here, they would receive common-core training in ethics, leadership, and the warrior ethos, to name a few subjects. Afterward, they would attend Basic Officer Leader Course Phase Two at a branch school for branch-specific training. Altogether, the two-phase course would not exceed 19 weeks and four days of instruction (the current length of the Officer Basic Course) as mandated by the Army to get second lieutenants to the operational forces as quickly as possible.[18]

For the Field Artillery School and other TRADOC branch schools, the Basic Officer Leader Course Phase Two format meant decreased technical training in an increasingly technical environment. Directed by TRADOC, the Field Artillery School created a Basic Officer Leader Course Phase Two program of instruction in 2001 by squeezing 19 weeks and four days of training from its Field Artillery Officer Basic Course into 13 weeks and four days.[19]

To reach the directed course length, a school working group abolished instruction in some tasks entirely, reduced the time allotted to some tasks, such as manual gunnery, and cut back on the time devoted to some TRADOC common core subjects, among other things. Even though this program of instruction of 13 weeks and four days met TRADOC and Army guidelines concerning course length, it would not produce second lieutenants with competency in branch skills because critical field artillery tasks would not be taught to standard. This generated concern among school leaders about the quality of second lieutenants being graduated under this format and sent to operational units and prodded them to press for more training time before implementing Basic Officer Leader Course Phase Two in Fiscal Year 2003.[20]

Although the basic philosophy of the Basic Officer Leader Course remained constant, critical changes reshaped it in 2002 before TRADOC could consider the school's plea for more training time. Basic Officer Leader Course Phase One became the pre-commissioning phase. Basic Officer Leader Course Phase Two became the common core portion of basic leader training; and Basic Officer Leader Course Phase Three became branch-specific training.[21]

The lack of resources soon prompted the Army to move implementing the revamped basic course from Fiscal Year 2003 to Fiscal Year 2006. Initially, the Army had hoped to pull resources from the Captain's Career Course by making it more reliant upon distance learning and less dependent upon institutional training in the school house. Such a move would free up money and instructors for the Basic Officer Leader Course which would require more resources than the existing basic course. When it became clear that the proposed Captain's Career Course reforms would not produce captains to meet the desired standards and were designed for a peacetime environment and not wartime conditions, such as OIF and OEF, the Army put more resources into it by withdrawing them from the basic course. This forced TRADOC to push implementing the Basic Officer Leader Course back until resources could be found.[22]

After obtaining the requisite resources, the Army officially announced on 5 November 2003 that Basic Officer Leader Course Phases One, Two, and Three would start during Fiscal Year 2006. As explained in a Basic Officer Leader Course conference in 2004, the course would develop a corps of mature, confident, and competent second lieutenants who would have a common bond with their combined arms peers and would be ready to lead small units at their first assignment.[23]

Upon receiving official notification late in 2004 that it would be a Basic Officer Leader Course Phase Two site, Fort Sill started developing a six-week pilot course. Based upon guidance, phase two would be tough, rigorous, and physically demanding with 80 to 90y percent of the training being executed in a field environment. To support training, Fort

Sill and the Field Artillery School built and renovated the required facilities and procured equipment and texts.[24]

As Fort Sill worked in 2005 to furnish the facilities and equipment necessary for phase two, to identify requirements to support the training, and to build a forward operating base that would increase training time, facilitate continuous operations, reduce down time, and replicate the contemporary operational environment, TRADOC furnished additional guidance. On 19 July 2005, it announced that the number of sites for Basic Officer Leader Course Phase Two had been reduced from four (Fort Benning, Georgia; Fort Knox, Kentucky; Fort Bliss, Texas; and Fort Sill) to two because the Base Realignment Commission 2005 recommended transferring air defense artillery training from Fort Bliss to Fort Sill and armor training from Fort Knox to Fort Benning. This meant that a Basic Officer Leader Course Phase Two would be moved from Fort Bliss to Fort Sill and that the Field Artillery School would train more phase two students than initially planned and had to increase the number of classes per year from eight to 16 to accommodate the load.[25]

The Basic Officer Leader Course Phase Two became a reality in 2006. On 4 June 2006, the school implemented phase two training developed by TRADOC and the Infantry School. During the first week, the lieutenants assumed leadership responsibilities for in-processing. The cadre issued them an operational order that required them to draw new equipment, participate in medical screening and physicals, update their financial and medical records, complete pre-combat inspections and counseling, and close with an after action report. In the second week, the students went through troop leading procedures and basic marksmanship rifle training. The following week, they learned about US small arms weapons and other equipment and became proficient in firing the M2 Browning .50 caliber heavy machine gun. In the fourth week, the lieutenants received combat orders while living in a realistic forward operating base. They went through decentralized operations by platoons or squads and learned to protect the force during tactical movements. In week five during the urban operations exercise, the lieutenants had hand-to-hand combat training (combatives), while they conducted 24-hour operations in the contemporary operational environment in week six.[26] According to the Field Artillery School, phase two accomplished its goal. It produced competent second lieutenants who were ready for leadership positions in small units and provided solid training in ethics, the warriors ethos, and other critical subjects.[27] Thus, its future appeared to be bright.[28]

In the meantime, the Field Artillery School developed the branch-oriented Basic Officer Leader Course Phase Three. After extensive analysis, the school outlined a 20-week (19 weeks and 4 days) course in its initial proposal to TRADOC. Such a length which was the same as the existing Field Artillery Officer Basic Course would permit training field artillery second lieutenants to standard in all critical tasks. This meant that field artillery second lieutenants would spend a total of 25 weeks and four days in phases two and three before reaching their operational units.[29]

Because this length exceeded the 20-week limitation for phases two and three set by the Army, the school had to reduce phase three training to 15 weeks and four days. The school eliminated less critical tasks and planned to furnish assignment-oriented training of varying lengths for second lieutenants who were projected to be assigned to a Paladin 155-mm. self-propelled howitzer, a Bradley Fire Support Team Vehicle, a Multiple-Launch Rocket System/High Mobility Artillery Rocket System, or a Stryker unit. Although the 15-week and four-day course meant that some critical tasks would not be taught to standard, TRADOC approved it in June 2005 and sent it to the Army for approval even though the Army still stood firm on 13 weeks and four days for phase three.[30]

The Field Artillery School clearly understood the challenges associated with the 15-week and four-day course. With the reduction in the number of hours from 724 to 629, the school focused the course on towed artillery to furnish a foundation for mechanized field artillery that would be taught through assignment-oriented training and had less time to train field artillery second lieutenants in core competencies of a platoon leader, fire support officer, and fire direction officer. With less training time, the school prioritized the tasks to be taught to produce leaders who would be capable of performing in the contemporary operational environment of OIF or OEF, would be adaptive leaders, and would be competent field artillery officers.[31]

At the end of 2005, the school acknowledged the need for further sacrifice because TRADOC had not yet approved assignment-oriented training even though it had tentatively approved the 15-week and four-day program of instruction for phase three and because the Army had not yet approved it. If TRADOC failed to endorse assignment-oriented training, the school planned to provide tracked training of two weeks for the Paladin, Bradley Fire Support Team Vehicle, Multiple-Launch Rocket System, High Mobility Artillery Rocket System, and towed artillery during the 15 weeks and four days. This training would be based upon the first unit of assignment following phase three and meant cutting additional time from critical tasks. If the Army did not approve the 15-week and four-day course, the school outlined dedicating the 13-week and four-day variant to only field artillery core competencies of field artillery platoon leader, company fire support officer, and fire direction officer and eliminating tracked training, among other tasks. For the school, the 13-week and four-day course created unacceptable risk and would not produce competent field artillery second lieutenants.[32]

Fortunately, the sacrifice did not have to be made. Recognizing that the Field Artillery School would take a 33 percent cut in length for phase three, the Assistant Commandant of the School, Colonel James M. MacDonald (2005-2006), petitioned TRADOC for 15 weeks and four days of training time. In January 2006, TRADOC agreed and permitted two weeks of assignment-oriented training. Subsequently, the Army approved the 15-week and four-day Basic Officer Leader Course Phase Three with assignment-oriented training courses on the Paladin, Multiple-Launch Rocket System, High Mobility Artillery Rocket System, or Bradley Fire Support Team Vehicle that would come afterward. While phase three's program of instruction would center on light or towed artillery, the assignment-oriented training would furnish the required training for mechanized systems. Ultimately, the reduction in course length from 19 weeks and four days to 15 weeks and four days degraded manual and automated gunnery training. Field Artillery School conducted its first Basic Officer Leader Course Phase Three in September 2006 to replace the Field Artillery

Officer Basic Course that ended when class 4-06 graduated on 23 August 2006.[33]

Even though Basic Officer Leader Courses Phases Two and Three produced adaptive leaders, rising costs prompted the Commanding General of TRADOC to eliminate them, to transfer phase two tasks to phase three or the future unit of assignment, and to create a Basic Officer Leader Course B. In August 2009, TRADOC e-mailed subordinate commands, including the Field Artillery School, that the last phase two classes would report on 1 November 2009 and graduate on 19 December 2009, that the last phase three classes would report on 10 January 2010, and that phase three would be converted to the Basic Officer Leader Course B in February 2010. As of 2011, the Field Artillery School's Basic Officer Leader Course B which started in February 2010 included common core subjects, branch-specific training, and some tasks transferred from the Basic Officer Leader Course Phase Three and lasted 19 weeks and four days.[34]

As the Field Artillery School pressed to introduce Basic Officer Leader Course Phases Two and Three, the Army released its Warrant Officer Education System Study on 18 July 2002 conducted by the Army Training and Leader Development Panel. Among other things, the study pointed out the Army's reliance upon the expertise of warrant officers for many years and the need to make fundamental changes in the warrant officer corps to support full spectrum operations and the imperative of building upon the Warrant Officer Leader Development Action Plan of 1992 that had improved training, personnel management, and leader development programs.[35] The heart of the study's recommendations focused on integrating warrant officers completely into the officer corps, a process that had begun in 1985 with the Total Warrant Officer Study. However, integration was never completed because warrant officers were still recruited, assessed, managed, educated, and retained separately from commissioned officers.[36]

Although the panel's study of 2002 outlined various options for integrating warrant officers into the officer corps, it centered on developing a shared training experience with officers.[37] Following up upon this and the Army Modernization Plan's proposal to produce warrant officers and officers who were bonded and grounded in the fundamentals of leadership and possessed sound conceptual and interpersonal skills, the Army Training Directorate and TRADOC developed a plan of action. On 9 November 2005, the Chief of Staff of the Army announced the Army's intention of integrating warrant officers into Basic Officer Leader Course Phase Two training. While TRADOC wanted integration initiated in Fiscal Year 2010 to give time for study and implementation, the Army proposed Fiscal Year 2009.[38]

Regardless of when integration would begin, the Commander of the 428th Field Artillery Brigade in the Field Artillery School which would be responsible for the training, Colonel Kevin M. Batule, explained in 2007 as planning moved into high gear about the need for more resources. Integrating warrant officers into the Basic Officer Leader Course Phase Two would require adding two more phase two companies at Fort Benning and Fort Sill and more battalion staff to support the increased student load that would grow by about 1,000 students. Despite the requirement for more resources, the Army Deputy Chief of Staff, G3/5/7, signed a memorandum in May 2008 directing incorporating warrant officers into the Basic Officer Leader Course Phase Two in the third quarter of Fiscal Year 2009 to end all speculation about when it would happen.[39]

Rising costs made this decision moot when the Commanding General of TRADOC announced in July 2009 its intention to cancel Basic Officer Leader Course Phases Two and Three to save money. Thus, efforts to integrate warrant officer training into officer training came to a haltwhen the Field Artillery School started the Basic Officer Leader Course B in February 2010 that was a merger of Basic Officer Leader Courses Phases Two and Three.[40]

Concurrently, the school reexamined educating field artillery warrant officers for the first time since 1996 when it conducted an extensive job and task analysis for the Warrant Officer Basic Course. As Chief Warrant Officer Four Stephen A. Gomes, the Program Manager for the Warrant Officer Education System in the school, explained in January 2003, the job and task analysis would determine what should be eliminated from the course's program of instruction, what should remain, and what Army Training and Leader Development Panel recommendations should be included in the course.[41]

After completion of the job and task analysis, restructuring the basic course moved forward in a significant way. Late in 2005, the Commandant of Field Artillery School, Major General David C. Ralston (2005-2007), approved forming a team to revise the program of instruction for the Warrant Officer Basic Course and the Warrant Officer Advance Course to make them more relevant. Of the two, the basic course received higher priority and more attention and underwent greater change.[42]

For the most part, the recommendations centered on shifting the basic course's focus. The most significant recommendations included increasing the emphasis on targeting and intelligence integration, reducing the emphasis and training on the duties and responsibilities on the AN/TPQ-36 and AN/TPQ-37 radars, and providing more training on managerial responsibilities of a suite of systems in general, such as the duties of the newly created target acquisition platoon leader position. Besides implementing the team's recommendations, the school added instruction on collateral damage estimation and precision targeting to prepare students for the operational environment of Afghanistan and Iraq. Other classes, such as electronic warfare to defeat suicide bombers and improvised explosive devices in a counterinsurgency environment, were added to the basic course to shift it from its previous focus on radars.[43]

The most significant reform expanded the basic course's targeting phase from nine to 17 weeks for enhanced training. Lengthening the targeting phase meant adjusting the basic course's three training phases of targeting, radar operations, and radar maintenance over a period of time. In 2006, the school increased the targeting phase from nine to 12 weeks. Early in 2007, the school lengthened the targeting phase from 12 to 15 weeks. Subsequently, the school adopted the objective 17-week model in February 2008. Adjusting the length of the targeting phase came at a cost. To furnish 17 weeks of targeting training without increasing course length, the school gradually reduced radar maintenance training from 20 weeks in 2006 to 12 weeks in June 2007. Reducing maintenance training continued over the next several years. In 2010 the school decreased radar operations and radar maintenance to seven weeks, added a target acquisition platoon leader module, expanded the capstone exercise to two weeks, and planned to implement the changes in July 2011.[44]

Meanwhile, the Field Artillery School revamped its noncommissioned officer courses. Directed by the Chief of Staff of the Army, General Eric K. Shinseki, in June 2000, Abrams formed the Army Training and Leader Development Panel to review, assess, and provide recommendations for training and developing 21st century Army leaders, including noncommissioned officers. Among other issues addressed, the panel's noncommissioned officer study of May 2002 indicated the need to improve the Noncommissioned Officer Education System.[45]

In view of the disaster with shake-and-bake noncommissioned officers with little training and experience during the Vietnam War, the Army established the Noncommissioned Officer Education System in 1970 to prepare noncommissioned officers to lead and train soldiers and designed it as a progressive, sequential, task-based training system to prepare them for assignments at their grade level. Although the system satisfied Cold War requirements and taught the technical and tactical skills needed for the noncommissioned officer's role on the conventional battlefield, it did not adequately teach the conceptual and interpersonal skills for full-spectrum operations in the 21st century's operational environment. Basically, the Noncommissioned Officer Education System was a rigid, task-based system and designed around the select-train-promote model with a one-size-fits-all approach to training and educating. The Noncommissioned Officer Education System, according to the panel, had to provide more hands-on, performance-oriented, field-based, practical-exercise, scenario-based training and education than presently offered.[46]

Early in 2004, the Commanding General of TRADOC, General Kevin P. Byrnes, directed redesigning the Noncommissioned Officer Education System to satisfy the panel's recommendations, to be relevant to an Army at war, to integrate combat experience into its program of instruction, and to be synchronized with Army initiatives. This meant training and educating noncommissioned officers in full-spectrum operations and the operational environment of Afghanistan and Iraq and including the appropriate training and education on combined arms warfare. Moreover, Byrnes wanted the system to be modular so that training could be supplied in TRADOC's schools or through distance learning to soldiers anywhere in the world through the Internet and to furnish assignment oriented training to prepare the soldier for the next assignment.[47] Subsequently on 27 February 2004, the Commanding General of the Combined Arms Center, a subordinate command to TRADOC, issued more specific guidance. Lieutenant General William S. Wallace wanted programs of instruction to reflect lessons learned from OIF and OEF by 1 October 2004 to ensure currency.[48]

To satisfy the guidance, the Noncommissioned Officer Academy revamped training. In 2004-2005, it integrated lessons learned from Iraq and Afghanistan into lesson plans for each military occupational specialty in the Primary Leadership Development Course, the Basic Noncommissioned Officer Course, and the Advanced Noncommissioned Officer Course and introduced cultural awareness training. The academy also added improvised explosive device training in the basic course and the primary course in the form of a slide presentation and a practical exercise and introduced training on traffic control points. In the primary course the academy initiated combative training (hand-to-hand combat), pugilistic stick fighting, and training on entering and clearing buildings, among other tasks. For training on the operational environment, the academy provided classroom instruction in the three courses and later established field training on the contemporary operational environment in all courses.[49]

Based upon after action reviews with students with recent combat experience in OIF and OEF about the need to integrate lessons learned into the programs of instruction more thoroughly and the need to ensure technical competency in core field artillery skills, the Field Artillery School under the Assistant Commandant, Colonel James M. McDonald, continued reforming noncommissioned officer education in 2005-2006. This endeavor involved refining tactics, techniques, and procedures for the war on terrorism and ensuring the preservation of technical competency that was being lost because of the non-standard missions, such as patrolling, in OIF and OEF. To prevent increasing the length of the courses, the school and Noncommissioned Officer Academy made some of the instruction self-study, such as the Army sexual assault prevention and response program, and reduced the time spent on other training, such as on the precision lightweight receiver. This permitted integrating live-fire training in Military Occupational Specialties 13B30/13B40 (Cannon crewmember) and 13M (Multiple-Launch Rocket System Crewmember) in the Basic Noncommissioned Officer Course in 2007.[50]

As the training and educational reforms of the first decade of the 21st century indicated, the school moved from its Cold War orientation of the last years of the 20th century to supporting the war on terrorism. Although officer, warrant officer, and noncommissioned officer training still taught core field artillery competencies of fire support, among other subjects, it became increasingly focused on training field artillerymen for OIF and OEF.

Resetting the Force and New Competencies

Introducing a live-fire exercise into the noncommissioned officer basic course in 2007 reflected a growing concern on the part of the school, the academy, and the Army about the competency of field artillerymen. During the first years of the 21st century, the Field Artillery performed a wide variety of missions during OIF and OEF. Initial operations in OIF and OEF in 2001-2003 provided field artillery units with opportunities to perform their traditional missions of synchronizing and delivering timely cannon, rocket, and missile fires to support the maneuver forces. After 2003, patrolling, providing base defense, and convoy operations, generally called non-standard missions, dominated the Field Artillery's time with only a few units furnishing fire support missions.[51]

As outlined in the Army Campaign Plan Update of 20 July 2006, the Vice Chief of Staff of the Army recognized that field artillerymen were not performing their traditional missions and feared the deterioration of their fire support skills. He responded by directing TRADOC and the Field Artillery School to assess the state of competency of field artillery lieutenants to determine if non-standard missions in Iraq and Afghanistan had degraded their basic branch skills and if they required additional or refresher training.[52]

Tasked to look at the state of training for lieutenants by the Army and TRADOC, the Field Artillery School surveyed field artillery tactical commanders, school instructors, and students at the Field Artillery Captain's Career Course in July 2006 to determine how seriously field artillery skills had been degraded and issued its findings and solutions. The school found that non-standard mission assignments had an adverse impact on the junior officers' ability to retain branch core competency skills in both the Army and Marine Corps. Lieutenants had lost branch technical skills of fire direction, fire support, and weapon-specific platoon leader skills as a result of the non-standard missions. Thus, junior officers lacked tactical and technical proficiency to be promoted to more senior levels of responsibility. On the positive side, non-standard missions reinforced leader skills.[53]

The same survey also took the liberty of examining the impact of non-standard missions on noncommissioned officers, majors, and sections, platoons, batteries, and battalions. As the Commanding General of the US Army Field Artillery Center and Fort Sill, Major General David C. Ralston (2005-2007), wrote in a memorandum to the Vice Chief of Staff of the Army on 7 August 2006, leaders at all levels have experienced the atrophy of field artillery-specific skills. Field grade officers and senior noncommissioned officers also experienced diminished field artillery skills. The ability of field artillery officers and noncommissioned officers to perform core tasks was questionable after executing non-standard missions and being away from traditional field artillery missions.[54]

In that same memorandum, Ralston outlined ways of addressing the problem by retraining (resetting) soldiers, officers, and units in field artillery core competencies. The Field Artillery School could increase the length of the Field Artillery Captain's Career Course. This would furnish more time to retrain senior first lieutenants and captains in branch core competencies after having limited or no tactical experience with these functions in their first assignment. Also, the school could bring entire battalions back to proficiency after spending 18 or more months performing non-field artillery missions. This could be accomplished by sending mobile training teams to unit locations as necessary or using the Fires Knowledge Network to provide "reach back" capability through lesson plans, interactive multimedia training products, and other materials via the computer and Internet to soldiers and units in the field.[55]

As a means of implementing retraining options, Ralston chartered the Field Artillery War on Terrorism Reset Task Force on 23 August 2006 to develop a concept plan to reset the Field Artillery force. Assigned this mission, the task force envisioned institutional and unit training as the primary means of resetting the Field Artillery. From the task force's perspective, the Noncommissioned Officer Education System, Officer Education System, and Warrant Officer Education System had to focus more on core field artillery and leader skills than they had done in recent years, while unit training had to be tailored to each unit's needs. In a briefing to the TRADOC Deputy Commanding General, Lieutenant General Thomas F. Metz, on 2 October 2006, the task force outlined using paper-based training support packages, mobile training teams, video teleconferences, and web-based distance learning packages, among other things, for unit reset training. For unit-oriented reset training to succeed, however, each unit had to determine its needs so that the school could identify the training products, assets, and methods, obtain funding, and prioritize training (Who gets what and when.).[56]

While institutional training was still basically a one-size-fits-all approach, unit training support required a totally different methodology. This training revolved around "reach-back" services and mobile training teams. "Reach-back" capabilities exploited the Internet. By logging onto the Army Knowledge Network, soldiers could access more than 1,000 hours of interactive multi-media training subdivided by military occupation specialty and skill level. For more robust training needs, the school provided mobile training teams. Unlike the normal mobile training team designed for new equipment training that taught a specific program of instruction, reset mobile training teams geared their training to the unit's needs. For example, one team taught refresher training on manual and automated gunnery to the 18th Fires Brigade at Fort Bragg, North Carolina. Another team trained the 2d Battalion, 8th Field Artillery Regiment at Fort Wainwright, Alaska, on manual gunnery, survey, the Advanced Field Artillery Tactical Data System, and the countermortar radar.[57]

Reset efforts continued unabated in 2008. Reset mobile training teams supplied training to noncommissioned officers in all field artillery military occupational skills, instructed the trainer, and developed subject matter expertise to help field artillery units to regain their core skills. One team trained master gunners to ensure that the commander had a weapon system expert on training, safety, ammunition, resupply, and maintenance operation. Having a qualified master gunner gave a battalion an individual with the skills to help reset the unit. Besides training master gunners, teams trained 15 active component and National Guard field artillery battalions as well as 18 batteries at unit home stations and in theater on tasks ranging from manual and automated gunnery to crew drill for the M198 towed 155-mm, howitzer.[58]

With help from TRADOC, the Commandant of the Field Artillery School, Major General Peter M. Vangjel (2007-2009), funded two contract mobile training teams – the Battery and Below Mobile Training Team and the Collective Training Evaluation Team – at the end of 2008. For the reset effort, this was a major breakthrough. Through 2008, the school took resources from other activities to fund the teams. In some instances, the school employed instructors from the instructional base to fill out teams.[59]

Both teams pressed to restore fires warfighting skills and field artillery core competencies and began unit training in 2009. While the battery and below mobile training team focused on leader training and train-the-trainer instruction covering cannon battery operations, the collective training evaluation team concentrated on collective and leader training on core field artillery skills and tasks at the platoon, battery, and battalion levels. Specifically, the collective training evaluation team deployed to the home station and developed, planned, and executed platoon, battery, and battalion fire support element/fire support team, combat observation lasing team, and fire direction center training. Such training through 2011 enhanced a unit's ability to operate within a full-spectrum environment.[60]

The need to reset officer and noncommissioned officer fire support skills also led to expanding the length of the Captain's Career Course, the Basic Noncommissioned Officer Course, the Advanced Noncommissioned Officer Course, and the Pre-Command Course for fires brigade and brigade combat team commanders in 2008. The same year, the Captain's Career Course went through its third major redesign in as many years to keep it relevant. The first redesign of February 2006 met the challenges, demands, and skill sets required by the operating environment. Implemented in February 2008, the second met the challenges of a corps of young officers who lacked field artillery experience and aligned the program of instruction with emerging doctrine, incorporated lessons learned from past redesigns, and revamped training to stay abreast of the changing operating environment. This involved adding a new command and control module, more in-depth instruction on coordinating non-lethal fires, updated counterinsurgency operations theory, planning and application instruction, and practical exercises to furnish the students with instruction and training that could serve in lieu of fire support and field artillery experience that they might have missed in their initial assignments.[61] Atrophy of skills drove the second redesign. Surveys performed by the school in December 2007 identified that two out of three captains who reported to the career course had not performed traditional company-grade field artillery tasks or basic fire support skills that they had learned in the Basic Officer Leader Course Phase Three or the Field Artillery Officer Basic Course.[62]

Even though the redesigns of the Captain's Career Course since 2006 had kept pace with emerging doctrine, three critical gaps still existed in 2008. Because captains had not been performing traditional field artillery skills and had been conducting non-standard missions in OIF or OEF, they lacked competency in core field artillery skills. Also, the course did not provide assignment-oriented training to prepare officers for their next assignment. Last, officers did not have the skills to integrate non-lethal fires required in *Army Field Manual 3-0*. Basically, they required additional training in core competencies and instruction in lethal and non-lethal integration, and needed assignment-oriented training.[63]

To eliminate these training gaps, the Field Artillery School under Vangjel's direction expanded the length of the Captain's Career Course in 2008 (the third redesign) with the first class conducted under the new format starting in 2009. The existing 20-week course did not get past the familiarization level of instruction in many skills and did not reset core field artillery skills. As a result, Vangjel pushed a two-phase expansion program. The first phase or short-term fix expanded the course to 24 weeks. The additional weeks permitted immersing the student officers in practical applications to become experts at coordinating lethal fires at the battalion level and delivering lethal fires at the battery level. Basically, the first phase of expansion fixed two of the three gaps – core competency and assignment-oriented training. The second phase or long-term solution would extend the course to 36 weeks and address the gap of integrating non-lethal fires. According to Vangjel, furnishing non-lethal fires was a field artillery core competency which was supported by the Combined Arms Center Commander, Lieutenant General William B. Caldwell IV, at the Fires Seminar in 2008.[64]

The non-standard missions of OIF and OEF also caused noncommissioned officers' core skills to atrophy. Pre- and post-course surveys conducted by the Quality Assurance

Office at Fort Sill with the students at the Noncommissioned Officer Academy validated this. In fact, some noncommissioned officers felt that they could perform a critical task only with the help of another leader or a graphic aid. As General Richard A. Cody, Vice Chief of Staff of the Army, testified before the US Senate Armed Forces Services Committee on 31 March 2008, soldiers were training for counterinsurgency operations and focusing on the mission of the brigade where they would be serving in Iraq or Afghanistan and were not training for full-spectrum operations.[65]

Because of this, the Noncommissioned Officer Academy at Fort Sill revamped training. Supporting the Field Artillery Campaign Plan of Vangjel, leaders from the Directorate of Training and Doctrine in the Field Artillery School and Noncommissioned Officer Academy submitted a plan through Vangjel to TRADOC to increase the length of Field Artillery Noncommissioned Officer Education System courses to reset soldiers in core skills, to improve skill proficiency, to incorporate additional training, such as non-lethal fires, to address current and emerging core-competency requirements, and to compensate for the reduction in time for unit and self-development training. On 10 July 2008 the Commanding General of TRADOC approved implementation.[66]

Depending upon the Field Artillery military occupational specialty, Noncommissioned Officer Education System courses expanded from one to three weeks. Expansion was the most critical for Military Occupational Specialties 13B, Cannon Platoon Sergeant, and 13D, Field Artillery Tactical Data Systems Specialist, in the Advanced Noncommissioned Officer Course and in Military Occupational Specialties 13B, Cannon Section Chief, and 13F Fire Support Specialist, in the Basic Noncommissioned Officer Course. This expansion promoted mastery of skills rather than familiarization and built adaptive, flexible, and critical-thinking leadership. According to Command Sergeant Major Dean J. Keveles, the Commandant of the Noncommissioned Officer Academy, expanding the courses helped reset core field artillery skills and made graduates more adaptable to the complex operating environment of the 21st century.[67] With pilot courses beginning in May 2009, the expanded courses played a vital role in transforming noncommissioned officer education TRADOC-wide. On 1 October 2009 as directed by TRADOC, the academy's Basic Noncommissioned Officer Course was redesignated as the Advanced Leader Course and Advanced Noncommissioned Officer Course as the Senior Leader Course. Beyond the name changes and the increase in course lengths, the courses shifted the focus from squad to squad/platoon training in the advanced course and from platoon to platoon/battery training in the senior course while 35 hours of the First Sergeant Course were incorporated in the Senior Leader Course with the First Sergeant Course being phased out in January 2010.[68]

As expanding officer, including developing branch-specific training in 2009 for majors before they started the Command and General Staff College, and noncommissioned officer courses and forming mobile training teams to reset units suggested, the Field Artillery School rose to the challenge of training soldiers and units. Responding to the adverse impact that OIF and OEF had upon the Field Artillery, the school initiated aggressive action to restore lost skills by tailoring instruction and training so that field artillerymen could furnish effective fire support.⁶⁹

To adjust to the new warfighting environment in OIF and OEF, the Army meanwhile tasked the US Army Field Artillery Center and Fort Sill to take the lead in the integration of lethal (kinetic) and non-lethal (non-kinetic) fires and effects planning. With the extension of fire support beyond its traditional battlefield role with the addition of non-lethal effects, the Field Artillery School took on the mission of preparing field artillery officers to defend or influence information and information systems and to shape decision making through electronic warfare, psychological operations, military deception, information operations, public affairs, civil affairs, and other non-lethal means to complement lethal means.⁷⁰

For the school, this involved integrating non-lethal instruction in its warrant officer, officer, and noncommissioned officer courses beginning in 2004-2005. School instruction taught officers how to collect and use information and covered tactical information operations, information superiority, effects-based operations, effects-based thinking, the purpose and scope of information operations, offensive and defensive information operations, and the effects planning cycle, among other topics.⁷¹

With information operations growing steadily in importance, the school went beyond adding information operations in its programs of instruction when it created a three-week Tactical Information Operations Course. First offered in 2006 and still taught in 2011, the course trained officers, warrant officers, and noncommissioned officers, including those from the active and reserve components and other military services, to serve as members of an information cell at the brigade combat team and lower, gave them a working knowledge of tactical information operations integration, and provided a practical exercise to validate the students' learning.⁷²

Concurrently, the Army also renewed its interest in electronic warfare as a part of information age warfare and non-lethal warfare. On 30 October 2003, the Department of Defense concluded that electronic warfare capabilities had to be improved to meet advances in the application and the use of the electromagnetic spectrum to deny adversarial situational awareness, to disrupt command and control, and to develop targeting solutions to defeat weapons while protecting the United States' electronic capabilities from being successfully attacked. Subsequently on 15 May 2004, the Commanding General of TRADOC designated the Commanding General of the Combined Arms Center, Fort Leavenworth as the specified proponent for electronic warfare in the Army. Later on 23 November 2004, the Combined Arms Center Commander, Lieutenant General William S. Wallace, designated the Commander of the US Army Field Artillery Center and Fort Sill, renamed US Army Fires Center of Excellence and Fort Sill late in 2005, as the lead for the Army's electronic warfare attack for the brigade, division, and corps and for doctrine, organization, training, material, leadership, personnel, and facilities requirements.⁷³

Under the direction of the Combined Arms Center, and the US Army Intelligence School and Center at Fort Huachuca, Arizona, the Field Artillery School created an electronic warfare course in 2006. The school's Army Operational Electronic Warfare Course awarded an additional skill identifier of 1J upon graduation and trained electronic warfare officers to plan, integrate, synchronize, and execute electronic warfare according to the commander's scheme of maneuver and to assess electronic warfare operations of the brigade combat team, division, and corps electronic warfare cells.[74]

As of 2011, the Army Operational Electronic Warfare Course was one of four electronic warfare courses taught. The Functional Area 29 pilot course began in January 2009 for officers in the career field to train them to be experts in electronic warfare and to be a part of an electronic attack team. Courses for warrant officers and enlisted soldiers began in April 2009.[75]

Developing electronic warfare courses and the Tactical Information Operations Course to train field artillerymen and military personnel from the other US armed services took the Field Artillery School in a new direction. Over the years, field artillery officers and soldiers employed cannon, rocket, and missile fires, close air support, and mortars as lethal fires but had not been doctrinally involved with non-lethal fires, such as information operations and electronic warfare. This changed during the first decade of the 21st century with the creation of non-lethal effects instruction in officer, warrant officer, and noncommissioned officer courses and functional courses. At the 2008 Fires Seminar, the Commander of the Combined Arms Center, Lieutenant General William B. Caldwell IV, told participants that non-lethal fires were now a requirement for the Field Artillery. Reinforcing General Caldwell's position, Vangjel made non-lethal fires a vital part of his vision of the branch. Field Artillery officers and soldiers had to be comfortable integrating information operations, electronic warfare, and psychological operations into the targeting process. Providing non-lethal effects became a core field artillery competency in 2008, continued to be in 2011, and complemented lethal effects according to Brigadier General Thomas S. Vandal (2011-present), the Commandant of the Field Artillery School..[76]

The creation of non-lethal fires as a field artillery competency with accompanying training reflected the imperative of adjusting to the international political scene of the first decade of the 21st century and the war on terrorism. As OIF and OEF revealed, the Field Artillery School could no longer focus on developing field artillerymen whose sole reason for being was providing lethal fires in support of the maneuver arms. The school had to break that paradigm of delivering responsive, lethal fires for a new one of training field artillerymen for full-spectrum operations against an adaptive foe. Twenty-first century field artillerymen required the ability of providing lethal and non-lethal effects to achieve the commander's objective. By training field artillerymen to supply lethal and non-lethal effects, the school introduced a new dimension to the branch and no longer focused solely on kinetic effects in 2011 as it had done through most of its existence.

Base Realignment and Closure 2005, The Fires Center of Excellence, and The Field Artillery School

During the first decade of the 21st century, the base realignment and closure process had a profound impact on the Field Artillery School and Fort Sill. From 1988 through 1995, the Department of Defense closed 112 Army installations and realigned 26 others to create more efficiency and effectiveness within the Army's installation infrastructure. Combined with more than 230 minor actions undertaken during four base realignment and closure rounds, the major closures or realignments reduced much of the Department of Defense's infrastructure and saved billions of dollars through 1995. In view of this resounding achievement, three successive Secretaries of Defense during the remaining years of the 20th century urged further trimming of the military's infrastructure through more base realignment and closure actions. This would save additional billions of dollars annually, free up excess capacity, permit funding facilities that were actually required, support warfighting, and furnish quality-of-life improvements for men and women in the military services. Basically, another base realignment and closure would improve the Department of Defense's ability to improve its warfighting capabilities.[77]

Although the George W. Bush administration wanted to conduct a base realignment and closure in 2003, Congress opposed such action but later approved one in the National Defense Authorization Act for Fiscal Year 2002. This permitted one to be conducted in Fiscal Year 2005. On 15 November 2002, Secretary of Defense Donald Rumsfeld explained that Base Realignment and Closure 2005 would permit reconfiguring the department's infrastructure into one that would maximize warfighting capability and efficiency. Equally important, it would help reshape the military, create multi-mission and multi-service bases, help optimize military readiness, and produce significant monetary savings.[78]

In May 2005, the Base Realignment and Closure 2005 issued its recommendations about Fort Sill's future. Besides closing and relocating Fort Sill's Defense Finance and Accounting Service, moving the installation's Regional Confinement Facility to Fort Leavenworth, Kansas, and relocating the 95th Division (Training) to Fort Sill, the Base Realignment and Closure 2005 proposed moving a fires brigade from Fort Sill to Fort Bliss, Texas, to locate it with existing maneuver units there or those scheduled to be moved there. This action would create space at Fort Sill for transferring an air defense artillery unit from Fort Bliss.[79]

Equally important, the Base Realignment and Closure 2005 recommended relocating the Air Defense Artillery Center and School at Fort Bliss to Fort Sill and co-locating it with the Field Artillery Center and School to form the heart of the Net Fires Center. This would consolidate field artillery and air defense artillery training and doctrine development at a single location, would fit with the TRADOC Maneuver Support Center model at Fort Leonard Wood, Missouri, where the Military Police, Engineer, and Chemical Centers and Schools were co-located, and would functionally align two related branch centers and schools at one location to foster consistency, standardization, and training proficiency. At the same time creating the Net Fires Center would permit the Army to reduce the number of military occupational skills training locations, support Army Transformation by co-locating institutional training, and gain synergy for the two artillery branches.[80]

Upon notification of the Base Realignment and Closure 2005 recommendations for creating a Net Fires Center, renamed the Fires Center of Excellence late in 2005, at Fort Sill, Fort Bliss and Fort Sill quickly developed a plan by mid-July 2005 to co-locate the Air Defense Artillery Center and School with the Field Artillery Center and School at Fort Sill.

The plan proposed merging some functions and organizations if manpower savings could be created while keeping others separate. In keeping with TRADOC Maneuver Support Center model, the draft plan envisioned creating one center staff under a major general and merging the Air Defense Artillery's and Field Artillery's combat development functions into one organization.[81]

Other functions, however, would remain separate. For example, the Air Defense Artillery School and Field Artillery School would remain as separate organizations with each having a brigadier general as a commandant even though some of their training activities would be integrated.[82]

The plan consisted of three phases. During phase one (Fiscal Year 2006), Fort Sill and Fort Bliss would activate a virtual Fires Center of Excellence, would expand the Fires Center of Excellence's staff functions to receive an advance party from the Air Defense Artillery Center, and would start constructing the required facilities for air defense artillery training based upon the availability of the funding. This phase would also include the creation of a collaborative capabilities development integration function for air defense and fire support combat developments. In phase two (Fiscal Year 2007) or the initial operational capability, the Air Defense Artillery School headquarters and elements of initial military training for noncommissioned officers, officers, and warrant officers would move to Fort Sill. Equally as important, a commanding general for the Fires Center of Excellence would be designated. In phase three (Fiscal Year 2008) or full operational capability, Fort Sill and Fort Bliss would complete the realignment of the Air Defense Artillery Center's functions to Fort Sill. In the meantime, one Air Defense Artillery brigade would move from Fort Bliss to Fort Sill while Fort Sill would receive the 95th Training Division (Institutional Training), close its Regional Confinement Facility and Defense Finance and Accounting Service, and transfer a fires brigade to Fort Bliss to enhance training and force stabilization.[83]

As this work began unfolding, TRADOC established a multi-branch Center of Excellence model and a single branch Center of Excellence model in mid-2005. With the colocation of the Air Defense Artillery Center and the Field Artillery Center, Fort Sill would fit into the multi-branch model where the alignment of functions or combined functions would exist. Basically, the multi-branch model provided for a center commander (major general), a general staff that would consolidate the center and installation staffs, and two separate branch schools for functional training. The model also emphasized combining functions and organizations where commonality existed and permitted variance if appropriate.[84] Additionally, the multi-branch Center of Excellence model provided for a basic combat training unit, a Directorate of Training, a Directorate of Training Support, a Directorate of Doctrine and Training Development, and a Capabilities Development and Integration Directorate for combat developments.[85]

Later in 2005, Fort Sill and Fort Bliss announced that their proposed organization for the Fires Center of Excellence deviated from the approved model. First, they merged the center Directorate of Training and Directorate of Training Support functions into one center-level Directorate of Training and Support. This would allow for additional savings in personnel and resources and would execute joint, Army capstone training, doctrine, and lessons learned issues. Second, they created a Directorate of Training and Doctrine at the branch school level. With the current structure of the two schools, merging the separate Directorates of Training and Doctrine into one center-level function as outlined by the TRADOC model would not be practical because the two branches were unique and divergent and because branch-specific lessons learned and training development and doctrine needed to be in the two schools. Their proposal, therefore, provided for a center-level Directorate of Training and Doctrine equivalent and branch-level Directorates of Training and Doctrine. However, Fort Sill and Fort Bliss envisioned merging the two branch-level directorates into one center directorate sometime in the future where all training development and doctrine and lessons learned would be done. Also, they planned to rotate the assignment of the center's commanding general between the Field Artillery and Air Defense Artillery branches on a regular basis.[86]

Subsequently in 2006, Fort Sill and Fort Bliss added a Joint and Combined Integration Directorate at the center. It represented the Army on all joint fires matters, coordinated air support for Army training exercises, instructed all air courses for the Officer Education System, Warrant Officer Education System, and Noncommissioned Officer Education System, and was the proponent for the Joint Fires Observer Course, the Joint Operational Fires and Effects Course, the Joint Theater Air Missile Defense Course, and the Battlefield Coordination Detachment.[87]

As of mid-2006, the Fires Center of Excellence model which was approved by the TRADOC Commanding General, General William S. Wallace, on 14 March 2006 consisted of seven primary center-level organizations that would be capable of executing combined field artillery and air defense artillery missions and were not branch-specific. They included a Noncommissioned Officer's Academy that would be formed by combining the Field Artillery and Air Defense Artillery Noncommissioned Officer Academies to furnish functional training and leader development for noncommissioned officers in Career Management Fields 13 (Field Artillery) and 14 (Air Defense Artillery). Center-level organizations also included the Directorate of Training and Support for center-level administrative tasks; the Directorate of Training and Doctrine for air defense artillery and field artillery doctrine, joint doctrine, and training instruction, among other services; the Capabilities Development and Integration Directorate for capabilities development (combat developments); the Joint and Combined Integration Directorate to link the center to all aspects of joint fires; the Army Training Center for initial military training for all entry-level soldiers and the Basic Officer Leader Course Phase Two; and the branch schools. This organization would give the center three brigades (the 6th Air Defense Artillery Brigade as part of the Air Defense Artillery School, the 428th Field Artillery Brigade as part of the Field Artillery School, and the 434th Field Artillery Brigade for initial military training) and abandoned the multiple Directorates of Training and Doctrine initially proposed late in 2005 in favor of a single center-level Directorate of Training and Doctrine.[88]

Although this model satisfied Base Realignment and Closure 2005 guidance, was approved by the Field Artillery School and Air Defense Artillery School commandants and the Commanding General of TRADOC, and achieved 396 of the TRADOC-directed 412 personnel savings with their three-brigade model, the US Army Manpower Analysis Agency and the TRADOC Deputy Chief of Staff for Resource Management challenged it. Directed by the Secretary of the Army and the Chief of Staff of the Army, the US Army Manpower Analysis Agency visited Fort Sill in March 2006 to study workload and to recommend the most efficient and effective Fires Center of Excellence organization. The agency proposed cutting 614 personnel spaces and creating a one-brigade center. Subsequently, TRADOC's resource management directorate outlined a two-brigade Fires Center of Excellence model in October 2006 to save personnel spaces. It included a noncommissioned officer academy, a basic combat training office for initial entry training, a Directorate of Training, a Directorate of Training Support, a Directorate of Training Development, and a Capabilities Development and Integration Directorate on the center staff.[89]

Because the US Army Manpower Analysis Agency's and Deputy Chief of Staff for Resource Management's proposals saved even more resources, the Field Artillery School and Air Defense School had to justify their Fires Center of Excellence model of three brigades. In a briefing to the Deputy Commanding General of TRADOC, Lieutenant General Thomas F. Metz, on 15 November 2006, the two schools told him that the cuts, especially that suggested by the US Army Manpower Analysis Agency, would create unacceptable risks because the student load would be increasing as the center's personnel strength would be declining. Also, TRADOC resource management directorate's two-brigade proposal would create significant risk in training and combat developments, eliminate subject matter experts from the schools, and jeopardize branch identity. Besides exceeding higher headquarters' savings guidelines, the US Army Manpower Analysis Agency's one-brigade organization would eliminate training and doctrine core functions, dissolve branch identity, among other key issues, and create unacceptable risk. Despite the options that outlined greater savings, Wallace subsequently reaffirmed his approval of the three-brigade organization on 26 January 2007 and the 396 personnel savings.[90]

By mid-2007, Fort Sill and Fort Bliss had their Fires Center of Excellence of three-brigade design in place. The design created a center-level staff consisting of the commanding general, chief of staff, center staff (G-1, G-2, G-3, G-4, G-6/Command Information Officer and Knowledge Management, G-8/Strategic Communications, and Quality Assurance Office), headquarters detachment, Noncommissioned Officer's Academy, the Joint and Combined Integration Directorate to supervise all joint training and activities, and directorates of activities. The design merged the training and doctrine development functions of the Field Artillery and Air Defense Artillery into the Directorate of Training and Doctrine, provided for the Directorate of Training Support to oversee common training support and other functions. This organization also consolidated the branches' combat development functions under the Capabilities Development and Integration Directorate, including the TRADOC Capabilities Managers, formerly called TRADOC System Managers, who oversaw system acquisition. The design also provided for the Field Artillery School, the Air Defense Artillery School, and the Army Training Center for basic military training.[91]

Concurrently, the Fires Center of Excellence movement plan changed. Late in 2005 and early 2006, Wallace concluded that implementing the Fires Center of Excellence movement plan of 2005 was unfeasible. The lack of funding precluded achieving the overly ambitious full operational capability of 2008 as originally intended. As directed by Wallace, Fort Bliss and Fort Sill developed a new implementation plan with a full operational capability in 2009. Continuing budgetary problems, however, moved starting facilities construction from early 2007 to late 2007 which caused a difference of opinion in September 2007 on the proposed movement timeline between Fort Sill and Fort Bliss to arise. The Air Defense Artillery School suggested delaying the move of the main body because construction had just started at Fort Sill. Under the revised plan the center-level staff move would be postponed from January 2009 to July 2009, while the 6th Air Defense Artillery Brigade's move would be pushed from the spring of 2009 to the spring of 2010. In comparison, the Field Artillery School preferred retaining the basic movement schedule of 2009 believing that Fort Sill would be able to accommodate the Air Defense Artillery School even though some of the facilities would not be complete.[92]

Although the two schools did not resolve the movement dates by the end of 2007, both sides finally decided early in 2008 to execute the move on the delayed timeline. The new initial operating capability would be the fourth quarter of 2009; the new full operational capability date would be moved from 2009 to the third quarter of 2010. Based upon the new timetable, advance parties from the Air Defense Artillery center staff, the 6th Air Defense Artillery Brigade, and the Noncommissioned Officer Academy would arrive late in 2008. In June 2009, the Air Defense Artillery Commandant, Deputy Assistant Commandant, and the command group staff would come to Fort Sill. They would be followed closely by the center-level staff elements and the Noncommissioned Officer Academy in the summer of 2009. Fort Sill and Fort Bliss anticipated that the first Air Defense Artillery class would be taught late in 2009. Yet, they candidly noted the requirement of conducting dual Air Defense Artillery School operations until the move had been completed. The Air Defense Artillery School would be shrinking at Fort Bliss while growing in size at Fort Sill.[93]

In January 2008, the Air Defense Artillery School's new Commandant, Major General Howard B. Bromberg, modified the arrival date of the Air Defense Assistant Commandant at Fort Sill. Bromberg directed Fort Bliss to be proactive by moving elements as soon as possible and gave guidance to move the Air Defense Artillery Assistant Commandant in January 2009.[94] Subsequently, the commandants of the Field Artillery and Air Defense Artillery Schools briefed the Vice Chief of Staff of the Army on 21 February 2008 about the urgency of approving the movement plan. Coming out of this briefing, all parties agreed that a significant Air Defense Artillery Center and School advance party would start arriving at Fort Sill around June 2008 with the new Air Defense Artillery Commandant arriving at Fort Sill sometime between January 2009 and June 2009 based upon the one-star slating. The Air Defense Artillery center-level main body moves would start late in the spring of 2009, while the bulk of the 6th Air Defense Artillery Brigade would move in November 2009-May 2010. Approved by the Army on 16 April 2008, the movement plan established an initial operational capability for the Fires Center of Excellence in the fourth quarter of Fiscal Year 2009 and the full operational capability in the third quarter of Fiscal Year 2010. Meanwhile, the Air Defense Artillery School would continue to look at what classes and agencies could move earlier as the buildings became available at Fort Sill.[95]

As 2008 wore on, more information about the class moves emerged although classroom space might be constrained. At a Base Realignment and Closure 2005 movement briefing on 4 September 2008, the Air Defense Artillery School indicated that 18 courses would move from Fort Bliss to Fort Sill. Five would move in Fiscal Year 2009, and 13 would move in Fiscal Year 2010. Specifically, professional military education courses for Air Defense Artillery noncommissioned officers would begin at Fort Sill in August 2009. The Air Defense Artillery Warrant Officer Advanced Course would start in October 2009; and the Air Defense Artillery Captain's Career Course for the active component would begin in August 2009. Initial military training courses for Air Defense Artillery would start in January 2010, while the Basic Officer Leader Course Phase Three would begin in March 2010. The first air defense artillery advance individual training classes would start at Fort Sill in January 2010 with all being taught at Fort Sill by April 2010.[96]

Although the Fires Center of Excellence three-brigade model remained constant during the discussions of the movement plan, a proposal in mid-2008 to modify it arose as leaders at Fort Sill and Fort Bliss started questioning the need for a Directorate of Training Support. To maintain similarity with the TRADOC model, they initially adopted the Directorate of Training Support which co-located smaller, distinct agencies and functions that supported both schools into one organization but left training execution to the school brigades. This organization gave the Directorate of Training and Doctrine the responsibility for training and doctrine development and placed support organizations that could stand alone in the Directorate of Training Support. With this in mind and the issue of the overhead required to support the Directorate of Training Support, serious discussions led to the decision in September 2008 to abolish the directorate because the Directorate of Training and Doctrine already performed many of the former's proposed functions. This would free up positions for redistribution to other directorates and permit building a robust center G-3.[97]

Although additional work was still required, the base realignment and closure process reached a critical milestone in 2009. On 4 June 2009, Major General Peter M. Vangjel, the Commandant of the Field Artillery School and Chief of Field Artillery, passed authority to Brigadier General Ross E. Ridge to be the Commandant of the Field Artillery School and Chief of Field Artillery.[98]

Subsequently, the official transition of authority from Fort Bliss to Fort Sill for the Air Defense Artillery Center and School occurred on 23 June 2009. That day, Major General Howard B. Bromberg, the Commandant of the Air Defense Artillery School and Chief of Air Defense Artillery, conveyed authority of the Chief of Air Defense Artillery and Commandant of the Air Defense Artillery School to Brigadier General Rodger F. Matthews. Subsequently, the Air Defense Artillery School which trained soldiers, Marines, sailors, civilians, and allied forces on air defense artillery systems and taught a curricula that ranged from the Patriot missile, the Avenger, and man-portable Stinger systems to command, control, computers, and intelligence systems to basic noncommissioned officer courses to warrant officer courses to the Patriot Master Gunner Course opened with its first Captain's Career Course class taught at Fort Sill beginning in August 2009. With these actions, Fort Sill no longer served solely as a field artillery post as it had since the early years of the 20th century. It now provided field artillery and air defense artillery training as the US Army Fires Center of Excellence.[99]

As a result of the initial operational capability of 2009 and the full operational capability of August 2010, the Field Artillery School became a part of the Fires Center of Excellence under Major General David D. Halverson. As a preferred fires training location for international partners, the Center's key joint initiatives and innovative training and education methods established the conditions for growing proficient officers and soldiers. Conducted by the Center's Joint and Combined Integration Directorate, the Joint Fires Observer Course, for example, grew from 500 graduates in 2008 to 1,000 in 2010. This course and other joint courses, such as the Joint Fires and Effects Course, reflected the Center's and the Field Artillery School's commitment to joint operations.[100]

Meanwhile, as a part of an Army initiative to improve cultural and foreign language capabilities, the Fires Center of Excellence established the Cultural and Foreign Language Program to help soldiers and leaders understand how culture influenced military operations. To this end, the Field Artillery School and the Air Defense Artillery School revised officer, warrant officer, and noncommissioned officer courses to provide cultural and foreign language training to make their graduates more effective in dealing with a local populace and launched an all-volunteer language and cultural awareness orientation class in July 2010, among other initiatives in 2010 and 2011, to assist learning a foreign language.[101]

As the cultural and foreign language program indicated, the Fires Center of Excellence and the Field Artillery School took bold steps to improve training. They embraced new programs to produce proficient officers and leaders for full-spectrum operations and demonstrated their ability to adapt to changing conditions.

Molding the Future

In the midst of the Base Realignment and Closure 2005 endeavor, the Field Artillery School pushed to modernize the Field Artillery for the future but not the one that it had initially anticipated.[102] Upon becoming the Chief of Staff of the Army in June 1999, General Erik K. Shinseki expressed the need for the Army to eliminate the deficiencies underscored by the Task Force Hawk deployment to Kosovo early in 1999. The deployment underscored that the Army's heavy forces were too heavy, took too long to deploy, and were too difficult to maneuver in areas of the world where they might have to deploy. At the same time, Army's light forces were too light and lacked sufficient staying power and lethality.[103] Shinseki observed in June 1999, "[The] Heavy forces must be more strategically deployable and more agile with a smaller logistical footprint, and [the] light forces must be more lethal, survivable, and tactically mobile."[104]

Shinseki later advocated the need to erase the distinction between the heavy and light forces and to build a totally new force structure for future warfare around combat systems with the survivability of the Abrams tank and the Bradley fighting vehicle but with the strategic mobility of the light systems. Such capabilities would permit the Army to deploy an independent combat brigade anywhere in the world within 96 hours, a division within 120 hours, and five divisions within 30 days.[105]

Based upon his thinking, Shinseki unveiled his Transformation of the Army vision in October 1999. He laid out retaining a Legacy Force of existing Cold War systems to preserve current capabilities that would be upgraded or modernized as required and transforming the rest of the Army in three phases beginning with creating an Initial Force with off-the-shelf equipment, including vehicles. The Interim Force would follow and be equipped with the interim armored vehicle, commonly called an IAV. After February 2002, the vehicle was designated as the Stryker in honor of two Medal of Honor recipients: Private First Class Stuart S. Stryker who had served in World War II and Specialist Robert F. Stryker who had served in Vietnam. In some cases, Initial Force units would be retrofitted with the Stryker to become Interim Force units. Finally, the Army would field the Objective Force beginning in 2008. The Objective Force would be equipped with the Future Combat System, a family of vehicles with the capabilities of heavy and light forces.[106]

Upon replacing Shinseki as the Chief of Staff of the Army in August 2003, General Peter J. Schoomaker pointed out the imperative of accelerating the Transformation of the Army, improving Army's wartime relevance and readiness, and institutionalizing a joint and expeditionary mindset. Echoing Shinseki's concerns about the lack of strategic mobility with heavy systems and staying power of light systems and understanding the requirements surrounding the nation's war on terrorism caused by the terrorist attacks on the Twin Towers in New York City and the Pentagon in September 2001, Schoomaker recognized the need to respond to a threat rapidly. Equally as important, the Army's forces had to commence operations immediately upon arrival in distant theaters of operations.[107]

However, the post-Cold War Army lacked the required flexibility and responsiveness to meet such demands. In support of military operations during the past five years, for example, the Army had to dismantle its corps and divisions for operations in the Balkans, Afghanistan, and Philippines. The difficulty of using existing formations coupled with the need to employ land forces immediately with little time to reorganize caused Schoomaker to step up the pace of transformation started with Shinseki. He abandoned the Initial Force and Interim Force for the Current Force and the Objective Force for the Future Force that would be designed around the Future Combat System family of vehicles. He also pressed to speed up fielding select Future Force capabilities to the Current Force to make it relevant and ready and to have the ability to conduct major combat operations across the full spectrum of conflict.[108]

Additionally, Schoomaker pushed to redesign the Army's force structure, adding a dimension that Shinseki had not considered. Beginning in late 2003 and early 2004, he initiated modularizing the Army's forces to provide land combat power that could be task organized for any combination of offensive, defensive, stability, or support operation as part of a joint campaign with the Field Artillery School becoming deeply immersed in the effort.[109] Thus, Schoomaker's plans set in motion a comprehensive effort to transform the Army at the tactical, operational, and strategic levels by replacing existing echelons-above corps, corps, divisions, and brigades with new organizations. The Army intended to create modular organizations. Modularization would move the Army from dependence upon large, powerful, fixed organizations to reliance upon smaller, self-contained, lethal organizations with the capabilities of the full range of missions.[110]

As outlined in the Unit of Employment Operations White Paper of 23 January 2004 and refined in the Unit of Employment White Paper of 20 March 2004, the Army planned to create a modular corps and division. Most likely commanded by a lieutenant general, the corps would consolidate most functions performed by the corps and Army service component commands into a single operational echelon and would be the primary vehicle for Army support to the regional component commander's area of responsibility. Approved in November 2004 for standing up, the corps could be tailored for any mission and supported the modular.[111]

Commanded by a major general or a lieutenant general and approved for standing up in mid-2007, the division would serve as the Army's primary tactical and operational warfighting headquarters. The division did not have a fixed structure beyond its headquarters because it was completely modular and could be deployed as a pure headquarters without subordinate units. Its supporting brigades – an aviation brigade, a maneuver enhancement brigade, a fires brigade, a battlefield surveillance brigade, and a battlefield sustainment brigade – could be attached or assigned depending upon the operations.[112]

Restructuring the Army's main combat unit formed another major part of the Transformation of the Army. Throughout most of the 20th century, the division was the Army's primary fighting organization. Formed with a standard number of brigades or regiments and a division base of specialty troops, the division fought battles under a corps. Although the battles typically took place over considerable space, the division's brigades operated close to each other and reinforced each other as needed. Normally, the brigade had three or four combat maneuver battalions and received its specialty support from the division, such as division artillery. Even though doctrine stressed flexibility in brigade organization, the tendency for habitual relationships between the combat brigades and their supporting units, such as the field artillery battalion, led to *de facto* fixed organizations that proved to be valuable in combat.[113]

To build upon the tactical experience of the last years of the 20th century and the practice of habitual association and to provide more flexibility, the Army abandoned the division during the first decade of the 21st century as its primary fighting unit for the brigade combat team of battalion-size and company-size subunits that would be controlled by a division. One brigade combat team variant was a standard armored (heavy) brigade, and another was the standard infantry (light) brigade. The Stryker brigade combat team that employed the Stryker vehicle was the third. These three modular maneuver brigades were stand-alone warfighting elements and had an organic maneuver, fires (field artillery), reconnaissance, and logistics subunits.[114]

As the Field Artillery School participated in designing the fires battalion for the brigade combat teams, it also worked on developing the fires brigade to support the division. Although it might or might not be stationed with the division, the fires brigade played a critical role in the division. It could plan, prepare, execute, and assess combined arms operations to provide close support and precision strike for the joint force commander, the division, or the brigade combat teams. Even though the fires brigade could be tasked organized with additional units, such as rocket and cannon battalions, depending upon the situation, its organic units included a headquarters and headquarters battery, a fires and effects cell for planning and executing lethal and non-lethal effects, a rocket/missile battalion, a support battalion, a signal company, and a target acquisition battery. The fires brigade had the capability of providing long-range fires to support the division and brigade combat team employing organic and assigned assets as required and conducting counterstrike.[115]

As anticipated, the Field Artillery immediately felt the impact of the Transformation of the Army with the emergence of modular units and the demand for lighter but still lethal weapons to equip them.[116] Late in 1999, the Army terminated the Multiple-Launch Rocket System Smart Tactical Rocket and Army Tactical Missile System Block IIA programs to help fund forming brigade combat teams and procuring the appropriate weapon systems. The Army made the Army Tactical Missile System Block II the carrier for the Brilliant Antiarmor submunition and even contemplated discontinuing work on the futuristic Crusader 155-mm. self-propelled howitzer because many senior Army officers found it to be too heavy and more closely attuned to the Cold War battlefield than future operations.[117]

With support from Shinseki who liked the Crusader and its resupply vehicle, disliked their collective weight of more than 100 tons, and wanted them to be an integral member of the Army's dominant maneuver force, the Crusader which had been under development since the early 1990s temporarily survived being eliminated because the Army restructured its development and acquisition program. In December 1999, the Army outlined reducing the howitzer's and resupply vehicle's weight to make them more strategically deployable without losing their key capabilities and moved fielding from 2005 to 2008 to make the necessary modifications to the program. The Army also projected using the Crusader as a technology base for future systems and planned to field the lighter Crusader to modernize the heavy forces that had been organized and equipped during the Cold War.[118]

In comparison, the Lightweight 155-mm. towed howitzer (M777), the High Mobility Artillery Rocket System (M142), and the Advanced Field Artillery Tactical Data System developmental programs did not require revamping to satisfy Shinseki's vision of the future. With its strong emphasis on deployability, the Transformation of the Army made the Lightweight 155-mm. towed howitzer and the High Mobility Artillery Rocket System part of Shinseki's Interim Force (Schoomaker's Current Force), while the Objective Force (Schoomaker's Future Force) would be designed around the multi-functional Future Combat System that would include a cannon system (Non-Line-of-Sight Cannon) and a rocket system (Non-Line-of-Sight Launch System), among other systems. However, the Lightweight 155-mm. towed howitzer and the High Mobility Artillery Rocket System which were fielded in the first years of the 21st century would eventually be phased out along with the Crusader and Cold War vintage systems in favor of the Future Combat System cannon and rocket systems. In contrast, the stress on digitization that was a critical aspect of the transformation effort guaranteed a place for the Advanced Field Artillery Tactical Data System and hand-held command and control systems in the long-term.[119]

Despite support from some quarters in the Army, the Crusader fell victim to transformation. Although the redesign made it lighter, the debate over the system's future arose again in 2002. As some critics in the Department of Defense suggested, the system represented a Cold War weapon and "old-think approach to warfare" and should be abolished. In contrast, advocates in the Field Artillery School and the Field Artillery community still maintained that Crusader had a place in the Army's inventory of weapons.[120]

In the midst of this debate, the Secretary of Defense Donald Rumsfeld canceled the Crusader program on 8 May 2002. From his vantage point, it did not suit the new threats of cyberwar and terrorism of the 21st century with their requirements for more nimble and mobile forces. After terminating the Crusader developmental program, the Department of Defense and the Army allocated the money saved to accelerate development of the Non-Line-of-Sight Cannon, also called the Future Combat System Cannon, the Excalibur family of precision 155-mm. munitions, the Guided Multiple-Launch Rocket System rocket, the Non-Line-of-Sight Launch System, the High Mobility Artillery Rocket System, and the M777. Basically, the emphasis on developing such munitions and systems reflected the lessons learned from military operations in OEF where light, mobile weapons and precision munitions had been critical and impressive.[121]

Although work on Future Combat System Cannon, properly known as the Non-Line-of-Sight Cannon, started in earnest in 2002, funding eventually became an issue.[122] Congressional funding reductions in 2007 for the Future Combat System program prompted the Army to revamp its modernization efforts, to reduce the number of Future Combat System family of systems platforms from 18 to 14, and to extend the timeline for buying and fielding them to stay within budget.[123] Pressed to support the war on terrorism, the Department of Defense, headed by Robert Gates, eventually cancelled the Future Combat System program, including Future Combat System Cannon, in May 2009, replaced it with the brigade combat team vehicle modernization program, and shifted the funding saved to counter-terrorism. This caused the Army and Field Artillery School to shift their focus to the Paladin Integrated Management program which had been underway since 2007 to improve the readiness and sustainability of the M109 family of vehicles – M109A6 Paladin 155-mm. self-propelled howitzer, the M992A2 ammunition resupply vehicle, and the Paladin Operations Center Vehicle. Later in 2009, TRADOC stripped the Paladin Operations Center Vehicle from the Paladin Integrated Management program and tied it to a new command and control vehicle.[124]

Determined to increase the range of its cannon artillery without sacrificing accuracy, the Army meanwhile investigated adopting the Excalibur Extended Range Guided Projectile. As outlined in February 1996, Excalibur would be a fire-and-forget precision projectile with a Global Positioning System receiver and a guidance package to permit flying extended ranges (50 kilometers) and to hit within six meters of the target. The projectile's modular design would permit carrying the Dual-Purpose Improved Conventional Munition for area targets, the Search-and-Destroy-Armor Munition for counterfire, or the Unitary munition for hard or soft targets. According to the Field Artillery School, Excalibur would improve fire support, would be compatible with all digitized 155-mm. howitzers, such as the M109A6 (Paladin), the M777 under development, and the Crusader under development, and would reduce fratricide.[125]

However, the fear of duds and collateral damage, the need for precision, the cost of the Search-and-Destroy Armor Munition, and the Transformation of the Army process that was underway prompted the Commandant of the US Army Field Artillery School, Major General Toney Stricklin (1999-2001), to sign a decision paper in December 2000 to recommend switching Excalibur's initial development from the Dual-Purpose Improved Conventional Munition with its bomblets to the Unitary munition. Concurring with Stricklin, the Program Manager for Excalibur subsequently deferred work on the Dual-Purpose Improved Conventional Munition in January 2001 because it caused collateral damage by scattering sometimes unexploded bomblets upon detonation. He made the Unitary the primary warhead because it produced low collateral damage, causing it to rise in importance after being a low priority for years.[126]

In August 2004, an urgent needs statement for the Excalibur Unitary endorsed by the Coalition Forces Land Component Command accelerated fielding the precision munition but with reduced capabilities with the idea that the fully capable or objective munition would be fielded later.[127] The reduced capabilities Excalibur Unitary quickly demonstrated its value in combat. On 5 May 2007, the 1st Cavalry Division conducted the first operational firing of the munition in Bagdad, Iraq. Elements from the 1st Squadron, 7th Cavalry Regiment teamed with the 1st Battalion, 82d Field Artillery Regiment to destroy a prominent insurgent safe house with one Excalibur Unitary round. Through the end of 2009, Army and Marine field artillery units had fired 76 Excaliburs in Operation Iraqi Freedom and 41 in Operation Enduring Freedom in Afghanistan[128]

Recognizing that Excalibur Unitary and Search-and-Destroy-Armor Munition were expensive and that the requirement to curtail collateral damage was intensifying, the Army meanwhile searched for less expensive precision munition.[129] This led to developmental work on the Course Correcting Fuse, renamed Precision Guidance Kit. Based upon analysis during the first part of 2004, the Field Artillery School concluded that the Precision Guidance Kit would vastly improve the accuracy of 105-mm. and 155-mm. projectiles and reduce the number of rounds required for each engagement. Technical difficulties pushed fielding back into the second decade of the 21st century.[130]

In "Fires: The Cutting Edge for the 21st Century" in the *Field Artillery Magazine* in the May-June 1998 edition, the Assistant Commandant of the Field Artillery School, Brigadier General Toney Stricklin, meanwhile, outlined the school's vision of the future of fire support. Among other things, the vision proposed an advanced fire support system of a family of precision missiles with the capability of attacking with precision or loitering over the target area before attacking with precision. However, the missiles would not require a large, heavy, expensive, and crew-intensive launch platform.[131]

Out of this vision evolved NetFires. Basically, NetFires, later renamed the Non-line-of-Sight Launch System, would consist of a container/launch unit with 15 containerized missiles and an on-board computer and communications system. The system would deliver the Loiter Attack Missile with a range of 70 kilometers plus a search time of about 30 minutes and the Precision Attack Missile with a maximum range of 40 kilometers.[132]

After the termination of the system had been considered, the Defense Authorization Bill for Fiscal Year 2005 modified the system's acquisition program. The bill accelerated work on the Precision Attack Missile and slowed down work on the Loiter Attack Missile. Although the Loiter Attack Missile was deemed capable of meeting all of its threshold requirements, the bill returned it to the science and technology base for further maturation and permitted moving the Precision Attack Missile further into the developmental cycle because it was easier to integrate with existing command and control systems than Loiter Attack Missile.[133]

With the intent of fielding the Precision Attack Missile and container/launch unit by 2010, the Army accelerated development. As one of the first Future Combat System systems to be employed, the Non-Line-of-Sight Launch System with the Precision Attack Missile would be incorporated into the fires battalion of the heavy brigade combat team and then fielded to the other modular brigades. In 2008, the Army decided to field the system to the infantry brigade combat team rather than heavy brigade combat team to give the former additional situational awareness and self-protection capabilities and organic precision fires which it lacked.[134]

Because a detailed analysis of alternatives in 2009 determined that the Non-Line-of-Sight Launch System did not provide a cost-effective precision fire capability, the Army concluded that it was no longer required. Based upon this, the Secretary of the Army recommended canceling the program. The Undersecretary of the Department of Defense concurred and authorized terminating the program on 13 May 2010, thus, bringing an end to a futuristic field artillery system.[135] In contrast, the Guided Multiple-Launch Rocket System rocket, another precision munition, proved its utility. Together, the proliferation of rocket systems with greater ranges than the Multiple-Launch Rocket System rocket with its unacceptable dud rate of often unexploded bomblets during Operation Desert Storm of 1991 led to the requirement for an Extended-Range Multiple-Launch Rocket System rocket with a range of 45 kilometers. This would increase the commander's ability to influence the battlefield at depth, would increase the survivability of the launcher, and would permit firing across boundaries.[136]

After the Army started production of the extended range rocket in 2001 to meet the range requirements identified in Operation Desert Storm, it turned its efforts to a Guided Multiple-Launch Rocket System rocket that would be fired from the M270A1 Multiple-Launch Rocket System launcher under development and the High Mobility Artillery Rocket System launcher also under development and supplant the Extended-Range Multiple-Launch Rocket System rocket. Unlike the accuracy of the traditional free-flight Multiple-Launch Rocket System rocket that degraded as the range to the target increased, the guided rocket's Global Positioning System aided navigation system would provide consistent, improved accuracy from a minimum range of 15 kilometers to a maximum of 60 to 70 kilometers to attack area and point targets. The guided rocket would also enhance the ability to conduct precision strikes, would reduce the number of rockets required to defeat a target, and would give an additional 15 kilometer range beyond the Extended-Range Multiple-Launch Rocket System rocket's range. Such a range would permit hitting more targets and make the Multiple-Launch Rocket System launcher more survivable because it could be positioned farther from the target according to the Field Artillery School.[137]

Looking at the need to reduce damage to civilian property and the loss of lives during combat operations and to deliver organic fires in all types of terrain and weather, the Army turned to the Guided Unitary Multiple-Launch Rocket System rocket as its preferred precision rocket. It would have a fuse with the capabilities of a proximity fuse, a point-detonating fuse, or a time-delay fuse capability. While the proximity fuse would provide a large burst over the target area, the point-detonating fuse would reduce the size of the burst and collateral damage because of the ground burst. The time-delay fuse would permit the rocket to penetrate certain types of structures or targets and then detonate the rocket.[138]

Even before operational testing could be done on the Guided Unitary Multiple-Launch Rocket System rocket, Lieutenant General Thomas F. Metz, the Commander of the Multi-National Forces in Operation Iraqi Freedom and also Commander of the III US Corps, sent the Army an operational needs statement on 28 March 2004 for the rocket. After the Army denied the request on 13 September 2004, Metz forwarded an urgent needs statement for the rocket to the Army on 12 October 2004. His forces required a precision, all-weather, low-caliber, high-explosive Multiple-Launch Rocket System munition to integrate into joint fires in an urban environment to attack high pay-off targets and provide large area coverage at the same time; the Guided Unitary Multiple-Launch Rocket System rocket met those requirements.[139]

On 6 January 2005, the Army validated Metz's request and accelerated work on the Guided Unitary Multiple-Launch Rocket System rocket. To get it to the field sooner than planned, the rocket would have a point-detonating and time-delay fuse and be less capable than the objective rocket which would be fielded later.[140]

Combat operations soon confirmed the less capable Guided Unitary Multiple-Launch Rocket System rocket's accuracy. On 9 and 10 September 2005, B Battery, 3d Battalion, 13th Field Artillery Regiment fired a six-rocket mission at an insurgent safe house in a Baghdad at 53 kilometers and demolished it, killing insurgents, and shot another two-round mission in the same area, killing more insurgents. One day later, A Battery, 3d Battalion, 13th Field Artillery Regiment shot six rockets at a bridge in Tal Afar, Iraq, and destroyed it to prevent insurgents from using it. In all instances, collateral damage to surrounding buildings was almost non-existent according to participants. By the end of 2007, US field artillery units in Iraq had fired more than 300 Guided Unitary Multiple-Launch Rocket System rockets, playing an important part in a critical paradigm shift with the advent of precision field artillery munitions.[141]

With the advancements in precision delivery systems and precision munitions, accurate target location assumed greater importance. Forward Observer Software coupled with the

Precision Strike Suite-Special Operation Forces software provided commanders with a precision targeting tool. A forward observer or a soldier using the Precision Strike Suite-Special Operation Forces software employed the Global Positioning System to find his own location. Then, he lased a target. The software then would draw a three-dimensional image so that the forward observer could determine the exact location of the target to be sent to fire support command, control, and communications systems, the Advanced Field Artillery Tactical Data System. Without Precision Strike Suite-Special Operation Forces software and Forward Observer Software tied to sophisticated fire support command, control, and communication systems, Excalibur Unitary and Guided Multiple-Launch Rocket System Unitary would be less effective because exact target locations could not be determined. Besides reducing the delivery time and providing an exact location, precision targeting software and precision munitions gave the Field Artillery a role in OIF and OEF where limiting collateral damage was critical to maintain the public opinion support in those countries.[142]

The M270A1 launcher and the M142 High Mobility Artillery Rocket System launcher fired the Guided Unitary Multiple-Launch Rocket System precision munition. Based upon after-action reports from Operation Desert Storm of 1991, the Army realized that the M270 launcher required a faster response time and improvements to its fire control system and launcher drive system. The Army modernized the launcher during the 1990s to create the M270A1 which was fielded early in the 21st century.[143]

Designed for the Cold War battlefield, the M270A1 launcher did not have the ability to support light, airborne, and air assault divisions and forced/early entry contingency force operations and also lacked inter-theater tactical deployability. In contrast, the M142 High Mobility Artillery Rocket System launcher which began to be fielded in 2005 provided the Army with a critical precision deep fires capability for light and early entry forces. The M142 not only replaced the aging M198 towed 155-mm. howitzer but also would replace the M270 and M270A1 launchers as they reached the end of their service life. The High Mobility Artillery Rocket System launcher which fired Multiple-Launch Rocket System rockets and missiles supplied field artillery medium and long-range rocket and long-range missile fires.[144]

Without state-of-the-art target acquisition systems, the new weapon systems and munitions would be less effective. During the middle years of the 1990s, modernizing the AN/TPQ-36 radar produced its first fruits in 1993. The effort yielded the Q-36 (Version 7) radar for towing on a trailer behind a High Mobility Multi-purpose Wheeled Vehicle. Subsequently, the Army fielded the Q-36 (Version 8) in 2001 with electronic upgrades that increased memory and possessed the ability to process up to 20 targets a minute.[145]

Meanwhile, the Army and the school modified its AN/TPQ-37 counterfire radar modernization program in 1990. Because the Q-37 lacked the required capabilities, they decided to replace it with the Advanced Target Acquisition Counterfire System that would take advantage of leap-ahead technology to detect more targets and have greater range, among other desired characteristics. As it fielded the AN/TPQ-37 block one as an interim upgrade measure, the Army initiated work on the Advanced Target Acquisition Counterfire

System late in the 1990s. Using advanced technology to furnish dramatically improved capabilities over the Q-37, the Advanced Target Acquisition Counterfire Radar would replace all Q-37s, including the Q-37 block one.[146]

Challenges soon altered the Advanced Target Acquisition Counterfire System program. In 1999 the Army redesignated the program as the AN/TPQ-47. Technological problems and schedule delays necessitated modifying the Q-47 program several times. In 2002, the Army redesignated the radar program as the Phoenix Battlefield Sensor System which would provide increased capability in range and accuracy and would be a 90-degree sensing system when it was becoming increasingly apparent that a 360-degree sensing capability was necessary as indicated in OIF and OEF during the first decade of the 21st century. Technological problems and the systems limitations caused the Army to end the Q-47 program in 2005.[147]

Because of the termination of the Phoenix, the Army deferred long-range counterfire target acquisition capability requirements. However, the medium range threat set of cannon and rockets and the 360-degree medium range coverage defined a capability gap with no fielded solution that neither the modernized Q-36 nor Q-37 addressed. The Field Artillery School defined a change to the Q-36 radar to incorporate new technology to close that gap. The Enhanced Q-36 (EQ-36) radar would reduce crew size and footprint, would increase range and accuracy against cannon and rockets in a 90-degree mode, and would eventually incorporate a 360-degree capability for mortars, cannon, and rockets.[148] Through the efforts of the Field Artillery School, the Army redesigned its field artillery target acquisition assets. New technology transformed radar target acquisition to make it more responsive to the requirements of modern warfare with the new AN/TPQ-48 countermortar radar, also called the Lightweight Countermortar Radar, being developed for counterinsurgency warfare to complement other sensors, such as the Bradley Fire Support Team vehicle.[149]

As the radar and sensor systems indicated, the Transformation of the Army at the beginning of the 21st century moved the Field Artillery School and the Field Artillery beyond their Cold War orientation of the last half of the 20th century to focus on strategic mobility which the Cold War ignored. Although rising costs led to the termination of the Non-Line-of-Sight Cannon and Non-Line-of-Sight Launch System which were the cornerstones of cannon and rocket system modernization, transformation caused the school to become involved with developing and fielding new light mobile systems, such as the M777 and High Mobility Artillery Rocket System, and precision munitions for the emerging 21st century battlefield to replace field artillery systems designed for the Cold War and to reduce collateral damage.

While transformation prompted the school to adopt advanced information technology to enhance training and to give the Army's field artillery expeditionary capabilities with lighter weapon systems, OIF and OEF reinforced the requirement for precision munitions and simultaneously broadened the Field Artillery's mission beyond its traditional emphasis on lethal capabilities. The wars in Iraq and Afghanistan highlighted the requirement to integrate non-lethal effects, such as electronic warfare and tactical information operations, and lethal effects to defeat a resourceful threat. In response, the school added non-lethal effects as core field artillery competencies and introduced electronic warfare and tactical information operations into programs of instruction and even created specialized courses on those topics.

Ironically, the wars in Iraq and Afghanistan where field artillerymen generally conducted non-standard missions of patrolling, among others, caused their fire support skills to atrophy. To overcome this problem the Field Artillery School lengthen its Captain's Career Course and noncommissioned officer courses to reset field artillerymen in fire support skills. This created an interesting situation. The school had to retrain field artillerymen in their core fire support competencies while also training them for non-standard missions.

Notes

1   2000 US Army Field Artillery Center and Fort Sill (USAFACFS), Annual Command History (ACH), pp. 41-42.

2   E-mail, subj: School Reorganization, 28 Feb 2003, Historical Research and Document Collection (HRDC), Command Historian's Office, USAFACFS; Memorandum for Students, CCC, subj: Overview of Field Artillery Captain's Career Course (FACCC), 28 May 2002, HRDC; 2000 USAFACFS ACH, pp. 41-42; Interview with atchs, Dastrup with Dan L. Scraper, Program Manager, Officer Education System (OES), Directorate of Training and Doctrine (DOTD), 27 Jan 2004, HRDC. Interview, Dastrup with Dan Scraper, Program Manager, OES, DOTD, 13 Jan 2004, HRDC; E-mail with atch, subj: OBC and CCC Input to 2003 Annual Command History, 17 Feb 2004, HRDC. The first US Marines arrived at Fort Sill in 1917 to attend the School of Musketry. Eight years later in 1925, the first Marine entered the Field Artillery School. In the 1950s, the US Marine Corps established the billet of the Senior Marine Corps Representative and created a small detachment in 1952 under Brigadier General Wilburt Scott "Big Foot" Brown who had received a Silver Star for his actions in the Korean War. In 1977, the Marine Corps representative was designated as the commanding officer of Marine Corps detachment. The detachment supervised Marines assigned to the Air Training Command at Sheppard Air Force Base, Texas, and Fort Sill. After the decision to centralize all Marine Corps field artillery training at Fort Sill in 1978, the number of Marines more than doubled at the school. In 1989, the detachment was redesignated as the Marine Corps Artillery Detachment and later designated the fire support doctrinal proponent for the Marine Corps. See "History of the USMC Artillery Detachment at Fort Sill," *Field Artillery Magazine*, Sep-Oct 2006, p. 19.

3   Briefing, subj: Leader Development Campaign Plan OES Workshop, 9-11 Jan 2002, HRDC; Briefing, subj: Leader Development Transformation, 8 Nov 2001, HRDC.

4   Memorandum for Commandants, TRADOC Service Schools, subj: Senior Leader Institutional Transformation Conference (SLITC) II After Action Report, 7 Dec 2000, HRDC.

5   Memorandum for Commandants, TRADOC Service Schools, subj: Senior Leader Institutional Transformation Conference (SLITC) II After Action Report, 7 Dec 2000.

6   E-mail with atch, subj: FACCC-Proposed Changes, 8 Feb 2001, HRDC; Point Paper, subj: SLITC II, 17 Jan 2001, HRDC; Memorandum for Record, subj: FACCC, 26 Jan 2001, HRDC; Memorandum for Commandants, TRADOC Service Schools, subj: SLITC II After Action Report, 7 Dec 2000, HRDC; Msg, FSCAOD to Command Historian, subj: Annual Command History, 16 Apr 2001, HRDC.

7   Memorandum for CG, subj: Trip Report – TRADOC Leader Development Campaign Conference, 1-3 Oct 2001, HRDC; Briefing, subj: Leader Development Transformation, 8 Nov 2001, HRDC.

8   See Note 7.

9   Interview, Dastrup with MAJ Alvin Peterson, Chief, Integration Division, DOTD, 13 Jan 2003, HRDC; E-mail, subj: School Reorganization, 28 Feb 2003, HRDC.

10 Interview, Dastrup with CPT Paul J. Payne, Canadian Army Exchange Officer, FSCAOD, 27 Jan 2002, HRDC; Briefing, subj: Leader Development Plan OES Workshop, 9-11 Jan 2002, HRDC.

11 E-mail, subj: School Reorganization, 28 Feb 2003, HRDC; Briefing, subj: Captain OES Transformation Update, 13 Jan 2003, HRDC.

12 See Note 11.

13 E-mail with atch, subj: OBC and CCC Input to 2003 Annual Command History, 17 Feb 2004, HRDC; Interview, Dastrup with Dan Scraper, OES Program Manager, DOTD, 13 Jan 2004, HRDC; Briefing, subj: CPTs OES, 21 Aug 2003, HRDC; Memorandum for See Distribution (Draft),

subj: Captains' Officer Education System Guidance, 22 Aug 2003, HRDC; Executive Overview of CPTs OES Video Conference, 25 Aug 2003, HRDC.

14 Briefing (Extract), subj: Field Artillery School Update, Summer 2004, HRDC; Interview, Dastrup with Dan Scraper, OES Program Manager, DOTD, 7 Jan 2005, HRDC; "Combined Arms and Services Staff School to Merge with Officer Advanced Course," US Army News Release, 12 Apr 2004, HRDC; E-mail, subj: Basic Officer Leader Course (BOLC) and CCC, 25 Feb 2005, HRDC.

15 2006 USAFCOEFS ACH, p. 34; Interview, Dastrup with Dan Scraper, OES Branch Manager, DOTD, 16 Jan 2008, HRDC; Briefing, subj: 428th FA Brigade, Jun 2007, HRDC; LTC Loyd A. Gerber, "Reset: Rebuilding FA Core Competencies for Future Full-Spectrum Operations," *Field Artillery Magazine,* Mar-Apr 2007, pp. 14-18; MAJ Scott A. Shaw, "COIN in the FACCC," *Fires Magazine,* May-Jun 2007, pp. 8-9; Briefing (Extract), subj: Field Artillery School Update, 31 Jul 2007, HRDC.

16 "Army Acts on Training and Leaders Development Panel Findings," US Army News Release, 25 May 2001, HRDC; "Survey Says Balance Army Needs with Army Beliefs," ArmyLink News, 25 May 2001, HRDC; "Study Suggests Fixes for Officer Development," ArmyLink News, 25 May 2001, HRDC; ATLDP Officer Study, 25 May 2001, pp. 7, 11, 12, HRDC; Briefing, subj: Leader Development Campaign Plan OES Workshop, 9-11 Jan 2002, HRDC.

17 See Note 16.

18 Briefing (Extract), subj: One-Site Officer Basic Combat Training, 5 Jun 2000, HRDC; Memorandum for Record, subj: Untitled, 26 Jan 2001, HRDC; Interview, Dastrup with Melvin R. Hunt, Warfighting Integration and Development Directorate (WIDD), 26 Jan 2001, HRDC; Memorandum for Record, subj: FAOBC and OBCT Concept, 26 Jan 2001, HRDC; E-mail, subj: FAOBC, 29 Jan 2001, HRDC; E-mail with atch, subj: Field Artillery Officer Basic Course - (FAOBC) Proposed Changes, 8 Feb 2001, HRDC; LTC Gordon K. Rogers, "Transforming Institutional Training and Leaders Development," *Army AL&T*, Nov-Dec 2001, p. 7-8, HRDC; Memorandum for CG, subj: Trip Report – TRADOC Leaders Development Campaign Plan Conference, 17 Oct 2001, HRDC.

19 Interview, Dastrup with MAJ Alvin Peterson, Chief, Cannon Division, Gunnery Department, 24 Jan 2002, HRDC; Briefing, subj: BOLC Phase II, 2001, HRDC; Briefing, subj: BOLC Course Description, 11 Jan 2002, HRDC; Memorandum for CG, subj: Trip Report – TRADOC Leader Development Campaign Plan Conference, 1-3 Oct 2001, HRDC.

20 Interview, Dastrup with Peterson, 24 Jan 2002, HRDC; Briefing, subj: BOLC Phase II, 2001, HRDC; Briefing, subj: BOLC Course Description, 11 Jan 2002, HRDC; Memorandum for CG, subj: Trip Report – TRADOC Leader Development Campaign Plan Conference, 1-3 Oct 2001, HRDC; Memorandum for Dir, DOTD, subj: Coordination of Annual Command History, 3 Mar 2003, HRDC; E-mail msg, subj: School Reorganization, 28 Feb 2003, HRDC; Report, subj: School Update, May 2002, HRDC; Interview, Dastrup with MAJ Alvin Peterson, Chief, Integration Division, DOTD, 13 Jan 2003, HRDC; "Field Artillery Training Command," *Field Artillery Magazine*, Nov-Dec 2002, p. 32, HRDC; Memorandum, subj: None, 19 Mar 2003, HRDC; 2002 USAFACFS ACH, p. 33; 2005 USAFACFS ACH, p. 31; Briefing, subj: BOLC E-mail History, Jun 2005, HRDC.

21 E-mail, subj: School Reorganization, 28 Feb 2003, HRDC; Interview, Dastrup with Peterson, 13 Jan 2003, HRDC; Report, subj: Directorate of Resource Management (DRM) Sigacts, 13 Nov 2002, HRDC; Report, subj: School Update, May 2002, HRDC; Report, subj: DRM Sigacts, 21 Oct 2002, HRDC; Report, subj: DRM Sigacts, 27 Jan 2003, HRDC; Briefing, subj: Transforming Leader Development, 8 Apr 2003, HRDC; Msg, DA to AIG 7406, subj: Officer Education System Transformation, 041338Z Feb 2003, HRDC; Memorandum for See Distribution, subj: Memorandum of Instruction for Ft. Sill BOLC II Development, 11 Mar 2004, HRDC; E-mail,

subj: BOLC and CCC, 22 Feb 2005, HRDC.

22 Briefing (Extract), subj: Basic Officer Leader Course Update, 14-15 Jan 2004, HRDC; Interview, Dastrup with Dan Scraper, OES Manager, DOTD, 7 Jan 2005, HRDC; Memorandum for See Distribution, subj: Request for Four Directed Military Overstrength for the Basic Officer Leader Course Phase II, 5 Nov 2003, HRDC; Interview with atchs, Dastrup with Dan Scraper, OES Manager, DOTD, 27 Jan 2004, HRDC; E-mail msg with atch, subj: OBC and CCC Input to 2003 Annual Command History, 17 Feb 2004, HRDC.

23 Interview with atchs, Dastrup with Scraper, 27 Jan 2004, HRDC; "Changes Approved to Officer Education System," US Army News Release, 4 Feb 2003, HRDC; "Army to Transform Officer Education," ArmyLink News, 4 Feb 2003, HRDC; E-mail with atch, subj: OBC and CCC Input to 2003 Annual Command History, 17 Feb 2004, HRDC; Interview, Dastrup with Scraper, 7 Jan 2005, HRDC; E-mail, subj: BOLC and CCC, 22 Feb 2005, HRDC.

24 E-mail with atch, subj: FY05 Command History, 25 Apr 2006, HRDC.

25 SIGACTS, DRM, 22 Nov 2005, HRDC; SIGACTS, DRM, 27 Oct 2005, HRDC; SIGACTS, DPTM, 30 Sep 2005, HRDC; E-mail, subj: 17 Aug 2005 Biweekly Report, 15 Aug 2005, HRDC; SIGACTS, DRM, 30 Mar 2005, HRDC; SIGACTS, DRM, 16 Mar 2005, HRDC; SIGACTS, DRM, 4 Mar 2005, HRDC; SIGACTS, DRM, 1 Feb 2005, HRDC; K.W. Hillis, "BOLC II Mission Doubles," Fort Sill *Cannoneer*, 29 Sep 2005, p. 1a, HRDC; Lisa Alley, "BOLC Gets Green Light for Officer Education," ARNEWS, 25 Feb 2005, HRDC; Briefing, subj: BOLC Update, 5 Oct 2005, HRDC; Memorandum for Cdr, US Army Accessions Command with atchs, subj: BOLC II Assessment for Fort Sill, HRDC; Memorandum for Deputy Commanding General, TRADOC, with atchs, subj: Concept Plan - BOLC II, 4 May 2004, HRDC; Memorandum for LTG Robert L. Van Antwerp, CG, US Army Accessions Command/Deputy Commanding General Initial Entry Training, subj: BOLC II Implementation, 21 Sep 2005, HRDC; Memorandum for See Distribution, subj: BOLC Common Core Tasks, 18 May 2004, HRDC.

26 Briefing (Extract), subj: 30th Field Artillery Regiment, 2006; MAJ M. Shayne Mullins, "New BOLC II at Fort Sill," *Field Artillery Magazine*, May-Jun 2006, pp. 28-30.

27 E-mail with atch (FOUO), subj: FRAGO 23, 28 Jul 2009, information used is unclassified, HRDC; E-mail, subj: TRADOC Campaign Plan, 3 Aug 2009, HRDC; Interview, Dastrup with Dan Scraper, Officer Education System Manager, DOTD, 8 Jan 2010, HRDC.

28 See Note 27.

29 Interview, Dastrup with Dan Scraper, OES Program Manager, DOTD, 7 Jan 2005, HRDC; Briefing, subj: 15 Week 4 Day BOLC III with Tracked Follow-on Courses, 9 Dec 2004, HRDC; E-mail with atch, subj: Biweekly Report, 23 Nov 2004, HRDC; E-mail with atch, subj: G3 Biweekly Input, 20 Dec 2004, HRDC; E-mail with atch, subj: Bi-weekly Update, 12 Oct 2004, HRDC; E-mail with atch, subj: G3/G4 Biweekly Update Report, 27 Oct 2004, HRDC; E-mail, subj: BOLC and CCC, 22 Feb 2005, HRDC; Briefing to CG, subj: Transition of FAOBC to FA BOLC III, 19 Dec 2005, HRDC; Briefing, subj: BOLC E-mail History, Jun 2005, HRDC; Interview, Dastrup with Dan Scraper, Program Manager OES, DOTD, 11 Jan 2006, HRDC; Briefing, subj: BOLC III AOT Strategy, 5 Jan 2006, HRDC.

30 See Note 29.

31 Briefing (Extract), subj: 30th Field Artillery Regiment, 2006, HRDC.

32 Briefing (Extract), subj: 30th Field Artillery Regiment, 2006; Fact Sheet, subj: ATRRS Course Catalog, 11 Jan 2007, HRDC; MAJ Todd R. Peery, "The Changing Face of Field Artillery Officer Training," undated draft article, HRDC; Briefing, subj: Approved FA Lieutenant Critical Tasks, Apr 2006, HRDC.

33 Briefing (Extract), subj: 30th Field Artillery Regiment, 2006, HRDC; Fact Sheet, subj: ATRRS Course Catalog, 11 Jan 2007, HRDC; Peery, "The Changing Face of Field Artillery Officer

Training," undated draft article, HRDC; Briefing, subj: Approved FA Lieutenant Critical Tasks, Apr 2006, HRDC.

34   E-mail with atch (FOUO), subj: FRAGO 23, 28 Jul 2009, information used is unclassified, HRDC; E-mail subj: TRADOC Campaign Plan 3, Aug 2009, HRDC; Interview, Dastrup with Dan Scraper, Officer Education System Manager, DOTD, 8 Jan 2010, HRDC.

35   Memorandum for Chief of Staff, Army, and Commanding General, US Army Training and Doctrine Command, subj: Army Training and Leader Development Panel Report (Warrant Officers), 17 Jul 2002, in The Army Training and Leader Development Panel (ATLDP) Phase III - Warrant Officer Study, 18 Jul 2002, HRDC; Memorandum for Chief of Staff, Army and Commanding General, US Army Training and Doctrine Command, subj: ATDLP Phase III (WO Study) Report, 17 Jul 2002, in ATLDP Phase III - Warrant Officer Study, 18 Jul 2002, HRDC; ATLDP Phase III - Warrant Officer Study, 18 Jul 2002, pp. WO-22-23, HRDC.

36   "Army Training and Leader Development Panel Completes Warrant Officer Study," US Army News Release, 22 Aug 2002, HRDC; "Study Recommends 63 Changes for Warrant Officers," ArmyLink News, 22 Aug 2002, HRDC; Memorandum for CSA, subj: Army Training and Leader Development Panel, Phase III (WO Study) Report, 17 Jul 2002, in Final Report, subj: ATLDP Phase III--Warrant Officer Study, 18 Jul 2002, HRDC; Fact Sheet, subj: History of the Army Warrant Officer, 2 May 2001, HRDC; Information Paper, subj: TWOS, WOLDAP, 29 Dec 1999, HRDC; Fact Sheet, subj: History of the Warrant Officer Corps, HRDC; Final Report, vol 1, subj: TWOS, Jun 1986, HRDC; E-mail, subj: WOES Input to 2002 Annual Command History, 3 Feb 2003, HRDC.

37   Memorandum for Chief of Staff, Army, and Commanding General, US Army Training and Doctrine Command, subj: ATDLP Report (Warrant Officers), 17 Jul 2002, in ATLDP Phase III - Warrant Officer Study, 18 Jul 2002, HRDC; Memorandum for Chief of Staff, Army and Commanding General, US Army Training and Doctrine Command, subj: ATDLP, Phase III (WO Study) Report, 17 Jul 2002, in ATLDP Phase III - Warrant Officer Study, 18 Jul 2002, HRDC; ATLDP Phase III - Warrant Officer Study, 18 Jul 2002, pp. WO-22-23, HRDC.

38   Memorandum for Record, subj: 9 Feb 2007 BOLC II Warrant Officer Work Group Minutes, 17 Feb 2007, HRDC; Briefing, subj: Warrant Officer Integration into BOLC II, 11 Apr 2007, HRDC; Memorandum for Record, subj: Accessions Command Takeaways, undated, HRDC; Briefing (Extract), subj: Warrant Officer Integration into BOLC II, 10 Jan 2007, HRDC; Briefing, subj: Ft Sill BOLC II Warrant Officer Implementation Planning Committee, 2 Apr 2007, HRDC; E-mail with atch, subj: Summary of 21 Feb 2007 VTC, 23 Feb 2007, HRDC; Memorandum for See Distribution, subj: FY 2008 Commander's Training Guidance, 26 Jun 2007, HRDC; CW5 David P. Welch, "Warrant: The Legacy of Leadership as a Warrant Officer – 90 Years of Technical Expertise in the Army," *On Point*, Summer 2008, pp. 6-13, HRDC.

39   See Note 38.

40   E-mail with atch, subj: FRAGO 23, 28 Jul 2009, HRDC; E-mail, subj: TRADOC Campaign Plan, 3 Aug 2009, HRDC.

41   Interview, Dastrup with CW4 Stephen A. Gomes, Program Manager, Warrant Officer Education System (WOES), DOTD, 21 Jan 2003, HRDC; E-mail, subj: WOES for Annual Command History, 24 Jan 2003, HRDC; Welch, "Warrant: The Legacy of Leadership as a Warrant Officer," pp. 6-13, HRDC.

42   E-mail with atch, subj: NCOES and WOES Redesign for 2006 Annual Command History, 31 Jan 2007, HRDC; E-mail with atch, subj: WOES Redesign, 2 Mar 2007, HRDC.

43   E-mail with atch, subj: WOES Redesign, 2 Mar 2007; Briefing, subj: 428th FA Brigade, Jun 2007, HRDC; Briefing, subj: Warrant Officer Basic Course, 26 Mar 2008, HRDC.

44   Interview, Dastrup with CW4 Richard Gonzales, 26 Mar 2008, HRDC; Briefing, subj:

Warrant Officer Basic Course, 26 Mar 2008, HRDC; E-mail with atch, subj: WOES and OES Input to 2010 Annual Command History, 25 Feb 2011, HRDC; E-mail with atch, subj: 428 FAB Portion of 2010 Annual History, 4 Apr 11, HRDC.

45   "Army Study IDs NCO Concerns," ArmyLink News, 2 May 2002, HRDC; "Army Training and Leader Development Panel Reports on the NCO Study," US Army News Release, 2 May 2002, HRDC; "TRADOC Responding to Training Needs from NCO Study," ArmyLink News, 2 May 2002, HRDC; Memorandum for Chief of Staff of the Army, subj: ATLDP Phase II (NCO Study) Final Report, 2 Apr 2002, in Final Report, subj: The ATLDP Report (NCO), 2 Apr 2002, HRDC.

46   Final Report, subj: The ATLDP Report (NCO), 2 Apr 2002, HRDC, pp. 24, 26, 39.

47   Briefing, subj: BNCOC/ANCOC Adjustments and NCOES Redesign, 9 Apr 2004, HRDC; Fact Sheet, subj: NCOES Executive Summary, 14 Apr 2004, HRDC; Memorandum for See Distribution, subj: FY05 TRADOC Commander's Training Guidance, 22 Jul 2004, HRDC, for TRADOC training guidance for FY 2005.

48   E-mail with atch, subj: NCOES Redesign, 18 Mar 2005, HRDC; Briefing, subj: BNCOC/ANCOC Adjustments and NCOES Redesign, 9 Apr 2004, HRDC; Fact Sheet, subj: Noncommissioned Officer Education System (NCOES) Executive Summary, 14 Apr 2004, HRDC. Note that CG TRADOC reiterated incorporating lessons learned into NCOES POIs in July 2004, see Memorandum for See Distribution, subj: FY 2005 TRADOC Commander's Training Guidance, 22 Jul 2004, HRDC. Also see ATLDP Report, 2 Apr 2002, for background on previous reforms efforts, HRDC.

49   E-mail, subj: NCOES Redesign, 2 Feb 2005, HRDC; Interview, Dastrup with CSM Allie R. Ousley, Cmdt, NCOA, and SGM John M. Dorsey, 9 Feb 2005, HRDC; E-mail with atch, subj: NCOES Redesign, 18 Mar 2005, HRDC.

50   E-mail, subj: Redesign, 5 Feb 2007, HRDC; MSG William F. Johnson and LTC David J. Brost, "The Making of Redleg Pentathletes: Transforming Enlisted CMF 13," *Field Artillery Magazine*, Nov-Dec 2006, pp. 6-10; MG David C. Ralston, "State of the Field Artillery," *Field Artillery Magazine*, Nov-Dec 2006, pp. 1-5; Briefing, subj: 13M30 Requirements, undated, HRDC; Briefing, subj: 13B30/13B40 New Direction – Live Fire, 23 Oct 2006, HRDC; Interview, Dastrup with CSM Robert L. White, Cmdt, NCOA, and SGM Ikchin Kim, Asst Cmdt, NCOA, 14 Feb 2007, HRDC; E-mail with atch, subj: NCOES and WOES input to 2006 Annual Command History, 14 Mar 2007, HRDC; LTC Loyd A. Gerber, "Reset," pp. 14-18.

51   CSM (Ret) Jeffrey L. Moyes, "MTTs: Resetting FA Core Competencies," *Fires Bulletin,* Jul-Sep 2008, pp. 10-11; 2006 US Army Fires Center of Excellence and Fort Sill (USAFCOEFS) ACH, p. 15; Gerber, "Reset," pp. 14-18.

52   2006 USAFCOEFS ACH, p. 15; Gerber, "Reset," pp. 14-18.

53   Gerber, "Reset," pp. 14-18.

54   Memorandum thru TRADOC CAC Cdr and TRADOC Cdr for VCSA, subj: Response to VCSA Tasker to Assess FA Lieutenant Training, 7 Aug 2006, HRDC; Briefing, subj: Field Artillery Reset, 3 Oct 2008, HRDC; Briefing, subj: Field Artillery Reset, 3 Oct 2008 and HQ TRADOC Tasking Order, subj: TRADOC Task # IN 000564, 29 Aug 2006, HRDC.

55   CSM William E. High, "The FA Master Gunner and Reset of the Redeployed FA Battalion," *Field Artillery Magazine*, Jan-Feb 2007, pp. 1-3.

56   High, "The FA Master Gunner and Reset of the Redeployed FA Battalion," pp. 1-3; Briefing, subj: FA WOT Reset, 22 Nov 2006, HRDC.

57   Briefing, subj: Commander's Call 22 Feb 2007, HRDC; Interview with atch, Dastrup with LTC Loyd Gerber and LTC David Vineyard, Task Force Reset, 29 Jan 2008, HRDC; Briefing, subj: Restoring Core Competencies, undated, HRDC. In 2007, the Rand Corporation conducted a study about leader skill competencies and reached the same conclusions as the TRADOC and DA studies

of 2006. See E-mail with atch, subj: Reset Rand Study, 29 Jan 2008, HRDC; E-mail, subj: Reset Task Force, 6 Mar 08, HRDC; E-mail, subj: Reset Task Force, 6 Mar 2008, HRDC.

58 CSM Joseph D. Smith, "The FA NCO: Absolutely Mission Essential," *Fires Bulletin*, Jul-Sep 2008, pp. 4-5; Moyer, "MTTs: Resetting FA Core Competencies," pp. 10-11; Briefing, subj: Field Artillery Reset, 3 Oct 2008, HRDC.

59 E-mail with atch, subj: Reset Input to 2008 Annual Command History, 17 Feb 2009, HRDC; Interview, Dastrup with LTC David S. Lee, Chief, FA Lessons Learned/FA Reset, DOTD, 17 Feb 2009, HRDC.

60 MG Peter M. Vangjel, "State of the Field Artillery: Today and Tomorrow, Artillery Strong," *Fires Bulletin*, Oct-Dec 2008, pp. 1-8; Briefing, subj: Field Artillery Collective Training Evaluation Team (CTET), 5 Dec 2008, HRDC; Briefing, subj: Field Artillery Reset Assistance Training, 10 Dec 2008, HRDC; E-mail with atch, subj: Reset Input to 2008 ACH, 11 Feb 2009, HRDC.

61 Memorandum thru Cdr, 428th FAB, Chief, Field Artillery Proponency Office (FAPO), Dir, DOTD, and Asst Cmdt, for CG, US Army Fires Center of Excellence (USAFCOE), subj: Decision Brief for Expansion of the Field Artillery Captains' Career Course, 4 Sep 2008, HRDC; MAJ Peter M. Sittenauer and MAJ Cornelius L. Morgan, "FACCC: Redesigned for Today and Tomorrow," *Fires Bulletin*, Jul-Sep 2008, pp. 16-19; Interview, Dastrup with Dan Scraper, DOTD OES Manager, 9 Jan 2009, HRDC; Briefing, subj: Requirement, 30 May 2008, HRDC; Field Artillery Precommand Course Schedule, 14 Jan 2009, HRDC; E-mail, subj: Gap Mitigation Action, 15 Jan 2009, HRDC; E-mail with atch, subj: Pre-Command Course, 10 Feb 2009, HRDC; Memorandum (Draft) for CG, TRADOC, subj: Field Artillery Branch Assessment, 5 May 2008, HRDC.

62 Sittenauer and Morgan, "FACCC," pp. 16-19.

63 Memorandum thru Cdr, 428th FAB, Chief, FAPO, Dir, DOTD, and Asst Cmdt, for CG, USAFCOE, 4 Sep 2008, HRDC; Briefing, subj: FACCC Expansion: Preparing Leaders for the Future, 4 Sep 2008, HRDC; Interview, Dastrup with Scraper, 9 Jan 2009, HRDC.

64 Sittenauer and Morgan, "FACCC," pp. 16-19, HRDC; Memorandum thru Cdr, 428th FAB, Chief, FAPO, Dir, DOTD, and Asst Cmdt, for CG, USAFCOE, 4 Sep 2008, HRDC; Briefing, subj: FACCC Expansion: Preparing Leaders for the Future, 4 Sep 2008, HRDC; Briefing (Extract), subj: FA Branch Update, Nov 2008, HRDC; COL Frank J. Siltman and LTC John P. Frisbie, "Fire Support Just Got Harder: Adding Non-lethal Fires as a Core Competency," *Fires Bulletin*, Jul-Sep 2008, pp. 6-8; Interview, Dastrup with Scraper, 9 Jan 2009, HRDC.

65 CSM Dean J. Keveles, "NCOES: Restoring NCO Core Competency," *Fires Bulletin*, Jul-Aug 2008, pp. 20-21.

66 Keveles, "NCOES," pp. 20-21; Briefing, subj: NCOEs Expansion and Transformation, 5 Sep 2008, HRDC; Briefing, subj: The Requirement, 30 May 2008, HRDC.

67 Jim Tice, "NCO Training Overhaul," *Army Times*, 22 Dec 2008; Keveles, "NCOES:," pp. 20-21; Briefing, subj: NCOEs Expansion and Transformation, 5 Sep 2008, HRDC; Unit Award Recommendation, 30 Sep 2009, HRDC.

68 Keveles, "NCOES," pp. 20-21; Briefing, subj: NCOEs Expansion and Transformation, 5 Sep 2008, HRDC; Tice, "NCO Training Overhaul."

69 E-mail with atch, subj: Reset Input to 2008 ACH, 20 Feb 2009, HRDC; COL James L. Davis, "Intermediate Level Education: Helping Combat Artillery Atrophy," *Fires* Bulletin, Nov-Dec 2009, pp. 41-43.

70 Statement of Work, Development of Resident Tactical Information Operations Course, undated, HRDC; Memorandum for BG James C. Yarbough, DCG, US Army Infantry School, subj: Effects Based Operations, 31 Mar 2005, HRDC; Tactical Information Operations Course Brochure, undated, HRDC; Interview, Dastrup with CW3 Andre Williams, Warrant Officer Education System (WOES) Branch, 30th FA Brigade, 19 May 2005, HRDC.

71 Briefing, subj: Tactical Information Operations IPR, 17 Feb 2005, HRDC; Briefing (Extract), subj: LTG Wallace Update, 14 Jun 2004, HRDC; E-mail with atch, subj: Courses Instructing Non-lethal/Effects-based Operations, 19 May 2005, HRDC; Interview, Dastrup with CW3 John Watson, Warrant Officer Advance Course Instructor, 30th FA Battalion, 23 May 2005, HRDC.

72 Vangjel, "State of the Field Artillery: Today and Tomorrow, Artillery Strong," pp. 1-8; Information Paper, subj: Tactical Information Operations Course, 29 Jan 2009, HRDC; Information Paper, subj: Tactical Information Operations Course, 29 Jan 2009; Information Paper, subj: Course Information, 14 Feb 2006, HRDC; Information Paper, subj: Tactical Information Operations Course, undated, HRDC; Information Paper, subj: Tactical Information Operations Course, 14 Feb 2006, HRDC; Memorandum for Cdr, TRADOC, subj: Commander's Statement - FY06 TRADOC Budget Guidance, undated, HRDC; 2010 US Army Field Artillery School Annual History, p. 42.

73 Statement of Work, Development of Resident Tactical Information Operations Course, undated, HRDC; Memorandum for BG James C. Yarbough, DCG, US Army Infantry School, subj: Effects-Based Operations, 31 Mar 2005, HRDC; Tactical Information Operations Course Brochure, undated, HRDC.

74 Ralston, "State of the Field Artillery," pp. 1-5; Army Training Requirements and Resources System, Army Operational Electronic Warfare Course, 22 Jan 2007, HRDC; Vangjel, "State of the Field Artillery," pp. 1-8; Briefing, subj: Army Operational Electronic Warfare Course, US Army Field Artillery Center and School, 6 Jun 2008, HRDC; Jeff Crawley, "Class a Glimpse of Future," Fort Sill *Cannoneer*, 19 Feb 2009, p. 1a, HRDC; E-mail with atch, subj: Electronic Operational Warfare Course, 10 Mar 2009, HRDC..

75 Crawley, "Class a Glimpse of Future," p. 1a; E-mail with atch, subj: Electronic Operational Warfare Course, 10 Mar 2009, HRDC.

76 Siltman and Frisbie, "Fire Support Just Got Harder," pp. 6-8; E-mail with atch, subj: Adding Non-lethal Fires as a Core Competency, 14 Jul 2009, HRDC; Briefing, subj: Requirement, 30 May 2008, HRDC; Field Artillery Precommand Course Schedule, 14 Jan 2009, HRDC; E-mail, subj: Gap Mitigation Action, 15 Jan 2009, HRDC; E-mail with atch, subj: Pre-Command Course, 10 Feb 2009, HRDC; Memorandum (Draft) for CG, TRADOC, subj: Field Artillery Branch Assessment, 5 May 2008, HRDC; Briefing, subj: FA Commandant's Priorities, 14 Apr 2011, HRDC.

77 Statement before the Subcommittee on Military Construction, the Senate Appropriations Committee, by Raymond F. Dubois, Deputy Undersecretary of Defense for Installations and Environment, 18 Mar 2003, pp. 2-3, 15, 16, HRDC; Report (Extract), subj: Report to Congress on Base Realignment and Closure 2005, 22 Mar 2004, pp. 1, 3, HRDC.

78 National Army of the United States, Update for 9 Jan 2004, p. 1, HRDC; Memorandum for See Distribution, subj: Transformation through Base Realignment and Closure, 12 Dec 2002, HRDC; Memorandum for Secretaries of the Military Departments, subj: Transformation through Base Realignment and Closure, 15 Nov 2002, HRDC; Memorandum for Secretaries of the Military Departments (Extract), subj: Transformation through BRAC 2005 Policy Memorandum One – Policy, Responsibilities, and Procedures, 16 Apr 2003, HRDC; E-mail, subj: Public Affairs Guidance for BRAC 2005, 15 Jan 2004, HRDC; Federal Managers Association, Washington Report, 23 Dec 2002, HRDC; DOD Report to the Defense BRAC (Extract), DA Analysis and Recommendations BRAC 2005, Vol III, Executive Summary, pp. 3-17, HRDC.

79 BRAC Report (Extract), Vol I, Part 1 of 2, May 2005, Appendix A, p. 36-37, HRDC; BRAC Report (Extract), Vol I, Part 2 of 2, May 2005, Section 1, pp. 22-23, Section 4, pp. 12-13, Section 5, pp. 22-23, 37-38, HRDC; Base Summary Sheet for Defense BRAC Commission Visit, 11 Jun 2005, HRDC; Memorandum for Cdr, TRADOC, subj: BRAC Manpower Action Plan, 3 Aug 2005, HRDC; Talking Points for BRAC Commission Visit, 11 Jun 2005, HRDC; Ltr, Defense

BRAC, subj: Request Comment on Fort Sill related BRAC Recommendations, 11 Jun 2005, HRDC; Briefing, subj: Realignment and Closure Actions, Considerations and Analysis, 11 Jun 2005, HRDC; DOD Report to Defense BRAC, (Extract), DA Analysis and Recommendations BRAC 2005, Vol III, Executive Summary, May 2005, pp. 3-17; HRDC; Interview with atch, Dastrup with James H. Wollman, Fires Integration Division (FID), DOTD, 12 Feb 2008, HRDC.

80 See Note 79.

81 Interview with atch, Dastrup with Wollman, 12 Feb 2008, HRDC; BRAC Base Visit Report, 11 Jun 2005, HRDC; E-mail with atch, subj: Net Fires Brief, 13 Jul 2005, HRDC; Briefing, subj: Net Fires Center Staff, undated, HRDC; Briefing, subj: Realignment and Closure Actions, Requirements and Analysis, 9 Jun 2005, HRDC; Briefing, subj: Realignment and Closure Actions, Considerations and Analysis, 10 Jun 2005, HRDC; Briefing, subj: Fires Center of Excellence, Jan 2006, HRDC; James H. Wollman and David S. Henderson, "Fires Center of Excellence in 2011," *Field Artillery Magazine,* Jul-Aug 2007, pp. 16-20.

82 Briefing, subj: Realignment and Closure Actions, Considerations and Analysis, 10 Jun 2005; Interview, Dastrup with LTC William Pitts, Chief, FID, DOTD, 24 Jan 2006, HRDC; Briefing, subj: Plans Cell, Jan 2006, HRDC; Briefing, subj: Fires Center of Excellence, Jan 2006; Briefing, subj: Realignment and Closure Actions, Considerations and Analysis, 10 Jun 2005, HRDC; Briefing, subj: Army Net Fires Center Concept Brief, undated, HRDC.

83 2005 USAFACFS ACH, pp. 9-10; Department of the Army, Analysis and Recommendations BRAC 2005 (Extract), May 2005, HRDC; Defense Base Closure and Realignment Commission, Base Summary Sheet, Fort Sill, OK, 11 Jun 2005, p. 5, HRDC; Base Visit Report, 11 Jun 2005, HRDC.

84 E-mail with atch, subj: Latest Center of Excellence (COE) Design Slides, 25 Jan 2006, HRDC; E-mail with atch, subj: TAI #3 VTC Read Ahead Slides, 25 Jan 2006, HRDC; E-mail, subj: Personal Notes from Brief - FYI only - comment/ask questions as desired, 25 Jan 2006, HRDC; E-mail, subj: You'd Think I'd Learn, 25 Jan 2006, HRDC; E-mail with atch, subj: Fires COE - Historical Article, 11 Apr 2007, HRDC; US Army Field Artillery School Position Paper, 7 Dec 2005, p. 3, HRDC; Briefing, subj: Fires Center of Excellence Design and Implementation, 9 Mar 2006, HRDC.

85 E-mail with atch, subj: Latest COE Design Slides, 25 Jan 2006, HRDC; E-mail with atch, subj: TAI #3 Video Teleconference (VTC) Read Ahead Slides, 25 Jan 2006, HRDC; E-mail, subj: Personal Notes from Brief - FYI only - comment/ask questions as desired, 25 Jan 2006, HRDC; E-mail, subj: You'd Think I'd Learn, 25 Jan 2006, HRDC.

86 E-mail with atch, subj: Fires COE - Historical Article, 11 Apr 2007, HRDC; US Army Field Artillery School Position Paper, 7 Dec 2005, p. 3, HRDC; Briefing, subj: Fires Center of Excellence Design and Implementation, 9 Mar 2006, HRDC.

87 See Note 86.

88 Wollman and Henderson, "Fires Center of Excellence in 2011," pp. 16-20; Briefing, subj: Information Brief on Fires Integration Division, 22 Feb 2007, HRDC; Briefing, subj: Fires COE Update, 14 Mar 2007, HRDC; Briefing, subj: Fires Center of Excellence Manpower Review, 17 Jan 2007, HRDC.

89 Briefing, subj: Fires Center of Excellence Manpower Review, 17 Jan 2007, HRDC; Briefing, subj: Fires Center of Excellence Manpower Review, undated, HRDC; Interview with atch, Dastrup with John W. Reid, DRM Management Division, 6 Feb 2007, HRDC; E-mail with atch, subj: Fires COE - Historical Article, 11 Apr 2007, HRDC; Memorandum with atch, subj: Draft Fires Center of Excellence TDA, 17 Apr 2006, HRDC; Briefing (Extract), subj: Home-on-Home, 15-16 May 2006, HRDC; Briefing, subj: Fires Center of Excellence, 16 Oct 2006, HRDC; Briefing, subj: USAMAA Manpower and Organizational Study of TRADOC Center, ATC, and School, 28

Mar 2006, HRDC; E-mail with atch, subj: TRADOC Alternative Organization Design and Force Structure Reductions, 13 Oct 2006, HRDC; Memorandum for See Distribution, subj: Transforming TRADOC – Enabling the Army Vision, 15 May 2006, HRDC.

90 Interview, Dastrup with Reid, DRM Management Office, 6 Feb 2007, HRDC; E-mail with atch, subj: DRM's Portion of 2006 Annual Command History, 4 May 2007, HRDC; Memorandum for Record with atch, subj: Information Delivered by MAJ Williams, FID, 6 May 2008, HRDC; E-mail with atch, subj: DRM's Portion of 2007 Annual Command History, 22 Apr 2008, HRDC; Briefing, subj: Fires Center of Excellence Manpower Review, 17 Jan 2007, HRDC; Briefing, subj: Informational Brief on Fires Integration Division, 22 Feb 2007, HRDC; Briefing, subj: Fires COE Update, 14 Mar 2007, HRDC; Wollman and Henderson, "Fires Center of Excellence in 2011," pp. 16-20; Briefing, subj: USAFCOEFS, 21 Sep 2007, HRDC; E-mail with atch, subj: Assessment of Risks on BRAC Savings, 10 Oct 2007, HRDC; Briefing, subj: FCOE Update, 17 Apr 2007, HRDC; Information Paper, subj: Risks Assumed with Fires Center of Excellence, 5 Oct 2007, HRDC; Memorandum for Record, subj: BRAC Input to 2007 Annual Command History, 13 Mar 2008, HRDC; E-mail with atch, subj: Fires COE - Historical Article, 11 Apr 2007, HRDC; Briefing, subj: USAMAA Manpower and Organizational Study of TRADOC Alternative Organization Design and Force Structure Reductions, 13 Oct 2006, HRDC; Memorandum for See Distribution, subj: Transforming TRADOC – Enabling the Army Vision, 15 May 2006, HRDC.

91 Interview, Dastrup with John W. Reid, DRM Management Office, 29 Jan 2008, HRDC; Wollman and Henderson, "Fires Center of Excellence in 2011," pp. 16-20; Briefing (Extract), subj: Review of Concept Drill for Movement Plan, 30 Aug 2007, HRDC; E-mail with atch, subj: Assessment of Risks on BRAC Savings, 10 Oct 2007, HRDC; Briefing, subj: USAFCOEFS, 21 Sep 2007, HRDC; Briefing, subj: FCOE Update, BRAC Summit, undated, HRDC; Interview, Dastrup with James H. Wollman and LTC Matthew W. Youngkin, FID, DOTD, 18 Jan 2008, HRDC.

92 Briefing, subj: Fires Center of Excellence Update, 1 Aug 2007, HRDC; Briefing, subj: Stationing Management Office, 25 Oct 2007, HRDC; Briefing, subj: Key COE Milestones, 8 Feb 2007, HRDC; Memorandum for Record, subj: BRAC Input to 2007 ACH, 13 Mar 2008, HRDC; Interview, Dastrup with Wollman, 12 Feb 2008, HRDC.

93 Memorandum for Record, subj: BRAC Input to 2007 ACH, 13 Mar 2008, HRDC; Memorandum for Record with atch, subj: Information Delivered by MAJ Williams, FID, 6 May 2008, HRDC.

94 See Note 93.

95 Fires Review of Concept Drill summary of Discussions, 30 Aug 2007, HRDC; Briefing (Extract), subj: FCOE Update, 16 Jun 2008, HRDC; Interview, Dastrup with Youngkin and Wollman, 21 Jan 2009, HRDC.

96 Information Paper, subj: FCOE Range, Classroom, and Simulation Requirements, 8 Sep 2008, HRDC; Briefing, subj: Fires Center of Excellence, FY09 BRAC Course Movement, 4 Sep 2008, HRDC; Briefing (Extract), subj: Fires Center of Excellence FY09 BRAC Course Movement, 17 Sep 2008, HRDC; Briefing, subj: Fires Center of Excellence, BRAC Update, 6 Dec 2008, HRDC.

97 Briefing, subj: Structure Update, 13 Aug 2008, HRDC; Briefing, subj: Structure, 25 Aug 2008, HRDC; Briefing, subj: Current Fires COE Model, 22 Aug 2008, HRDC; Briefing, subj: BRAC Management Way Ahead, 29 Jul 2008, HRDC; Minutes, Fires Executive Council, 4 Sep 2008, HRDC; Interview, Dastrup with LTC Youngkin and James H. Wollman, FCOE FID, 21 Jan 2009, HRDC; Briefing (Extract), subj: Fires COE Fires Executive Council, 29 Aug 2008, HRDC; Briefing, subj: FCOE GAO Visit, 26 Jan 2009, HRDC; E-mail with atch, subj: DOTS Decision Brief PPT, 11 Aug 2008, HRDC.

98 Personal observation and attendance at transfer of authority ceremony; BG Rodger F. Mathews, "ADA and Fort Sill: New Horizons," *Fires Bulletin*, May-Jun 2009, pp. 1-2; Wilson

A. Rivera, "Air Defense Artillery School Moves to Fort Sill," *Fires Bulletin*, May-Jun 2009, p. 3; "Standing-up the Fires Center of Excellence," *Fires Bulletin*, May-Jun 2009, pp. 4-5.

99   See Note 98.

100 MG David C. Halverson, "2010 State of the Fires Center of Excellence," *Fires Bulletin*, Nov-Dec 2010, pp. 4-6.

101 Sharon McBride, "Creating Culturally Astute Leaders: Joint and Combined Fires University Providing Innovative Cultural Education," *Fires Bulletin*, Sep-Oct 2010, pp. 23-26; Memorandum for Record, subj: Cultural and Foreign Language Program, 17 Feb 2010, HRDC; Email with atch, subj: Cultural and Foreign Language Program, 19 Feb 2010, HRDC; Draft Concept Paper (Extract), subj: FCOE Cultural and Foreign Language Program Strategy, 19 Feb 2010, HRDC; Memorandum for Record, subj: Cultural and Foreign Language Program, 17 Feb 2010; Email with atch, subj: Cultural and Foreign Language Program, 9 Feb 2010, HRDC; Briefing, subj: Army Culture and Foreign Language Strategy, US Army Field Artillery School, 8 Jan 2009, HRDC.

102 "Army Announces Vision for the Future," US Army News Release, 12 Oct 1999, HRDC; Vision Statement, 23 Jun 1999, HRDC; CSA Remarks at Dwight D. Eisenhower Luncheon, AUSA, 22 Oct 2002, p. 5, CSA Remarks File, HRDC.

103 E-mail with atch, subj: Manuscript Review, 8 Dec 2003, p. 3, HRDC; E-mail with atch, subj: Transformation Activities in Congress, 14 Feb 2000, HRDC; Briefing, subj: Transformation Campaign Plan, 19 Jan 2000, HRDC; The Brigade Combat Team Organizational and Operational Concept, 6 Jan 2000, p. 4, HRDC; Intent of the Chief of Staff, Army (CSA), 23 Jun 1999, HRDC; E-mail with atch, subj: CSA Expands on Presentation to Association of the United States Army (AUSA) in Oct, 1 Feb 2000, HRDC; E-mail, subj: Initial Bde – Historical Reporting, 22 Dec 1999, HRDC; Briefing, subj: Transformation Campaign Plan, 19 Jan 2000, HRDC. See Quadrennial Defense Review Report, 30 Sep 2001, HRDC, for background on the Transformation of the Army and military forces.

104 Intent of the CSA, 23 Jun 1999, HRDC.

105 E-mail with atch, subj: CSA Expands on Presentation to AUSA in Oct, 1 Feb 2000, HRDC; "Army Announces Vision for the Future;" 1999 USAFACFS ACH, p. 63.

106 E-mail with atch, subj: Crusader, 5 Jan 2000, HRDC; E-mail with atch, subj: Special Report, 4 Jan 2000, HRDC; Interview, Dastrup with MAJ Stephen Hitz, TSM Cannon, 7 Mar 2000, HRDC; "Secretary of the Army Says Crusader Still Viable," Army Link News, 15 Nov 1999, HRDC; U.S Army Posture Statement for Fiscal Year 2001, p. 30, Posture Statement File, HRDC; 2000 USAFACFS ACH, p. 68; Briefing, subj: Equipping the Brigade Combat Team, 21 Jun 2000, HRDC; 2000 USAFACFS ACH, p. 68; 2002 USAFACFS ACH, p. 52; Mission Statement for FCS, 2 Nov 2001, HRDC; Briefing (Extract), subj: FCS Industry Day, 9 Nov 2001, HRDC.

107 "Focus Task Force 'Jump Starting' Future," Army Public Affairs, 27 Jan 2004; Fact Sheet, subj: Focus Areas, 25 Feb 2004, HRDC; Schoomaker Speech, Dec 2003; DA, "The Way Ahead," pp. 12-13; DA, 2003 US Army Transformation Road Map (Extract), undated, Executive Summary, p. 11, HRDC; Interview, Dastrup with Dan Bankston, Task Force XXI, Futures Development and Integration Center (FDIC), 2 Mar 2004, HRDC; Memorandum with atch for Dir, FDIC, 20 Apr 2004, HRDC; Army Comprehensive Guide to Modularity, Version 1.0, Oct 2004, pp. 1-1, 1-6, HRDC; Briefing, subj: Modular Army Overview, 5 Apr 2004, HRDC; Schoomaker Speech, Dec 2003, HRDC.

108 See Note 107.

109 Army Comprehensive Guide to Modularity, Version 1.0, Oct 2004, pp. 1-1, 1-6, HRDC; Briefing, subj: Modular Army Overview, 5 Apr 2004, HRDC.

110 2005 USAFACFS ACH, p. 45; Briefing, subj: Modularity Overview, 28 Apr 2006, HRDC; 2003 USAFACFS ACH, pp. 62-63; Interview, Dastrup with Daniel L. Bankston, FDIC, 3 Mar

2005, HRDC; White Paper, subj: Unit of Employment Operations, 20 Mar 2004, pp. 9-12, HRDC; Briefing, subj: US Field Artillery in Transformation, undated, HRDC; Army Comprehensive Guide to Modularity, Version 1.0, Oct 2004, pp. 1-7, 1-8, 1-9, 1-10, HRDC; Briefing, subj: Modular Army Overview, 5 Apr 2004, HRDC; 2004 USAFACFS ACH, p. 50; E-mail with atch, subj: Transformation Portion of the 2006 ACH, 30 Apr 2007, HRDC;. Briefing, subj: Modularity Overview, 28 Apr 2006, HRDC.

111 2003 USAFACFS ACH, pp. 62-63; Interview, Dastrup with Bankston, 3 Mar 2005, HRDC; White Paper, subj: Unit of Employment Operations, 20 Mar 2004, pp. 9-12, HRDC; Briefing, subj: US Field Artillery in Transformation, undated, HRDC; Army Comprehensive Guide to Modularity, Version 1.0, Oct 2004, pp. 1-7, 1-8, 1-9, 1-10, HRDC; Briefing, subj: Modular Army Overview, 5 Apr 2004, HRDC; 2004 USAFACFS ACH, p. 50; E-mail with atch, subj: Transformation Portion of the 2006 ACH, 30 Apr 2007, HRDC; Briefing, subj: Modularity Overview, 28 Apr 2006, HRDC; Briefing, subj: Modularity Overview, 28 Apr 2006, HRDC.

112 Report for Congress, Congressional Research Service, 20 May 2005, p. 6, HRDC. The Stryker brigade combat team was a brigade combat team equipped with the Stryker Interim Armored Vehicle. See 2002 USAFACFS ACH, p. 52.

113 2003 USAFACFS ACH, p. 63; Army Comprehensive Guide to Modularity, Version 1.0, Oct 2004, pp. 1-13, 1-14, HRDC; White Paper, subj: Unit of Employment Operations, 20 Mar 2004, p. 10, HRDC.

114 Briefing, subj: Chief of Field Artillery Update, Nov-Dec 2004, HRDC; White Paper, subj: Unit of Employment Operations, 20 Mar 2004, pp. 10-11, HRDC; "Army Announces FY05 and FY06 Modular Brigade Force Structure Decision," US Army News Release, 23 Jul 2004, HRDC; Briefing, subj: Modular Army Overview, 5 Apr 2004, HRDC; Briefing, subj: US Field Artillery in Transformation, undated, HRDC. E-mail with atch, subj: Transformation of the Army, 4 Apr 2005, HRDC; "Army to Reset into Modular Brigade-Centric Force," Army News Service, 24 Feb 2004, HRDC; Briefing, subj: US Field Artillery in Transformation, undated; Briefing, subj: Chief of Field Artillery Update, Nov-Dec 2004, HRDC; 2004 USAFACFS ACH, p. 53; 2005 USAFACFS ACH, p. 47; Report, subj: US Army's Modular Redesign: Issues for Congress, 24 Jan 2007, pp. 3, 10, HRDC; Briefing, subj: Fires Brigade, 16 Dec 2005; Operational Concept for Armed UAVs, 6 Dec 2004, pp. 1-5, HRDC; LTC Samuel R. White, Jr., "The Fires Brigade: Not Your Daddy's FFA HQ," *Field Artillery Magazine*, Nov-Dec 2005, pp. 14-19; Briefing, subj: Fires Brigade CONOP, Armed ER-MP in Support of CJFLCC, 2005, HRDC; Briefing, subj: Fires Brigade Mission, 2005, HRDC.

115 E-mail with atch, subj: Transformation of the Army, 4 Apr 2005, HRDC; Briefing, subj: Chief of Field Artillery Update, Nov-Dec 2004, HRDC; Briefing, subj: How the UEx Fights, 29 Mar 2004, HRDC; MG David P. Valcourt, "Issues and Answers," *Field Artillery Magazine*, Jul-Aug 2004, pp. 1-4; Briefing (Extract), subj: Fires Brigade, 4 Dec 2004, HRDC; Fires Brigade Organizational and Operational Plan (Extract), 9 Nov 2004, p. 12, HRDC; Briefing, subj: Modularity/Transformation, Jan 2005, HRDC; Briefing, subj: US Field Artillery in Transformation, undated; FA and Joint Fires and Effects Themes and Messages, 29 Dec 2004, HRDC; Msg, ca 18 Mar 2005, HRDC; 2004 USAFACFS ACH, p. 50; Fires Brigade Operational and Organizational Plan (Extract), 26 Jul 2005, pp. 12-29, HRDC; Briefing, subj: Fires Brigade, 16 Dec 2005, HRDC; Briefing, subj: Fires Brigade, 16 Dec 2005; Operational Concept for Armed UAVs, 6 Dec 2004, pp. 1-5, HRDC; White, "The Fires Brigade," pp. 14-19; Briefing, subj: Fires Brigade CONOP, Armed ER-MP in Support of CJFLCC, 2005, HRDC; Briefing, subj: Fires Brigade Mission, 2005, HRDC.

116 "Army Announces Vision for the Future;" Vision Statement, 23 Jun 1999, HRDC; CSA Remarks at Dwight D. Eisenhower Luncheon, AUSA, 22 Oct 2002, p. 5, CSA Remarks File, HRDC.

117 See Note 116.

118 E-mail with atch, subj: Manuscript Review, 8 Dec 2003, HRDC; Briefing, subj:

Recapitalization of the Legacy Force, 17 Oct 2000, HRDC; Briefing, subj: Army Transformation, 17 Oct 2000, HRDC; 2001 Army Modernization Plan (Extract), Executive Summary, pp. 11, 24, HRDC; Testimony, General Shinseki before Senate Armed Services Committee, 10 Jul 2001, HRDC; Information Paper, subj: CSA Remarks at AUSA Seminar, 8 Nov 2001, HRDC: BG William F. Engel, "Transforming Fires for the Objective Force," *Field Artillery Magazine*, Nov-Dec 2001, pp. 9-13; E-mail with atch, subj: Crusader, 1 Mar 2000, HRDC; E-mail with atch, subj: Crusader, 5 Mar 2000, HRDC; E-mail with atch, subj: Future of Heavy Systems, 6 Jan 2000, HRDC; Director of Operational Test and Evaluation, FY99 Annual Report (Extract), subj: Crusader, HRDC; MAJ Donald L. Barnett, "Crusader Target Weight: 38 to 42 Tons," *Field Artillery Magazine*, Mar-Apr 2000, pp. 34-36; Fact Sheet, subj: Crusader 155mm Self-propelled Howitzer, USA, 15 Aug 2002, Crusader File, HRDC.

119 1999 USAFACFS ACH, p. 67; 2000 USAFACFS ACH, pp. 74-79; 2001 USAFACFS ACH, pp. 55-65; E-mail with atch, subj: LegIntObj2, 1 Apr 2002, HRDC; Briefing, subj: None, 12 Oct 2001, HRDC; Interim Division Organizational and Operational Plan, Feb 2001, pp. 4, 10, 23, 25, HRDC; E-mail with atch, subj: LW 155 2005, 3 Mar 2006, HRDC; Interview, Dastrup with John Yager, TSM Cannon, 24 Feb 2006, HRDC; John Yager, TSM Cannon, Notes, undated, HRDC; CPT Waco Lane, "M777 Starts Fielding in the 11th Marines," *Field Artillery Magazine*, Mar-Apr 2005, p. 9; COL John A. Tanzi and LTC Robert D. Harper, "Field Artillery Cannon Systems Update," *Field Artillery Magazine*, Jan-Feb 2006, pp. 14-17; Memorandum for CG, Marine Corps Systems Command, subj: Initial Operational Capability for M777 Lightweight Howitzer, 19 Dec 2005, HRDC; 2006 USAFCOEFS ACH, p. 84; Interview with atch, Dastrup with MAJ Clinton Verge and MAJ Michael Bricker, TRADOC Capabilities Manager (TCM) Rockets and Missiles (RAMS), 25 Feb 2007, HRDC; E-mail with atch, subj: HIMARS 2005, 21 Feb 2006, HRDC; 2006 USAFCOEFS ACH, p. 84.

120 Rowan Scarborough, "Army Chief Crusades to Save New Howitzer Set from Axing," *Washington Times.com*, 2 May 2002, HRDC; E-mail msg with atch, subj: Prepared Opening Remarks for MG Maples, 20 Feb 2003, HRDC; E-mail msg with atch, subj: Crusader, 11 Mar 2003, HRDC; 2001 USAFACFS ACH, pp. 83-86; Fact Sheet, subj: Timeline of Events, undated, HRDC.

121 "Defense Discusses Crusader Alternatives," Defense Link, 15 May 2002, HRDC; "Pentagon Already Has Plans for How to Spend Crusader Billions," *Inside the Army*, 6 May 2002, pp. 1, 13, 14, HRDC; Interview, Dastrup with Doug Brown, Dep Dir, TSM Cannon, 6 Feb 2003, HRDC; Department of Defense, FY 2003 Budget Amendment for Crusader Termination (Extract), May 2002, HRDC; E-mail msg with atch, subj: Crusader, 11 Mar 2003; "Rumsfeld Pulls Plug on Big Gun," *Reuters.com*, 8 May 2002, HRDC; "Rumsfeld Dumps Crusader, Defends Decision," CNN.com, 9 May 2002, HRDC; "Crusader Howitzer Gets the Axe," ArmyLink News, 8 May 2002, HRDC; Briefing, subj: Field Artillery Discussion to the Crusader Alternative, May-Jun 2002, HRDC; "GAO, Crusader Needs Mature Technology, Not Weight Reduction," *Inside the Army*, 4 Mar 2002, pp. 1, 11, HRDC; Memorandum for Secretary of the Army, subj: Crusader Artillery Program Termination, 13 May 2002, HRDC; Memorandum for the Secretary of the Army, subj: Request for Extension of Submission of Crusader Information, 20 May 2002, HRDC; Fact Sheet, subj: Timeline of Events, undated; HRDC.

122 E-mail msg with atch, subj: Testimony, 20 Feb 2003, HRDC; E-mail msg with atch, subj: Testimony, 20 Feb 2003, HRDC; "Authorizers Grant $293 million for FCS Non-line-of-Sight Cannon," *Inside the Army*, 18 Nov 2002, pp. 14-15, HRDC; E-mail msg with atch, subj: FCS Cannon, 11 Mar 2003, HRDC; E-mail msg with atch, subj: Deputy Commanding General Sends, 4 Dec 2002, HRDC; Briefing, subj: FCS Cannon Concept Technology Demonstration Update, Dec 2002, HRDC.

123 E-mail with atch, subj: Historical Update, 31 Mar 2008, HRDC; Information Paper, subj:

FCS FY08 Program Adjustments, undated, HRDC; Briefing, subj: Cannon Smart Book, 30 Jan 2009, HRDC; BAE Information Paper, 13 Jun 2008, HRDC; BAE Information Paper, undated, HRDC; BAE Information Paper, 13 Jun 2008, HRDC; BAE Information Paper, 6 Oct 2008, HRDC; FCOE, Fort Sill on the Move, 15 Dec 2008, HRDC; E-mail with atch, subj: NLOS Cannon Apr 2009, 6 Apr 2009, HRDC.

124 2008 USAFCOEFS ACH, pp. 91-92; DOD News Release, 20 Jul 2009; DOD News Release 23 Jul 2009; 2009 US Army Field Artillery School Annual History, pp. 94-95.

125 E-mail with atch, subj: Excalibur's Role, 30 Apr 2004, HRDC; Information Paper, subj: Excalibur 155mm Precision-Guided Extended Range Artillery Projectile Family, 2001, HRDC; MAJ Danny J. Sprengle and LTC Donald C. Durant, "Excalibur: Extended-Range Precision for the Army," *Field Artillery Magazine*, Mar-Apr 2003, pp. 13-16; Interview, Dastrup with Doug Brown, Dep Dir, TSM Cannon, 8 Feb 2001, HRDC; Fact Sheet, subj: Excalibur, 21 Feb 2001, HRDC; Interview with atch, Dastrup with MAJ Danny J. Sprengle, TSM Cannon, 26 Feb 2001, HRDC; E-mail with atch, subj: Excalibur, 2 Mar 2001; E-mail msg, subj: Command History Coordination, 6 Apr 2001, HRDC.

126 E-mail, subj: None, 12 Mar 2002, HRDC; Scott Gourley, "XM892 Excalibur Warhead," *Army*, Nov 2001, pp. 56-57; Interview, Dastrup with MAJ Danny J. Sprengle, TSM Cannon, 6 Feb 2002, HRDC; Interview, Dastrup with Doug Brown, Dep Dir, TSM Cannon, 4 Feb 2002, HRDC; Information Paper, subj: Excalibur and Trajectory Correctable Munitions Program Merger, 21 Nov 2001, HRDC; E-mail msg with atch, subj: Excalibur, 20 Feb 2002, HRDC.

127 Interview, Dastrup with MAJ J. Riley Durant, TSM Cannon, 7 Mar 2005, HRDC.

128 Fact Sheet, subj: PM Combat Ammunition Systems, 23 May 2007, HRDC; Fact Sheet, subj: PM Excalibur, 9 May 2007, HRDC; Talking Paper, subj: XM892 Projectile, 5 Mar 2008, HRDC; E-mail with atch, subj: TCM Cannon Munitions Input, 4 Apr 2008, HRDC; Briefing, subj: TCM Cannon, 2 Nov 2009, HRDC.

129 Approved Precision Effects Study Plan, undated, HRDC; Memorandum for Cdr, USAFACFS, *et al*, subj: Precision Effects Study, 20 Nov 2003, HRDC; Precision Effects Study Announcement, undated, HRDC; Fact Sheet, subj: Precision Effects, undated, HRDC; Interview, Dastrup with Thomas Hills, Sr Analysis, Analysis Branch, FDIC, 23 May 2005, HRDC.

130 E-mail with atch, subj: Precision Effects Study, 23 May 2005, HRDC; Valcourt, "Issues and Answers," pp. 1-3; Routing Sheet, undated, HRDC; Briefing, subj: Phase II - Precision Effect Study Recommendation, undated, HRDC; Briefing, subj: Course of Action for Accelerated Course Correcting Fuse Development, 30 Apr 2004, HRDC; Interview, Dastrup with Don Durant, Munitions Branch, TCM Cannon, 18 Feb 2009, HRDC; Briefing, subj: Smart Book, Munition Programs, 30 Jan 2009, HRDC; E-mail with atch, subj: XM892 Excalibur Extended Range Guided Projectile 2008, 30 Mar 2009, HRDC; 2009 US Army Field Artillery School Annual History, pp. 71-73.

131 MAJ (Ret) George A. Durham and COL (Ret) James E. Cunningham, "Netfires: Precision Effects for the Objective Force," *Field Artillery Magazine*, Mar-Apr 2002, pp. 5-9.

132 Durham and Cunningham, "Netfires," pp. 5-9; Fact Sheet, subj: FCS NetFires, 17 Oct 2002, HRDC; Fact Sheet, subj: NetFires, undated, HRDC.

133 Interview, Dastrup with LTC William E. Field, TSM RAMS, 10 Feb 2006, HRDC; E-mail with atch, subj: NLOS-LS, 10 Mar 2006, HRDC.

134 Interview, Dastrup with Field, 10 Feb 2006, HRDC; E-mail with atch, subj: NLOS-LS, 10 Mar 2006, HRDC; E-mail with atch, subj: NLOS-LS Command History, 12 Mar 2009, HRDC; E-mail, subj: NLOS-LS ST, 12 Mar 2009, HRDC; E-mail with atch, subj: NLOS-LS 2008 Command History, 31 Mar 2009, HRDC; Information Paper, subj: Current Key Parameters for NLOS-LS, undated, HRDC.

135 Fact Sheet, subj: Army Cancels Non-Line-Sight Launch System, undated, HRDC; Fires

Center of Excellence CSM Newsletter, Jun 2010, p. 7, HRDC.

136 2000 USAFACFS ACH, p. 117; LTC Jeffrey L. Froysland, "Transformation: Bringing Precision to MLRS Rockets," *Field Artillery Magazine*, Mar-Apr 2003, pp. 17-19.

137 Froysland, "Transformation," pp. 17-19; See footnote 124, p. 119, 2000 USAFACFS ACH, for an extensive list of primary sources; Interview with atchs, Dastrup with Jeffrey L. Froysland, TSM RAMS, 8 Mar 2005, HRDC; Lockheed Martin News Release, 11 May 2004, HRDC.

138 2000 USAFACFS ACH, p. 120; 2001 USAFACFS ACH, pp. 95-96; 2002 USAFACFS ACH, pp. 73-74; 2003 USAFACFS ACH, p. 89; E-mail with atch, subj: MLRS Rocket and Missile 2007, 25 Mar 2008, HRDC.

139 Interview with atchs, Dastrup with Froysland, 8 Mar 2005, HRDC.

140 COLs Gary S. Kinne, John A. Tanzi, and Jeffrey W. Yaeger, "FA PGMs: Revolutionizing Fires for the Ground Force Commander," *Field Artillery Magazine*, May-Jun 2006, pp. 16-21.

141 Kinne, Tanzi, and Yaeger, "FA PGMs," pp. 16-21; Fact Sheet with atch, subj: History for Rockets and Missiles, 2007, 26 Feb 2008, HRDC; Fact Sheet with atch, subj: The Guided MLRS Unitary Rocket, 26Apr 2007, HRDC; Press Release (Lockheed Martin), subj: Lockheed Martin GMLRS Program Receives Certification and $125 Million US Army Production Order, 21 Jun 2007, HRDC; Press Release (Lockheed Martin), subj: Lockheed Martin successfully Concluded Phase II Tests of GMLRS Rocket, 25 Apr 2007, HRDC.

142 Fires Center of Excellence CSM Newsletter, Jun 2010, p. 9, HRDC; MG (Ret) David C. Ralston and Patrecia Slayden Hollis, "PGM Effects for the BCT Commander," *Fires Bulletin*, Jan-Feb 2009, pp. 22-27.

143 2000 USAFACFS ACH, p. 120; LTC Rocky G. Same, "M270A1: An MLRS Launcher with Leap-ahead Lethality," *Field Artillery Magazine*, Mar-Apr 2002, pp. 40-41.

144 Memorandum for Dir, TSM RAMS, with atch, subj: Coordination of 2002 ACH, 18 Mar 2003, HRDC; Memorandum with atch for Dir, TSM RAMS, subj: Coordination of 2002 ACH, 18 Mar 2003, insert, HRDC; E-mail with atch, subj: HIMARS 2005, 21 Feb 2006, HRDC.

145 Oral History Interview, Dastrup with COL David A. Ralston, former division artillery commander, 24th Infantry Division (Mechanized), 25 Aug 1992, pp. 4-5, HRDC; Oral History Interview, Dastrup and L. Martin Kaplan with COL Stanley E. Griffith, Dir, Target Acquisition Department, USAFAS, 24 Jul 1991, pp, 2, 3, 6, 7, 10, 13-16, HRDC; COL Vollney B. Corn, Jr., and CPT Richard A. Lacquemont, "Silver Bullets," *Field Artillery Magazine*, Oct 1991, p. 13; Fact Sheet, subj: Firefinder Radar Product Improvement Program, 23 Jun 1995, HRDC; Interview, Dastrup with Ron Anderson, TSM Target Acquisition, DCD, 11 Mar 1996, HRDC; Fact Sheet, subj: FF Q-36 Block II, 17 Mar 1997, HRDC; 1995 USAFACFS ACH, pp. 140-41; LTC Robert M. Hill, "Future Watch: Target Acquisition and Precision Attack Systems," *Field Artillery Magazine*, Jan-Feb 1996, pp. 18-21; 2001 USAFACFS ACH, pp. 102-04.

146 Fact Sheet, subj: ATACS, 31 Jan 1991, HRDC; "Field Artillery Equipment and Munitions Update," *Field Artillery Magazine*, Dec 1990, p. 55; Draft Operational and Organization Plan for ATACS, 30 Oct 1990, HRDC; USAFAS, Program and Project Summary Sheets, 5 Oct 1992, pp. 26-1 - 26-2, HRDC; USAFAS, Program and Project Summary Sheets, 1 Nov 1994, pp. 19-1 - 20-2, HRDC; Fact Sheet, subj: Firefinder Radar Product Improvement Programs, 25 Jan 1994, HRDC; Fact Sheet, subj: FF Q-37 Block II, 17 Mar 1997, HRDC; 2000 USAFACFS ACH, pp. 135-37; 2002 USAFACFS ACH, p. 84.

147 2005 USAFACFS ACH, p. 86; E-mail with atch, subj: TPO Sensors History, 27 Mar 2007, HRDC.

148 E-mail with atch, subj: TPO Sensors History, 27 Mar 2007.

149 2008 USAFCOEFS ACH, pp. 122-32.

Conclusion

As the Field Artillery School approached its centennial in 2011, it could look back on 10 decades of dedicated service to the United States during times of peace and war and boast of being part of the recently created, innovative Fires Center of Excellence. With the exception of being closed during the Pershing Expedition into Mexico in 1916-1917, it kept its doors continuously open, teaching the latest field artillery tactics, techniques, and procedures, developing fire support doctrine, participating in the acquisition of new equipment and weapon systems, and going through critical watersheds.

Although World War I provided the school with its first opportunity to showcase its graduates, World War II created its first important watershed. Constrained by a limited budget, the size of the US Army, and the absence of a real threat, the Field Artillery School operated at a leisure pace during the 1920s and 1930s. Through July 1940 when the school started expanding its operations for possible war, the graduation rate averaged around 200 per year, while classes ran from September to early June to avoid the searing Oklahoma summers. Mobilization for World War II abruptly changed the school. To meet the demand for trained field artillerymen during the war, the school started running classes the entire year, and graduations climbed to a yearly average of 22,000.

As much as the school envisioned returning to the pre-war years in 1945, the Cold War dispelled any lingering notions of that happening. From 1946 through 1999, the school averaged around 12,000 graduates annually, a far-cry from the 22,000 of the war years and the 200 of the 1920s and 1930s, and conducted classes all year.[1]

Unlike during the two decades prior to World War II when a discernable enemy did not exist, the Cold War provided the school with a real threat to national security. For more than 40 years, the school developed field artillery tactics and doctrine, participated in introducing weapon systems and equipment, and trained field artillerymen to defeat Soviet and Warsaw Pact ground forces. The Korean and Vietnam Wars furnished only a temporary diversion from the all encompassing focus on the Soviet Union and Warsaw Pact. Although the Berlin Wall fell in 1989 and the Cold War ended shortly afterward, the Field Artillery School continued preparing graduates for a war against a Soviet-style army through the end of the 20th century and participating in the development of weapons and equipment for such a conflict.

Together, General Eric K. Shinseki's initiative of 1999 to make the Army more mobile and the War on Terrorism during the first decade of the 21st century formed another critical juncture in the school's evolution by moving the school away from its Cold War paradigm. While Shinseki's effort emphasized worldwide deployability by developing systems with the lethality of Cold War heavy systems and the mobility of light systems and started the shift from the Cold War orientation, the 11 September 2001 terrorist attack where terrorists flew hijacked aircraft into the Twin Towers in New York City and the Pentagon completed the reorientation by prompting the United States to launch a war against a stateless enemy. Initially, the war permitted field artillerymen to mass and shift fires around the battlefield as they had been trained to do for years.

Operation Iraqi Freedom reflected this. In March 2003, field artillerymen furnished effective close support and counterfire to defeat the Iraqi ground forces with a minimal number of friendly casualties. Soon after Saddam Hussein's government fell, Operation Iraqi Freedom metamorphosed from a conventional effort into an insurgency where field artillerymen employed their fire support skills infrequently and took upon a variety of non-standard tasks, such as patrolling and convoy operations, as their major functions. This caused their field artillery skills to deteriorate and led to the Field Artillery School's aggressive effort to reset or retrain field artillerymen and field artillery units in core field artillery skills beginning in 2006 and continuing into 2011.

Likewise, the war on terror emphasized the need for non-lethal effects to complement lethal effects – the traditional focus of field artillerymen – and joint operations. As the requirement for non-lethal effects grew, the Field Artillery School assumed proponency for training field artillerymen in tactical information operations and electronic warfare by developing the appropriate courses to create specialists and integrated these topics, including psychological warfare, into programs of instruction for officers, warrant officers, and noncommissioned officers.

Although the Field Artillery School's mission of the early 2000s added non-lethal effects to complement the traditional lethal effects, it mirrored the School of Fire for Field Artillery's mission of the early 1900s. Both embarked upon creating a field artillery force for a new century. In the case of the School of Fire, it had the unprecedented task of building a field artillery from virtually nothing for fighting a highly trained enemy on a conventional battlefield and becoming part of a progressive educational system. Almost 100 years later, the Field Artillery School faced creating a field artillery with the capabilities of fighting across the full spectrum of conflict and employing lethal and non-lethal effects.

Of the two, the Field Artillery School of 2011 lived in a more complex world. It encountered conventional battles which could quickly turn into insurgencies and make complicated demands on field artillerymen to provide lethal and non-lethal effects. In comparison, the School of Fire focused its energy on training officers and soldiers to supply lethal effects on a conventional battlefield. Regardless of the different worlds that they faced, both schools graduated field artillerymen to satisfy their country's security needs.

Notes

1 Excel Spread Sheet of Graduates of FAS, HRDC.

Glossary

AFATDS, Advanced Field Artillery Tactical Data System

AGF, Army Ground Forces

AHIP, Army Helicopter Improvement Program

AIT, Advance Individual Training

ANCOC, Advance Noncommission Officer Course

ARTEP, Army Training and Evaluation Program

ARVN, Army of the Republic of Vietnam

ASF, Army Service Forces

ATACMS, Army Tactical Missile System

ATCCS, Army Tactical Command and Control System

BFIST, Bradley Fire Support Team Vehicle

BG, Brigadier General

BNCOC, Basic Noncommissioned Officer Course

BOLC, Basic Officer Leader Course

BRAC, Base Realignment and Closure

CAS3, Combined Arms Services Staff School

CDID, Capabilities Development and Integration Directorate

CD-ROM, Compact Disk-Read Only Memory

CCC, Captain's Career Course

CLASS, Closed Loop Artillery Simulation System

COL, Colonel

CONARC, Continental Army Command

CPT, Captain

CRAM, Counter Rockets and Missiles

CWO, Chief Warrant Officer

DCD, Directorate of Combat Developments

DPICM, Dual-purpose Improved Conventional Munitions

DOT, Directorate of Training

DOTD, Directorate of Training and Doctrine

DOTMLPF, Doctrine, Organization, Training, Material, Leadership, Personnel, and Facilities

DOTS, Directorate of Training Support

DPTM, Directorate of Plans, Training, and Mobilization

FACCC, Field Artillery Captain's Career Course

FACCC-DL, Field Artillery Captain's Career Course-Distance Learning

FADAC, Field Artillery Digital Automated Computer

FAOAC, Field Artillery Officer Advance Course

FAOAC-RC, Field Artillery Officer Advance Course-Reserve Component

FAOBC, Field Artillery Officer Basic Course

FAS, Field Artillery School

FIST, Fire Support Team

FISTV, Fire Support Team Vehicle

FM, Field Manual

FSCATT, Fire Support Combined Arms Tactical Trainer

FSCATT-T, Fire Support Combined Arms Tactical Trainer-Towed

FSCOORD, Fire Support Coordinator

FY, Fiscal Year

GEN, General

GLCM, Ground-launched Cruise Missile

GUARDFIST, Guard Unit Army Device Full Crew Interactive Simulation Trainer

HELP, Howitzer Extended Life Program

HIMARS, High Mobility Artillery Rocket System

HMMWV, High-mobility Multi-purpose Wheel Vehicle

IFSAS, Interim/Initial Fire Support Automated System

INF, Intermediate-range Nuclear Forces

IPADS, Improved Positioning Azimuth Determining System

JACI, Joint and Combined Integration Directorate

LT, Lieutenant

LTC, Lieutenant Colonel

LTG, Lieutenant General

MAAG, Military Assistance Advisory Group

MAJ, Major

MG, Major General

MLRS, Multiple-Launch Rocket System

MOS, Military Occupational Specialty

MSTAR, MLRS Smart Tactical Rocket

NATO, North Atlantic Treaty Organization

OCS, Officer Candidate School

OEF, Operation Enduring Freedom (Afghanistan)

OIF, Operation Iraqi Freedom

OPMS, Officer Personnel Management System

PAVN, People's Army of Vietnam

PLDC, Primary Leadership Development Course

PWA, Projects Works Administration

RETO, Review of Education and Training of Officers

ROAD, Reorganization Objective Army Division

ROTC, Reserve Officer Training Corps

SADARM, Search-and-Destroy-Armor Munition

SHOT, Student Highlights of Training

SOS, Services of Supply

TACFIRE, Tactical Fire Direction System

TADSS, Training Aids, Devices, Simulators, and Simulations

TDA, Tables of Distribution and Allowance

TRADOC, US Army Training and Doctrine Command

UAS, Unmanned Aerial System

UAV, Unmanned Aerial Vehicle

USAFAC, US Army Field Artillery Center

USAAMS, US Army Artillery and Missile School

USAFACFS, US Army Field Artillery Center and Fort Sill

USAFAS, US Army Field Artillery School

USAFCOEFS, US Army Fires Center of Excellence and Fort Sill

USAMAA, United States Army Manpower and Analysis Agency

WO, Warrant Officer

WOAC, Warrant Officer Advance Course

WOBC, Warrant Officer Basic Course

WOEC, Warrant Officer Entry Course

WPA, Works Projects Administration

Names of the Field Artillery School

School of Fire for Field Artillery, 1911-1919

Field Artillery School, 1919-1946

The Artillery School, 1946-1955

The Artillery and Guided Missile School, 1955-1957

US Army Artillery and Guided Missile School, January 1957-July 1957

US Army Artillery and Missile School, July 1957-1969

US Army Field Artillery School, 1969-Present

Field Artillery School Commandants

CPT Dan T. Moore, 19 Jul 1911-15 Sep 1914

LTC Edward F. McGlachlin, Jr., 15 Sep 1914-26 Jun 1916

School was closed 9 July 1916-2 July 1917.

COL William J. Snow, 27 Jul 1917-26 Sep 1917

BG Adrian S. Fleming, 26 Sep 1917-11 May 1918

BG Laurin L. Lawson, 11 May 1918-18 Dec 1918

BG Dennis H. Currie, 24 Dec 1918-10 Jun 1919

BG Edward T. Donnely, 30 Jun 1919-9 Jul 1919

MG Ernest Hinds, 25 Oct 1919-1 Jul 1923

MG George LeR. Irwin, 1 Jul 1923-1 Apr 1928

BG Dwight E. Aultman, 6 Apr 1928-12 Dec 1929

BG William Cruikshank, 8 Feb 1930-31 Jul 1934

MG Henry W. Butner, 17 Sep 1934-10 May 1936

BG Augustine McIntyre, 29 Jun 1936-31 Jul 1940

BG Donald C. Cubbison, 1 Aug 1940-22 Dec 1940

BG George R. Allin, 20 Jan 1941-31 Jun 1942

BG Jesmond D. Balmer, 1 Jul 1942-11 Jan 1944

MG Orlando Ward, 12 Jan 1944-30 Oct 1944

MG Ralph McT. Pennell, 31 Oct 1944-30 Aug 1945

MG Louis E. Hibbs, 30 Aug 1945-4 Jun 1946

MG Clift Andrus, 18 Jun 1946-9 Apr 1949

MG Joseph M. Swing, 1 Jun 1949-31 Mar 1950

MG Arthur M. Harper, 2 Apr 1950-16 Nov 1953

MG Charles E. Hart, 4 Jan 1954-28 May 1954

MG Edward T. Williams, 8 Jul 1954-23 Feb 1956

MG Thomas E. de Shazo, 12 Mar 1956-31 Jan 1959

MG Verdi B. Barnes, 15 Feb 1959-6 Mar 1961

MG Lewis S. Griffing, 6 Apr 1961-31 Mar 1964

MG Harry H. Critz, 1 Apr 1964-15 May 1967

MG Charles P. Brown, 5 Jul 1967-20 Feb 1970

MG Roderick Wetherill, 24 Feb 1970-31 May 1973

MG David E. Ott, 1 Jun 1973-24 Sep 1976

MG Donald R. Keith, 9 Oct 1976-21 Oct 1977

MG Jack N. Merritt, 22 Oct 1977-26 Jun 1980

MG Edward A. Dinges, 27 Jun 1980-27 Sep 1982

MG John S. Crosby, 28 Sep 1982-3 Jun 1985

MG Eugene S. Korpal, 4 Jun 1985-17 Aug 1987

MG Raphael J. Hallada, 20 Aug 1987-19 Jul 1991

MG Fred F. Marty, 19 Jul 1991-15 Jun 1993

MG John A. Dubia, 15 Jun 1993-7 Jun 1995

MG Randall L. Rigby, 7 Jun 1995-7 Jun 1997

MG Leo J. Baxter, 7 Jun 1997-11 Aug 1999

MG Toney Stricklin, 11 Aug 1999-23 Aug 2001

MG Michael D. Maples, 23 Aug 2001-9 Dec 2003

MG David P. Valcourt, 9 Dec 2003-4 Aug 2005

MG David C. Ralston, 4 Aug 2005-13 Sep 2007

MG Peter M. Vangjel, 13 Sep 2007-4 Jun 2009

BG Ross E. Ridge, 4 Jun 2009-1 Oct 2010

BG Thomas S. Vandal, 18 Jan 2011-present

Note: From World War I to 2009, the school commandant has also served as post commander of Fort Sill. On 4 June 2009, the Commanding General of Fort Sill passed authority for Chief of Field Artillery and Commandant of the Field Artillery School to Brigadier General Ross E. Ridge as part of standing up the Fires Center of Excellence mandated by the Base Realignment and Closure Committee recommendations of 2005. As a result, the school commandant no longer served as post commander. That responsibility fell to the Fires Center of Excellence Commander.

Chiefs of Field Artillery

*MG William J. Snow, 10 Feb 1918-19 Dec 1927

*MG Fred T. Austin, 20 Dec 1927-15 Feb 1930

*MG Harry G. Bishop, 10 Mar 1930-9 Mar 1934

*MG Upton Birnie, Jr., 10 Mar 1934-24 Mar 1938

*MG Robert M. Danford, 26 Mar 1938-9 Mar 1942

BG George R. Allin, 9 Mar 1942-31 Jun 1942

BG Jesmond D. Balmer, 1 Jul 1942-11 Jan 1944

MG Orlando Ward, 12 Jan 1944-30 Oct 1944

MG Ralph McT. Pennell, 31 Oct 1944-30 Aug 1945

MG Louis E. Hibbs, 30 Aug 1945-4 Jun 1946

MG Clift Andrus, 20 Jun 1946-15 Apr 1949

MG Joseph M. Swing, 9 Apr 1949-31 Mar 1950

MG Arthur M. Harper, 2 Apr 1950-16 Nov 1953

MG Charles E. Hart, 4 Jan 1954-28 May 1954

MG Edward T. Williams, 8 Jul 1954-23 Feb 1956

MG Thomas E. de Shazo, 12 Mar 1956-31 Jan 1959

MG Verdi B. Barnes, 15 Feb 1959-25 Mar 1961

MG Lewis S. Griffing, 6 Apr 1961-31 Mar 1964

MG Harry H. Critz, 1 Apr 1964-15 May 1967

MG Charles P. Brown, 5 Jul 1967-20 Feb 1970

MG Roderick Wetherill, 24 Feb 1970-31 May 1973

MG David E. Ott, 1 Jun 1973-24 Sep 1976

MG Donald R. Keith, 9 Oct 1976-21 Oct 1977

MG Jack N. Merritt, 22 Oct 1977-26 Jun 1980

MG Edward A. Dinges, 27 Jun 1980-27 Sep 1982

*MG John S. Crosby, 28 Sep 1982-3 Jun 1985

*MG Eugene S. Korpal, 3 Jun 1985-17 Aug 1987

*MG Raphael J. Hallada, 20 Aug 1987-19 Jul 1991

*MG Fred F. Marty, 19 Jul 1991-15 Jun 1993

*MG John A. Dubia, 15 Jun 1993-7 Jun 1995

*MG Randall L. Rigby, 7 Jun 1995-7 Jun 1997

*MG Leo J. Baxter, 7 Jun 1997-11 Aug 1999

*MG Toney Stricklin, 11 Aug 1999-23 Aug 2001

*MG Michael D. Maples, 23 Aug 2001-9 Dec 2003

*MG David P. Valcourt, 9 Dec 2003-4 Aug 2005

*MG David C. Ralston, 4 Aug 2005-13 Sep 2007

*MG Peter M. Vangjel, 13 Sep 2007-4 Jun 2009

*BG Ross E. Ridge, 4 Jun 2009-1 Oct 2010

*BG Thomas S. Vandal, 18 Jan 2011-present

Individuals with an asterisk by their name were officially recognized by the Department of War or Department of the Army as the Chief of Field Artillery. The War Department created the Office of the Chief of Field Artillery on 15 February 1918 to supervise the Field Artillery. On 9 March 1942, the War Department abolished the Office of the Chief of Field Artillery as part of wartime reorganization and placed the Field Artillery under the Army Ground Forces. When the War Department dissolved the Chief of Field Artillery on 9 March 1942, General Allin, who was serving as the Commandant of the Field Artillery School, became the unofficial Chief of Field Artillery until 31 June 1942.

In 1983, the Department of the Army reestablished the Chief of Field Artillery to oversee the development of Field Artillery tactics, doctrine, organization, equipment, and training. Although the War Department and later the Department of the Army did not recognize an official Chief of Field Artillery from 1942 through 1983, the Commandants of the Field Artillery School and its successors considered themselves to be the Chief of Field Artillery. See TRADOC Annual Command History for 1 Oct 1982-30 Sep 1983, pp. 57, 308.

On 4 June 2009, Vangjel officially transferred authority for Commandant of the Field Artillery School and Chief of Field Artillery to Ridge as part of the creation of the Fires Center of Excellence.

Note: The article, "Three Chiefs," *Field Artillery Journal*, Mar-Apr 1931, p. 115, lists Snow's date of tenure as Chief of Field Artillery as 10 February 1918 to 19 December 1927. USAFAS's records list 15 February 1918 to 19 December 1927. The same article lists Austin's tenure as 22 December 1927 to 15 December 1930. USAFAS's records list 20 December 1927 to 15 February 1930.

Bibliography

For e-mails, studies, reports, memoranda, letters, oral history interviews, pamphlets, and other primary source material, please see notes.

Manuscript Collections

Historical Research and Document Collection, Field Artillery Branch Historian's Office, Fort Sill
Morris Swett Technical Library, US Army Field Artillery School, Fort Sill.

Books

Addington, Larry H. *The Patterns of War since the Eighteenth Century.* Bloomington, IN: Indiana University Press, second edition, 1994.
Ambrose, Stephen E. *Undaunted Courage: Meriwether Lewis, Thomas Jefferson, and the Opening of the American West.* New York: Touchstone Books, 1996.
Arms, Larry R. *A Short History of the NCO*, edited by Patricia Rhodes. Fort Bliss, TX: US Army Sergeant Major Academy, 1991.
Bailey, J.B.A. *Field Artillery and Firepower.* Oxford: The Military Press, 1989.
_____. *Field Artillery and Firepower.* Annapolis, MD: Naval Institute Press, 2004.
Barnes, G.M. *Weapons of World War II.* New York: D.Van Nostrand Company, Inc., 1947.
Bethel, H.A. *Modern Artillery in the Field.* London: Macmillan and Company, Limited, 1911.
Bidwell, Shelford and Dominick Graham. *Firepower: British Army Weapons and Theories of War, 1904-1945.* London: George Allen and Unwin, 1982.
Billington, Ray M. *Westward Expansion: A History of the American Frontier.* New York: Macmillan Publishing Company, Inc., 1974.
Bishop, Harry G. *Field Artillery: King of Battle.* Boston: Houghton Mifflin Company, 1936.
Coffman, Edward M. *The Old Army: A Portrait of the American Army in Peacetime, 1784-1898.* New York: Oxford University Press, 1986.
_____. *The Regulars: The American Army, 1898-1941.* Cambridge, MA: The Belknap Press of the Harvard University Press, 2004.
Comparato, Frank E. *Age of Great Guns: Cannon Kings and Cannoneers Who Forged the Firepower of Artillery.* Harrisburg, PA: The Stackpole Company, 1965.
Conn, Stetson. *Highlights of Mobilization, World War II, 1938-1942.* Washington, D.C.: US Army Center of Military History, n.d.
Cosmas, Graham A. *An Army for Empire: The United States Army in the Spanish-American War.* Columbia, MO: University of Missouri Press, 1971.
Craig, Reginald S. *The Fighting Parson: The Biography of Colonel John M. Chivington.* Los Angeles: Westernlore Press, 1959.
Dastrup, Boyd L. *King of Battle: A Branch History of the US Army's Field Artillery.* Fort Monroe, VA: Office of the Command Historian, US Army Training and Doctrine Command, 1992.
_____. *Modernizing the King of Battle: 1973-1991.* Fort Sill, OK: Office of the Command Historian, US Army Field Artillery Center and School, 1994, reprinted by the US Army Center of Military History, 2003.
_____. *The Field Artillery: History and Sourcebook.* Westport, CT: Greenwood Press, 1994.
Department of the Army, *Historical Summary for Fiscal Year 1971.*
_____. *Historical Summary for Fiscal Year 1972.*
_____. *Historical Summary for Fiscal Year 1974.*

_____. *Historical Summary for Fiscal Year 1975.*
_____. *Historical Summary for Fiscal Year 1977.*
_____. *Historical Summary for Fiscal Year 1978.*
_____. *Historical Summary for Fiscal Year 1979.*
_____. *Historical Summary for Fiscal Year 1980.*
_____. *Historical Summary for Fiscal Year 1982.*
_____. *Historical Summary for Fiscal Year 1984.*
_____. *Historical Summary for Fiscal Year 1986.*
_____. *Historical Summary for Fiscal Year 1987.*
_____. *Historical Summary for Fiscal Year 1989.*
_____. *Historical Summary for Fiscal Years 1990 and 1991.*
_____. *Historical Summary for Fiscal Year 1992.*
_____. *Historical Summary for Fiscal Year 1993.*
_____. *Historical Summary for Fiscal Year 1996.*

Foreman, Grant. *Indian Removal: The Emigration of the Five Civilized Tribes of Indians.* Norman, OK: University of Oklahoma Press, 1972.

_____. *The Five Civilized Tribes: Cherokee, Chickasaw, Choctaw, Creek, and Seminole.* Norman, OK: University of Oklahoma Press, 1974.

Franks, Kenny A. *Citizen Soldiers: Oklahoma's National Guard.* Norman, OK: University of Oklahoma Press, 1984.

Friedman, Norman. *Desert Victory: The War for Kuwait.* Annapolis, MD: Naval Institute Press, 1991.

Green, Constance M., Harry C. Thomson, and Peter C. Roots, *The Ordnance Department: Planning Munitions for War.* Washington, D.C.: Office of the Chief of Military History, 1955.

Greene, Jerome A. *Washita: The US Army and the Southern Cheyennes, 1867-1869.* Norman, OK: University of Oklahoma Press, 2004.

Griffith, Paddy. *Forward into Battle: Fighting Tactics from Waterloo to Vietnam.* Sussex, UK: Antony Bird Publications, Limited, 1981.

Griswold, Gillette. "Fort Sill, Oklahoma: A Brief History," unpublished manuscript, Historical Research and Document Collection, US Army Field Artillery School.

_____. "Fort Sill, Oklahoma: A Chronology of Key Events," unpublished manuscript, Historical Research and Document Collection, US Army Field Artillery School.

Groteleuschen, Mark E. *Doctrine under Trial: American Artillery Employment in World War I.* Westport, CT: Greenwood Press, 2001.

Gugeler, Russell A. *Major General Orland Ward: Life of a Leader.* Oakland, OR: Red Anvil Press, 2009.

Herbert, Paul H. *Deciding What Has to be Done: General William E. Depuy and the 1976 Edition of FM 100-5.* Fort Leavenworth, KS: Combat Studies Institute, US Army Command and General Staff College, 1988.

Hewes, James E. *From Root to McNamara: Army Organization and Administration, 1900-1963.* Washington, D.C.: Center of Military History, US Army, 1975.

History of the Field Artillery School: World War Two. Fort Sill, OK: Fort Sill Printing Plant, n.d.

History of the US Army Artillery and Missile School, 1945-1957. Fort Sill, OK: Fort Sill Printing Plant, 1957.

History of the US Army Artillery and Missile School, 1958-1967. Fort Sill, OK: Fort Sill Printing Plant, 1967.

Hoig, Stan. *The Battle of the Washita: The Sheridan-Custer Indian Campaign of 1867-69.* Lincoln, NB: University of Nebraska Press, 1976.

Holloway, O. Willard. *Post Commanders of Fort Sill: 1869-1940*. Fort Sill, OK: US Army Artillery and Missile Center, n.d.

Hutton, Paul H. *Phil Sheridan and His Army*. Lincoln, NB: University of Nebraska Press, 1985.

Kennedy, Paul. *The Rise and Fall of the Great Powers: Economic Change and Military Conflict from 1500 to 2000*. New York: Random House, 1987.

Lawrence, Arthur R. *Lawton: A Golden Anniversary, 1901-1951*. Lawton, OK: Arthur R. Lawrence, 1951.

Leckie, William H. *The Buffalo Soldier: A Narrative of the Negro Cavalry in the West*. Norman, Oklahoma: University of Oklahoma Press, 1967.

Looney, Joe and Vivian Wilson Looney. *The History of Comanche County, Oklahoma*. Lawton, OK: Southwest Genealogical Society, 1985.

Malone, Henry O., ed. *TRADOC Support to Operations Desert Shield and Desert Storm*. Fort Monroe, VA: Office of the Command Historian, 1992.

Matloff, Maurice. ed. *American Military History*. Washington, D.C.: US Army Center of Military History, 1985.

McNeill, William H. *The Pursuit of Power: Technology, Armed Force, and Society since A.D. 1000*. Chicago: University of Chicago Press, 1982.

McReynolds, Edwin C. *Oklahoma: A History of the Sooner State*. Norman, OK: University of Oklahoma Press, 1964.

Morando, Paul S. and David J. Johnson. *Fort Monroe*. Charleston, SC: Arcadia Publishing, 2008.

Morgan, H. Wayne and Anne Hodges Morgan. *Oklahoma: A Bicentennial History*. New York: W.W. Norton and Company, Inc., 1977.

Morris, John W. and Edwin C. McReynolds. *Historical Atlas of Oklahoma*. Norman, OK: University of Oklahoma Press, 1965.

Nye, Wilbur S. *Carbine and Lance: The Story of Old Fort Sill*. Norman, OK: University of Oklahoma Press, 1974.

Odom, William O. *After the Trenches: The Transformation of US Army Doctrine, 1918-1939*. College Station, TX: Texas A&M University Press, 1999.

On the Way: First Class, School of Fire for Field Artillery, Fort Sill, Oklahoma. Salt Lake City, UT: The Deseret News Publishing Company, n.d.

Ott, David E. *Field Artillery: 1954-1973*. Washington, D.C.: Department of the Army, 1975.

Palmer, Robert R., Bell I. Wiley, and William R. Keast. *The Procurement and Training of Ground Combat Troops*. Washington, D.C.: Office of the Chief of Military History, Department of the Army, 1948.

Raines, Edgar F., Jr. *Eyes of Artillery: The Origins of Modern US Army Aviation in World War II*. Washington, D.C.: Center of Military History, US Army, 2000.

Romjue, John L. *From Active Defense to Airland Battle: The Development of Army Doctrine, 1973-1982*. Fort Monroe, VA: US Army Training and Doctrine Command Historical Office, 1984.

_____. *History of Army 86: Division 86, The Development of the Heavy Division*. Fort Monroe, VA: TRADOC Historical Office, 1982.

_____. *The Army of Excellence: The Development of the 1980s Army*. Fort Monroe, VA: Office of the Command Historian, US Army Training and Doctrine Command, and US Army Center of Military History, 1997.

Romjue, John L., Susan Canedy, and Anne W. Chapman. *Prepare the Army for War: A Historical Overview of the Army Training and Doctrine Command, 1973-1993*. Fort Monroe, VA: Office of the Command Historian, United States Army Training and Doctrine Command, 1993.

Roosevelt, Theodore. *An Autobiography.* New York: The Macmillan Company, 1919.

Scales, Robert H., Jr. *Certain Victory: United States Army in the Gulf War.* Washington, D.C.: Office of the Chief of Staff, US Army, 1993.

Schubert, Frank N. and Theresa L. Kraus, ed. *The Whirlwind War: The United States Army in Operations Desert Shield and Desert Storm.* Washington, D.C.: Center of Military History, United States Army, 1995.

Snow, William J. *Signposts of Experience: World War I Memoirs.* Washington, D.C.: United States Field Artillery Association, 1941.

Stevens, M. David. *Lawton-Fort Sill: A Pictorial History.* Norfolk, VA: The Donning Company, 1990.

Stockel, H. Henrietta. *Shame and Endurance: The Untold Story of the Chiricahua Apache Prisoners of War.* Tucson, AZ: University of Arizona Press, 2004.

Strachan, Hew. *European Armies and the Conduct of War.* London: George Allen and Unwin, 1983.

Sunderland, Riley. *History of the Field Artillery School: 1911-1942.* Fort Sill, OK: Fort Sill Printing Plant, 1942.

Swett, Morris. "History of Artillery School in the United States (extract)," unpublished manuscript, 1938, Historical Research and Document Collection, US Army Field Artillery School.

_____. "History of Artillery Schools in the United States (Extract)," unpublished manuscript, pp. 42-43, Historical Research and Document Collection, US Army Field Artillery School.

_____. *Fort Sill: A History*, photocopy, Fort Sill, OK: 1921, Historical Research and Document Collection, US Army Field Artillery School.

The Field Artillery School, *Field Artillery Materiel.* Fort Sill, OK: The Field Artillery School, 1934.

Turcheneske, John A. *The Chiricahua Apache Prisoners of War: Fort Sill, 1894-1914.* Boulder, CO: University Press of Colorado, 1997.

Walters, Raymond, *et al. The Story of the Field Artillery Central Officers Training School, Camp Zachary Taylor, Kentucky.* New York: The Knickerbocker Press, 1919.

Watson, Mark Skinner. *Chief of Staff: Prewar Plans and Preparations.* Washington, D.C.: Historical Division, US Army, 1950.

Weigley, Russell F. *History of the United States Army.* Bloomington, IN: Indiana University Press, 1984.

Weinert, Richard P., Jr. *A History of Army Aviation: 1950-1962.* Fort Monroe, VA: Office of the Command Historian, United States Army Training and Doctrine Command, 1991.

Articles

"A Brief History of Fort Sill and the Field Artillery School," *Field Artillery Journal,* Nov-Dec 1933, p. 528.

"AAA Now Air Defense Artillery," *Artillery Trends,* Jun 1958, p. 59.

"A Proposed Scheme of Officers' Schools for Field Artillery," *Field Artillery Journal*, Apr-Jun 1919, p. 207.]

Abrams, Creighton W. "The Gulf War and European Artillery," *Journal of Royal Artillery*, Autumn 2001, p. 41.

"Active Army and Marine Units in OCONUS," *Field Artillery Journal*, Nov-Dec 1999, p. 21.

"Air Assault," *Artillery Trends*, Jul 1960, p. 20.

"Air Assault to Air Mobile," *Artillery Trends*, Nov 1965, p. 27.

Alley, Lisa. "BOLC Gets Green Light for Officer Education," ARNEWS, 25 Feb 2005, HRDC.

Anderson, John B. "Are We Justified Discarding 'Pre-War' Methods of Training," *Field Artillery Journal*, Apr-Jun 1919, p. 222.

"Army Acts on Training and Leaders Development Panel Findings," US Army News Release, 25 May 2001, HRDC.

"Army Announces FY05 and FY06 Modular Brigade Force Structure Decision," US Army News Release, 23 Jul 2004, HRDC.

"Army Announces Vision for Future," US Army News Release, 12 Oct 1999, HRDC.

"Army Study IDs NCO Concerns," ArmyLink News, 2 May 2002, HRDC.

"Army to Reset into Modular Brigade-Centric Force," Army News Service, 24 Feb 2004, HRDC.

"Army to Transform Officer Education," ArmyLink News, 4 Feb 2003, HRDC.

"Army Training and Leader Development Panel Completes Warrant Officer Study," US Army News Release, 22 Aug 2002, HRDC.

"Army Training and Leader Development Panel Reports on the NCO Study," US Army News Release, 2 May 2002, HRDC.

Arnold, Robert W., Ira E. Greeley, and Lawrence O. Zittrain. "Aerial Rocket Artillery," *Artillery Trends*, Apr 1965, p. 20.

"ARTEP," *Field Artillery Journal*, Jan-Feb 1975, p. 52.

"Authorizers Grant $293 Million for FCS Non-line-of-Sight Cannon," *Inside the Army*, 18 Nov 2002, HRDC.

Aultman, Dwight E. "Maps and Map Firing," *Field Artillery Journal*, Jul-Aug 1920, p. 380.

"Automatic Data Processing Systems," *Trends in Field Artillery for Instruction*, Feb 1958, p. 33.

"Azimuth Check: FAOAC Update," *Field Artillery Magazine*, Feb 1994, p. 42.

Bailey, J.B.A. "The First World War and the Birth of Modern Warfare," in Macgregor Knox and Williamson Murray, eds. *The Dynamics of Military Revolution, 1300-2050.* New York: Cambridge University Press, 2004.

Barnett, Donald L. "Crusader Targetweight: 38 to 42 Tons," *Field Artillery Magazine*, Mar-Apr 2000, p. 34.

Baxter, Leo J. "Honing the Edge: State of the Branch 1997," *Field Artillery Magazine*, Nov-Dec 1997, p. 1.

_____. "Meeting the Future: State of the Field Artillery 1998," *Field Artillery Magazine*, Nov-Dec 1998, p. 1.

Becker, William A. "A Bold New Look," *Artillery Trends*, Apr 1965, p. 6.

Belknap, Leslie. "The Unsung Heroes: Redleg Advisory Efforts in Vietnam, 1965-1969," *Field Artillery Journal*, Apr 1991, p. 14.

"BFIST is on the Way," *Field Artillery Magazine*, May-Jun 1997, p. 45.

Bilo, William C. "A Decisive Victory for Strategic Victory," *Field Artillery Magazine*, Mar-Apr 1995, p. 22.

Bray, Britt E. and William J. Raymond. "Redleg Mentor Program: Sharpening the Sword, Nurturing the Spirit," *Field Artillery Magazine*, Mar-Apr 1999, p. 1.

Breitenbach, Daniel L. "The Command and NCO Professional Development," *Field Artillery Magazine*, Aug 1989, p. 7.

Bronfeld, Saul. "Fighting Outnumbered: The Impact of the Yom Kippur War on the US Army," *The Journal of Military History*, Apr 2007, p. 465.

Brown, Sam A. "EPMS and the Field Artillery," *Field Artillery Journal*, May-Jun 1977, p. 29.

Burdick, Donald. "An Essential Element of National Strategy," *Army*, Oct 1990, p. 116.

Burleson, Richard C. "Some Observations Concerning the Use of Accompanying Batteries During the World War with Some Personal Experiences," *Field Artillery Journal*, Dec 1921, p. 525.

Burt, W.H. "Notes on the Course at the School of Fire," *Field Artillery Journal*, Apr-Jun 1912, p. 235.

Cahalane, Robert C. "Field Artillery Gun Data Computers," *Trends in Field Artillery for Instruction,* Feb 1958, p. 32.

Cavitt, David W. and Melvin R. Hunt. "Captains Professional Military Education: New Technology for the New Millennium," *Field Artillery Magazine,* Nov-Dec 1999, p. 11.

Chapman, Berlin B. "Establishment of the Wichita Reservation," *Chronicles of Oklahoma,* Mar-Dec 1933, p. 1044.

Coffman, Donna. "OPMS to OPMS XXI: Then, Now, and the Future: What Does It Mean to the Quartermaster Officer," *Quartermaster Professional Bulletin, online edition,* Aug 1997, HRDC.

Corn, Vollney B. and Richard A. Lacquemont. "Silver Bullets," *Field Artillery Magazine,* Oct 1991, p. 13.

"Counterfire," *Field Artillery Journal,* Nov-Dec 1975, p. 14.

"Counterinsurgency Operation Classes," *Artillery Trends,* Jul 1965, p. 27.

"Courses of Instruction," *Field Artillery Journal,* Jun 1946, p. 348.

"Current Notes," *Field Artillery Journal,* Jul-Sep 1918, p. 427.

Crawley, Jeff. "Class a Glimpse of Future," Fort Sill *Cannoneer,* 19 Feb 2009, p. 1a.

Crecelius, Richard A. and Henry A. Pedicone. "Nuclear Firepower," *Artillery Trends,* Jul 1965, p. 30.

Crisco, Telford E. "The Modular Force: Division Operations," *Military Review,* Jan-Feb 2006, p. 95.

Crosby, John S. "On the Move," *Field Artillery Journal,* Mar-Apr 1984, p. 1.

"Crusader Howitzer Gets the Axe," ArmyLink News, 8 May 2002, HRDC.

Curtis, Myron F., Thomas B. Brown, and John C. Hogan. "Pershing: It Gave Peace a Chance," *Field Artillery Magazine,* Feb 1991, p. 29.

Custer, Robert G. "Air Assault Artillery Finale," *Artillery Trends,* Nov 1965, p. 12.

Dale, Burris C. "Atomic Targets of Opportunity – Definition and Brief Discussion," *Trends in Artillery for Instruction,* Oct 1957, p. 100.

"Dan Tyler Moore: Captain Field Artillery," *Field Artillery Journal,* Oct 1945, p. 600.

Danford, Robert M. "Morris S. Simpson," *Field Artillery Journal,* Nov-Dec 1944, p. 765.

Dastrup, Boyd L. "School of Application for Cavalry and Light Artillery," in William E. Simon, ed., *Professional Military Education in the United States: A Historical Dictionary.* Westport, CT: Greenwood Press, 2000.

Davis, James L. "Intermediate Level Education: Helping to Combat Artillery Atrophy," *Fires Bulletin,* Nov-Dec 2009, p. 41.

"Defense Discusses Crusader Alternatives," Defense Link, 15 May 2002, HRDC.

Denson, Andrew, "Unite with Us to Rescue the Kiowas: The Five Civilized Tribes and Warfare on the Southern Plains," *Chronicles of Oklahoma,* Winter 2003-2004, p. 458.

"Department of Combat Development," *The Artillery Quarterly,* Jan 1957, p. 2.

Department of Gunnery, "American Drill Regulation and Artillery Firing," *Field Artillery Journal,* Jul-Sep 1918, p. 363.

De Shazo, Thomas E. "The Artillery School," *Field Artillery Journal,* Mar-Apr 1947, p. 95.

Devers, Jacob L. "Artillery Integration," *Field Artillery Journal,* Sep-Oct 1947, p. 303.

Dinges, Edward A., "On the Move," *Field Artillery Journal,* Jan-Feb 1981, p. 1.

"Discussions," *Field Artillery Journal,* Apr-Jun 1919, p. 218.

"Division AWE Will Be Basis for 21st Century Fighting Force," Army Link News, 28 Oct 1997.

Dorsey, James J. "This Patch Needs A Sleeve," *Artillery Trends,* Dec 1963, p. 34.

Downing, Jim. "Ft. Sill's Future is Keyed to Expansion," Tulsa *Tribune,* 8 Aug 1959.

"Drones in the Future," *Artillery Trends,* Mar 1959, p. 61.

Dubia, John A. "Force XXI and the Field Artillery: State of the Branch 1994," *Field Artillery Magazine*, Dec 1994, p. 1.

Duitsman, Leighton L. "Army TACMS," *Field Artillery Magazine*, Jan-Feb 1991, p. 38.

Durham, George A. and James E. Cunningham. "Netfires: Precision Effects for the Objective Force," *Field Artillery Magazine*, Mar-Apr 2002, p. 5.

Durette, E. "Fort Sill in Wartime," *Field Artillery Journal*, May-Jun 1923, p. 239.

Engel, William F. "Transforming Fires for the Objective Force," *Field Artillery Magazine*, Nov-Dec 2001, p. 9.

"EPMS," *Field Artillery Journal*, Nov-Dec 1977, p. 39.

"FAOBC Enhancements," *Field Artillery Magazine*, Feb 1994, p. 44.

"Field Artillery Equipment and Munitions Update," *Field Artillery Magazine*, Dec 1990, p. 55.

"Field Artillery Equipment and Munitions Update," *Field Artillery Magazine*, Jan-Feb 1996, p. 18.

"Field Artillery School," *Field Artillery Magazine*, Dec 1991, p. 13.

"Field Artillery School Builds 'Classrooms' without Walls," Fort Sill *Cannoneer*, 2 Feb 1995, p. 6a.

"Field Artillery Training Command," *Field Artillery Magazine*, Dec 1994, p. 30.

"Field Artillery Training Command," *Field Artillery Magazine*, Nov-Dec 1996, p. 32.

"Field Artillery Training Command," *Field Artillery Magazine*, Nov-Dec 1997, p. 32.

"Field Artillery Training Command," *Field Artillery Magazine*, Nov-Dec 1998, p. 32.

"Field Artillery Training Command," *Field Artillery Magazine*, Nov-Dec 1999, p. 32.

"Field Artillery Training Command," *Field Artillery Magazine*, Nov-Dec 2002, p. 32.

"Field Artillery Training Command Telephone Directory," *Field Artillery Magazine*, Nov-Dec 1995, p. 10-11.

"Field Artillery Training in the United States," *Field Artillery Journal*, Jul-Sep 1918, p. 427.

"Field Artillery Units Worldwide," *Field Artillery Magazine*, Dec 1989, pullout.

"Fire Direction in the Battalion," *The Digest of Field Artillery Developments*, 1935.

"Firing Schools," *Field Artillery Journal*, Apr-Jun 1911, p. 187.

"First Round Hits with FADAC," *Artillery Trends, Sep 1960, p. 8.*

"Focus Task Force 'Jump Starting' Future," Army Public Affairs, 27 Jan 2004, HRDC.

"Force XXI: A Revolution and Evolution in Military Affairs," ArmyLink News, 17 Jul 1996, HRDC.

"Forces Committed," *Military Review*, Sep 1991, p. 80.

Ford, William W. "Wings for St. Barbara," *Field Artillery Journal*, Apr 1941, p. 232.

"Fort Sill to be Permanent Home of the Field Artillery School," *Field Artillery Journal*, Jan-Feb 1931, p. 96.

"Fort Sill Soldiers Train Guard," *MLRS Dispatch*, 3rd Quarter, 1998, p. 3.

Foss, John W. "AirLand Battle-Future," *Army*, Feb 1991, p. 20.

Fox, Donald C. "Automatic Data Processing Systems," *Trends in Artillery for Instruction*, Feb 1958, p. 14.

Froysland, Jeffrey L. "Transformation: Bringing Precision to MLRS Rockets," *Field Artillery Magazine*, Mar-Apr 2003, p. 17.

Fuller, Harrison. "The Apache Gate Sector," *Field Artillery Journal*, Jan-Mar 1919, p. 7.

Gage, Duane. "Oklahoma: A Resettlement Area for Indians, *Chronicles of Oklahoma,* Autumn 1984, p. 284.

Gaither, Virgil. "Sill's Vietnam Village Shows What It's Like," Lawton *Constitution-Morning Press*, 5 Nov 1967, p. 10b.

"GAO, Crusader Needs Mature Technology, Not Weight Reduction," *Inside the Army*, 4 Mar 2002, HRDC.

Gerber, Loyd A. "Reset: Rebuilding FA Core Competencies for Future Full-Spectrum Operations," *Field Artillery Magazine*, Mar-Apr 2007, p. 14.

Goedkoop, Thomas R. and Barry E. Venable. "Task Force XXI: An Overview," *Military Review*, Mar-Apr 1997, p. 71.

"Going to That School," *Field Artillery Journal*, Mar-Apr 1947, p. 92.

Gourley, Scott. "M7 Bradley Fire Support Team Vehicle," *Army*, Jul 2002, p. 51.

_____. "XM892 Excalibur Warhead," *Army*, Nov 2001, p. 56.

"Guerrilla, Jungle Instruction Increased," *Artillery Trends*, Aug 1961, p. 30.

Haes, Brenda L., "Fort Sill, The Chiricahua Apaches and the Government's Promise of Permanent Residence," *Chronicles of Oklahoma*, Spring 2000, p. 28.

Hall, Lawrence T. and Michael A. Sharp, "MLRS NET for the ARNG," *Field Artillery Magazine*, Mar-Apr 96, p. 44.

Halverson, David C. "2010 State of the Fires Center of Excellence," *Fires Bulletin*, Nov-Dec 2010, p. 4.

Hamilton, John. "Common Ground: The Antiaircraft and Field Artillery Merger of 1950," *Air Defense Artillery Journal*, Apr-Jun 2006, p. 23.

Hanna, Mark. "Task Force XXI: The Army's Digital Experiment," *Strategic Forum*, Jul 1997.

Harrison, William J. "Malor," *Field Artillery Journal*, Mar-Jul 1975, p. 30.

Hart, Charles E. "Integration of the Artilleries," *Military Review*, Nov 1949, p. 17.

Heller, Charles E. "Educating the Army for the 21st Century," *Military Review*, Jul-Aug 1996, p. 86.

"HELP Program Continues," *Field Artillery Journal*, Jan-Feb 1983, p. 47.

Hernandez, Rhett A. and Terry M. Lee. "OPMS XXI: What Does It Mean for Your Future," *Field Artillery Magazine*, Sep-Oct 1997, p. 16.

High, William E. "The FA Master Gunner and Reset of the Redeployed FA Battalion," *Fires Bulletin*, Jan-Feb 2007, p. 1.

Hill, Robert M. "Future Watch: Target Acquisition and Precision Attack Systems," *Field Artillery Magazine*, Jan-Feb 1996, p. 18.

Hillis, K.W. "BOLC II Mission Doubles," Fort Sill *Cannoneer*, 29 Sep 2005, p. la.

Hinds, Ernest. "Graduation Address to the Classes at the Field Artillery School, June 14, 1924," *Field Artillery Journal*, Sep-Oct 1924, p. 469.

_____. "The Training of Artillery in France," *Field Artillery Journal*, Sep-Oct 1919, p. 381.

House, Jonathan M. "Designing the Light Division," *Military Review*, May 1984.

Hustead, Michael W. "Fire Support Mission Area: Impact of Precision Guided Munitions," *Field Artillery Journal*, May-Jun 1981, p. 19.

Jackson, Charles W., Jr. "Adjust by Sound," *Artillery Trends*, Jan 1968, p. 28.

Janda, James F. "Getting HELP and HIP," *Field Artillery Journal*, Sep-Oct 1985, p. 20.

Jennings, Richard M. "Special Warfare," *Artillery Trends*, Aug 1961, p. 22.

Johnson, David E. "From Frontier Constabulary to Modern Army: The US Army Between the Wars," in Harold R. Winton and David R. Mets, eds. *The Challenge of Change: Military Institutions and New Realities, 1918-1941*. Lincoln, NE: University of Nebraska Press, 2000.

Johnson, William F. and David J. Brost. "The Making of Redleg Pentathletes: Transforming Enlisted CMF13," *Field Artillery Magazine*, Nov-Dec 2006, p. 6.

Keller, Morris J. "Little John: The Mighty Mite," *Artillery Trends*, Jul 1960, p. 20.

Kinne, Gary S., John A. Tanzi, and Jeffrey W. Yaeger. "FA PGMs: Revolutionizing Fires for the Ground Force Commander," *Field Artillery Bulletin*, May-Jun 2006, p. 16.

Kirby, John. "Colonel Carter Explains Aims of Artillery School," *Field Artillery Journal*, Jul-Sep 1918, p. 374.

Klinger, Donald R. "The Field Artillery Board," *Field Artillery Journal*, Sep-Oct 1982, p. 13.

Keveles, Dean J. "NCOES: Restoring NCO Core Competency," *Fires Bulletin*, Jul-Aug 2008, p. 20.

Koch, Andrew. "General Dynamics to Develop TAD System," *Jane's Defense Weekly*, 27 Sep 2000, p. 8.
Kyne, Peter B. "The Artillery Mill at Old Fort Sill," *The Saturday Evening Post*, 9 Nov, 1918, p. 15.
Lane, Waco. "M777 Starts Fielding in the 11th Marines," *Field Artillery Magazine*, Mar-Apr 2005, p. 9.
LaPorte, Ryan J. "Paladin Platoon Operations versus Battery Operations," *Field Artillery Magazine*, Jan-Feb 2001, p. 16.
Leach, C.R. "Special Warfare," *Artillery Trends*, Aug 1961, p. 16.
Leahy, Todd. "Beef Instead of Bayonets: Cultural Mores and the Failure of Assimilation on the Kiowa-Comanche Reservation," *Chronicles of Oklahoma*, Winter 2005-2006, p. 490.
Lee, Terry M. "OPMS XXI: What Does It Mean for Your Future," *Field Artillery Magazine*, Sep-Oct 1997, p. 16.
Lee, William B. "US Army Training Center, Field Artillery," *Artillery Trends*, Feb 1960, p. 28.
Leonard Steven M. "One Man's Vision: The Evolution of Airmobile Artillery," *Field Artillery Journal*, Jul-Aug 1999, p. 24.
"Let's Shoot, Lieutenant," *Field Artillery Journal*, Nov-Dec 1975, p. 24.
Loudenslager, Kerry J. and Ryan J. LaPorte. "Paladin Platoon Operations versus Battery Operations," *Field Artillery Magazine*, Jan-Feb 2001, p. 16.
Lowitt, Richard. "Fort Sill Enters the Missile Age," *Chronicles of Oklahoma*, Winter 2005-2006, p. 389.
Madison, William W. "The First Round," *Artillery Trends*, Oct 1958, p. 30.
Maples, Michael D. "Ready and Relevant: The FA Now and in the Future," *Field Artillery Magazine*, Nov-Dec 2003, p. 1.
_____. "2002 State of the Field Artillery," *Field Artillery Magazine*, Nov-Dec 2002, p. 4.
Markestad, James A. "Warrant Officers: The New WOs for the Total Force," *Field Artillery Magazine*, Dec 1990, p. 39.
Markovetz, Robert F. "Distance Learning: MLRS 3x6 Conversion for the Army National Guard," *Field Artillery Magazine*, Sep-Oct 1999, p. 42.
Marschhausen, John C. "New Eyes for the Countermortar Team," *Artillery Trends*, Jun 1958, p. 3.
Marston, O.F. "The Camp Roberts Replacement Center," *Field Artillery Journal*, Mar 1941, p. 178.
Marty, Fred F. ""Deep Operations," *Field Artillery Magazine*, Apr 1993, p. 1.
_____. "Developing Soldiers and Leaders for the Future," *Field Artillery Magazine*, Aug 1992, p. 1.
_____. "State-of-the-Branch Address," *Field Artillery Magazine*, Dec 1991, p. 2.
_____. "State-of-the-Branch Address," *Field Artillery Magazine*, Nov-Dec 1992, p. 1.
_____. "Train to Win – Make the Most of Fires and Maneuver," *Field Artillery Magazine*, Oct 1992, p. 1.
Mathews, Rodger F. "ADA and Fort Sill: New Horizons," *Fires Bulletin*, May-Jun 2009, pp. 1-2.
McBride, Sharon. "Creating Culturally Astute Leaders: Joint and Combined Fires University Providing Innovative Cultural Education," *Fires Bulletin*, Sep-Oct 2010, p. 23.
McClung, Paul. "Lawton, Fort Sill Forge Early Successful Combination," Lawton *Constitution*, 5 Aug 1976, p. 9g.
McKenney, Janice. "More Bang for the Buck in the Interwar Army: The 105-mm., Howitzer," *Military Affairs*, Apr 1978, p. 82.
McKinney, James C. "Advice to NCOs Today: Be Patient and Professional," *Field Artillery Magazine*, Oct 1993, p. 6.
McPhee, Richard R. "The Divisional MLRS Battalion in DAWE," *Field Artillery Magazine*, May-Jun 1998, p. 38.
"Medium-weight Units to Take Advantage of Effects-based Operations," *Inside the Army*, 10 Apr

2000, p. 6, HRDC.
Menoher, Paul E. "Force XXI: Redesigning the Army through Warfighting Experiments," *Military Intelligence*, 1996.
Merriam, Wheeler G. "The Ground General School," *Field Artillery Journal*, Mar-Apr 1947, p. 93.
"M198 Production Rolling," *Field Artillery Journal*, Sep-Oct 1978, p. 15.
Morrison, W.B. "Fort Arbuckle," *Chronicles of Oklahoma*, Mar 1928, p. 26.
Moyes, Jeffrey L. "MTTs: Resetting FA Core Competencies," *Fires Bulletin*, Jul-Sep 2008, p. 10.
Mroczkowski, Dennis P. "Artillery School at Fort Monroe," in William E. Simon, ed. *Professional Military Education in the United States: A Historical Dictionary*. Westport, CT: Greenwood Press, 2000.
Mullins, M. Shayne. "New BOLC II at Fort Sill," *Field Artillery Magazine*, May-Jun 2006, p. 28.
"Multimedia Technologies to Train the Total FA," *Field Artillery Magazine*, Oct 1993, p. 44.
"Name-that-Howitzer: Crusader, A Knight for the 21st Century," *Field Artillery Magazine*, Dec 1994, p. 3.
Naugher, William A. "ROCID Artillery FDC," *Trends in Artillery for Instruction*, Feb 1958, p. 36.
"Need for Electronic Computers," *Trends in Field Artillery for Instruction*, Jun 1957, p. 19.
Neuwien, R.A. "How You Got It and What You Got," *US Army Aviation Digest*, Mar 1982, p. 6.
"New Family of Weapons," *Trends in Artillery for Instruction*, Apr 1957, p. 17.
Nichols, Roger L., "Stephen H. Long," in Paul A. Hutton, ed. *Soldiers West: Biographies from the American Frontier*. Lincoln, NB: University of Nebraska Press, 1987.
Nizolak, Joseph P., Jr., William T. Drummond, Jr., and Michael J. Zyda. "FOST: Innovative Training for Tomorrow's Battlefield," *Field Artillery Magazine*, Feb 1990, p. 46.
"Notes on the Course at the School of Fire," *Field Artillery Journal*, Apr-Jun 1912, p. 235.
"Nuclear Weapons Department," *Artillery Trends,* Jul 1960, p. 3.
"1951-1961: "The Korean Threat," Lawton *Constitution,* 5 Aug 1976, p. 2h.
"OBC: Training the New Lieutenant," *Field Artillery Magazine*, Mar-Apr 1999, p. 35.
O'Connell, John P. "Organization and Tactics for Field Artillery Missile Units," *Artillery Trends*, Feb 1959, p. 11.
Odierno, Raymond T. and Thomas L. Swingle. "AFATDS: Digitizing Fighting with Fires," *Field Artillery Magazine*, Sep-Oct 1996, p. 12.
"OH-58D," *Army,* Aug 1990, p. 54.
Ott, David E. "Forward Observations," *Field Artillery Journal*, Nov-Dec 1975, p. 6.
_____. "Forward Observations," *Field Artillery Journal*, May-Jun 1976, p. 6.
_____. "Forward Observations," *Field Artillery Journal*, Jul-Aug 1976, p. 3.
Parker, Edwin P., Jr. "Field Artillery Replacement Centers," *Field Artillery Journal*, Feb 1941, p. 83.
_____. "New Construction at Fort Sill," *Field Artillery Journal*, Jan-Feb 1934, p. 5.
_____. "The Regular Course, The Field Artillery School," *Field Artillery Journal*, May-Jun 1934, p. 202.
_____. "They Start to Roll," *Field Artillery Journal,* May 1941, p. 273.
Parker, Ellis. "This Vision of LHX," *US Army Aviation Digest,* Dec 1986, p. 5.
Pearson, Paul. *"FIST,"* *Field Artillery Journal,* May-Jun 1976, p. 7.
"Pentagon Already Has Plans for How to Spend Crusader Billions," *Inside the Army*, 6 May 2002, p. 1, HRDC.
Pierce, Linda G. and Walter W. Millspaugh. "Simulations to Train and Develop the 21st Century FA," *Field Artillery Magazine*, Jul-Aug 1997, p. 39.
Peterson, Felix, Jr., and Charles Morris. "Small Group Instruction in the Field Artillery School," *Field Artillery Magazine*, Apr 1989, p. 45.
Pokorny, Anthony. "Take the Tech," *Field Artillery Journal*, Sep-Oct 1984, p. 21.

"Portrait of BG Albert J. Bowley," *Field Artillery Journal*, Sep-Oct 1921, p. 426.

Rains, Roger A. "Readiness: The Field Artillery Takes Aim," *Army*, Mar 1985, p. 41.

Ralston, David C. "State of the Field Artillery," *Field Artillery Magazine*, Nov-Dec 2006, p. 6.

Ralston, David C. and Patrecia Slayden Hollis. "PGM Effects for the BCT Commander," *Fires Bulletin*, Jan-Mar 2009, p. 22.

Ratliff, Frank G. "The Field Artillery Battalion Fire-Direction Center – Its Past, Present, and Future," *Field Artillery Journal*, May-Jun 1950, p. 117.

"Redlegs' Career Update: Officers, Warrant Officers, and Noncommissioned Officers," *Field Artillery Magazine*, Dec 1987, p. 48.

Reeder, Thomas. "Exercise Your Radar," *Artillery Trends*, Jun 1959, p. 38.

Reitz, John W. "A Fire Supporter's Guide to FM 100-5," *Field Artillery Magazine*, Dec 1993, p. 10.

"Reorganization of the War Department and the Army," *Field Artillery Journal*, Jun 1946, p. 339.

"Reorganized AGF School System," *Field Artillery Journal*, Nov-Dec 1946, p. 644.

Rigby, Randall L. "AFATDS: Learning to Interoperate – Not Just Interface," *Field Artillery Magazine*, Sep-Oct 1996, p. 1.

_____. "CG Reflects, Reviews 1996 Goals at Fort Sill," Fort Sill *Cannoneer*, 4 Dec 1996, p. 6a, HRDC.

_____. "Fires for Division XXI: State of the Branch 1995," *Field Artillery Magazine*, Nov-Dec 1995, p. 1.

_____. "Mapping the Future: FA State of the Branch," *Field Artillery Magazine*, Nov-Dec 1996, p. 1.

_____. "1996 Senior Fire Support Conference: Focusing Fires for Force XXI," *Field Artillery Magazine*, May-Jun 1996, p. 18.

_____. "3x6-2x9 MLRS Transition," *Field Artillery Magazine*, Sep-Oct 1996, p. 18.

Riley, Robert S. "AOE: What is It?" *Field Artillery Journal*, Sep-Oct 1985, p. 22.

Rittenhouse, C. William. "Fire Support on the Non-Linear Battlefield: The Shape of Things to Come," *Field Artillery Magazine,* Oct 1990, p. 36.

_____. "Operation FireStrike," *Field Artillery Magazine*, Feb 1991, p. 33.

Rivera, Wilson A. "Air Defense Artillery School Moves to Fort Sill," *Fires Bulletin*, May-Jun 2009, p. 3.

Rogers, Gordon K. "Transforming Institutional Training and Leaders Development," *Army AL&T*, Nov-Dec 2001, p. 7.

Rogers, Patrick F. "The New Artillery," *Army*, Jul 1980, p. 31.

Roshell, Robert W. and Lawrence M. Terranova, "Education for ARNG FA Officers and Noncommissioned Officers," *Fires Bulletin*, Jan-Feb 2009, p. 31.

"Rumsfeld Dumps Crusader, Defends Decision," *CNN.com*, 9 May 2002, HRDC.

"Rumsfeld Pulls Plug on Big Gun," *Reuters.com*, 8 May 2002, HRDC.

Russell, Theodore S., Jr., and Harold H. Worrell, Jr., "Focus on Light Force XXI: AWE Warrior Focus," *Field Artillery Magazine*, May-Jun 1996, p. 36.

Samek, Rocky G. "M270A1: An MLRS Launcher with Leap-ahead Lethality," *Field Artillery Magazine*, Mar-Apr 2002, p. 40.

Scarborough, Rowan. "Army Chief Crusades to Save New Howitzer Set for Axing," *WashingtonTimes.com*, HRDC.

Schowalter, W.E. "An All Around Problem," *Trends in Artillery for Instruction*, Jun 1957, p. 16.

Schroeck, Thoren J. "Developing Future Artillery," *Artillery Trends*, Dec 1959, p. 3.

Schucker, Jean. "Henry Post Army Airfield: First Home of Army Aviation," *US Army Aviation Digest*, May-Jun 1992, p. 18.

"Secretary of the Army Says Crusader Still Viable," *ArmyLink News*, 15 Nov 2000, HRDC.

Shaw, Scott A. "COIN in the FACCC," *Field Artillery Magazine*, May-Jun 2007, p. 8.
Shearer, Robert L. "Development of Pershing II," *Field Artillery Journal,* May-Jun 1980, p. 31.
Shiemann, Heinz A. "Fire Support for the Light Division," *Field Artillery Magazine,* Oct 1987, p. 19.
"Silhouettes of Steel," *Field Artillery Magazine*, Nov-Dec 1999, p. 32.
Siltman, Frank J. and John P. Frisbie. "Fire Support Just Got Harder: Adding Nonlethal Fires as a Core Competency," *Fires Bulletin*, Jul-Sep 2008, p. 6.
Sittenauer, Peter M. and Cornelius L. Morgan. "FACCC: Redesigned for Today and Tomorrow," *Fires Bulletin*, Jul-Sep 2008, p. 16.
Smith, Joseph D. "The FA NCO: Absolutely Mission Essential," *Fires Bulletin*, Jul-Sep 2008, p. 4.
Snow, Joe, "CAS3 Anyone?" *Field Artillery Journal*, Jul-Aug 1985, p. 34.
Snow, William J. "Origin of the Field Artillery School," *Field Artillery Journal*, Feb 1941, p. 102.
_____. "Field Artillery Firing Centers," *Field Artillery Journal*, Nov-Dec 1940, p. 450.
"Snow Hall Burns Down," *Field Artillery Journal*, Sep 1929, p. 584.
Sprengle, Danny J. and Donald C. Durant. "Excalibur: Extended-Range Precision for the Army," *Field Artillery Magazine*, Mar-Apr 2003, p. 13.
"Standing-up the Fires Center of Excellence," *Fires Bulletin*, May-Jun 2009, p. 4.
Stark, Kenneth B. "Methods of Deploying Cannon and Missile Field Artillery," *Artillery Trends*, Jun 1958, p. 5.
_____. "Revision of Field Manual 6-20, Artillery Tactics and Technique," *Trends in Artillery for Instruction*, Feb 1958, p. 19.
Stebbins, Steven A., "To Teach a Man to Shoot: Dan T. Moore and the School of Fire, 1909-1914," *Field Artillery Magazine*, Aug 1994, p. 10.
Steffen, Jerome O., "William Clark," in Paul A. Hutton, ed. *Soldiers West: Biographies from the Military Frontier.* Lincoln, NB: University of Nebraska Press, 1987.
Stricklin, Toney. "Fires: The Cutting Edge for the 21st Century," *Field Artillery Magazine*, May-Jun 1998, p. 22.
"Striker/Reconnaissance Team," *Field Artillery Magazine*, Jan-Feb 1996, p. 38.
Strobridge, Truman R. and Bernard C. Nalty. "The Roar of the 8-Incher," *Field Artillery Journal*, Mar-Apr 1980, p. 36.
"Study Recommends 63 Changes for Warrant Officers," ArmyLink News, 22 Aug 2002 HRDC.
"Study Suggests Fixes for Officer Development," ArmyLink News, 25 May 2001, HRDC.
Stump, Michael M. "4th ID Stands Up Army's First Fires Brigade," *Field Artillery Magazine*, Jan-Feb 2005, p. 27.
Sunderland, Riley. "Massed Fire and the FDC," *Army*, May 1958, p. 56.
"Survey Says Balance Army Needs with Army Beliefs," ArmyLink News, 25 May 2001, HRDC.
Swett, Morris, "The Forerunners of Sill: A History of Artillery Schools in the United States," *Field Artillery Journal,* Nov-Dec 1938, p. 453.
"TA Warrant Officer Restructured Approved," *Field Artillery Magazine*, Aug 1993, p. 37.
Tanzi, John A. and Robert D. Harper, "Field Artillery Cannon Systems Update," *Field Artillery Magazine*, Jan-Feb 2006, p. 14.
"Technological Advances in Training," *Field Artillery Magazine*, Mar-Apr 1997, p. 27.
"The Computer Story: Speed and Accuracy," *Artillery Trends*, Sep 1960, p. 30.
"The Field Artillery Central Officers' Training School," *Field Artillery Journal*, Jul-Sep 1918, p. 370.
"The Flying Artillery," *Artillery Trends*, May 1960, p. 12.
"The H-2C in Artillery Employment," *Artillery Trends*, Jul 1962, p. 42.
"The Mission of the School of Fire for Field Artillery," *Field Artillery Journal*, Oct-Dec 1917, p. 383.

"The Needs of the School of Fire," *Field Artillery Journal*, Apr-Jun 1915, p. 459.

"The Radar Technician and His Role," *Field Artillery Magazine*, Jul-Aug 1996, p. 2.

"The Regular Course, The Field Artillery School," *Field Artillery Journal*, May-Jun 1934, p. 202.

"The School of Fire for Field Artillery and the School of Musketry," *Field Artillery Journal*, Jul-Sep 1915, p. 630.

"The School of Fire for Field Artillery," *Field Artillery Journal,* Jan-Mar 1912, p. 116.

"The XM777 Lightweight 155-mm. Howitzer," *Army*, Oct 2000, p. 303.

Tice, Jim. "NCO Training Overhaul," *Army Times*, 22 Dec 2008, HRDC.

Todd, John J. and James M. Holt. "Army Science Board Study: How Much Field Artillery is Enough," *Field Artillery Magazine*, Jun 1995, p. 20.

"TRADOC Responding to Training Needs from NCO Study," ArmyLink News, 2 May 2002, HRDC.

"Training Command: FA School, FATC, and NCOA," *Field Artillery Magazine*, Dec 1993, p. 30.

"Training the Targeting Technician," *Field Artillery Magazine*, Jan-Feb 1997, p. 26.

"Transition," *Field Artillery Magazine*, Sep-Oct 1996, p. 18.

Tredway, R.N. "The H-2C in Artillery Employment," *Artillery Trends*, Jul 1962, p. 42.

Unger, F.T. "Special Weapons Instruction," *Trends in Artillery for Instruction,* Apr 1957, p. 22.

"USAAMS Extension Courses Provide Many Benefits," *Artillery Trends*, Apr 1965, p. 2.

"USAFAS Curriculum Revisions," *Field Artillery Magazine*, Sep-Oct 1995, p. 45.

"US Army Field Artillery School," *Field Artillery Magazine*, Dec 1990, p. 13.

"US Army Field Artillery School," *Field Artillery Magazine*, Dec 1991, p. 13.

"US Army Field Artillery School," *Field Artillery Magazine*, Dec 1992, p. 14.

Valcourt, David P. "Issues and Answers," *Field Artillery Magazine*, Jul-Aug 2004, p. 1.

Vangjel, Peter M. "State of the Field Artillery: Today and Tomorrow, Artillery Strong," *Fires Bulletin*, Oct-Dec 2008, p. 1.

Voigt, Suzann W. "Much Ado About Something," *Field Artillery Journal*, Jul-Aug 1986, p. 29.

Vuono, Carl E. "Change, Continuity, and the Future of the Field Artillery," *Field Artillery Magazine*, June 1991, p. 6.

Walters, Raymond. "Field Artillery in American Colleges," *Field Artillery Journal*, Nov-Dec 1919, p. 543.

Ward, William F. "Performance in Panama Underscores Readiness," *Army*, Oct 1990, p. 104.

Ward, William H. "The Army's First Fires Brigade," *Field Artillery Magazine*, Nov-Dec 2005, p. 20.

Warren, Ross B., "Advanced Course (Special) Number Two," *Field Artillery Journal,* Aug 1941, p. 554 "Weapon System: 1970," *Artillery Trends*, Feb 1962, p. 4.

Weaver, Vince C. "Fires in AWE Focused Dispatch: A Step Toward Task Force XXI," *Field Artillery Magazine*, Mar-Apr 1996, p. 38.

Welch, David P. "Warrant: The Legacy of Leadership as a Warrant Officer – 90 Years of Technical Expertise in the Army," *On Point*, Summer 2008, p. 6, HRDC.

Wharton, Richard W. "The Cannon Still the King on Battlefield," *Army*, Jul 1989, p. 55.

Whelihan, William. "M198," *Field Artillery Journal*, Jan-Feb 1978, p. 9.

_____. "We've Got 30," *Field Artillery Journal*, May-Jun 1979, p. 9.

White, David C. "Cutting Edge Training Prepares Soldiers for Changing Future," Fort Sill *Cannoneer*, 27 Nov 1996, p. 6a.

White, David C. and Clyde W. Ellis. "Army Training XXI," *Field Artillery Magazine*, Mar-Apr 1996, p. 8.

White, Samuel R., Jr. "The Fires Brigade: Not Your Daddy's FFA HQ," *Field Artillery Magazine*, Nov-Dec 2005, p. 14.

Willebrand, Guy E. "FA Training Devices for the 1990s and Beyond," *Field Artillery Magazine,* Mar-Apr 1995, p. 11.

Willis, Browder A. "HELP for the M109 Self-Propelled Howitzer," *Field Artillery Journal*, May-Jun 1982, p. 35.

Wollman, James H. and David S. Henderson," Fires Center of Excellence in 2011," *Fires Bulletin*, Jul-Aug 2007, p. 16.

Wood, William J. "Tactical Employment of the New Division Artillery," *Artillery Trends*, Mar 1959, p. 23.

Zabecki, David T. "Dan T. Moore: Founder of the Field Artillery School," *Field Artillery Journal*, Nov-Dec 1981, p. 58.

Theses

Brand, William F., Jr. "A Re-examination of the Integration of the Artilleries," thesis, US Army War College, 1963.

Collins, Monta Rae. "The History of the City of Lawton, Oklahoma," master's thesis, University of Oklahoma, 1941.

Pierce, Richard L. "A Maximum of Support: The Development of US Army Field Artillery Doctrine in World War I," master's thesis, Ohio State University, 1983.

Snow, William J. "The Functions and Training of Field Artillery," thesis, Army War College, 1908.

Stebbins, Steven A. "Indirect Fire: The Challenge and Response in the US Army, 1907-1917," master's thesis, University of North Carolina, 1993.

Turtentine, Luanne Aline. "Intermediate-Range Nuclear Force Modernization and Soviet-West German Relations," master's thesis, Naval Postgraduate School, 1984.

Index

Abrams, John N., 252
Adams, Granger, 31, 34
Adams, Paul D., 148
Advance Course of 1920s and 1930s, 78, 80
Aerial observation, 120-23
Ainsworth, Fred C., 21
Air Defense Artillery Center and School, 269-75
    See Antiaircraft Artillery School
Air-Ground Procedure Board of 1939-1940, 122
AirLand Battle, 189, 231
AirLand Operations, 231-233
Air Service School, 48
Air Training School, 137
Akers, Albert B., 177
Allin, George R., 90, 111, 118
American Expeditionary Forces, 51, 60
Anderson, John B., 74
Andrews, Henry M., 21
Andrus, Cliff, 47, 133, 134
Antiaircraft Artillery School, 132, 133, 134, 137, 138, 139
    See Air Defense Artillery School
Apache Tribe, 8, 9, 10
Arapaho Tribe, 5, 7, 8
Army Aviation School, 137
Army Campaign Update of 2006, 262
Army Correspondence Course Program, 214
Army Medical School, 16
Army Modernization Plan, 259
Army Reorganization Act of 1950, 140
Army Science Board of 1995, 228, 229, 230
Army Training and Evaluation Program, 181, 182, 197
Army Training and Leader Development Panel Study of 2000-2001, 252, 254
Army War College, 16, 71, 76
Arnold, Henry H., 122
Artillery Branch Study of 1967, 153
Artillery Center, 132-34
    See consolidating artillery schools, 132-34
Artillery School, 16, 18
Aultman, Dwight E., 73
Austin, Fred T., 25, 47, 59

Bagnal, Charles W., 182
Base Realignment and Closure 2005, 251, 269-75
    See Fires Center of Excellence, 269-75, 301

Basic Course of 1920s and 1930s, 77, 78, 80
Basic Officer Leader Course, 255, 256, 257, 258, 259
Battery Officer Course of 1920s, 77
Batule, Kevin M., 259
Baxter, Leo J., 211, 216, 221
Beal, Mattie, 11
Bell, J. Franklin, 17, 18
Benton, David L. III, 215
Birnie, Upton, Jr., 89, 91, 116
Bishop, Harry G., 85, 86, 121
Blatchford, Richard M., 31, 32, 46
Bliss, Tasker H., 59, 60
Boggy Depot, 8
Boiseau, Louis T., 25
Boone, Albert Gallatin, 8
Bowley, Albert J., 77, 120
Brigade firing centers, 59, 60
Brewer, Carlos, 89
Bromberg, Howard B., 273, 275
Brown, Charles P., 160
Brownlee, Les, 254
Bruchmüller, Georg, 54
Bush, George H., 197
Bush, George W., 269
Butner, Henry W., 27, 78, 79
Byrnes, Kevin P., 253, 261

Caldwell, William B., 265, 268
Calhoun, John C., 70
Camp Benning, Georgia, 78
Camp Bragg, North Carolina, 70, 71, 77, 78
Camp Doniphan, Oklahoma, 48, 59, 60, 110, 115, 143
    See Concurrent Camp Area, 110, 143
Camp Jackson, South Carolina, 59
Camp Knox, Kentucky, 59, 70, 72, 76, 77, 78
Camp McClellan, Alabama, 59
Camp Supply, Indian Territory, 6, 7
Camp Wichita, Indian Territory, 8
Camp Zachary Taylor, Kentucky, 59, 61, 70
Captain Professional Military Education Study, 212
    See officer training
Career Management Field 13, 175, 220
Carr, Eugene A., 6
Carter, Arthur H., 61
Chaffee, Adna R., 16

Cheyenne Tribe, 5, 8
Chief of Field Artillery, 57, 58, 69, 71, 81, 83, 85, 90, 103, 106, 115, 116, 122
    See Protective Mobilization Plan of 1939, 108
    See Baxter, Leo J.; Birnie, Upton, Jr.; Bishop, Harry G.; Danford, Robert M.; Dubia, John A.; Hallada, Raphael F.; Marty, Fred F.; Ralston, David C.; Ridge, Ross E.; Snow, William J.; Stricklin, Toney; Vangjel, Peter M.
Chiricahua Apache, 9, 10, 21, 22, 49
Chisholm Trail, 9
Chivington, John M., 5
Chrystie, Phineas P., 51
Chouteau, Jean Pierre, 3, 4
Churchill, Marlborough, 32
Clark, Mark W., 142, 147
Clark, William, 2
Clarke, Bruce C., 133
Classroom modernization, 220-21, 224, 225
Clear Boggy, 8
Coast Artillery School, 18, 19
Cody, Richard A., 266
Colbern, William H., 143
Cold War, 136-37, 142, 143
Collins, Leroy P., 106
Comanche Tribe, 4, 5, 6, 7, 8, 9, 10
Combined Arms Battle Command Course, 252, 253
    See officer training
Combined Arms Center, 182, 183
Combined Arms Leader Course (Combined Arms Staff Course), 253
    See officer training
Combined Arms Service Staff School, 212, 213, 251, 254
Command and General Staff College, 71, 76, 213
Conner, Fox, 20
Consolidating the artillery branches (Coast Artillery, Antiaircraft Artillery, and Field Artillery), 131-34, 140, 141
Counterinsurgency warfare, 159, 160
Craig, Daniel F., 79
Craig, Malin, 103
Cross training (integrated), 137-42, 146-54
Cruikshank, William M., 80, 82, 83, 84
Cubbison, Donald C., 110, 111
Custer, George A., 6, 8, 31

Danford, Robert M., 47, 49, 59, 71, 85, 103, 104, 107, 110, 118, 119, 123
Department of Defense, 268
Depuy, William E., 186
de Shazo, Thomas E., 133, 138, 146, 149, 150
Devers, Jacob L., 132, 133, 138
Digitization, 220
    See classroom modernization
Distance learning, 222-23, 225, 226
Dodge, Henry, 5
Doniphan, Alexander W., 48
Dubia, John A., 221, 224
Dunbar, William, 2

Eddy, Manton S., 152
Eddy Board, 152
Eisenhower, Dwight D., 132
Elliott, Joel, 8
Engineer School of Application, 16
Enlisted Personnel Management System, 180, 181
Enlisted Specialists' School, 72
Enlisted training, 72, 73, 179-81, 184-85, 219, 261-62
    See Noncommissioned Officer Education System
Ennis, William P., 88, 89
Evans, Andrew W., 6, 7

Farnsworth, Charles S., 48
Field artillery advisory teams, 158
Field Artillery Captain's Career Course-Distance Learning, 214, 215
    See Field Artillery Officer Advance Course-Reserve Component
Field Artillery Drill Regulations for 1916, 47
Field Artillery Journal/Magazine, 19, 32, 34, 50, 52, 122, 138, 199
Field Artillery Officer Advance Course/Field Artillery Captain's Career Course, 177, 178, 184, 209, 210, 211, 212, 213, 251, 252, 253, 254, 264, 265
Field Artillery Officer Basic Course, 174, 175, 176, 177, 184, 211, 215, 216, 217, 254
Field Artillery Officer Candidate School (Artillery Officer Candidate School), 103, 109, 111, 112, 113, 114, 115, 116, 117, 118, 119, 120, 124, 161, 173
    Closing in 1946

Closing in 1973, 173
Opening in 1941,
Opening in 1951, 143
Preparatory course, 118
Salvage course, 119
Field Artillery Officer Advance Course-Reserve Component, 214, 215
Field Artillery Replacement Center (Korean War), 143
Field Artillery Replacement Center (World War II), 118, 119
Field Artillery School, 70, 71, 72, 73, 76, 81, 85, 87, 88, 104, 107, 108, 109, 111, 112, 116, 120, 121, 134, 135, 136, 138, 154-62, 173, 174, 175, 176, 178, 182, 183, 186, 187, 190, 192, 193, 197, 212, 218, 219, 223, 230, 234, 235, 255, 256, 257, 258, 259, 261, 262, 263, 265, 268, 301
   Aerial observation, 120-23, 137
   Atomic and nuclear weapon courses, 144, 145
   Cold War, 136-37, 144-46
   Combat developments, 86-92, 154-62, 185-197, 228-235, 278-85
   Construction program, 80-82, 85-86
   Cross training (integrated), 137-42, 146-54
   Depth and Simultaneous Attack Battle Laboratory, 232
   Digest of Field Artillery Developments, 90-91
   Digitization, 220-23, 232, 233
   Distance learning strategy, 221, 222, 223
   Expansion for Vietnam War, 161
   Field Manual 6-20, Fire Support for Combat Operations, 188, 189
   Fire Direction Center, 87-90
   Fire Support Team, 188
   Horses, 123-24
   Instructor shortages, 136-37
   Polo, 91
   Renamed Artillery and Guided Missile School, 144
   Renamed The Artillery School, 133
   Renamed US Army and Missile School, 144
   Renamed US Army Artillery and Guided Missile School, 144
   Renamed US Army Field Artillery School, 154
   Training aids, devices, simulators, and simulations, 226
   Transformation of the Army, 275-79
   Vietnam War, 157-62, 173
Field Artillery School Commandants
   See Allin, George R.; Andrus, Cliff; Baxter, Leo J.; Brown, Charles P.; Butner, Henry W.; Cruikshank, William M.; Cubbison, Donald C.; Dubia, John A.; de Shazo, Thomas E.; Fleming, Adrian S.; Griffing, Lewis S.; Hallada, Raphael J.; Harper, Arthur M.; Hinds, Ernest; Irwin, George LeR.; Keith, Donald R.; Marty, Fred F.; McGlachlin, Edward T.; McIntyre, Augustine; Moore, Dan T.; Ott, David E.; Pennell, Ralph McT.; Ralston, David C.; Ridge, Ross E.; Snow, William J.; Stricklin, Toney; Vangjel, Peter M.
Field artillery tactics, 51-55, 73-76, 88-90
   Gunnery, 73-76
   Observed indirect fire, 51-55, 73-76
   Unobserved indirect fire, 73-76
Field artillery training
   Consolidating training at Field Artillery School in 1920s, 76-78
   Cross training (integrated), 137-42, 146-54
   Korean War, 142-43
   Operations Desert Shield and Storm, 197-99
   Vietnam War, 157-62, 173
   World War I, 56-62
   World War II, 103-19
Field Artillery Central Officers' Training School, 59, 60, 61
Fires Center of Excellence, 269-75, 301
   Base Realignment and Closure 2005, 251, 269-75
   Full operational capability, 275
   Initial operational capability, 275
   Organizational design, 271, 272, 274
   Five Civilized Tribes, 4, 5
Fleming, Adrian S., 47, 50, 56, 120
Ford, William W., 122, 137
Fort Arbuckle, Indian Territory, 5, 6
Fort Bascom, New Mexico Territory, 7
Fort Bliss, Texas, 268-75
Fort Cobb, Indian Territory, 6, 8
Fort Dodge, Kansas, 6
Fort Gibson, Indian Territory, 4, 5, 6, 8
Fort Harkness, Kansas, 8
Fort Larned, Kansas, 6
Fort Leavenworth, Kansas, 71

Fort Reno, Indian Territory, 9
Fort Riley, Kansas, 16, 19, 34
Fort Sill, Indian Territory/Oklahoma, 5, 8, 9, 10, 11, 15, 17, 18, 21, 22, 31, 45, 48, 70, 78, 79, 81, 82, 84, 105, 110, 111, 112, 119, 145, 147, 198, 253, 256, 268-75
    Apache Prisoners of War, 9, 10
    Construction of New Post, 18
    Expansion of boundaries in 1895, 9
    Expansion of boundaries in 1901, 10
    Expansion of boundaries in 1957, 145, 146
    Lottery Opening Act of 1901, 10, 11
    Water supply, 23, 84, 109-10
Fort Smith, Arkansas, 3
Fort Towson, Indian Territory, 4, 5
Foss, John W., 198, 230, 231
Franks, Tommy, 209, 210
Freeman, Thomas, 2
French liaison officers, 53
Future Army Schools Task Force Twenty-One, 223
    See Total Army School System/The Army School System

Garrison, Lindley M., 32
Gates, Robert, 279
Gayle, Edward E., 16
General Staff and Service College, 16
German Field Artillery School, 20, 29, 92
Geronimo, 9
Gerow Board, 152
Gerow, Leonard T., 152
Givens, Joshua, 10
Gomes, Stephen A., 260
Grant, Ulysses S., 8
Grierson, Benjamin H., 8, 16
Griffing, Lewis S., 150, 156
Griffith, Stanley E., 197
Gruber, Edmund L., 59
Guyer, George D., 48
Haines Board, 152, 153
Haines, Ralph E., 152
Hallada, Raphael J., 192, 198
Halverson, David D., 275
Handy, Thomas T., 131
Hanson, P.N., 122
Harney, William S., 5
Harper, Arthur M., 140, 141
Hartshorn, Edwin S., 151

Hartzog, William W., 211, 222
Hazen, William B., 6
Helmick, Eli A., 81
Hendrick, Wayne, 110
Henry B. Post Field, 48, 55, 81, 115
Hero Board (1918-1919), 120, 121
Hinds, Ernest, 27, 72, 74, 75, 76, 77, 79, 81, 120
Hodges, Courtney H., 113
Hogan, Thomas R., 198
Honeycutt, Francis W., 49
Hopkins, F.E., 46
House, R.W., 212
Howe, Walter, 16
Hurley, Patrick J., 84

Indian Removal Act of 1830, 4
Indian Territory, 2, 3, 4, 5, 6, 7, 8, 9, 11, 84
    Battle of Washita (Massacre), 6, 7
    Explorers, 2, 3, 5
    Indian Removal Act of 1830, 4
    Medicine Lodge Creek Peace Treaty, 5
    Red River Campaign of 1874-1875, 9
    Reservations, 5, 6, 8, 9
    Traders, 3, 4
    Winter Campaign of 1868-1869, 6, 7
Irwin, George LeR., 79, 81, 82, 83

Jackson, Andrew, 4
Jefferson, Thomas, 2, 4
Jennings, Richard M., 159
Jerome, David H., 10
Jones, H.L.C., 90

Keith, Donald R., 189, 191
Kerr, Robert S., 145
Ketch, Frank L., 111
Kennedy, John F., 157
Key, William S., 109
Kiowa-Apache Tribe, 5, 9, 10
Kiowa Tribe, 4, 5, 6, 7, 8, 9
Korean War, 141, 142, 143, 144, 149
Kreyenbuhl, Craig, 119

Lafarge, André, 54
Lake Lawtonka, 23, 109, 110
Langdon, Jesse, 21
Lassiter, William J., 20
Lawton, Henry W., 11

Lawton, Oklahoma, 10, 18, 22, 109, 110
Leach, C.R., 158, 159
Leavenworth, Henry, 2, 5
Lennox, William J., 216
Lewis, Meriwether, 2
Long, Stephen, 3
Lottery Opening Act of March 1901, 10, 11
Louisiana Territory, 2

MacArthur, Douglas A., 103
Macomb, M.M., 30
MacDonald, James M., 258, 262
Mann, William A., 32, 33
March, Peyton C., 60, 75
Marcy, Randolph B., 5
Marshall, George C., 87, 90, 113
Marty, Fred F., 199, 210, 218
Matthews, Rodger F., 274
Maul, John C., 27
McCain, Henry P., 34, 49, 58
McGlachlin, Edward T., 15, 30, 31, 32, 33, 34, 77
McIntyre, Augustine, 27, 74, 85, 104, 107, 109
McKinley, William H., 11
McNair Hall, 115, 143
McNair, Lesley J., 53, 85, 113
McNamara, Robert S., 196
Medicine Creek/Bluffs, Indian Territory, 8, 22
Medicine Lodge Creek Peace Treaty, 5, 6
Medicine Park, 23
Mellon, John M., 85
Mentoring (Small Group Instruction), 182, 183, 184, 185, 210, 211
Metz, Thomas F., 272, 282
Meyer, Edward C., 189
Mitchell, Billy, 121, 122
Mobilization, 45-50, 103-12, 159-61
Monko, Joseph P., 198
Monroney, Mike, 145
Moore, Dan T., 15, 20, 21, 22, 23, 24, 25, 26, 28, 29, 30, 34, 85, 91
Morris, Charles A., 184
Mounted Service School, 19
Murray, Arthur, 17, 20, 21
National Defense Act of 1916, 45, 46
National Defense Act of 1920, 70, 71, 103, 104
Net Fires Center
    See Fires Center of Excellence
New Mexico Territory, 9

New Post, Fort Sill, 18, 31, 85
Noncommissioned Officer Education System, 179, 180, 181, 197, 219, 261, 263
    Advanced Noncommissioned Officer Course/ Senior Leader Course, 180, 181, 184, 219, 261, 266
    Basic Noncommissioned Officer Course/ Advance Leader Course, 180, 181, 184, 219, 261, 266
    Primary Leadership Development Course/ Warrior Leader Course, 180, 181, 219, 261, 266
Nonlethal instruction, 267-68, 302
    Electronic warfare, 267, 268, 302
    Tactical information, 268, 302

Office of the Chief of Field Artillery, 58, 71
Officer Personnel Management System, 174, 175, 177
Officer training, 71, 72, 73, 78, 80, 146-54, 174-76, 182-85, 209-17, 251-59
    See Advance Course, Basic Course, Field Artillery Officer Advance Course/Field Artillery Captain's Course, Field Artillery Officer Basic Course/Basic Officer Leader Course, Regular Course
Old Post, Fort Sill, 31, 49, 110, 115
Old Trader's Store, Fort Sill, 32, 46, 50
Operation Desert Shield, 197-99, 220, 221, 228
Operation Desert Storm, 197-99, 209, 215, 220, 228, 234, 281, 282
Operation Enduring Freedom (Afghanistan), 251, 253, 254, 256, 261, 262, 265, 266, 267, 268, 279, 282, 284, 285
Operation Iraqi Freedom, 251, 253, 254, 256, 261, 262, 265, 266, 267, 268, 282, 284, 285, 302
Orleman, L.H., 8
Ott, David E., 177, 187, 188

Palmer, W.B., 148
Parker, Quanah, 9, 10
Parrott, Roger S., 27
Patch, Alexander M., 131
Patch Board, 131, 132
Patterson, Robert T., 131
Pennell, Ralph M., 25, 27
Peck, George M., 85
Pershing, John P., 52, 53, 77
Peterson, Felix, Jr., 184

Pickard, A.D., 153
Pike, Zebulon Montgomery, 2
Post, Henry B., 58
Potter, W.C., 109
Protective Mobilization Plan of 1937, 103
Protective Mobilization Plan of 1939, 103, 105, 106, 116

Quay, Matt, 10
Quinnette, William H., 31

Ralston, David C., 260, 263
Randolph, William F., 16
Red River Campaign/War of 1874-1875, 9
Reimer, Dennis, 213, 232
Regular Course of the 1930s, 80
Reorganization Act of 1821, 16
Reserve Component Captain Professional Military Education, 214
    See Field Artillery Officer Advance Course-Reserve Component
    See Field Artillery Captain's Career Course-Distance Learning
Reset (Retraining), 263-66
    Classroom instruction, 263-64, 265-66
    Mobile training teams, 264
    See Operation Enduring Freedom (Afghanistan)
    See Operation Iraqi Freedom
Review of Education and Training of Officers, 175
Richardson, William R., 178
Ridge, Ross E., 274
Rogers, Bernard, 175
Roosevelt, Franklin D., 104
Roosevelt, Theodore, 20
Root, Elihu, 15
    Reforms, 15, 16
Rumbaugh, D.J., 21
Rumsfeld, Donald, 269, 279
Russo-Japanese War of 1904-1905, 27, 54

St. Greble, Edwin John, 21, 22, 23, 24, 25, 28, 30, 48
Sayre, Warren G., 10
School for Aerial Artillery Observers, 48, 50, 55
School of Antisubmarine Defense, 16
School of Application for Cavalry and Field Artillery, 16

School of Fire for Field Artillery, 15, 16, 18, 19, 20, 21-25, 26, 27, 28, 29, 30, 31, 32, 33, 34, 35, 45, 46, 48, 52, 53, 55, 56, 57, 59, 61, 62, 69, 70, 71, 77, 84, 143
    Closing the school in 1916, 33-34
    Dan T. Moore, 21-25, 27-29
    Edward T. McGlachlin, 30, 34
    First facilities, 31-32
    Founding the school, 18-20
    Renamed Field Artillery School, 71
School of Musketry, 16, 31, 33, 48, 49
School of Practice for Cavalry and Field Artillery, 19
Schoomaker, Peter J., 276
Scott, Hugh L., 9, 10, 30, 49
Seacoast Artillery School, 132, 133, 134, 139
Selective Service Act of 1940, 112
Selective Service Act of 1948, 136
Separation of Coast Artillery and Field Artillery, 16, 17
Sheridan, Philip H., 6, 7, 8
Sherman, William T., 6
Shinseki, Eric K., 254, 261, 275, 276, 301
Showalter, W.E., 155
Sibley, George C., 3
Signal Mountain, Fort Sill, 18
Sill, Joshua W., 8
Simpson Board, 132
Simpson, William H., 131
Small group instruction (mentoring), 182-85
Snow Hall, 49, 83, 84, 143
    Construction of first Snow Hall, 49
    Destruction of first Snow Hall by fire, 84
    New Snow Hall of 1954, 143
Snow, William J., 20, 46, 47, 48, 49, 51, 53, 55, 56, 57, 58, 59, 60, 61, 62, 69, 75, 77, 79, 82, 83, 84, 143
Soldier's Springs, Indian Territory, 7
Somerville, Brehon B., 113
Southern Cheyenne Tribe, 5, 6
Spanish-American War of 1898, 15, 17, 19, 20, 34
Spaulding, Oliver S., 52
Starbird, Alfred A., 58
Starry, Donn A., 189
Story, Joseph P., 17
Stricklin, Toney, 280
Styron, James C., 146
Sullivan, Gordon R., 230

Sully, Alfred M., 6
Summerall, Charles P., 52
Swett, Morris, 46

Taft, William H., 18
Taylor, Maxwell, D., 148
Teletraining Network, 221, 222, 223
    See classroom modernization
Terry, Alfred H., 5
Total Army School System, 223, 224
    Renamed The Army School System, 223
Total Army Training System, 223
Total Warrant Officer Study, 218
Training aids, devices, simulations, and simulators, 226-27
Training reforms
    See enlisted training, officer training, Noncommissioned Officer Education System, and Warrant Officer Education System 1920s, 78, 79, 80, 81
    Cross (integrated) training, 137-42, 146-54
    Small group instruction, 182-85
    Vietnam War, 157-62
    World War I, 47-56
    World War II, 103-09, 112-20
Transformation of the Army, 276-78, 284
Truman, Harry S., 48, 131, 136

US Military Academy, 26
US Army Training and Doctrine Command, 173, 174, 175, 176, 177, 178, 180, 182, 183, 186, 189, 190, 198, 209, 210, 212, 218, 221, 251, 252, 255, 256, 257, 258, 260, 262, 266, 270, 272

Vangjel, Peter M., 264, 265, 266, 268
Vietnam War, 157-62, 173
    Field artillery advisory teams, 158
Vuono, Carl E., 198, 230, 231
Wallace, William S., 267, 271
    War Department, 4, 8, 15, 16, 17, 19, 22, 24, 25, 26, 29, 33, 34, 48, 49, 59, 62, 70, 73, 86, 103, 104, 105, 106, 108, 110, 111, 112, 113, 114, 116, 117, 119
Ward, Orlando, 89
Warrant Officer Education System, 178, 179, 184, 185, 197, 217, 218, 219, 259-61, 263
    Warrant Officer Advance Course, 179, 218, 219, 260, 261
    Warrant Officer Basic Course, 178, 179, 218, 219, 260, 261
    Warrant Officer Entry Course, 178, 179, 218
Warrant Officer Leader Development Action Panel of 1992, 259
    Integrating warrant officers into Basic Officer Leader Course, 259
Washita River, Indian Territory, 5
Waters, John K., 151
Westerfelt (Caliber) Board, 86
Westerfelt, William I., 86
Wichita Mountains, Indian Territory, 7
Wichita Tribe, 5
Wickham, John A., 176
Wilkinson, James, 3
Williams Board, 152
Williams, Edward T., 152
Wilson, Alfred M., 10
Wood, James T., 11
Wood, Leonard, 21
Wood, Robert J., 149

www.ingramcontent.com/pod-product-compliance
Lightning Source LLC
Chambersburg PA
CBHW080437170426
43195CB00017B/2810